THE INDIAN ENGINEERS
1939-47

INDIAN ENGINEERS

Left to right:

    A Naik of   A Sapper of   A Sapper of
    The Madras Group   The Bengal Group   The Bombay Group

THE
INDIAN ENGINEERS
1939-47

BY

LIEUT.-COLONEL E. W. C. SANDES,

D.S.O., M.C., R.E. (*Ret.*)

LATE PRINCIPAL, THOMASON CIVIL ENGINEERING COLLEGE, ROORKEE, INDIA.

AND AUTHOR OF

"IN KUT AND CAPTIVITY", "TALES OF TURKEY", "THE MILITARY ENGINEER IN INDIA", VOLS I AND II, "THE ROYAL ENGINEERS IN EGYPT AND THE SUDAN", "THE INDIAN SAPPERS AND MINERS" AND "FROM PYRAMID TO PAGODA (HISTORY OF THE WEST YORKSHIRE REGIMENT)".

The Naval & Military Press Ltd

Published by

The Naval & Military Press Ltd
Unit 5 Riverside, Brambleside
Bellbrook Industrial Estate
Uckfield, East Sussex
TN22 1QQ England

Tel: +44 (0)1825 749494

www.naval-military-press.com
www.nmarchive.com

In reprinting in facsimile from the original, any imperfections are inevitably reproduced and the quality may fall short of modern type and cartographic standards.

TO

THE INDIAN ENGINEERS

WHO DIED FOR FREEDOM

IN

THE SECOND WORLD WAR

FOREWORD

By Lieut.-General Sir HAROLD WILLIAMS, K.B.E., C.B., late Engineer-in-Chief, India, and Colonel Commandant, Corps of Engineers, India.

THIS history of the Indian Engineers covers the period from the outbreak of the Second World War in 1939 to Independence Day in 1947, an era fraught with great changes everywhere. At the outset, the Army in India was unprepared for war. Its Divisions existed largely on paper and it had no plans for Corps or Armies. Its administrative services were elementary, its fire power was meagre and its transport mainly animal; and although it was one of the largest voluntary armies in the world, well-trained and finely disciplined, it was ill-organized and ill-equipped for modern warfare. But when the war ended, it had fought with great distinction in Africa, Europe and Asia, using every known weapon and type of equipment. It had played a decisive part in the defeat of Germany, Italy and Japan. Its officers and men had shown themselves undaunted in adversity and courageous and magnanimous in success.

In 1939 the Indian Engineers formed but a small proportion of the Army in India. They comprised a handful of field units with their headquarters at Bangalore, Roorkee and Kirkee. They had no transportation or survey units and practically no L of C units. They had little or no bridging equipment, no mines or mine detectors and, with the exception of a few bulldozers and compressors, very little mechanical equipment. Indeed, so urgently were they in need of re-equipping that the Chatfield Committee which met in 1938-39 considered the possibility of making funds available for this purpose by reducing them to one Group with its headquarters at Mathura. Finally, the Committee recommended a reduction to two Groups; but fortunately this was not done because, only a few years later, the three existing Groups had to be reinforced by the formation of three more Groups at Lahore and others at Jullundur, Sialkot and Deolali, and all these Groups were soon fully occupied in recruiting and training personnel for Engineer units of every type in the field.

Lieut.-Colonel E. W. C. Sandes' book describes the work of the Indian Engineers during the period covered. His selection as author was amply justified for, in addition to other military histories, he had already written the histories of the Military Engineers of India from the earliest times and of the Indian Sappers and Miners up to 1939, and had carried out much research into the record of the Second World War when writing the history of The West Yorkshire Regiment. His task was not an easy one. Entries in War Diaries are not always as informative as the historian would like, and for security reasons officers no longer write personal diaries on active service. In the rush and hurry of post-war reconstruction few officers had time to record their experiences, and accordingly the material available to Lieut.-Colonel Sandes was disappointingly limited. Nevertheless, the number and variety of the references in the text show that he has left no source of information untapped. His book gives not only an accurate chronicle of the course of events but also some account of those who played a part in them and of the atmosphere in which they trained and fought.

Future generations of engineers seeking to know how these large formations of engineer troops were raised and trained in so short a time, and how they confronted the tasks which they were called upon to perform, will find the answers interestingly and vividly recorded in these pages. They will learn with pride of the ready acceptance of responsibility and the undaunted resolution of those who trained and led these units, and of the fine courage, imperturbable cheerfulness and unquestioning loyalty of the men. They will read with professional pride of the great resources in engineer personnel, machines and material which were organized and controlled, and of the wide range of technical difficulties successfully overcome. They will find here grounds for confidence that if they maintain and enhance the traditions they have inherited they need not fear comparison with the military engineers of any other nation.

Throughout the Second World War, British, Indian and Pakistani engineers served together in the same units and formations until they separated on Independence Day to serve their own free and independent countries. The author rightly takes the partnership for granted, for, strange as it may seem to future generations, the partnership was widespread and genuine. Officers and men were proud of their Corps because there existed between them a bond of affection and the comradeship of arms. Each respected the traditions of the other; each held the other in esteem. Many longed for Independence, but the partnership which had developed over many years held firm under the strenuous and searching test of war and was dissolved only when political considerations made a breach inevitable.

The joint endeavours of the last years of this partnership are here faithfully recorded, and it is fortunate that this has been done by so competent and experienced an historian. It is a record of which all who were privileged to share in the partnership may justly be proud; a record of boldly conceived plans, of tactical and technical brilliance, of boundless energy in execution and patient endurance under difficulties, of military engineering on a vast scale, of personal courage and of ungrudging service.

Roorkee,
August 19th, 1956.

PREFACE

EVERY military historian faces a serious dilemma. Should he compile a detailed record in the current official style which many may consult but few will read? Or should he concentrate rather on describing great achievements or gallant deeds in battle which will attract and hold the attention of all? In this volume I have tried to strike a mean by coating the pill of facts, figures and dates with the sugar of adventure and occasional humorous anecdote and thus to produce something more than a book of reference. Any record of engineering exploits in the field loses half its value unless provided with a background showing the purpose of the operations. Hence I have felt bound to deal occasionally with matters of strategy and tactics or even to encroach upon the dangerous ground of policy. After all, engineering in war is no more than a means to an end. That end is victory. And victory can be secured only through the achievements of all arms in combination.

Nearly thirteen years have elapsed since the question of a sequel to *The Indian Sappers and Miners* was first raised in January 1944. The writing of the latter volume, which I had begun in February 1938, was shelved in March 1940 in the interests of war work. It was resumed in March 1944 and finished in August 1947, but meanwhile the subject of a sequel had been revived. Early in 1945, the British Commandants of the three Engineer Groups in India considered the proposal and decided that, if a sequel was written, the author should be a serving officer of one of the Groups. Much to my disappointment I was informed accordingly that my services would not be required. However, no serving officer could be found who was prepared to attempt the task and in consequence the scheme remained in abeyance for more than three years. In July 1948, after I had been invited to write the history of The West Yorkshire Regiment in the Second World War, I thought it might be well to afford the Indian Commandants of the three Groups an opportunity to reconsider the decision reached by their British predecessors. They agreed that I should write a sequel, but unfortunately my negotiations with The West Yorkshire Regiment were so advanced when the reply arrived from India that I was obliged to suggest a postponement until the West Yorkshire history had been completed. The prospects of a sequel to *The Indian Sappers and Miners* then seemed rather dim. Nevertheless, in September 1949 the Commandants agreed that I should write the sequel after I had completed *From Pyramid to Pagoda*. That occurred in April 1951, and in October 1951 I wrote the first words of *The Indian Engineers, 1939-47*. Six chapters dealing mostly with the Middle East, North Africa and Italy were finished by April 1953, and the remaining nine chapters on Burma, Malaya and post-War India, by September 1955. Thus the actual writing of the narrative occupied about four years although the project had been under consideration for more than seven years previously.

In India the moving spirit throughout has been Lieut.-General Sir Harold Williams who was mainly concerned in the revival of the project and, as Engineer-in-Chief, in co-ordinating and supervising its progress. My thanks are due to Mr. H. A. Cordery, Librarian and Archivist of the Historical Section of the Cabinet Office, for affording me office accommodation while in London and allowing me to consult hundreds of War Diaries. The Mapping Section under Colonel T. M. M. Penney has also given me valuable assistance. All the maps have been drawn by me and faired by Captain A. C. Jenner. A number of them have appeared already in *From Pyramid to Pagoda* and have been reproduced by kind permission of The West Yorkshire Regiment. In order to avoid a bulky end pocket, each chapter has been given its relevant maps. The Appendices have been written by the Commandants of the Groups in India, and the Index has been compiled by Lieut.-Colonel E. E. N. Sandeman, Head Librarian of the R.E. Corps Library at Chatham, from which I have had many books on loan. I am indebted to Major-General R. P. Pakenham-Walsh for allowing me to consult several documents used by him in writing the latest volumes of *The History of the Corps of Royal Engineers*, and my thanks are due also to Brigadier C. C. Phipps, Secretary of the Institution of Royal Engineers, for managing the financial and other arrangements in England and for undertaking much correspondence in connection with the work. Under the supervision of Major K. O. Stiffle, Secretary of the Institution of Military Engineers, the printing and publication of this history have been carried out very efficiently by the small Press forming part of the College of Military Engineering in Kirkee.

Finally I should like to acknowledge the help given by some officers of the Royal or Indian Engineers and particularly by the following who forwarded personal notes :— Lieut.-General Sir Lionel Bond;

Major-General C. de L. Gaussen; Brigadiers L. O. Clark, R. E. Holloway, Partap Narain, C. R. Mangat Rai, A. McGregor Stewart and B. E. Whitman; Colonels Arjan Singh, D. B. Chopra, T. H. F. Foulkes, G. F. Hutchinson, M. M. Jeakes, R. A. Loomba and Shamsher Singh; Lieut.-Colonels G. A. Clayton, J. R. Connor, R. Dinwiddie, J. R. S. W. Elkington, A. G. Hellicar, Kuldip Singh, A. F. Toogood, B. P. Wadhera and J. B. Wilson; Majors W. B. J. Armstrong, T. D. Badhani, T. Beaumont, P. M. Bennett, N. H. Bower, J. F. Butlin, O. Callaghan, J. H. Clark, D. De Souza, L. S. Dubashi, R. C. Gabriel, B. G. Goodier, G. Horne, P. M. Leslie-Jones, D. W. McGrath, B. D. Neame, A. B. Rhodes and A. H. W. Sandes; Captains G. M. Birse, R. Kiff and T. Le M. Spring-Smyth; and the Rev. R. T. Urwin, formerly a Major R.E.

As a Bengal Sapper and Miner in the First World War I commanded men who were the forbears of some of the Indian Engineers figuring in this narrative; and between the two World Wars, until I left India in 1930, I was in close touch with the Bengal Sappers at Roorkee. It is sad therefore to have reached the end of a long story about those whose ancestors I knew so well. Methods and conditions of warfare have changed out of all recognition since the far off days of 1914-18; yet I hope that I have shown that the Indian Sapper remains the same—a brave and intelligent soldier, upholding the traditions which he has inherited and ready to meet any emergency which the future may hold in store.

E. W. C. SANDES

Ryelands,
   Weymouth.
October 19*th*, 1956.

CONTENTS

CHAPTER I
INDIA 1939-43

Pre-War conditions in India—Roorkee News Letters (1939-40)—History of Indianization—Increased responsibilities of Sapper units—Expansion during Second World War—S & M Groups—Recruitment—A.I.R.O.—O.C.T.Us.—E.O.T.S. established—Formation of Engineer Training Centres (1940)—History of Transportation Services—Transportation Training Centres—Transportation units—Survey Group—Military Engineer Services—Mobilization in 1939—Many units despatched overseas (1940)—New units raised (1941-42)—S & M Groups adopt suffix "Indian Engineers" (1942)—Subsequent changes in title—Regimental Centres—N.W. Frontier operations (1940-41)—Indian States Sappers—Bangalore (1941-43)—Roorkee News Letters (1942-43)   1

CHAPTER II
EGYPT, THE WESTERN DESERT, THE SUDAN AND ERITREA, OCTOBER 1939 - MAY 1941

Indian Divs sent overseas in 1939—Gen. Wavell in Middle East—4th Div (Gen. Heath) in Egypt—4th Div Engrs train in Nile Delta—First Libyan Campaign—Gen. Wavell attacks Italians in Western Desert (June '40)— Defeats Marshal Graziani—Italian counter-offensive (Sept. '40)—Matruh fortified—Second Libyan Campaign—Gen. O'Connor attacks Marshal Graziani (Dec. '40)—Battle of Sidi Barrani—Italians defeated—Sollum and Tobruk occupied—O'Connor advances beyond Benghazi—Work of 4th Div Engrs—Experiences of 12 Fd Coy—4th Div transferred to Sudan to reinforce 5th Div (Jan. '41)—Voyage of 5th Div Engrs from India (Sept. '40)—5th Div on Atbara R.—"Gazelle Force" under Col. Messervy—10th Bde under Brig. Slim—Engineer work—Gen. Platt invades Eritrea (Jan. '41)—2nd Lt. P. S. Bhagat, I.E., wins V.C. near Gondar—Exploits of 2, 4 and 12 Fd Coys—4th Div (Gen. Beresford-Peirse) held up at Keren (Feb. '41)—Battle of Keren—4th and 5th Divs penetrate Keren Gorge (March '41)—Sappers clear obstacles—Battle of Ad Teclesan—Asmara and Massawa occupied—5th Div (Gen. Mayne) takes Amba Alagi (May '41)—Duke of Aosta surrenders all Italian forces in Eritrea—Operations of African Divs under Gen. Cunningham from Kenya—Third Libyan Campaign—Afrika Korps under Gen. Rommel attacks with Italian support in Western Desert (April '41)—Gens. O'Connor and Neame, V.C., captured—Tobruk isolated—Rommel halts at Egyptian frontier—4th Div Engrs at Sollum—Fate of 35 Fd Sqn—5th Div arrives from Eritrea—Failures in Greece and Crete   20

CHAPTER III
THE LEVANT, IRAQ AND PERSIA, 1941-46

10th Div (Gen. Fraser) lands in Iraq (April '41)—Germans capture Crete—Hitler invades Russia (June '41)—Col. Roberts defends Habbaniya on Euphrates against Iraqis—Iraq Campaign ends (June '41)—Work of 10th Div Engrs—More I.E. units reach Iraq—Campaign in Syria against Vichy French—Gen. Maitland Wilson takes Damascus—French Gen. Dentz surrenders (July '41)—10th Div (Gen. Slim) sent to Persia—41 Fd Pk Coy in advance up Euphrates—Life in S. Iraq—Campaign in Persia—8th Div (Gen. Harvey) advances to Ahwaz (Aug. '41)—Work of 8th Div Engrs—Shatt-al-Arab floating bridge at Basra—Teheran entered (Sept. '41)—6th Div (Gen. Thomson) arrives in Iraq—Work of Sapper units in Persia—Defensive area prepared around Mosul by 8th Div Engrs and 3rd Corps Tps Engrs—Other Sapper units build defences elsewhere—Experiences of 52 A.T. Coy—"Paiforce" formed—Middle East situation (Sept. '42)—Ind. Railway units on Trans-Iranian Railway—Americans take over charge (Dec. '42)—5 Fd Coy in Iraq and Persia—Amusing incidents—Benga Sapper units in Gulf of Oman (Dec. '43)—Most I.E. units leave Iraq (1944)—Employment in Cyprus—Det. of 9 Fd Coy lost in Dodecanese Is. (Oct. '43)—Experiences in Syria (1945)—4th Div Engrs in Greece (1944-45) 51

CHAPTER IV
THE WESTERN DESERT, MAY 1941 - AUGUST 1942

4th Div Engrs in Bagush (May '41)—Western Desert Force prepares to attack (June '41)—Battle of Sollum—Attack fails—Gen. Wavell transferred to India as C.-in-C.—Succeeded in Middle East by Gen. Auchinleck—Bagush defences strengthened—70th (Br) Div holds Tobruk—Eighth Army formed under Gen. Cunningham (Nov. '41)—Composed of 15th Corps (Gen. Godwin-Austin) and 30th Corps (Gen. Norrie)—German-Italian army under Gen. Rommel much superior in armour and A/T guns—Fourth Libyan Campaign—Cunningham attacks (Nov. '41)—Checked by German armour—Gen. Cunningham replaced by Gen. Ritchie—Tobruk relieved—Rommel withdraws beyond Benghazi (Jan. '42)—Fifth Libyan Campaign—Rommel attacks—He recaptures Benghazi but halts on Gazala Line—Sappers destroy crippled enemy tanks—Minelaying on Gazala Line—Experiences of 4 and 12 Fd Coys—5th Div Engrs fortify El Alamein Line (July '41)—20 Fd Coy sent to Iraq and Cyprus—2 and 21 Fd Coys remain—18 Fd Coy in action near Tobruk (Dec. '41)—Gen. Messervy appointed Comdr, 1st (Br) Armoured Div (Jan. '42)—Country around Benghazi—M.T. in bad condition—12 Fd Coy in actions beyond Benghazi—5th Div Engrs in Tobruk Area—Sixth Libyan Campaign—Rommel attacks Gazala Line (May '42)—Capture and escape of Gen. Messervy—Tank battles around "Knightsbridge"—Our tanks outmatched—Gen. Ritchie orders withdrawal beyond Egyptian frontier—Gen. Auchinleck takes personal command in field—Tobruk garrison surrenders (June 21st, '42)—Rommel by-passes Matruh but halts before Alamein Line (June 30th)—Engineer units in retreat—31 Fd Sqn overrun—Experiences of 2 and 4 Fd Coys and 41 Fd Pk Coy—9 and 61 Fd Coys at Matruh—10 Fd Coy suffers heavily in break-out—61 Fd Coy suffers also—Lt.-Col. Saegert captured—Italian treatment of prisoners—20, 21, 58 and 66 Fd Coys at work on defences (July' 42)—El Alamein Line strengthened—5th Div on Ruweisat Ridge—Mr. Winston Churchill visits Western Desert (Aug. 5th)—Gen. Montgomery appointed Comdr., Eighth Army—Gen. Alexander succeeds Gen. Auchinleck as C.-inC., Middle East—Montgomery reorganizes Eighth Army—Engineer units trained in minelaying and minelifting 82

CHAPTER V
THE WESTERN DESERT AND NORTH-WEST AFRICA, AUGUST 1942 - MAY 1943

Gen. Rommel attacks El Alamein Defence Line (Aug. '42)—Battle of Alam-el-Halfa—German armour thrusts towards coast—Operation fails with heavy loss—Rommel withdraws (Sept. 3rd)—5th Div Engrs strengthen Ruweisat positions—Relieved by 4th Div Engrs—Rommel flies to Berlin to consult Hitler—Enemy reinforcements checked by Allied air and sea superiority—Eighth Army strongly reinforced—Gen. Montgomery prepares to attack with 10th, 13th and 30th Corps—Enemy now under Gen. Von Stumme—Montgomery's message to his troops—Seventh Libyan Campaign—Battle of El Alamein opens (Oct. 23rd, 1942)—Vast artillery bombardment—30th and 10th Corps advance in northern sector—Gen. Von Stumme killed—Replaced by Gen. Von Thoma—13th Corps in southern sector—Rommel arrives from Berlin (Oct. 27th)—He counter-attacks in north—Montgomery regroups Eighth Army—30th Corps resumes offensive in north (Nov. 2nd)—Last minefields penetrated—10th (Armoured) Corps pours through gap—German armour defeated—Von Thoma captured—Enemy routed—Pursuit begins (Nov. 5th)—I.E. units open gaps in minefields and destroy abandoned enemy tanks—Diary of 12 Fd Coy—Methods of mine clearance—Problems of pursuit—I.E. units kept at El Alamein clearing up battlefield—9 Fd Coy lifts mines along Tobruk railway—Matruh reoccupied (Nov. 6th)—Heavy rain interferes with pursuit—Panzer Divs escape—Tobruk reoccupied (Nov. 13th)—Benghazi entered (Nov. 20th)—Rommel halts at El

Agheila—He resumes retreat into Tripolitania (Dec. 11th)—British - American First Army already landed in Tunisia—115 Railway Coy, I.E., on Tobruk Railway—7th Armoured Div enters Tripoli (Jan. 23rd, '43)—4th Div Engrs in Benghazi—They follow towards Tripoli—German booby-traps—Mr. Winston Churchill at Tripoli (Feb. 3rd)—Rommel retreats into Tunisia—He tries to prevent junction of Eighth and First Armies—He fails and turns back to face Eighth Army—He occupies Mareth Line in Tripolitania—German armour attacks 51st Div and 7th Armoured Div at Medinine (March 6th)—Attack repulsed—Montgomery assaults Mareth Line (March 20th)—50th Div fails at Wadi Zigzaou—Left hook by 2nd N.Z. Div outflanks Mareth Line—Advance of 4th Div through mountains—Exploits of 4 and 12 Fd Coys at Wadi Zigzaou—Lt.-Col. Blundell—4 Fd Coy in Hallouf Pass—Gen. Montgomery attacks enemy under Gen. Messe at Wadi Akarit (April 5th)—Lt. Col. Blundell mortally wounded—Brig. Kisch (C.E. 30th Corps) killed—Germans withdraw—Wholesale surrender of Italians—Eighth and First Armies link up—Montgomery captures Enfidaville (April 20th)—Axis forces, now under Gen. Von Arnim, reinforced from Sicily—Gen. Alexander commands all forces in Tunisia as Gen. Eisenhower's deputy—4th Div in new 9th Corps (Gen. Horrocks)—Allies capture Tunis and Bizerta (May 7th)—Von Arnim withdraws to Cape Bon (May 9th)—4th Div Engrs in final operations—German capitulation (May 11th)—F.M. Alexander on Tunisian Campaign—4th Div moves back towards Egypt—Review by King George VI at Tripoli (June 19th)—4th Div Engrs reach Alexandria (July 8th, '43) .. .. ,. .. .. ..· 110

CHAPTER VI
ITALY, 1943 - 45

Plans for invasion of S. Europe—Invasion of Sicily and Italy by Eighth Army and American Seventh Army (Gen. Patton) approved—Gen. Alexander in chief command—Air-borne landing in Sicily (July 9th, '43)—Sea-borne invasion (July 10th)—Patton occupies Palermo (July 22nd)—Montgomery checked at Catania—Patton enters Messina (Aug. 16th)—Germans escape to Italy—Mussolini resigns—Marshal Badoglio agrees to Italian surrender—Germans pour 13 divisions into Italy—F.M. Rommel in command in north—F.M. Kesselring in south—Eighth Army crosses Messina Straits into Italy (Sept. 3rd)—Invasion of Italy by Eighth Army under Gen. Montgomery and American-British Fifth Army under American Gen. Mark Clark—Eighth Army to advance up east coast—Fifth Army (American 6th Corps and British 10th Corps) to land on west coast and capture Naples—Natural obstacles—Inadequate communications—Air-borne Div lands at Taranto and Fifth Army at Salerno (Sept. 9th)—Eighth Army moves up Adriatic coast—British 10th Corps occupies Naples (Oct. 1st)—Kesselring withdraws to Volturno R.—Fifth Army attacks (Oct. 12th)—Kesselring retires to Garigliano R.—Alexander aims at Rome—Fifth Army Engrs begin to restore Naples—Work of Eighth Army Engrs—List of I.E. units in Italy—8th Div Engrs land at Taranto (Sept. 24th, '43)—Arrive near 'Gustav' Line, south of Biferno R.—7 Fd Coy bridges Biferno—Trigno R. crossing—Sangro R. reached—Eighth Army captures Sangro (Nov. 28th)—8th Div Engrs bridge flooded Sangro R.—'Montgomery' Bailey bridge—Russian Mission—Eighth Army crosses Moro R. (Dec. 10th)—"Impossible Bridge" built by 69 Fd Coy—Mr. Winston Churchill visits front—Changes in high commands—Gen. Eisenhower transferred to U.K. as Supreme Commander for Allied invasion of France—Gen. Montgomery follows to command 21st Army Group—Gen. Maitland Wilson succeeds Eisenhower in Mediterranean—Gen. Leese appointed Eighth Army Commander—Montgomery's farewell message (Dec. 31st)—4th Div Engrs arrive in Taranto (Dec. 8th)—Move north of Sangro R.—Fifth Army operations—American 6th Corps (3rd U.S. and 5th British Divs) and British 10th Corps involved—No I.E. units present—Plans for Anzio landing—Attack across Garigliano on 'Gustav' Line—Anzio landing (Jan. 22nd, '44)—6th Corps held up—Bitter fighting at Cassino on Rapido R.—Reinforcements from Eighth Army—4th Div at Cassino—Diary of 21 Fd Coy—Subedar Subramaniam, 11 Fd Pk Coy, wins George Cross (Feb. 24th)—Bridging under fire by 8th Div Engrs on Rapido R.—Polish troops storm Cassino Monastery (June '44)—'Gustav' and 'Hitler' Lines broken—Fifth Army occupies Rome (June 4th)—Allied landings reported in Normandy—General advance towards 'Gothic' Line—Rapid bridging by 8th Div Engrs—10th Div Engrs arrive in

Italy (Feb. '44)—Move to Ortona on east coast in April—Other I.E. units present—10th Div transferred to west coast (June 22nd)—Then to Perugia region—German mines—Mine detection by 10 Fd Coy—Exciting adventures—Ten divisions ordered from Italy to France—Advance towards 'Gothic' Line retarded—Eighth Army masses on Adriatic coast—4th, 8th and 10th Divs begin Operation "Vandal" (Aug. 3rd)—5 Fd Coy rescues Italian Countess—"Lovers' Lane"—Eighth Army assaults 'Gothic' Line (Aug. 26th)—Fifth Army attacks south of Pisa—Kesselring abandons positions—Alexander reaches R. Po plain (Sept. 21st)—Employment of I.E. units—'Houdini' submersible bridge—Repair of mountain roads—4 Fd Coy bridges Rubicon R.—8th and 10th Div Engrs in the Apennines (1944-45)—Much Bailey bridging—Eighth Army enters Faenza (Dec. 15th)—Halts on Senio R.—Fifth Army south of Bologna—Country flooded—Eighth Army crosses Senio (April 10th, '45)—Bridging by 2nd N.Z. Div Engrs—8th Div Engrs at Santerno crossing (April 12th)—2nd N.Z. Div and Eighth Army reach Po R. (April 23rd/24th)—Po crossed by rafting—Advanced troops arrive on Adige R.—German resistance now negligible—8th Div Engrs build F.B. bridge across Adige (April 29th)—Padua occupied—13th Corps enters Trieste (May 2nd)—5th Corps already in Venice—Complete victory attained—Decorations won by Sapper officers—Adventures of Lt. Shamsher Singh in Italy—Work of I.E. units after German capitulation—Last I.E. unit (97 Fd Coy) leaves Italy (Nov. '45)—Gen. Alexander's farewell message 140

CHAPTER VII
MALAYA, 1941-42

Losses of Bombay Group in Singapore surrender—Singapore defences in 1941—Nature of Malayan Peninsula—Situation in Far East after First World War—Naval base started at Singapore—Defences designed only against sea-borne attack—Remainder of Malaya virtually undefended—Haphazard progress of defences—Air forces expected to guard Singapore against land attack—Japan withdraws from League of Nations (April 1933)—Col. Dobson improves sea-ward defences of Singapore Island—Three aerodromes built on east coast of Malaya—Gen. Dobbie appointed G.O.C. Malaya (Nov. '35)—Col. Perceval as G.S.O.I—Dobbie envisages probable land attack from north—He plans defensive zone north of Singapore I.—Gen. Dobbie succeeded by Gen. L. V. Bond (1939)—Singapore sea-defences completed—Defence policy against Japan based on prompt arrival of British fleet—Period extended to 180 days—Consequent need to hold Thailand frontier with 2½ divisions—Reliance placed on French in Indo-China—Malaya garrison only one division—12th Ind. Inf. Bde arrives with 15 Fd Coy (Aug. '39)—Brig. Partap Narain describes Sapper work—War declared on Germany (Sept. 3rd, 1939)—Vichy French admit Jap troops to Indo-China (Sept. '40)—Two Bdes of 11th Ind. Div. (Gen. Murray-Lyon) arrive Singapore (Nov. '40)—8th Australian Div (Gen. Gordon Bennett) begins to arrive (Feb. '41)—Two Bdes, 9th Ind. Div. (Gen. Barstow) reach Singapore (April '41)—3rd Ind. Corps in Malaya commanded by Gen. Heath—Troops untrained in jungle warfare—Equipment unsuitable—Few A/A guns or aircraft—No tanks—Defence schemes prepared—Many I.E. units arrive (1940-41)—Mostly Bombay Sappers—Brig. Simson, C.E. Malaya Command—Brig. K. B. S. Crawford, C.E. 3rd Corps—Lt.-Col. Lindesay, C.R.E. 9th Div Engrs—Lt.-Col. Steedman, C.R.E. 11th Div Engrs—Australian Engrs and Fortress Engrs—Frontier Operation 'Matador' planned—Jitra defence line started in N. Kedah—9th Div Engrs on east coast beach defences—11th Div Engrs on frontier defence work—War against Japan appears imminent (Nov. '41)—Jitra Line incomplete—Jap planes sink U.S. fleet at Pearl Harbour in Hawaii Is. (Dec. 7th, 1941)—War declared forthwith—Japs attack Hongkong—Surrender of Hongkong (Dec. 25th)—Experiences of Lt.-Col. J. B. Wilson, R.E.—Jap forces in Indo-China and Thailand (Dec. 8th)—Landings on E. coast of Malaya—Operation 'Matador' cancelled—I.E. units on raids into Thailand—Bridge demolitions—Withdrawal of 11th Div—9th Div evacuates Kota Bahru (Dec. 9th)—Withdraws from Kelantan State—Diary of 1 A.W. Coy—Jap equipment and tactics—Gen. Perceval, G.O.C. Malaya, describes situation—Jitra Line crumbles—Demolitions by 11th Div Engrs—Jitra Line abandoned (Dec. 12th)—H.M.S. *Prince of Wales* and H.M.S. *Repulse* sunk by enemy aircraft (Dec. 10th)—Withdrawal of 11th Div continues—Muda R. bridge destroyed by 46 A.T. Coy—17 Fd Coy at Perak R. bridge (Dec. 22nd)—Battle of Kampar

CONTENTS   xix

begins (Dec. 28th)—Jap landings on west coast—Kampar evacuated (Jan. 3rd '42)—3 Fd Coy at Dipang bridge—9th Div withdrawing down east coast—Kuantan airfield abandoned (Jan. 4th)—22nd Bde reaches Jerantut (Jan. 7th)—Exploits of 22 Fd Coy—Ferry demolition—11th Div reaches Slim R. (Jan. 6th)—Suffers heavily in Slim R. battle—Enemy advances through Kuala Lumpur against 8th Australian Div on Johore State border—Australians defend Muar R. positions (Jan..15th-19th)—Positions abandoned after heavy losses—13 Fd Coy almost wiped out—Jap brutality to prisoners—Batu Pahat and Mersing abandoned (Jan. 26th)—Kluang airfield lost—Withdrawal ordered to Singapore Island (Jan. 26th)—Brig. Paris organizes defences—Engineer work on defences—Distribution of defence forces—Final Jap offensive begins (Feb. 8th)—Enemy cross Johore Strait into N.W. Sector—They capture vital water reservoirs (Feb. 10th)—Composite Engineer Bn formed—Retirement to Singapore Town (Feb. 13th)—Positions violently attacked—Gen. Perceval surrenders Singapore to Japanese (Feb. 15th, 1942)—Subsequent adventures of 2nd Lt. M. M. Pillai, I.E.—Escape of two ships—Disastrous effect of loss of Singapore   175

CHAPTER VIII
RETREAT FROM BURMA, DECEMBER 1941 - MAY 1942

Japanese invade S. Tenasserim (Dec. 14th, 1941)—Rangoon bombed (Dec. 23rd)—Gen. Chiang Kai-Shek sends Chinese armies into Toungoo region under American Gen. Stilwell—1st Burma Div (Gen. Bruce-Scott) defends eastern frontier—Mergui and Tavoy evacuated (Jan. 17th, '42)—17th Ind. Div (Gen. Smyth, V.C.) reinforces 1st Burma Div—16th Bde at Martaban—46th Bde at Bilin—2nd Burma Bde at Moulmein—Japs attack Moulmein (Jan. 30th)—Moulmein evacuated—17th Div on Salween R. line—Japs push up Salween—Martaban evacuated (Feb. 9th)—Enemy cross Salween—17th Div withdraws to Kyaikto and Bilin R.—Gen. Wavell approves further withdrawal to Sittang R. line (Feb. 19th)—Poor communications—Australia refuses to send reinforcements to Burma—I.E. units in early operations—1st Burma Div Engrs (Lt.-Col. Swan)—17th Ind. Div Engrs (Lt.-Col. Ward)—Ferrying at Moulmein by 60 Fd Coy—18 A.W. Coy during withdrawal—Demolitions by Malerkotla Fd Coy—Gen. Smyth orders demolition of Sittang R. bridge—Bridge demolished by Malerkotla Fd Coy (Feb. 23rd)—Troops remaining on Mokpalin bank swim across—Lt.-Col. Orgill describes demolition—Problem confronting Gen. Smyth—Gen. Cowan assumes command of 17th Div—Gen. Alexander replaces Gen. Hutton in chief command (March 4th)—Alexander orders counter-offensive—Japs penetrate to Pegu—Evacuation of Rangoon—Alexander plans withdrawal up Irrawaddy R. to Prome—70 Fd Coy in withdrawal—Lack of explosives and M.T.—Japs enter Rangoon (March 8th)—Gen. Slim appointed Comdr 1st Burma Corps (March 19th)—Corps redesignated later '4th Ind Corps'—Subsequent career of Gen. Slim—Allied air force destroyed near Prome (March 21st)—Defeat of Chinese armies—Enemy occupy Toungoo (March 29th) and Prome (April 1st)—Mandalay suffers air raid—Burma Corps covers Yenangyaung oilfields—Work of Burma Div Engrs—Diary of 60 Fd Coy during retreat—Experiences of 24 Fd Coy and 18 A.W. Coy—Burma Corps evacuates Allanmyo and Thayetmyo (April 6th)—Operations north of Yenangyaung—Oilfields destroyed—Gen. Alexander continues withdrawal northwards—Chinese again defeated in Shan States—Japs occupy Mandalay—70 Fd Coy destroys bridges at Kyaukse (April 29th)—24 Fd Coy blows Ava Bridge (April 30th)—Malerkotlas at Monywa—Story of dog "Gemma"—60 and 70 Fd Coys in withdrawal to Shwegyin—Gen. Cowan crosses Chindwin R. at Kalewa (May 10th)—Troops march towards Tamu—Road choked by refugees—Diary of 24 Fd Coy—Unit reaches Kanglatongbi beyond Imphal (May 18th)—Joined by other I.E. units—Work of 59 Fd Coy on Tamu Road—Burma Army under Gen. Alexander dissolved (May 20th, '42)—4th Ind Corps under Gen. Slim assumes control   210

CHAPTER IX
THE BUILD-UP IN ASSAM, JUNE 1942 - MARCH 1944

Situation at Imphal in May 1942—Stalemate during ensuing monsoon—Gen. Wavell plans counter-offensive—Tehri-Garhwal Fd Coy on Tamu Road—114 Works Bn repairs Imphal damage—Det. 91 Fd Coy ordered to Fort Hertz—Order cancelled—Det. 71 Fd Coy at Fort Hertz—Bridging on Lokchao R.—Tamu Road opened (Dec. '42)—Elephants assist in bridging—Alternative routes to Chindwin R.—Difficulties of Tiddim route—Brahmaputra L. of C.—Air supply—Airfield construction—G.R.E.F. formed—362 Fd Coy prepares airfield—4th Corps Engrs extend Tamu Road—Operations of Gen. Orde Wingate's 'Chindits' (March '43)—Myitkyina Railway cut—Chindits withdrawn (June '43)—Bengal Sappers on Tamu Road—Madras and Bombay Sappers in Tamu area—24 Fd Coy builds first Bailey bridge—Organization of work on Tamu Road—Brig. Partap Narain describes conditions and methods—Changes in higher commands —Gen. Wavell appointed Viceroy (June '43)—Gen. Auchinleck becomes C.-in-C., India—Creation of S.E.A.C. under Admiral Lord Mountbatten—Tiddim route given priority—Exercise "Navvy"—Tehri-Garhwal Fd Coy builds Manipur R. bridge—17th Div Engrs in Exercise "Navvy"—Description by Brig. Horsfield, C.E. Fourteenth Army—Experiences of 70 Fd Coy—Tiddim Road opened to Manipur R. (May 1st, '43)—West Yorkshires on Tiddim Road—Extension towards Tiddim—Manipur R. suspension bridge—Lord Mountbatten arrives in Delhi (Oct. 7th, '43)—Contacts Americans in China—Visits Imphal—Eastern Army (Gen. Giffard) split into Eastern Command, India (Gen. Mayne) and Fourteenth Army, Burma (Gen. Slim)—Gen. Giffard to command 11th Army Group including Fourteenth Army—Fourteenth Army comprises 4th Corps (Gen. Scoones) and 15th Corps (Gen. Christison)—Mountbatten decides on land offensive into Burma during monsoon—Disposition of forces—Gen. Wingate's L.R.P. Force (formerly Chindits)—I.E. 'Special Sections' formed for L.R.P. Force but not used—Japanese dispositions in Burma—Thailand-Burma 'Railway of Death'—Enemy plans for invasion of India—4th Corps (17th, 20th and 23rd Divs) on Manipur front—Progress of Americans and Chinese (Gen. Stilwell) along Ledo Road—33rd Jap Div begins offensive against 17th Ind Div on Tiddim Road (Oct. '43)—Brig. Partap Narain on experiences of 428 Fd Coy—Tiddim water-supply scheme—Method of demolishing enemy bunkers—70 Fd Coy in close fighting—Brig. Partap Narain on action near Kennedy Peak—Sapper gallantry—Engineer build-up in Assam and Arakan (Dec. '43)—4th Corps awaits enemy offensive in Manipur—15th Corps attacks in Arakan (Jan. '44)—Wingate's L.R.P. Force lands in Upper Burma by air (Feb. '44)—Wingate killed in air crash (March 24th)—Gen. Lentaigne assumes command—Jap offensive against Imphal launched (March 8th, '44)—17th Div (Gen. Cowan) retires from Tiddim—5th Div summoned by air from Arakan—17th Div almost cut off—20th Div withdraws up Tamu Road—33rd Jap Div advances up Tiddim Road—15th Jap Div up Tamu Road—31st Jap Div makes right hook against Kohima in rear—Japanese so-called 'March on Delhi' begins 240

CHAPTER X
ARAKAN, 1942-45

First Arakan Campaign (1942-43)—Dense jungle—Heavy rainfall—Bad communications—14th Ind. Div (Gen. Lloyd) occupies Maungdaw and Buthidaung (Oct. '42)—Engineer units available—Diary of 26 Fd Coy—14th Div advances down Mayu Peninsula (Dec. '42)—Re-occupation of Akyab planned—Work of I.E. units—Maungdaw-Buthidaung Road—'Tunnels' Section—Razabil Fortress—14th Div consolidates south of road (Dec. 27th)—47th Bde attacks Donbaik positions and fails (Jan. 18th, '43)—123rd Bde repulsed at Rathedaung (Feb. 3rd)—55th Bde fails at Donbaik (Feb. 17th)—Japs under Col. Tanahashi begin counter-offensive—6th (British) Bde repulsed at Donbaik (March 18th)—26th Ind. Div (Gen. Lomax) relieves 14th Div—Gen. Wavell admits responsibility for failure—Withdrawal to Maungdaw-Buthidaung Road—Maungdaw evacuated (May 13th)—Withdrawal to Bawli Bazar—Experiences of 74 Fd Coy—26th Div Engrs take over—Diary of 26 Fd Coy—28 Fd Coy leaves Buthidaung (May 7th)—Roadmaking during monsoon—Sappers take part in raids—26th Div relieved by 7th Ind. Div (Gen. Messervy)—26th Div moves into Kalapanzin Valley (Sept. '43)—5th Ind. Div (Gen. Briggs) arrives at front—Gen. Christison (15th Corps) plans to recapture Maungdaw-Buthidaung Road—5th Div on coast —7th Div in Kalapanzin Valley—81st West African Div further inland—25th and 26th Ind. Divs in support—36th (British) Div in reserve—62 and 77 Fd Coys improve Ngakyedauk Pass lateral track—Second Arakan Campaign—Offensive by 15th Corps—5th Div occupies Maungdaw (Jan. 9th, '44)—74 Fd Coy at

Razabil Fortress—7th Div advances on Buthidaung—Checked at Letwedet—
Japs launch counter-offensive—'Tanahashi Force' advances up Kalapanzin R.—
15th Corps Forward Base at Sinzweya threatened—7th Div HQ overrun at
Laungtaung (Feb. 6th)—Admin. Box at Sinzweya prepared for defence—62 and
303 Fd Coys and 17 Bridging Section present in Box—Admin. Box invested—
"Ascot Car Park"—"Blood Nullah"—Life in Admin. Box—123rd Bde (5th Div)
arrives through Ngakyedauk Pass—Siege ends (Feb. 22nd)—Work of I.E.
units with Relief Forces—7th Div recaptures Buthidaung (March 11th)—5th
Div takes Maungdaw and Razabil—25th Div (Gen. Davies) replaces 5th and
7th Divs at front during monsoon—26th Div in reserve—Goppe Pass ropeway—
425 Fd Coy on Maungdaw-Buthidaung Road—Sappers demolish bunkers—
63 and 425 Fd Coys cut tracks—Third Arakan Campaign—Gen. Christison
resumes offensive (Dec. '44)—15th Corps advances down Mayu Peninsula and
valleys to east—25th Div (Gen. Wood) on coast—51st Bde (Brig. Thimayya)
reaches Foul Point (Dec. 25th)—Rafting by 63 and 425 Fd Coys on Kalapanzin
R.—Landings on Akyab Island (Jan. 3rd, '45)—Japanese gone—History of Indian
Beach Groups—Duties of a Beach Group—78 Fd Coy (Major Beaumont) in
41 Beach Group—Unit disembarks at Akyab (Jan. 9th)—Lt. Sandes describes
air attack on shipping—Myebon Peninsula occupied (Jan. 21st)—Landings on
Cheduba and Ramree Islands—Experiments by Lt. Sandes with Jap mines—
26th Div Engrs on Ramree Island—Improvement of airfields—Heavy fighting
at Kangaw landing (Jan. 22nd)—Enemy routed—63 Fd Coy and det. 78 Fd Coy
at Kangaw—25th Div lands at Ru-ywa (Feb. 16th)—Experiences of 425 Fd
Coy—Landing at Letpan (March 16th)—Lt. Raymond, R.E., wins V.C.—
Operation "Dracula"—26th Div (Gen. Chambers) sails from Ramree Island
for Rangoon (April 27th)—Lands in Rangoon Estuary and re-embarks (May
2nd)—Occupies Rangoon (May 4th)—28, 72, 73 and 98 Fd Coys begin repairs—
Lt. Sandes on condition of Rangoon 274

CHAPTER XI

THE DEFENCE OF IMPHAL, MARCH-JULY 1944

Japanese plans for invasion of Assam—Advance of 33rd, 15th and 31st Jap
Divs against 4th Ind Corps—23rd Div guards Imphal—Strategic advantages and
disadvantages of Imphal—17th Div begins withdrawal up Tiddim Road—Jap
tanks destroyed in minefield—Lt.-Col. A. J. R. Hill reported missing—23rd Div
helps 17th Div on Tiddim Road—Experiences of 428 Fd Coy—Jap road-blocks—
Tehri-Garhwal Fd Coy demolishes Manipur R. bridge (March 26th, '44)—
17th Div reaches Imphal (April 3rd)—Operations from Bishenpur along Silchar
track—Diary of 24 Fd Coy—24, 362 and 429 Fd Coys improve Silchar track
—Isolated by enemy—Improvised bridging—Operations of 20th Div on Tamu
Road—Japs attack Tamu (March 22nd)—20th Div withdraws to Shenam (April
5th)—92 and 424 Fd Coys in withdrawal from Moreh—Extensive demolitions—
Diary of 481 Fd Coy—402 and 429 Fd Coys in fighting at Shenam—Experiences
of 422 Fd Coy—Lt. Pearson on Bengal Sapper units at Shenam—Work of 23rd
Div Engrs—Experiments by 323 Fd Pk Coy—Withdrawal from Ukhrul—
Operations around Kohima against 31st Jap Div—5th and 7th Divs flown to
Dimapur from Arakan—Emplaning mules—33rd Ind Corps concentrates at
Dimapur (April '44)—4th Corps isolated at Imphal—Description of Kohima—
Japanese strategical error—Japs attack Kohima (April 5th)—Defence of
"Garrison" and "Summerhouse" Hills—Desperate fighting on Commissioner's
tennis court—Garrison relieved by 6th Bde, 2nd (Br) Div (April 20th)—Monument
on "Jail" Hill—31st Jap Div retreats towards Imphal—2nd (Br) Div
pursues—Work of 5th Div Engrs at Kohima—Kohima area finally cleared
(May 29th)—Sapper work during pursuit—33rd and 4th Corps meet north of
Imphal (June 22nd)—Kanglatongbi Box episode in April—Bridging by 20, 62
and 422 Fd Coys—Battles on the Tiddim Road—17th Div opposes 33rd Jap
Div—Fighting at Potsangbam (May 8th)—Heavy rain—Supplies at Imphal
almost exhausted—Imphal saved by air supply—Bitter struggle at Ningthoukhong
on Tiddim Road (July 16th)—33rd Jap Div driven out (July 16th)—Pursued
towards Tiddim—92 Fd Coy in operations near Bishenpur—Cutting hill tracks
for tanks—70 Fd Coy in outflanking march—5th Div takes over the lead in
pursuit (July '44)—5th Div Engrs repair Tiddim Road—Re-grouping of
Fourteenth Army—4th Corps and 33rd Corps to unite at Kalemyo on Chindwin
R.—Operations to continue throughout monsoon—23rd Div Engrs clear Tamu
Road—Description of modern Imphal 313

CHAPTER XII
THE ADVANCE TO MEIKTILA AND MANDALAY, AUGUST 1944 - MARCH 1945

Japanese retreating on all Burma fronts (Aug. '44)—Americans under Gen. Stilwell in Myitkyina and approaching Mogaung—Chinese armies across Salween R. and nearing eastern frontier of Burma—23rd Div and 2nd (Br) Div on Chindwin R.—11th E. African Div in Kabaw Valley—5th Div advancing down Tiddim Road—Japs killing their wounded—Hundreds dying of starvation and disease—Character of "Vinegar Joe" Stilwell—4th Corps withdrawn to India—33rd Corps to conduct pursuit—E. Africans reach Kalemyo (Nov. 15th) —I.E. units build Tamu-Kalewa Road—Role of Sappers in large river crossings —2 and 20 Fd Coys at crossing of flooded Manipur R. (Sept. '44)—5th Div occupies Tiddim (Oct. 18th)—Reaches Kalemyo (Nov. 13th)—19th Div arrives at front—Div Engrs build rafts for crossings of Chindwin R.—Ramped Cargo Lighter assembled—Kalewa boat-building yard—Chindwin fleet—Kalewa floating bridge—Difficulty of bringing boats to site—Kalewa bridge completed and opened (Dec. 10th)—Gen. Slim at bridge site—"Christmas" Bailey bridge on L. of C.—361 Fd Coy floats jeeps down Chindwin—75 Fd Coy reaches Kalewa on rafts—Changes in higher commands (Nov. 44)—Gen. Stilwell replaced by American Gen. Sultan—Gen. Leese becomes Supreme Comdr, Land Forces, Burma—Gen. Messervy takes over 4th Corps from Gen. Scoones —Gen. Stopford continues to command 33rd Corps—Lord Mountbatten's plans for the reconquest of Burma—Fourteenth Army (Gen. Slim) to invade Central Burma and capture Mandalay—Gen. Slim decides to cross Irrawaddy R. at several points south of Mandalay after 19th Div has crossed to north—Problems of advance—Operations north of Mandalay—36th (Br) Div coming down from north meets 19th Div from west (Dec. 16th)—Road transport deficient—Corduroy road-making—Sappers repair Mogaung railway—Jeep trains improvised—36th (Br) Div arrives Katha and crosses Irrawaddy on rafts—58 Fd Coy at Shweli R.—Crossing attempted at Myitson (Feb. 1st, '45)—Gallantry of Lt. Rajwade, I.E. —Crossing succeeds (Feb. 9th)—36th (Br) Div advances towards Maymyo— Sapper fleet of bamboo rafts on Indawgyi Lake—19th Div enters Shwebo (Jan. 7th, '45)—2nd (Br) Div arrives—Work of 19th Div Engrs—Story of derelict steam-roller—33rd Corps employs water-diviners—Jap mines operated by suicide men—Procedure in airstrip construction—19th Div begins crossing of Irrawaddy near Shwebo (Jan. 15th)—Experiences of 64 Fd Coy—Crossing completed by 29 and 429 Fd Coys (Feb. 16th)—19th Div advances on Mandalay —2nd (Br) Div crosses Irrawaddy at Nzagun (Feb. 23rd)—Captures Ava Fort (March 17th)—Moves towards Meiktila—20th Div crosses Chindwin R. by Kalewa bridge (Jan. '45)—Concentrates at Myinmu—Experiences of 92 Fd Coy—Mules swim rivers—"Elephant Bill" (Col. J. H. Williams) provides elephants for bridging work—422 Fd Coy ferries stores down Chindwin R.—Lt. Wright mortally wounded—20th Div begins crossing Irrawaddy R. at Myinmu (Feb. 13th)—92 Fd Coy under fire—Gallantry of Lt. Balston—Crossing completed (Feb. 27th)—20th Div advances towards Kyaukse—Ferrying at Myinmu by 481 Fd Coy—422 Fd Coy prepares exits—Kyaukse captured (March 30th)— Operations of 4th Corps (7th and 17th Divs and 255th Tank Bde)—Advance directed towards Meiktila—Elaborate methods of deception—4th Corps transferred across rear of 33rd Corps—Surprise crossing of Irrawaddy planned at Nyaungu—7th Div to lead—Sappers improve L. of C.—Drawbacks of Nyaungu site—Equipment brought by air—7th Div Engrs in approach to Irrawaddy—Equipment collected at three beaches near Nyaungu (Feb. 13th)— Trouble with sandy approaches—7th and 17th Div Engrs combine—Leading infantry paddled across in assault boats (Feb. 13th/14th)—Heavy enemy fire —Reinforcements taken across—36 Fd Sqn ferries tanks—Diary of 62 Fd Coy —Gallantry of Lt. Goodall—Crossing transferred to another beach—Difficult approaches—Sommerfeld track awaited by air—Story by Gen. Cobb—"The Irrawaddy Regatta"—4th Corps takes Taungtha and Mahlaing (Feb. 24th/25th) —Assault on Meiktila begins (Feb. 28th)—Meiktila almost cleared (March 7th)—Stories of Gen. Slim—Japs launch counter-offensive—9th Bde (5th Div) flown in (March 18th)—Meiktila cleared (March 28th)—19th Div enters outskirts of Mandalay (March 9th)—Capture of Mandalay Hill (March 11th)— Fort Dufferin bombed—Infantry assaults fail—Hole blown in wall by bombing —Fort Dufferin entered (March 20th)—Work of 19th Div Engrs—Reconnaissances—Scaling ladders—Union Jack hoisted over Fort Dufferin, Mandalay. 346

CHAPTER XIII

THE RECONQUEST AND RESTORATION OF LOWER BURMA, APRIL 1945 - OCTOBER 1947

Fourteenth Army regroups for thrust to Rangoon—Use of atom bomb against Japan approved by Cabinet (July 24th, '45)—Closely guarded secret—Gen. Slim's plans—4th Corps to move southwards from Meiktila—33rd Corps to use Irrawaddy route through Prome—Advance of mechanized 4th Corps (Gen. Messervy)—17th Div leaves Meiktila (March 30th)—5th Div follows—17th Div captures Pyawbwe (April 10th)—5th Div takes Yindaw—5th Div now assumes lead—Yamethin occupied—Shwemyo falls (April 16th)—Fighting at Shwemyo Bluff—Armour reaches Pyinmana (April 19th)—Lewe Airfield seized—Pyinmana captured (April 21st)—Armour sweeps into Toungoo (April 22nd)—Toungoo cleared (April 24th)—Airfield repair started—Armour occupies Pyu (April 25th)—17th Div resumes lead—I.E. units make airstrips—Japanese begin to evacuate Rangoon—17th Div makes for Pegu—Tanks race along main road—"Burma National Army" mops up Jap stragglers—4th Corps now on reduced rations—Jap resistance at Moyingyi Reservoir—Armour reaches Pegu (April 28th)—Bde of 17th Div occupies part of town (April 30th)—Remainder of Div continues towards Rangoon—News that 26th Div from Ramree Island is already in Rangoon (May 3rd)—Work of 4th Corps Engrs and Forward Airfield Engrs during advance—Rapid bridging and airstrip construction—362 Fd Coy at Pyinmana bridge—Experiences of 36 Fd Sqn with 255th Tank Bde—Use of Scissors Bridge tanks—Bomb dropped down well—Pyu Chaung crossing—Bailey bridging—Jap suicide men with 'Lunge' mines—36 Fd Sqn in attack at Pyinbongyi (April 27th)—Lt. Cooper killed in gallant exploit—Casualties from road mines and booby traps—60, 70 and Tehri-Garhwal Fd Coys in Pegu—Repair of timber bridge over Pegu R.—Monsoon breaks—Floating bridge destroyed by floods (May 5th)—Gap in steel railway bridge repaired (May 8th)—70 Fd Coy bridges Lagunbyin Chaung near Hlegu—Existing bridge repaired—American Colonel uses flooded airstrip for take-off—Summary of Engineer work up to capture of Rangoon—Allied Ps. of W. recovered from Japanese—Operations of 33rd Corps (Gen. Stopford) on Irrawaddy axis—Kyaukpadaung captured by 7th Div (April 12th)—Yenangyaung taken (April 22nd)—Taungdwingyi occupied by 20th Div (April 13th)—Magwe and Myingun captured (April 19th)—Allanmyo occupied (April 28th)—Prome entered (May 2nd)—20th Div advances towards Rangoon—7th Div mops up near Prome—20th Div contacts 26th Div from Rangoon on Rangoon Road (May 20th)—Experiences of 422 Fd Coy (20th Div) on Irrawaddy—Yin Chaung crossing—Bwetgyi Chaung tank crossing—Bridging flooded Nawin Chaung near Prome (May 2nd)—Medium artillery taken across—Further bridging on Rangoon Road—422 Fd Coy halts at Hmawbi (May 25th)—Work of 7th Div Engrs—Ferrying at Kyaukye and Magwe—62 Fd Coy in pursuit down west bank—Ferrying at Allanmyo—Repair work in Prome—7th Div Engrs concentrate in Pegu area (June '45)—33rd Corps Engrs raft stores down Irrawaddy (April '45)—"Red" and "White" fleets—Formation of 34th Corps under Gen. Roberts (May '45)—15th and 34th Corps to comprise Fourteenth Army under Gen. Dempsey—Fourteenth Army destined for invasion of Malaya—4th and 33rd Corps to comprise new Twelfth Army under Gen. Stopford in Burma—Gen. Slim becomes C.-in-C., A.L.F.S.E.A., vice Gen. Leese, and controls both Armies—Twelfth Army disposed along Toungoo-Rangoon Road—Rehabilitation of Rangoon—Airfields at Mingaladon—Japanese dispositions in Burma—4th Corps deployed between Toungoo and mouth of Sittang R.—Ordered to prevent escape of Jap forces eastwards—"Battle of the Break-out" (July '45)—Few Japs escape—Sapper work in Pegu—"Messervy" suspension bridge built (Aug. '45)—Jeep trains operated—Dukw service on canals—Airfield construction around Rangoon—64 Fd Coy (19th Div Engrs) on Thazi-Kalaw Road—29 and 65 Fd Coys on Toungoo-Mawchi Road—"Ramshackle Bridge"—Tarpaulin raft designed for tanks—Bridging under fire—Mawchi reached (Aug. 15th, '45)—72 Fd Coy repairs Rangoon water-supply—7th Div Engrs in Sittang R. bend—"V.J. Day" (Aug. 15th)—Gen. Kimura orders Jap surrender in Burma—Brig. Armstrong accepts surrender for Gen. Stopford (Sept. 15th)—17th Div replaces 7th Div in Sittang bend—Lt.-Col. Foulkes on Japanese attitude in defeat—Post-war experiences of 17th Div Engrs in Tenasserim—Jap engineers co-operate fully—Road construction between Moulmein and Ye—17th Div Engrs begin to leave Tenasserim (March '46)—19th Div Engrs extend Thazi-Kalaw-Hopong

Road beyond Salween R. (Jan. '46)—Reconnaissance to Kentung—New Myitnge R. bridge near Mandalay—4th Corps Engrs provide temporary pontoon bridge —Existing Bailey bridge removed (July '46)—Sapper officers work in diving suits—New bridge finished by P.W.D.—Title "Royal" bestowed on Corps of Indian Engineers (Feb. '46)—Few R.I.E. units remaining in Burma—7, 19 and 64 Fd Coys detailed for Burma garrison (Feb. '47)—19 Fd Coy secures evidence against murderer of Gen. Aung San—Last R.I.E. units recalled to India (Oct. '47)—History of connection of Corps with Burma 383

CHAPTER XIV

POST-WAR OPERATIONS IN MALAYA, THE EAST INDIES AND THE FAR EAST

Malaya and Indonesia ravaged by Japanese during occupation—Operations "Zipper" and "Mailfist" planned—Fourteenth Army to invade Malaya—34th Corps (Gen. Roberts) to land on west coast—15th Corps (Gen. Christison) to follow up—No opposition expected after Japanese surrender—15th Corps therefore to proceed to Singapore—25th Div to disembark south of Port Swettenham on Sept. 9th, '45—23rd Div to land later south of Port Dickson—5th Div to follow 25th Div—Expedition sails from India and Burma late in Aug. '45—Lt. Sandes on voyage of 78 Fd Coy (41 Beach Group)—Coy disembarks at Port Dickson (Sept. 12th)—Nature of coast—Few good beaches—Landings unopposed—5th Div therefore continues to Singapore—Many vehicles stuck in mud—Episode of bogged bulldozer—23rd and 25th Div Engrs prepare routes inland—23rd Div ordered to Java (Sept. 22nd)—25th Div Engrs improve communications and provide accommodation north of Johore State—Many additional Engineer units arrive in Malaya—Large bridges rebuilt at Gedong and Juru—Bridging on railways—Construction of Kuantan-Kota Bahru Road on east coast—93 Fd Coy commences bridging (Feb. '46)—472 A.G.R.E. starts main undertaking (June '46)—Ten I.E. Coys and an Engineer Bn employed—Also four Bns of Japanese Ps.-of-W.—Work nearly completed (Nov. '46)—Events at Singapore—5th Div (Gen. Mansergh) nears Singapore Island (Sept. 4th, '45)—Arrival of Jap delegates awaited in H.M.S. *Sussex*—Gen. Itagaki signs surrender document—Terms of Malaya surrender—5th Div lands in Singapore (Sept. 5th, '45)—Allied Ps.-of-W. liberated—Shocking condition of prisoners—Repair work by 5th Div Engrs in Singapore and Johore State—Official general surrender at Singapore of all enemy forces in S.E. Asia (Sept. 12th, '45)—Admiral Lord Mountbatten presides at ceremony—Senior officers of Allied nations present—Jap delegation headed by Gen. Itagaki—Surrender terms signed—Union Jack hoisted—Boundaries of S.E.A.C. greatly extended—15th Corps redesignated "A.F.N.E.I."—Ordered to Java and Sumatra—Brig. Swan as C.E.—1st and 37th Bdes, 23rd Div, arrive Batavia (Oct. '15)—49th Bde diverted to E. Java—Bde reaches Sourabaya (Oct. 25th)—Situation in E. Java—Indonesians under Dr. Soerkano—Brig. Mallaby occupies Sourabaya and Darmo suburb—Armed revolt of Indonesians—Mallaby murdered—Decision to send 5th Div to E. Java—Description of Sourabaya—9th Bde (5th Div) disembarks (Nov. 7th)—Darmo evacuated—123rd Bde arrives—161st Bde diverted to W. Java—Gen. Mansergh begins clearance of Sourabaya (Nov. 10th)—Town cleared (Nov. 28th)—Subsequent operations—5th Div leaves E. Java (Jan. '46)—Experiences of 71 Fd Coy with 49th Bde—Massacre of Dutch women and children—71 Fd Coy besieged in Darmo barracks (Oct. 29th, '45)—Gallantry of Capt. Floyer—Convoy of women and children leaves Darmo (Nov. 2nd)—71 Fd Coy follows (Nov. 6th)—Embarks with 49th Bde for W. Java (Nov. 25th)—5th Div Engrs remain in Sourabaya—Damaged installations repaired—Diverse duties of 44 Fd Pk Coy—Dutch troops arrive Sourabaya (Feb. 4th, '46)—Last 5th Div troops leave E. Java (June '46)—23rd Div in W. Java—Indonesians troublesome—R.A.P.W.I. organisation—Dutch internee camps guarded—161st Bde (5th Div), 36th Bde (26th Div) and 5th Para Bde arrive (Dec. '45)—Operations at Bandoeng (March '46)—Dutch troops begin to arrive—Convoy heavily attacked on Buitenzorg-Bandoeng Road (March 15th)—Dutch troops assume control in W. Java—Last British-Indian forces leave Batavia (Nov. 30th)—Engineer work in W. Java—Dutch units trained—68 Fd Coy prints newspaper—Operations in Sumatra by 26th Div (Gen. Chambers) —Description of Sumatra and inhabitants—26th Div sails from Madras (Oct. '45)—HQ established at Padang—Occupation of Medan and Palembang—Dutch Engineer Platoon raised—Dutch units arrive (Sept. '46)—26th Div embarks for India—Operations in Thailand—7th Div (Gen. Evans) flown in from Burma (Sept. '45)—Japanese subservient—Jap methods of discipline—Composite 62/421 Fd Coy arrives Bangkok (Sept. 7th)—77 Fd Coy follows by air (Oct. '45)—331 Fd Pk Coy and 402 Fd Coy come later by sea—Amusing diary of 62 Fd Coy—Japanese Generals surrender swords to Gen. Evans (Jan. 11th, '46)—Brig. Cobb commands troops on parade—7th Div begins to leave Thailand for Malaya (Feb. '46)—421 Fd Coy remains till July—Operations in French Indo-China—20th Div (Gen. Gracey) detailed to occupy Saigon area (Sept. '45)—Div Engrs study French—Description of Saigon—Annamese population hostile—Bravery of Major Lawler, R.A.E.—20th Div arrives mostly by sea—422 Fd Coy flown in from Burma (Sept. 29th)—Other I.E. units come by sea—Sappers guard wells and repair installations—Col. Loomba on assistance given by Jap engineers—Experiences of 422 Fd Coy—French troops arrive—Japs interned at Cap St. Jacques—Mahrattas of 92 Fd Coy billeted in Grand Hotel—92 Fd Coy assists French column—Coy transferred to Borneo (Dec. '45)—Coy returns to India (May '46)—422 Fd Coy leaves Saigon (Jan. 21st, '46)—Voyages to Celebes Island—Repairs airfield near Macassar—Takes over stores from Australians—Malino hill station—422 Fd Coy embarks for India (July 1st)—481 Fd Coy and 332 Fd Pk Coy leave Saigon (Feb. 9th, '46)—Re-occupation of Hongkong—Mixed Force under Gen. Festing sails from Madras—Arrives Hongkong (Nov. 19th, '45)—Work of 96 Fd Coy in Hongkong—Coy returns to India (April '46)—Occupation of Japan by Allied Force under American Gen. MacArthur—British Commonwealth Contingent under Australian Gen. Northcott includes British-Indian Div under Gen. Cowan—268th Ind. Inf. Bde under Brig. Thimayya represents Indian Army—Div Engrs include 429 Fd Coy, R.I.E.—429 Fd Coy lands at Kure (March 2nd, '46)—HQ of "Brindiv" transferred to Okayama (June 4th)—Australian Gen. Robertson succeeds Gen. Northcott as "Brindiv" Comdr—363 Fd Coy and other R.I.E. units arrive in Japan—Assisted by Jap civilian labour—Ceremonial guard duties in Tokyo—Severe earthquake (Dec. 21st)—"Brindiv" reduced to 268th Bde Group under Brig. Shrinagesh (May 1st, '47)—363 Fd Coy embarks for India (Sept. 14th)—429 Fd Coy follows (Oct. 20th)—Last Indian units sail from Japan (Nov. '47)—Malaya in 1947—Most R.I.E. units depart before Independence Day (Aug. 15th)—Their services urgently needed in India 422

CHAPTER XV

INDIA, 1944-47

Corps of Indian Engineers enormously expanded in 1944-45—N.W. Frontier fairly quiet until 1947—Small expedition against Hazara gang beyond Oghi—Approach track bulldozed—Hazaras surrender (Jan. '47)—Rioting and arson in Dera Ismail Khan (April '47)—9 Fd Coy lays pipe-line—Gurkhas ambushed in Shahur Tangi (Sept. '47)—Non-combatants evacuated by air—Earlier events further south—14th and 39th Training Divs formed (Aug. '43)—Sappers attached for training in jungle warfare—Lt.-Col. Lindsell on Bangalore in 1943-44—Boys Bn formed (Oct. '43)—Training Bns—Instructional courses—Visit by Gen. Charles, Chief Royal Engineer (Dec. '43)—Bangalore News Letter revived (July '44)—Posthumous award of George Cross to Sub. Subramaniam—Training of Boys—Boxing—Visit by Gen. Auchinleck (April '44)—Strength of Madras Group (Sept. '44)—Engineer Officers' Training School—Jungle Training Camp —Indian Families' Hospital—Women's Club—Boys Bn moved to Jalahalli Camp (Jan. '45)—Boys' Boxing team sent to Delhi—Senior officers in Madras Centre—Demobilization Centre formed (Aug. '45)—Resettlement training—Madras Sapper Officers' Association formed (Nov. '45)—Three Training Bns reduced to one—Lt. Pearson on events in Roorkee in 1944—Bengal Group totals 23,850 ranks (March '44)—School of Military Engineering established at Roorkee—Jungle training with 39th Training Div near Hardwar—33 Fd Sqn and 40 Fd Pk Sqn with 44th Armd Div in 1943 to defend east coast against invasion—44th Div converted to Airborne Div (April '44)—33 Fd Sqn personnel train as parachutists—Airborne role cancelled—Three Training Bns and Boys Bn at Roorkee (Jan. '44)—Depot Wing formed (March '44)—Battle School—Two O.C.T.Us.—Extracts from Roorkee News Letter (Jan. '44)—Visit by Gen. Charles (Nov. '43)—Gen. C. A. Bird—Corps Parade—Lt.-Col. Connor on life in Roorkee in 1945—Remarks by Brig. Holloway—Kirkee in 1944-45—Three Training Bns at Dighi—Jungle Training School started—Brig. L. O. Clark on life in Kirkee—Clubs and Messes—Disbanding war-time Fd Coys—Condition

CONTENTS

of ex-Ps-of-W.—Few Regular R.E. officers remaining—Major Leslie-Jones on Boys Bn (1946)—Leadership training encouraged—Physical standards improved—Boxing popular—History of Engineer Groups in Punjab—Nos. 1, 3, and 6 Groups at Lahore—No. 4 Group at Sialkot—No. 3 (Construction) Group raises 165 units—Remarks by Brig. Partap Narain—Disbandment ordered (May '45)—Demobilization begins (Nov. '45)—No. 4 Group provides nucleus for R. Pakistan Engineers after Partition in 1947—Gen. Gaussen on improvements noted in 1945 in Boys Bns and Sapper equipment and training—Value of 14th and 39th Training Divs—Keen young officers—K.C.I.Os. already in many senior posts—Fateful years 1946 and 1947—Gen. H. Williams on the role of the Engineer in the defence of modern India—Gen. Roome as E.-in-C., India—Succeeded by Gen. Hasted (Jan. '46)—Reception accorded to home-coming units—Capt. Spring—Smyth on welcome given to Sirmoor Fd Coy at Nahan (June '46)—7 Fd Coy re-formed as Sikh unit (Oct. '46)—Muslim second-in-command very popular—Welcome given to 65 Fd Coy at Bangalore—Col. Loomba on process of demobilization—Lt.-Col. Lindsell on events in Bangalore in 1946—Title "Sappers and Miners" abolished—"Regimental Centre" substituted—Brig. R. C. R. Hill as first Col. Commandant of Madras Group—Gen. Roome for Bengal Group, and Gen. Nosworthy for Bombay Group—First re-union of Madras Sappers Officers Association (May 31st, '46)—Victory Parade in London—R.I.E. contingent under Lt.-Col. Kochhar (June '46)—Madras Boys Bn wins All-India Boys Boxing Championship—Madras Sapper headgear ("Doopta") abolished (Sept. '46)—Origin of the "Doopta"—Process of demobilization at Roorkee—Story of C.O. Demob Bn and inspecting General—Title of "Royal" conferred on Corps of Indian Engineers (Feb. '46)—Post-war Class Composition of Bengal Group—Impressions of Roorkee in 1946 by Brig. Duke—Many new buildings—Kirkee in 1946—Description in News Letters—Witty poem by Commandant—Communal feeding in Boys Bn—Sub.-Major Taj Din dined out—Self-Government for India—Cabinet Mission in 1946—Lord Mountbatten appointed Viceroy *vice* F. M. Wavell (Feb. '47)—Partition of India from Pakistan to be carried out—Gen. Tuker on attitude of troops—Army to be re-organized into communal classes—Impartially controlled contingent advocated—Problems of Partition—Retention of British volunteers—Transfer of most Muslim officers to Pakistan—Replacements needed—Gen. Steedman as E.-in-C., India—Gen. Hasted as E.-in-C., Supreme HQ—Partition decided—Announced by Prime Minister in Parliament (Feb. 20th, '47)—Character of Lord Mountbatten—Partition Committees appointed (June 16th)—Partition date fixed as August 15th, 1947—Basis of division of Army between India and Pakistan—Allotment of available units—Joint Defence Councils—F.M. Auchinleck in administrative control of Forces—Lord Mountbatten on speed of Partition—Army remains staunch—Effects of Partition on R.I.E. Groups—Madras Centre almost untouched—Bengal Centre loses half its strength—Bombay Centre loses 40%—New Class Composition of Bengal and Bombay Centres—Bengal Centre to supply bulk of equipment for R. Pakistan Centre at Sialkot—Disposal of silver and assets of R.E. Mess, Roorkee—Disposal of Thomason College workshop equipment—Thomason College becomes an University—History of S.M.E. in Thomason College—Transfer of S.M.E. to Kirkee begins (Aug. '47)—Commandant (Brig. H. Williams) appointed C.E. Southern Command—S.M.E. established in Kirkee (Dec. '47)—Instruction commences (Feb. '48)—List of Bengal units transferred to Pakistan—List of those remaining in Roorkee—Equipment and transport sent to Sialkot (July '47)—Seven British officers and nine Muslim officers elect transfer—Bengal Centre almost crippled—Regimental funds halved—Messes denuded—No instruments for Band—Floods add to difficulties—Col. Loomba on Partition at Madras Centre—Uncertainty among British officers—Short Term Commissions proposed for V.C.Os.—Few Muslim Sappers elect for Pakistan—Events at Bombay Centre—Bombay News Letter (July '47)—Announcement that all British officers will have left India by June 1948—Shortage of I.C.Os.—Regular Commissions for V.C.Os.—Demob Bn abolished (March 31st, '47)—Total released is 16,519 by June 16th—Almost all B.W. & N.C.Os. gone—General effects of sudden Partition—Junior Indian officers have to fill high appointments—Lack of Coy Commanders—R.I.E. units help to restore order in Sialkot and Lahore Districts (July-Aug. '47)—India and Pakistan declared Independent Sovereign States (Aug. 15th, '47)—Farewell Message from F. M. Auchinleck to British troops—Partnership of British and Indian Armies—British withdrawal from India—R.A.F. sail from Bombay (Aug. 17th)—F. M. Auchinleck closes

Supreme Headquarters and leaves for U.K. (Nov. '47)—HQ British Troops in India transferred to Bombay (Dec. 22nd)—Gen. Whistler in command—Only 1st Bn, Somerset L.I., remaining in India by Feb. '48, and 2nd Bn, The Black Watch, in Pakistan—Somersets embark at Bombay (Feb. 28th, '48)—Impressive Ceremonial Parade—Farewell Message from Gen. Bucher, C.-in-C., India—Good feeling between Indian and Pakistan troops during Partition period—Independence Day celebrations peaceful—Union Jack lowered at Lucknow Residency—Indian National Flag hoisted—Last British units in Lucknow and Delhi—Transfer of military control—Indian Government agrees that Lord Mountbatten should remain as Governor General for seven months—Gen. Lockhart hands over command as C.-in-C., India, to Gen. Cariappa (Jan. '48)—Lord Mountbatten leaves India (June '48)—Gen. H. Williams remains as E.-in-C. for eight years—Last British Commandants at R.I.E. Centres—2nd Lt. Rane wins Param Vir Chakra in Kashmir operations (April '48)—Equivalent to Victoria Cross—Last R.E. officers leave Corps of Indian Engineers in 1948—"Sarvatra" (everywhere) the motto of the modern Corps—Corps Day celebrated annually on Jan. 28th 463

APPENDIX A

MADRAS ENGINEER GROUP 501

APPENDIX B

BENGAL ENGINEER GROUP .. 506

APPENDIX C

BOMBAY ENGINEER GROUP 511

ILLUSTRATIONS

INDIAN ENGINEERS. A NAIK OF THE MADRAS GROUP; A SAPPER OF THE BENGAL GROUP; A SAPPER OF THE BOMBAY GROUP .. .. *Frontispiece*

	Facing page
RECRUITS GOING THROUGH AN ASSAULT COURSE	14
SAPPERS AND MINERS REPAIRING THE ROAD TO BARENTU	34
COLONEL P. S. BHAGAT, V.C.	36
SAPPERS AND MINERS CLEARING A ROAD BLOCK BETWEEN ASMARA AND MASSAWA	44
INDIAN ENGINEERS LAYING RAILWAY TRACK IN IRAQ	56
SAPPERS AND MINERS RUSH MINE DETECTING APPARATUS THROUGH A GAP IN ENEMY WIRE CLEARED BY A BANGALORE TORPEDO	108
MINE DETECTION IN TUNISIA	120
USING A PNEUMATIC DRILL WHILE ROADMAKING IN TUNISIA	132
SUBEDAR SUBRAMANIAM, G.C.	154
INDIAN AND BRITISH ENGINEERS OF THE EIGHTH ARMY SPANNING THE RIVER PO WITH A 1,370 FEET PONTOON BRIDGE, THE LONGEST MILITARY BRIDGE IN ITALY	170
JUNGLE TRAINING IN MALAYA	182
TRANSPORT ON THE TAMU-PALEL ROAD	236
OIL TANK UNDER CONSTRUCTION BY GENERAL RESERVE ENGINEER FORCE AT DIBRUGARH	248
LANDING AT AKYAB	300
REINFORCEMENTS AND EQUIPMENT ARRIVING IN KOHIMA	334
FERRYING ARMOUR AND TRANSPORT ACROSS THE IRRAWADDY	368
INDIAN TROOPS IN ACTION AT SEYWA DURING THE ADVANCE TO MEIKTILA	376
65 FIELD COMPANY OPENING THE GATES OF FORT DUFFERIN AT MANDALAY, MARCH 20TH, 1945	380
SUNSET OVER RANGOON HARBOUR	404
CONSTRUCTING THE KEMAJARAN AIRFIELD NEAR BATAVIA	442

MAPS

	Facing Page
N. E. Africa	
Eritrea and Sudan-Abyssinia Border	50
Battle of Keren	
Middle East	80
North Africa	138
Tunisia	
Central and Southern Italy	174
N. E. Italy	
Malaya	208
Waw Area	238
Tiddim Road, Chindwin R. Area	272
Arakan	
Maungdaw Area	312
7th Ind. Div. Admin Box, Sinzweya	
Lower Arakan	
Imphal	344
Tiddim Road, Milestones 32 to 83	
Tiddim Road, Milestone 109 to Kalemyo	382
Central Burma	
Upper Burma	
Lower Burma	420
Toungoo-Rangoon Area	
South-East Asia	
Landings in Malaya	462
Sourabaya	

THE INDIAN ENGINEERS 1939-47

CHAPTER I

INDIA, 1939-43

IT is a far cry from Delhi to Munich, and farther yet to Rome or Tokio. Though the unprovoked invasion of Abyssinia by the Italians in 1935 had shown that Mussolini might follow Hitler, and subsequent Japanese training in amphibious landings and jungle warfare had given rise to much speculation, India seemed so distant from any possible danger zone that it might reasonably be supposed that she would not be drawn, to any great extent, into an armed conflict with Germany. Nevertheless, in 1938, long before cipher messages had begun to reach Simla with increasing frequency, preparations were put in hand and 15 Field Company was detailed to go to Malaya, although little of this filtered through to the man in the ranks. Indeed, in 1939 the normal round of daily work continued everywhere as if no clouds were gathering on the western horizon. Some acceleration in a process of mechanization could be noted at the Sapper and Miner Headquarters at Bangalore, Roorkee and Kirkee, but on the North-West Frontier the construction of fortified camps, bridge-building on the Kabul River and occasional demonstrations against recalcitrant tribesmen, continued in accordance with the usual routine.

Perhaps the general atmosphere at the Sapper and Miner Headquarters immediately before the war may be illustrated by some extracts from the Adjutant's News Letter written in Roorkee on the fateful morning of September 3rd, 1939. "We have received no warning orders of any impending mobilization and it is not clear what effort the Bengal Corps will be expected to produce in any war. Cipher wires have been arriving fairly frequently and everyone likely to be mobilized has been medically examined. All leave has been stopped, and all ranks have been recalled from leave. In the meantime, work proceeds on plans for modernization. 1 and 2 Field

Companies and 43 Divisional Company are due for modernization this cold weather and will get a large increase of motor transport and mechanical tools. 43 Divisional Company will become a Field Park Company after being modernized. 3 Field Company expect to have their work on the Wana Project completed by the end of December. Their destination after that is uncertain, but they hope to go to Nowshera in place of 15 Field Company which has gone overseas. In the meantime, they have been busy winning the Wana Brigade hockey tournament. We don't know when to expect any officers from home, if at all. We had hoped to see Lieut-Colonel K. J. Lee (Commandant) about September 20th and Lieut-Colonel C. L. B. Duke some ten days earlier. They may be on their way now, *via* the Cape, but we have not heard. 4 Field Company, as a practice for the Mobile Column, marched through Saharanpur the other day and returned wearing gas-masks. The inhabitants were slightly taken aback, and the Mobile Column got extremely hot! The Training Battalion now do all their drill in threes, and other units have been practising the new drill although it has not yet been generally adopted. We have two Indian Commissioned Officers here for training—2nd Lieuts. Shiv Dial Singh and Arjan Singh. Major H. Williams is commanding a Field Squadron at Aldershot and writes that he is hard-worked but happy."

It is almost incredible that this could have been written only a few hours before news of the outbreak of a World War. Yet, at the end of the same letter is a short but momentous postscript. "Since writing the above, war has broken out with Germany. Viceroy's Commissioned Officers and N.C.Os listened to the King's broadcast on September 3rd, 1939, in the V.C.Os' Club." Thus the terrible news reached the little station on the bank of the Solani River within sight of the Himalayan snows.

On October 9th, the Roorkee Adjutant resumes his story. "4 Field Company, the first to go overseas in the last war, has maintained its reputation and has just started for an unknown destination. One Section, left behind, has been experimenting with a mat bridge, a sort of magic carpet which floats on water. Most officers who were on leave in the United Kingdom have now rejoined. A cryptic cipher message reached Army Headquarters the other day stating that there were a large number of officers "in the Duchess's bed"! This, however, proved to be merely a corruption of the name of the ship in which they sailed. We expect Ievers and Mangat Rai to return soon from an E. and M. Course at home. We were very glad to welcome General C. A. Bird on October 2nd. He had just arrived in India to take over as Engineer-in-Chief. The Faridkot Field Company of the Indian States' Forces is now in Roorkee, training with us. They are a fine body of men. The Malerkotla Field Company is at Rawalpindi. 5 Field Company is now fully Indianized and all the V.C.Os have left it".

The next letter, written early in November 1939, states that the war had not yet made much difference in Roorkee; and another dated January 3rd, 1940, records that the only item of major importance during December had been the conversion of 41 and 43 Divisional Companies into one-class units, all Sikhs and all Mussulmans respectively. There is much about Sport. A Sapper team had reached the final of the Meerut Polo Tournament and five officers had gone to Gulmarg in Kashmir for ski-ing. The News Letters, however, necessarily give a rather one-sided picture, and lest it should be imagined that the Sappers and Miners at Roorkee, Kirkee and Bangalore were taking the war too lightly it may be well to emphasize that intensive training and expansion filled every hour of a long working day and that the Adjutant's apparent fondness for social and sporting events was due to steadily increasing censorship. Polo began to languish, and after April 1940, when 35 Field Troop was mechanized, it became difficult to mount a team for any tournament. Social life declined. By July 1940, the Roorkee Club, which had been closed fifteen months earlier, had become a derelict cattle-byre, and No 1 Bungalow, once the Commandant's residence, had lain unoccupied for years. As in Bangalore and Kirkee, the war was leaving its mark. Everything was being subordinated to military needs. The Sapper polo ground was converted into hockey and football grounds for the rapidly increasing garrison. New buildings were springing up in all directions. No 1 Bungalow was to be renovated to provide an additional Officers' Mess. The New Year's Parade on January 1st, 1941, saw all officers on foot for the first time and the men in field service dress in place of the former tunic, knickerbockers and blue putties. It would have been difficult for any pre-war Sapper to recognize the Roorkee of 1941.

The enormous expansion of the three Corps after 1939 would have been impossible had not Indianization of the King's Commissioned Officer ranks been started during the summer of 1934 when three Field Companies—5 (Bengal), 15 (Madras) and 22 (Bombay) —were selected for the purpose. The history of this process is described briefly in *The Indian Sappers and Miners* to which this volume is a sequel, but some recapitulation may be advisable. Indianization of other branches of the Indian Army had been initiated as early as 1923 as a natural consequence of political evolution and in recognition of gallantry displayed in the First World War, but for some reason it was withheld from the Sappers and Miners. In 1932 an Indian Military Academy was opened in Dehra Dun to train cadets for commissions in the Indian Army, including the newly formed "Corps of Indian Engineers." The Commandant was Brigadier L. P. Collins; and the Assistant Commandant, Colonel A. J. G. Bird, was a former Commandant of the Bengal Sappers and Miners. This institution was designed to replace the R.M.A. Woolwich and the R.M.C. Sandhurst in catering for the needs of the Indian Army. Half the cadets came through an open competition, whilst the remainder were from the ranks. A number came from the Prince of Wales' Royal Indian Military College at Dehra Dun, where boys were already being educated on military lines. Major H. Williams, R.E., joined the Staff of the Academy, and thus the Engineer element was well represented; but only those young Indian Officers of the Engineer Branch who returned to India after qualifying at Woolwich and the School of Military Engineering, Chatham, held King's Commissions (K.C.I.Os), the entries from the Dehra Dun Academy being denominated I.C.Os (Indian Commissioned Officers). The latter had to undergo a further course of 3 years training in civil engineering at the Thomason College, Roorkee, before being posted to one of the three Sapper and Miner Corps. The first K.C.I.O., Lieut. R. E. Aserappa, reached India in 1935 and others followed. 2nd Lieuts. N. S. Bhagat and A. N. Kashyap, I.E., arrived in Roorkee from Dehra Dun in February 1935, and 2nd Lieut. Anant Singh in August, being followed, in February 1936, by 2nd Lieuts. J. S. Dhillon and A. D. Verma, I.E., and later by other I.C.Os. In October 1936, Major H. Williams took charge of the I.C.Os studying at the Thomason College. He was followed by Major C. D. Reed in November 1938. Only six officers completed the full training at the College, the remainder being withdrawn due to the outbreak of the war. The Officers' Mess formed at the Thomason College may well be regarded as the first "Indian Engineers' Mess". It can be said to have been revived when the School of Military Engineering was established later during the war in the College buildings. When the Royal Military Academy at Woolwich was closed suddenly on the outbreak of the Second World War, the Academy at Dehra Dun became the sole means of normal entry for Indians to the King's

Commissioned ranks of the Indian Engineers. It supplied hundreds of young officers who were often called upon to command Field Companies, or even higher formations, in battle and did so with marked ability and success. Several Indian officers had qualifed, long before the war, in the Staff Colleges at Camberley or Quetta, the most notable being Captain K. M. Cariappa, 7th Rajput Regiment, who was a Staff Captain in the Deccan District in 1937 and later became a General Officer and Commander-in-Chief of the Indian Army.

Some details of the vast expansion which took place in the Corps of Indian Engineers from September 1939 onwards can be studied in the Appendices at the end of this volume which have been compiled by the Commandants of the three Sapper and Miner Groups. They need hardly be repeated in this narrative, for the average reader requires only a general picture; but before embarking on a brief voyage through the ever changing channels of a stream of reorganization which soon developed into a mighty flood, we may pause to consider the contrast between the duties required of Sappers and Miners (or Indian Engineers) in the First and Second World Wars. In the 1914-18 War, the Sappers and Miners had to be expert in all forms of field works, bridging and demolitions, to be skilled in various trades, and to have considerable knowledge of water-supply, road and railway construction and electrical and mechanical plant. But in the 1939-45 War, far more was demanded. In addition to all their former accomplishments they had to be able to construct and maintain airfields, build large permanent bridges, lay and lift minefields, operate bulldozers and cranes, and provide and operate oil-pipe lines. They had also to be familiar with the technique of chemical, tank, amphibious and jungle warfare, and to have a working knowledge of surveying, forestry, quarrying, and docks for shipping. It is obvious that no Engineer soldier could hope to be even moderately efficient in all these branches, and hence the diversity of the new technical formations which appeared after 1939, bringing about an expansion in strength and an elaboration in training which none could have foreseen.

When war was declared, the Madras Sappers and Miners comprised only 11 field units—9 and 10 Field Companies, 11 Army Troops Company, 12, 13, 14 and 15 Field Companies, 16 Army Troops Company, 32 Field Troop (later re-designated "Squadron"), 44 Divisional H.Q. Company (later re-designated "Field Park") and 51 Printing Section. Including a Training Battalion and Depot formations, the total strength amounted to only 51 Officers, 55 British Warrant and Non-Commissioned Officers, 65 Viceroy's Commissioned Officers (V.C.Os), 3 Indian Warrant Officers and 3,300 Indian Other Ranks. It is interesting to note that, when Japan surrendered, the Madras Group of the Indian Engineers was represented by 101 units including 667 Officers, 217 B.W. and N.C. Officers, 607 V.C.Os and no less than 30,630 Indian Other Ranks.[1] In 1939, the Bengal Sappers and Miners had 11 field units—1, 2, 3, 4 and 5 Field Companies, 6 and 8 Army Troops Companies, 41 and 43 Divisional H.Q. Companies, and 31 and 35 Field Troops. With a Training Battalion and Depot formations, the total strength was 3,242. But in March 1944, when it reached its peak, the Bengal Group had 73 units and a strength of 23,800 ranks, or roughly seven times the 1939 figure. The Bombay Sappers and Miners started the war with 7 field units —18, 19, 20, 21 and 22 Field Companies, 42 Divisional H.Q. Company and 55 Printing Section. Including a Training Battalion and Depot formations, the strength was 3,006. Yet in spite of losing two-thirds of the regular units in the disaster at Singapore early in 1942, the Bombay Group comprised nearly 25,000 officers and men before the end of the following year. When the war ended, exclusive of the Transportation and Survey Branches but including the Military Engineer Services, the Corps of Indian Engineers totalled more than 7,000 Officers and 235,000 Other Ranks. The field units numbered 482 and were of 54 different types.[2] Statistics, though irksome, are sometimes very revealing.

"Expansion for the war started initially in the Sapper and Miner Corps", writes the Engineer-in-Chief,[3] "and such units as a Workshop and Park Company and a Railway Construction Company were raised. It was realized in 1940 that it would be difficult for the three Corps to undertake the whole production of the many and various types of Engineer units which would be required by the rapidly expanding Indian Army, so recourse was had to civilian tradesmen for the raising of Technical Corps and Army Engineer units, including Transportation units, and six Engineer Depots were formed to raise the new types of Indian Engineer units. These were No 1 Depot

---

[1] Bangalore News Letter, Sept. 1945.

[2] "India's Engineer War Effort", by the E-in-C., India, appearing in *The R.E. Journal*, June 1946.

[3] "The Corps of Indian Engineers", by the E-in-C., India, appearing in *The R.E. Journal*, March 1945.

for E. and M. Companies, Workshops and Stores units; No 2 for Railway units; No 3 for Artisan Works Companies and Heavy Bridging Companies; No 4 for Pioneer (later re-named Engineer) Battalions; No 5 for Docks and Inland Water Transport (I.W.T.) units; and No 6 for Excavating Machinery units. Towards the end of 1941, the various categories of Indian Engineers were renamed "Groups", including not only the Sappers and Miners but also Nos 1, 3, 4 and 6 Depots. Transportation units, which originally were formed under the Engineer-in-Chief, had meantime passed to the control of the Quarter-Master-General, and the original Nos 2 and 5 Engineer Depots had been re-designated Nos 2 and 1 Transportation Training Centres (T.T.Cs) respectively."

The Engineer-in-Chief adds that under his own orders were placed the three Sapper and Miner Groups, Nos 1, 3, 4 and 6 Groups and the Military Engineer Services (M.E.S.): under the Quarter-Master-General, the Railway Construction and Maintenance Groups, Railway Operating Groups, Railway Workshop Groups, Transportation Stores Groups, Docks Groups and I.W.T. Groups: and under the Chief of the General Staff, the Survey Group. The Sapper and Miner Groups comprised all Divisional Engineer units such as Field Companies, etc, and units of similar types with Corps or Army Troops, and also Quarrying Companies, Pipe-line Operating Units and Army Troops Companies. So great was the complication of this organization that it must suffice merely to touch the fringe of the subject before embarking in later chapters on a narrative of front line operations and the experiences of field units.

Since rapid expansion depends on properly organized recruitment, urgent steps had to be taken to obtain the necessary personnel. Prior to 1932, each Sapper and Miner Corps was responsible for its own recruitment. This was a simple matter because there was no lack of applicants of the very best type to supply the modest needs of the comparatively small establishments centred on Roorkee, Kirkee and Bangalore. When recruits were required, all that was necessary was to send postcards to the *Umedwars*, or aspirants for entry, each of whom had previously come to the Headquarters at his own expense to be medically examined and interviewed and, if found satisfactory, placed on a waiting list for enrolment. Some had travelled hundreds of miles to receive this honour. Every man was vouched for by some relative or connection who was serving, or had served, in the Corps, and thus recruitment was, in fact, a family affair. But in 1932 the old system was abolished. Orders were issued that in future all recruiting was to be done through Recruiting Officers controlled by the Adjutant-General's Branch. Family tradition and personal selection were to go by the board and be replaced by a cold, though highly efficient, regime which was better designed, no doubt, to meet increasing demands or any sudden emergency. Nevertheless the Sappers and Miners, and particularly the Madras Corps, continued to do a considerable amount of their own recruiting.

In September 1939, recruitment was accelerated to meet war requirements, but not to the extent that might have been expected in view of the bellicose attitude of Japan, and although all Reservists were called up, the real flood of recruits did not begin until 1941. Boys Battalions were then formed in each Corps, and after 18 months' training, these youths were admitted as Sappers. They were excellent material, well educated, good tradesmen and suitable for promotion from the ranks. The classes of men enlisted into the Bengal Sappers and Miners were Mussulmans (Punjabi Mussulmans, Pathans and Meos), Hindus (Brahmins and Chathris) and Sikhs (mostly Jats). The Bombay Corps enlisted Punjabi Mussulmans, Hindus (Mahrattas) and Sikhs (Mazbis and Ramdasias); while the Madras Corps enlisted Hindus, Mussulmans, Christians and Bhuddists who, even in these early days, fed together and ignored all class distinctions. In this respect the administration and maintenance of the Madras Corps was greatly simplified on active service, and it is happy to record that the system has now spread to both the other Corps.

The initial slowness of expansion in the three Sapper and Miner Corps may be attributed not only to the neutrality of Japan and the improbability that Indian troops would be used against Germany in Europe, but also to a general shortage of equipment. In addition, there was the acute problem of finding the necessary number of officers. As in the 1914-18 war, the Army in India Reserve of Officers (A.I.R.O.) came to the rescue so far as possible, and young civilian engineers from Government Departments or firms flocked to the three Headquarters for training before being posted to units. Early in 1940, Officer Cadets Training Units (O.C.T.Us.) were established for all three Corps, and the intake from the Indian Military Academy at Dehra Dun was increased. Promotion of suitable Indian V.C.Os to I.C.O. rank was encouraged and helped to some extent to ease the situation though not many such promotions were made during the war. The O.C.T.Us were soon replaced by an Engineer Officers' Training School (E.O.T.S.) in Bangalore, affiliated to the Madras Corps and responsible for training all A.I.R.O. officers, and also cadets, for direct commissions. In addition, the School conducted special classes for officers and N.C.Os from West Africa, Burma and Afghanistan. Many of the cadets were Indians, though most were British who were drawn from the civil population of India; but when this source dried up, parties of British cadets were sent from England. The School had an excellent Mess which could accommodate 120 cadets, and the catering was usually all that could be desired. But not invariably, for in the Mess records can be seen a chit written by a certain cadet to the Mess Steward. "I am going out this evening", it runs. "So whatever Officer Cadet Smith can eat of my dinner, please let him do so."

During 1940, a number of Engineer Training Centres (E.T.Cs) were formed throughout India. They were well equipped with workshops and trained Other Ranks in all branches of military engineering. Additional Training Battalions were formed during 1941, and also Forming Troops Battalions to supervise the training of new units. The Engineer Training Centres were located at Rawalpindi, Secunderabad, Quetta, Jhansi, Sialkot, Lucknow, Meerut, Nowshera, Dighi (Kirkee) and Kohat, and undertook the training of some new units and of tradesmen of all new field units. In 1941 the Commandant at Bangalore was Colonel P. A. Tucker, who was succeeded in April 1942 by Colonel J. F. D. Steedman. At Roorkee, the Commandant was Colonel H. N. Obbard, who had taken over from Colonel K. J. Lee in August 1940; and at Kirkee the Commandant was Colonel H. E. Horsfield, who was succeeded by Colonel H. P. Cavendish in September 1942.

We come now to the enormous field of Transportation in all its various aspects. Although the Indian Army Transportation Services were controlled during the greater part of the war by the Quarter-Master-General, they were officered and manned largely by the Indian Engineers and consequently require some notice.

In Napoleon's days, armies were said to move on their bellies; now they move more comfortably, and much more rapidly, by every form of land, sea and air transport. Long before armies became mechanized, the science of military logistics had begun to occupy the minds of commanders in the field. For instance, the first transportation unit in the British Army appeared in Egypt in 1882 when 8 Company, R.E., was converted into a Railway Company[1]. In

---

[1] Paper by Brigadier R. Gardiner, C.B.E., Director of Transportation, India Command, 1942-43.

India, a Military Railway Company was raised at Sialkot in 1902 as a result of experience gained during the Third China War.[1] The original proposal was to raise six companies; but only one more appeared and this was formed in 1905. The two units, known as 25 and 26 Railway (Construction) Companies, were vaguely affiliated to the Bengal and Bombay Corps respectively. In 1914 they proceeded to East Africa and, with the addition of three more companies (27, 28 and 29), developed into a Railway Battalion, Sappers and Miners, which rendered good service in Africa and elsewhere until abolished in 1921. 25 and 26 Companies remained in being as part of the Royal Bombay Sappers and Miners, but they also were disbanded in 1931. Thus, at the outbreak of the Second World War, the Army in India had no Transportation service whatever! There was no organization similar to those to be found in the British, American or Russian armies, nor even a nucleus from which such an organization could be expanded. Mr. Winston Churchill once said that Transportation was the greatest problem of the war. For India, the problem seemed well nigh insoluble; yet by enormous exertions, it was solved.

A beginning was made in 1940 when two Railway Companies and two small Dock Companies were raised under the Engineer-in-Chief whose responsibilities for military transportation extended at that time from the shores of the Mediterranean to the Far East. The first to be formed was 101 Railway Construction Company of the Madras Corps. Early in 1941, No 2 Engineer Depot was established at Jullundur and the raising of a further eleven Railway companies was sanctioned[2]. In October, this Depot became No 2 Transportation Training Centre (T.T.C.) and was made responsible not only for raising all Railway units but also for their training and reinforcement. One month earlier, No 1 T.T.C. responsible for Docks units and Inland Water Transport units, had been established in Bombay and Deolali, having originated from No 5 Engineer Depot[3]. These reorganizations were undertaken by the Quarter-Master-General's Branch to which all responsibility for military transportation had been transferred in May 1941, much to the relief, no doubt, of the Engineer-in-Chief. No less than 37 different types of transportation

---

[1] *The Indian Sappers and Miners*, by Lieut-Colonel E. W. C. Sandes, D.S.O., M.C., p. 689, Appendix F.

[2] "Indian Army Transportation Service," by Major Sharma, Engineers, appearing in *The Journal of the Institution of Military Engineers (India)*, April 1950.

[3] No 5 Engineer Depot had been formed in July 1941.

units were raised in India during the war, and in October 1945, excluding a "Defence of India Corps", the Transportation Service had 217 units and a strength of 1,463 officers and 89,000 other ranks.[1] The Defence of India Corps was formed in 1943 to help in the maintenance of communications for the war against the Japanese who seemed likely at that time to attempt an invasion of India. It expanded gradually until it included most of the civilian employees of the Indian railways and ports and of the I.W.T. companies operating against the enemy, and in time it reached a strength of more than 200,000. The men were mostly Railway and Port employees.

Some idea of the complexity of the Military Transportation Service may be gained from a list of the main types of units. The Railway units comprised Survey, Bridging, Construction, Maintenance, Telegraph Maintenance, Operating, Yard Operating, Control and Workshop Companies. The Transportation Stores units included Stores Companies and Docks Liaison Sections. The Docks and Ports units comprised Docks Operating and Docks Maintenance Companies, Stevedore Units, Boat Companies and Port Operating and Port Construction Companies; and the Inland Water Transport branch was represented by Operating Companies, Workshop Companies, Floating Workshop Companies, River Salvage Companies, "Z" Craft[2] Operating Companies, Craft Erection Companies and Riveting Companies. The list almost staggers the imagination.

The Survey Group formed a small but important branch of the Indian Engineers during the war. Before 1940 there was no Military Survey service in India, all such work being undertaken by the Survey of India Department when occasion demanded. This arrangement had proved satisfactory in the 1914-18 War but was inadequate for the conditions of the 1939-45 War, and accordingly steps were taken to raise some Military Survey units resembling those of the British Army. A Survey Depot, formed in 1940, soon brought satisfactory results and during the following year a number of Survey units were sent overseas. In 1942, after the entry of Japan into the war, the Survey Directorate was expanded and units of many different types were formed including not only Field Survey Companies but also Air Survey Companies and formations dealing with Drawing, Map Reproduction and other branches. By 1945, the Directorate was

---

[1] "India's Engineer War Effort, 1939–45", by the E-in-C., India, appearing in *The R.E. Journal*, June 1946.

[2] "Z" Craft were powered barges of shallow draft.

employing 206 officers and nearly 4,000 men, and most of the Field Survey Companies were busily engaged in mapping the wilder parts of Burma.

The Military Engineer Services, an indispensable part of the Corps of Indian Engineers, did yeoman work behind the fighting fronts during the Second World War. They constructed and maintained buildings, defences and airfields on the lines of communication, together with roads, electrical and mechanical installations, water supply and drainage systems and a thousand and one other requirements of the armies in the field, and not only for them but also for the Naval and Air Forces. The work was done mostly by contract. When the war ended, the Military Engineer Services had spent more than £260 million. They had provided living accommodation for nearly one million men and hospital accommodation for 150,000 and had completed 26 large bases and docks for the Royal Navy, and 215 large airfields, 60 smaller ones and 260 hangars, for the Royal Air Force, not to mention a great number of Prisoner-of-War camps. They had constructed 1,600 miles of roadway and laid 1,191 miles of oil-pipe line. These statistics are sufficient to show that, together with the Transportation Services, they did everything possible to ensure that the forces in the field should lack nothing to ensure victory.

After this outline of the organization and war expansion of the Indian Engineers we can revert to the events during the first half of the war which concerned the Sapper and Miner units still remaining on Indian soil. As already recorded, 4 Field Company of the Bengal Corps was mobilized at Roorkee in the middle of September 1939 and 12 Field Company of the Madras Corps at Bangalore. Each was to have only three Sections instead of four, and no animals were to be kept; but the number of mechanical transport vehicles per unit was to be raised from four to no less than thirty-five. India had offered two brigades for service overseas, and each brigade was to be allotted one Field Company. Accordingly, in October 1939, 4 Field Company departed from Roorkee soon after 12 Field Company had set out from Bangalore, heavily garlanded and much envied by those they left behind. They were bound for Egypt, though they did not know it. 11 Army Troops Company also started for Egypt from Bangalore, and 18 Company of the Bombay Corps had already gone from Kirkee. There was little unusual activity at any of the Sapper Headquarters at this early stage except that all reservists had been called up and intensive training was in progress in trades and mechanical transport. The idea still persisted at Army Headquarters that a whole year would be needed to produce an efficient field unit, primarily because of the very high standard of skill in trades demanded for modern warfare. "The M.T. training was pursued with vigour and a great deal of smoke", writes Lieut. G. Pearson.[1] "The most up-to-date types of vehicles being unavailable, fabulous prices were paid to contractors to supply what they could. As a result, an exciting circus of ancient buses, old private cars and a few lorries were gathered together, and these, puffing and shaking, made disjointed progress around the M.T. School's training pitch. Many of them burnt too much oil, and some connections were made with string, all of which was good training for the smokescreens and hastily improvised repairs of the future." Similar scenes might have been observed at the Headquarters of the Madras and Bombay Sappers, where only by the most strenuous efforts could the lag in mechanization be retrieved. The immediate problems facing all the Sapper units destined for battle fronts were shortages of motor transport and equipment. In this connection one calls to mind Mr. Winston Churchill's description of a Democracy entering a major war. He said that during the first year the rate of munitions' production was nothing at all; during the second year, very little; during the third year, quite a lot; and during the fourth year, 'all that you want.'[2] Such was the experience of India.

By the middle of 1940, in spite of problems of transport, equipment and training, the Sappers and Miners were able to despatch a number of field units overseas.[3] The fall of France, and the entry of Italy as an ally of Germany, had widened the area of commitments, and the attitude of Japan was causing grave concern. Speed, and yet more speed, was demanded. In August 1940, 2 Field Company, 6 and 8 Army Troops Companies and 2 Bridging Train (formed from the fourth Section of 4 Field Company) were mobilized by the Bengal Corps and set out for the Sudan to join the 5th Indian Division in fighting the Italians. 44 Field Park Company and 16 Workshop and Park Company went also from Bangalore; and in September, Roorkee began to assemble the Divisional Engineer units of an 8th Indian Division in Iraq, these being 7 and 66 Field Companies and

---

[1] *Brief History of the K.G.V's O. Bengal Sappers and Miners Group, R.I.E.*, by Lieut. G. Pearson, R.E., p.2.

[2] *A Short History of the Q.V's O. Madras Sappers and Miners during World War II, 1939-45*, by Lieut.-Colonel R. A. Lindsell, R.E., p. 3.

[3] In Bangalore the first new unit to be formed was 56 Field Company, which came into being on April 15th, 1940.

47 Field Park Company. Then, at the end of the year and early in 1941, the Bombay Corps made its great effort and despatched to Malaya no less than six field units—17, 19, 22 and 23 Field Companies, 42 Field Park Company and 45 Army Troops Company—or more than two-thirds of its regular units, none of which was destined to return for they were lost in the tragedy of Singapore.

The year 1941 saw a steady stream of units under formation, and as soon as they were ready they left for the various theatres of the war. Men were being trained everywhere, on the ranges, parade grounds and field works grounds, in the workshops, in boats on rivers and canals and in the jungles. Some units were on the North-West Frontier practising with Inglis and Hamilton bridges at Akora on the Kabul River; others were engaged on water supply schemes or building fortified camps; others again were in the Central Provinces or Southern Indian jungles, working under novel conditions. All were desperately busy. More than a dozen new Field Companies were raised in Roorkee alone during 1941 and 1942, and as fast as they were trained at Headquarters they disappeared eastwards to learn the more advanced technique of the jungle before meeting the Japanese. "To the Bengal Corps, early in the war", writes Lieut. G. Pearson,[1] "fell the lot of raising various specialist units such as Road Roller Platoons, Bridge Construction Sections and Line of Communication units; but soon the enlarging scope of the war forced the Corps to concentrate on the provision of Companies for the field." The same may be said of the Madras and Bombay Corps. From directives, pamphlets and intelligence summaries, and the experiences of units at the front, it became possible to instruct new units in the latest methods of warfare, the use of new weapons, enemy tactics, and the best means of defence against air attack. When the Japanese entered the field and produced their elaborate 'bunker' system of defence, the Sappers and Miners had to experiment on similar lines and evolve a technique for demolishing the subterranean labyrinths. The experiments were not always successful. For instance, a certain Field Company, having decided to try the effect of 'bee-hive' charges on a bunker, placed a few chickens inside it to determine the amount of concussion and blast. The charges exploded grandly and everyone pressed forward to see the result. Out ran a few excited but uninjured fowls, and nothing was proved except that either the bunker

---

[1] *Brief History of the K.G. V's O. Bengal Sappers and Miners Group, R.I.E.*, by Lieut. G. Pearson, R.E., p. 39.

Recruits going through an assault course

was exceptionally well built or that the charges were insufficient or wrongly placed. Yet perhaps, after all, there was a lesson—the toughness, in more senses than one, of the average Indian *murghi*.

At the beginning of 1942, in accordance with orders issued in October 1941, the three Corps of Indian Sappers and Miners were re-named "Groups". Previously, Sapper and Miner units had not been shown as belonging to the Indian Engineers, but now they were required to adopt the suffix "I.E." And here it may be appropriate to describe briefly the subsequent changes in nomenclature. In February 1946, in recognition of their services in the war, the Indian Engineers were honoured with the title "Royal", and so continued for several years; but at the same time all the field units had regretfully to relinquish the time-honoured designation "Sappers and Miners." The "Q.V's O. Madras Sappers and Miners Group, Indian Engineers" became, for instance, the "Q.V's O. Madras Group, Royal Indian Engineers." The appointments of "Colonels" of the three Sapper Groups were abolished and replaced by those of "Colonels-Commandant", these being Brigadier R. C. R. Hill (Madras Group), Lieut-General Sir Ronald Charles (Bengal Group) and Brigadier-General G. H. Boileau (Bombay Group) who had previously held office as Colonels. The Regimental Centres[1] at Bangalore, Roorkee and Kirkee also relinquished the title of "Sappers and Miners" on adding the prefix "Royal", that at Bangalore becoming the "Q.V's O. Madras Regimental Centre, R.I.E." But this was not the end, for in 1947 the word "Regimental" was changed to "Engineer." The next important alteration occurred on January 25th/26th, 1950, the prefix "Royal" being discontinued some $2\frac{1}{2}$ years after the partition of India from Pakistan when India was declared a Republic. The "Royal Indian Engineers" then became the "Corps of Engineers."

Several Sapper and Miner units had some experience of active service conditions on the North-West Frontier before they were transferred to one or other of the major theatres of the war. The operations took place chiefly in Waziristan. On February 21st, 1940, our troops attacked a hostile gathering at the Tangai Algad in the Ahmedzai territory, and at the end of the year, and early in 1941, further operations were launched from Nowshera in the north and

---

[1] The term "Centre" indicated the organization under the direct command of the Commandant, including not only Group H.Q. the Depot Wing and any Training Battalions but also such field units at H.Q. as were not attached to higher formations. The term "Group" meant the Centre *plus* all field units.

against the Mahsuds around Tauda China in Western Waziristan. The Sappers were engaged also in strengthening the defences of the Khaibar Pass against a possible invasion by Russia because of the Russo-German treaty of friendship, though happily the invasion never materialized. In June 1941, some columns were despatched into the Tochi Valley of Northern Waziristan. They remained in the field until the end of August, and further operations were undertaken subsequently from Razmak against the Datta Khels. The unsettled state of Waziristan, however, was not allowed to interfere with the progress of several large Frontier projects, notably the Wana Project in Southern Waziristan on which 9 Field Company and 16 Army Troops Company of the Madras Corps were engaged. This was completed before the two companies returned to Bangalore in June 1940. It was fortunate that no large rising of the Frontier tribes occurred early in the war to interfere with the despatch of regular Sapper and Miner units to the Middle East and Far East, and also that considerable assistance could be afforded on the Frontier by Engineer units of the Indian States' Forces.

Before the outbreak of the Second World War, five Indian States had their own Sapper and Miner formations, these being Faridkot, Malerkotla, Sirmur, Tehri-Garhwal and Mandi. Each maintained one Company, and these varied in strength between 233 and 129 officers and men. Although their combined strength was less than 1,000, the Indian States' Sappers, under their own officers assisted by British 'Special Service Officers', were well trained and most enthusiastic. After the war started, recruits flocked in, and thus many of the Indian States' Sappers were able to take their share in fighting the Japanese in Burma as well as working on the North-West Frontier, and consequently they will figure from time to time in this narrative. In 1940-41, a Mandi State Sapper Section was serving with the Zhob Independent Brigade at distant Fort Sandeman in Baluchistan. This Section was amalgamated in January 1942 with a newly formed 95 Royal Bombay Mandi Field Company, raised at Nowshera, which was transferred later to the Bengal Corps. As at the beginning of the First World War, the Rulers of the Indian States offered all they had to further the war effort, and their soldiers made a very welcome addition to the regular forces.

Colonel M. M. Jeakes, who was in Bangalore during most of the war, gives some interesting details of life in the Madras Sapper

Headquarters. "Towards the latter part of 1940", he writes,[1] "the Mess filled up rapidly and bungalow accommodation became very scarce. Cadets, as well as officers, were accommodated in the Mess, and there were two overcrowded sittings for every meal. There was little time for games or recreation. Early in 1941, when new camps were occupied at Jalahalli, the worst of the congestion in the Meannee and Assaye Lines was over. Expansion then went ahead steadily. Early in 1942, when the Japanese threat to Madras developed, things began to move quickly in Southern India, and by the end of the year there were camps and establishments all over the countryside. Few troops were stationed in Madras itself, and not many in Bangalore, so the Sappers were called upon to raise a "Brigade" to defend Madras. Three battalions of men were collected and armed with all the rifles available. These, however, were only sufficient for half the number, so the remainder carried picks, pick-helves, 'Molotov cocktails' and all manner of other weapons. Bangalore soon began to change completely. Canteens, Rest Camps, Leave Camps, P. of W. Camps, Hospitals, etc, appeared in every direction. Indeed, most of Southern India became a training ground for formations destined for the recapture of Burma and Singapore. Although many improvised Companies had to be provided in aid of the Civil Power, the formation of new Sapper units continued steadily and the standard improved perceptibly. As regards amenities, the Bangalore Hunt functioned throughout the war, and the Sunday morning meets were much enjoyed. The efforts of young Polo enthusiasts to knock a ball about were most amusing, as also those of the budding tent-peggers under instruction by a few veteran Field Troop Reservists. These old Sappers were thrilled when put in charge of riding classes of young officers and cadets. With the advent of petrol rationing in 1942, pony-traps reappeared on the scene and also some small Rudge motor-cycles. Occasional snipe and duck shoots were possible, and Brigadier R. C. R. Hill, our Colonel, who lived at the Club throughout the war, used to drive his trap out to the snipe grounds with a change of horses half-way. Overcrowding in the Headquarter Mess ceased when a new Mess was opened at Jalahalli. Guest Nights could then be held fairly regularly, the Christmas Party was revived, and periodical dances were arranged. About 1942 it was decided that all the beer from the Bangalore Brewery should be reserved for British troops; but fortunately this decision was modified after protest so

---

[1] Notes by Col. M. M. Jeakes, M.C., dated January 18th, 1952.

that beer continued to be available for the Sapper Canteens. The Corps Hockey and Football Tournaments caused great enthusiasm, and in 1943 the first war-time Corps Athletic Sports Meeting was held. A very good Tamil Concert Party was organized which entertained Tamil troops in many places. The officers' wives, and one officer's mother, were indefatigable in their war activities. Three were awarded the Kaisar-i-Hind Medal. The Families' Hospital continued to flourish, and in 1943 a Women's Club was started to teach industries and provide relaxation. Canteen work, St. John's Ambulance, W.V.S. activities, dispensing, car driving and W.A.C. duties were a few of the ways in which the women assisted the war effort. The British officers' mother must have cut out thousands of garments for female working parties in addition to instructing Indian women in the Club. There was some criticism at the time about the so-called lack of effort displayed by British women in India, but this certainly could not be said of Bangalore. Push-biking along hot and dusty roads for considerable distances was no joke. To sum up about affairs at Bangalore. From 1939 to the middle of 1940, there was not much change. Thence to the middle of 1942, everything was hectic; and afterwards, to the end of 1943, there was steady improvement all round."

This brief sketch of India in the first few years of the war may be concluded, as it was begun, with some extracts from the Roorkee News Letters. In January 1942, the Adjutant writes: "Six months have elapsed since the last News Letter went out. The trouble was that at the end of September 1941 there was really nothing to record except the weather and some notable departures. Veitch and G. C. Clark were whisked away from us, the former to be C.R.E. of a Division and the latter to a Staff job overseas, but Veitch's present address is Delhi. Stenhouse and Ievers returned to the fold and Murray (J.) was added to it, not to mention some very welcome drafts from the U.K. Rumours were floating around that Bill Williams was also returning, but he failed to make the last 100 miles except for a brief visit when the complete Orderly Room Staff of 1932 were once again assembled. I should like to give you some idea of our expansion to date, but I am afraid it would only get me into trouble. However, I can say that most of the empty spaces in the Cantonments are now built over, as also is the Grass Farm and right out to the Rifle Ranges. Our units overseas seem to be in good heart and doing excellent work. New units in India spend most of their time in intensive training. Shikar has been rather limited owing to petrol rationing and the decreased number of cars."

In July 1942, he writes: "Another six months have slipped by, and each time it becomes harder to write anything of real interest. The Bengal Group continues to expand and we have units everywhere. Here in Roorkee we grow and grow and have even had a new railway siding built. Among the decorations and New Year and Birthday honours are a K.B.E. for Major-General L. V. Bond, a C.B.E. for Brigadier E. L. Farley, a D.S.O. for Colonel O. L. Roberts, and O.B.Es. for Lieut.-Colonels A. H. G. Napier and N. E. V. Patterson. Of sport, I fear, I have little to report as since the New Year only one party of four guns has managed to get to the jheels. No one has got a tiger, and two or three people who had blocks were unable at the last minute to get out to them. Polo has struggled on with reduced numbers and has been restricted to the odd day when sufficient players were forthcoming. An innovation in aid of War Funds was a Race Meeting on Sunday afternoon in which all the horses in the Station turned out. Some refused to start, some decided to run the course the wrong way, and some just parked their riders on the ground. However, sufficient finished to ensure a decision in each race and the War Funds benefited by Rs. 1,032." In January 1943, the Adjutant records that polo, played on the College *maidan* and often with only three a side, was made possible by the inclusion of a lady player. The old monsoon polo ground near the Malikpur estate could no longer be used as it was covered with Thomason College buildings. New married quarters had appeared in the area between the *maidan* and the Garrison Church and also on the spur above the Slaughter House. A branch of the Women's Voluntary Service organization had been established and was doing excellent work.

The Roorkee News Letters afford a glimpse of life in India far from any battle front, and they show that, even after four years of war conditions, the Sapper and Miner Headquarters had occasional relaxations from the wear and tear of intensive training and wholesale expansion. Such diversions kept them tuned to concert pitch and thus enabled them to send rapidly to many theatres of the war those highly skilled units without which our armies could have made little progress.

CHAPTER II

EGYPT, THE WESTERN DESERT, THE SUDAN AND ERITREA,
OCTOBER 1939 - MAY 1941

DURING the autumn of 1939, long before Italy entered the war, India began to reinforce the overseas defences of the Empire. First to leave her shores was the 4th Indian Division which sailed for Egypt, and shortly afterwards the 12th Indian Infantry Brigade left for Singapore. This was the commencement of a steady flow of reinforcements to both East and West at a time when every man in Great Britain was needed for home defence. The 5th Indian Division was sent to the Sudan, the 3rd Indian Motor Brigade to Egypt, the 6th, 8th and 10th Indian Divisions to Iraq, the 9th and 11th Indian Divisions to Malaya, and other formations to Burma to form eventually the 17th Indian Division. Units voyaged to Kenya, Aden, British Somaliland, Borneo and Hongkong, and all this was accomplished while the Indian Army was in the throes of an expansion without precedent.

It was fortunate that Great Britain had, in the Middle East, a master of strategy in the person of General Sir Archibald Wavell. Operating on interior lines against Italian armies vastly superior in numbers and armament, Wavell accomplished in 1940 and 1941 a bluff unequalled in military annals. On June 10th, 1940, after Italy had announced that from June 11th she would consider herself at war with Great Britain and France though not with Egypt,[1] Wavell had at his disposal only 36,000 troops in Egypt and 9,000 in the Sudan, in addition to 5,500 in Kenya and 1,475 in British Somaliland. It is true that there were a further 27,500 in Palestine, 800 in Cyprus and 2,500 in Aden, but these could not be withdrawn for operations in Africa because the fall of France and the ascendancy of the Vichy Government had changed the entire situation in the Middle East. Facing Wavell in Libya were 215,000 Italians under Marshal Balbo, while a further 200,000 under the Duke of Aosta threatened the Sudan from Eritrea, Abyssinia and Italian Somaliland. Our armour in Egypt was represented by the 7th Armoured Division comprising two poorly-equipped brigades. Our air-force was pitifully weak

---

[1] Egypt, however, broke off relations with Italy on June 12th.

and obsolete in nature. Our sea communication through the Mediterranean was precarious, and that round the Cape and through the Red Sea entailed enormous delay. Yet, isolated and out-numbered, Wavell struck and struck again, and thus retrieved a desperate situation and broke the strength of a ponderous and boastful enemy.

The Engineer units originally with the 4th Indian Division were 4 Field Company (Bengal), 12 Field Company and 11 Field Park Company (Madras) and 18 Field Company (Bombay), the whole being under Lieut.-Colonel R. V. Cutler, R.E., as C.R.E. In 1940, 6 Army Troops Company (Bengal) joined the Division. After an uneventful voyage from Bombay, the 4th Division disembarked at Suez during the autumn of 1939 and prepared to defend the Nile Valley in the event of Italy entering the war. The first Sapper and Miner unit to leave India for Egypt was 18 Field Company, under Major H. P. Cavendish, R.E., which sailed on August 3rd and landed at Suez on the 15th. Next came 12 Field Company, under Major J. B. Sutherland, R.E., and 11 Army Troops Company, under Major E. Waring, R.E. These sailed on September 22nd and landed on October 4th. Bringing up the rear was 4 Field Company, under Major A. H. G. Napier, R.E., which sailed on October 10th and reached Suez on the 21st.

Before 4 Field Company left Roorkee it was inspected by the local District Commander, none other than Major-General (afterwards Field-Marshal) C. J. E. Auchinleck under whom it was destined later to see much service. At Cairo it camped under peaceful conditions within sight of the famous Pyramids and began a course of training in the rudiments of desert warfare and the handling of motor vehicles and new weapons. "Men who had driven a lorry for the first time only a few weeks earlier", writes Lieut G. Pearson,[1] "had now to pilot their vehicles through the terrifying Cairo traffic and then to drive over soft desert sand, a lesson which involved hours of laborious 'unbogging' with portable steel channels and canvas mats. Then came formation driving, manoeuvring from column into fans and back again according to signal. Near the Nile delta, the desert was simply sand, but further west it was rock, sparsely covered with soil and tufts of shrub. Everywhere there was dust, as fine as flour, which gathered in the food and bedding, rifle barrels and lorry engines; while periodically, over the desert,

---

[1] *Brief History of the K.G.V's O. Bengal Sappers and Miners Group, R.I.E., August* 1939-*July* 1946, by Lieut. G. Pearson, R.E., pp. 3, 4.

blew the Khamseen, a wind which filled the air with sand, blotting out vision beyond twenty yards and making life thoroughly miserable. In 1939, Cairo had not yet felt the full impact of war, and one of the features of the Christmas festivities was a big concert in aid of the Red Cross, organized by a Royal Princess and attended by leaders of Egyptian Society. At this, some Pathans of 4 Field Company performed with great *éclat* what the programme described as "Danses Indiennese-Khattak des Bengalis!" A relief from training came early in 1940 when the Company was ordered to Fayid in the Suez Canal Zone to assist in preparing structures for the equivalent of two divisions. This camp was the nucleus of the enormous Reinforcement Camp of a few years later." While 4 Field Company was thus engaged, 12 Field Company had been undergoing similar desert training, and afterwards, with 11 Army Troops Company, built hutted camps at several places and worked on an extensive defence system in the desert.

At the beginning of May 1940, 4 Field Company moved westwards to Bagush, 30 miles short of Mersa Matruh, to develop a water-supply system from an oasis and to help the 11th Brigade to build a defensive position within 10 miles of Matruh.[1] This work was interrupted in June by the declaration of war against Italy and the start of what may conveniently be called the 'First Libyan Campaign.' Surprisingly enough, the campaign was initiated by General Wavell, the weaker of the two opponents, from a line of small defensive works stretching southwards from the Matruh area and facing Marshal Balbo's army which lay in positions along the Egyptian frontier from Bardia far into the desert. Released by the fall of France from any menace from Tunis, Balbo had hurried six divisions eastwards along the North African coast in motor transport and stood ready to invade the Nile Valley. The British forces had one all-important standing order. They were to make one man appear to be a dozen, a single tank to look like a squadron, and a raid to seem a general advance.[2]

Soon after the middle of June, Wavell attacked in small units, swiftly and by night, and although the campaign was really little more than a series of raids, it upset the Italian plans completely. Strong point after strong point fell in the enemy's line. Fort Maddalena was occupied, then Fort Capuzzo. British vehicles roamed

---

[1] See the map of North Africa included in Chapter V.

[2] "*African Trilogy*", by Alan Moorehead, p. 22.

along the enemy's lines of communication. All was confusion and disorder, and Balbo called excitedly for reinforcements from Rome. This was almost his last act, for on June 28th he perished during a British air raid on Tobruk. His successor, Marshal Graziani, who arrived in August, was prepared to listen to Mussolini's urging that he should launch a counter-offensive from the elaborate frontier line of wire and forts extending southwards from Bardia, and accordingly, on September 13th, the Fascist divisions rolled down the escarpment at Halfaya. Graziani occupied Sollum and advanced cautiously to Sidi Barrani, 75 miles west of Matruh, while our meagre forces fell back in good order, mining the coastal road and spoiling the sources of water-supply. At Sidi Barrani the Italians halted and proceeded to build another chain of defensive posts south-westwards into the desert. The 7th Armoured Division, Wavell's striking force, had lost many tanks during the withdrawal and the enemy was much closer to Cairo, but the British had gained an all-important respite.

During this brief campaign, which gave time for the arrival in Egypt of a large number of fairly powerful Infantry Tanks ("I" Tanks),[1] the Sapper companies of the 4th Indian Division and the R.E. companies of the 7th Armoured Division were exceedingly busy. The Armoured Division Engineers accompanied every raid behind the enemy's lines, lifting mines, clearing obstacles and demolishing defences. They also reconnoitred frequently for water. The 4th Division Engineers, other than those employed on camp construction and water-supply, assisted the infantry in preparing the defences of a 'Bagush Box' and consequently they were seldom in close contact with the enemy. The Engineer troops of the Matruh garrison, under Lieut.-Colonel P. A. Ullman, R.E., constructed concrete defences and anti-tank obstacles and laid extensive minefields using Egyptian pattern mines which were dangerous to lay and still more dangerous to lift.[2] When the situation had become more stable, 4 Field Company was withdrawn to Fuka to resume its training.

Before leaving the Western Desert to describe the operations already in progress on the Sudan-Abyssinia frontier, it may be well to deal with the Second Libyan Campaign which started with a victorious battle at Sidi Barrani and ended after a hot pursuit of

---

[1] Previously, three types of tanks had been available—the Support Tank carrying a light howitzer; the Cruiser Tank, fast, lightly armoured and carrying a 2 pr. gun; and the Light Tank, with a 2 pr. gun but little protection. The "I" Tank, though slow, was better armoured, but it mounted only a 2 pr. gun.

[2] Notes by Lieut.-Colonel P. N. M. Moore, R.E., dated Sept. 1st, 1947.

the enemy throughout the length of Cyrenaica. In October 1940, Lieut.-General Sir H. M. Wilson, commanding the British troops in Egypt, was instructed to examine the possibilities of an air attack; but early in November, Mussolini declared war on Greece, and General Wavell was then ordered to occupy Crete and send several air squadrons to help the Greeks. Consequently, an offensive in the Western Desert had to be postponed until December. At that time the Western Desert Force, the precursor of the famous Eighth Army, was commanded by Lieut.-General R. N. O'Connor and consisted of the 7th Armoured Division, the 4th Indian Division, two brigades of the 6th Australian Division and a regiment of "I" Tanks, in all about 31,000 men with 120 guns and 275 tanks. Opposing O'Connor was Graziani's army distributed along a line of seven fortified camps to the east and south of Sidi Barrani. These were at Maktila near the coast, 'Point 90', Tummar East, Tummar West, Nibeiwa, Sofafi East, and in the south, Sofafi West. The enemy numbered about 80,000 men with 120 tanks, a powerful artillery and three times as many planes as the British. Our patrols, however, had discovered a wide undefended gap in the Italian line between Nibeiwa and the two Sofafis, and this gave O'Connor his opportunity. Supplies were pushed forward across the desert, and after dark on December 7th, 1940, the advance began. During the 8th, the troops hid as best they could, and at dawn on the 9th our armour broke through the gap, swung northwards, and rolled up the enemy's defensive line. The Matruh garrison attacked from the east while the 4th Indian Division followed the Armoured Division through the gap and the Royal Navy and Air Force bombarded and bombed the Maktila fortress and the enemy defences at Sidi Barrani. Complete success attended the operations. At dusk, the 4th Division was on the coastal road to Buq Buq, 20 miles beyond Sidi Barrani, and the garrison of the latter place surrendered on the 10th. The Battle of Sidi Barrani cost the enemy the greater part of five divisions, and O'Connor captured 38,000 men, 400 guns and a number of tanks.

Sollum was occupied on December 16th. The demoralized Italians made no stand of any importance until our troops reached the escarpment beyond that place, and then their efforts failed to stem the tide. Bardia and Tobruk became the next objectives. Though both had been strongly fortified, Bardia was carried by assault on January 22nd, producing a further haul of 75,000 prisoners, 689 guns and 100 tanks. The advance on Tobruk was hindered by a terrific sandstorm on January 20th which completely blotted out the landscape.

So violent was the wind that it uprooted telegraph poles and overturned dozens of vehicles, while the troops had to huddle on the ground, covered with blankets. Tobruk was no easy nut to crack. On high white cliffs above a small harbour lay the town itself, capable of housing many thousands of men. The outer defensive perimeter of forts, wire and minefields was 30 miles in length with both flanks resting on the sea: the inner perimeter was 19 miles long. Powerful artillery commanded every approach. Since the railway ended at Matruh, almost all our supplies had to be brought up to the front by road, mostly in captured Italian lorries, for little could be landed from ships at Sollum.

After the fall of Tobruk, Marshal Graziani had only two strong detachments in Cyrenaica—part of his 60th Division at Derna, and a brigade, with 160 tanks, at Mekili, south of that port, the whole being under General Bergonzoli, a capable and very elusive commander familiarly known as 'Old Electric Whiskers'. "O'Connor decided to contain the Derna position and attack the Mekili Group", writes Major-General Fuller,[1] "but during the night of 26th/27th January that group withdrew towards Barce. Thereupon Wavell saw O'Connor, and together they decided that while the 7th Armoured Division was to move across the desert by way of Mekili and cut the coastal road south of Benghazi, the rest of the Desert Army was to press the enemy along the road towards Benghazi. Early on the 30th, the enemy began falling back on Barce, whereupon it was decided to move at once across the desert. The 7th Armoured Division set out from Mekili to Msus which was occupied by armoured cars at daybreak on February 5th. A few hours later, Major-General M. O'M. Creagh sent two detachments to cut the coastal road in two places some 50 miles south of Benghazi at a point called Beda Fomm. On the same evening, an enemy column, 5,000 strong, retreating southwards from Benghazi, suddenly came upon the 4th Armoured Brigade on the coastal road and forthwith surrendered. Next, on the 6th, the main enemy column appeared, including a large number of tanks; but coming into action piece-meal, it was destroyed piece-meal, 84 of its tanks being put out of action. Pinned down on almost 20 miles of road, blocked in front and attacked in rear, the 60th Division was so completely trapped that at dawn next day General Bergonzoli surrendered unconditionally, and 20,000 prisoners, 120 tanks and 190 guns were added to the captures of the

---

[1] *The Second World War*, 1939-1945, by Major-General J. F. C. Fuller, p.97.

Desert Army. Thus ended one of the most audacious campaigns ever fought. In all, though never more than two full divisions were employed, an army of nearly ten divisions was destroyed between December 7th and February 7th, and 130,000 prisoners, 400 tanks and 1,240 guns were captured at a cost of 500 killed, 1,373 wounded and 55 missing."

O'Connor swept on to Agedabia and Agheila, nearly 200 miles south of Benghazi. Graziani's army had disintegrated and no less than 19 Fascist Generals were in our hands. An area as large as England and Wales had been swept clear of the enemy. The Suez Canal was no longer in danger. The victory appeared complete, irrevocable. But appearances are often deceptive. Germany was already preparing to rescue her fallen ally, and our front in Cyrenaica had to be starved or reinforcements because of the urgent demands of the campaign in Greece. Thus the ground which we had won so rapidly, and more besides, was destined to be lost in the Third Libyan Campaign which is outlined later in this chapter.

The Indian Sappers and Miners played a useful though unspectacular part in the Second Libyan Campaign. When General O'Connor set out from rail-head at Mersa Matruh on December 7th, 1940, the 4th Division Engineers were occupied in normal duties. 4 Field Company assisted the 5th Brigade in the capture of Tummar East and Tummar West, while 12 Field Company, 11 Field Park Company and 18 Field Company lifted mines, demolished obstacles, repaired desert tracks or worked on water-supplies. Owing to the mobile character of the operations, the featureless nature of the ground and the poor resistance offered by the enemy, there were few opportunities for the Sappers to come into the limelight. A detachment of 4 Field Company moved with the "I" tanks which were primarily responsible for the victory at Sidi Barrani, but no formidable obstacles were encountered. As soon as the Italian camps were entered, the Sappers began to collect and drive off enemy lorries piled high with equipment and stores. They also took spare parts from many vehicles. After two days of such work, during which a Khamseen raged and filled the air with sand, 4 Field Company was detailed to guard some 4,000 Italian prisoners who were only too glad to be out of danger and had not the least inclination to escape. The 4th Division Engineers also undertook water-supply duties and assisted the infantry in clearing away minefields around Sidi Barrani. Italian officers helped them by indicating the positions of the mines. Some of these officers must have been sorry to exchange their deep dug-outs for the stark realities of a prisoner-of-war cage, for the furniture, fittings and stores of wine and food in their subterranean quarters were luxurious and profuse. Silver-topped jars and bottles of scent adorned their dressing-tables, and gold-braided uniforms filled their wardrobes.

Colonel D. B. Chopra, who was serving as a subaltern in 12 Field Company, has much to say about his experiences during the Battle of Sidi Barrani. "The Company", he writes,[1] "was in support of the 16th British Infantry Brigade which formed part of the 4th Indian Infantry Division. After the capture of the objectives by the 5th and 11th Indian Infantry Brigades, our Brigade was to be launched during the early morning of December 9th, having completed the approach march the previous evening. To our surprise we found our night bivouac were uncomfortably close to the enemy positions, and as soon as we started moving, our vehicles came under fire. We dismounted and took up positions, and enemy planes began to 'strafe' us. They flew so low that I wanted to engage them with the small arms of my Section, but I found that our rifles and Light Machine Gun had been left in the vehicles. Running to one vehicle, I retrieved the L.M.G. and began to engage the enemy, and the men then rushed to the other vehicles and got their rifles. Never again did I allow them to be separated from their arms! The 16th Brigade suffered heavy casualties in the initial stages of the battle when it was caught on the move in vehicles close to the enemy positions; but after the arrival of our tanks and Divisional Artillery, things began to improve. Before dark, we had over-run the Italian defences facing south and south-west. Streams of prisoners started pouring in, and I was told to take charge of them. I had a few thousands to look after and only my Section as escort. As I was marching them away from the front line, enemy planes again came overhead and began to 'strafe' us. My escort took cover and the prisoners ran in all directions, while I shouted myself hoarse in efforts to check the stampede. However, after the air attack was over, I got the column re-assembled and marched it back some distance from the front line, where we hurriedly constructed a cage with concertina wire. I handed over the prisoners to another unit while my Section was sent to rejoin 12 Field Company, which was not far off; but afterwards I was unable to locate the Company in the dark so I decided to spend the night where I was. In the morning, to my great surprise, I found myself within 200

---

[1] Notes by Colonel D. B. Chopra, dated March 15th, 1951.

yards of my own Section! After this incident, I made a habit of always recording compass bearings to important landmarks before darkness fell. Day dawned with the usual blinding sandstorm, reducing visibility at times to zero, and the entire Company, except Major Sutherland, myself and my Section lost its way and failed to arrive until the afternoon when the storm had abated".

The scene now shifts from the Western Desert to the Sudan, whither the 4th Indian Division was sent early in January 1941, shortly after the Battle of Sidi Barrani, to join the 5th Indian Division while General O'Connor was chasing the defeated Italians to Benghazi. The 4th Division moved partly by sea to Port Sudan and partly by rail and boat up the Nile. The transfer was made by order of General Wavell in whose perspicacity and ability the Prime Minister had the greatest confidence. "Without this far-reaching decision," writes Mr. Winston Churchill,[1] "the victory of Keren could not have been achieved and the liberation of Abyssinia would have been subject to indefinite delays". That Mr. Churchill was resolved to support General Wavell to the utmost is proved by a telegram which reached the Headquarters in Cairo on December 18th, 1940. "See St Matthew, Chapter VII, Verse 7", it ran. A reference to the Bible will show that the message was "Ask, and it shall be given to you: seek, and ye shall find: knock, and it shall be opened unto you."

The political and military situation in the Sudan in the autumn of 1939, before Italy entered the war, was fantastic. Nobody wanted to fight, and least of all the Italians. Backed by small British and Egyptian garrisons far inland, the Sudan Defence Force, the local police and some irregular formations were responsible for watching 1,200 miles of frontier as well as guarding Khartoum, Atbara, Port Sudan and other important centres.[2] Friendly relations with the Italians in Eritrea and Abyssinia persisted long after Germany started the Second World War. For instance, on the last day of 1939, the Commander of the Troops in the Sudan dined with the officers of the Italian garrison at Metemma opposite our frontier post at Gallabat, and as late as May 1940, officers of the Sudan Defence Force in Gedaref and Kassala were receiving invitations to visit Asmara. It came as a shock, therefore, when friendships of many years standing had to be broken suddenly through the folly of a Dictator in Rome.

---

[1] *The Second World War*, by the Rt. Hon. Winston Churchill, Vol. II.

[2] See the map of North-East Africa included in this chapter.

In August and September 1940, the 5th Indian Division under Major-General L. M. Heath voyaged from India to the Middle East. One of its three brigades, the 7th, was detached to join the 4th Indian Division in Egypt, while the 9th and 10th Brigades, under Brigadiers A. G. O. M. Mayne and W. J. Slim respectively, were sent up-country from Port Sudan to join a 29th Brigade under Brigadier J. C. O. Marriott, formed after a redistribution of the three British battalions already in the Sudan. The Engineer formations with the Division consisted of 2 Field Company (Bengal), 20 and 21 Field Companies (Bombay), 44 Field Park Company (Madras) and 6 and 8 Army Troops Companies[1] and 2 Bridging Section (Bengal). Later additions were 16 Workshop and Park Company (Madras) under Major J. F. C. Reilly, R.E., and 101 Railway Construction Company (Madras) under Major R. Gardiner, R.E. The forces in the Sudan were commanded by Lieut.-General Sir W. Platt whose anxieties must have been considerable before the advent of the 5th Division, the odds against him being 10 to 1. On December 2nd, 1940, shortly before he initiated the attack on Sidi Barrani, General Wavell summoned to Cairo Lieut-General Platt and also Lieut.-General Sir Alan Cunningham who commanded the forces in Kenya. He told them that he wanted them to foster rebellion in Abyssinia and afterwards to carry out a gigantic pincer movement against the Italians in that country and Eritrea. The movement was to be from north and south simultaneously, one force being based on Khartoum and the other on Nairobi. African Divisions would advance from Kenya, and the 4th and 5th Indian Divisions from the Sudan. Hence the sudden transfer of the 4th Division from the Western Desert. Both pincers would encounter exceptionally difficult country—in the north, precipitous mountains, and in the south, immense and arid plains—and both would meet vastly superior strength. Daring and speed must overcome all obstacles. The enemy, however, could not be prevented from securing some early successes. They had occupied Kassala and Gallabat on the Sudan frontier. Columns had marched deep into Kenya, and in August 1940, British Somaliland had been over-run. They had secured from the Vichy French the use of the Red Sea port of Djibuti, far south of their main port of Massawa, and thus they could interfere with our line of communication to Suez. East Africa presented a dark and depressing picture.

---

[1] The Os. C. Companies were Majors R. H. Platt, R.E., H. E. G. St. George, R.E., G. E. H. Philbrick, R.E., R. W. W. How, R.E., H. Grattan, R.E., and F. K. Moodie I.E.

The voyage of the 5th Indian Division Engineers to Port Sudan was accomplished safely, though not without minor difficulties. Colonel Arjan Singh, who was serving with 6 Army Troops Company under Major H. Grattan, writes as follows:— "The date of sailing and the destination were kept closely guarded secrets, and even the Captain of our ship did not know his destination until after he had left Bombay. As Quartermaster, I had to arrange for many different types of kitchens in the restricted space available in a ship not specially built for Indian troops, for in those days Hindus, Mussulmans, Sikhs, Madrassis, Bengalis and Mahrattas were each entitled to have a separate kitchen. The ship's Chief Officer, however, had never heard of any such arrangement. "There is the galley" said he. "Get on with it." He recognized only two divisions in his crew—the Engineer group and the Deck hands—for which two galleys were sufficient. But after I had told him that I was myself an ex-sailor, he was persuaded to make certain alterations and, as it was impossible to have separate kitchens for every caste in each unit, it was decided that all cooking should be done in combined central community kitchens. Our convoy consisted of forty ships, some of which sailed from Karachi or Cochin. They all met in the Arabian Sea and were escorted by two warships. It was surprising that the Italians, who were in a strong position along the Somaliland and Red Sea coasts, made no attempt to interfere with us. Either their system of intelligence was poor or they lacked initiative. In any case, we arrived undamaged in Port Sudan where unloading from the ships and loading into trains was done at night to avoid air raids."

Both Kassala and Gallabat had been occupied by the enemy on July 4th, 1940; but Khartoum, though subjected to occasional air attack, was never seriously threatened, and with the advent of the rainy season a period of watching and waiting developed along the entire length of the Sudan-Abyssinia frontier. This was much to our advantage since it gave time for the 5th Indian Division to arrive and concentrate for offensive action. Artillery also began to reach the Sudan to supplement the single battery of 3.7" howitzers which till then had been the sole representative of that arm. Haile Selassie, the exiled Emperor of Abyssinia, was back in Khartoum, ready for an opportunity to return to Addis Ababa, whence he had been driven by Mussolini in 1935. His presence did much to encourage the patriots in his country and forced the Italians to increase their precautions against a rising in their rear.

In October 1940, the 9th and 10th Brigades of the 5th Indian Division took post on the frontier, the former on the Atbara River opposite Kassala and the latter in the Gallabat area to the south.[1] A mobile force, known as "Gazelle", composed mostly of Sudan Defence Force armoured cars, was formed under Colonel (later General) F. W. Messervy to harry the enemy north of Kassala. The level of the Atbara was falling and consequently the river was fordable in many places. These fords were important in the defensive scheme, and the 5th Division was fully occupied in watching them. General Heath was obliged for a time to remain on the defensive because an advance into Eritrea was impossible until he was reinforced. Nevertheless, his brigades frequently took the initiative in local actions. On November 6th, for instance, Brigadier Slim's 10th Brigade attacked and entered the fort at Gallabat, though it had to withdraw later under heavy bombing. The Sappers and Miners in this affair were represented by 21 Field Company, of the Bombay Group, which remained in the fort to the last moment to destroy buildings and stores. Slim's policy was not to re-occupy Gallabat but to patrol vigourously and deny the fort to the enemy. His troops re-entered the place on November 9th, and again on the 10th before retiring to their defensive positions. The Brigadier was recognized as a brilliant leader. There is a story that a Scottish soldier once shouted to him "Don't you worry, Sir. We'll follow you anywhere", to which Slim replied "Don't you be so b.... sure of that. I'm going to follow *you*!"[2]. In the middle of December, the 10th Brigade was relieved in the Gallabat area by the 9th Brigade which continued the policy of denying Gallabat to the enemy.

During October, several units of the Bengal Sappers were busily employed further north. At Gedaref, which was second only to Kassala in road and rail importance, 2 Field Company provided a water-supply, carried out road reconnaissances and prepared bridges for demolition, and in November, it was at work on ford crossings of the Atbara south of Kassals.[3] 2 Bridging Section dug trenches at Gedaref and established an Engineer dump. 6 Army Troops Company began to improve the road communication between Port Sudan and

---

[1] See the map of Eritrea and the Sudan-Abyssinia Border included in this chapter.

[2] "*Ball of Fire*. The 5th Indian Division in the Second World War", by Antony Breet-James, p. 30.

[3] *Brief History of the K.G.Vs O. Bengal Sappers and Miners Group, R.I.E. Aug. 1939-July 1946*, by Lieut. G. Pearson, R.E., p. 7.

Kassala. A railway ran from Port Sudan to Atbara on the Nile, where it joined the main line connecting Khartoum with Wadi Halfa; but Kassala could be reached only along a branch line taking off at Haiya on the Port Sudan-Atbara line. There was no road connection between it and Haiya, and a new road, away from the coast, was needed between Port Sudan and Haiya. Accordingly, 6 Army Troops Company was stationed at Gebeit, in the Red Sea Hills, to prepare for the transit of the 4th Division coming from the Western Desert. A Section under 2nd Lieut. Arjan Singh, I.E., though assisted by 300 labourers, could not cope with some of the work, so Arjan Singh asked the commander of the Advance Party of the 4th Division (a Lieut.-Colonel) for the loan of three infantry companies. He met with a blank refusal, and it was only after he had appealed to his Chief Engineer and induced the senior infantry officer to examine the route in person that he got the working parties and was able to push a temporary road through with rapidity. The incident shows the difficulties which may arise on active service through a disparity in rank. While at Gebeit, 6 Army Troops Company, assisted by a detachment of 8 Army Troops Company of the 5th Division, built a very fine causeway, 500 yards long, through a sandy river bed.

At Atbara, where the Atbara River joins the Nile, the main line of railway from Wadi Halfa to Khartoum crosses the tributary river by a large steel bridge, and as this structure was liable to damage by bombing, 8 Army Troops Company was detailed to build a boat bridge. The project was completed successfully with the help of local labour, though there was some delay because the water-level fell so rapidly that half the bridge had to be supported on piers instead of boats. The unit then moved southwards to a place about 20 miles from Gedaref to build an advance base depot for the 5th Division. The design was ingenious for the depot was made to resemble a native village by the extensive use of circular grass huts known as *tukls*. Other Sapper units with the 5th Division were 44 Field Park Company and 16 Workshops and Park Company, both of the Madras Corps. 20 Field Company, under Major H. E. G. St George, R.E., and 21 Field Company, under Major G. E. H. Philbrick, R.E., were present also. 44 Field Park Company was stationed at first at Gebeit where it was employed in making a road to the old port of Suakin, preparing landing grounds, improving water-supplies and arranging for stores' dumps.[1] Later, it went to Gedaref to remove

---

[1] *Bangalore News Letter*, January 1946.

unexploded enemy bombs; and still later, in February 1941, it was at Barentu in Eritrea, engaged in salvaging stores from gold mines abandoned by the enemy during the British offensive.[1] The greater part of 16 Workshop and Park Company went to Khartoum to prepare Engineer Stores Base Depots (E.S.B.Ds.) in various large centres. A detachment left in Port Sudan suffered some casualties on December 16th through enemy bombing. After the general advance into Eritrea, the unit opened an E.S.B.D. at Kassala and finished the campaign at Asmara, where it took over a number of civil installations and quantities of abandoned enemy stores. Such employment, though unspectacular, should be given due credit, for without it the progress of the military operations would have been gravely hampered.

Colonel R. A. Loomba, who served as a Captain in 16 Company during this period, writes as follows:— "It was not until May 1940 that it was decided to reorganize a Divisional HQ Company into a Workshop and Park Company for service overseas, and the establishment and organization of the new unit was almost the same as it is today. The Stores element was found from the M.E.S. and consisted of some 9 or 10 British Warrant Officers and about 20 Indian subordinates who were hurriedly given elementary military training and put into uniform. They were on special terms and conditions of service but unfortunately had no Depot until an M.E.S. Depot was formed later. The unit supported the operations in the Sudan and Eritrea, during 1940 and 1941, under most favourable conditions. There was no language problem, and the Stores' procedure resembled that in the M.E.S. A British civilian Stores Officer from the Sudan P.W.D. was attached to the Chief Engineer's Office for the local purchase of stores and liaison duties. Immediately on arrival, the Workshop and Park Company was split into two parts to run E.S.B.Ds. and E.B.Ws. at Port Sudan and Khartoum, and as operations developed, advanced depots were established and run efficiently by detachments ably assisted by MES storekeepers. After the fall of Eritrea and Abyssinia, large stocks of captured Engineer stores had to be taken over and sent to Egypt. In addition, sabotaged workshops had to be re-established quickly in order to produce articles needed by the occupying forces. The bulk of the unit was therefore concentrated in Eritrea, and the depot and workshops at

---

[1] *A Short History of the Q.V's O. Madras Sappers and Miners during World War II*, 1939-45, by Lieut.-Colonel R. A. Lindsell, R.E., p. 5.

Khartoum were run almost entirely by civilians. During the operations the unit undertook tasks far beyond its normal role because of the shortage of manpower. For instance, at one period it established 4 E.S.B.Ds. and ran 3 E.B.Ws. This was only possible because of the skilled labour available and the high quality of the M.E.S. staff posted to the unit."

The first contingent of the 4th Indian Division having landed at Port Sudan on January 7th, 1941, General Platt was able to assume the offensive and strike at Eritrea. The risk was great but he took it, for the tide was flowing against the Italians. Harassed continually by Messervy's "Gazelle Force", General Frusci, the enemy commander on the northern front, had begun to withdraw to a defensive line along the edge of the high plateau running from Agordat and Keren, past Adowa, to Gondar, and this retrograde movement spread from north to south till it reached the Gallabat area. On January 19th, Platt marched into Eritrea and occupied Kassala, Sabderat and Tessenei, all of which the enemy had evacuated under cover of darkness. This was a bold stroke for he had at the moment only the 10th and 29th Brigades of the 5th Division and the 11th Brigade of the 4th Division. The role of the 5th Division was to take Tessenei and Aicota, while the 4th Division, with "Gazelle" under command, was to push through Sabderat towards Keru on the road leading to Agordat and Keren.[1] The troops made good progress through minefields and demolitions, and early on January 21st the 5th Division occupied Aicota while "Gazelle" entered the Keru Gorge. Considerable resistance was encountered in this rugged defile until the enemy melted away after being attacked in rear by the 10th Brigade and the Sudan Defence Force operating from Aicota. On the 28th, the 5th and 11th Brigades of the 4th Division met bitter opposition in an attack on Agordat, but the "I" tanks knocked out the Italian armour on the 31st and cut the enemy's line of communication to Keren. Though now thoroughly demoralized, the Italians were saved from immediate collapse by the arrival of reinforcements from Abyssinia and by the terribly difficult nature of the country through which our troops had to advance. Nevertheless, Mussolini's African Empire needed only one strong push to send it tottering to ruin, and that push might have been given by

---

[1] "*From Pyramid to Pagoda*", (History of the West Yorkshire Regiment, 1938-48), by Lieut.-Colonel E. W. C. Sandes, D.S.O., M.C., Chapter VI. See also the map of Eritrea and the Sudan-Abyssinia Border included in this chapter.

Sappers and Miners repairing the road to Barentu

General O'Connor's forces, then rushing on Benghazi, had it not been for the despatch from Egypt of three divisions under General Wilson to help Greece. It is an object lesson in the effect of operations in one theatre on those in another. War is indeed a tangled skein which few can unravel.

Although several Sapper and Miner companies took part in the general offensive which culminated in the Battle of Keren, a few were denied that privilege and among them 21 Field Company which had to remain with the 9th Brigade at Gallabat to hold the enemy in the south while General Platt delivered his blow in the north. The minor operations around Gallabat ebbed and flowed during most of January 1941. The Italians were now in Gallabat Fort and were holding tenaciously to Metemma on the other bank of the Atbara, but on January 30th they vacated the fort after dark as the first step in a general withdrawal. A small Mobile Column was then sent out to probe towards Metemma and beyond it to Wahni on the road to Gondar. The column included a detachment of 21 Field Company under the command of 2nd Lieut. Premendra Singh Bhagat, I.E. At first, it met with no resistance, though progress beyond Metemma was slow because the retreating enemy had mined the track extensively, but it would have been much slower had it not been for the gallantry of young Bhagat which brought the award of the first Victoria Cross earned by an Indian Commissioned Officer in the Second World War. The citation runs as follows:— "During the pursuit of the enemy following the capture of Metemma on the night of 31st January-1st February, 1941, 2nd Lieut. Bhagat was in command of a section of a Field Company, Sappers and Miners, detailed to accompany the leading mobile troops (Bren Carriers) to clear the road and adjacent areas of mines. For a period of 4 days and over a distance of 55 miles, this officer led the column in the leading carrier. He detected and supervised the clearing of 15 minefields, working at high pressure from dawn till dusk. On two occasions his carrier was blown up, with casualties to others; and on a third occasion, when ambushed and under close enemy fire, he carried straight on with his task. He refused relief when worn out with strain and fatigue (and with one ear-drum punctured by an explosion) on the grounds that he was now better qualified to continue his task to the end. His coolness over a period of 96 hours, and his persistence and gallantry not only in battle but throughout the long period during which the safety of the column and the speed at which it could advance were dependent on his personal efforts, were of the highest order". A senior British Officer records that not until February 3rd did Bhagat relinquish his dangerous post, and then only on a peremptory order from the Column Commander who rightly decided that the young subaltern should be sent back for medical treatment. The column reached and bombarded Wahni and returned to Gallabat on the 7th, and so ended a very successful raid. The coveted Cross was presented to Lieut. Bhagat at a ceremony held in New Delhi early in November 1941 in the forecourt of the Viceroy's House.[1] It was bestowed by the Viceroy himself in the presence of General Wavell, then Commander-in-Chief, India, and a large gathering of military and civil officers. Lieut.-Colonel H. E. Horsfield, R.E., Commandant of the Royal Bombay Sappers and Miners, conducted Lieut. Bhagat to the dais, and an official account of the action for which the Victoria Cross was awarded was read in English and Urdu. This was a great day for the Corps of Indian Engineers, and particularly for the Bombay Group of the Indian Sappers and Miners.

The exploits of some of the other Sapper companies during the operations preceding the Battle of Keren deserve more than passing mention. In December 1940, when the offensive against the Kassala-Tessenai position was being planned, 2 Field Company intensified its work on the approaches to ford crossings over the Atbara, and on January 15th, 1941, moved towards the River Gash, south of Kassala, in support of the 10th Brigade. The bed of the Gash, at that time, was a dry expanse of soft sand, but the Company soon laid steel-mesh track across the sand and thus enabled the 5th Division to reach Aicota rapidly. On January 19th, when the enemy withdrew from Kassala, the first unit to enter the place was 6 Army Troops Company. Led by "Gazelle Force", the 4th Division passed through the town in pursuit of the enemy, the objective being Agordat. 4 Field Company, which arrived in Kassala on the 21st, set to work immediately to improve the dry-weather track through the Keru Defile leading to Bishia and Keren, and cleared the defile of many anti-tank mines and obstructions. Meanwhile, 2 Field Company, with the 10th Brigade, was moving southwards to a position on the Agordat-Barentu Road, arranging water-supplies, laying track across sandy ravines and removing rocks. Next it was called upon to deal with a huge road-block, 8 miles north of Barentu, which was holding up the advance of the 5th Division. Masses of rock, many as large as a 3-ton lorry, had been blown down onto the road from an

---

[1] Supplement to *The R.E. Journal*, December 1941.

Colonel P. S. Bhagat, V.C.

overhanging cliff. The obstruction was 200 yards in length and was often under enemy machine gun fire and sniping as well as dive bombing; but with some assistance, 2 Field Company got through at last after several days of furious labour, though the final clearance could not be completed until after the enemy had abandoned Barentu.

4 Field Company did well while the 4th Indian Division, under Major-General N. M. Beresford-Peirse, was trying to annihilate the enemy entrenched in the hills around Agordat. On January 29th, when the 11th Brigade gained a hold on the crest of Mount Cochen, a lofty feature east of the town, 4 Field Company prepared tracks up the rough and thorny hill-side for the maintenance of the infantry and afterwards carried up ammunition and water. "On the evening of January 30th" writes Pearson,[1] "the position was critical as the brigade was in imminent danger of being driven off the hill. A Section of 4 Field Company was ordered to reoccupy positions covering the direct approach to Brigade Headquarters which had been evacuated by the infantry, and O.C. Company was told to take charge and organize the defence of the summit still held by our hardpressed infantry. Later, other sections were used as infantry, and a detachment under Jemadar Kirat Singh led a bayonet charge to capture a machine gun post.[2] Mount Cochen was held, and Agordat fell on January 31st". 4 Field Company received high praise for its exploits on this occasion, for it had contributed in a large degree to the success of the operation. It was followed to Agordat by 6 Army Troops Company which took over the power house, pumping plant and water-points in the captured town and afterwards repaired bridges, improved roads and collected masses of abandoned enemy equipment.

A detachment of 12 Field Company, under 2nd Lieut. D. B. Chopra, I.E., served for a time with the mobile "Gazelle Force" after the Company had arrived with the 4th Division from the Western Desert. "We moved up to the front immediately after landing at Port Sudan", writes Chopra.[3] "The enemy, in his withdrawal, had laid extensive minefields through which passages were cleared by my Section which was always with the leading brigade. The advance was so rapid that the Sappers worked literally 24 hours a day for several days, making

---

[1] *Brief History of the K.G.V's O. Bengal Sappers and Miners Group, R.I.E., August 1939-July 1946*, by Lieut. G. Pearson, R.E., p. 10.

[2] Jemadar Kirat Singh was subsequently awarded the I.O.M. for bravery at Cochen and at the road-block at Keren, this being the first decoration won by a Bengal Sapper and Miner in the war.

[3] Notes by Colonel D. B. Chopra, dated March 15th, 1951.

diversions through *nalas* which were always mined. I disarmed every new type of mine myself and showed the mechanism to the men before allowing mine clearance to proceed. As the advance outstripped the maintenance capacity of our transport columns, we had to make full use of the railway, but unfortunately the enemy had removed all rolling stock. Consequently, it was decided to deposit a small Sapper detachment behind the enemy lines in the hope of securing some rolling stock. I volunteered for the job and selected two Sappers from my Section to accompany me. We were to be picked up in the evening by a tank; but after waiting till midnight at the *rendez-vous*, we were told that as the enemy had withdrawn our mission was impracticable, and so we returned to the Company. Early next morning, I was ordered to join "Gazelle Force" with one Sub-Section, and in a few hours we overhauled it and were placed at the tail of the column. Though I pointed out that it was desirable that my detachment should be well forward in order to deal quickly with mines and obstacles, I was over-ruled. Later, when there was an abnormally long halt, I went forward and found that a bridge called the "Ponte Mussolini"[1] had been partly demolished and its approaches heavily mined and covered by fire. As both approach roads were on high embankments and the river was wide and sandy, I recommended a diversion and said that this would take at least 8 to 10 hours. Work was started at once, and by the following day we had the entire "Gazelle Force" across the obstacle. I remained with "Gazelle" until contact was effected with the main enemy position near Keren".

In order to reach the Italian capital at Asmara, General Platt had to force a passage through the Keren Gorge situated in country so fantastically rugged and mountainous that it was once described as 'a stormy sea moved by the wrath of God'. Early attempts by General Beresford-Peirse's 4th Division to penetrate this defile unaided in the face of strong resistance had met with little success. The Italians were determined to hold it to the end and threw into it their last strategic reserves of any importance. Here, General Frusci massed a powerful force of artillery, and with his infantry securely entrenched on every height and having superb facilities for observation, he could afford to await the issue with some confidence. On the left of the road climbing up through the deep and winding

---

[1] The Ponte Mussolini spanned the Baraka River about 12 miles from Agordat. The events described took place about February 2nd, after Agordat had been captured.

gorge were the hills known as Cameron Ridge, Sanchil, Brig's Peak, Samanna and Mount Amba: on the right, Dologorodoc crowned by a fort, Falestoh, Zelale and Zeban[1]. "The whole mass of mountains, like a bleak and jagged screen", writes Antony Brett-James,[2] "looms up into the sky some 2,500 feet above the green valley of the approach. It is steep, high, immense, forbidding. The soil crumbles beneath your feet, and the rocks are easily dislodged if used as a lever to pull yourself up. At every step, spear-grass stabs through the toughest clothing and the skin is torn by prickly thorn-trees. It is no wonder that those of our soldiers, laden with equipment, rifles, ammunition and shovels, who actually reached the almost unclimable heights were momentarily too exhausted to make further effort. It was this moment of breathless exhaustion and strain that the Italians chose so often for delivering a counter-attack".

The story of the long and desperate struggle in and around the Keren Gorge begins on the night of February 3rd/4th, 1941, when the 11th Brigade of the 4th Indian Division failed in a gallant attempt to capture and hold the Sanchil height to the west of the road and railway. Italian guns fired down on the attackers and grenades were tossed among them, but the Cameron Highlanders managed to establish themselves on a ridge below the summit which thereafter bore their name. On the following night, the 3/14th Punjabis reached the crest of Brig's Peak and held it for a few hours, but in the end they had to withdraw under intensive bombardment. The 5th Brigade now appeared on the scene and General Beresford-Peirse sent it against the Acqua Ridge to the right of the gorge between Falestoh and Zelale and at the head of the wide Happy Valley. Again he failed; but on February 10th he prepared to try once more, this time on both flanks simultaneously with the 29th Brigade of the 5th Division in reserve. Sanchil and Brig's Peak on the left were stormed, but neither could be held, and the Acqua attack fared no better. So the 4th Division, with only Cameron Ridge to show for much blood and sweat, settled down to await the arrival of the remainder of the 5th Division. The enemy made good use of the respite so gained. They had already blocked the road by a huge demolition at the most difficult spot and now they proceeded to pour reinforcements and guns into their elaborate defences.

---

[1] See the map of the Battle of Keren included in this chapter.

[2] "*Ball of Fire*", by Antony Brett-James, pp. 51, 52.

With the 5th Brigade at Keren was 12 Field Company of the Madras Corps which, with 4 Field Company of the Bengal Corps and 18 Field Company of the Bombay Corps, had to bear the heavy burden of the engineering operations before the 5th Divisional Engineers began to arrive. Colonel D. B. Chopra, then a subaltern with 12 Field Company, gives the following description of his experiences:—
"The enemy had blown up a long stretch of road and had incorporated with it a strong road-block, and after seeing it in a tank from some distance, I reported the details of this obstacle. Meanwhile, the 4th Division had come up and it became apparent that a full-scale attack would have to be launched to capture the enemy positions guarding the obstacle before the main line of communication could be used. The 5th Brigade was detailed to take a ridge on the right and to get behind the enemy's position at Keren, and I was sent with a reconnaissance party to find a route by which transport especially tanks, could get as close as possible to the objective. The reconnaissance was conducted in broad daylight and in full view of the enemy. We had scarcely finished when the forward elements of the Brigade began to arrive in the area. I told the Brigade Major that there was a route further ahead which could be developed for transport without much labour, and he directed me to go as far as possible along it towards the enemy position and report exactly where the route met the ridge we were to attack. After obtaining this information, I was returning along the route when I was challenged suddenly by troops whose language I could not understand. It was very dark, so my Naik and myself took cover behind an embankment. I then told the Naik to find a way round the flank, but as soon as he started we were challenged again from barely 20 yards away. I replied in a few words of Arabic which I had picked up in Egypt and thereupon we were recognized and allowed to pass. It turned out that the men were Sudanese, and to this day I believe that I owe my life to those few Arabic words".

Deeply involved in the tragic experiences of the 4th Division at Keren was 4 Field Company which was in support of the 11th Brigade, the first to attack. The tanks which accompanied the Brigade found the road through the gorge blocked by hundreds of tons of rock covered by fire from enemy positions in the hills. After Cameron Ridge had been secured, 4 Field Company began to make paths and mule tracks up the hill-side so that the infantry could be maintained in their exposed position by carriers and by pack transport which General Platt had been collecting for some time. The unit accompanied the 3/1st Punjabis when that battalion seized and tried to hold Brig's Peak on February 10th. By day, the Sappers laboured on the paths and tracks: by night, they fought as infantry on the crest. This continued for 36 hours until, in the early hours of February 12th, the peak was lost and the troops withdrew to Cameron Ridge. 4 Field Company suffered many casualties and among them a Jemadar who died bravely while leading a bayonet charge. During the lull of nearly a month which followed the failure of all attempts by the 4th Division, consolidation proceeded steadily on Cameron Ridge. Early in March, the 9th and 10th Brigades of the 5th Division arrived from the Tessenai area, and 2 and 4 Field Companies of the Bengal Corps met for the first time at the front and together prepared to take their part in opening the Keren Gorge road.

Some weeks earlier, General Platt had initiated a subsidiary movement from the north which was designed to draw off a considerable part of General Frusci's force at Keren. On February 9th, part of the 7th Brigade of the 4th Division, together with some French formations, had crossed the Eritrean frontier near the Red Sea coast and had taken Karora, 150 miles north of Keren. A few days later, this column, under Brigadier H. R. Briggs, occupied Kubkub, only 40 miles from Keren, and on March 1st, broke through the Mescelit defile only 15 miles away. This threat to his communications with Asmara and Massawa forced General Frusci to look over his right shoulder and keep a reserve near the coast. As the coastal route was long and rough, it was decided to disembark a Company of infantry and a Section of 12 Field Company at an advanced point down the coast to improve landing facilities and receive supplies for the column. A jetty was built, washed away in a storm, and rebuilt, and by improvised means the Sapper detachment contrived to keep the force properly supplied until the race for Massawa started after the fall of Keren. The race was won by the advanced troops of the 5th Division; but some of the Sappers of the coastal column were only a few minutes behind. Havildar-Major Sampangi Raju of 12 Field Company gained the Indian Order of Merit for gallantry shown in the coastal expedition and on many other occasions between March 27th and 30th. The citation records that he displayed great courage, initiative, skill and devotion to duty in the destruction of well concealed minefields, in one of which, containing a new type of mine, he personally dismantled the first mine and cleared the most dangerous area after three men had been killed.[1]

---

[1] Some of Havildar-Major (later Captain) Sampangi's experiences are given in an article entitled "I will never forget."

The assault at Keren opened with a roar at dawn on March 15th, 1941, every gun being concentrated on a vital target. On the left, the 4th Division was to advance once again from Cameron Ridge against the heights of Sanchil and Brig's Peak. On the right, the 9th Brigade of the 5th Division was to take Fort Dologorodoc and Falestoh beyond it, after which the 29th Brigade would capture Mount Zeban and advance on the town of Keren, which the 10th Brigade would occupy later. The 4th Division attack met with only limited success, yet enough was gained to warrant the start of the operations to the right of the road. By 6.15 a.m., Dologorodoc had fallen to the West Yorkshires, but the success of any further advance depended upon whether they could hold the place. This they did for several days under heavy bombardment and repeated counter-attacks and thus enabled the area of conflict to be extended.[1] 2 Field Company, with infantry working parties, was busily employed in building a mule-track up to the captured fort. In the words of Brigadier F. W. Messervy, who was now in command of the 9th Brigade, the occupation of Fort Dologorodoc virtually sealed the fate of Keren, although the attempt by the 29th Brigade against Falestoh and Zeban on March 17th was unsuccessful. On March 19th, the West Yorkshires were still hanging on grimly in Fort Dologorodoc under heavy fire from Sanchil, which the 4th Division was trying once more to capture. The 3/18th Garhwalis lost all their British officers, except one, in a desperate but abortive attack. Nothing then remained but to make a final thrust up the road through the gorge which the enemy had obstructed by an enormous block of rocks and rubble, thus effectively preventing the advance of our "I" tanks which were to lead the way to Keren and Asmara.

The Keren road-block was more than 100 yards in length and cleverly sited at a spot where the road turned a corner and entered the narrowest part of the gorge. A cliff had been blown down onto the highway, and the obstacle was well covered by fire. The enemy, moreover, had perfect observation posts overlooking it. After the capture of Dologorodoc, a closer reconnaissance became possible, and on the night of March 16/17th an officer of 2 Field Company went out to examine the breach. He reported that there were two craters in the road, each about 20 yards long, and between them and beyond them, lengths of debris including many large rocks, but he

---

[1] "*From Pyramid to Pagoda*", by Lieut.-Colonel E. W. C. Sandes, D.S.O., M.C., Chapter VI.

estimated that a path of some sort for tracked vehicles might be opened in 48 hours. On the following night, Lieut.-Colonel A. H. G. Napier, R.E., now C.R.E. 4th Division, made a personal reconnaissance with a detachment of 2 Field Company and some Indian infantry. He had hoped to be able to start clearing the debris at once and had arranged a programme of artillery and small arms' fire; but the enemy were on the alert, and after the little force had come under fire, the work had to be postponed.

On the evening of March 18th, 2 Field Company tried to break up some of the largest boulders but was prevented by heavy fire from an enemy picket beyond the block, and after another failure under still heavier fire from several directions on the 19th, it became apparent that no progress was possible until the surrounding ground had been captured and the enemy artillery subdued. A Divisional operation was therefore staged and it was arranged that all the 5th Divisional Engineers available, assisted by 4 Field Company, should be employed in turn on the road-block. By March 25th, the infantry had succeeded in clearing all small arms' fire from the area and were over-running the lower slopes of Mount Sanchil so that 2 Field Company was able to start work at 6.30 a.m., on clearing the block. Thereafter, four Sapper companies relieved each other at 5-hour intervals, toiling night and day with picks and shovels and even bare hands. 2 and 4 Companies of the Bengal Corps, and 20 and 21 Companies of the Bombay Corps, vied with each other in this stupendous task, and after 32 hours a track fit for "I" tanks was opened. Night was falling, however, so it was decided to use the hours of darkness to improve the track in order to allow the passage of a complete mobile column, including wheeled vehicles, and work continued accordingly. At last, on the morning of March 26th, "I" tanks, troops and transport poured up the Keren Gorge, entered Keren itself and pursued the enemy towards Asmara until held up for a time by a position, with further road-blocks, at Ad Teclesan. Keren was one of the few occasions on which the Italians fought with tenacity. They kept up the battle for 53 days and lost it mainly because they wore themselves out in eight fruitless attempts to retake Fort Dologorodoc. They left more than 3000 dead on the rugged heights and signed the death-warrant of their Empire in East Africa.

At Ad Teclesan, where the road from Keren descends to the Asmara Plain, General Frusci made a last effort to stem our advance. The bulk of the 4th Division being already under orders to return to the Western Desert to reinforce the troops then retreating before

General Rommel, the task of opening a way to Asmara fell to the 5th Division. After an attack by the 28th Brigade on the Teclesan positions had failed, the West Yorkshires of the 9th Brigade carried them by assault on March 31st and, on the following day, General Platt occupied Asmara. 20 Field Company distinguished itself during the advance to Teclesan by clearing a long road-block to help the 29th Brigade, and 2 Field Company also removed many obstructions. Their work was typical of that of all the Sapper and Miner units in which officers and men constantly risked death or disablement as they formed the spear-head of every advance; and yet, unlike the other arms, they were seldom able to retaliate. No duty could demand greater courage.

Thousands of Italian soldiers laid down their arms at Asmara. Vast quantities of equipment fell into our hands in addition to 1,500,000 shells and masses of small arms' ammunition. The Italian Army in East Africa was broken. Only General Frusci and a handful escaped to the south to help the Duke of Aosta to muster the remnants holding out in Abyssinia. Already, the Emperor Haile Selassie was on his way back to Addis Ababa, where he resumed his rule on May 5th. The only remaining operation in Eritrea was now the occupation of Massawa. Admiral Bonetti, who was in command at the port, had been ordered to resist to the end, and accordingly, early on April 4th, the entire 10th Brigade started on a 60-mile march down the 7,000 feet descent to the sea. Already, 2 Field Company, with infantry working parties, was hard at work in the Nefasit Gorge clearing the winding road of obstructions, one of which was 700 yards in length. The railway line had also to be cleared and mine-fields removed. A deliberate attack was planned on the Massawa defences which were held by 10,000 men, but little resistance was offered, and the town, and the harbour full of scuttled shipping, were seized by the 10th Brigade on April 8th shortly before the arrival of the 7th Brigade by the coastal route from the north. Reconstruction in an abnormally hot and humid climate claimed for a time the energies of 2 Field Company, while the detachment of 12 Field Company which had been with the 7th Brigade column cleared the surrounding country of mines until it embarked with the 4th Division for Egypt and the Western Desert. The work of reconstruction on the Eritrean railway system was accelerated by the assistance afforded by 101 Railway Construction Company, of the Madras Corps, under Major R. Gardiner, R.E., which spent two months in the country before being transferred to Iraq in May.

Sappers and Miners clearing a road block between Asmara and Massawa

After Massawa had fallen, the remnants of the Italian forces withdrew southwards along the roads leading from Asmara to Amba Alagi and Gondar, and the task of attacking the immensely strong enemy position at Amba Alagi, 235 miles from Asmara, was allotted to the 5th Division, now commanded by Major-General A. G. O. M. Mayne. This position was on a precipitous mountain, over 10,000 feet in height, surrounded by subsidiary peaks and ridges. The chief burden of the engineering work fell on 2 Field Company. The rapid advance of the African troops under General Cunningham from Kenya had resulted in the capture of Dessie on April 28th; but the leading formation—the 1st South African Brigade—was too distant to co-operate until General Mayne was close to Amba Alagi. It was planned accordingly that the main attack on the mountain fortress should be carried out at dawn on May 4th by the 29th Brigade against the enemy's western flank. A subsidiary force was to operate along a road further east which led to the Falaga Pass and thence swing westwards for the assault, while a third force made a direct approach along a main road in a valley. Each force had a detachment of 2 Field Company. The intricate manoeuvres which followed are fully described in the 5th Indian Division History,[1] and it must suffice to record here that they were eminently successful. The Sappers had to lay a special track up the mountain side, marked with white stones, to enable animal transport to carry supplies to the forward troops, and also to clear road-blocks, lift mines and arrange for water-supply; and when the South African brigade joined in the fray, they used Bangalore torpedoes to blow lanes through barbed wire. On May 16th, driven into his last defences, the Duke of Aosta asked for terms of surrender. The terms were generous, and on May 17th, 1941, 4,700 Italian officers and men, including many Generals, laid down their arms. Most of the prisoners were marched away, but 1,200 were kept for a time to help 2 Field Company in opening roads, clearing the battlefield and repairing captured lorries. The amount of transport, munitions and supplies which fell to the 5th Division was enormous. The Duke of Aosta was removed to Kenya where, worn out by the stress and anxiety of his campaigns against the British, Indian and African forces, he died of tuberculosis within a year.

The 5th Indian Division soon began to retrace its steps northwards, and with it went 2 Field Company. 8 Army Troops Company

---

[1] "*Ball of Fire*," by Antony Brett-James, pp. 101-136.

remained in Abyssinia throughout the summer, being stationed for a time at Dessie. A Section assisted in the capture of Debra Tabor, and others kept open the road to that place. At Adowa, the unit re-opened an airfield for the South Africans, who were assembling for an assault on Gondar, and in August it took part in an attack on a very strong position on the Wolchefit Pass. Fortunately, the enemy surrendered and the Company was then able to clear the road. It moved with other troops to capture Gondar at the end of November 1941, and finally, after the last pocket of Italian resistance had been liquidated, it followed the 5th Division to Egypt.

Little need be recorded about the southern arm of the great pincer movement against Eritrea and Abyssinia because no Sapper and Miner units were concerned in it. While the northern arm under Lieut.-General Sir William Platt was clearing Eritrea, the southern arm under Lieut.-General Sir Alan Cunningham was making history by a wonderful march from the Indian Ocean. In September 1939, Kenya, Uganda and Tanganyika were defended by only 6 front-line battalions of the King's African Rifles. They had no field artillery, no armour, no engineers, no medical organization and hardly any motor transport. However, by the end of 1940, our forces had reached a strength of 3 divisions (1st South African and 11th and 12th East African Divisions) and on January 24th, 1941, General Cunningham crossed the Kenya frontier into Italian Somaliland at the head of the 11th and 12th Divisions. He went from success to success. Forcing a passage over the Juba River on February 18th, he entered the port of Mogadishu a week later. Then he swung north across the desert, heading for Jijiga on the border of British Somaliland, which we had lost in August 1940. He entered Jijiga on March 17th, having averaged 37 miles a day since leaving Mogadishu. The Italians had been thrown out of British Somaliland on the previous day by a force from Aden. Next, with Berbera as a base, Cunningham turned south-westwards and set out for Addis Ababa. On March 27th, the 11th East African Division captured Harar at the moment when General Platt broke through at Keren, and on April 6th the advanced troops entered Addis Ababa in triumph only 40 days after starting from Mogadishu, 1,100 miles away. The 1st South African Brigade, then moved northwards, captured Dessie and, as already related, combined with the 5th Indian Division in the attack on Amba Alagi. Thus, through the exercise of a mobility never before attained in war, the great pincer movement reached a successful conclusion. The 12th East African Division was already mopping up far inland in the region of the Great Lakes, and soon a triangle of country round Gondar was all that was left to the Italians. Gondar surrendered on November 27th, and with its fall the operations in East Africa came to an end. A million square miles of country had been occupied and 220,000 Italians accounted for; but it should be remembered that, except at Keren, the enemy rarely fought as the Germans did. Another phase of the great struggle, that in the Western Desert to which we now return, forms an object lesson in the unpredictable vagaries of modern mechanized warfare.

In March 1941, the striking force in Cyrenaica, comprising the 2nd Armoured Division (less one brigade in Greece) and the 9th Australian Division (less one brigade in Tobruk), was holding Benghazi and the coast to the south. The troops were in high fettle. Ably led by Lieut.-General O'Connor, they had smashed the Italians, and with adequate reinforcement there seemed to be nothing to prevent them from advancing to Tripoli or even to Tunis. But they counted without the Germans. The destruction of Marshal Graziani's army had compelled Hitler to look towards Africa, and while General Wavell was depleting his reserves in order to find troops for Greece, General Erwin Rommel's 'Afrika Korps' began to land in Tripolitania. German aircraft commenced to bomb Benghazi so persistently that shipping had to be unloaded at Tobruk, whence all supplies were transported for 200 miles in such vehicles as were available. The number of vehicles being insufficient to meet an emergency, a system of supply from large forward dumps was established, the main petrol reserve being at Msus in the desert. Logistics began to govern strategy, a situation often encountered in war.

The Third Libyan Campaign was opened by Rommel at the end of March 1941 when the bulk of our advanced forces under Lieut.-General Sir Philip Neame, V.C., who commanded in Cyrenaica, were in position near El Agheila, a coastal town south of Benghazi. Rommel had the 90th Light Motorized Division of the Afrika Korps, an Italian Armoured Division, an Italian Motorized Division and several weak divisions of Italian infantry. Cutting across the desert behind Neame and over-running our petrol store at Msus and a number of supply dumps, he quickly re-occupied Benghazi. Generals O'Connor and Neame were captured by a German patrol, and although most of the Australian Division managed to reach Tobruk on April 7th, the 2nd Armoured Division, hopelessly out-gunned and often out-manoeuvred, was virtually annihilated. Rommel's armour swept forward. By April 11th, Tobruk was isolated and besieged and a German-Italian army stood on the Egyptian border above Sollum. Thus, in the brief space of twelve days, all our gains were swept away. It was a disaster of the first magnitude.

Both sides now paused, exhausted; but the first to recover was Rommel. On May 1st, he tried to take Tobruk by storm. He failed and then resorted to siege operations and bombing. The Nile Valley, however, was once more in acute danger and it was fortunate that, owing to the success of the Eritrean operations, General Wavell was able to reinforce the Western Desert front with the 4th Indian Division. He decided to hold Tobruk, and consequently Rommel was obliged to invest that place with a large force which might otherwise have been available for an advance on Alexandria and Cairo. The strategical position developed into a stalemate and a race for reinforcements. But in this, Rommel held a great advantage. His reinforcements traversed an excellent road through Tripolitania, while Wavell's had to voyage round the Cape.

Few Sappers and Miners were concerned in this lightning campaign, for Rommel had already reached the Sollum escarpment before the 4th Indian Division, now under Major-General F. W. Messervy, could arrive at the front. Such engineering work as was possible during the rapid withdrawal was carried out by the 2nd Armoured Division Engineers under Lieut.-Colonel A. C. Mitchell, R.E., and the 9th Australian Division Engineers under Lieut.-Colonel T. Mann, R.A.E. The 4th Indian Division Engineers, under Lieut.-Colonel H. P. Cavendish, R.E., moved out to Mersa Matruh soon after they reached Egypt from Eritrea and were engaged principally in laying mine-fields near the coast and developing a standard method of setting and recording them, known as the 'Indian Rope Trick.'[1] They were concerned also with communications and with the improvement of the water-supply at Buq Buq, between Sollum and Sidi Barrani. In action against the Germans near Sollum, 12 Field Company helped to bring up ammunition and evacuate casualties. The only Sapper and Miner unit involved in heavy fighting was 35 Field Squadron of the Bengal Corps, attached to the 3rd Indian Motor Brigade, which had landed at Suez from India on February 7th and arrived in Mersa Matruh on March 9th.

The sad story of 35 Field Squadron may be given in brief. Towards the end of March, shortly before Rommel started his sudden offensive, the Squadron was at El Adem, in the desert south of Tobruk, and

---

[1] Notes by Lieut.-Colonel P. N. M. Moore, R.E., dated September 1947.

was ordered westwards to Mekili to 'new training grounds'. The information available at the time indicated that no enemy patrols were within 250 miles of the place. Arrived at Mekili, "A" Troop went out to reconnoitre for water while "B" Troop laid mines. Neither got very far, for Rommel's armour was already flooding in and Mekili was soon surrounded. The little fort, with its cluster of huts and a few water cisterns, was in no way suited for a long and stubborn defence even if that had been possible against overwhelming numbers. Not realising the proximity of the enemy tanks, orders had been made out for the day's march of the Motor Brigade; but being low in the order of march, the officers and men of 35 Field Squadron were still waiting near their vehicles when five German tanks appeared south of the fort. The OC Squadron, Major P. F. Hayes, R.E., promptly went forward with Captain A. G. Hellicar, R.E., to stalk the tanks, though armed only with an anti-tank rifle and an ordinary rifle, and when the Mark III tanks rushed upon and over-ran the Brigade Headquarters and the remainder of the Squadron, they were completely isolated. Yet, in the general confusion, they managed to seize a stranded vehicle, and in it they escaped to Tobruk, where they helped to reorganize a few men and vehicles from another Squadron. All the other officers and men of 35 Field Squadron were captured and spent the remainder of the war in prison camps.

The 5th Division Engineers reached Egypt too late to assist in stemming Rommel's onrush to the frontier. For instance, 20 and 21 Field Companies did not disembark at Suez from Massawa until July. The burden of the early defensive preparations by Indian troops fell accordingly on the 4th Division Engineers — 4, 12 and 18 Field Companies, 11 Field Park Company and 6 Army Troops Company—and right well did they carry out their various tasks. The 4th Division had lost no time in reaching the Desert front. The 5th Brigade arrived in Suez only eight days after leaving Keren and went straight through by rail. It was followed by the other two brigades, and by the end of April 1941 the Division was concentrated in the Bagush area, east of Mersa Matruh, where, with New Zealand troops, it had built a defended position some months earlier before it was transferred to Eritrea. The 5th Brigade, however, did not remain long in Bagush, for it was called away for service against the Vichy French in Syria and did not return until November.

By the end of April 1941, the Germans were in Athens and the Greek adventure had failed dismally. Of the 60,000 British and

Dominion soldiers landed there, 15,000 never returned. And after Greece came the disaster in Crete, for by the end of May, Crete had succumbed to an air-borne invasion. In spite of Keren, in spite of Amba Alagi, British fortunes in the Middle East had reached their nadir. The fate of a large part of the British Empire hung precariously in the balance. But happily, such depressing considerations did little to lower the buoyant spirits of the average Indian Sapper and Miner, who was not much affected by matters of high strategy. He laboured as stoutly as ever for the welfare and protection of the other arms of the Service and remained always confident in ultimate victory.

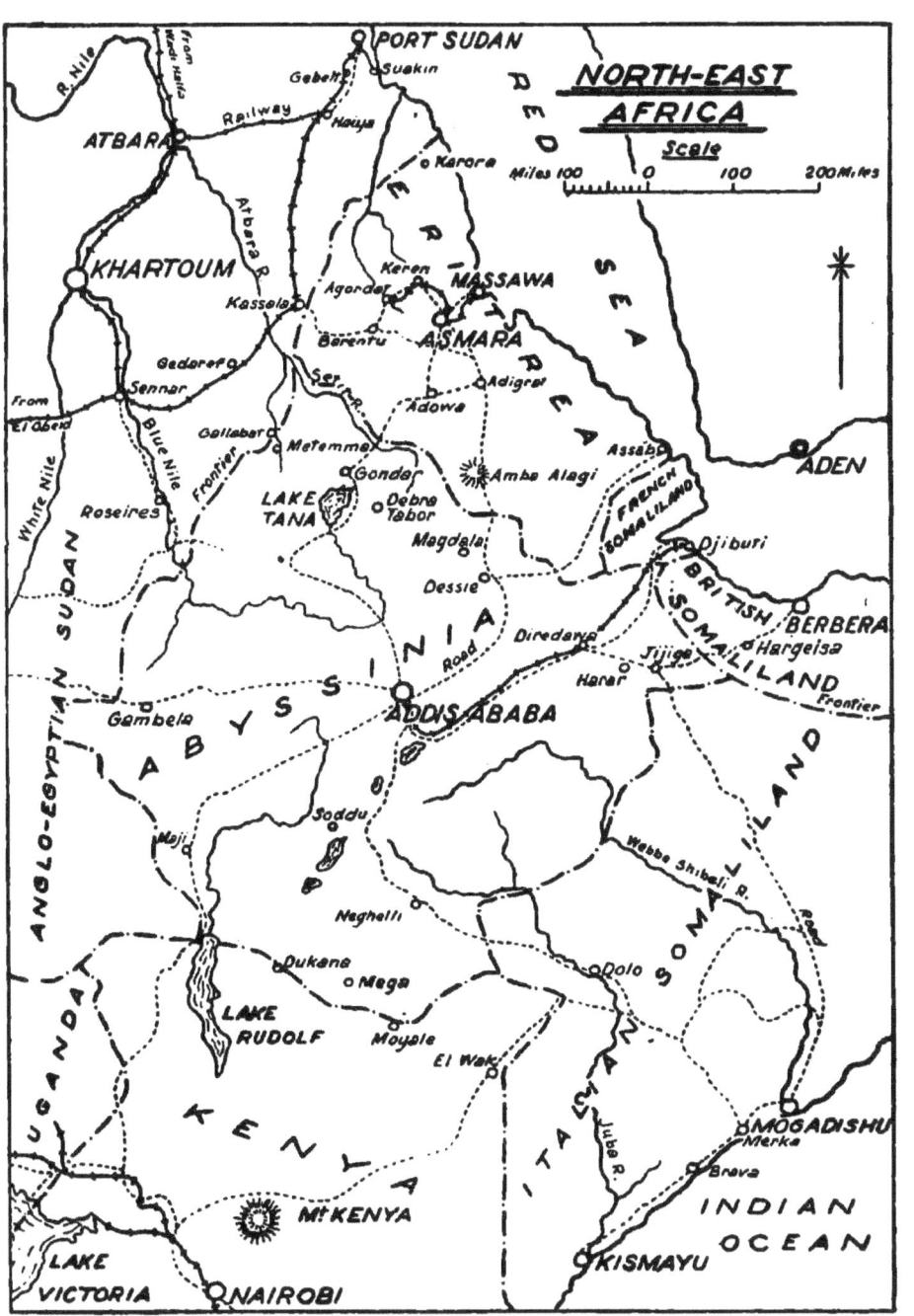

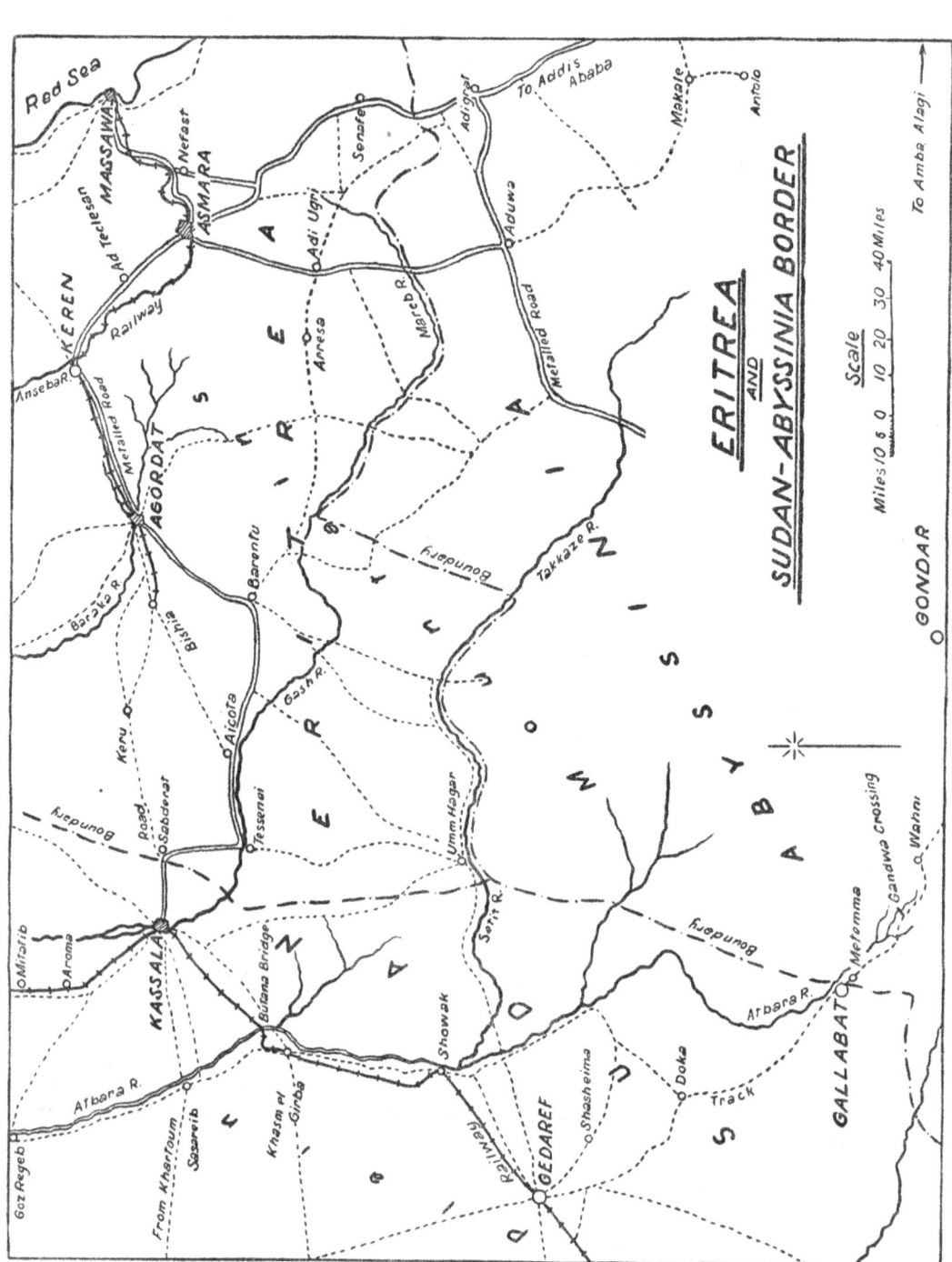

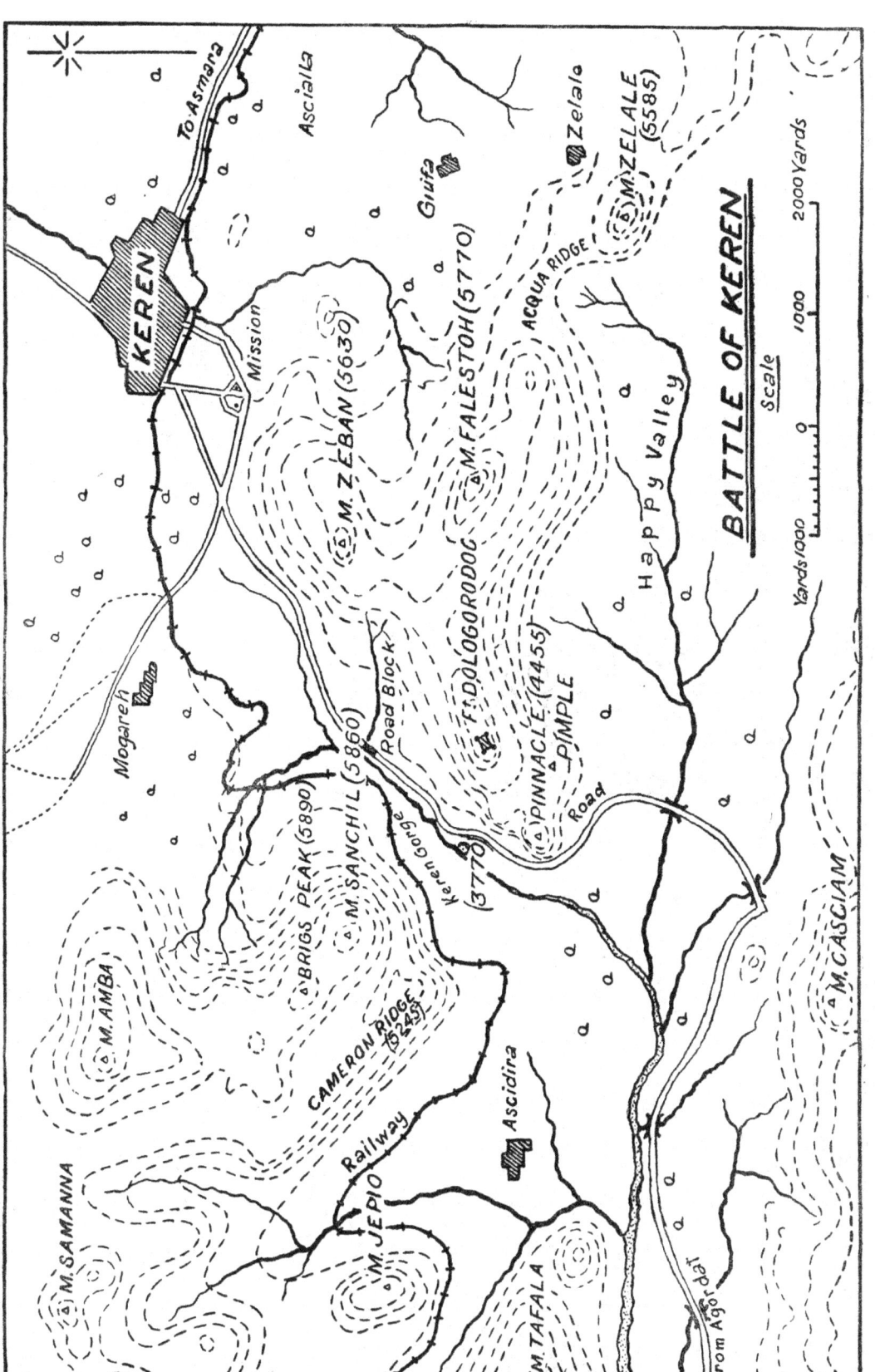

CHAPTER III

THE LEVANT, IRAQ AND PERSIA, 1941-46

BEFORE the collapse of Greece, the Government of India had agreed to send a force to Iraq to counter German aggression in the Balkans, to checkmate enemy designs against neutral Turkey and to safeguard the valuable oilfields of Iraq and Persia, and accordingly, on April 19th, 1941, the 20th Indian Infantry Brigade was landed at Basra as the forerunner of the remainder of the 10th Indian Division under Major-General W. A. K. Fraser. Another brigade disembarked on April 28th, and on May 7th Lieut.-General E. P. Quinan arrived by air to assume the supreme command in Iraq. The Germans were then in Athens and had crossed the Aegean Sea to occupy several Greek islands. It was hoped that we should be able to hold Crete, where Major-General B. C. Freyberg, V.C., was in command, but events soon proved otherwise. Despite great sacrifices by the Royal Navy and a dour defence on the ground, Crete succumbed to a mass air-borne assault during the last fortnight of May and thus the German tide crept still closer to the Syrian coast. The Vichy French forces in Syria, under General Dentz, amounted to about 35,000 men with 120 guns and 90 tanks. These misguided deserters from the Allied cause welcomed the German aeroplanes flying continually eastwards towards Iraq to support a rebel called Rashid Ali who had overthrown the Iraqi Government. Baghdad simmered with intrigue. German agents were busy in Persia. It was obvious that Iraq would soon be occupied by German forces unless forestalled by British and Indian troops. Nevertheless, General Wavell viewed the situation in Syria as more immediately dangerous than that in Iraq and consequently, on May 25th, he forwarded a plan for the invasion of Syria from the south by Australian, British and Free French forces under General Maitland Wilson, the chief objectives being Damascus, Beirut and Rayak, a few miles inland from Beirut.

The situation in the Eastern Mediterranean was further complicated by the strategic importance of the Dodecanese Islands which controlled the entrance to the Aegean Sea. This archipelago, held by the Italians, had many good harbours and airfields from which the Germans could interfere with our sea traffic and isolate Turkey, and therefore it was advisable that we should occupy the islands as soon as possible. By June 18th, the Axis threat to Turkey had become so great that the Turks actually ratified a treaty of mutual assistance with Germany, though this was promptly annulled when Hitler invaded Russia a few days later and thus disclosed the direction of his main bid for world domination. Russia had then to be assisted against her former ally, Germany, and the Turks, relieved of the threat of a Muscovite invasion, could be considered as friendly to the Allies. But could Wavell find sufficient forces on the shores of the Mediterranean to checkmate enemy designs both in Syria, Iraq and Persia? It was soon apparent that he could not, and therefore assistance, and still more assistance, was needed from India.

We turn first to the events in Iraq, where Rashid Ali opened the ball. On April 30th, 1941, two Iraqi brigades, supported by artillery and armoured cars, began to concentrate around the British Cantonment and R.A.F. Station at Habbaniya on the Euphrates to the west of Baghdad. Hostilities started on May 2nd. The Cantonment and Station were bombed and machine-gunned for several days by the Iraqi Air Force and there was a considerable amount of shelling. While some of our planes evacuated women and children to Basra, the remainder retaliated by bombing the enemy positions overlooking the area. The situation was serious, for the sole defenders on the ground were 1,200 R.A.F. Levies, comprising loyal Arabs, Kurds and Assyrians. Luckily, Colonel (now General Sir) O. L. Roberts, an ex-Bengal Sapper and Miner, was present and organized a stout defence. Nevertheless, even after the arrival by air of a British battalion from Basra, the garrison was greatly outnumbered. The enemy occupied Rutba on the oil-pipe line to Haifa and various oil stations and refineries elsewhere. Additional reinforcements could not be expected to reach Habbaniya quickly. A mechanized cavalry brigade group from Palestine arrived on May 18th, only to find that the small garrison had already defeated the enemy, twelve days earlier, capturing 26 Iraqi officers and 408 men and driving the remainder in disorder towards Falluja and Baghdad. The Iraqi Air Force had been practically eliminated by the R.A.F in spite of some intervention by German and Italian planes. Assisted by loyal Iraqis, our troops entered Falluja on May 19th. Rashid Ali and most of his supporters were then in flight, and on May 31st an armistice was signed in Baghdad.

In the Basra district, there was little fighting, though some bombing was necessary to induce the rebel Iraqis to withdraw northwards. By May 7th, we had restored order in the port and its surroundings.

The most pressing task was, of course, to reach Baghdad and Habbaniya. A Gurkha battalion was sent to the latter place by air, and on May 27th the 20th Brigade Group began to advance up the railway, reaching Samawa on June 10th and Baghdad on the 12th. The line had been badly damaged but was re-opened as the troops progressed. The 20th Brigade Group set out by the Tigris River route and arrived in the capital on June 19th. This expedition had a salutory effect on the riverain tribes who were inclined to be hostile. Afterwards, no time was lost in despatching troops northwards by air and road to Mosul, where pro-Axis influence was particularly marked, and also to Kirkuk, Haditha, Rutba, and Falluja,[1] and the Iraq Campaign may be said to have ended on June 24th, 1941.

We can now turn to the part taken by some Indian Sapper and Miner units in these operations. With the 20th Brigade was 41 Field Park Company (Bengal) under Major C. R. Mangat Rai, I.E. This unit disembarked at Basra on April 29th, being followed next day by 10 Field Company (Madras) under Major C. M. Bennett, I.A.R.O. The next to arrive was 9 Field Company (Madras) under Major L. A. B. Paten, R.E., which landed on May 19th, and on June 5th 5 Field Company (Bengal), under Major I. G. Loch, R.E., came ashore. With this unit was Captain J. S. Dhillon, I.E. The 10th Indian Division, whose C.R.E. was Lieut.-Colonel L. I. Jacques, R.E., was short of one Field Company during the most critical period before the signing of the armistice, and hence 41 Field Park Company had to act for a time as a Field Company in addition to its normal workshops and stores duties. The remarks of its Commander are therefore of special interest.

"The 10th Indian Division was the first to arrive in Iraq", writes Brigadier Mangat Rai,[2] "and this being a relatively undeveloped country, there was much engineer work to be done. For the first month and a half, the Company stayed in Shaiba (Basra) with Divisional H.Q. and remained fully occupied with a miscellany of jobs at the base, the most important of which was the laying of a piped water system for Army camps. The unit built two slaughter-houses and a sun-stroke centre, but the latter did not receive many patients despite a temperature of 124 degrees in the shade. Outside Shaiba there was a big and interesting work. This was the repair of the

---

[1] See the map of the Middle East included in this chapter.

[2] "With 41 Field Park Company", by Brig. C. R. Mangat Rai, appearing in *The Journal of the Institution of Military Engineers*, January 1951.

railway line from Basra to Ur. The form the sabotage had taken was the removal of sleepers and the destruction of small culverts. The repair party, consisting of the Workshops Section under Lieut. Devonald, began work at the Basra end and moved up the line with a train following close behind. Work continued throughout the day under a blistering sun, but the party lived in comfort at night for the train was equipped with shower baths and electric fans. As the job took longer than had been expected, the party ran short of food. More food was then dropped from the air, and this is probably one of the earliest instances of supply-dropping in the war. When the task of repairing the line up to Ur was completed, the party was complimented by General Quinan, the Force Commander. It then returned to Shaiba after three weeks' absence, the men being in very good heart though their bodies were covered with insect bites. In the middle of June, the 10th Division moved up to Baghdad and 41 Field Park Company was a part of the first big convoy of 400 vehicles to leave Shaiba. Many of the unit's M.T. drivers had received only a hurried training in India, but they acquitted themselves well. At Ur and at Diwaniya, the two intermediate stages in the journey of 325 miles, the unit was responsible for providing water for the column. A water party, with canvas tanks and pumps, was sent with the leading vehicles and, on arrival at the destination, set up a water-point on the bank of a canal. This had to be kept open till late at night because stragglers among the vehicles kept coming in till morning. At Diwaniya the water party got no sleep at all, for the water-point had to be kept open all night. The cooks also got little rest. Immediately on arrival they had to start their work, and as food was demanded till late at night, and again in the early morning before starting the day's run, there was not much time for sleep except while on the move."

These extracts give a good idea of the experiences of all the Sapper units when traversing this arid land. The Sappers had to open a way for the troops and transport and to provide them with water, and although they saw little fighting, their work was essential to the success of the military operations.

10 Field Company advanced with a Brigade Group to Ur at the end of May, reaching Baghdad on June 12th and Mosul on June 16th. 9 Field Company entered Baghdad on June 14th after one Section had suffered a few casualties while accompanying a reconnaissance on the Basra-Baghdad road.[1] Later, it joined the 21st Brigade at

---

[1] "Short Histories of Units", given in *Bangalore News Letter*. December 1946.

Habbaniya. 5 Field Company remained for the most part in Basra as the advance party of the 3rd Corps Troops Engineers. This formation included also 1 Field Company (Bengal) under Major S. H. M. Battye, R.E., which arrived in September, and in addition, at later dates, 14 Field Company (Madras) under Major D. K. S. Cameron, I.E., and 301 Field Park Company (Bombay) under Captain J. G. Wood, R.E. Other Sapper units appeared during 1941 and were employed mostly on defences, improving communications and expanding supply bases. Among these was 52 Army Troops Company (Madras), under Major F. H. R. French, R.E., which landed on June 16th. 32 Field Squadron (Madras) under Captain D. J. Middleton-Stewart, I.A.R.O. arrived on July 3rd, 61 Field Company (Madras) under Major C. C. F. Russell, R.E., on August 9th, and 49 Army Troops Company (Bombay) under Major C. G. Caffin, R.E., on September 11th. During July and August certain Bengal Sapper units reached Basra as 8th Divisional Engineers, for the 8th Division' was reinforcing the 10th Division in Iraq. These were 7 Field Company (Major H. A. H. Radcliffe-Smith, R.E.), 66 Field Company (Major H. G. A. Elphinstone, R.E.), 69 Field Company (Major W. G. A. Lawrie, R.E.) and 47 Field Park Company (Captain W. H. Cooper, R.E.). In addition there was 1 Bridging Platoon of the Madras Sappers under Lieut. R. T. Gerrard, R.E. In August and September, 27 Field Company of the Bombay Corps (Major H. W. Kitson, R.E.) and 57 and 58 Field Companies of the Madras Corps (Majors W. M. S. Lillie and G. C. Richards, R.E.) disembarked as 6th Divisional Engineers under Lieut.-Colonel A. E. Armstrong, R.E. 6 Army Troops Company of the Bengal Corps under Major H. Grattan, R.E., came from the Sudan in September, and 302 Field Park Company, of the same Corps, arrived under Captain D. H. Bardell, R.E., in November. Many specialist units were added during the summer and autumn of 1941. Among these were 101 Railway Construction Company (Major R. Gardiner, R.E.) and also 105 Railway Construction Company and 104 Transportation Stores Company. Other specialist units followed in 1942 and 1943, such as Electrical and Mechanical, Workshops and Excavating formations, but these cannot be dealt with in this narrative. At least 9 Railway units worked in Iraq or Persia during or after the military operations[1] and by repairing

---

[1] In an article entitled "My Experiences in Paiforce" Capt. Harbans Singh mentions 101, 105, 106, 120, 136 and 137 Railway Construction Companies and 121, 129 and 145 Railway Maintenance Companies.

damaged lines and laying new ones helped to consolidate our position. So much for the technical aspect of a vast programme of rehabilitation.

When the Regent of Iraq returned to Baghdad at the beginning of June 1941 the first task was to establish, at all main centres, sufficient forces to keep order while preparations were made to deal with a possible German invasion through Persia. Two battalions reached Mosul on June 3rd, and by June 18th the 20th Brigade H.Q. were at that place and a battalion was guarding the oilfields at Kirkuk. The 10th Division H.Q. were in Baghdad, and there were Gurkha detachments at Haditha, Rutba and Falluja. The 21st Brigade was posted at Kut-al-Amara, the scene of the historic siege in 1915-16.[1] At Shaiba, near Basra, were the 17th and 25th Brigades, and another brigade was in the process of landing. The lines of communication were adequately protected and it seemed that our forces should be able to devote all their energies to strengthening their positions, particularly around Mosul. But events dictated otherwise. Serious trouble had been brewing for some time in Syria, where the Axis powers were establishing powerful air-bases within two hours' flying distance of Baghdad, and thus the process of pacifying and strengthening Iraq suffered its first interruption and the war spread to the Levant.

The situation in Syria under the French mandate was most peculiar. Before France fell, General Weygand had massed a strong army there, and even after the surrender it was hoped that he would return to help the Allied cause. The country was honeycombed with intrigue. The Vichy French wanted to maintain their mandate; the British wanted a new ally; the Germans wanted a spring-board in the Middle East. The Vichy Government tried a series of administrators all of whom failed. Then they appointed the pro-German General Dentz and the enemy took virtual control of the country. They passed their aircraft through to help Rashid Ali in Iraq and start the encirclement and isolation of neutral Turkey.

The Syrian Campaign under General Maitland Wilson opened on June 8th, 1941, when the 7th Australian Division, less one brigade in Tobruk, began to advance northwards from Palestine with the assistance of a British brigade and a formation of Free French. "The essence of this campaign was tragedy", writes Alan Moorehead,[2]

---

[1] See *In Kut and Captivity*, by Major E. W. C. Sandes, M.C., R.E., (the present author).

[2] *African Trilogy*, by Alan Moorehead, p. 47.

Indian Engineers laying railway track in Iraq

"for in fighting their enemies the British were forced to fight also men who had been their friends." And worse still. Frenchmen fought against Frenchmen. At first there was little resistance on the road to Damascus and Beirut, but bitter warfare soon developed as casualties began to mount. The tough Algerians and Foreign Legion soldiers under Dentz took a heavy toll of the Australians and British on the Litani River, south of Tyre. To the east, a mobile British column fought its way into the desert city of Palmyra. Sidon was captured and the Australians, British, Indians and Free French drove onwards up the coast towards Damascus supported by the British fleet and many squadrons of bombers. The Vichy French then counter-attacked and regained much ground south of Damascus. Two weeks of stubborn fighting ensued before reinforcements enabled General Wilson to capture Damascus by a three-way thrust. At last, General Dentz asked for terms and an armistice was arranged on July 7th. The brief campaign ended on July 12th, 1941, after which Dentz withdrew his battered troops northwards to Tripoli. He was soon interned by the British and thus the second phase of the war in the Middle East was brought to a conclusion. It left behind it a legacy of much bitterness; but German machinations had been defeated, and not alone by the troops sent from Palestine but also by others despatched from the recently subdued territory in Iraq.

It had been decided that troops from Iraq should undertake the protection of the portion of the railway from Anatolia to Iraq which ran through Syrian territory, and that two Indian Infantry Brigade Groups should advance into Syria from the east. Accordingly, orders were issued that the 21st Brigade Group, then at Baghdad, and the 25th Brigade Group and 13th Lancers at Basra, should move up the Euphrates valley. The 21st Brigade, under Brigadier C. J. Weld, was to protect the line of communication between a forward base at Haditha and an advanced base to be formed at Deir-ez-Zor, which had to be occupied as quickly as possible. By June 30th, the 21st Brigade and 13th Lancers were at Abu Kemal, and the advance from that place began on the following day. Meanwhile, a small column from Mosul was driving the Vichy French from Ras-el-Ain in order to secure the use of the railway as far as the Turkish frontier near Nisibin. On July 6th, the 17th Brigade (Brigadier D. D. Gracey) arrived in Mosul from Basra, and three days later Ras-el-Ain was clear of Vichy troops. The 10th Division, less the 20th Brigade, remained for several weeks in Syria until required for operations in

Persia. It may be remarked here that its commander was Major-General (now Field-Marshal Sir) W. J. Slim, who had assumed the appointment on June 1st, 1941, and held it until March 29th, 1942, when he became Commander, 4th Indian Corps, in India.

9 Field Company (Madras), under Major L. A. B. Paten, R.E., took part in the Syrian Campaign and was with the 21st Brigade Group when Deir-ez-Zor was captured on July 3rd after a battle lasting three days. The unit remained there until the middle of the month and then moved up the Euphrates to Meskene where it stayed until it returned to Basra in August. Another Engineer unit which shared in the Syrian Campaign was 18 Field Company of the Bombay Corps. This unit left Bagush in Egypt on May 16th and reached Deraa in Trans-Jordan on June 8th with the 5th Brigade. It took part in an attack on enemy positions at Mezze, west of Damascus, on the night of June 18/19th, when the brigade was trying to cut the Beirut road and railway, and one Section was over-run when the Vichy French re-captured their lost positions. 31 Field Squadron and 41 Field Park Company, both of the Bengal Corps, also served in Syria. The former moved from Egypt through Deir-ez-Zor to the Turkish frontier where it remained until required in August, 1941, to support the operations against Persia near the Pai Tak Pass at Khaniqin.[1]

As regards the experiences of 41 Field Park Company, Brigadier Mangat Rai writes as follows[2]:— "The 10th Indian Division did not get the opportunity of halting long at Baghdad. It arrived there at Taji Camp on June 18th and began its advance into Syria on the 30th. It was to attack the Vichy forces from the east along the Euphrates valley. Fawzi Quwachi, who had come to help Rashid Ali in Iraq, had retreated to his base in Syria along this line, leaving a trail of sabotage in his wake. The bridge over the Khan Naquta canal, 10 miles outside Baghdad on the way to Habbaniya, had been destroyed. An F.B.E. bridge had been erected, but something stronger was needed and this task was given to 41 Field Park Company. Only two days were allowed for the work. We were able to get most of the stores from the Iraq railways, and working round the clock by the light of vehicle headlamps at night, a 42-feet bridge of sleeper trestles and rolled steel joists, capable of taking Class 30 loads, was

---

[1] *Brief History of the K.G.V's O. Bengal Sappers and Miners Group, R.I.E., (August 1939-July 1946)*, by Lieut. G. Pearson, R.E., p. 17.

[2] "With 41 Field Park Company", by Brig. C. R. Mangat Rai, appearing in *The Journal of the Institution of Military Engineers*, January 1951.

ready in time for the advance of the Division. During the advance to, and capture of, Deir-ez-Zor, the main work of the unit was to supply water to the troops, mostly by repairing sabotaged pumping stations. Among these was that at Al Qaim (beyond Haditha) from which water was pumped to Station T.1, 13 miles from the Euphrates, where Divisional H.Q. were established for some days. The Vichy French had air superiority and we had no anti-aircraft guns, so our Anti-Tank Battery Commander conceived the idea of using his 18-pounders in an anti-aircraft role on fixed lines. To do this, he needed help from the Sappers in making emplacements and special fittings to enable the guns to fire at high elevation. This we did for him, and soon his guns were in a circle round Divisional H.Q. pointing in the air. Not long after the capture of Deir-ez-Zor, the fighting in Syria came to an end and the Division was able to pause for about three weeks. Deir-ez-Zor is a pleasant place on the Euphrates and more habitable than Iraq in the summer. The Division held a Sports Meeting in which the Company did best among the smaller units. It was a fitting finale to a hard-fought campaign."

Life in Southern Iraq for those Sapper and Miner units whose fate it was to be stationed there during the summer of 1941 can best be described by quoting from the official story entitled "Paiforce."[1] "Men can exist and work prodigiously for a long time when they lack nearly all of what are usually considered necessities, but they cannot exist without water and food. No 1 Engineer Base Workshops Company at Basra, consisting largely of raw recruits, was hardly ashore before it was required to lay an 8-inch water pipeline for the R.A.F. compound at Maqil, across the desert to Shaiba, a distance of 15 miles. Sections of pipe were arriving a few at a time. Each joint required one pound of yarn and twelve pounds of lead. Neither yarn nor lead was available, and there was nothing like the necessary equipment of tools. "The impossible we do at once. Miracles take a little longer." The O.C. unit, Major Adcock, started to comb the bazaars, buying out of his own pocket every appropriate tool he could see and trusting that the Army would refund the money (which the Army did). He discovered Captain John Morris, Chief Engineer of the Port of Maqil. Morris lent his own tools, all suitable stores he could find, and even his own skilled tradesmen. The task of laying 700 tons of pipe, with 20 tons of lead, went ahead, the men working from 5 a.m. till 4 p.m. and camping

---

[1] *Paiforce. The Official Story of the Persia and Iraq Command*, 1941-46, pp. 55-59.

at the point the pipe had reached. The shifting camp grew till it contained 1,350 men. The shade temperature rose to 128 degrees, but in 25 working days the whole job was done. The size of the main base increased steadily and the centre of gravity moved forward. Depots were opening in and about Baghdad, at Haditha, at Kirkuk, as far as Mosul. An advanced base was started at Musaiyib, 40 miles south of Baghdad. It was Shaiba over again. There were dust-storms on five days out of seventeen. Work was impossible then. Men wrapped themselves in blankets and waited through the hours for the storm to subside. Tents were sent scurrying across the desert, iron roofs were torn from walls and pitched a hundred yards away. As long as the office-tent remained in its place, the O.C. and his Adjutant sat in pools of sweat at either side of the folding table, took papers from the heaped 'Action' tray and tried to think of an answer before the paper was blown away or covered with liquefying sand. The sweat ran in rivers down their faces, down chest, back and legs, and the sand, driven hard against these dripping surfaces, turned instantly to mud. The nights were free from storm, but at dawn the flail of sand began again. And when the storm was finally over, there were the heat and sandflies and the arrears in the programme to contend with." Many of the Sapper field units had similar experiences. It is indeed a matter of some wonder that the War Diaries of the various companies could be faithfully and clearly written up day by day. Yet such was the case.

Long before they were thwarted in Iraq and Syria, the Germans had coveted Persia, and when Great Britain and Russia became allies, it was obvious that their first joint task must be to establish contact through that difficult country. Persia offered a valuable prize to either side. Outside America, her oilfields were the largest in the world and they supplied the Allied armies and navies in the Middle East. Persia was, in fact, a country in which the Germans might almost win the war outright. It became necessary, therefore, to consolidate our position by operations within it, both in the south-east and south-west, and accordingly a very brief campaign was launched in August 1941 against the pro-Axis elements in the country. As early as July 22nd, General Quinan had been ordered to occupy Abadan and the Naft-i-Shah oilfields at the head of the Persian Gulf, and later, those further north and north-west, and early in August he made certain preparations. The 24th Brigade of the 8th Indian Division (Major-General C. O. Harvey) was to seize the Abadan Refinery and an adjacent village called Khurramshahr, while the 25th Brigade and 13th Lancers advanced northwards through Ahwaz. Simultaneously, the 2nd Indian Armoured Brigade (Brigadier J. A. Aizlewood) was to begin an advance on Kermanshah from Northern Iraq, joined later by the 9th Indian Armoured Brigade which was expected shortly from Palestine. Bandar Shahpur, a port at the head of the Perisan Gulf, was to be occupied by a small naval and military force. Little opposition was expected anywhere.

The 18th Brigade from India joined the 8th Division on August 10th, 1941, in time to assist in the operations which began before dawn on August 25th. At Abadan the 24th Brigade found Persian troops asleep in their barracks and captured many of them while the remainder fled in lorries. The 18th Brigade was soon in Khurramshahr. On the 26th, a ferry was established across the Karun River, and the brigade crossed on the 27th and advanced beyond Dorquain Pumping Station to a point half-way to Ahwaz. Meanwhile, the 25th Brigade had occupied Qasr Shaikh. Bandar Shahpur also was in our hands. On the 28th, the 25th Brigade moved up the west bank of the Karun to within 25 miles of Ahwaz. Both brigades then advanced on that town, astride the river. They met some resistance *en route*, but as they were approaching their objective the news arrived that the Shah of Persia had ordered his troops to cease fire and consequently the operations ended suddenly. 1 Bridging Platoon of the Madras Corps, under 2nd Lieut. R. T. Gerrard, R.E., was concerned in the ferrying operations over the Karun, and 9 Field Company, under Major L. A. B. Paten, R.E., accompanied the 18th Brigade and ferried vehicles across the wide stream on improvised equipment. On the 27th, 9 Field Company handed over the ferry to 7 Field Company of the Bengal Corps (Major H. A. H. Radcliffe-Smith, R.E.) and rejoined the 18th Brigade before the occupation of Ahwaz. The stores and spikes for the ferrying rafts were supplied by 47 Field Park Company (Bengal) under Captain W. H. Cooper, R.E.

The operations between Abadan and Ahwaz were facilitated by the provision of a floating bridge across the Shatt-al-Arab at Basra. This was accomplished in about a week by 5 Field Company under Major I. G. Loch, R.E., with Captain J. S. Dhillon, I.E., as second-in-command. Loch had the assistance of one Section of 7 Field Company, an Indian Pioneer Battalion, and two Indian Artisan Works (or Army Troops) Companies.[1] The bridge was composed of *mahailas*

---

[1] Notes by Colonel I. G. Loch, O.B.E., dated June 5th, 1952.

(Arab dhows), and progress depended largely on the rapidity with which suitable craft could be secured. The structure was in two sections, 970 feet and 830 feet in length, on either side of Coal Island, and not only was it the first bridge to span the Shatt-al-Arab but also, at that time, the longest boat-bridge in the world. The section to the west of Coal Island was attached, upstream and downstream, to steel wire cables, while that to the east was secured by anchors in order to allow a navigation cut. Gunwale loading, using short joists, had to be adopted at first because of a scarcity of long rolled-steel joists for central loading, and consequently the roadway needed much stiffening to prevent excessive rolling of the *mahailas* under heavy traffic.[1] The bridge was opened on August 14th, 1941, shortly before the Persian Campaign, and within a few weeks no less than 1,000 vehicles a day were rolling across the wide river instead of a possible 80 vehicles carried by ferry. Thus 5 Field Company played a notable part in expediting the supplies needed by Russia. It may be remarked here that, as soon as the necessary materials became available, the bridge was remodelled to provide central loading. Railway sleepers were used for the decking.

The *mahaila* bridge did not remain long in existance for in January 1942 a Section of 57 Field Company, under 2nd Lieut. G. Horne, R.E., which had been maintaining it and working the cut, was engaged in dismantling it while the rest of the unit was employed on a defensive position at Pul-i-Tang, north of Andimishk in Persia.[2] Some months later it seemed probable that if large-scale operations opened against German forces in Persia about 2,000 tons of war material would have to go forward daily from Basra across the Shatt-al-Arab. Ferrying in barges to the railway terminus at Tanuma, near Abadan, could not meet the situation, nor could a *mahaila* bridge cope with the demand, and accordingly General Maitland Wilson ordered the rapid construction of a more permanent structure, to take both road and rail traffic, and a site was selected close to the Basra airport.[3] The work was directed by Brigadier G. B. G. Hull.[4] This bridge, like the *mahaila* bridge (afterwards converted to pontoons), was in two sections divided by Coal Island. The bridge had to provide for

---

[1] The author was faced with the same problem in 1915 when bridging the Tigris at Kurna and Amara. (See *In Kut and Captivity*.)

[2] Notes by Major G. Horne, R.E., dated August 5th, 1952.

[3] *Paiforce. The Official Story of the Persia and Iraq Command, 1941-46*, p. 120.

[4] Brig. Hull held an R.E. Regular Emergency Commission.

the passage of river traffic, but lack of time and materials prevented the incorporation of a rising centre span. An ingenious solution was therefore adopted. The centre span in the eastern section was made to sink instead of rise so that vessels could pass over it when it was submerged. Most of the pile-driving was done by Engineer units, and the new bridge was opened for use on August 20th, 1943, after considerable delay caused by floods. It was still operating successfully in 1947.[1]

Although the operations in the Abadan-Ahwaz area between August 24th and 28th, 1941, were necessary as a safety precaution, the major operations in the brief Persian Campaign took place further to the north-west in the Naft-i-Shah—Pai Tak region. The Persian forces in that area had been strongly reinforced, but in the nick of time the 9th Armoured Brigade reached Khaniqin from Syria to support the 2nd Armoured Brigade under Brigadier Aizlewood. "Hazel" Force was then formed from the two brigades and two battalions of Gurkhas. On August 24th, Major-General W. J. Slim, Commander, 10th Indian Division, was placed in charge of the operations planned for the capture of Naft-i-Shah and an advance on Shahabad through Gilan. He was reinforced by the 21st Brigade which he decided to employ against the Pai Tak Pass positions in co-operation with a turning movement through Gilan. The Naft-i-Shah oilfields and Qasr-i-Shirin were seized early on August 25th, and on the following day Gilan was entered and the advance continued unopposed towards Shahabad through a number of roadblocks. Shahabad was occupied on the 27th. The 21st Brigade, having found the Pai Tak Pass empty, had moved on to Karind, where patrols of the 9th Armoured Brigade were met. Forward reconnaissance showed that Persian troops were holding positions overlooking the route to Kermanshah, and on the 28th, they shelled the road. However, when General Slim was preparing to attack, a Persian officer appeared and asked for a truce. This was approved by General Quinan, and General Slim was instructed to occupy the oil refinery at Kermanshah forthwith. When "Hazel" Force had accomplished this task, a column under Brigadier Aizlewood was sent forward to contact the Russians who were advancing on Kermanshah from Senna, and on Hamadan from Kasvin. They were

---

[1] "A Short Description of the Hull Bridge across the River Shatt-al-Arab at Margil (Basra), Iraq," by G. B. G. Hull, C.B.E., M.I.C.E., appearing in *The Civil Engineer in War*, Vol I.

met at Senna on August 29th, and near Kasvin on the 31st. As there were indications that the Persians did not intend to satisfy our demands for the surrender of Axis nationals, it was then arranged that a joint Anglo-Russian advance to Teheran should be undertaken and should culminate in a simultaneous entry into the capital on September 17th. Cordial relations were established with our new allies and the plan was duly carried out. The campaign in North-West Persia ended in prolonged festivities in Teheran for those officers and men who were fortunate enough to be present. Our casualties had been negligible. Indeed, in the fighting in both theatres in Persia, we lost only 22 killed and 42 wounded.

The 6th Indian Division, under Major-General Thomson, began to arrive in Basra on September 12th, 1941, and was ordered to relieve the 8th and 10th Indian Divisions in the Mosul area and Western Persia. During October, however, after the abdication of Raza Shah Pahlevi and a combined British-Russian parade in Teheran, our troops withdrew gradually to Sultanabad and Hamadan. Persia had been thoroughly subdued and Axis agents rounded up, but there was still considerable unrest and some danger of a German invasion. Many rifles, abandoned by the Persian troops, had fallen into the hands of recalcitrant tribesmen who now had the finest products of the German arsenals to help them in their traditional occupations of blood-feuds and highway robbery, and we were saddled with the task of restoring confidence and security in a country larger than South Africa.

Several Sapper units took part in the advance to Kermanshah and Teheran in August 1941. One of these was 41 Field Park Company, of the Bengal Corps, and others were 32 Field Squadron, 61 Field Company and 1 Bridging Platoon of the Madras Corps. "The Persian campaign was in the nature of a holiday" writes Brigadier Mangat Rai.[1] "The unit was not involved in any fighting, and after the deserts of Iraq and Syria, the mountains of Persia, with their cool breezes and crystal streams, were a paradise. There was not a great deal of work to do, and water-supply presented no problems. The unit carried out several road reconnaissances, and there were the usual workshop jobs. Special mention must be made of our workshop lorry. This was an old Thornycroft which could not stand the pace of ordinary convoy running and always had to move

---

[1] "With 41 Field Park Company", by Brig. C. R. Mangat Rai, appearing in *The Journal of the Institution of Military Engineers*, January 1951.

by itself. It was affectionately known as "Lizzie." With an attendant 15 cwt. truck, "Lizzie" usually started well before dawn, and moving at a maximum speed of 10 m.p.h., arrived just before dark at the night's staging place."

32 Field Squadron, which had disembarked at Basra early in July, joined the 2nd Armoured Brigade and crossed with it into Persia. It was fully occupied in removing road-blocks and mines. On August 30th, after the Persian surrender, it took part in a triumphal entry into Kermanshah and subsequently pushed on with the armoured forces to Hamadan which was reached before midnight after covering 120 miles of very rough road in 4 hours. This was considered to be a record at that time. The unit participated in festivities with the Russians at Kasvin, when it is recorded that "there was much eating and drinking."[1] After some road reconnaissances, the Squadron was present at Teheran at the Victory Parade on October 17th before moving back to the Mosul area. 61 Field Company reached Khaniqin on August 25th, just in time for the advance into Persia. It repaired roads, and one platoon worked with the leading column which entered Karind. The unit reconnoitred routes and arranged water-supplies at Khaniqin, Kermanshah and Senna before returning to Iraq in the middle of October 1941 with the 25th Brigade. 1 Bridging Platoon was also with the advance, repairing culverts and undertaking a variety of other engineering duties.

The link with Russia having been forged, attention could be concentrated on defence. The defensive area selected in the summer of 1941 in Northern Iraq was shaped like an inverted triangle with its apex on Baghdad, the Tigris and Diyala rivers as its two sides, and its base, in the north, running along the Turkish border. Mosul, and Kirkuk thus came within the triangle. General Quinan had estimated that he would require 10 divisions to defend Iraq, but he had only the 6th, 8th and 10th Divisions in addition to the 2nd Armoured Brigade, and the 6th and 8th Divisions had each only two brigades.[2] Meanwhile, Hitler's armies were driving hard towards Kharkov and into the Crimea north of the Black Sea. Time was very short. When the 6th Division arrived, it assumed responsibility in Persia, but with only one brigade as the other was detailed to help a brigade of the 10th Division on protective duties throughout

---

[1] "Short Histories of Units", appearing in *Bangalore News Letter*, December 1946.

[2] The 5th Indian Division made a brief appearance in September 1941 but soon returned to fight in the Western Desert.

Iraq. The remainder of the 10th Division prepared defence works in the Baghdad area and two brigades of the 8th Division took over the defence works around Mosul. A perimeter had to be constructed at Mosul from which armoured forces could advance and operate freely. General Harvey planned originally to prepare positions for two brigade groups on the west side and one on the east, while a fourth group was to be centred on Zakho, 80 miles to the north. At each sector there were to be obstacles, sited in depth, at which the enemy could be checked and then counter-attacked. The plan had to be modified because of lack of man-power, but even so it involved a huge programme of digging in very hard ground.

The lay-out finally adopted for the Mosul fortress involved the provision of a wide defensive ring around the city, together with a subsidiary fortified area at Qaiyara about 20 miles to the south, and the construction of 1,181 concrete pill-boxes and gun emplacements, 110 miles of anti-tank ditch (much of which was in solid rock), 186 miles of road and 23 air-strips. Works units, Engineer battalions, Sapper units, Pioneer and civil labour were all busily engaged. The Infantry also were called in to help the overworked Sappers who concentrated rapidly after the conclusion of the Persian campaign. Civilian labour was recruited mostly from the local tribes, and at the peak some 20,000 labourers were at work. These men had to be fed and housed in addition to being taught their job. The troops lived in tents, and when rain began to fall in the autumn, their camps became deep in mud. This titanic defensive scheme was the most pressing Engineer task in Iraq during 1941 and 1942, and it was of the utmost importance because rumour had it that by May 1942 the Germans might have no less than five divisions poised on the border and ready to sweep into the country. General Quinan had not only to defend Iraq but had also to help the Russians. "You will take steps" ran an order from General Wavell, "to develop such road, rail and river communications as are necessary to ensure the maximum possible delivery of supplies to Russia." As ever, logistics had a far-reaching effect on operational planning.

The Deputy Chief Engineer, Defences, Northern Iraq, at this period was Colonel L. D. Grand, (late R.E.) under whom were Lieut.-Colonel C. M. MacLachlan, R.E., C.R.E. 8th Division, who was responsible for the right bank sector at Mosul, and the C.R.E. Army Troops, responsible for the left bank sector. By September 1941, most of the Sapper units were able to apply themselves to oilfield defence. The 3rd Corps was made responsible for the oil-fields. Its Engineer Troops, whose headquarters were composed wholly of Bengal Sappers, came to Iraq in September. They included 1 and 5 Field Companies (Bengal), 14 Field Company (Madras) and 301 Field Park Company (Bombay), and all four units moved up to the Mosul area in support of the 8th Divisional Engineers. Mosul, one of the world's greatest oil reservoirs, and Kirkuk, whence the oil was pumped across 550 miles of desert to Haifa and Tripoli, had natural protection on the north and east afforded by successive ranges of almost trackless hills. The only approach from the northeast was through the precipitous Ruwandiz Gorge on the Persian frontier, and from the north, through the lofty Zakho Pass. The Sappers were required to improve these natural obstacles by adding artificial ones, blasting hill-sides for defence works, repairing and making roads, and demolishing any structures which might help an invader. "It was the special task of the Engineers", writes Lieut. G. Pearson,[1] "to supervise large parties of infantry and local coolie labour and to plan the technical work. No bulldozers were available, and digging was difficult in ground which was often solid rock. Work was always against time, and the men were eternally trying to make themselves understood by people who spoke another language and had not the slightest notion of how or why the job was to be done. 69 Field Company was placed in charge of camouflage. Meanwhile the other 8th Divisional Engineers (7 and 66 Field Companies), together with the 3rd Corps Engineers, built concrete defence works and dummy weapon posts and spread camp roads with shingle." The winter, that year, was the bitterest in living memory. Some quotations from 1 Field Company's War Diary will show the extreme discomfort experienced in January 1942. "Snow started to fall early and continued all day. This was a miserable day for everyone and work was called off at 10 a.m....... The next few days were bitter, being especially hard on those men who had not yet received woollen underclothing. There were 20 degrees of frost one night and great trouble was experienced in keeping the M.T. vehicles going. Ten coolies died one night. By day, the sun shone and melting snow turned roads into a quagmire, but work continued though at a slower pace." In spite of these hardships, however, the men remained in good spirits and indulged in many snow-ball fights. They slept soundly at night although the lorry engines had to be kept running most of the time.

---

[1] "*Brief History of the K.G.V's O. Bengal Sappers and Miners Group, R.I.E., August 1939-July* 1946", by Lieut. G. Pearson, R.E., p. 19.

The chief task of 47 Field Park Company, apart from building up dumps, consisted in providing steel shuttering for concrete defences. Meanwhile, 5 Field Company built camps, shingled camp roads, completed demolitions in the Zakho Gorge and made mined roadblocks in the Mosul area. Also, with the assistance of 1 Field Company and 301 Field Park Company (Bombay), it provided a ferry across the Tigris at Qaiyara. At Habbaniya, in March 1942, 41 Field Park Company began defence work in the Falluja area. Rifles had to be closely guarded, for many thieves prowled around at night. Indeed on one occasion the C.S.M. felt his greatcoat being drawn off him! The winter cold had been very severe. Five men had been frost-bitten during wet bridge training. April opened with sandstorms and a plague of sandflies, so it was with much relief and satisfaction that in May 1942 the unit left Iraq for Egypt. By that time, the northern defences were far advanced and demolition charges were in position at all strategic points.

Other Sapper units engaged on road or defence work during 1941 and the first half of 1942 were 9, 10, 57 and 58 Field Companies, 32 Field Squadron, 39 Field Park Squadron and 52 Army Troops Company, all of the Madras Corps, and 20 Field Company and 49 Army Troops Company of the Bombay Corps.[1] On September 7th, 1941, after the occupation of Ahwaz, 9 Field Company returned to Iraq to build defences at Habbaniya and the Hindiya Barrage on the Euphrates, and from March till May 1942, when it left for Egypt, it was employed on a defensive position at Taji near Baghdad. 10 Field Company reached Mosul on June 16th, 1941, and prepared defences at Zakho, Qaiyara and other places until March 1942. In April, the unit built a pontoon bridge over the Euphrates, and having handed over to 52 Army Troops Company, departed for Egypt where it met its fate in the Western Desert on June 28th, 1942. The greater part of 57 Field Company worked on defences at Pul-i-Tang in Persia, and 58 Field Company supervised the labour of large gangs of Arabs on the Pai Tak Pass defences until April 1942. In July, 58 Field Company was transferred to Egypt, but it was back in Iraq by the end of the year. 32 Field Squadron worked during the winter of 1941-42 on defences between Nisibin and Qaiyara, and in June 1942, moved to Kermanshah in Persia where it was joined by 39

---

[1] The Os.C. were Majors L. A. B. Paten, R.E., C. M. Bennett, I.A.R.O., W. M. S. Lillie, R.E., G. C. Richards, R.E., D. J. Middleton-Stewart, I.A.R.O., W. B. J. Armstrong, R.E., F. H. R. French, R.E., C. G. Caffin, R.E., and J. C. Winchester, R.E., respectively.

Field Park Squadron, newly arrived from India. These units then built tank tracks towards the Russian zone in North Persia as part of a defensive system in case Stalingrad succumbed to the Germans. 20 Field Company, arriving in Iraq from Egypt on September 3rd, 1941, reconnoitred routes into Persia from Kirkuk before returning to Egypt in October *en route* for Cyprus. 49 Army Troops Company, arriving also in September, worked mostly in the Basra and Baghdad areas.

Some of the experiences of 52 Army Troops Company are worthy of record. After landing at Basra on June 16th, 1941, the unit was employed on water-supply until it moved by road to Baghdad in October. In November, it joined 14 Field Company at Mosul for work on the "Wavell" Defence Line near Faida Village. The line ran for about 35 miles, mostly along a high ridge, and included an anti-tank ditch with pill-boxes on the forward slope. Water was pumped from springs in the plain to storage tanks on the ridge. The only explosives available were dynamite and gunpowder, and, as fuses were scarce, gunpowder-trains were often used. The cold during the winter was so severe that five men lost fingers and toes through frost-bite. There were no fires except in the cookhouses and the men had to live in widely spaced tents. When the defence line was practically completed in March 1942, 52 Army Troops Company moved to Altun Kupri near Kirkuk to construct an underground hospital for 800 beds distributed in 12 wards, each 60 feet by 16 feet.[1]

Afterwards, the unit worked on staging camps in the desert along the Kirkuk-Haifa oil-pipe line, and September 1942 found it building a 900 feet floating bridge across the Tigris, two miles downstream of the Maude Bridge at Baghdad—a 5 months' job. Then it went to Kut-al-Amara to erect workshops, and before it left Iraq in April 1943 it had rafted 250 tons of Engineer stores down the Euphrates for 200 miles to Habbaniya. Such diverse employment was typical of that which fell to the lot of many Sapper units.

Throughout the summer of 1942, the situation in the Middle East remained serious and even menacing. The Russians were still retreating and in Egypt it was doubtful whether the Alamein line could be held. By September, Rommel was within 50 miles of Alexandria and planning to sweep up the Nile Valley. Stalingrad was invested, and

---

[1] A still larger underground hospital was built at Mosul during the winter. It was designed for 1,450 beds and had every convenience. The wards were extensions of some marble quarries. This hospital was in use for some years.

German troops were thrusting towards the Caucasus region, whence they might reach Northern Persia by November. It was possible also that Hitler might invade Anatolia and enter Iraq from that direction. The burden placed on General Quinan as Commander, 10th Army, was obviously becoming too great, for while he was engaged in operational planning he could not administer properly the immense lines of communication behind his forces. Consequently, in August 1942, it was decided that the Persia and Iraq Command, represented by the 10th Army, should be designated "Paiforce" and that General Sir Henry Maitland Wilson should be in command. An Inspector General of Communications was to take over the general administration, while an area command, known as "Pibase", dealt with internal security and local administration on the lines of communication. General Wilson, with headquarters in Baghdad, was then able to integrate the activities of both the 10th Army and L. of C. formations and thus, in September 1942, "Paiforce" was born. By that time, the defence systems in Northern Iraq and the adjacent tracts of Persia were far advanced and the over-riding consideration had become the acceleration of aid to the hard-pressed Russians.

Much has been written about the convoys which gallantly fought their way from Great Britain round the North Cape to Archangel, but little has been recorded about the supplies sent by land along the 3,000-mile road from North-West India through Duzdab and Meshed in Persia to Askabad on the nearest railway in Russia, or about the supplies poured northwards along the Trans-Iranian Railway from Bandar Shahpur on the Persian Gulf, and Tanuma opposite Basra, through Ahwaz, Andimishk, Dorud, Sultanabad and Qum to Teheran and thence to Bandar Shah on the Caspian. The Trans-Iranian Railway had been built, before the war, by engineers of several nations. From Bandar Shahpur the main line crossed 150 miles of desert and then climbed into the mountains to a height of 7,000 feet, reached through 130 tunnels. Next it dropped 3,000 feet to Teheran, 500 miles from its start, and finally ran for another 300 miles through difficult country to Bandar Shah, whence supplies could be carried to Russia by ship or lorry. Branch lines were under construction towards Tabriz and the Caucasus region, and eastwards to Meshed and south-eastwards to Yezd. In October 1941, the railway could carry only 200 tons a day. Twelve times that tonnage was needed for Russia. Colonel Sir Godfrey Rhodes, late R.E., then General Manager of the Kenya and Uganda Railways, was appointed to secure this result with the assistance of Lieut.-Colonels H. A. Davis and A. R. Mais, R.E., and a staff of British and Indian railwaymen who had been engaged in the original construction. The magnitude of the problem facing Colonel Rhodes is shown by the following extract from "Paiforce."[1] "There were no train control offices, no system of controlling the distribution of wagons, no arrangement for classified yard working. The freight time-table was largely ornamental. Wagon doors were fastened with bits of string. Thieves haunted the line. Brakesmen had a habit of screwing down their hand-brakes and going to sleep. On one stretch it was the custom of the driver and fireman of the second locomotive (when two were drawing the train) to alight for a glass of tea at the lowest loop, leaving their locomotive to make its own way, with regulator fully open, to the station at the top loop where, by moving smartly across 300 yards of country, they resumed control."

The winter cold was cruel in the mountains traversed by the line, and the summer heat of 1942 was terrible in the plains. At Andimishk, the shade temperature by day stayed at 130 degrees F. for weeks, and water left outside a tent was too hot for washing, even after the blazing sun had gone down. Road supply supplemented railway transport both in East and West Persia. In the west, hundreds of lorries carried supplies from the rail-head at Khaniqin through Kermanshah and Hamadan. The names of Brigadier J. L. French and Lieut.-Colonels A. J. R. Hill and G. W. Kirkland, R.E., will always be associated with the road-supply to Russia. Supplies also flowed in by road along the route from Quetta through Duzdab (Zahidan) to Meshed.[2] Then came the treacherous attack by the Japanese at Pearl Harbour on December 7th, 1941, which brought America into the war. American engineers soon began to assume responsibility for the eastern supply routes through Persia, and when Field-Marshal Von Paulus surrendered at Stalingrad in February 1943 our American Allies were pouring in supplies and munitions by the Trans-Iranian line which British and Indian engineers had done so much to develop.

Units of the Indian Engineers (prior to October 1941 called 'Sappers and Miners') accomplished a great deal during some stages of the railway supply to Russia and in all stages of the road supply. For

---

[1] *Paiforce. The Official Story of the Persia and Iraq Command*, 1941-46, pp. 94, 95.

[2] See "The Supply Road to Russia" appearing in *The Journal of the United Service Institution*, May 1948.

instance, 105 Railway Construction Company under Captain Harbans Singh, I.E., which was transferred to Andimishk in February 1943, did useful work in remodelling railway yards and providing crossing stations. Other railway units were similarly engaged. Until the likelihood of a German invasion decreased, the Field Companies of Indian Engineers were employed chiefly on defence works, but afterwards they were able to help road supply by repairing bridges and keeping road surfaces in reasonably good condition.

As an example of the experiences of many Indian Engineer field units in Iraq and Persia in 1942-43, some extracts may be given here from a description of the adventures of 5 Field Company, written by Brigadier Mangat Rai,[1] who then commanded the unit. The Brigadier, at that time a Major, was one of the earliest Regular officers of the Corps of Indian Engineers and among the few K.C.I.Os. and I.C.Os. serving in the Corps at the outbreak of war. Others in the same category, who appear in the records of "Paiforce", are Brigadiers R. E. Aserappa, J. S. Dhillon and A. D. Verma, and Colonels R. A. Loomba, Shiv Dial Singh and A. L. Gomes. Some of the remainder—Brigadiers Harkirat Singh, Partap Narain, R. K. Kochhar, K. N. Dubey and D. B. Chopra, and Colonels N. S. Bhagat, A. P. Nanda and A. N. Kashyap—were spared the hardships of service in Iraq though they had their share elsewhere.[2] Major Mangat Rai took over command of 5 Field Company from Major I. G. Loch, R.E., on April 10th, 1942, when the unit was constructing a defensive area at Baquba on the Diyala River above Baghdad. "The works consisted entirely of field defences" writes Mangat Rai. "No concrete was used. We carried out some of the more complicated work, but the remainder was done by contract labour. It was unpleasant because of the intense heat and the difficulty of controlling a large body of heterogeneous composition. The coolies were mainly Iraqis but also included Persians, Kurds, Armenians and Jews. Simultaneously with this work the unit prepared demolitions in the area Diltawa-Baquba-Shahraban-Kifri which was more interesting. All the major bridges, both road and railway, were prepared for demolition. After finishing the Baquba defences, the unit moved to Kirkuk and on June 26th into Persia to Kermanshah for more training. The change

---

[1] Notes by Brig. C. R. Mangat Rai, dated March 1951.

[2] Others among the earliest officers (ranks as held in October 1941) were the following: Capts. L. M. H. Wadia and M. G. Bewoor, T/Capts. Mahomed Anwar Hussain, V. Panch and J. S. Paintal, and Lieut. Anant Singh.

was very welcome because of the cool summer climate of Kermanshah. A chain of defensive positions was to be made in Persia, and we went finally to Sarwandhar to construct a position on a mountain pass. There we remained from July 14th to November 20th, 1942, working under the 8th Division whose H.Q. were at Charaveshah, 20 miles away, on the main road from Ahwaz to the Caspian. The C.R.E. 8th Division, Lieut.-Colonel C. M. Machlachlan, R.E., had been a Bengal Sapper for many years and knew the unit well. Our camp was at 6,000 feet and pleasantly cool throughout the summer, though before we left in November it had become wet and cold. We had to work against time, yet we enjoyed it as there was little interference from above. The defensive position was sited by a team of all arms from the 8th Division. Major-General C. O. Harvey, the Commander, stayed with us for about a week to give his approval. He was very popular and took the keenest interest in the smallest detail. Before work was started, Lieut.-General A. G. O. M. Mayne, the Corps Commander, inspected the site and stayed with the unit for a couple of days, living in a caravan which was parked below the Officers' Mess. A small 'ablutions' tent used by officers had been pitched below the Mess, and one morning, while General Mayne was in it, it was pelted with a fusillade of earthen clods thrown from higher up the hill. The whole tent shook. Naturally surprised, the General emerged from it only to discover that the culprit was the junior subaltern of the unit who, on seeing him, was greatly alarmed. However, the subaltern apologized and explained that he had thought it was a friend of his who was in occupation and the General received his apologies with good humour. Nevertheless, when he went to the tent next morning, he placed his 'brass hat' carefully on the apex."

5 Field Company had the assistance of two companies of auxiliary Pioneers, but the actual work on the defences was done as usual mainly by contract labour. Early in November 1942, the defensive position was nearing completion. Meanwhile, the threat to the Persian oilfields had diminished owing to the increasing Russian resistance to Hitler's armies. Rain and cold retarded digging operations and finally, on November 15th, it was decided to stop work. All defences were covered up as far as possible to protect them from snow, and the unit motored back to Iraq, reaching Tuz Khurmatli, near Kirkuk, on November 26th. Early in April 1943, after spending the winter months in training and the erection of camp structures, it moved to Egypt. A hard fate seemed to dog the footsteps of 5 Field Company

Year by year passed and it saw no fighting, but the men were not discouraged and looked forward confidently to what the future might hold in store for them.

The amusing incident in which General Mayne figured has its counterpart in another in which Brigadier F. W. T. Hards, Chief Engineer 3rd Corps, was concerned. Major A. B. Rhodes, R.E., who commanded 97 Field Company of the Royal Bombay Engineers writes as follows:— "After the unit reached Basra in November 1942 it moved to Qasr-i-Shirin in Persia to join temporarily the 6th Indian Division, and early in 1943 it became part of the 3rd (British) Corps Troops Engineers under Brigadier 'Daddy' Hards, an old Bombay Sapper. The Brigadier paid us a surprise visit and spent the night, and as we had no Guest tent, the Canteen tent was emptied and made available for him. After dinner, when we had all retired to our tents, we were horrified to hear a very loud-voiced Sapper beating on the Canteen tent with a stick and shouting "Oh! Canteen wallah! Give me some cigarettes." Brigadier Hards kept silent for a few minutes, but the beating was resumed and the Sapper started to undo the tent fly and looked inside. He must have been considerably skaken when, instead of the Canteen wallah, he came face to face with the irate occupant. However, by breakfast time next morning, the Brigadier was prepared, in his usual kindly way, to overlook the incident."

During April and May 1943, the 8th Division moved from Iraq into Syria for further training, and with it were 1 and 5 Field Companies who had been in winter quarters at Khaniqin near the Persian border. Despite the considerable exodus of Engineer units which followed news of the relief of Stalingrad, there was still much to be done in Iraq, especially in building up supply depots, improving communications and expanding airbases, though units of the Bengal Group took little part in the work. However, Lieut. Pearson records some of the doings of two Bengal units from the autumn of 1942 onwards. "In September 1942", he writes,[1] "8 Army Troops Company arrived in Khaniqin from Egypt and began to build water-supply tanks, sheds and hutting and to provide electric installations. 6 Army Troops Company was already in the country, engaged on a great variety of jobs such as workshops at Andimishk in Persia, ice-plants and sheds for the R.A.F., Hamilton and Inglis bridges in Basra, and the re-erection of wireless masts for the R.A.F. In December

---

[1] *Brief History of the K.G.V's O. Bengal Sappers and Miners Group, R.I.E., August 1939-July 1946*, by Lieut. G. Pearson R.E., pp. 44-46 and 93-95.

1942, a more united effort was required of 6 Army Troops Company. It sailed for some islands beyond the Persian Gulf to complete R.A.F. aerodromes. A detachment was dropped at Ras-al-Hadd and the main party went on to Masirah Island,[1] where stores had to be landed in Arab dhows. The aerodromes were already in use, but hard standings and camps for the R.A.F. and American personnel were yet to be built. By March 1943, the Wireless Telegraph Station and the Operations Block were nearly finished and a power house was under construction. At Ras-al-Hadd, an extension to the runway was continued. In April, the accommodation at Masirah was completed, and in the following month 6 Army Troops Company left for Suez. Meanwhile, in February 1943, 8 Army Troops Company had been occupied mainly in improving two tented General Hospitals at Khaniqin and building an ice-factory. It was given a hundred ice-chests and some inadequate drawings and told to prepare ice! In September it moved to Basra to erect wireless masts at a Naval Station while detachments travelled round the Persian Gulf for a similar purpose. It re-assembled, in May 1944, in Bahrein Island to build a R.A.F. Station and worked there throughout the summer in extremely trying climatic conditions. In November 1944 it moved to Kermanshah. The cold of the Pai Tak Pass was but an introduction to a winter of snow, rain and hard work."

The transport of material to Russia came to an end in 1945 when five million tons had passed through Persia alone. "Paiforce" had nobly fulfilled its mission, not only in this great undertaking but in protecting and developing Iraq. Many Indian Engineer units had shared in the work besides those already mentioned—so many, in fact, that a mere outline of their movements must suffice. Of the Bombay units, 20 Field Company was in Iraq during the spring of 1943 before returning to India and 27 Field Company in Persia throughout the year. 31 Field Squadron (Bengal) spent the greater part of 1943 in Iraq before transfer to Egypt, as also did 32 Field Squadron (Madras). 39 Field Squadron (Madras), 44 Field Park Company (Madras) and 47 Field Park Company (Bengal) were also there for a time in 1943, and 57 and 58 Field Companies (Madras) were in Iraq or Persia for most of the year. Early in 1943, 69 Field Company (Bengal) was in Iraq and 97 Field Company (Bombay) in Iraq and Persia. 301 Field Park Company (Bombay) spent part of

---

[1] Ras-al-Hadd is a cape, 120 miles south-east of Muscat at the entrance to the Gulf of Oman. Masirah Island lies 150 miles further south on the shore of the Indian Ocean.

1943 in Iraq, and 302 Field Park Company (Bengal, formerly Bombay) and 322 Field Park Company (Bengal) were in Iraq or Persia throughout the year. 16 Workshop and Park Company also served in Iraq and Persia where it arrived early in 1942 after employment in Syria on organizing the stores required for defensive works. In general, however, it may be said that in 1944 the services of the Field Companies of Indian Engineers were more urgently needed in Italy or Burma than in the Middle East and consequently most of these units were to be found in one or other of those theatres.

Sapper units in the Middle East enjoyed an occasional but very welcome change of scene in the island of Cyprus which became an important bastion in our Mediterranean defences after the German invasion of Greece and consequently required much fortification. But long before the fall of Greece, Cyprus had been used as a rest centre for troops who had fought in the Western Desert. Its defences had not been neglected by the 50th British Division, which was there in the summer of 1941; but when the 5th Indian Division relieved the 50th Division in November 1941, the possibility of an air-borne attack had to be envisaged. Major-General Mayne, the Divisional Commander, was told by General Auchinleck that the island must be held at all costs and that there must be no repetition of the fiasco in Crete. It was considered that an air-borne invasion of Cyprus might be possible from Southern Anatolia as well as from Crete and the Dodecanese Islands in the Aegean Sea. The 5th Divisional Engineers, under Lieut.-Colonel A. H. G. Napier, R.E., prepared accordingly to demolish the runways of all aerodromes and the installations at all harbours, particularly on the south coast, and to block all vital roads. Plans were drawn up for the destruction of dumps. Prohibited areas were announced. Camouflage began. New camps and new roads were prepared and existing roads widened. Great attention was given to coast defences. The Sapper companies of the 5th Division were assisted by infantry and civilian labour. It was a very busy scene. Cyprus is a large island, 140 miles in length and 60 miles wide at the centre. Two parallel mountain ranges traverse it from east to west with a wide alluvial plain between. With the exception of Nikosia, the capital, the largest towns, such as Famagusta, Larnaka and Limassol, lie on the southern coast, and the population numbers about half a million. The island is a British colony and a very important one. 2 and 20 Field Companies and 44 Field Park Company were there in 1941, and during the following year, for varying periods, 11 Field Park Company, 12, 20 and 21

Field Companies, 41 and 44 Field Park Companies and 61 Field Company. In 1943, 9, 10, 14, and 21 Field Companies were present and also 41 Field Park Company and 61 Field Company. Thus many units of the three Groups of Indian Engineers helped to garrison and strengthen Cyprus during the war and found the island invaluable also as a training centre.

We come now to the tragic fate which overtook most of 9 Field Company of the Madras Group in 1943 in the Dodecanese Islands. Since June 1940, when Italian aircraft from these islands had bombed our fleet in Alexandria, the Italian forces holding the Dodecanese archipelago embracing Rhodes, Kos, Leros, Samos, Kalymnos, Symi, Stampalia and Kastelorizo (the last named being close to the Anatolian coast at the eastern end of the group) had closed the Aegean Sea to our shipping. "E" Boats and submarines infested the small harbours, especially in Leros, and after the fall of Crete in 1941 it was reported that landing craft were being massed for the invasion of either Cyprus or Syria. Early in 1943, the possibility of capturing Rhodes and opening up the Aegean was considered most carefully by our High Command, but the scheme had to be abandoned because of the demands of our advance in North Africa, and later, the assault on Sicily. At the beginning of September 1943, Italy having surrendered, we tried to encourage the Italians in the Aegean Islands to resist any German incursions until we could reinforce them with British and Indian troops in small parties, and some of the islands, including Kos, Leros and Kastelorizo, were thus reinforced at considerable hazard; but in Rhodes our emissaries were unable to prevent the Italian Governor from surrendering unconditionally to the Germans. It was considered that, even if Leros could be strongly occupied by us and the Kos airfields seized and defended, we should not be in a sufficiently secure position unless Rhodes was also in our possession, and this we were unable to accomplish.

However, the 234th Brigade had been training for some time for landings in the Dodecanese Islands as the major component of a Beach Landing Group known as "Brick Force." A programme of combined training was carried out in the Suez Canal area by composite formations of British and Indian troops known as "36 Brick" and "37 Brick". 5 Field Company had joined "36 Brick" from Syria in June 1943 to prepare for landing operations in September, and 1 Field Company from Iraq had joined "37 Brick". 97 Field Company was also posted to "Brick Force". Vehicles were waterproofed, equipment marked, and loading tables prepared for ships.[1] The mechanical transport was to be loaded at Beirut and Haifa and the personnel at Egyptian ports, but 5 Field Company had just completed its final exercise in Suez Bay when news came that the operation was postponed and in October that it had been abandoned. The reason was the failure of the initial attempts to defend Cos and Leros, the story of which may now be told.

Before dawn on October 3rd, 1943, part of an invading force of Germans, bound apparently for Rhodes, had landed at Kos and captured the small island in spite of the stubborn resistance offered by a British battalion which had been installed there. The loss of the Kos airfields, whence fighter cover could be given to our warships, prevented the transit by sea of adequate supplies to our small garrison on Leros. This garrison, consisting of another British battalion and some details, was slightly reinforced at the end of October; but in November a large enemy convoy began to move into the Kos-Kalymnos area and the German invasion of Leros started on November 12th. Our garrison resisted stoutly, though ammunition was running short. By November 16th, the situation was critical. Incessant bombing and fighting had reduced our men to the last stages of exhaustion and during the afternoon of that day they were obliged to surrender. A few only managed to escape in native boats. After the fall of Leros, the small British garrison of Samos was withdrawn, and the greater part of the still smaller garrison of Kastelorizo was also removed, leaving only an outpost for observation purposes.

On September 17th, 9 Field Company under Major P. G. O. Landon, R.E., was in support of the 234th Brigade of "Brick Force", then embarking at Haifa, but owing to transport shortages only three platoons and a Tactical H.Q. accompanied the brigade. No. 1 Platoon was landed on Kastelorizo, No. 2 on Cos and No 3 on Leros, and soon afterwards Major Landon perished when the flyingboat in which he was returning from Cos to Leros was shot down by enemy fighters.[2] An Order of Battle shows that 9 Field Company had 60 other ranks and perhaps one officer on Cos,[3] and 62 other ranks and 3 officers on Leros, when the garrisons were forced to surrender. Of these, only 3 other ranks escaped by boat to Anatolia

---

[1] "History of 5 Field Company, April 10th, 1942 - January 6th, 1944," by Brig. Mangat Rai, dated April 1951.

[2] "*A Short History of the Queen Victoria's Own Madras Sappers and Miners during World War II, 1939-45*", by Lieut-Colonel R. A. Lindsell, R.E., p. 13.

[3] Also on Cos were 32 other ranks of 74 Field Company, R.E.

and thence made their way to Syria. All communications between the Company H.Q. at Haifa and the platoons on Cos and Leros ceased on September 17th; but although there was no communication with No 1 Platoon on Kastelorizo, the greater part of the detachment was evacuated in December 1943, and 9 Field Company, then under Major P. A. D. Radcliffe, R.E., began to re-form at Haifa preparatory to joining the 10th Indian Division at Gaza. It was not sufficiently strong, however, to accompany that division to Italy in March 1944 and accordingly joined the 9th Army in Syria. The small party left behind on Kastelorizo rejoined in September 1944 when 9 Field Company, reinforced by drafts from 57 and 58 Companies, was at last reunited and could efface all traces of the Aegean tragedy.

The Company served in May 1945 with an Armoured Division detailed to intervene in a Franco-Syrian dispute, and the O.C., then Major N. M. R. Moody, R.E., was placed in command of the British garrison at Palmyra. An interesting, and occasionally very entertaining, account of the operations in this region has been written by Brigadier A. Mc. G. Stewart, who was the C.R.E. at that time.[1] 9 Field Company built a road in the mountains, and the other Engineer units were concerned chiefly in making hard-standings. While in Palmyra, 9 Field Company had to keep the peace between the few remaining French and the local inhabitants. All the French were supposed to leave as soon as possible, except the officers of a camel unit, so Moody was much annoyed one day when he saw two European women strolling in the town. He sent a subaltern to find out who they were; but the youngster, having used his best French, got a very caustic reply in his native tongue. The ladies turned out to be the English wives of two engineers from one of the desert pumping stations. Later, the main task of the Divisional Engineers was to pass French convoys through Homs on their way to evacuation from Beirut. 31 Field Squadron had to picket some corners in the road. There was considerable opposition from the Syrians, so a Subedar who knew some Arabic addressed the hostile crowd and pointed out that it did not help the proceedings if they threw stones. The leaders then explained quite amicably that they had no real intention of offending and would therefore throw over-ripe tomatoes instead, which they accordingly did! 9 Field Company and 39 Field

---

[1] "Notes on the Divisional Engineers, 31st (later 1st) Armoured Division, 1945-46", by Brig. A. Mc. G. Stewart, dated July 15th, 1951.

Park Squadron were both at Homs early in August 1945. The former returned to Egypt in September and to India in October.

The last active operations in the Levant in which units of the Indian Engineers took part were those in Greece in 1944. Ever since the British evacuation in April 1941, the Germans had held Greece in an iron grip, but in August 1944 they began to leave the country. They were then everywhere on the defensive. General Eisenhower's armies were sweeping through France, General Alexander's armies were struggling through the mountains north of Rome, and the Russians were driving through Rumania and Bulgaria. In September 1944, "Arkforce" was born, a force designed for the re-occupation of Greece, and in it, as the only Indian Army unit and also the only Engineer formation, was 6 Army Troops Company of the Bengal Group. The Company left the Suez Canal in October and entered the Piraeus harbour through many minefields. The enemy had damaged the dock area very badly. Sunken ships blocked the waterways: quays were cratered and littered with debris. However, 6 Army Troops Company soon cleared the quays and wharves sufficiently to enable General Scobie's troops to disembark and spread into Athens and beyond. Other Engineer units appeared gradually from Italy with the 4th Indian Division. These were 4 Field Company (Bengal) under Major H. C. Colter, R.E., 11 Field Park Company (Madras) under Major L. C. Hall R.E., 12 Field Company (Madras) under Major E. B. Wheaton, R.E., 21 Field Company (Bombay) under Major J. R. G. French, R.E., and a Bridging Platoon.[1] The Chief Engineer was Brigadier F. W. T. Hards. In December, after the withdrawal of the Germans, civil war broke out between the rival Greek factions known as "E.L.A.M." and "E.L.A.S.", the latter being hostile to the Allies. 6 Army Troops Company was entrusted with the defence of the dock area at Piraeus and the maintenance of the existing electric system. 4 Field Company arrived in the nick of time, when the fighting was at its height, and was employed on wiring and road-block clearance. It re-embarked in January 1945 and sailed for Volos where it was the first unit ashore. Meanwhile 21 Field Company had repaired the Patras-Corinth Road.

The main Engineer operations in Greece during 1944 and 1945 were based on Salonika in the northern province of Macedonia, and

---

[1] 12 Field Company landed at Salonika on November 8th and 11 Field Park Company on the 12th. 21 Field Company landed at Patras on November 24th and 4 Field Company at Piraeus on December 12th.

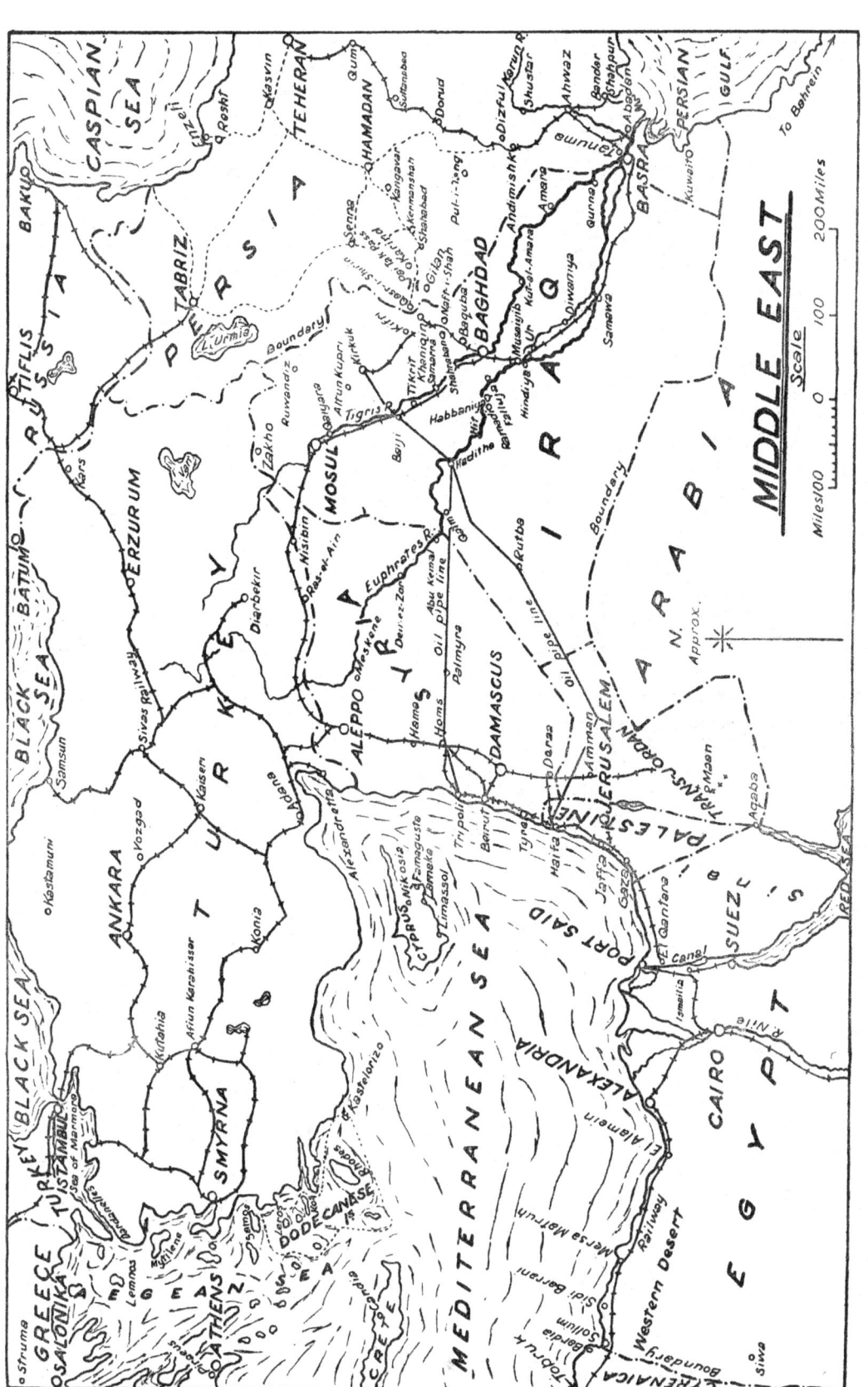

a full account of them has been given in *The R. E. Journal*.[1] "During November and early December 1944", writes the C.R.E. (Lieut.-Colonel Paten), "reconnaissances were pushed out as far as the Axios Plain to the west and to beyond the Struma Valley to the east. Sapper interests were focussed on two major physical obstacles, the Strimon (Struma) River and the Axios (Vardar) River, which offered bridging problems of the first order." E.L.A.S. commenced hostilities in Athens early in December, and by the 15th the 4th Indian Division was hemmed in at Salonika. This state of affairs persisted till the middle of January 1945 when, as a result of a truce with E.L.A.S., the Division was able to send out patrols to a distance of about 18 miles in all directions. Peace terms were accepted on February 12th. This was the signal for greatly increased Sapper activity, and by the end of the month all roads leading out of Salonika, with the exception of the Axios route, had been opened up. A major work demanding instant attention was the repair of the Axios River Bridge. 4 Field Company and 21 Field Company arrived from the south during March to help the other Engineer units. By providing a ferry across the Aliakmon River near the Serbian border a route for light traffic was restored between Salonika and Athens. During April, work was in progress over most of Macedonia. Five bridges were opened across the Aliakmon and Strimon Rivers in July 1945 and others elsewhere. In fact, the Sapper units excelled themselves in bridging and road making. They built or repaired 15 permanent structures and erected 5 large timber bridges and 18 Bailey bridges, and thus they helped materially to restore the communications in Northern Greece.

The war in the Middle East, with which this chapter has dealt, was fought in extremes of heat, cold and terrain and usually with quite inadequate forces. The story is one of improvisation and yet more improvisation. Nevertheless, complete victory was secured. Who knows what might have happened had Germany succeeded in overrunning Persia and Iraq? The Indian Engineer units which fought in those countries, and on the shores of the Mediterranean, have reason to be proud of their achievements.

---

[1] "The 4th Indian Divisional Engineers in Macedonia," by Lieut.-Colonel L. A. B. Paten, R.E., appearing in *The R.E. Journal*, March 1946.

CHAPTER IV

THE WESTERN DESERT, MAY 1941 - AUGUST 1942

IN Chapter II we left the battered Western Desert Force, the precursor of the Eighth Army, holding precariously a position to the east of the Egyptian frontier after Rommel had swept through Cyrenaica during May 1941 and had failed to take Tobruk by storm. By that time the 4th Indian Division, under Major-General F. W. Messervy,[1] had reached the Desert front from Eritrea and was concentrated in the Bagush area where a defensive position had been constructed in the previous autumn. On arrival with the 11th Brigade, 4 Field Company began at once to prepare anti-tank obstacles in the Bagush Box and to clear the old defences and dug-outs of sand. The weather was extremely hot. Indeed, one day the temperature rose to 137° F. The other Divisional Engineers—12 and 18 Field Companies, 11 Field Park Company and 6 Army Troops Company —followed in due course and were soon very busy at the front or behind it. Both the opposing armies needed reinforcements and equipment before they could attack; but General Wavell, taking a considerable though justifiable risk, was able to forestall Rommel in the offensive and nearly succeeded in relieving the beleaguered garrison of Tobruk. To quote a well known doggerel "Twice blest is he who has his quarrel just; but three times he who gets his blow in fust". Working on this principle, Wavell launched an attack early in June. The primary objective was the destruction of all the enemy forces east of Tobruk, but it was hoped also that time would be gained for the arrival of important reinforcements from overseas. The main body of the enemy was grouped around Tobruk and obviously preparing to renew the assault, for the fortress was like a festering sore in Rommel's side. The German armour roamed the desert between Tobruk and the Egyptian frontier while an advanced screen of Axis infantry and artillery was entrenched at Bardia and Sollum on the coast, at the Halfaya Pass, and on the high escarpment at Fort Capuzzo.[2]

---

[1] Major-General Sir Noel Beresford-Peirse had been promoted to the chief command of the Western Desert Force.

[2] See the map of North Africa included in Chapter V but referring also to this chapter.

The Western Desert Force was organized for the attack as a 'Coast Force' and a 'Plateau Force.' The former was to storm the Halfaya Pass, while the latter, which had most of the armour, was to sweep round westwards and northwards and cut the enemy's communications. With the Coast Force, comprising the 11th Brigade Group, was 4 Field Company. On June 14th, the Plateau Force, consisting of the 22nd Guards Brigade Group, set off with the 7th British Armoured Brigade and during the ensuing night our tanks penetrated deep into enemy territory; but shortly after dawn, when Plateau Force had taken Fort Capuzzo and was pressing on along the escarpment towards the top of the Halfaya Pass, it began to meet heavy resistance. On the 16th, many of the tanks were knocked out by enemy 88 m.m. guns and gradually the force was brought to a standstill. Tank battles developed, always in favour of the German heavy armour, and raged around Sidi Omar until the morning of the 17th. Meanwhile, Coast Force had also run into trouble. It had failed repeatedly to force a passage up the Halfaya Pass, and on the 16th its few 'I' tanks entered an uncharted minefield under heavy enemy fire. "It now became a Sapper's job", writes the official historian.[1] "Before the tanks could be removed, the extent of the minefield had to be discovered. Yet there were the tanks, stuck among the mines and only 500 yards from the enemy. Lieut. N. B. Thomas of 4 Field Company carried out a reconnaissance alone under intense fire. Coolly and deliberately he searched the ground, the tank commander being killed while actually hearing his report. Then the Sappers came forward and removed the mines—dangerous, cold-blooded work—and during the following night the tanks were recovered." Thomas was awarded an immediate M.C. for his gallantry on this occasion and he brought back with him the first 'Tellermine' seen by our troops. 12 Field Company, with Plateau Force, was also concerned in the attack. It distinguished itself during the capture of a key point called Omar Nuovo and did useful work in minelifting and improving communications.[2] Late in the evening of June 17th, the last parties of Plateau Force descended the escarpment and Coast Force also withdrew. Both forces then made their way to Sofafi and finally returned to the Bagush Box.

---

[1] "*The Tiger Kills.*" (M.O.I. Publication), p. 16.

[2] "*A Short History of the Q.V's O. Madras Sappers and Miners during World War II, 1939-45*", by Lieut.-Colonel R. A. Lindsell, R.E., p. 7.

The Battle of Sollum, as it is sometimes called, was a tactical failure, though perhaps it may be deemed a strategical success because it undoubtedly gave a respite to hard-pressed Tobruk. Yet it resulted in a very serious situation. We had lost almost all our tanks, we had no reserves, and Egypt lay wide open to invasion. This was General Wavell's last Middle East campaign, for in July he was transferred to India as Commander-in-Chief in place of General Sir Claude Auchinleck who came to relieve him in Cairo. Happily for Auchinleck, the change coincided with a gradual improvement in the aspect of the war in the Middle East. Iraq was subdued, Syria rescued, Tobruk furnished with supplies, and the Western Desert Force strengthened. East Africa gave no anxiety, and the threat to Cyprus had ceased when Germany declared war on Russia on June 22nd. Auchinleck needed only look to the west to find his enemy. His responsibilities, however onerous, were far less intricate than those of his distinguished predecessor, but he shouldered them bravely and competently and soon confirmed his previous reputation as a dour fighter whom nothing could dismay.

Much was learnt from the Battle of Sollum, and the 4th Divisional Engineers began to cogitate deeply on the question of anti-tank mines, how the Germans laid them and the best method of clearing them. "At that time", writes Pearson,[1] "mine-detectors were not available and there was little conception of the size to which the mine problem would grow. 4 Field Company evolved a drill for locating mines by prodding with bayonets which was provisionally adopted by the Division, and from study of suspected German methods of laying mines the C.R.E. 4th Division (Lieut.-Colonel H. P. Cavendish, R.E.) got the idea of the 'knotted cord drill' for minelaying which eventually became the standard method of the British Army. For two months, 4 Field Company worked again on the defences of the Bagush Box, building concrete pill-boxes and laying minefields, and late in August it moved forward to build sandbagged protective pens for fighter aircraft and buildings for Royal Air Force personnel at Sidi Barrani. On September 20th, work was begun on an extensive minefield in the Sofafi area in defence of an advanced base. This minefield was over 9 miles in length with more than 50,000 mines laid according to the new drill. Apart from an early alarm, work continued without incident into November 1941 and flame fougasses were installed to cover gaps."

---

[1] *"Brief History of the K.G.V's O. Bengal Sappers and Miners Group, R.I.E., August 1939-July 1946"*, by Lieut. G. Pearson, R.E., pp., 82.

The story of the Western Desert during the summer and autumn of 1941 is really the story of Tobruk where the first British experiment in the theory of fortress areas was proving highly satisfactory. When Auchinleck succeeded Wavell on July 5th he decided to maintain a defensive policy and did so until October, although he had no intention of awaiting passively a renewed attack by Rommel. He watched his enemy carefully, patrolled the frontier wire incessantly, occupied the desert oases of Siwa, Jarabub and Jalo, far inland from his southern flank, and covered the small port of Mersa Matruh and its airfields with belts of minefields situated about 125 miles east of Sollum. In Tobruk, the 70th British Division, with the 32nd Tank Brigade and some Polish troops, stood firm as a rock under Major-General R. Mac K. Scobie, late R.E., a very able commander; but as the Indian Army was represented by only one cavalry regiment and no Indian Engineers were present, the defence of Tobruk hardly comes within the scope of this narrative. It must suffice to record that with the support of the Royal Navy and Royal Air Force the garrison was able to frustrate every attempt at infiltration until relief came in November 1941.

Meanwhile, General Auchinleck was busy with preparations for a winter offensive. The campaign was given the code name "Crusader", and with the arrival of reinforcements a new army came into being. At the end of September the "Western Desert Force" became known as the "Eighth Army", and on November 18th, Lieut.-General Sir Alan Cunningham, the victor of East Africa, was appointed as its Commander. The Eighth Army was born at a critical period in Britain's fortunes. On it depended the fate of the Middle East, perhaps of the British Empire. It had first to be trained and then to turn defeat into victory over an experienced enemy provided with powerful armour and operating in a desert which has been aptly described as the tactician's paradise and the quartermaster's hell. The saviours of the troubled quartermaster have often proved to be Engineer troops, and so it was in the Fourth Libyan Campaign when units of the British, Indian, and Dominions' Engineers enabled the transport to reach the battle front while others accompanied the forward troops into the fight.

The new-born Eighth Army comprised the 13th Corps under Lieut.-General Godwin-Austin (4th Indian Division, New Zealand Division and 1st Army Tank Brigade) and the 30th Corps under Lieut.-General W. Norrie (7th Armoured Division, 4th Armoured Brigade, 1st South African Division and 201st Guards Brigade

Group). In addition, there was the Tobruk garrison, and in Army Reserve, the 2nd South African Division and the 29th Indian Infantry Brigade. Rommel's army was roughly one-third German and two-thirds Italian. He had the German Afrika Korps (15th and 21st Panzer Divisions and 90th Light Motorized Division) and a German Infantry Division, and also the Italian Ariete Armoured Division and six Italian Infantry Divisions. He was superior in air strength and much superior in armour, not numerically but in gun-power, for Cunningham's 2 pr. tank and anti-tank guns were almost useless against Rommel's 50 m.m. and 75 m.m. weapons and the British 'I' tanks had inadequate protection and were generally unsuitable for desert warfare.[1]

Cunningham opened the ball with a surprise attack on November 18th, 1941, against Rommel's right flank in the desert and during the next few days there was fierce fighting which culminated on the 22nd and 23rd in one of the largest tank battles of the war. This took place in the Sidi Rezegh - El Adem region, south of Tobruk. The beleaguered garrison tried hard to co-operate but could make little headway. Victory went to the German armour, and the vital escarpment of Sidi Rezegh, occupied for a time by Norrie, had to be abandoned. Rommel now launched his Panzers eastwards to smash Norrie's communications and so great was the resulting confusion in what may be called the "Battle of the Omars" that Cunningham wished to withdraw to Mersa Matruh; but Auchinleck promptly flew to the desert, forbade any withdrawal, removed Cunningham from the chief command and appointed in his place Lieut.-General N. M. Ritchie, a very forceful but rather junior leader. Yet the choice seemed justifiable, for after Sidi Rezegh had changed hands twice Rommel began to retreat westwards on December 5th and Tobruk was disengaged four days later. This event was the occasion of a wise-crack by Godwin-Austin. "Tobruk is relieved", said he, "but not half so relieved as I am!"

Rommel continued to withdraw rapidly along the coast of Cyrenaica and by the middle of January 1942 was back at his starting point at El Agheila. Italian garrisons, left behind on the Egyptian frontier, had been mopped up by our troops and Sollum and Halfaya re-occupied. It seemed now that Auchinleck was within an ace of complete victory. But Rommel thought otherwise. Ritchie was too

---

[1] "*From Pyramid to Pagoda*" (History of The West Yorkshire Regiment, 1938-48), by Lieut.-Colonel E. W. C. Sandes, D.S.O., M.C., p. 124.

far from Egypt to be adequately supplied, yet he decided to stand where he was, and Rommel, a master tactician and an able strategist, saw his opportunity and seized it with his customary vigour. On January 21st, 1942, he rushed his armour across the desert, overran our forward dumps of petrol and supplies, struck northwards towards the coast and re-captured Benghazi on the 28th. Ritchie rallied his army to the east of Gazala and finally brought the enemy to a halt on the Gazala Line consisting of a number of defended localities or 'Boxes' with minefields between them. Thus the end of the Fourth Libyan Campaign found us far into Cyrenaica though in a very exposed position. Both sides proceeded to consolidate and reinforce, but men and materials reached Rommel more rapidly than Ritchie. Nevertheless, despite the withdrawal in January, the campaign seemed to have ended in our favour. Tobruk had been rescued and the immediate threat to Egypt removed. Also, the Gazala Line was much stronger than the Sollum Line.

During the confused fighting between armoured formations in the early stages of this campaign a new task devolved on the Divisional Engineers. This was the complete destruction of crippled enemy tanks to prevent their recovery and repair during Axis counter-offensives. Any German tank which was not blown absolutely to pieces might soon be in use again for Rommel's tank-recovery units were very efficient and highly trained. Except during an assault on Sidi Omar by the 4th Indian Division and the capture of Bardia by the 2nd South African Division, there was very little mine clearance to be done. Both Divisional Engineers and Corps Troops Engineers were employed mostly in constructing forward airfields and in opening up ports such as Tobruk, Derna and Benghazi. When the withdrawal eastwards began, the 4th Divisional Engineers carried out extensive demolitions in Benghazi, and when they reached the Gazala Line they laid mines and helped the infantry to prepare anti-tank defences. After half a million mines had been laid, mine-laying outstripped production at the base, so the Divisional Engineers were able at last to devote some time to training.

The experiences of 4 Field Company of the Bengal Corps, under Major J. G. A. J. O'Ferrall, R.E. are described by Lieut. G. Pearson. "With great foresight", he writes,[1] "the new Commander-in-Chief, General Auchinleck, had selected a position at El Alamein in which

---

[1] "*Brief History of the K.G.V's O. Bengal Sappers and Miners Group, R.I.E., August* 1939-*July* 1946", by Lieut. G. Pearson, R.E., pp. 32, 33.

the Army could cover the Delta if ever again the desert fighting went against us. During the preparatory stages of the new offensive, 4 Field Company patrolled and laid mines on the frontier. There followed a short period of training with the 7th Brigade with special attention to the breaching of minefields. The advance began on November 19th. 4 Field Company cleared mines to get the 7th Brigade into the Sidi Omar camps, but in the desert warfare that followed there was little engineer work. Long and confused battles raged between Tobruk and the frontier until the Eighth Army, joined by the Tobruk garrison, eventually swept into Derna on December 18th. Next day, the Derna airfield was reconnoitred by 4 Field Company and the northern perimeter was cleared of some 800 mines. The water supply in Derna was restored and cratered roads were repaired. The advance continued and on December 24th the Company was called forward to remove road-blocks holding up our armoured cars. In miserable rain it moved to Cyrene, to Barce and into the Benghazi area. There was a huge road-block to be cleared at the Tocra Pass, and it was not until January 5th, 1942, that all the sections reached Benghazi. The place was a dismal sight. Bombing had wrecked the large installations in the town, and the harbour facilities had been ruined. While the tanks fought out a great battle at Ajedabia, 4 Field Company worked on the power station and pumping plant at Barce and began to restore the harbour facilities in Benghazi. Then, on January 26th, it heard that the tank battle had gone against us. A rapid withdrawal had become necessary. Some demolitions were done in Benghazi before leaving, and in the Tocra Pass the road was mined and the whole route left full of blown culverts. In particular, very successful demolitions were carried out on February 1st to the west of Cyrene. A new defence zone was formed, east of Derna, on the Gazala-Bir Hacheim line. The Company remained in this line for several days, laying extensive minefields. During one night, 3,000 mines were laid in just over 12 hours, and many thousands more were put down before the unit was relieved on February 22nd. An interval then occurred in the fighting. 4 Field Company returned to Sollum for defence work and in April moved with the 4th Division to Kabrit, on the west side of the Bitter Lakes, for a period of rest, refitting and training. Kabrit was a large tented camp area forming part of a group of huge base camps and depots stretching north from Suez along the west bank of the Canal. The Company remained in Kabrit until May 1942 and then moved to Palestine." However, 4 Field Company's stay in pleasant surroundings at Hadera on the Palestine coast was destined to be very brief for within a few weeks the unit was ordered back to the Desert where, as will be seen later, it shared in the desperate efforts to halt a renewed enemy offensive.

A Madras Sapper unit which did Trojan work in the Fourth Libyan Campaign was 12 Field Company under Major J. B. Sutherland, R.E. While confused fighting was in progress on December 5th around El Gubi, south of Tobruk, a large dump of German ammunition, petrol, oil and food was discovered a few miles away and 12 Field Company, with some Sappers of an Armoured Division, was sent to destroy it. The stores were widely scattered, and sometimes buried to avoid air observation, so that it was quite possible to drive right through the dump and be none the wiser. For many days the Company was busy on this demolition job and the blazing petrol and exploding ammunition made a wonderful spectacle. The work was interrupted on one occasion by the arrival of enemy tanks in search of fuel and the Madras Sappers wisely withdrew; but they were soon back again to continue the process of destruction until nothing was left in the dump. There can be no doubt that the loss of this vast quantity of supplies must have had a marked effect on the mobility of the enemy's armour and may even have been the primary cause of the Axis retreat to the west.

Although the 5th Division, under Major-General A. G. O. M. Mayne, had reached the Western Desert in April 1941 too late to assist in stemming Rommel's first rush to the frontier it was soon giving full support to the hard-pressed 4th Indian Division. By July 1941, it was concentrated in the Bagush area with the exception of the 5th Brigade which had been called away for service in Syria. The 5th Divisional Engineers, under Lieut.-Colonel A. H. G. Napier, R.E., (2, 20 and 21 Field Companies and 44 Field Park Company) worked in two positions near El Alamein. These were known as "Fortress 'A' " on the edge of the Qattara Depression and "Fortress 'B' " midway between the Depression and the coast. However, on August 22nd, digging and mine-laying were interrupted suddenly when the Division was ordered to Iraq for possible operations in Persia. Only the 29th Brigade, with which was 2 Field Company, was left behind to guard some desert oases. The other two brigades returned to Egypt at the beginning of October 1941 but were transferred, early in November, to Cyprus. These divisional or brigade transfers did not necessarily involve the attached Engineer units. For instance, 21 Field Company (Major R. W. W. How, R.E.) did not move with the 5th Division to Iraq in August 1941, nor to Cyprus in November. It arrived in Bagush from Eritrea on August 6th and worked there for several months on landing grounds and defences. Rest and relaxation were rarities for the Engineer soldier until the threat to Egypt was removed.

The fighting capabilities of the Bombay Sappers were strikingly shown in an action at a spot called 'Point 204', south of Gazala, on December 15th, 1941, the unit concerned being 18 Field Company commanded by Major N. L. Stuart, R.E. The Company, while attached to the 5th Brigade, had worked in the Bagush region until it moved with the brigade to Palestine, Trans-Jordan and Iraq in May and June, but on October 5th it was back at Sofafi in the Western Desert and early in December it was advancing with the 5th Brigade Group west of Tobruk. The garrison of Point 204 consisted of a battalion of The Buffs, some artillery, a few tanks and No. 3 Section of 18 Field Company. At 2 p.m. the enemy opened a furious artillery bombardment and then attacked with 40 heavy tanks supported by guns and lorried infantry. Our tanks were knocked out. Our gunners had no proper cover and were soon mowed down. The guns were literally rolled into the ground by the German armour. When the Panzer rush had passed, small parties of the Buffs, Sappers and Gunners were still fighting gallantly and met the advancing enemy infantry with a blaze of fire, but by nightfall all was silent at Point 204. The War Diary records "No. 3 Section destroyed in action with the Buffs by enemy tanks after heavy shelling all day. Nine men came back, of whom three were wounded. Remainder, including Lieut. E. G. Cox, R.E., and all N.C.Os., are missing. It is hoped that most of these are prisoners-of-war." The desperate resistance at Point 204 probably saved the bulk of the 5th Brigade from complete destruction and so enabled the 4th Division to resume the pursuit along the coast towards Benghazi while the 7th Armoured Division followed up the enemy armour retreating through the desert by way of Mekili.

When Barce was occupied on December 22nd, 18 Field Company was at Derna aerodrome. Benghazi fell to the 4th Division on December 24th. On Christmas Day, General Messervy is said to have received an intriguing message. It ran as follows. "C. I. H. patrols reached Benghazi 1800 hrs yesterday. Dancing girls arrived three hours previously." Entrancing expectations, however, were destined to be unfulfilled for the 'dancing girls' proved later to be merely the advanced elements of the Kings Dragoon Guards. The year 1941 ended with the 4th Division elated by recent victories though scattered widely along the rain-sodden ridges of Western Cyrenaica. Rommel had escaped annihilation and his armour had even struck back at Antelat midway in the desert between Fort Msus and Ajedabia. On January 2nd, 1942, Major-General F. W. Messervy handed over command to Major-General F. I. S. Tuker on appointment as Commander, 1st British Armoured Division, and thus resumed the mobile role which he had filled so capably when leading the small 'Gazelle' Force of armoured cars in the Sudan and Eritrea.

The nature of the country traversed by the Indian Engineer units before they reached the more fertile Jebel region around Benghazi is described most graphically by Antony Brett-James in his history of the 5th Indian Division.[1] "The landscape of the Desert was painted in colours of brown, yellow and grey, and the fighting men learned to hide themselves by the skilful use of these same colours in the paints and camouflage nets that adorned their vehicles. It was a land of fawn and black rocks, of beige sand: a scene without interest, being drab in its slight undulations, its occasional low ridges, its steep escarpments. If you wanted to go to a certain point on the map, you could go there on a straight course provided your navigation was sound. Sometimes the ground was firm and rocky, sometimes it was powdered dust that swirled up when a vehicle's wheels rolled through it. The Desert has been described as 'miles and miles and bloody miles of absolutely damn all.' There was a seeming eternity of barren inhospitable nothingness. This lack of physical features was particularly baffling to the newcomer. You learned to move by map, compass and speedometer. You were never really certain that you were actually at the point from which you thought you were starting and you had to take your map reference on trust: there was no guarantee. It was hard to tell how far away the horizon was. Your sense of direction was befuddled. You were haunted by the constant risk of losing your way. After a time you developed a sense of direction in daylight; but at night it was no light matter to pin-point a unit or a *rendezvous*. You might search for a group of tanks reputed to be leaguered at a certain map reference and spend hours driving around, when all the time the tanks were only a mile distant. Unless it was extremely urgent that they should be found, it was wiser to camp for the night and wait until daybreak, for usually the tanks were then visible towards the horizon." Campaigning under

---

[1] "*Ball of Fire*", by Antony Brett-James, pp. 164, 165.

such conditions, and in fast moving vehicles, was a completely novel form of warfare. Each side groped for the other. Surprise assumed a new importance. Wireless communication was paramount. Every locality had to be prepared for all-round defence. Existence depended on water: safety, on petrol. The 'Desert Rats' of the Eighth Army lived a spartan life, sometimes lonely, often exhausted and always exposed to extremes of heat or cold, but it was a life that bred a camaraderie unequalled in military history.

As was only natural in such a country and under such conditions, the Indian Engineer units in the field experienced the greatest difficulty in maintaining their mechanical transport. No motor vehicle, however well built and well tended, could be expected to survive for long when driven hard, day in day out, in swirling clouds of dust or cloying mud, over the roughest of rough tracks. "Vehicles in very bad state" runs 18 Field Company's War Diary of January 9th, 1942, when the unit was at Barce. "We have 13 different types, which makes spares hard to obtain. Only 38 vehicles present. Thirteen are more than two years old and worn out. Seven others are relics which towed trucks up the Keren railway in Eritrea and were not replaced as promised. Their engines are finished. Steering is deplorable and frames are out of alignment. Six more are a year old and have been in the Sudan, Syria and Libya. Of the remainder, one is a captured French lorry of uncertain vintage, one was recovered and repaired after being blown up on a minefield, and another had a shell burst under it and is still full of holes." The Company transport on the move must have presented a sorry sight. Indeed, it is wonderful that it ever succeeded in moving anywhere; but move it did, and quite rapidly too so long as the vehicles held together.

A Sapper unit closely involved in the sudden counter-offensive with which Rommel opened the Fifth Libyan Campaign in January 1942 was 12 Field Company of the Madras Corps, under Major E. Waring, R.E. At that time, General Tuker's 4th Indian Division was much scattered as only the 7th Brigade was at the front. The 11th Brigade was still in Tobruk waiting for transport, and the battered 5th Brigade was reorganizing in Derna. Tuker was also short of guns, for his artillery was being transferred piece-meal to the armoured formations. On January 21st, Rommel burst out from El Agheila, and on the 22nd, having reached Antelat in force, he decided to exploit to the limit in the desert what was originally intended to be only a demonstration. The next two days were fateful ones for the Eighth Army. The 1st Armoured Division clashed with the German armour and was badly mauled. Our 2 pr. guns were outranged and outweighted by the German weapons. Only the 25 pr. guns of the artillery could cope with the powerful Panzers. Rommel caught us at the precise moment when our dumps in the desert were piling up nicely and had few troops to protect them, and at a time when our attention was concentrated on solving problems of supply in preparation for an advance into Tripolitania. Just as Rommel's projected invasion of Egypt in June 1941 had been forestalled by Wavell's offensive, so Ritchie's projected advance beyond El Agheila was forestalled by Rommel, but at considerably less risk. The Sapper units were repairing the desert tracks, now inches deep in mud, and much of our meagre transport was unfit for use. The 7th Brigade of the 4th Division took up positions along a series of minefields some 12 miles south of Benghazi. A battalion was sent forward by the 5th Brigade. The 11th Brigade was summoned from Tobruk. Some guns and tanks were rushed to the front. The plan now was that the 4th Division should hold a line inland from the coast through Beda Fomm, a place about 60 miles south of Benghazi, but at midday on the 25th news came that the 1st Armoured Division could no longer defend the Msus dump area in the desert. Nevertheless, the 7th Brigade, and with it 12 Field Company, advanced southwards from Benghazi to Soluch, half-way to Beda Fomm, though its safety depended largely on the ability of our armour to hold the Germans east of Msus.

On the morning of January 28th, the 7th Brigade was operating in three mobile groups, two forward and the other in reserve at Soluch, where 12 Field Company was in position. Just as the brigade was about to ascend the escarpment to attack eastwards it was learned that German tanks and lorried infantry were advancing up the coast and might reach Benghazi in a few hours if unopposed. Brigadier H. R. Briggs, who afterwards commanded the 5th Indian Division, immediately turned his brigade southwards to meet the enemy, and 24 German tanks then cut in behind his left flank, making for Soluch. Meanwhile, the Armoured Division had been forced back further into the desert beyond Msus. It was obvious that Benghazi could not be saved and consequently the destruction of all supplies and installations was started and a general withdrawal ordered. A group of the 7th Brigade had reached a point on the coast near Beda Fomm when news came that both roads leading eastwards out of Benghazi had been cut by the enemy and that the desert offered the only route of escape. 12 Field Company and some other troops joined this group which then marched further southwards, hid for the day, and finally turned eastwards to by-pass Msus and make for Mekili. The column of 300 vehicles avoided many roving enemy tanks and reached El Adem on the afternoon of February 1st, but by that time 12 Field Company had lost 40 men. Indeed, it was lucky to be still in existence.

The break-out from Benghazi showed our troops at their best, and it succeeded because of the boldness and determination displayed by all ranks. No less than 4,100 officers and men escaped from the place and brought with them 800 vehicles. But until January 30th, General Tuker could get no news of the wandering 7th Brigade. It was obvious that he must withdraw, yet not too rapidly because the Sappers must be given time to destroy the roads and blow up all dumps of stores and ammunition. 18 Field Company did this most effectively, and when the enemy pressure on the 11th Brigade became almost insupportable, the unit volunteered to go into the line and fought for a whole day alongside the infantry. Thus, after a series of stubborn rearguard actions, Tuker was able to assemble the 5th and 11th Brigades at Tmimi on February 3rd, and on the following day both brigades arrived in a position at Acroma, west of Tobruk and well behind the Gazala Line. The retreat was over, and the 4th Divisional Engineers resumed their usual tasks of mine-laying and defence work.

The 4th Indian Division was now due for relief in the Desert by the 5th Indian Division and its three brigades were soon scattered far and wide—the 5th Brigade in Palestine, the 7th in Cyprus and the 11th in the Canal Zone. 4 Field Company left the Gazala Line on February 22nd for defence work at Sollum, and later, after spending a month at Kabrit, was transferred in May to Palestine. 12 Field Company moved in February to Cyprus. 18 Field Company reached Sollum towards the end of March, and after handing over to 2 Field Company of the 5th Division, went to the Canal Zone for training, but at the end of May it was back at Sollum with Captain N. B. Thomas, R.E., in command. In May 1942, the Engineer units of the 5th Indian Division were all present in the Western Desert under the able leadership of Lieut.-Colonel A. H. G. Napier, R.E., as C.R.E. They comprised 2 Field Company (Bengal), 20 and 21 Field Companies (Bombay) and 44 Field Park Company (Madras). 20 Field Company (Major J. C. Winchester, R.E.) arrived in Alexandria from Cyprus on April 8th after relief by 12 Field Company and reached Tobruk with the 9th Brigade on May 1st. 21 Field Company (Major R. W. W. How, R.E.) which had been working on the Tobruk defences during March, joined the 29th Brigade in the Sollum area in the middle of May and moved with it to the El Adem Box at the end of the month. 44 Field Park Company (Lieut. J. H. Partridge, I.E.) was there also, having come from Cyprus in April. The 5th Indian Division was now being reinforced in the Western Desert by the 10th Indian Division whose Engineer units were 9, 10 and 61 Field Companies (Madras) and 41 Field Park Company (Bengal), the whole being under the command of Lieut.-Colonel J. M. Saegert, R.E. as C.R.E. 9 Field Company (Major P. G. O. Landon, R.E.) came to Sollum at the end of May with the 21st Brigade from Iraq and took over the Gambut defences from 2 Field Company. 10 Field Company (Major C. M. Bennett, I.A.R.O.) and 61 Field Company (Major C. C. F. Russell, R.E.) arrived in due course, the latter reaching Mersa Matruh on June 4th but the former not until June 25th. 41 Field Park Company (Major G. T. Roche, R.E.) came also in June. Another unit which appeared about the same time was 66 Field Company of the Bengal Corps, under Major H. G. A. Elphinstone, R.E. 31 Field Squadron of the Bengal Corps, under Major J. M. Griffith, R.E., which had moved from Syria in February, went far up into the Western Desert, towards the end of May 1942, with the unfortunate 3rd Indian Motor Brigade. These details must suffice for the present to show the kaleidescopic changes in Sapper representation in the field before and after Rommel struck.

Suddenly, on May 27th, 1942, the opening of the Sixth Libyan Campaign changed the whole aspect of the war in North Africa. Heavily reinforced from Italy and full of confidence, Rommel launched a powerful offensive against the Gazala Line, aiming at a locality called "Knightsbridge", a road junction on General Ritchie's main line of supply. Having by-passed a French desert outpost at Bir Hacheim during the night, the Axis armour plunged due north in three columns in rear of the Gazala defences, on the left the Italian Ariete Division, in the centre the 21st Panzer Division, and on the right the 15th Panzer Division. The enemy plan was to take "Knightsbridge" and the Sidi Rezegh-El Adem defences, then to wheel westwards to overrun the Gazala Line from the rear, and finally to turn about and storm Tobruk. While the armour struck, the Italian infantry divisions were to pin down the Gazala defenders and their engineers were to open a passage through the Gazala minefields to shorten the supply line to the roaming Panzers. This bold design, if successful, might have meant the annihilation of the Eighth Army. The fact that it did not succeed fully was due to the gallantry and self-sacrifice shown by our own armour and particularly to the stubborn resistance offered by the small garrison of Free French in Bir Hacheim on our left flank in the desert. At 7.30 a.m., the Panzers crushed out of existence the 3rd Indian Motorized Brigade and soon afterwards drove back the 4th Armoured Brigade, the nucleus of the 7th Armoured Division. Then, rushing onwards in clouds of dust, they surprised the 7th Divisional Headquarters and captured the Divisional Commander, Major-General F. W. Messervy.[1] They ended the day by engaging the 1st Armoured Division in bitter tank battles around "Knightsbridge." It seems that they had not yet begun to feel the lack of petrol which was later to prove a very severe handicap.

The unique story of General Messervy's lightning capture and escape must not go unrecorded. Before he and his staff were taken prisoners, they took the precaution of tearing off their badges of rank. Soon they found themselves in a German lorry following hard behind the enemy tanks. At a dressing station a German doctor looked at 'Private' Messervy with some surprise and said "You are old to be serving in the desert." "Yes, yes", replied the General, "but you see I am a very good batman." Later, in the heat of battle, Messervy and two of his officers jumped from the lorry and hid under a tarpaulin in an old gun emplacement. The Germans did not trouble to waste much time in hunting for a few 'other ranks' and so, after three hours under cover, the party crept out, found some water and threaded their way for sixteen miles through enemy-infested country until they met a British unit. Thus, in less than eighteen hours, the 7th Armoured Division regained its commander and the enemy let slip a captured General.

By the evening of May 27th, the German advanced forces had reached Acroma, El Duda and Sidi Rezegh, but the Gazala Line still stood firm and Bir Hacheim had not yet fallen. Desperate fighting ensued in the "Cauldron" area, west of "Knightsbridge", and armoured clashes continued for several days. On the 28th, the enemy succeeded in clearing two lanes through the Gazala minefields and protected them with anti-tank guns. The tank battles reached a climax on the 29th when the British suffered very heavily. On June 1st, Rommel overwhelmed a Brigade Box between the two lanes in the minefields and so widened his corridor of direct supply from the west, and finally Ritchie decided to pinch out the German bulge into the

---

[1] General Messervy, orginally appointed Commander, 1st Armoured Division, had assumed command of the 7th Armoured Division.

"Cauldron" by a vigorous counter-attack. On June 5th, part of the 50th Division, supported by tanks, attacked the bulge from the north, and the 9th and 10th Brigades of the 5th Indian Division, also with tank support, attacked from the east. The northern venture failed completely; the 5th Division made some headway; but both brigades were heavily counter-attacked and almost wiped out. Disaster stared us in the face. Over confidence was exacting a dire penalty. The French under General Koenig, after a glorious stand at Bir Hacheim, were forced to retire on June 10th, and four days later, "Knightsbridge" was evacuated. The loss of this position uncovered the coastal road and exposed the 1st South African and 50th Divisions to attack from the rear as planned by Rommel. Ritchie therefore ordered the entire Eighth Army, with the exception of the Tobruk garrison, to withdraw to the Egyptian frontier, and the manoeuvre was accomplished successfully under strong air cover and after desperate fighting on the part of the 1st Armoured Division. The 1st South African Division carved a way past Tobruk, and the 50th Division, under the redoubtable General 'Straffer' Gott, escaped by first attacking westwards and then marching southwards into the desert and finally eastwards. Until June 17th, the 30th Corps kept open the exits from Tobruk. Then it had to withdraw and Tobruk was isolated once more. On this occasion there was no long siege. By heavy air attack and engineer co-operation, Rommel blasted a way through the minefields on June 20th. His armour rushed in and spread throughout the fortress area. Resistance ceased on the following day and Tobruk was his together with 25,000 prisoners and immense booty. The news of this disaster was one of the greatest shocks experienced by the Allies in the Second World War. It rivalled that of the fall of Singapore only a few months earlier.

Auchinleck reacted strongly and energetically. He flew at once to the Western Desert and took over personal command from Ritchie. The fragments of the Eighth Army fell back sullenly into Egypt, leaving only some outposts at Halfaya, Sollum and further out in the desert. On June 23rd, Rommel crossed the frontier between Fort Maddalena and Sidi Omar and Auchinleck ordered a withdrawal to Mersa Matruh screened to the south by the 9th and 29th Brigades of the 5th Indian Division, the 2nd New Zealand Division and an Armoured Car Brigade. On the 26th, the Panzers were south of Matruh and Italian infantry was closing in on the place. The enemy armour by-passed Matruh, swung northwards, and tried to isolate the defenders, but most of the 5th Division and New Zealanders fought their way out. Rommel pressed on furiously, and on the afternoon of June 30th began to arrive before the El Alamein Line. The next four days were critical. Though exhausted and with little serviceable armour, the Germans launched a powerful attack only to be promptly counter-attacked and repulsed. This was the turn of the tide. Static operations replaced mobile warfare. The race for reinforcements was resumed with the British no longer at a disadvantage. So ended the Sixth Libyan Campaign. Our prestige was now at its lowest ebb throughout the Middle East, and a situation had arisen which only the most rigorous measures and the most determined leadership could retrieve. Happily, a man was found who was prepared to take those measures and could give that leadership.

The experiences of the Indian Engineer units in this campaign afford some interesting reading. The chaotic conditions of a general withdrawal in desert country forbade any constructional work, and often the units suffered severe losses. Such, for instance, was the fate of 31 Field Squadron of the Bengal Corps which was with the 3rd Indian Motorized Brigade when the latter was overrun. Early on May 27th, the Squadron was warned that action was imminent on the south face of the Brigade Box and all vehicles prepared to move to a 'B' Echelon area. Shelling started and a large number of enemy tanks appeared on the sky line. Major J. M. Griffith, R.E., at Brigade H.Q., asked for orders and was told that his Squadron was to retire at once to the 'B' Echelon. A few minutes later, Lieut. Bennett, who had been at a mine-dump, arrived and reported that a large column of tanks was actually entering the Squadron position from the east. These tanks opened machine-gun fire before Bennett could reach Griffith and before orders to withdraw could be passed back to the Squadron lines, where Captain Johnson was in charge. The unit's vehicles were widely dispersed, ready to move. They started for 'B' Echelon, but the Panzers were now scouring the area and fire was coming from all directions. "B" Troop was soon surrounded and captured. The remainder escaped with the loss of a valuable water-truck. Orders then came from 'B' Echelon to move with them some 10 miles north-eastwards towards Fort Capuzzo, and on the 28th the Brigade was directed to collect at Buq Buq, east of Sollum. Meanwhile, a truck which had been sent forward for Major Griffith was hit as it arrived and went up in smoke. The occupants lay down behind a bush while the enemy tanks passed to right and left and the crews threw grenades at them. One tank rolled right over a shallow trench containing three men without harming any of them. Major

Griffith, with Lieut. Black, collected fourteen men of the Squadron and a few from other units and got them into slit trenches where they remained until the tanks roared away. The whole party then piled into the only two carriers available and with great difficulty induced the engines to start. One carrier, with Havildar Rahmat Khan, went ahead and was not seen again. It was captured, with other Brigade vehicles, while trying to find a way through the enemy's tank formations. Nevertheless, the Havildar and 6 men rejoined at Buq Buq on June 23rd with a party of 24 others of the unit who had escaped after being taken prisoner. The second carrier, with Major Griffith aboard, joined a Gunner column which weaved an erratic course hither and thither until nearly midday when a Bofors tractor, with gun in tow, was hit. The carrier then took the gun in tow and the crew crowded onto the already grossly overloaded vehicle. The remainder of the column was now out of sight ahead. This was lucky for Griffith's party because the column was soon surrounded and captured. As a result of attempting to tow the gun and at the same time to carry 23 passengers, the long-suffering carrier now developed engine trouble, so it was parked, with the gun, behind the smoke from two burning tanks until the fault could be located and remedied. The party remained undetected by the enemy although a German officer was observing them at times through field glasses from a car only a short distance away. Not until the carrier consented to move and the men made a dash to get on board it did the enemy open fire, and finally, long after darkness had fallen, the small party reached the 30th Corps Headquarters.

Despite recent heavy losses in men and equipment, 31 Field Squadron was able to move forward again on June 16th after receiving suitable reinforcements. It left Buq Buq with the Brigade, operating in three columns. Each column had a detachment of Sappers in three trucks and another detachment accompanied Brigade H.Q. Between June 22nd and 25th, the columns were heavily engaged. A party under Lieut. Black was caught west of a minefield and split up while trying to get through a gap. Black was reported missing but rejoined on July 1st in Egypt after an exciting 5 days' trip with an armoured column. A detachment under Major Griffith shot up the tail end of an enemy column passing through a gap and destroyed 2 guns and 3 vehicles. At the end of June, 31 Field Squadron was back in the Canal Zone, its adventures, for the time being, ended. The story of this unit has been given at some length because it shows that Sapper units were not always relegated to technical work in support of other troops. Often they were in the thick of the fighting, and then it was that their careful training in infantry duties stood them in good stead.

Other Bengal Sapper units concerned in the fighting were 2 and 4 Field Companies and 41 Field Park Company. On June 2nd, 2 Field Company, under Major W. H. D. Wakely, R.E., moved into the 'Cauldron' in support of an infantry attack.[1] Its task was to clear enemy minefields and destroy enemy equipment and stranded tanks. The attack failed, and while withdrawing the Company lost some men and vehicles. After the fall of Tobruk the unit thickened various minefields and finally arrived in the Bagush Box. On the 26th it was fortunate enough to be transferred to El Alamein and so avoided encirclement when the enemy cut the road behind Bagush on the following day. 4 Field Company, under Major J. G. A. J. O'Ferrall, R.E., was not so lucky for it was at Bagush when the attack came; but most of the officers and men succeeded in making their way singly or in small parties to El Alamein. 41 Field Park Company, formerly under Major C. R. Mangat Rai, I.E., but now under Major G. T. Roche, R.E., was the greatest sufferer. Many of its officers and men were engaged at the time on demolitions in Matruh itself. These were cut off and less than half got through to El Alamein. Not a single officer or V.C.O. reached that place. The survivors were collected and withdrawn to Cairo, whence they followed the 10th Division later to Cyprus.

Here is the story of part of 41 Field Park Company as told by Havildar Chanan Singh. "On June 26th we were moving towards Tobruk when we were ordered to camp at Mersa Matruh. On the 27th we were given the task of demolishing supply dumps. On the 28th our O.C. ordered the H.Q. Platoon and Office (later captured) to move back while two other platoons began to net the supplies with electric wire and charges. The enemy was now quite near and began to shell the supply area continuously. At 4 p.m., German bombers set all the petrol dumps on fire, but we continued our work. By 8 p.m., the supplies had been prepared for demolition and we were cut off by the enemy east of Matruh. Our Platoon Commander, Lieut. N. S. J. Devonald, told us that we had to withdraw without support but that in any case the enemy was not to benefit by the supplies. The demolitions were then started. Terrible

---

[1] *"Brief History of the K.G.V's O. Bengal Sappers and Miners Group, R.I.E., August 1939-July 1946"*, by Lieut. G. Pearson, R.E., p. 34.

explosions rent the sky. There was fire all around us. The water-supply system was destroyed and we withdrew, having orders to push straight towards the desert for forty miles and then seek the main road. This had to be done in impenetrable darkness, lit only by huge enemy fires, and without maps as we had received no maps from Headquarters. Every track, road and field was new to us. We started with heavy hearts but determined to slip through the enemy lines. The 50th Division and 10th Indian Division fought many dispersed battles that night. Every man had to act on his own initiative. There was no link, no organization. Three times, I, with my party of five in a truck, found ourselves very close to the enemy and pushed our way through in hand to hand fighting, but we never failed to regain the truck though we lost two men. By 4 a.m., most of the 10th Division columns had been captured. Many times our troops clashed with each other. Exhausted Germans and Italians were attacked while asleep. The thick morning fog added to our difficulties and sometimes we had to stop to regain direction. At dawn I found myself leading four other vehicles of my unit about 20 miles south of the main road to El Alamein, the rest of the convoy having vanished. I stopped the vehicles and went to each one. I found two wounded Sappers, so we did first aid and then pushed on. We had covered only a few more miles when two armoured cars were seen standing 400 yards away to the right. This made us believe that the road was near and that we had contacted our own troops, but as my vehicle passed the cars it was fired upon heavily. Those in rear promptly turned back and I told my driver to do the same; but all in vain, for my truck was immobilized. The enemy cars approached and we were taken prisoners. The other four vehicles managed to escape. We were taken back to Mersa Matruh, reaching it by nightfall, and I saw the supplies still burning. When we asked for food and water the Germans took us round the devastated area and asked whether we were worthy of being given anything at all. 'You should die of hunger' they said. Yet, in spite of all this, we survived."

9 Field Company, another unit of the 10th Division, reached Tobruk from Gambut early in June 1942 and began to mine the beaches in relief of 20 Field Company of the 5th Division. On June 5th it was at Sidi Rezegh, whence it moved forward towards the 'Cauldron.' However, it was soon turned back owing to the German breakthrough and retired to Sidi Rezegh where it found 18 Field Company at work. From the 9th till the 14th it laboured on the defences of the Gambut aerodrome. Then it moved through Sidi

Omar to Halfaya to prepare defences along the southern face of the Sollum-Halfaya Box and to thicken the existing minefields to a density of one mine per yard. It also blasted many gun-pits out of solid rock. News of the fall of Tobruk changed the policy of defence to one of evacuation and complete demolition, and during the night of June 23/24th the unit destroyed 25 tons of 25 pr. ammunition, 6,000 E.P. mines, 50,000 gallons of bitumen and the water-supply system for the 21st Brigade. After dark on the 24th, Lieut. J. L. Banerjee, I.E., was unfortunately killed when an anti-personnel mine was detonated accidentally. Apparently, 9 Field Company had no serviceable mine-detectors and Banerjee's party was withdrawing after clearing and marking a gap when the mishap occurred. By 11 p.m., the 5th, 21st and 25th Brigades were on the move and the Sollum defences were blown a quarter of an hour later. The defences at Halfaya Pass went up soon after midnight. The demolition parties of 9 Field Company, together with those of 4 and 61 Field Companies and two Australian companies, then made their way back to Mersa Matruh to block gaps in our minefields and prepare further demolitions.

The decision to abandon and demolish Matruh was reached on June 26th. 9 Field Company set to work to prepare bridges for crossing anti-tank ditches and place explosive charges in barracks. These jobs were handed over on the 28th to 61 Field Company which was helping the 25th Brigade in a rearguard action. The same evening, 9 Field Company received orders to break out of Matruh and make for Fuka which, unknown to Headquarters, was already in enemy hands. Preceded by some infantry it started on its perilous journey, but after covering only ten miles it ran straight into Rommel's Headquarters which was lining both sides of the road. The column was swept with machine-gun and anti-tank gun fire. It was almost impossible to distinguish friend from foe for the Germans were mostly using captured British vehicles. Those of the Company's vehicles which escaped immediate destruction scattered in all directions and then turned southwards into the desert and finally eastwards; but as the enemy now held the entire coastal plain for a distance of 90 miles to El Daba, the chances of evading capture were poor. Yet a fair number got through the enemy cordon and on July 1st trickled gradually into Amiriya, near Alexandria, where Major Landon proceeded to reorganize the unit. Although the known casualities were only 3 killed and 3 wounded, no less than 69 were missing, including 2 officers and 2 V.C.Os. The Company had also lost 16 trucks, a lorry, a compressor and 2 motorcycles and was therefore unfit to take the field; yet when the 10th Divisional Engineers moved to Cairo on July 4th to re-equip, no equipment could be obtained and consequently all the companies were immobilized for some time. It was not until July 23rd that 9 Field Company was able to return with the 21st Brigade to the Alamein Line where it laid mines near the Ruweisat Ridge until the middle of August before moving back to the Alexandria-Cairo Road to protect aerodromes and build desert tracks.

10 Field Company, under Major C. M. Bennett, I.A.R.O., suffered more heavily even than 9 Field Company in the break-out from Matruh. It arrived just in time to be involved in the catastrophe for it did not reach Matruh from Iraq until June 25th. Two days later, a Section under Captain Spencer was sent forward towards Bagush. After dark on the 28th the Company got the order to break out from Matruh and moved off at once, leaving a party of 2 officers and 14 men to complete the work of destruction. Its experiences were very similar to those of 9 Field Company. Only 1 Officer, 2 B.N.C.Os., 3 V.C.Os., 125 men and 25 vehicles reached El Alamein for it had lost 4 officers, 2 V.C.Os. and 102 men *en route*. In July it went to Cyprus, where it remained till the end of the year.

61 Field Company, under Major C. C. F. Russell, R.E., also suffered severely. After reaching Matruh from Iraq on June 4th it did defence work in the Bel Hamid-Sidi Rezegh area until it moved back to Sollum on the 21st for water-supply duties. On June 22nd it prepared to demolish the defences and dumps in Sollum and the Halfaya Pass and to arrange booby-traps in the Sollum Box, and after dark it began to withdraw with the exception of one Section which stayed behind for a time to carry out final demolitions. Three days later, the Company was in position behind the minefields at Matruh engaged in clearing gaps and laying additional mines. Its experiences on June 28th are recorded as follows in the War Diary. "Capt. Locock, with "B" Echelon and 1 Section, left at 1400 hrs along coast road to *rendezvous* with Brigade "B" Echelons at Kilo. 29. All were found later halted at Kilo. 26, enemy tanks and guns being in position across the road and firing. At about 21.30 hrs, "B" Echelons moved back towards Matruh and attempted to break out through minefields and behind enemy. Rear party of remaining 4 officers and 1½ Sections, after acting as infantry, were warned to move at 21.00 hrs. Lieut. Shamsher Singh was detailed for demolition work near coast road west of Matruh but did not return.

Company tried to break out to the south, being completely cut off in the dark. Major Russell was last seen under heavy fire about midnight. 2nd Lieut. Stevenson was not seen after leaving Matruh." The casualities in 61 Field Company were 3 officers, 1 B.W.O., 1 B.N.C.O., 1 V.C.O., and 93 men. On the following evening, part of the unit reassembled at El Alamein and on the 30th it moved to Amiriya.

Everything goes to show that the 10th Divisional Engineers were very severely mauled in the retreat from Mersa Matruh and, incidentally, they lost their C.R.E., Lieut.-Colonel J. M. Saegert, R.E. Saegert had been supervising in person the final demolitions at Matruh and was wounded and captured during the withdrawal. The circumstances are recorded by Havildar Clerk G. Francis.[1] "The C.R.E's staff became prisoners in three different places in the desert and at different times. In the third group was a station wagon containing the C.R.E., Lieut. Nash and two Sappers. The C.R.E. found it was too late to escape in his vehicle, so after setting fire to it he and the Sappers tried to get away on foot by the coastal route. They walked by night and hid during the day; but on the third day they were sighted by the 'Jerries' while hiding in a cave and were captured." Francis goes on to record his personal adventures. "I was travelling in a truck in the first group and followed another until we came to a large minefield and sighted some vehicles in flames. It was here that the enemy started a terrific bombardment from the air. My truck got blown up by a mine, but luckily I was not injured though thrown out of the vehicle. We loaded our stuff into the other two vehicles and tried to keep contact with the main convoy which in the meanwhile had gone out of sight. All our efforts failed, and when daylight came we found ourselves surrounded by enemy tanks and had to surrender when they opened fire. We were taken first to Tobruk and then to Benghazi. The British officers were evacuated by air to Italy. There were about 30,000 prisoners of war at Benghazi where the camp was run by the Italians. The 'Ities' themselves did not have sufficient rations so it is no wonder that the prisoners were poorly fed. Our day's ration consisted of a loaf of bread (about 10 ozs.), ½ oz of fish and half a teaspoonful of coffee. We were given no baths, clothing or blankets. From Benghazi the 'Ities' began to evacuate the prisoners gradually when shipping permitted. A batch of 2,900 men was evacuated to Italy in August. Their ship

---

[1] Notes by Havildar Clerk G. Francis, dated January 5th, 1943.

was torpedoed and sunk by a British submarine and, as usual, the escorting vessels did not attempt to pick up survivors. My own plan was to escape when a British 'push' started, and therefore I tried to remain in Libya until the spring for I could not walk the distance to El Alamein. We dug a cave below our tent, and when the 'Ities' began to empty the camp we hid in it, buried under some planks and sand and breathing through small tubes. After dark we emerged and in pouring rain and cold walked for six days without food before meeting British troops."

Two units of the Bombay Corps, belonging to the 5th Indian Division, were involved in the withdrawal from Mersa Matruh. On June 20th, 20 Field Company (Major J. C. Winchester, R.E.) moved to Sofafi and on the following day to Bagush. There it learned that Major R. W. W. How, R.E., who commanded 21 Field Company, was missing. 20 Field Company laid a number of mines and early on the 26th withdrew about five miles eastwards. During the afternoon, when the enemy had penetrated south to Matruh, the Company withdrew again to a 5th Division *rendezvous* where it was dive-bombed and split up. On the 27th, in small parties, it reached the Rear Headquarters and, on the 29th, proceeded through Hammam to Amiriya. Not until July 17th was it fit to return to the front where it rejoined the 9th Brigade on the Ruweisat Ridge at El Alamein.

21 Field Company, under Major How, was in the El Adem Box in the middle of June engaged in blasting gun-pits under considerable artillery bombardment. On June 17th it moved back in small parties to Bir Gibni, when How and 22 men were found to be missing. Two days later, the unit reached Sofafi with the 29th Brigade, and on the 21st it arrived in the Bagush Box where Major P. P. Miles, R.E., took over command. Next it went to a place called Hamza, 15 miles south of Matruh, to close a 10-mile gap with minefields. Then came the enemy break-through and the 29th Brigade withdrew 20 miles eastwards. 21 Field Company reached Fuka with the brigade, and July 3rd found it in the Nile Delta reorganizing and training. 18 Field Company was fortunate enough not to be involved in the Mersa Matruh affair, and thus, as a whole, the Bombay Engineer units escaped more lightly than their comrades of the other two Corps.

66 Field Company of the Bengal Corps, under Major H. G. A. Elphinstone, R.E., was rushed to the Western Desert from Iraq in June 1942 with a brigade of the 8th Division and after a journey of nearly 700 miles reached Bagush on June 26th. According to

Elphinstone, the amount of traffic on the road to Bagush was beyond anything his drivers had ever seen. Heavy lorries, driven at high speed and at 25 yards intervals, streamed without a break in both directions. On the 27th the unit was ordered to move to El Alamein through 160 miles of desert as the coastal road had to be kept clear. Alamein was reached on the following day. No food was available there, and the column in which the unit marched was ordered to proceed 10 miles southwards to take up a defensive position at Ruweisat, which it did under periodical bombing. On the 29th, Elphinstone writes "Most of the morning we tried to find out what was happening, but failed. We have been allotted 400 yards of front. Ground mostly solid rock and weapon pits require blasting. No explosives to be got, but fortunately we have brought 100 lbs of 808 Gelatine from Iraq. Compressors at work all night. The South African Sappers are magnificent. They won't stop working." On June 30th he adds "All our men are flat out digging. Heartbreaking work in the rock." This heavy labour, often interrupted by raids and alarms, lasted until August 25th when the unit was sent to the Delta to assist in preparing a position covering Cairo. Two months later, it returned to Iraq.

A Madras unit present at this period was 58 Field Company under Major G. C. Richards, R.E. It arrived in Amiriya from Iraq on July 13th after the retreat of our forces to the Alamein Line and began at once to lay ten miles of minefield belts to cover Alexandria. During August it laid more than 20,000 mines and, with infantry assistance, built 13 miles of double wire fencing. In September it left Egypt for Syria. No clearer proof of the defensive policy which gripped the Eighth Army at this period is needed than that supplied by the stupendous number of mines laid by Engineer units not only at the front but far behind the line. This was a policy which, as will be seen later, was soon to be changed suddenly and dramatically.

After July 5th, 1942, mobile warfare gave place gradually to static operations and the initiative in the Western Desert passed slowly but surely to the British, now firmly based on the Alamein Line in which the predominant natural features were two low ridges of considerable length. The Ruweisat Ridge, about 12 miles from the coast and only 200 feet above sea-level, ran east and west, while the Alam el Halfa Ridge, further to the southeast, was slightly higher and trended in a north-easterly direction. General Auchinleck's plan of defence was to hold strongly the area between the sea and the Ruweisat Ridge and to establish a powerful defensive position on the Alam el Halfa Ridge from which he could threaten any advance round his left flank between that ridge and the deep and practically impassable Qattara Depression to the south. He had not sufficient troops to hold firmly the entire line from the sea to the Depression, but neither had Rommel sufficient strength to mass his forces all along that line. The vital section was in the north, near the sea, where lay the main road and railway; but the security of that section depended on the defence of the two ridges in the central sector and hence the bitter fighting on the Ruweisat Ridge, the more advanced of the two. On July 1st, hurrying towards the western tip, the newly arrived 18th Brigade had been over-run, though the Germans had been thrown back, two days later, by supporting troops. Then, on the night of July 14/15th, the 5th Brigade attacked westwards along the ridge, gained some ground and repulsed an enemy counter-attack. The 5th Brigade attacked again on the 17th, supported by the 9th Brigade, and made a slight advance, and on the 18th it renewed the attack, repelled another counter-attack, and gained half a mile. Into this ding-dong battle came 20 Field Company whose unenviable job it was to lay a minefield around our forward positions. The unit went forward to 'Point 63', a locality on the Ridge which the 2nd Battalion, The West Yorkshire Regiment, had just captured, and attempted to lay E.P. Mark III mines to the west and north. The mine-laying lorries, however, were illuminated at once by German flares and four of them blew up when struck by small-arms fire. Curiously enough, the driver of one lorry was unhurt except for a slight cut on his head. 20 Field Company erected 1,100 yards of fencing on the Ridge and throughout the remainder of the month parties were daily in the front line mine-laying and improving the defences. 66 Field Company, further to the rear, was also busily employed on defence work.

After the end of July 1942, both the 5th Indian Division on the Ruweisat Ridge and the Germans ensconced in the Deir el Shein Depression beyond it led a trogdolytic existence. Both sides had fought themselves practically to a standstill. Flies swarmed everywhere. A sickening odour of unburied corpses polluted the air. The sun beat down pitilessly on trenches and *sangars*. The slightest movement brought down intense artillery fire. Sleep was almost impossible by day owing to the glare, the flies and frequent dive-bombing. By night it was interrupted by dazzling flares and heavy bombs. Nerves were stretched to breaking point and sickness took its toll. Ruweisat was a very near approach to hell. Yet the defenders carried on with grim determination, knowing that such a purgatory could not last for ever.

On August 5th, Mr. Winston Churchill, with Lord Alanbrooke and Generals Wavell and Smuts, visited the Western Desert, and soon afterwards many changes took place in the higher Army commands. Lieut.-General Gott was appointed to command the Eighth Army, only to be killed within a few days by a bullet from a Messerschmidt. Lieut.-General B. L. Montgomery was then given the chief command in the field and arrived in Cairo by air from England on August 12th. General Sir Harold Alexander, of Dunkirk and Burma fame, succeeded General Auchinleck as Commander-in-Chief, Middle East. Montgomery, full of confidence and enthusiasm, immediately toured the front and addressed his officers. He said that, under Alexander, he was going not only to hold the enemy at El Alamein but to defeat and utterly destroy all the Axis forces in North Africa. If anyone doubted this, he must go. Further retreat was out of the question. They would stand and fight where they were. All plans dealing with withdrawal and the defence of the Nile Delta were to be burnt forthwith. Every man, aeroplane, gun and tank was to be used to strengthen the front. Living conditions in the desert must be improved without delay. Two fine divisions—the 44th and 51st—and also two armoured divisions—the 8th and 10th—were arriving. Given a fortnight's respite, the Eighth Army would be secure. Given a month's grace, victory was certain. Thus the new commander brought confidence and hope to troubled minds and dispelled the melancholy sense of isolation which the desert is apt to breed. The Eighth Army became in a night an instrument of victory.

Towards the end of August 1942, Rommel made his last bid for Egypt by opening what may be called the Seventh Libyan Campaign. Alexander had four armoured and seven infantry divisions as against Rommel's four armoured and eight infantry divisions, but most of Rommel's infantry was Italian and of little fighting value. The German plan was to break through our lightly held line of observation on the southern flank of the Alamein defences and then, turning north, to drive to the sea and encircle our centre and right. This plan, when put into operation, led to the Alam el Halfa Battle, or First Battle of Alamein, which took place in September. Then, in October, followed the Battle of Alamein itself, and finally the glorious pursuit of the beaten enemy through the length of Cyrenaica and Tripolitania and the surrender in Tunisia which ended the war in North Africa in May 1943. These stirring events, however, must

Sappers and Miners rush mine detecting apparatus through a gap in enemy wire cleared by a Bangalore torpedo

form the subject of another chapter. We are concerned for the present only with the experiences of the Indian Engineer units up to the time when Montgomery began to prepare for his great offensive.

When the 10th Division was evacuated to Cyprus in July and the 4th Division was relieved at the front by the 5th Division, some of the Indian Engineer units in the Ruweisat region were left behind to continue their work of blasting gun-pits, laying mines, putting up barbed wire and covering desert tracks with wire netting. This was hard luck but was accepted as the fortune of war. The Alamein Line had to be held at all costs, and held it was though with much blood and sweat. The fighting in July emphasized the problem of opening passages for vehicles through minefields immediately behind the leading infantry. It was apparent that the existing haphazard methods of clearing mines were unsatisfactory when the ground was swept by enemy fire and that a proper drill must be evolved. A 'breaching' drill was therefore invented and instruction given in it, and the advent of a large number of really efficient mine-detectors (Polish Mark III) simplified matters. All the Engineer units soon became expert in both mine-clearance and mine-laying. In the preliminary stages of the attacks along the Ruweisat Ridge, 4 Field Company gapped many minefields and then helped to protect the forward troops by laying new minefields and extending earlier ones; and on August 1st, 2 Field Company, now under Major A. Selkirk, R.E., laid 900 mines south of the ridge. These are but two examples of the fine performances of Indian Engineer units.

The Ruweisat Ridge position, the key to the Alamein Line, was gradually rendered almost impregnable. The line itself, once no more than groups of weary and desperate men, was now as tight as a bowstring with an arrow on it, an arrow which Montgomery would soon loose and would follow by a *coup de grace* for the enemy in North Africa. The atmosphere in the sweltering desert was one of profound suspense. Who could foresee what the next few months, even the next few weeks, might hold in store? Yet hope reigned supreme, and impatience too, for the Eighth Army was straining at the leash.

CHAPTER V

THE WESTERN DESERT AND NORTH-WEST AFRICA,
AUGUST 1942 - MAY 1943

WHEN the El Alamein Line was finally stabilized towards the end of July 1942, it extended for about 40 miles between the Mediterranean coast in the north and the impassable Qattara Depression in the south.[1] The country was bare, stony and featureless except for a few low ridges. In the north, close to the coastal road and railway, was the Tel el Eisa Ridge, and 5 miles further south, the Miteiriya Ridge. Ten miles from the coast and slightly in rear of the Miteiriya Ridge was the Ruweisat Ridge, a hotly disputed position, and still further to the south and rear the more commanding Alam el Halfa Ridge, the key to the whole defensive line since it could be used to defeat any threat to our communications with Alexandria. Reinforcements were now pouring into Egypt, and Rommel was well aware of that fact. Montgomery was being pressed by the Cabinet to take the offensive but would not be hurried. "If the attack starts in September", he replied, "it will fail. If we wait until October, I will personally guarantee a great success and the destruction of Rommel's army. Am I to attack in September?" Thereupon, the Cabinet agreed to a postponement. They could hardly do otherwise.

Now was Rommel's opportunity. On August 29th he determined to make a final attempt to burst the line which covered Egypt. He announced to his troops that within two or three days they would be in Alexandria, and on August 30th, strengthened by new divisions, he began his attack 'for the final annihilation of the enemy.' He intended to cut Montgomery's communications, but he knew that the first step must be the occupation of the Alam el Halfa Ridge. So on August 31st, 1942, the Battle of Alam el Halfa, sometimes called the 'First Battle of Alamein', developed with three simultaneous enemy thrusts. Montgomery had then had a fortnight's grace in which to make his plans. Also, he had two new divisions in position. He was ready for the fray, and not only ready but eager.

---

[1] See the map of North Africa included in this chapter.

The Axis thrusts developed in the north, centre and south, the most serious being the southern attack. This was launched between the left flank of the 2nd New Zealand Division and an isolated hill called Himeimat near the Qattara Depression. The 15th and 21st Panzer Divisions and the 90th Light Motorized Division broke through our minefields and three Italian divisions tried to follow. Once clear of the mines, the German armour swung northwards against our positions on the Alam el Halfa Ridge. This was exactly the move anticipated by Montgomery whose Staff had succeeded in 'planting' a faked map on the enemy. It had been arranged that one of our scout cars should get blown up on a mine near the enemy's minefields and the crew rescued by another car. Stuffed away in a dirty haversack in the abandoned car was a falsified map, covered with tea stains, which showed a patch of sandy ground as 'good going.' An enemy patrol pounced on that map, and the consequence was that Rommel's tanks, on their way to the Alam el Halfa Ridge, used gallons of precious petrol and wasted hours of valuable time in floundering through deep sand. That, at least, is the story, and it bears the hall-mark of probability. Why else should the tanks have taken such an uninviting route?

Once Montgomery was sure that the main attack was directed against Alam el Halfa he moved the bulk of his available armour to fill a gap between the New Zealanders and the rest of the Alamein Line. Soon he had 400 tanks concentrated in the gap, and the ridge itself strongly held. Under heavy artillery fire and continuous bombing, the floundering Panzers were brought to a halt and Rommel realized that he had failed. Early on September 3rd, he began to withdraw westwards. Much of his armour got away, but nevertheless the battlefield was littered with damaged tanks and vehicles which he could not retrieve. By the morning of September 6th, no large enemy concentrations remained east of our minefields although some Axis forces still clung to a few strong points in certain gaps. Montgomery then decided to break off the action and resume the process of building up a powerful striking force for a major offensive. He had got the bulk of the enemy forces concentrated in the south where he wanted them, for he intended to launch his offensive in the north. So ended Alam el Halfa, Montgomery's first battle as Commander of the Eighth Army. Some regard it as his greatest, for it won him the complete confidence of his men.

Several units of the Indian Engineers helped to pave the way to victory in this critical struggle although the main battle raged far to the south of the Ruweisat Ridge where they were stationed. The War Diary of 2 Field Company, under Major W. H. D. Wakely, R.E., records that on September 1st enemy tanks were reported as approaching the Ridge from the south, and the Company, together with 20 Field Company under Major J. C. Winchester, R.E., laid mines till dark. The Sappers had to do this almost unaided for the infantry were not then accustomed to the work. 4 Field Company, under Major J. G. A. J. O'Ferrall, R.E., had recently moved up to the Ridge. 11 Field Park Company (Captain A. C. Cooper, R.E.), and 12 Field Company (Major J. A. Cameron, R.E.), were on their way from Cairo after a few months in Cyprus and therefore they were not present when Rommel attacked. Thus the brunt of the engineering work in strengthening the Ruweisat positions in the centre of the Alamein Line fell on 2, 4 and 20 Field Companies of the 5th Indian Division. After Rommel's failure, the 5th Indian Division was pulled out of the line and replaced by the 4th Indian Division, but 2, 4 and 20 Field Companies remained at Ruweisat to continue their work of minelaying and mine-lifting. Lieut.-Colonel A. H. G. Napier, R.E., C.R.E. 5th Indian Division, handed over charge to Lieut.-Colonel J. H. Blundell, R.E., C.R.E. 4th Indian Division, and Major A. Selkirk, R.E., became O.C. 4 Field Company. By September 9th, the Sapper companies at the front were 2, 4 and 12 Field Companies and 11 Field Park Company, the first two being Bengal units and the last two Madras units. Parties frequently supported the infantry in raids and reconnaissances but they were not involved in any set battle.

The remainder of September passed without major incident. Both sides were feverishly active in preparations for battle. Rommel took the opportunity to fly to Berlin where he was duly lionized by the Press. "I have not advanced to El Alamein", said he, "with any intention of being flung back. You may rely on my holding fast to what I have got." With the General Staff, however, he took a very different line, asking for reinforcements and refusing to attack unless he got them. To Hitler himself, he was completely subservient. The Fuhrer had decreed that there must be no retreat and therefore there could be none. So Rommel had to stay and be slaughtered. In the end he was grudgingly promised a division from Crete, but only one battalion arrived because the rest were sent to the bottom of the Mediterranean. During the first three weeks of October, Allied air superiority accounted for three-quarters of the Axis sea transport. Very little could get through to any port east of Benghazi.

On October 11th, the Germans and Italians renewed their violent air attacks on Malta in a desperate attempt to protect their sea-route between Sicily and Tripoli. They did great damage but the effort came too late to affect the balance of power in the Western Desert before Montgomery put his fortunes to the final test.

The Eighth Army was now almost ready to open the Seventh Libyan Campaign from the El Alamein Line. The Axis forces in position amounted to 4 armoured and 8 infantry divisions, in all about 96,000 men, of whom more than half were Germans. They had nearly 600 tanks, of which more than half were Italian. Montgomery had three Corps at his disposal — the 10th, 13th and 30th — commanded respectively by Lieut.-Generals Sir Herbert Lumsden, B.C Horrocks and Sir Oliver Leese. They comprised 3 armoured divisions, 7 armoured brigades and 7 infantry divisions, a total of about 150,000 men with 1,114 tanks. Montgomery therefore had a marked superiority on the ground and his strength in the air was overwhelming. The Royal Navy protected his right flank: the Qattara Depression, his left flank. In the absence of General Rommel the Axis forces were commanded by General von Stumme who had committed the egregious error of spreading his troops evenly along the whole front instead of concentrating his armour in rear in readiness to counter-attack.[1] Nevertheless, the Axis line was most formidable. Barriers of mines and wire provided the deepest defence system ever constructed in Africa and one which could not be outflanked. In front of the main position, consisting of a number of great fortified enclosures, was a forward system joined to the main line by a series of minefields resembling the rungs of a ladder. These 'rungs' were designed to 'canalise' any assault into low ground where it could be destroyed by murderous artillery fire before it came up against the main position. Actually, many of the enemy's minefields had been laid originally by us and altered subsequently by the Germans to suit their own requirements. There was, however, a notable difference between the enemy's technique and our own. The Germans concealed their minefields and used their mines as weapons. We made our minefields easily visible and used them chiefly as deterrents, the edges being marked with single strands of wire on which were hung scores of tin triangles which glinted in the sunlight.[2] One

---

[1] *The Second World War*, 1939-1945, by Major-General J. F. C. Fuller, p. 235.

[2] See "Tin Triangles" by Col. J. M. Lambert, O.B.E., late R.E., appearing in *The R. E. Journal*, December 1952, pp. 329-338.

advantage of our method was that we could mark an area as mined when not a mine had been laid and thus force an attacking enemy either to sweep it laboriously with detectors or to risk the destruction of his infantry and tanks.

Montgomery, being obliged to attack frontally, decided to break through in the north, where the road and railway lay, using the 30th Corps in the area between the Tel el Eisa and Miteiriya ridges. The Corps formations, reading from north to south, were the 9th Australian Division near the coast, 51st Highland Division, 2nd New Zealand Division, 9th Armoured Brigade and 1st South African Division. The 30th Corps was to make gaps by infantry attacks supported by heavy tanks. Then the 10th Corps, consisting of the 1st and 10th Armoured Divisions, was to advance from well behind the northern sector, go through the gaps and deal with the enemy armour in the open country beyond. Further to the south, the 13th Corps and the 7th Armoured Division were to attack also in order to pin down any enemy forces opposite them. The forward movement of the 10th Corps was to be most carefully concealed, and every possible measure was to be taken to make the enemy imagine that the main attack would be made in the south. The 4th Indian Division of the 13th Corps was to raid the enemy posts on the Ruweisat Ridge in the centre, while the remainder of the Corps—50th Division, 44th Division and Free French—prolonging the line southwards to the Qattara Depression, carried out the deceptive role assigned to it and if possible opened a way for the advance of the 7th Armoured Division. The general offensive was to be preceded by a fortnight of intensive bombing by 700 aircraft in order to ground the Axis air forces and destroy the enemy's ports along the coast. The massed artillery was to remain silent, awaiting the zero hour. Such in general was the plan of attack. The hostile front at Alamein has been compared to a door, hinged at its northern end. To push at the face might make the door swing back some way before serious damage was done; but a successful blow at the hinge would dislocate the whole front and throw the doorway wide open. Montgomery therefore concentrated at first on the hinge in the north.

No more than a mere outline of El Alamein can be given in these pages, but some description is needed to explain the movements and record the experiences of the Indian Engineer units at the front. On the eve of battle, Montgomery issued a stirring message to his troops. "When I assumed command of the Eighth Army", he wrote, "I said that the mandate was to destroy Rommel and his army and that it would be done as soon as we were ready. We are ready NOW. The battle which is now about to begin will be one of the decisive battles of history. It will be the turning point of the war. The eyes of the whole world will be on us, watching anxiously which way the battle will swing. We can give them their answer at once. It will swing *our* way. We have first class equipment, good tanks, good anti-tank guns and plenty of artillery and ammunition, and we are backed up by the finest air striking force in the world. All that is necessary is that each one of us, every officer and man, should enter this battle with the determination to see it through, to fight and kill, and finally, to win. If we do all this, we will hit the enemy for 'six' right out of North Africa ...... Let no man surrender so long as he is unwounded and can fight, and let us pray that the Lord Almighty will give us the victory".

Up to 9.40 p.m. on the fateful day October 23rd, 1942, the battlefield at El Alamein lay strangely still and quiet under a brilliant moon. The silence was broken only by occasional desultory shelling and the noise of aircraft. The infantry crouched in their trenches. Gun crews were grouped closely around their weapons. Then, with a crash which seemed to rend the sky, 800 guns opened fire simultaneously on a six-mile frontage in the northern sector against the enemy batteries. A vast crescent of flame illuminated the rolling clouds of dust which soon blotted out the landscape. For 20 minutes the barrage continued and then switched to the support of the advancing infantry. Meanwhile, the artillery in the centre and southern sectors had followed suit. The infantry of the 30th Corps, accompanied by engineers, followed the northern barrage and by 5.30 a.m. on October 24th had made two gaps through the main belt of enemy minefields. At 7.0 a.m. they occupied the Miteiriya Ridge, whereupon the 1st and 10th Armoured Divisions advanced up to it. The subsidiary operations of the 13th Corps in the south not having met with much success, the 7th Armoured Division was ordered to the north. In the northern sector, the 51st Highland Division, 1st South African Division and 2nd New Zealand Division poured through the southernmost of the two gaps with two Armoured Brigades in close support and the 10th Armoured Division following. The 9th Australian Division went through the northern gap, followed by the 1st Armoured Division. A narrow wedge was thus driven into the enemy's line, but the armour could not penetrate to the open country. The line was merely dented, not pierced. Von Stumme had withdrawn most of his troops and guns from their forward positions and had thus in effect turned his original front line into an outpost position. The bulk of his forces, and his guns, had still to be dealt with. This was his last action, for on the 25th he was killed in an air raid and the command of the Axis forces then devolved on General von Thoma. The operations of the 13th Corps in the south, though not spectacular, had the desired effect of holding the 21st Panzer Division and an Italian Armoured Division for a time in that sector and thus diminished the resistance encountered by the 30th and 10th Corps in the north. Indeed, it was not until the night of October 26/27th that the enemy moved these armoured divisions to the northern sector, a concentration which may have been due to the controlling hand of Rommel himself, for he had just arrived post-haste from Berlin to resume command. By that time, the battle was raging all along the line but with particular fierceness in the north where the Australians had attacked northwards from the narrow salient and had almost reached the sea.

On October 27th, Rommel launched a series of violent counter-attacks against the 30th and 10th Corps in the northern sector. Under cover of these offensives he wished to withdraw westwards for some miles; but Hitler intervened again and ordered him to stand and fight, and accordingly he stayed and fought and thereby signed the death warrant of his army. Yet the resistance which he offered was so stubborn that, as day succeeded day, it became more and more evident that a British break-through in the Miteiriya region, followed by a drive southwards as planned, could not succeed and Montgomery therefore decided to re-group his army and alter his strategy. His new plan was to strike westwards and then northwards. The 30th Corps was to deepen the salient already established, the 10th (Armoured) Corps was to withdraw and reorganize for the final thrust, and the 13th Corps was to revert to a defensive role. The 2nd New Zealand Division was pulled out of the line and its place taken by the 1st South African Division which moved northwards. The South Africans were relieved in turn by the 4th Indian Division, the next in the line. Thus the Indian Division found itself nearer to the centre of fighting in the north.

On October 28th, Rommel attacked once more and sent part of his armour to extricate his 90th Light Division which had been almost surrounded by the 9th Australian Division on the coast. Heavy fighting continued in this area until November 1st. During the night of November 1st/2nd, the 30th Corps resumed the offensive north of the Miteiriya Ridge and a feature beyond it called "Kidney", making an advance of 4000 yards at the point of junction of the German and Italian forces and penetrating the final Axis minefields though at heavy cost. The 10th Corps then advanced through the opening and throughout November 2nd fought a series of violent tank battles in comparatively open country against the 15th and 21st Panzer Divisions. When dawn broke on November 3rd, the German armour had at last been thoroughly beaten and shortly afterwards General von Thoma was captured. Rommel now began to abandon his line, at the same time plugging the yawning gap with all the anti-tank guns he could muster. But Montgomery had another trump in hand. The 4th Indian Division came into the picture once more, together with the 51st Division. The Indians broke south-west through two Italian divisions and into this new gap poured the 7th Armoured Division. "With one final shattering and cataclysmic blow", writes Alan Moorehead,[1] "the entire Axis army collapsed and fell to pieces. Thousands upon thousands of exhausted and bewildered Italians simply gave themselves up. The rest, with the Germans in the van (because they had grabbed most of the vehicles) set off pell-mell in wild disorder down the coast road in the long and dangerous attempt to escape into Libya".

The victory was absolute and complete. On November 5th, Montgomery's armour was streaming along the coast road to capture the enemy's dumps at Daba and beyond and if possible to encircle the roaring Panzers before they could climb the escarpment west of Mersa Matruh. Only 80 German tanks remained and they were pursued by 600 British tanks. Nose to tail and two deep, the vehicles of the Eighth Army poured westwards and in the other direction marched seemingly endless columns of German and Italian prisoners, the Germans sullen and dejected, the Italians happy to be out of it all. The Battle of Alamein cost the enemy 59,000 casualties, of whom 34,000 were Germans, while the British lost only 13,500 men. Each side lost between 400 and 500 tanks, but the enemy had in addition to abandon hundreds of guns and thousands of vehicles, none of which could be recovered. Italian morale was completely broken and German morale greatly lowered. Thus in every respect, Alamein stands out as one of the most decisive land battles in history.

It is time now to see in what way the Indian Engineers shared in this great struggle. Rarely were they in any heavy fighting, but they took an honourable part with the remainder of the 4th Indian Division

---

[1] *Montgomery*, by Alan Moorehead, p. 138.

in holding the ring while the main battle was fought in the north. Yet they were no mere spectators. Raiding and patrolling proceeded unceasingly, and such activities required the services of parties of Engineer troops. Sometimes there were more extensive operations. For instance, on the night of October 23rd, when the battle began, a full scale attack was launched against 'Point 62' on the Ruweisat Ridge and a detachment of 12 Field Company advanced with the 2nd Gurkhas to lift mines. On November 1st, when the final breakthrough in the north had begun, some Indian Engineers helped the 5th Indian Infantry Brigade to cut a lane through the enemy minefields and defences to a depth of 8,000 yards so that the tanks could go forward. At Alamein, for practically the first time in the North African campaigns, Divisional Engineers were employed as a whole, directly under the command of their C.R.E., on specified tasks instead of being attached to, and at the disposal of, brigades. Better co-ordination of work was thus secured, and 2, 4, 11 and 12 Companies of the 4th Indian Division, under Lieut.-Colonel J. H. Blundell, R.E., proved themselves equal to the best. Their main efforts during the battle were concentrated on opening gaps in minefields behind the assaulting infantry so that vehicles could pass through quickly. A 'gapping' drill was used which proved very successful. The Sappers were called upon also to complete the destruction of dozens of crippled and abandoned enemy tanks and guns and they became exceedingly quick and expert in this work. Previous training and experience had taught them exactly the sizes of the necessary explosive charges and where these should be placed to secure the best results.

Some extracts from the War Diary of 12 Field Company will show the general nature of the work of all the Indian units. Major J. A. Cameron, R.E., writes as follows:— "23rd October 1942, 1600 hrs. 12 Field Company moves to battle positions north of 4th Div. HQ. 2130 hrs. A compressor of 11 Field Park Company is going full blast on the front wire. Its object is to preserve the normal atmosphere up to the last possible moment and to drown the noise of the carriers. 2140 hrs. Counter-battery fire begins. The compressor is as loud as ever. 2155 hrs. "C" Company, 1/2nd Gurkha Rifles, pass through the wire in brilliant moonlight. The Sappers follow. The compressor reaches a crescendo of noise on the hardest rock it can find. 2200 hrs. 600 guns open fire from Ruweisat to the sea. The compressor packs up, its task accomplished. Meanwhile the Gurkhas, led by Capt. Carrick, have pulled away the wire with grapnels and their leading platoon has reached its objective. The following platoon is not so lucky and the men with made-up charges are halted—so also the Sappers behind them—and this state of affairs continues for the allotted 10 minutes of the operation until the leading Gurkhas return and the Sappers with them".

The chief obstacles at Alamein were enemy anti-tank minefields laid in great depth but containing relatively few anti-personnel mines or booby traps. It was thus possible to pass infantry through a minefield without serious casualties and then to clear the mines under their protection. After Alamein, the enemy used much larger quantities of anti-personnel mines and it became almost impossible for infantry to move through a minefield at night without heavy loss. This necessitated the fitting of mine-clearing devices to our tanks. At Alamein, however, the infantry were able to make their own way readily through the enemy wire and minefields, assisted by small detachments of Sappers to deal with occasional booby traps and blow gaps in the wire with Bangalore torpedoes if required. Behind the infantry came minefield task forces to widen the gaps for the passage of tanks and vehicles. Once the main minefields had been traversed, a difficult problem arose. This was to locate the forward edges of any minefields further in rear, for if sweeping with detectors was begun when the first mine was encountered much time might be wasted because the mine might merely be one of a few scattered haphazard between the fields. Nevertheless, the method of mine-clearance usually adopted at Alamein was that of employing a detachment of engineer troops provided with detectors and it was found that one Section could clear a 16-yard gap to a depth of 400 yards in 2 hours. If detectors were not available, the engineers and infantry had to resort to prodding with bayonets. An Engineer Mine-clearance Detachment was divided into a number of parties. First came a Reconnaissance Party following close behind the leading infantry to determine the exact extent of the minefield and the best starting point for the gap. Next came a Tape Party to mark an initial gap 8 yards wide, and behind it a Detector Party of three men, each of whom swept a width of 3 yards assisted by a man who marked any mines discovered. A Mine Disarming and Lifting Party followed, and then a Gap Marking Party to mark the edges of the gap with metal signs by day or screened lamps by night. A Control Party remained at the entrance and also a Reserve Party to replace any casualties. This elaborate organization shows how carefully the Sappers had to be trained and how many men were needed for mine clearance. Fortunately, they were not usually required to clear gaps in our own minefields before an attack. That task fell to the infantry, but the Sappers had to determine the sites and mark them. Mine clearance was dangerous work and the Indian Engineer units in the Ruweisat region had their fair share of it, particularly when they had to make gaps for the break-through of the 7th Armoured Division late in the battle.

The pursuit of Rommel's broken army out of Egypt, across Cyrenaica and into Tripolitania, was maintained at a prodigious speed so long as the weather permitted. Yet only four of Montgomery's twelve divisions were immediately available for the chase. These were the 51st Highland Division, the 2nd New Zealand Division and two Armoured Divisions. Others had to be re-equipped or had to provide garrisons along the route, and the unfortunate 4th Indian Division was soon left behind to clear up the Alamein battlefield. The main problem was to arrange that the pursuit did not outstrip the supplies. Tobruk is 360 miles from El Alamein, Benghazi 300 miles further on, and El Agheila another 160 miles. The meagre water-supplies along the coast road had been spoilt by contamination with bone-oil, and the pipe-line from Alexandria was unreliable and did not extend very far. Until the railway could be restored, the leading troops had to be supplied entirely by road and the number of lorries available was strictly limited. Our shipping could not use the various small ports along the coast until these had been cleared of mines and wrecks. Such obstacles, however, did not affect the Indian Engineer units tied to El Alamein. There was much disappointment among them for they felt that they deserved something better than picking up scrap. Yet they did it with a will for they knew that the sooner they completed the tedious job the sooner they might rejoin the forward troops. The Sapper units cleared the smaller minefields, marked the larger ones, destroyed enemy tanks and vehicles and gave advice on the salvage of no less that 1500 tons of material daily. These labours continued until December 1942 when 4 and 12 Field Companies and 11 Field Park Company began to move westwards and 2 Field Company left for Iraq *en route* to Burma.

Another Indian Engineer unit which now came into the picture was 9 Field Company, under Major P. G. O. Landon, R.E., which afterwards met disaster in the Dodecanese Islands.[1] Until November 5th it had been guarding aerodromes in the Nile delta, but on the 6th it was detailed to work with a Bomb Disposal Company on the

---

[1] See Chapter III.

Mine detection in Tunisia

clearance of mines and booby traps along the railway line from El Alamein to Tobruk. This single-track line, which ran for 500 miles along the route of the pursuit, had been extensively mined and damaged by the retreating Germans. Our forces advanced much more rapidly than the line could be repaired and cleared, but 9 Field Company completed the work along the 360 miles to Tobruk in 10 days during which it lifted 141 mines, 3 booby traps and 39 unexploded charges. Subsequently it continued mine-lifting on the roads as far as Derna before leaving in December for Egypt and Cyprus.

By November 5th it had become clear that Rommel's thoughts were centred solely on saving the remnants of his armour comprising his two depleted German Panzer Divisions and the survivors of two Italian Motorized Divisions. He tried to make a stand on the Fuka escarpment, and our 1st and 7th Armoured Divisions, in hot pursuit, prepared to deal with it. Early on the 6th they broke through the enemy's rearguard and then, resuming the race westwards, reached the escarpment south of Mersa Matruh and re-occupied that port. At this moment, when Rommel's armour might well have been totally destroyed, heavy rain began to fall. It was an outrageous piece of bad luck. Our tanks, whirling through the desert to cut off the retreating enemy, became bogged down in thick mud while the Panzers continued to pound along the coast road, and when the weather cleared on November 8th, Rommel had escaped. The vile weather had interfered also with the operations of our air force. Afterwards, however, the 10th Corps made rapid progress. Tobruk was entered on November 13th, Gazala on the 14th, and by the 15th we had seized the important airfields around Martuba beyond Tmimi. This was a notable achievement because our planes could then give cover to a vital sea convoy due to leave Alexandria for Malta. That island was in desperate need of supplies, and if the garrison had had to surrender, the enemy could have safely poured troops into North Africa from Sicily. The convoy got through and so a major disaster was avoided by the narrowest of margins. It is a lesson in the intricate pattern of war strategy. Benghazi was entered on November 20th, and three days later the 7th Armoured Division forced the enemy out of a position at Ajedabia. Rommel then retired to El Agheila, whence he had launched his counter-offensive on January 21st,[1] and there he prepared to make a resolute stand in an exceptionally powerful position in a narrow gap between a marsh

---

[1] See Chapter IV.

and the sea. The approaches were packed with anti-personnel mines, and in addition to anti-tank mines, some of the minefields had belts of 'S' mines seven rows deep, each mine being only 2 feet from the next. A pause of three weeks was therefore necessary for reconnaissance and to allow time in which to build up a strong force for a major attack. On December 11th, after we had made some probing attacks, the enemy completed his withdrawal from El Agheila and our advance was resumed along the now heavily mined coast road into Tripolitania. The delay had enabled Rommel to dig and mine another position at Buerat further along the coast.

The general situation in North Africa had recently undergone a startling change, for on November 8th, 1942, British and American troops had landed in the extreme west as the forerunners of a great army under General Eisenhower. On November 11th, the leading formations of the British First Army under Lieut.-General K. A. N. Anderson were re-embarked and transferred further eastwards from Algiers. They landed in Tunisia and on November 25th one division was at Medjez el Bab only 30 miles south-west of Tunis.[1] The Germans reinforced their Tunisian garrison by air, and by Christmas, although Medjez el Bab was still held by the First Army, difficulties of supply had brought about a stalemate which persisted until the middle of February 1943. Thus it became more and more necessary that the Eighth Army should break the deadlock by invading Tunisia, and the question was whether this was possible without outrunning its supply services. During the first week of January, a terrific storm wrecked the ships in Benghazi harbour, the only large supply port on the long line of communication. The Eighth Army was then facing the enemy in position at Buerat, 600 miles beyond Benghazi, and it was doubtful whether the land supply line could be stretched to cover the further 200 miles to Tripoli, the next large port. If not, the army would have to turn back, which was unthinkable. Such was the difficult problem which confronted Montgomery at this stage. The Army Commander wisely decided to reduce his striking force by immobilizing the entire 10th Corps at Benghazi so that its vehicles could carry supplies forward from the railhead at Tobruk. The railway from Alexandria to Tobruk was working to its utmost capacity. Closely concerned with this undertaking was 115 Railway Operating Company, R.I.E., under Major D. Robathan, the only Indian Railway Company to be awarded the Eighth Army clasp. The line was

---

[1] See the map of Tunisia included in this chapter.

operated with old Diesel locomotives which were kept running by using spare parts taken from still older ones.[1] It was a triumph of ingenuity.

On January 12th, reorganized and properly supplied, the Eighth Army was ready to attack at Buerat. A personal message was issued by Montgomery. "The Eighth Army is going to Tripoli" it ran. "Nothing has stopped us since the Battle of Egypt began on October 23rd. Nothing will stop us now. Some must stay back to begin with, but we will all be in the hunt eventually. ON TO TRIPOLI!" But already Rommel had begun to withdraw, and soon the Eighth Army was on the move again. Before dawn on January 23rd, 1943, the leading elements of the 7th Armoured Division entered Tripoli. The Army had advanced 1,400 miles in three months and its independent mission had ended. Henceforth its strategy would be controlled by General Eisenhower from Algiers and not by General Alexander from Cairo.

After the Battle of Alamein the 4th Indian Divisional Engineers, commanded by Lieut.-Colonel J. H. Blundell, R.E., included 2 Field Company under Major A. Selkirk, R.E., with Captain A. E. Scott, R.E., as second-in-command, 4 Field Company under Major W. J. A. Murray, R.E., with Captain R. D. Penney, R.E., as second-in-command, 11 Field Park Company under Captain T. E. Potts, R.E., and 12 Field Company under Major J. A. Cameron, R.E. The Bombay Group was not represented. Of these units, 2 Field Company took no share in the pursuit into Tripolitania for, as already stated, it was transferred in December 1942 to Iraq, so that when the Divisional Engineers were allowed to leave El Alamein and follow the other troops westwards the chief burden of the field work fell on 4 and 12 Field Companies. The men had suffered a keen disappointment soon after the end of the battle. "The desert is full of vehicles" runs the 4th Company War Diary of November 5th. "It is a grand sight. We march until almost dark and halt below a steep escarpment. There are lots of Verey signals going up all round us". Then came the unwelcome order to return to clear up the battlefield and the 4th Divisional Engineers sadly retraced their steps. However, in mid-December, 4, 11 and 12 Companies moved forward to the Tobruk area and on January 5th, 1943, 4 Field Company was approaching Benghazi in heavy rain. "The going is very bad", writes Murray.

---

[1] See "Accounts about 119 Railway Workshop Company", by Lieut.-Colonel Kuldip Singh, I.E., dated January 1951.

"Right from the start, vehicles are getting bogged. At one point the advance party are stuck 7 miles in rear of the Brigade column. At the lunch halt, only 17 vehicles of the Company transport are together in position, but after that the going is not too bad and we halt for the night about 2 miles from Msus. The drivers are not choosing their routes but following rigidly the vehicle in front. If it gets bogged and has to be pulled out, the driver behind thinks it is his inevitable fate to be bogged and pulled out too! The ground has become a complete quagmire through rain."

On January 8th, 4 Field Company arrived in a pleasant camp at Benghazi and was soon busily employed on harbour works and water-supply. "We are asked to open up a water-point at the Lete Grotto, 6 miles from here" continues Murray. "It is a wonderful place, an underground reservoir composed of three lakes about 120 feet below the surface. It is quite dark down there and it would be easy to get lost if one pushed off in a boat without a life-line for retracing one's route. We have found a well-shaft on the surface leading down to the lakes and have decided to have our pumping engine on the surface and to use the flex drive on the unit pumps down to the water. The maximum head is about 90 feet. The 'Waters of Lete' (or Lethe) are famous, and it is said that anyone partaking of them forgets everything."[1] 4 Field Company brought the first water to the surface on January 18th and we can only hope that the efficiency of those who drank it did not suffer!

At the end of the month, Murray received some shoulder emblems with the new Divisional sign—a Red Eagle on a black background. These were issued at once to the British and Indian officers pending the arrival of a full supply for all ranks. They had been secured through the good offices of Sir Sikandar Hayat Khan, Premier of the Punjab. Each was mounted on a piece of cardboard bearing the V sign and the words "The Punjabis are proud of you. With best wishes for final victory". The emblems and the accompanying message were greatly appreciated.

4 Field Company left Benghazi in the middle of February, and before the end of the month 11 Field Park Company and 12 Field Company arrived from the El Adem region. A fortnight later, they also took the road towards Tripoli. During March, 21 Field Company

---

[1] According to Greek mythology, the Lethe was a river of the nether regions from which departed spirits drank to obtain forgetfulness of the past. The name itself implies forgetfulness.

under Captain P. H. Fraser, R.E., appeared from Egypt and soon followed the others. All the Sappers units were very busy while in Benghazi for there was a great variety of work to be done and little time in which to do it. Barges driven ashore during the great storm were refloated, roads built or repaired and wireless masts erected. Courses of instruction in mine-laying and mine-lifting were run for the benefit of recruits. Relaxation was provided by occasional E.N.S.A. entertainments and by Indian films. "It was a very pleasant interlude" writes Pearson.[1] "Benghazi's white buildings glistened in the sun and the two domes of its cathedral dominated the sky-line. The blue skies overhead were dotted with silvery balloons, about twenty-two in all, the only outward signs of war."

Beyond El Agheila, 4 Field Company found many examples of the latest German booby-traps. According to Murray, the retreating enemy had shown the utmost ingenuity in planning these devilish devices. Large craters would be blown in the coastal road and 'S' mines buried beneath the metal splinters lying around the edges. These splinters prevented the use of mine-detectors. Again, an abandoned vehicle might have traps fixed to the brake or gear levers so that when an attempt was made to tow the vehicle clear of the road a mine exploded beneath it. Alternatively, the vehicle might be left clear of traps and several mines buried in the only empty space off the road to which it might be towed. To make certainty doubly sure, a mine might be buried just in front of a front wheel. Sometimes the enemy prepared a sham grave near the road with a cross leaning crazily to one side. The short path to that grave was sown with 'S' mines and any attempt to straighten the cross caused a mine beneath it to explode. Yet again, the side of the road would be undermined and a couple of Tellermines inserted beneath the metalling. A few vehicles might then pass safely, but when the crust of the undermined portion collapsed under further traffic the mines exploded. Occasionally, trip wires, as fine as gossamer threads and almost invisible, were attached to a barbed wire barrier across the road. The wires led to 'S' mines buried beneath the barrier. Oil drums, half filled with rubbish, were often strewn across the road, each with a pull-ignition arrangement attached to a Tellermine below. The lessons learned on the Agheila Road made the Sappers so suspicious that it is surprising that they could ever bring themselves

---

[1] *Brief History of the K.G.V's O. Bengal Sappers and Miners Group, R.I.E., August 1939-July 1946*", by Lieut. G. Pearson, R.E., p. 37.

to move anywhere or touch anything, but move they did and with remarkable rapidity. Fortunately, they were no novices at the game and consequently they suffered few casualties, but the leading troops, now far ahead, could have told a different tale.

While at Tripoli, the Eighth Army was honoured by another visit from Mr. Winston Churchill who took the salute on February 3rd at a great parade. The countryside afforded a welcome change from the arid stretches of the Western Desert. Flowers gladdened the eye, and fresh water from rippling streams eased many a parched throat. The coastal belt was well cultivated, but it was not so picturesque as Tunisia whose rolling downs and springy turf still lay far ahead beyond Rommel's army. Wadis galore, running down to the fertile coast from inhospitable inland tracts, afforded Rommel a series of ideal positions in which he might attempt to prevent a junction of the Eighth and First Armies, and as he had now received reinforcements of tanks and guns, he was determined to make a resolute stand. His Germans were still the same dour fighters: his new Italian divisions were composed mostly of enthusiastic youngsters. Knowing that Montgomery was not yet ready to move forward from Tripoli, Rommel marched a large part of his army onwards into Tunisia, encountered the Americans on February 14th and six days later broke through them to the Kasserine Pass, whence he advanced in two columns, one northwards towards Thala and the other north-westwards towards Tebessa, where the First and Eighth Armies might be expected eventually to meet.[1] He was repulsed after some fierce fighting, but not until he had succeeded in creating considerable disorganization in Tunisia. Then he turned back to face Montgomery in Tripolitania. He occupied the formidable Mareth Line of fortifications, about 200 miles west of Tripoli, which had been built originally by the French to guard against a possible Italian invasion from Libya. When France fell, the Italians had stripped this line, but it had recently been re-equipped by the retreating Axis forces. On February 17th, though much delayed by bad weather, Montgomery's advanced troops captured Medinine, 18 miles short of the Mareth Line, and he then proceeded to extend his position southwards. The 51st Division, 7th Armoured Division and 22nd Armoured Brigade had reached the front, and during the next fortnight the 2nd New Zealand Division, 8th Armoured Brigade, 201st Guards Brigade and some units of the 50th Division were rushed forward. On March

---

[1] See the map of Tunisia included in this chapter.

6th, Rommel attacked our positions at Medinine with massed armour but was repulsed with the loss of 52 tanks. Yet the situation had been sufficiently serious for Montgomery to issue stringent orders that there must be no withdrawal anywhere and, of course, no surrender.

The 4th Indian Division soon began to arrive on the scene and with it 4, 11 and 12 Companies under Lieut.-Colonel J. H. Blundell, R.E. After Divisional Headquarters had been set up a few miles north-east of Medinine, the 7th Brigade moved forward to take over a sector of the front from the 7th Armoured Division.[1] The Mareth Line was exceedingly strong. Its left lay on the sea coast, along its front ran the Wadi Zigzaou, a formidable obstacle 50 feet deep and 70 yards wide with a muddy bottom, and its right rested on the Matmata Hills which were believed to be impassable to wheeled traffic. South of Medinine, a pass in the hills led to a village called Foum Tatahouine, and 40 miles west of Mareth there was a strongly fortified gap called 'Plum' Pass. To outflank the Mareth Line by way of Foum Tatahouine and Plum Pass would entail a journey of 150 miles over broken ground. "Nevertheless", writes General Fuller,[2] "Montgomery decided to attempt it. While the 30th Corps pinned the enemy down by a frontal attack against his left flank, the 2nd New Zealand Division and the 8th Armoured Brigade were to move over the Foum Tatahouine Pass, link up with General Leclerc's small French force which had come up from Lake Chad, storm the Plum Pass and then fall upon the enemy's rear. Heavy air support was to be used not only against the enemy airfields and in a preliminary bombardment but also in closest co-operation with the troops attacking the narrow frontage at the Plum Pass. At 10.30 p.m. on March 20th, 1943, the 50th Division of the 30th Corps, under cover of a tremendous artillery barrage, stormed the Wadi Zigzaou and gained a footing on its western side but was driven back across it on the 22nd by the 15th Panzer and 90th Light Divisions. Next day Montgomery ordered the 10th Corps H.Q. and the 1st Armoured Division to move after dark and join the 2nd New Zealand Division, and reinforcing the 30th Corps with the 7th Armoured Division, he ordered it, after withdrawing the 50th Division, to open a new attack against the enemy's centre".

Meanwhile, the 2nd New Zealand Division had successfully traversed the Foum Tatahouine Pass but was held up at the Plum

---

[1] *The Tiger Kills*. (M.O.I. publication), pp. 159-160.

[2] *The Second World War*, 1939-1945, by Major-General J. F. C. Fuller, pp. 246, 247.

Pass until the way was opened on the 26th by an overwhelming air and artillery barrage. On the 27th the New Zealanders met increasing opposition, and when they had nearly reached El Hamma, a few miles west of Gabes on the coast, they were stopped by anti-tank gun fire. However, they were now far out on the Gabes plain and well in rear of the Mareth Line. This left hook was a fine achievement, but it succeeded mainly because of the energetic action of the 4th Indian Division, under Major-General F. I. S. Tuker, in finding an intermediate and shorter way to the Gabes plain through the Matmata Hills along almost unknown tracks.

The 4th Division had started out on March 24th. The mountain tracks which it followed meandered between rocky heights and across deep ravines. Everywhere they were sown with mines. Cliffsides had been blown down to block the tracks, and the Sappers and infantry had to clear the debris, day and night and often under heavy fire, so that the advance could proceed. The pace increased gradually and the retreating enemy was overhauled until a Sapper officer with our forward patrols was able to observe some Italian engineer troops actually mining a track after their rearguard had passed through and thus could send his men to lift the mines without further search. On the 27th, the Division was almost through the mountainous country. The Sappers continued to clear the tracks and bridge the worst gaps, and on the afternoon of March 28th the 5th Brigade burst out into the Gabes plain and joined the New Zealanders. By that time, Rommel's armour had been defeated and our tanks were in Gabes. The Mareth Line was open. This was Rommel's last battle in North Africa. He was a sick man, a mere shadow of his former self, and handing over command of the Axis forces to the Italian General Messe, he flew to Berlin. Some say that he left before the battle, though the energetic handling of the German armour would seem to indicate his presence.

Mareth was certainly a transcendent victory, but that it was nearly a disastrous defeat is shown by the story of the struggle to cross the Wadi Zigzaou at the opening of the battle. The Wadi resembled the *fosse* of an old-fashioned fortress of feudal times and our troops advanced to the assault carrying fascines and scaling ladders as some of their forbears had done at the storming of Badajoz in the Peninsula War. On the night of March 20th/21st a brigade of the 50th Division forced its way across the wadi in the face of direct and enfilade fire and established a precarious bridgehead. The 5th Brigade of the 4th Indian Division then moved up to pass through, but it was decided not to send it across until the bridgehead was more secure. Some Valentine tanks had cut up the bottom and banks so badly that no more vehicles could pass until the crossing sites had been repaired. In the pitch darkness before the moon rose some R.E. units of the 50th Division tried to make a causeway for vehicles but suffered such heavy casualties that they had to be withdraw. Prominent at every danger point was Brigadier F. H. Kisch, the Chief Engineer, who was always to be found directing the engineering operations in person on such occasions.

During the afternoon of March 22nd, the 15th Panzer Division counter-attacked in heavy rain and almost obliterated the bridgehead. This set-back resulted in a decision not to commit the 4th Indian Division to a direct attack across the wadi but to leave the task to the 50th Division after proper crossing places had been made. These, however, were to be prepared by the 4th Divisional Engineers, a decision which led to some heroic efforts by 4 and 12 Field Companies. A reconnaissance had been made by Lieut.-Colonel Blundell and some of his officers, and as a result, 11 Field Park Company had been ordered to prepare 150 fascines, each about 10 feet long and 2 feet in diameter. These were to be placed in position in the wadi and covered with steel mesh to form a causeway for vehicles. Cuttings were to be dug in the steep banks, and ramps built as required. 4 and 12 Field Companies would have to complete the crossing begun by the 50th Divisional Engineers and prepare a second crossing about 150 yards away.

11 Field Park Company had been very hard at work during March 21st and 22nd. Two bulldozers were parked in 12 Field Company's lines to help with the earthwork if the enemy's fire could not be subdued sufficiently, and every available man was busy collecting brushwood or making fascines. On the 22nd, Blundell ordered 11 Field Park Company to load up all available fascines, reserve tools and explosives and during the afternoon 100 fascines were despatched in lorries to a forward dump whence they were guided by men of 12 Field Company to the bank of the wadi. This was done between dusk and moonrise. Considerable shelling was in progress and one lorry was hit and the driver killed. It had been decided that the causeways must be built before the infantry could renew the assault and that therefore the Indian Engineer units must lead the way.

In the early hours of March 23rd, 1943, under the light of a full moon, 4 and 12 Field Companies approached the wadi and dropped down into it through gaps in the precipitous eastern bank. Above their heads sped thousands of tracer bullets and hundreds of mortar shells from which happily they were screened, but they could not avoid a certain amount of enfilade fire from concrete pill-boxes on the far bank. British and German guns were both laying down heavy barrages. Between these two walls of shell, the Sappers worked like beavers in the muddy depths. Blundell was there, of course, exhorting his men and pointing out how safe they were when one of his height could walk upright without risk. But he did not display a bullet hole already showing in the peak of his cap. The eastern approaches to the wadi soon became blocked with vehicles bringing up infantry for the assault and the lorries carrying the steel mesh for the causeways could not get through. Consequently, the assault had to go in over surfaces unsuitable for tanks and armoured cars. Having done all they could, 4 and 12 Field Companies were withdrawn, carrying their tools and marching slowly and in good order through the barrage and past the waiting infantry who were much impressed by their cool and confident bearing. The infantry rushed down into and across the wadi. Dust and flames spouted from it far up into the sky. The gallant Tynesiders established themselves on the further bank, and vehicles began to stream across over the rapidly deteriorating surface. However, it soon became evident that further Sapper assistance would be needed if progress was to be maintained so 4 and 12 Companies returned into the holocaust and set to work to repair the causeways with fascines and stones as the steel mesh had not yet arrived. For another hour and a half they sweated and floundered in the mud until at last they were satisfied that the causeways would bear wheeled traffic, and dawn was breaking when for the second time they withdrew from the wadi. Yet all their labour was wasted. A heavy storm broke over the areas, and under cover of the downpour the Panzers bore down again on the infantry and tanks on the far bank. This was the end of a bitter struggle. With the exception of a small foothold maintained for a time and subsequently relinquished, the infantry and tanks had to withdraw and both sides settled down to a fire-fight across the swirling flood. We were back where we had started. The Sapper units rejoined the remainder of the 4th Indian Division and moved with it into the Matmata hills, making for the Gabes plain.

A curious incident at the Wadi Zigzaou must not go unrecorded. While 4 Field Company, under Major W. J. A. Murray, was laying fascines in the bottom, a British officer of another unit asked for help to extricate a wounded Indian soldier who was buried beneath

Using a pneumatic drill while roadmaking in Tunisia

a blown-up truck. A Sapper dressed in an overcoat, and with his face covered with mud, immediately volunteered to rescue the man and did so at considerable risk. A few days later, Murray received a message from Divisional H.Q. stating that Army H.Q. wanted to know the name of this Sapper. He made enquiries but could not trace any such man in his unit and replied accordingly. However, the British officer who had asked for help insisted that there was such a man and an indentification parade was arranged so that the wounded man could pick out his rescuer. Still there was no result; but as the wounded man was leaving the parade ground he happened to pass an officer whom he saluted smartly. Then an expression of the utmost amazement came over his face. "*Wuh Admi* !", he shouted, and pointed to Lieut.-Colonel J. H. Blundell. The 'Sapper' who had saved him was the C.R.E. 4th Indian Division.[1]

During the advance through the Hallouf Pass in the Matmata Hills, the Division was held up by a huge demolition in a narrow gorge. "It was here", writes Pearson,[2] "that 4 Field Company further distinguished themselves. Their work with two compressors and a bulldozer was recorded in a B.B.C. despatch from Cairo. The machines were gingerly taken down the narrow trail, watched anxiously by officers on the heights above, and as the bulldozers filled the hole and the compressor drills cut away the overhang, swarms of men, directed by the Sappers, brought up stone from the bottom of the ravine to build the retaining wall, and slowly a new road grew, both there and further down the gorge. After eight hours, the first twelve thousand men and two thousand vehicles edged their way along the path and thus the 4th Division came down from the mountains to link up with the other division". On one day the Sapper companies worked continuously for no less than eighteen hours in getting the other troops and their transport along the mountain tracks. The E. and M. Section of 11 Field Park Company distinguished itself while operating with the 7th Brigade in the advance. On March 25th, when a large minefield was encountered covering the whole of a valley, a young Sapper drove a pilot vehicle through it in order to help 12 Field Company to clear it. The mines were deeply buried and therefore difficult to locate, and the Sapper had never before

---

[1] Notes by Lieut.-Colonel N. B. Grant, R.E., (undated).

[2] *Brief History of the K.G.V's O. Bengal Sappers and Miners Group, R.I.E., August 1939-July* 1946, by Lieut. G. Pearson, R.E., p. 38.

driven a pilot vehicle into a minefield, yet he carried on with the utmost coolness and bravery until the concrete rollers of his vehicle were blown to pieces.

Having been driven from the Mareth Line, the enemy had to build a new defensive bastion against the advance of the Eighth Army. The battle in Tunisia was not going too badly for the Germans and Italians. The British First Army was held up in the Medjerda Valley west of Tunis, and the Americans had been defeated at Kasserine, west of Sbeitla in the central region. In the south, and only 80 miles north-west of Gabes, the American 2nd Corps was trying with little success to force a passage past Gafsa towards the Eighth Army. Unfortunately for us, a replica of the Mareth position, so far as the physical features were concerned, existed about 20 miles north of Gabes. Here the coastal plain narrowed again to a few miles and was crossed by the Wadi Akarit, a deep and wide chasm running inland for a distance of ten miles. This natural obstacle had been prolonged for another two miles by an anti-tank ditch, the approaches to which were flanked by some low hills, and in rear towered a lofty range with two groups of peaks, Roumana to the north and Fatnassa to the south. The ditch linked up with the northern escarpment of Fatnassa. The enemy therefore had two lofty features for observation and fire control, and the approaches to his defences could be raked by oblique fire. In such a case Montgomery could not adopt his favourite 'left hook' tactics. He had to burst through in strength on the coastal plain itself, but to accomplish this he must first secure the heights beyond. He met General Eisenhower and explained his plans. The scheme was to storm the Fatnassa peaks, which lay directly north of the main road, and afterwards to over-run the 'hog's-back' which connected them with the Roumana group. Fatnassa was a tangle of ridges, escarpments and deep ravines. Every approach was under direct observation and fire and could be enfiladed by guns on the hog's-back. Montgomery re-grouped his forces and was ready by April 5th. The 50th, 51st and 4th Divisions were to breach the defences, after which the 10th Corps, supported by the 2nd New Zealand Division, would burst through and make for the enemy's airfields beyond. The most difficult role was that of the 4th Division which was to secure command of Fatnassa. General Tuker considered that infiltration under cover of darkness offered the best chance of success and therefore proposed to attack silently, without artillery preparation, some hours before the assault by the 50th and 51st Divisions. His 7th Brigade was to be directed straight on Fatnassa, and if it succeeded, the 5th Brigade would then press swiftly through and turn the strongly held anti-tank ditch positions which defended the hog's-back.

Accordingly, after dark on April 5th, 1943, the Battle of the Wadi Akarit began with the 4th Indian Division moving silently across the rolling country below the main peaks. In the ensuing fight the Gurkhas, Royal Sussex and 16th Punjabis of the 7th Brigade performed prodigies of valour in bloody hand-to-hand combat. They won Fatnassa at heavy cost and the 5th Brigade turned the anti-tank ditch. At 8.45 a.m., General Tuker was able to report that he had captured 6,000 yards of the enemy's position. "The gate is open" said he. "Turn your armour loose". On the coastal plain, the 51st Highland Division had already crashed through and taken 5,000 prisoners, but unfortunately there was some delay in launching the armour through the gap, so the enemy took new heart and bitter fighting ensued in the hills.

On April 6th, while the enemy guns were bombarding the northern slopes of an escarpment called Ras-el-Zouai, already captured by the Gurkhas, and also some tracks through the hills behind a length of abandoned anti-tank ditch, the 4th Divisional Engineers were sent forward to finish a half-completed crossing of the ditch and to construct another. This dangerous operation was marked by a most tragic event. According to the War Diaries, 4, 11, and 12 Companies were working on the crossings, when, shortly after 4.0 p.m., Lieut.-Colonel J. H. Blundell, the C.R.E., came to the ditch and stood on the bank talking to Major W. J. A. Murray, O.C. 4 Field Company and Lieut. J. R. S. Baldwin of the same unit who were watching the Sappers at work. The crossings were in a bowl in the hills, and our tanks had just started to move through when the enemy began to shell the area. Two shells in quick succession struck the Sapper group. Murray, Baldwin, an American officer and several men were killed outright and many others wounded, among whom was Blundell himself. He lived only a short time and characteristically his last words were a message for his successor. Blundell was universally acknowledged as a first rate officer in every way and had already won a D.S.O. for his exploits at the Wadi Zigzaou. "His death is the greatest individual loss this Corps has so far suffered" wrote the Commandant of the Bengal Group. Another deplorable casualty at the Wadi Akarit was Brigadier F. H. Kisch, the brilliant Chief Engineer of the 30th Corps, who was killed by a mine while examining the enemy's defences after the battle. Major J. A. Cameron,

R.E., O.C. 12 Field Company, took over as C.R.E. 4th Division and Major E. B. Wheaton, R.E., relieved him as Company Commander. The command of 4 Field Company fell to Major R. H. Eagan, R.E., from 21 Field Company.

In the opinion of General Alexander, the battle at the Wadi Akarit was heavier and more savage than any since El Alamein. Attack and counter-attack clashed unceasingly in the hills, and the Germans, and many Italians too, showed ruthless determination and unimpaired morale. Alexander gives the major credit for the victory to the 4th Indian Division. Only through a number of vigorous counter-attacks launched by the 15th Panzer and 90th Light Divisions was General Messe able to extricate his army after dark in some sort of order. His casualties were very heavy, particularly in prisoners. No less than 7,000 of the more peace-minded Italians laid down their arms. Major-General de Guingand, Montgomery's Chief of Staff, relates an amusing incident in connection with one of these mass surrenders. "During the fighting", he writes[1], "we received a report that the enemy were forming up in considerable strength for a counter-attack, so we at once started laying on an air attack. But just as the aircraft were about to take off, we were asked to cancel the bombers. It transpired that this alleged 'counter-attack' was in reality a formation of Italians preparing themselves for surrender. They had been paraded and had marched over to us, each carrying a little suitcase packed as if for a week-end visit. "Sir. I beg to report my unit all present and correct for surrender". It was indeed surrender *par excellence* !"

During the afternoon of April 7th, 1943, an American patrol met a Gurkha patrol of the 4th Indian Division on the road between Akarit and Gafsa, and thus at last the two armies from east and west made contact. The men shook hands, grinned at each other, and exchanged cigarettes. Though they had made history, they took it as a matter of course. The Eighth Army was now part of a continuous Allied front. Long convoys felt their way to the north along the coastal road while the advanced troops fought several minor actions against the enemy's rearguards. Sfax was occupied on April 10th and Sousse on the 12th, and by the evening of April 13th the leading troops were up against the powerful anti-tank defences of the Enfidaville position. But by now the wear and tear of a long

---

[1] *Operation Victory*, by Major-General Sir Francis de Guingand, K.B.E., C.B., D.S.O., p. 267.

campaign had sadly reduced the strength of the Eighth Army. Instead of the eight infantry divisions arrayed at El Alamein there remained only a single British division, a British brigade, and the 4th Indian Division consisting of two brigades. Elements of three armoured divisions, with their lorry-borne infantry, were also to hand, but it was recognized that in the mountains of Tunisia the role of armour would be very restricted. On April 19th, in order to pin the enemy down in the south and thus ease the difficulties of the Britsh First Army and the Americans in the north and centre, Montgoimery was ordered to attack Enfidaville which he did on the following day, carrying the defences and advancing a few miles beyond them. Enfidaville proved to be a pleasant little place at the entrance to a narrow strip of coastal plain. Behind it, among olive groves and fields strewn with buttercups and poppies, the 4th Division enjoyed a brief rest and prepared for its next task.

The Axis forces, now under the German General von Arnim, were in a bad way though they had been strongly reinforced by air from Sicily. The British, Indian and American forces in the field were commanded by General Alexander, who had become General Eisenhower's deputy. On April 26th, the British First Army captured 'Longstop' Hill overlooking the Medjerda Valley west of Tunis, and on May 3rd the American 1st Armoured Division took Mateur only 20 miles from Bizerta. Meanwhile, as the Eighth Army had been unable to make further progress in the Enfidaville sector, Montgomery had suggested to Alexander that a part of his command might be more usefully employed elsewhere. Alexander agreed, and the result was a very long march for the 4th Indian Division. For the final drive on Tunis, Alexander assembled on his left the American 2nd Corps and on his right most of the Eighth Army. In the centre, for the main thrust, he organized a new 9th Corps composed of the 4th British Infantry and 6th Armoured Divisions of the First Army and the 4th Indian Division, 201st Guards Brigade and 7th Armoured Division of the Eighth Army, the whole being under the command of Lieut.-General B. G. Horrocks. This assault force was supported by overwhelming air strength.

The plan for the final attack was simple and straightforward. After pressure had been applied along the whole front, the two infantry divisions of the 9th Corps were to break through in the Medjerda Valley, and when the enemy's anti-tank defences had been over-run, the two armoured divisions were to head straight for Tunis from Medjez el Bab. The battle opened during the early hours of May 6th with intense bombing by the Allied air forces and a concentrated bombardment by more than 1,000 guns. At 3.30 a.m. parties of Sappers went forward to lift mines and cut gaps in the wire. Masses of infantry followed and by 11.0 a.m. had penetrated the main defensive belt. Then came the tanks. By nightfall they were far ahead, and on the afternoon of May 7th they were in the streets of Tunis. On the same day, Bizerta fell to the Americans. Yet even now von Arnim continued the hopeless contest. He withdrew into the Cape Bon Peninsula, the base of which was guarded by a range of hills with only two entrances; but during the night of May 8th/9th the 6th Armoured Division broke through the northern entrance and roared towards Cape Bon past German airfields, workshops, dumps and gun positions. "In a contagion of doubt and fear", writes Alan Moorehead,[1] "the German army turned tail and made up the Cape Bon roads looking for boats; and when on the beaches it became apparent to them at last that there were no boats, nor aircraft either, the army became a rabble". Fighting ceased on May 11th, 1943. The last shot had been fired in Africa.

The Indian Engineers were in at the death although they were unable to take an active part in the final stages of the hunt. On April 19th, 4 and 12 Field Companies and 11 Field Park Company were happy to welcome 21 Field Company of the Bombay Group. This unit arrived shortly before the Eighth Army became engaged in a battle on Mount Garci near Enfidaville which is said to have equalled Keren in violence but provided no immediate tasks for engineer troops. "In April we moved some 200 miles nearer to Tunis", writes Cameron as C.R.E., "and though there was no lack of work for the companies, we were not heavily committed in any operation and suffered few casualties. May has opened with the 4th Divisional Engineers making a forced march by night from the Eighth Army at Enfidaville to the First Army at Teboursouk. Both the 4th Indian and 7th Armoured Divisions have been switched over at a few hours' notice to take part in what we hope will be the final breakthrough to Tunis. Our vehicles are old and decrepit and many have no lights. There is no moon, so we are floundering along unknown roads in closest column, and every time a vehicle stops, those following bump noisily into each other like the trucks of a goods train. The nightmare journey comes to an end at last and H.Q. R.E. sort themselves out in a cornfield at Teboursouk". On May 5th he continues "The

---

[1] *The End in Africa*, by Alan Moorehead, p. 201.

battle has begun. The 4th Indian and 4th British Divisions are to advance side by side and capture certain hill features near a farm, and the 6th and 7th Armoured Divisions are then to go through and take Tunis. Sappers are to be prepared to deal with pill-boxes and mines and have 'Scorpions' and pilot vehicles under command. Tracks are to be made as we advance. At first there is heavy shelling and opposition, but suddenly the enemy seems to melt away and further objectives are taken without difficulty. Little or no Sapper work is needed". On May 7th, the 4th Indian Division advanced a short distance, and on the following day 11 Field Park Company moved up behind it. On the 12th, when Cameron visited 12 Field Company, which was operating with the 7th Brigade, he was an eye-witness of the historic surrender of General von Arnim to Major-General Tuker. Major Wheaton, the Company Commander, afterwards claimed that, but for a stroke of bad luck, 12 Field Company would itself have had the honour of capturing the German Army Commander.[1]

The main German capitulation began during the night of May 11th/12th when Colonel Nolte of the Panzer Grenadier Regiment came into the lines of the Royal Sussex Regiment seeking terms of surrender for his unit. He was given his instructions and 3,000 German Grenadiers capitulated soon after dawn on the 12th. The Royal Sussex moved on, and later in the morning a German Staff Officer arrived in a car with a personal letter from von Arnim which was passed on at once to Divisional H.Q. The 2nd Gurkhas, under Lieut.-Colonel L. J. Showers, who had been mopping up from another direction, came suddenly upon nearly 1,000 Germans forming up on parade while a Staff Officer waved a white flag. These men, veterans of the Afrika Korps, were smartly dressed, clean shaven and with boots nicely polished. They did not appear in the least down-hearted for they seemed to consider that they had done quite enough for their Fuhrer and that others could now bear their share of the burden. A senior German approached Showers and informed him that Colonel Nolte had already left to sue for terms of surrender, so Showers and some German envoys proceeded in a German staff car to 7th Brigade H.Q., meeting on the way a British officer who was returning to place a guard over von Arnim's Headquarters. Soon afterwards, Lieut.-General Sir C. Alfrey, the 5th

---

[1] *A Short History of the Queen Victoria's Own Madras Sappers and Miners during World War II*, 1939-1945, by Lieut.-Colonel R. A. Lindsell, R.E., p. 12.

Corps Commander, and Major-General F. I. S. Tuker, the 4th Indian Division Commander, arranged the terms of capitulation. Von Arnim emerged before sunset from his caravan to surrender to Tuker. His staff had already lined up and gave a punctilious display of Prussian military etiquette. The German Commander-in-Chief then entered an open car and was driven away, standing in true Hitler fashion and acknowledging the salutes of his men.

Some years after the great events described in this chapter, Field Marshal Viscount Alexander of Tunis wrote as follows:— "The campaign which culminated in the Battle of Tunis was the first wholly successful one against the Axis. The final victory in Africa was a complete example of the battle of annihilation. Never before had a great army been so totally destroyed. A quarter of a million men laid down their arms in unconditional surrender; 663 men escaped. Immense stock of arms, ammunition and supplies of all natures were the booty of the victors. Our own casualties in the final battle were less than 2,000 men. At 2.15 p.m. on May 13th, 1943, I sent the following signal to the Prime Minister:— "Sir. It is my duty to report that the Tunisian Campaign is over. All enemy resistance has ceased. We are masters of the North African shores". In all, the Axis casualties in Africa had amounted to nearly a million men. And what had our enemies to show for this stupendous wastage? Nothing whatever, except perhaps a brief respite for Hitler.

The Tunisian Campaign having ended, the 4th Indian Division was withdrawn by easy stages to Egypt, and with it went the Divisional Engineers. They left the Tunis area about May 18th, and on June 1st most of the Sappers were getting very sunburnt on the pleasant beaches at Misurata, 140 miles east of Tripoli. They had well earned this brief and delightful interlude. On June 13th, however, Major H. W. Kitson, R.E., who was commanding 4 Field Company, heard that his unit was to take part, with the others, in a big parade at Tripoli, and accordingly 4, 11, 12 and 21 Companies all vacated their palm-grove camps at Castel Benito and set off westwards along the well-known coast road. The parade, held on Saturday June 19th, was the occasion of a review of the 4th Indian Division by H. M. King George VI. The Royal car passed slowly along the ranks of 11 and 12 Companies and stopped opposite Lieut.-Colonel J. A. Cameron. The King shook hands with him and Cameron asked permission to present Subedar Narinder Singh. "Can he speak English?" asked the King, and being assured that this was so, enquired how many year's service he had. "Seventeen years, Sir", replied the

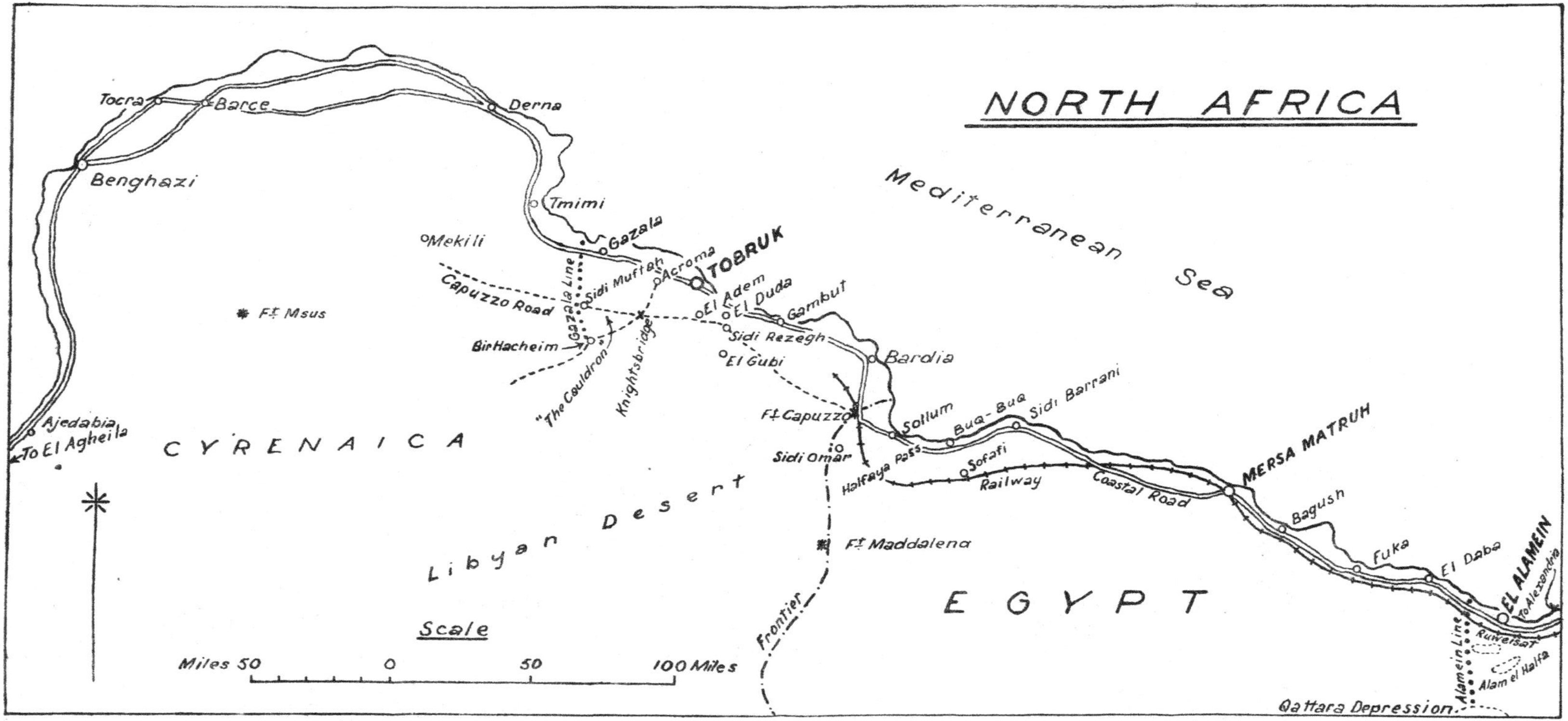

Reproduced by permission of
The West Yorkshire Regiment

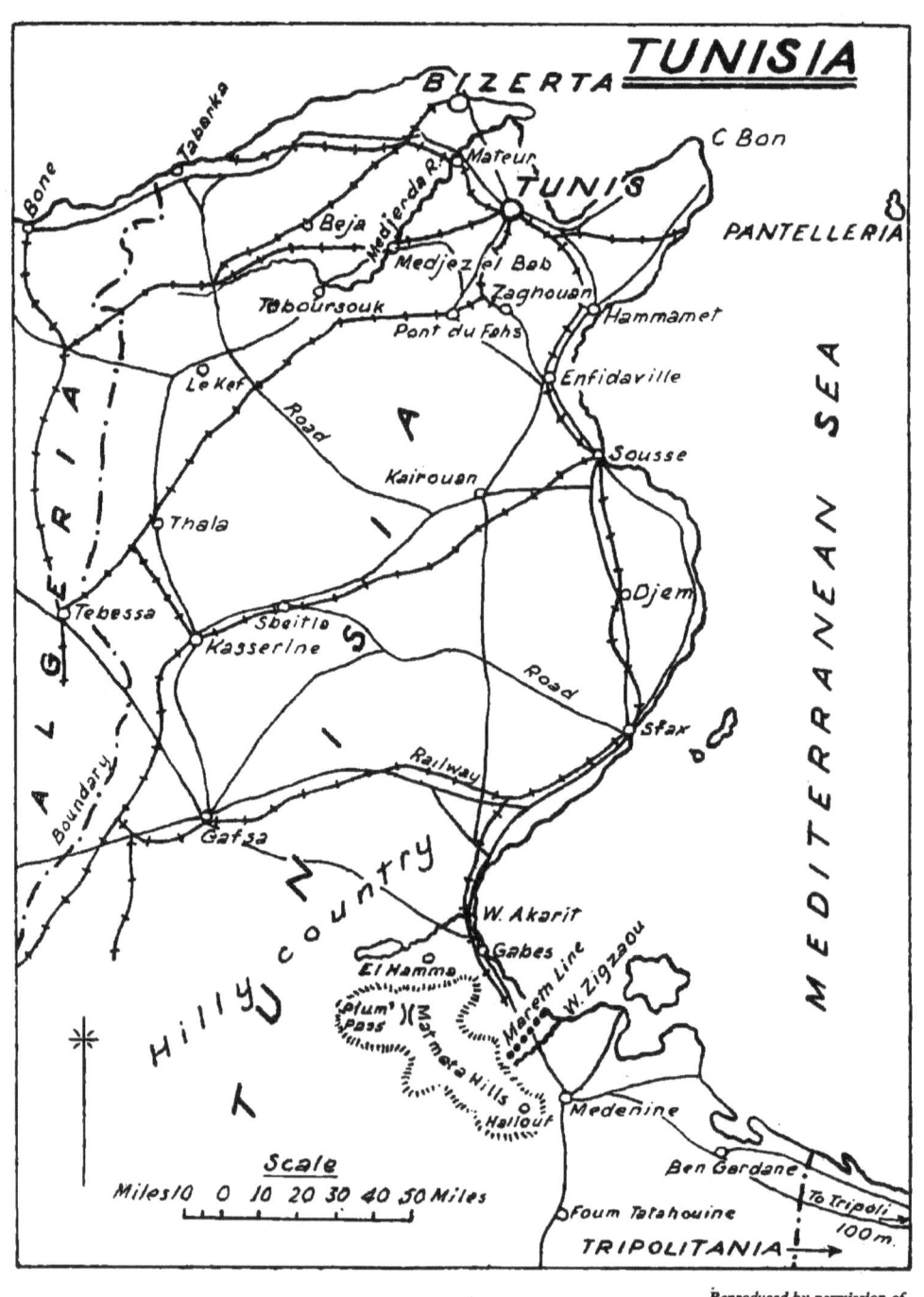

Subedar. "A good lot" said the King. Cameron then called for three cheers for His Majesty, which the King acknowledged standing up at the salute in his car. He was wearing a bush shirt without medal ribbons, a matter of some disappointment to a few of the men who had expected to see him in ermine robes and wearing a crown! As the cheers died away, the Royal car moved on, the King still standing and looking at the Sappers as he passed. It was an occasion the men never forgot.

On June 20th, the Sapper companies returned to Misurata and a few days later started on a journey of 1,500 miles to the Nile Delta. They reached Benghazi at the end of the month. On July 4th they were at Tobruk and four days later came to rest outside Alexandria. Their work in Africa was done. Many of their comrades lay buried on the battlefields between El Alamein and Tunis, and among those who returned, many wore proudly the ribbons for gallant conduct in the field; but all, living and dead alike, had maintained the high reputation of their Corps in a life and death struggle under terrible conditions against the pick of the German and Italian armies and had helped to secure an overwhelming victory for the Allies which changed the whole aspect of the Second World War.

CHAPTER VI

ITALY, 1943 – 45

IN the middle of April 1943, some weeks before the German surrender in Tunisia, the Allies were discussing plans for the invasion of the 'soft under-belly' of the Axis powers in Europe. Time was all-important, and Marshal Stalin was calling insistently and peremptorily for the opening of a second front. Three plans were considered—the invasion of Southern France, the invasion of Greece as a prelude to entry into the Balkans, and the invasion of Sicily and Italy. The French route was abandoned because of lack of shipping and air cover, and the Greek route because of uncertainty regarding the success of the Russian drive through Rumania and Marshal Tito's partisan movement in Jugoslavia. There remained the Italian route, much favoured by Mr. Winston Churchill and his advisers. Success here would make the Mediterranean safe for our convoys and bring Southern Germany within easy bombing range. So the invasion of Italy was approved. But unfortunately there was considerable delay in launching the operation. Landing craft were scarce, and the repercussions which might follow a repulse were unthinkable. The Allies therefore played for safety and bombed the small island of Pantellaria, south of Sicily, until it surrendered tamely to a sea-borne force on June 11th.

The invasion of Sicily, a necessary prelude to that of Italy, was to be carried out by the American Seventh Army ($2\frac{1}{2}$ divisions) under General Patton and the British Eighth Army ($4\frac{1}{2}$ divisions) under General Montgomery, the whole being under General Alexander. After a change in the original plans, it was decided that both armies should land near the south-east point of the island, Patton advancing north-westwards to Palermo and then swinging eastwards along the northern coast to Messina while Montgomery pushed up the east coast through Syracuse and Catania to the same destination. Sicily was garrisoned by five Italian infantry divisions and a similar number of inferior Italian coastal divisions, so that the only really stubborn resistance was likely to be from the German 15th Panzer and Hermann Goering Divisions which lay in reserve in the western part of the island. But once again it was considered advisable to spend some weeks in heavy bombing as a preliminary to assault, and consequently it was not until July 9th that a powerful air-borne force was able to land, followed on the 10th by the main sea-borne invasion. The Eighth Army met little serious opposition until it neared Catania, and the Americans occupied Palermo on July 22nd. Montgomery was held up at Catania for about three weeks; but after the 78th Division had come across from Tunisia to help him, he was able to fight his way slowly northwards. The race to Messina was won by Patton who entered the place on August 16th, 1943, after the Germans had made good their escape across the straits. Thus Sicily was conquered in about five weeks. It was a most propitious start.

Italy presented a very different proposition. Mussolini had resigned, and Marshal Badoglio was trying to gain time by negotiations. The Germans used this respite to pour thirteen divisions into the country. Not until September 3rd did Badoglio agree to surrender unconditionally, and by that time Field-Marshal Rommel held Northern Italy in a powerful grip and Field-Marshal Kesselring controlled Rome, Naples and all the territory to the south. Italy had become, in fact, a German province. The Allies had hoped that as soon as an armistice was announced, the Italian Army would change sides and help them in ejecting the Germans. Few Allied commanders envisaged a campaign throughout the winter of 1943-44, and none imagined that the fighting could possibly last until 1945. It was expected that Kesselring would withdraw at once to the Po Valley in the far north. Instead, within a month of Montgomery's crossing the Messina straits at Reggio on September 3rd, it became clear that the German commander had no such intention. Thus, as Alan Moorehead puts it,[1] the whole character of the Mediterranean war and the Italian campaign was changed, and all possibility of a quick run through Italy and the release of the Balkans vanished. The Allied forces were committed to a war of rivers and mountains in bitter icy rain, a winter campaign along some of the highest ranges in Europe.

The primary object of the invasion was the destruction of the German armies; but another, almost as important, was the establishment of strategic air bases in the Foggia district, on the Adriatic coast level with Naples, from which those parts of German Europe which were inaccessible from England might be heavily bombed. The Eighth Army, under General Montgomery, was to advance up

---

[1] *Eclipse*, by Alan Moorehead, p. 51.

the east coast, and the Fifth Army, under the American General Mark Clark, composed of the American 6th Corps and the British 10th Corps, was to land shortly afterwards on some beaches near Salerno on the west coast in order to capture Naples, which lay a few miles to the north.[1] An advanced sea-base would thus be secured. After the Italian surrender, it was decided also that a British Air-borne Division, followed by the 78th Division, should occupy Taranto in the heel of Italy and the other southern ports of Brindisi and Bari on the Adriatic coast.

If ever there was an Engineer war, this was it. "The advance up Italy was a veritable Calvary" writes Major-General de Guingand, Montgomery's Chief of Staff.[2] "Our speed was determined by the capacity of the Sappers to repair bridges and other demolitions. The country was ideal for delay and the Germans had evidently worked out a most efficient plan". Let us consider for a moment the configuration of the peninsula. If it had been flat, Alexander's task would have been fairly simple, for both his flanks rested on the sea and he had command of the sea and air. But unfortunately the country had a central and increasingly lofty spine composed of the Apennine range with peaks rising to 7,000 feet or more. An invading army advancing up the 600 miles' length of Italy had to negotiate an endless succession of rivers, ravines and spurs at right angles to the central spine, each offering a natural line of defence which could only be stormed frontally. "It made no difference if you captured some river valley" writes Moorehead. "Another lay just beyond, and beyond that, more mountains, more valleys, more impossibly entrenched positions. Huge convoys were bogged along the roads, and sometimes were halted altogether for hours or even days. A piercing wind kept sweeping down from the Apennines, and the Adriatic turned from cobalt blue to a sullen grey. Success seemed to be forever just round the corner; but each time the commanders reached forward to grasp it, something went wrong". There were few good tarmac roads in Italy in 1943: on the east coast, only one. On the west, from Naples onwards, two main roads led to Rome, and thence several others ran northwards to Florence, but they were often steep and winding and had long stretches still untarred. The Italians were among the best road-builders in the

---

[1] See the map of Central and Southern Italy included in this chapter.
[2] *Operation Victory*, by Major-General Sir Francis de Guingand, K.B.E.,C.B.,D.S.O., p. 318.

world, but money was scarce. The railway system was fairly elaborate though easily rendered unserviceable. Some of the rivers presented formidable obstacles. To the west of the Apennine backbone were the Volturno (350 feet), Garigliano (350 feet), Tiber (600 feet) and Arno (450 feet), all perennial and with high banks: to the east, the Biferno, Trigno, Sangro and a host of smaller streams, each liable to become a raging torrent after a storm of rain.[1] Lack of shipping and landing craft prevented General Alexander from attempting any extensive by-passing of the land obstacles ahead of him. He had to burst through each in turn.

On September 9th, 1943, six days after the bulk of the Eighth Army had crossed the narrow Straits of Messina unopposed, the Air-borne Division landed at Taranto and the Fifth Army began to disembark on the western beaches near Salerno. The Eighth Army advanced rapidly up Calabria, the southernmost province of Italy, in spite of many wrecked bridges and cratered roads, and by the middle of the month it was in contact with the right flank of the Fifth Army and co-operating with it in opening up the first important lateral communication through Potenza, a road and railway junction 60 miles east of Salerno. The Fifth Army met stubborn opposition soon after landing at Salerno, but on September 22nd it broke out from its beach-head in the direction of Naples, which fell to the British 10th Corps on October 1st. At once, the Germans began to draw in their horns. They had already evacuated Sardinia, and now they proceeded to abandon Corsica. Kesselring stood firm on the Volturno River, where the Fifth Army attacked him on October 12th and accomplished its first major river crossing. The fighting lasted four days and the Engineer units excelled themselves in bridging exploits. Kesselring then retreated to the Garigliano where he had decided to make a more determined stand. Meanwhile, on the Adriatic coast, the Eighth Army had occupied Bari and Foggia in spite of countless demolitions and steadily increasing resistance. Alexander had now got the airfields which he needed for strategic bombing, and also a major port on the west coast; but it was decided that, in order to safeguard these acquisitions and secure an adequate defence in depth, his armies should advance still further, say to a line running across the peninsula from Pescara to a point south of Rome, and if to that

---

[1] "An outline of Engineer Work in the Italian Campaign", by Major-General N. A. Coxwell-Rogers, C.B.,C.B.E.,D.S.O., appearing in *The R.E. Journal*, September 1946, pp. 189-206.

line, of course he must have Rome itself. Thus the lure of Baghdad, which led to the loss of the 6th Indian Division at Kut-el-Amara in 1916,[1] found its counterpart in Italy in 1943, though happily without such a disastrous result. Politically, the occupation of the Italian capital was certainly very important.

For some time after the fall of Naples, the Fifth Army could make little use of its facilities as a port. The place had been cruelly bombed. Most of the inhabitants were starving. Ragged children swarmed everywhere, crying for food. Looting was rampant: murder, commonplace. The black market, and vice of every sort, flourished exceedingly. All the public services had broken down. The sewers discharged into the streets. Typhus had begun to take its toll. The docks were a shambles. Wharves, sheds and cranes had been demolished by the Germans. Wrecks filled the harbour. The Fifth Army engineers had to produce order out of chaos, and they did it with remarkable speed in spite of time-bombs left behind by the enemy in such places as post-offices and telephone exchanges which exploded weeks later and killed hundreds of men, women and children. Gradually, Naples became a port in more than the name and after a few months was able to handle most of the supplies and munitions for the armies further north. But meanwhile came the first warnings of a very severe winter. Soon, half the elaborate paraphernalia of modern war was to become almost useless. The burden then fell on the infantry, "the man crawling in the mud" to quote a modern writer.

Such was the position in Italy shortly after the first units of the Indian Engineers had set foot on its soil in September 1943. The units were 7, 66, and 69 Field Companies and 47 Field Park Company, all of the Bengal Corps, under Lieut.-Colonel C. M. Maclachlan, R.E., as C.R.E.,[2] and they arrived with the 8th Indian Division which, with the 78th British Division, was to form the 5th Corps of the Eighth Army. After the Tunisian campaign, the 4th and 8th Indian Divisions had been withdrawn at first to Alexandria and the 10th Indian Division to Cyprus, and all three had been put through an elaborate course of training in amphibious and mountain

---

[1] See *In Kut and Captivity*, by Major E. W. C. Sandes, M.C., R.E., (the present author).

[2] Lieut.-Colonel C. M. Maclachlan, R.E., was wounded on December 19th, 1943, and succeeded by Lieut.-Colonel P. L. Kirwan, R.E., who was killed on May 9th, 1944. Lieut.-Colonel B. M. Archibald, R.E., then became C.R.E. 8th Ind. Div. Engineers until relieved on November 21st, 1944, by Lieut.-Colonel H. B. Calvert, R.E.

warfare in Syria, Cyprus or elsewhere though the Engineers had still to carry on their normal duties in addition. The three divisions had been ear-marked for Italy where proficiency in mountain warfare was a *sine qua non*, and for the Engineers, proficiency also in bridging. "Among the 8th Divisional Engineers", writes Pearson,[1] "69 Field Company completed extensive camp structures at Burg-el-Arab. Later, while 66 Field Company and 7 Field Company did bridging training in various parts of Syria at Meskene, Hama and Litany camps, 69 Field Company began assault landing training at Burg-el-Arab. During the months that followed, the units were much on the move—to Kabrit for 'wet-shod' training, to Djedeide where 47 Field Park Company spent some time, to Damascus, Haifa and Suez, wherever there was bridging training or combined operations to be had. In September, however, all moves coincided, and the 8th Divisional Engineers went to Alexandria and sailed for Italy".

As the 4th and 10th Indian Divisions followed the 8th Indian Division later to Italy, it may be convenient at this point to enumerate the Indian Engineer field units which served with all these divisions or with other formations in that country. The list is as follows:— *8th Indian Division*, 7, 66, and 69 Field Companies (Bengal) and 47 Field Park Company (Bengal): *4th Indian Division*, 4 Field Company (Bengal), 12 Field Company (Madras), 21 Field Company (Bombay) and 11 Field Park Company (Madras): *10th Indian Division*, 10, 14 and 61 Field Companies (Madras) and 41 Field Park Company (Bengal). In 1944, however, 5 Field Company (Bengal) replaced 14 Field Company. A body called '466 Corps Troops Engineers' was formed in 1944 and included 1 Field Company (Bengal), 14 Field Company (Madras) from the 10th Division, 97 Field Company (Bombay) and 301 Field Park Company (Bombay). 52 Army Troops Company (Madras) rendered good service on the lines of communication from February 1944 to July 1945, and there were in addition some Artisan Works Companies, several technical units and two Indian Engineer Battalions. From the foregoing list it appears that 16 Field units of the Indian Engineers fought in Italy, a very small number compared with the total of about 120 such units of British, Dominions, Armoured and Allied formations. Nevertheless, though outnumbered by more than seven to one, the Indians gave a very good account of themselves under conditions completely foreign to their previous experience.

---

[1] *Brief History of the K.G.V's O. Bengal Sappers and Miners Group, R.I.E., August 1939-July 1946*, by Lieut. G. Pearson, R.E., p. 59.

On September 24th, 1943, the three Field Companies of the 8th Divisional Engineers disembarked at Taranto after an uneventful voyage from Alexandria and 47 Field Park Company landed a week later. 'Sunny' Italy belied its reputation by providing a light fall of snow. It was cold and rather dreary. 7 Field Company was commanded by Major G. V. J. M. Smith, R.E., 66 Field Company by Major W. H. Cooper, R.E., 69 Field Company by Major R. G. G. Higham, R.E., and 47 Field Park Company by Major J. McLean, R.E. Within the next few days the units reached the battle ground near the German 'Gustav' Line, south of the Biferno River, having moved up the east coast by rail through Bari and past the captured Italian airfields around Foggia. The 13th Corps of the Eighth Army had recently crossed the Fortore River under fire, and now, on October 11th, the 5th Corps (78th British and 8th Indian Divisions) was resuming operations in the coastal sector while the 13th Corps (5th British and 1st Canadian Divisions) battered its way northwards through the foothills of the Apennines to Termoli. "The Engineers brought new tools for battle" writes Pearson.[1] "Bulldozers began to push their way northwards, impressing everyone with the amount and speed of their work. The Bailey Bridge, whose versatility equalled the simplicity of its construction, began to create temporary diversions and roadways as well as crossing the river gaps with astonishing ease. Rain turned streams into torrents overnight, sodden roads crumbled under unaccustomed traffic, retaining walls slid away from steep hillsides, and earth was churned into mud. Every bridge had been destroyed, and the approaches to fords and likely diversions had been heavily mined. The programme of the Engineers was therefore filled with road-mending, mine-clearance and continual bridging from the very start, and 7 Field Company opened it by bridging the Biferno, a minor stream covering the approaches to the more substantial Trigno".

Late in October, heavy rain began to fall as the 5th Corps came up to the Trigno. A crossing was forced by the 78th British Division while the 8th Indian Division held the enemy in front, and early in November, the Eighth Army, with the 5th Corps on the right and the 13th Corps on the left, reached the River Sangro behind which the Germans had withdrawn. The Sangro presented a formidable obstacle. High ridges overlooked both banks, and to the north

---

[1] *Brief History of the K.G.V.'s O. Bengal Sappers and Miners Group, R.I.E., August 1939-July 1946*, by Lieut. G. Pearson, R.E., pp. 60, 61.

were greater heights which gave the enemy perfect observation over the whole valley. Near the coast the river bed was about 1,000 feet wide, narrowing to 400 feet some miles inland. There were a number of fordable channels, but after heavy rain these might combine suddenly to form a raging torrent. Here the enemy had established his 'Winter Line', making no attempt to defend the river itself but concentrating his attention on the ridge beyond it, and so the Battle of the Sangro was really a fight for this ridge. Four or five times Montgomery had to alter his plan of assault, for as soon as one scheme was drawn up the rain pelted down, transport was bogged, supplies were lost and the troops could not move from their start lines. At last, on November 28th, a fine day dawned, and from a bridgehead already established across the river, the assaulting forces carried the ridge and the heights beyond and the German Winter Line was broken.

During these operations, the 8th Divisional Engineers were occupied mostly in road maintenance and mine clearance though they did a certain amount of bridging. The approaches to the Sangro were improved by laying Sommerfeld track, often under considerable shellfire, and when the river had been crossed, the ground beyond it was found to be so thick with minefields that a small party of 47 Field Park Company removed no less than 261 Tellermines in two days. The scene during the Sangro battle is described most graphically by General Coxwell-Rogers. "On November 20th," he writes,[1] "heavy rain fell and the river rose quickly, putting all fords out of action. Only one folding boat ferry could be kept in operation. On the night of November 21st/22nd, work was started on low-level Bailey bridges and by next morning one crossing for vehicles had been completed and another to provide a tank crossing. On the following night, a third Bailey was built. Then came the first serious spate. Nothing could be seen of the bridges except the tops of the girders in the middle of a sea of water 1,000 feet wide. Next day, however, the water level dropped quickly and it was found that the only damage was to the approaches to the bridges. By November 26th, three low-level bridge crossings were in action. The main attack was launched that night and a fierce battle ensued, but it was not until November 30th that the enemy was driven off the high

---

[1] "An Outline of Engineer Work in the Italian Campaign", by Major-General N. A. Coxwell-Rogers, C.B.,C.B.E.,D.S.O., appearing in *The R.E. Journal*, September 1946, pp. 189-206.

ground. During this time, two of the bridges across the river were knocked out by direct hits and replaced. On December 4th a high-level bridge, 350 feet long, was opened to traffic, but two hours afterwards the river had risen 6 feet and was flowing at 10 knots. By midnight, one pier had collapsed and every other bridge had become impassable. The 8th Indian Division, the 78th Division and the 1st Canadian Division, who were relieving them, were thus cut off from road communication with the south bank. However, by the afternoon of the next day, December 5th, the river level had fallen sufficiently for the work of repairing the high-level bridge to be started, and at the same time, the construction of another 350 feet bridge (partly of folding boat equipment and partly of Bailey equipment) was begun. Both these bridges were in operation on December 7th and an anxious period came to an end". This record furnishes an example of the sort of crisis which so often faced the British, Indian and Dominions Engineers in Italy in 1943 and 1944. The field units, and the formations which followed them, worked together in perfect harmony and with only one end in view—to help the other arms in their long and painful pilgrimage to the north.

Reviewing in more detail the work of the 8th Divisional Engineers during the Trigno and Sangro crossings it is recorded that on the Trigno 7 Field Company started by making a skidway down to the river and then a diversion round a demolished bridge. Afterwards it moved forward with the 17th Brigade and repaired other diversions. 66 Field Company, with the 19th Brigade, built a trestle bridge over the river and cleared mines, while 69 Field Company made a road up to the river and built a 70 feet Bailey bridge across it and a larger one further in rear. On the Sangro, 7 Field Company prepared approach roads before the battle and then, with 47 Field Park Company, completed a 100 feet Bailey bridge across the river which was shelled heavily on November 21st. Afterwards, moving with the 17th Brigade to the far side, it made a diversion round two craters which were holding up the tanks supporting the assaulting infantry and then cleared the road ahead of mines. Meanwhile, 66 Field Company had been lifting road-mines under fire. On November 27th it worked for most of the night on a floating bridge until held up by heavy shelling, and it also carried out much Bailey bridging over gaps.

A notable bridge should be mentioned here although the Indian Engineers did not build it. This was the 'Montgomery' Bridge, a

1,200 feet Bailey across the Sangro erected at the site of a demolished structure. At that time it had the distinction of being the longest Bailey bridge in the world. Work began on December 7th, when the floods had subsided sufficiently, and continued day and night until December 17th when the bridge was opened to traffic. The project was remarkably well organized, for all the equipment, plant and stores had to be brought forward along a single narrow road crowded with the maintenance traffic of three divisions.

There is a story about a party of Russian officers who appeared during the Sangro battle as an official mission sent to view the Italian front. They arrived full of bravado, boasting about the heroism of the Soviet armies and the desperate nature of the fighting during the advance from Stalingrad. So they had to be taught a lesson. They were taken up to a particularly 'sticky' sector to see how the fighting in Italy compared with that in Russia. This had the desired effect. On the second day of being under heavy fire, their leader remarked "Thank you. We have seen enough bravery for one day. Now we should like to have a little sleep!" From which one may gather that they were prepared to admit at last that their 'capitalist' allies could and did fight.

Pushing steadily forward from the Sangro, the Eighth Army occupied Lanciano on December 3rd, 1943, and was soon faced with a crossing of the small river Moro which barred the way to the port of Ortona. It was not until December 10th that the Canadians were able to establish a bridgehead across the Moro, and thereafter the advance towards Ortona was fiercely contested, particularly by some German paratroops. The 8th Divisional Engineers were very busy during the approach to Lanciano, building or repairing bridges, making diversions and sweeping the roads clear of mines, but their most spectacular feat was the construction over the Moro of what came to be known as "The Impossible Bridge". This was accomplished by 69 Field Company on December 9th. The scheme was considered impossible because the Bailey equipment could not be launched from the near bank owing to a right-angle bend in the road, and therefore it had to be done from the enemy side where there was sufficient room. Although the work was most hazardous, some bulldozers at once cleared a space for the bridging lorries. Detachments of 69 Field Company then crossed the river, cleared an area of mines, and cut steps in the far bank. Others waded across with stores, and by the afternoon a 100 feet Bailey spanned the Moro. On the following day, 7 Field Company added a third truss and made the bridge a 'Class 30' structure capable of taking most medium tanks.[1] Afterwards, it was lengthened and improved by 66 Field Company. The "Impossible Bridge" brought great credit to the 8th Divisional Engineers.

69 Field Company was presented with the Army Commander's flag for its work on the Moro. Later, with the other companies, it co-operated with the infantry advance on Ortona by building bridges, clearing mines and supervising Italian labour gangs. Ortona fell at Christmas, and with that event the operations on the Eighth Army front came virtually to a standstill while preparations were made for the winter. Some Italian Engineer units were formed to provide additional labour for roadwork and skilled tradesmen to help in 47 Field Park Company's workshops.

After Mr. Winston Churchill had visited the battle front with Generals Eisenhower and Sir Alan Brooke (C.I.G.S.), some notable changes ensued in the high command in the Mediterranean. Eisenhower was transferred to England to become Supreme Commander for the invasion of Northern France, and Montgomery followed him to command the 21st Army Group, the spearhead of the invasion. General Sir Maitland Wilson assumed the post vacated by Eisenhower, and General Sir Oliver Leese became Eighth Army Commander in Italy where both the Fifth and Eighth Armies remained under General Alexander. On December 31st, 1943, Montgomery handed over charge to Leese. He had already said goodbye to his senior officers and had read aloud a Farewell Personal Message which was issued later to his troops. "It is difficult to express to you adequately what this parting means to me" ran the Message. "I am leaving officers and men who have been my comrades during months of hard and victorious fighting and whose courage and devotion to duty have always filled me with admiration. What can I say as I go away? When the heart is full it is not easy to speak. But this I would say to you. *You* have made this Army what it is. *You* have made it a household word all over the world. Therefore, *you* must uphold its good name and traditions. I would ask you to give to my successor the same loyal and devoted service that you have never failed to give

---

[1] In general terms it may be said that the Classification number given to a bridge represented the gross weight in tons of the vehicles which it could support when spaced at 50 yards intervals. Thus a Class 30 bridge could carry most medium tanks except Shermans; but heavy Churchill tanks needed a Class 40. A Class 9 bridge could take 3-ton lorries, and a Class 5 bridge, 30 cwt. lorries and cars of all sizes.

to me. And so I say Goodbye to you all. May we meet again soon and serve together again as comrades in arms". It was a stirring message and no doubt it helped the Eighth Army greatly in its hard passage to the north while engaged in operations so different from the open fighting of the Western Desert. Perhaps Montgomery was more fortunate than those he left behind. That was probably the opinion of most of his officers and men.

Shortly before General Montgomery's departure, another contingent of Indian Engineers had arrived in Italy with the 4th Indian Division, a veteran formation of Eritrea and the Western Desert. The Engineer units, under Lieut.-Colonel E. E. Stenhouse, R.E., were 4 Field Company (Bengal) under Major C. C. Fraser, R.E., 12 Field Company (Madras) under Major E. B. Wheaton, R.E., 21 Field Company (Bombay) under Major R. H. Eagan, I.A.R.O., 11 Field Park Company (Madras) under Major M. C. Butterfield, R.E., and 5 Bridging Section (Bengal). 4 and 21 Companies and the Bridging Section had embarked at Port Tewfik (Suez), and 11 and 12 Companies at Alexandria, and on December 8th, 1943, they all landed at Taranto. Thence, they moved with the Division to the Potenza area and spent some weeks in bridging, constructing diversions and removing road-blocks. In January 1944, they proceeded northwards to take over a sector on the Adriatic coast beyond the Sangro River. Another Indian Engineer unit disembarked at Taranto in February. This was 52 Army Troops Company (Madras) under Major J. G. Brown, R.E., and it was sent to the Foggia district to build camps. Later in the month, most of the 4th Divisional Engineers were transferred, with the Division, to the west coast to help General Mark Clark's Anglo-American Fifth Army in the bitter struggle which was raging at Cassino, 50 miles north of Naples.

After the Volturno crossing in October 1943, the Fifth Army had been faced by a crossing of the Garigliano River and the flooded Pontine marshes before Rome could be reached. With winter rapidly approaching it was evident that a direct advance would be both long and difficult, so a plan was evolved for a sea-borne landing by several divisions at Anzio, 30 miles south of the capital, in order to cut the enemy's communications behind the Garigliano and thus force his retreat. The American 6th Corps (3rd U.S. and 1st British Divisions) was to make the landing while the British 10th Corps attacked across the Garigliano and the American 2nd Corps across the Rapido, a tributary of the Garigliano which ran southwards through Cassino. Before the Anzio landing was launched the

5th British Division was sent across from the Eighth Army to replace the 1st British Division in the American 6th Corps. The ball was opened on January 12th, 1944, by an attack by a French Corps on the right of the Fifth Army in order to threaten Cassino, and three days later the American 2nd Corps reached the entrance to the Liri Valley, a few miles south of that vital point. On the 17th, the 10th Corps launched an attack against the right of the 'Gustav' Line across the Garigliano. The river had been strongly fortified, and on the 19th the attack was held up. The American 2nd Corps then tried to cross the Rapido to the right of the 10th Corps and failed, and thus the main body of the Fifth Army was unable to join hands with the troops already landed at Anzio. No units of the Indian Engineers were concerned in these abortive operations. The Anzio landing was made on January 22nd, 1944, and achieved a tactical surprise, but unfortunately this advantage was not pressed to the full extent. The enemy held commanding ground a few miles inland, and the Allied forces were held up after penetrating only ten miles. Gradually the initiative passed to the Germans, who had been strongly reinforced, and within a week the beachhead was effectively sealed off. Once again, no Indian Engineers were present for they had not yet arrived from the Eighth Army sector, and thus they were spared some very unpleasant fighting in bitterly cold weather. However, their turn was soon to come.

Cassino, on the Rapido River about 20 miles inland from the west coast, was undoubtedly the keystone of the 'Gustav' Line. Its famous monastery, crowning a steep hill above the town, dominated the Liri Valley which led northwards towards Rome. The 1st German Parachute Division, every man a fanatical Nazi, held the Monastery hill and the adjacent heights with the utmost determination. Cassino was bombed and shelled till it was nothing but a wilderness of rubble, but the parachutists had the deepest of dug-outs and could not be ejected. Bombing only increased the horrid conglomeration of shattered brick and stone until it became almost impassable for our tanks, and so the burden of the assault fell entirely on the infantry. Most of the Eighth Army moved gradually from the coast towards Cassino to help the Fifth Army, leaving only the 5th Corps on the Adriatic side, and soon the 4th Indian Division, 78th British Division and 2nd New Zealand Division were in the fight. Three unsuccessful attempts were made to capture Cassino, but the towering Monastery height, and the village below it, remained in German hands. During these attacks, the Engineer units laboured on the improvement of mountain tracks so that tanks might be brought into action. The enemy had inundated large areas of the valley below and had thus obstructed the passage of vehicles, and every piece of open ground was mined. For more than six weeks the 4th Indian Division was heavily engaged at Cassino. 4 Field Company came under concentrated shell-fire immediately on arrival, and then, after twelve days of digging in drenching rain, made mule tracks towards our hill positions and a jeep track known as 'Roorkee Road'. Meanwhile, 21 Field Company had been busy on another remarkable jeep track which was called 'Cavendish Road'. This work was finished on March 11th by 4 Field Company and a New Zealand Field Company. The track led through the mountains north of Cassino and in one place had a gradient of 1 in 4. It was decided to widen it for the passage of tanks and make a new alignment to avoid a hairpin bend. The process of widening began on March 1st, and with the aid of compressors and blasting it was completed within the next ten days.

Some entries in 21 Field Company's War Diary make depressing reading. "*February 29th.* Everyone wet through. Work called off. All slit trenches collapsed. C.R.E. holds conference in 12 Field Company's lines about future of widening the jeep track for tanks and general maintenance of tracks forward of the River Rapido". And later. "*March 8th.* Roadwork as before. Camp being shelled regularly during daylight. Decision made to keep all men out of camp from 1600 to 1830 hrs to avoid casualties". On the night of March 11th/12th, the shelling was so severe that the men had to move into an adjacent nullah in order to get any sleep. Shell and mortar fire continued day and night, and 12 Field Company, which was building a close support track up Monastery Hill, worked under incessant bombardment. Many brave deeds were performed by the officers and other ranks of all the Sapper units. For instance, Lieut. A. Murray, R.E., of 12 Field Company, actually entered the ruins of the Monastery itself and so earned a Military Cross. Accompanied by a New Zealand sergeant, he was leading a small party of his men on a night reconnaissance when he accidentally passed into the enemy's forward positions. Noticing that the armed men around him seemed to be Germans, he and the sergeant hid behind a house, and then, descending into a cellar, ran straight into a party of the enemy. The sergeant was killed, but Murray shot three men and escaped from the trap. Outside, he shot another German before making his way back to our positions below Castle Hill where 4 Field Company was working on a tank track. Murray and his men are believed to have been the only Allied soldiers ever to set foot in the Monastery until it was finally stormed by Polish troops in June 1944.

The first award of the George Cross to a member of the Indian Forces occurred at Cassino. This honour was accorded posthumously to Subedar Subramaniam of 11 Field Park Company who on February 24th, 1944, was in charge of a small party of Sappers engaged in locating and clearing mines on the 'Cavendish' track. The Subedar was operating a mine-detector and behind him was a Lance-Naik marking the path with white tape. The Lance-Naik trod on a Schumine, and the Subedar, hearing the small initial detonation and realising that within the next four seconds the canister would be thrown into the air and explode with great violence, turned instantly, pushed his companion aside, and deliberately flung himself onto the mine. As a result of the explosion he died a few minutes later, but his extraordinary heroism undoubtedly saved the lives of Lieut. Young and five others who were close to the spot. "Greater love hath no man than this, that a man lay down his life for his friends".

On March 25th, the 4th Indian Division left the stalemate at Cassino and returned to the Adriatic front to help the 5th Corps. It was now the turn of the 8th Indian Division to attempt to burst through the Cassino barrier by forcing a crossing of the Rapido River below the town and fighting north-eastwards to turn the Monastery defences. The enemy's 'Gustav' Line followed the west bank of the Gari, a part of the Rapido, behind which was hinged yet another series of defences forming what was known as the 'Hitler' Line. Three crossings of the Gari were needed on the right of the 8th Divisional front. Minesweeping parties from the Sapper units went forward to clear the approaches to the river, levelling and widening the rutted tracks and covering them with shingle. All the work had to be done at night, and through unmarked minefields, because the enemy on the heights above could observe every movement by day. "On the night of May 11th", writes Pearson,[1] "an artillery barrage set the plan in motion. A platoon of 66 Field Company swept the opposite bank for mines, and the rest of the Company, with 69 and 7 Field Companies, began rafting and bridging operations. The infantry went across and the sappers then turned to

---

[1] *Brief History of the K.G.V's O. Bengal Sappers and Miners Group, R.I.E.,* by Lieut. G. Pearson, R.E., p. 65.

Subedar Subramaniam, G.C.

solve the problem of supply. Three bridges, named 'Oxford', 'Cardiff' and 'Plymouth', were begun. 'Oxford' was thrown across under intense artillery and small-arms fire by 7 Field Company under cover of smoke. The first tanks rumbled across. 'Plymouth' bridge was a triumph of mechanical improvisation, the result of collaboration between 69 Field Company and the Canadian Engineers. Built and carried on a tank, with another to push, it was run into place at high speed. With these two bridges as supply routes, the infantry west of the Gari were saved from probable defeat. Work was carried out in smoke and thick mist, but when the mist cleared, the shelling became very severe and bulldozing was dangerously unpleasant. 'Plymouth' bridge soon became restricted in use, but at 'Cardiff' the prolonged efforts of 7 Field Company were at last successful, and despite further shelling this bridge was able to ease the congestion of traffic. Fierce fighting drove the enemy back, and after the capture of San Angelo, 'London' Bridge, built by the Corps Sappers, was taken over. The 8th Divisional Engineers then did road maintenance and mine clearance in and around Cassino. Previously, Jemadar Sher Ali of 69 Field Company had won the M.C. in rafting operations, and now, at the 'Oxford' bridge site, Havildar Balkaran Singh of 66 Field Company won the M.M. and at 'Plymouth' bridge Naik Shazada Khan and Sapper Ghosi Khan of the same Company gained similar awards. Shelling caused many casualties, particularly in 66 Field Company while doing maintenance work on the 'Oxford' and 'Cardiff' bridges, and in 7 Field Company also as the 8th Indian Division moved forward to the Liri River. The Battle of Cassino, however, was won, and the brigades began to leap-frog with the Field Companies in close support".

Before leaving the Cassino front it may be well to give some more details of the extraordinary 'Plymouth' bridge constructed by 69 Field Company and the Canadians, for this was the first Bailey assault bridge built in the field. It was a single-double Bailey, 100 feet long, carried forward on two Sherman tanks. On the front tank it rested on rollers so that when this tank reached the gap the bridge could be launched by the rear tank by pushing. To complete the launching, both tanks moved forward, the one in front descending into the gap. The operation was carried out successfully although the front tank toppled into the river and was lost. The site came under heavy fire, and in an effort to launch the landing ramp the tank officer and one of the crew were killed and three Sappers were killed and five wounded, but an improvised ramp was made and the tanks were then able to cross.[1]

The general plan after the rupture of the 'Gustav' Line was that both the Eighth and Fifth Armies should attack simultaneously. The Eighth Army was to advance with the Polish Corps on the right, to the north of Cassino, and the 13th Corps on the left, to the south of that place. Then the Canadian Corps would attack on the left of the 13th Corps, breach the 'Hitler' Line and drive forward up the Liri Valley. Meanwhile, the Fifth Army would press onwards nearer the coast. The attack was launched with spectacular results. On May 23rd, 1944, the 'Hitler' Line was broken and thence-forward the the two armies progressed side by side. On the 25th, General Mark Clark's Fifth Army linked up at last with the Anzio beachhead force, and on June 4th it occupied Rome, which was found to be quite undamaged. Thus American troops secured the honour of being the first to enter the Italian capital—an event which was not quite in accordance with General Alexander's plan of campaign— but the capture of Rome was too important from a political point of view to warrant any critical examination of the methods by which it was secured. Rome fell exactly two days before the Allied landings on the coast of Normandy. Those landings were destined to have very serious repercussions on the Italian front where a process which Mr. Winston Churchill described as "dragging the hot rake of war up the length of the peninsula" was to be slowed down almost to vanishing point through lack of men, equipment and material.

While the final mopping up at Cassino was being done by a special Task Force, the 8th Divisional Engineers were engaged in rapid bridging during the general advance northwards. The Germans had been very thorough in their demolitions. 7 Field Company cleared road-blocks at Veroli, a few miles north-east of Frosinone, and 66 Field Company built a Bailey bridge further on. On June 7th, 69 Field Company encountered extensive demolitions at Subiaco, 30 miles east of Rome, and 7 Field Company came up to assist in building a Bailey bridge across a gap and in clearing road-blocks cleverly sited at hairpin bends. Mine-sweeping parties were constantly at work, and many small Bailey diversions were made across craters while bulldozers cleared the rest of the road. The work was often very dangerous. 7 Field Company, for instance, lost twenty men

---

[1] *History of the Corps of Royal Engineers*, Vol. VIII, by Major-General R. P. Pakenham-Walsh, C.B., M.C.

when a scout car was blown up on a deep mine. The pursuit of the enemy now passed far beyond the region of Rome, the rate of advance being governed mainly by the speed with which the Sapper companies could clear the road of mines. Heavy rain fell unceasingly and added to the difficulties of the situation. However, when the 8th Division reached Terni, 50 miles north of Rome, the advance began to quicken and several bridges, prepared by the Germans for demolition, were captured intact. Near Foligno, another 30 miles to the north, enemy resistance increased. Every demolition was covered by fire and progress became slow and laborious. This was not surprising, for only 75 miles further north the Germans were already hard at work on their next fortified zone, the 'Gothic' Line. June 29th found the 8th Division in the mountains south of Perugia, and afterwards, having covered 220 miles in 5 weeks, it was withdrawn to the Foligno area for a well-earned rest.

A few months earlier, while the 4th Divisional Engineers were enduring a purgatory of shell-fire at Cassino, a third contingent of Indian Engineers had landed in Italy with the 10th Indian Division or as Corps or Army Troops. In the latter categories were 97 Field Company (Bombay) under W. F. Eason, R.E., and 52 Army Troops Company (Madras) under Major D. H. Boydell, R.E. The two units disembarked at Taranto in February 1944 and moved up the east coast, 97 Company repairing bridges and roads and 52 Company building camps and jetties in the Foggia region. With the 10th Indian Division on March 28th came 10, 14 and 61 Field Companies (Madras) under Majors R. A. Lindsell, F. F. Radford and A. C. Cooper, R.E., 41 Field Park Company (Bengal) under Major G. T. Roche, R.E., and "A" Bridging Platoon (Bengal) under Captain T. C. H. Bateson, R.E. The C.R.E. was Lieut.-Colonel G. F. Hutchinson, R.E. Towards the end of April, the Division went to Ortona on the east coast beyond the Sangro River and joined the 5th Corps of the Eighth Army. Alongside it was the 8th Division until the latter left for the Cassino operations. Another Indian Engineer unit which landed at Taranto in March 1944 was 5 Field Company (Bengal) under Major M. J. Youngs, R.E.. This Company was first classed as 'independent' and was later posted to 466 Corps Troops Engineers. In June, as already stated, it joined the 10th Divisional Engineers in place of 14 Field Company. Another unit arrived in Italy during the summer of 1944. This was 301 Field Park Company (Bombay), and on August 11th came 1 Field Company (Bengal) under Major J. G. Wood, R.E. Both these Companies were posted to 466 Corps

Troops Engineers, a formation which also included 14 Field Company and 97 Field Company.

Some very extraordinary tasks have occasionally to be undertaken by Sappers in the field, and as an illustration one may quote from the experiences of 97 Field Company as given by Major A. B. Rhodes, R.E., who was a subaltern with that unit in Italy. "While my platoon was converting a school at Asto into a hospital", he writes,[1] "the senior Surgeon performed an operation on a man's stomach and removed a large pathological specimen which he thought would interest the Royal College of Surgeons in London. He turned to me for help. The specimen was about 18 inches by 12 inches, so the manufacture of a waterproof glass-topped case to hold it gave my carpenter quite a headache. However, he made the case and handed it over, but I never heard whether the specimen got safely to its destination".

The story of the achievements of the 10th Indian Divisional Engineers in the Italian campaign is told very fully in a volume written by Lieut.-Colonel Hutchinson.[2] In the Foreword to that volume, Major-General D. W. Reid, the Divisional Commander, makes the following comments:— "Infantry and Artillery can on many occasions avoid and by-pass certain known or suspected places of danger. You, the Engineers, cannot. Yours is a task of service, one of the proudest tasks of all. You have always a shrewd idea of the cold-blooded hazard which you are to encounter, and it is with open eyes and a high sense of duty that you have faced the wicked and deadly artificial obstacles which the enemy has constantly laid in our path". This is a fine tribute, and it might apply with equal force to the Engineer units of the 4th and 8th Indian Divisions.

In May 1944, the 10th Divisional Engineers were busily engaged in roadmaking and bridging in the Ortona area on the east coast. 41 Field Park Company carried out a fine piece of improvisation in the form of a nullah causeway called "Rockery Ridge" which carried the entire maintenance traffic of the Eighth Army for many months. At the beginning of June, the 10th Indian Division was relieved by the 4th Indian Division and moved across to Venafro, near Cassino, where 5 Field Company replaced 14 Field Company on June 22nd.

---

[1] Notes entitled "Personal Experiences in the Indian Engineers", by Major A. B. Rhodes, R.E.

[2] *History of the 10th Indian Divisional Engineers in Italy*, by Lieut.-Colonel G. F. Hutchinson, D.S.O., R.E.

The end of the month saw the Division on the move to the neighbourhood of Perugia where the Germans had established a temporary line of resistance across the Peninsula, based on Lake Trasimene. The Fifth Army was then advancing up the west coast, the main body of the Eighth Army was moving forward in the central Apennine sector, and the 5th Corps of that Army was advancing in the east coast sector, where it was due to be relieved by the Polish Corps. The 10th Division now took over from the 8th Division astride the valley of the River Tiber and improved the communications. Both the 4th and 10th Divisional Engineers worked in constant danger from mines. On June 27th, for instance, 61 Field Company met for the first time the "Riegel" mine. Lieut. Fraser, R.E., managed to lift and dismantle one of these horrible contraptions without accident, but afterwards three Sappers were killed and three others wounded when collecting some lifted mines. So unaccountable was the behaviour of these mines that orders were issued that they were never to be handled but merely pulled to one side and afterwards destroyed where they lay. The Engineer units of both Divisions made numerous tracks up to the forward troops, a notable example being one called "Jacob's Ladder" constructed by the 4th Divisional and 10th Corps Troops Engineers. This track rose 1,150 feet at an average gradient of 1 in 10, and when the clouds were low, it seemed indeed to lead to heaven.

As a further example of the danger from mines, the experiences of 10 Field Company on the road to Umbertide (beyond Perugia) may be quoted here. This unit, working in conjunction with 61 Field Company, was making a diversion to by-pass a demolished reinforced concrete bridge whose metal-work and rubble were scattered around. The splinters of metal made electrical detection very uncertain, and the rubble impeded prodding with bayonets. After a bulldozer had been at work for some time, there was a violent explosion. The driver, blown into the air, landed at the feet of the C.R.E. and bravely rushed back at once to stop his machine which was thrashing around with one track gone. This accident occurred in the darkness preceding dawn. When daylight came and the site had been carefully examined, bulldozing was resumed with another machine; but within an hour this also was blown up, and although the driver again escaped damage, one Sapper was killed and six others wounded. Mine-lifting had become a daily feature in the life of the men. Every day and along every road, Sapper parties picked their way gingerly with detectors and prodders, first clearing the roadway itself and then dealing with the ground on either side. As a rule they followed close behind the leading infantry; but sometimes, when the infantry were off the road and engaged in occupying some adjacent point of vantage, they were quite unprotected and consequently liable to be ambushed. Wooden 'Schumines' were met in increasing numbers. With these, as already mentioned, electrical apparatus was useless and too vigourous prodding was liable to cause a detonation. Colonel Hutchison therefore suggested that a process of raking might be substituted for prodding, and a light rake, with strong wire prongs mounted on a long bamboo handle, was produced in 41 Field Park Company's workshops at Umbertide, the wire being obtained from local vineyards. Except on very hard ground, these rakes proved most efficient and became quite popular with all ranks except the pronounced 'die-hards' who still pinned their faith on prodding. The 'rakers' sometimes caused considerable surprise to newcomers to the front. For instance, a newly arrived R.E. subaltern records that he was greatly intrigued one day to notice a line of smart bearded men, each armed with what appeared to be a garden rake, marching up the road, and then, at a word of command, attacking the surface with the utmost ferocity. A squad of 'die-hards', with bayonets stuck in their belts, reminded him of Captain Kidd's pirates, so bloodthirsty did they look! [1]

A few other stories by young Royal Engineer officers in Italy are worthy of record. A Sapper subaltern, going out to meet an infantry patrol on a dark night, lost his way and walked straight through our forward defence localities. Arriving eventually at the headquarters of a unit, he asked a sentry "Are you the London Scottish?", and not till then did he notice that the man wore a German helmet. As the unit was a Panzer Grenadier Regiment, he was very lucky to be able to fade away without being shot, but he managed to do so and found his way back to his own folk. Again, as an example of how far forward the Sappers sometimes had to work, there is the story of the Tank Troop leader who was recommended for a Military Cross for making his way successfully to the far end of a much shelled village. When he arrived there, he found a party of Sappers intent on brewing their tea. They had swept the road clear of mines some three days before! The Indian Engineers invented a very effective method of deceiving the enemy as to the site of a bridge under construction. They dug a few slit trenches on the river bank

---

[1] Notes by Captain D. Gardiner, R.E., dated January 3rd, 1953.

at some distance from the site and placed in each a Sapper provided with a hammer and an empty tin or piece of scrap metal. These men hammered vigorously while the bridge was being built and thus distracted the enemy's attention. It was a ruse which appealed greatly to their sense of humour.[1]

The pursuit of the German forces towards Florence continued steadily during the summer of 1944 though increasingly hampered by the demands of the invasion of Normandy and preparations for a landing in Southern France. Shortly after the occupation of Rome, General Alexander was ordered to release the American 6th Corps of 3 divisions, a French Expeditionary Force of 7 divisions, and large numbers of landing craft and aeroplanes for the adventure into the south of France. The target date was to be August 15th, and more than 2,000 ships were ear-marked to transport the invading army. The loss of ten divisions was a serious blow to Alexander, and particularly at a time when the Germans were about to rally on their carefully prepared 'Gothic' Line beyond Florence. It is true that he was to be reinforced by some Greek, Italian and Brazilian formations, but these could not be expected to equal the American and French divisions which he had to release. All hope of ending the Italian campaign in 1944 then vanished. Our diminished forces were destined to become more and more 'bogged down', in more and more mountainous country, against a more and more easily reinforced enemy, until the valley of the Po was reached. Another winter would soon be on its way, and to reach the River Po Alexander would first have to fight through the Apennine defiles, then to force the crossing of a succession of small rivers, and finally to traverse a flat stretch of country intersected by innumerable irrigation and drainage channels ideal for delaying tactics. Yet his sorely tried troops were not dismayed by the prospect, and even after the 4th Indian Division was sent to Greece towards the end of the year and a further four British and Canadian divisions were withdrawn to France or the Eastern Mediterranean in February 1945, the cosmopolitan Fifth and Eighth Armies still waged their war in Italy with praiseworthy energy and valour and brought it at last to a successful conclusion.

On July 21st, 1944, 4 Field Company arrived in Arezzo, only 40 miles south-east of Florence, and four days later, every man who could be spared went to the neighbouring 10th Division sector to

---

[1] Notes by Captain J. D. Watson, M.B.E., R.E., dated January 6th, 1953.

see H. M. King George VI who was touring the front. Soon afterwards, the 10th Division axis was switched across the Tiber towards the Arno Valley, and by the end of the month the general line Ancona-Florence-Leghorn had been reached and the River Arno crossed and bridged by the Fifth Army.

The decision was now taken to move the Eighth Army back to the Adriatic coast and there to launch the main attack on the 'Gothic' Line which extended across the peninsula from beyond the River Arno to the east coast about Pesaro. The 13th Corps was to be transferred to the Fifth Army, which would press forward towards Bologna, while the Eighth Army, comprising the 5th and 10th British Corps, the 1st Canadian Corps and some other formations, would advance up the east coast. Meanwhile, preparations were made to thrust towards the 'Gothic' Line in the central or Apennine sector, and on August 3rd, 1944, the 4th and 10th Indian Divisions began Operation 'Vandal.' "This", writes Pakenham-Walsh,[1] "involved the Sappers and Miners in the opening of a mule track, the construction of a jeep track and the provision of a tank road. It is recorded that 'giant boulders, crumbling surfaces, rocky ledges, patches of scrub and heavy forest alike succumbed to the caterpillars, picks and shovels and high explosives of the urgent Sappers. Neither enemy shell-fire nor direct attack impeded their progress. The team work of the engineers triumphed over every obstacle, and the bare log of accomplishment does less than justice to a superb achievement'. Six miles of jeep track were completed in 66 hours, and the tank track in 36 hours. As a result of the labours of the Sappers, the tanks reached their assembly position on the heather-studded crests on August 7th when a change in the general plan caused the operation to be called off". This cancellation was due to orders for the withdrawal of the 4th Indian Division to the Adriatic sector and the consequent necessity of extending the 10th Indian Division over the whole Corps front.

An exploit by 5 Field Company should not be missed. This was the gallant rescue of an Italian Countess from her booby-trapped castle by a platoon engaged in filling in craters in full view of the enemy. So impressed was the lady with the bravery and *sang froid* of the Platoon Commander that she asked him to repeat the performance next day by rescuing her maid, and this was duly accomplished

---

[1] *History of the Corps of Royal Engineers*, Vol. VIII, by Major-General R. P. Pakenham-Walsh, C.B., M.C.

although there were a number of Germans in the castle. History does not record the relative attractions of mistress and maid and consequently which rescue afforded the greater satisfaction. Humour of a rough and ready kind often helps to relieve the monotony of war, so here is an example. The 10th Divisional Engineers had almost completed a long track through the mountains except for a few narrow defiles, one of which, a leafy glade, was known as "Lover's Lane." This title was most appropriate and encouraging. But a little further on there was another notice. "Virgins not checked beyond this point" it ran. *Honi soit qui mal y pense* !

Cheered no doubt by such crude witticisms, the 10th Indian Division moved slowly towards the outposts of the 'Gothic' Line with other formations on either flank, while in the west the 8th Indian Division made good progress northwards from Siena along heavily mined roads. As usual, there were occasional fatal accidents. In a single week, while clearing mines under fire, 69 Field Company lost three officers killed. Often, as many as fifteen 'Tellermines' were lifted at one spot, each ringed with intricate booby-traps. Engineer patrols entered Florence on August 11th, 1944. The only undamaged bridge was found to be the celebrated Ponte Vecchio, but the approaches to it were blocked with rubble and mines. However, by August 14th, 7 Field Company had cleared a way through and forded the River Arno before handing over charge to the engineers of a British Division. 47 Field Park Company had already contrived to lower the water-level by opening some sluice gates, and thus the infantry were able to ford the river without much difficulty for there was no opposition. On the Adriatic side, the Eighth Army was now ready to move against the left of Field-Marshal Kesselring's 'Gothic' Line. The Germans were well placed to offer a stubborn resistance. Fortifications and mine-fields protected their lateral communications across the peninsula and barred entry into the narrow and winding valleys by which alone the Fifth and Eighth Armies could reach the crest of the mountains and descend into the plain of the River Po.

The assault on the 'Gothic' Line was opened by General Leese's Eighth Army on the Metauro River, south of Rimini, on August 26th, 1944. Initial surprise was secured, but the fighting which followed was some of the bloodiest in British history. Bridging on an unprecedented scale was involved, and the "Ark", or bridging tank,[1]

---

[1] The "Ark" was a turretless Churchill tank to which were attached, fore and aft, two American treadway tracks. "Arks" could crawl over each other, if necessary, to make a longer or higher bridge.

was used by our armour with great effect. General Mark Clark's Fifth Army then attacked south of Pisa on the west coast, meeting extensive bridge demolitions and long stretches of broken road; but by August 29th, with the exception of a fraction in the west, the entire 'Gothic' Line had crumbled. Five days later, the Eighth Army was on the move, and with the crossing of the Marecchia River on September 21st, the plain of the Po was reached by the forward troops.

The work of the Indian Engineer units during the Eighth Army's advance was exceedingly heavy. Their first task was to open and maintain communications for the leading troops through a welter of demolitions and mud, and in this they showed much ingenuity and resource. 61 Field Company, for example, built and operated an aerial ropeway across a gap where its bulldozers could not provide a causeway. 10 Field Company developed a new type of bridge. This was the "Houdini", which could be used at night but rendered invisible by day. It consisted of a steel cable taken across a river, through a couple of snatch-blocks, and back again to some tackle on the near bank. Timber decking was lashed to the cables. At dawn, by slackening the cables, the bridge could be submerged, and when the shoremost decking had been removed at both ends and the anchorages properly camouflaged with brushwood, there was no sign of a crossing place. Yet, soon after dark, the bridge could be operating once more to full capacity. 41 Field Park Company carried the necessary cables and tackle.

Behind the Field Companies came a host of Corps and Army Engineers, replacing Bailey bridges by timber or brick structures, often with the help of Italian labour, so that the Baileys could be sent forward for further use. These units also built high-level bridges to guard against interruption of the road communications by sudden floods. The road maintenance problem became almost insoluble when a deluge of rain began to fall in September. Continuous traffic crowded the narrow roads, which were mostly gravelled. The foundations became waterlogged. Torrents attacked weak points. Low-level bridges and culverts simply disappeared. High-level bridge piers led a precarious existence. Yet between November 5th and December 17th, the 8th Divisional Engineers, reinforced by other troops, opened 34 miles of road, maintained 64 miles, built 23 Bailey bridges (some of which had piers 70 feet high), constructed two folding boat bridges, replaced seven Baileys by timber structures, made a number of mule and jeep tracks and several aerial ropeways, provided water-points galore and built up dumps of stores. Their achievements were matched by those of the 10th Divisional Engineers. They could hardly have been more diverse.

As road and bridge maintenance was a major duty of the Indian Engineers in Italy, especially those behind the front, it may be well to record briefly some of the problems it presented and how they were solved. 97 Field Company, under Major W. F. Eason, R.E., had very extensive experience in this department when serving in 466 Corps Troops Engineers.[1] According to Captain D. C. Browning, R.E.[2], the unit encountered all types of ground—plains, marshes and mountains—and worked in all kinds of weather. When a tar macadam road had to be repaired while under heavy traffic both ways—a very common state of affairs—the most that could be done was to throw tar-coated chippings into the pot-holes and trust to the traffic to roll them in. Non-tarred roads were more difficult to maintain. The first step was to get rain-water off the road as quickly as possible by cutting small channels in the surface. Ruts and potholes were then repaired and the channels filled in. In the mountains, catchwater drains had to be dug. Ice-bound roads in the winter brought their own troubles and the only solution was to have one-way traffic in convoys in one direction and later in the other direction. Drivers could then keep to the crown of the road, though this practice was liable to produce two deep ruts with an ice ridge between them. Bulldozers were very useful for removing snow. When 97 Field Company had to build masonry bridges or culverts on main roads without interrupting the flow of traffic, the usual procedure was to place a small Bailey bridge over the gap and build the permanent structure beneath it with the help of Italian labour. Materials were sometimes very difficult to obtain. On the plain south of Florence there was no stone whatever and trucks had to go 15 miles to fetch bricks and cement; but later, in the mountains, plenty of stone was available from a large quarry operated by 301 Field Park Company. Diversions on precipitous mountain slopes were sometimes so difficult that new alignments had to be blasted. On one occasion the problem was solved by taking the road through a convenient railway tunnel which 301 Field Park Company illuminated with its own electric lighting set. As the winter progressed, snow clearance from all main

---

[1] 466 Corps Troops Engineers was an independent Group working under 16 A.G. R.E. and commanded by Lieut.-Colonel C. A. N. Peglar, R.E.

[2] "Road Maintenance in Italy", by Captain D. C. Browning, R.E., appearing in *The R.E. Journal*, March 1950, pp. 61-71.

roads above the 2,000 feet level became a priority task. This was done by special teams of men equipped with snow-ploughs and operating a number of 'snow posts' which had Italian labourers for manual work. Most of the Indian Engineer units took part from time to time in these activities and thus helped forward the invasion of the Po Valley.

Seriously depleted by the departure of the 4th Divisional Engineers to Greece at the end of October after 4 Field Company had bridged the Rubicon, the 8th and 10th Divisional Engineers laboured manfully through the bitter winter of 1944-45 in the mountain fastnesses of the northern Apennines. 5 Field Company of the 10th Division had distinguished itself in October by converting an old aqueduct on the Ronco River[1] into a first-class bridge while under heavy fire, and other units of both Divisions had shown similar bravery and ingenuity, but now a weary period of more or less static warfare had to be endured. The road maintenance work was heartbreaking. "There was danger and doubt in every turn of the road", writes Pearson.[2] "Once a bulldozer fell over the side of a cliff and turned over ten times before it landed with engine and tracks undamaged". Many new jeep tracks were blasted and bulldozed, and in the 8th Divisional sector 47 Field Park Company pulled down a number of houses to supplement the supply of stone from quarries. In two months, 69 Field Company built three large Bailey bridges, (240, 180 and 140 feet), 7 Field Company contributed no less than five (270, 240, 210 and two of 140 feet), and 66 Field Company built two (210 and 190 feet). 47 Field Park Company also completed four small Baileys out of a total of twelve.

On November 25th, 1944, 5 Field Company made an "Ark" crossing under heavy fire on the small river Montone. Another stream, the Lamone, was crossed on December 15th and the troops entered Faenza. The occupation of this town, which lies south-east of Bologna, opened the way for subsequent attempts to cross the successive barriers offered by the rivers Senio, Santerno, Sillaro, Idice and Reno which the Eighth Army had to traverse in order to by-pass the Valli di Comacchio lagoon and reach Ferrara and the banks of the Po. Meanwhile, a general thaw in January 1945, accompanied by heavy rain, brought most preparations to a virtual standstill; but

---

[1] See the map of North-East Italy included in this chapter.

[2] *Brief History of the K.G.V's O. Bengal Sappers and Miners Group, R.I.E., August* 1939-*July* 1946, by Lieut. G. Pearson, R.E., p. 110.

in February, after the rain had ceased, the roads and tracks became usable once more. March came and the 10th Division resumed its share in the preparations for a great offensive. The terrain in the plains where it now found itself was most difficult. Every small road was flanked by deep irrigation ditches and crossed at short intervals by others of the same kind. The roads were untarred and had no foundations. If a vehicle slipped, it fell into a ditch and remained there for hours. Every bridge had been demolished. Every river was protected by minefields and elaborately entrenched. It was fortunate indeed that our troops had now been equipped with many new devices such as flame-throwers, the most modern artillery and new forms of bridges, for otherwise the casualties which they might have suffered in traversing this deep zone of fortification do not bear contemplation.

The general offensive which carried the Allied forces through the 'Gothic' Line was halted with the Eighth Army on the River Senio and the Fifth Army separated from Bologna only by the foothills of the Apennines. The Eighth Army, however, had now not only to circumnavigate the Valli di Comacchio on the east coast but also to cross the many small rivers near it. In addition, large areas had been flooded by the enemy by means of cutting the high river banks. These sheets of water extended far inland and could be traversed only by following two dry corridors, named the "Argenta Gap". The Fifth Army was to deliver the main assault from the mountains west of Bologna and come into line with the Eighth Army south of the River Po. The Po having been crossed, the Eighth Army was to move on Padua and the Fifth Army on Verona.

As no Indian Engineer units were now serving with the Fifth Army, this account is concerned mainly with the Eighth Army which was directed to attack north-westwards across the Senio and Santerno Rivers on a narrow front, the 5th Corps on the right and the Polish Corps on the left. The 56th British Division of the 5th Corps was to strike straight towards the Valli di Comacchio. The 78th British Division was then to pass through a bridgehead established on the Santerno and swing right to help the 56th Divison in forcing the Argenta Gap while the 2nd New Zealand Division and the Polish Corps made for Bologna. When the 56th and 78th Divisions had broken out of the Gap, they would advance to Ferrara, and the 6th Armoured Division, passing through, would swing left to contact the Fifth Army and trap all German forces south of the Po. It was a sound plan, but later it had to be modified in some respects owing to the withdrawal of certain formations from the Italian theatre. The Divisional Engineers, and Armoured Engineer units under Divisional command, were to prepare all assault crossings over rivers and canals including rafting, low-level Bailey bridges, "Ark" bridges, folding boat bridges and mobile Bailey bridges, while the Corps Engineers were made responsible for main communications and high-level bridges.

After some preliminary operations, the Eighth Army attacked across the Senio River during the night of April 9th/10th. In the 5th Corps sector, the 8th Indian Division was on the right and the 2nd New Zealand Division on the left. The banks of the Senio were 30 feet above the surrounding plain and the slopes heavily fortified. Early on April 10th, 7 and 69 Field Companies and 564 Field Company, R.E., built two Class 40 Baileys across the river without much difficulty, but further west there was trouble in finding a site for an "Ark" crossing to be made by another unit, and 66 Field Company was therefore called upon to provide a Bailey bridge instead. The New Zealanders established a bridgehead very quickly and built six bridges for tanks. So skillful were they at this work that their methods for assault crossings were adopted by the Indian Engineer units. The New Zealand Engineers first collected their Bailey bridging material under cover of the near flood bank after a bridgehead had been secured, and then carried it over by hand. The bridge took the form of a 50 feet single-single low-level Bailey erected as separate single girders on a folding boat raft. When ready, the girders were lifted by man-power and the bottom pins inserted. Transoms and decking followed, and the completed structure was sufficiently strong to take Sherman tanks. The first bridges across the Senio were soon followed by others constructed by Corps Troops Engineers, and meanwhile the attacking troops surged forward to the next obstacle, the Santerno River, which lay three miles ahead.

Our tanks reached the Santerno very swiftly, followed by 66 Field Company with bulldozers to clear the approaches and later by the other Companies with bridging equipment. The Santerno was even wider and deeper than the Senio, and the task of the 8th Divisional Engineers was to get the first tanks and anti-tank guns across by dawn on April 12th to hold a bridgehead and then to build bridges strong enough to carry the vehicles of the 78th Division and a Tank brigade. 7 Field Company was to build an assault Bailey bridge for the leading tanks and guns, and 66 Field Company to provide the first bridge for wheeled traffic. Under heavy mortar and shell fire, 7 Field Company carried out its task. 66 Field Company constructed a floating bridge, and thus the 78th Division and the Tank brigade were able to cross the river and swing northwards towards the Argenta Gap. After the Santerno crossing, the 8th Indian Division was withdrawn to a rest area and the Sapper units repaired roads between the Senio and Santerno and opened up routes northwards from Ravenna towards the Argenta Gap.

The 13th Corps and the Polish Corps were now advancing on the left of the 5th Corps, but on April 13th, the 13th Corps was relieved by the 10th Corps and, with the 10th Indian Division, began to move across the rear of the Polish Corps to take over the sector of the 2nd New Zealand Division which would then come under its command. Every Engineer unit of the 13th Corps was to open a way for the advance of the New Zealanders. The attack went home with great power. On the 14th, the New Zealanders reached the Sillaro River, and six days later, the Idice. The latter was crossed quickly, and by April 24th, the New Zealanders were on the banks of the River Po some 24 hours after the 5th Army, on their left, had reached that river at San Benedetto, 45 miles north-west of Bologna. The 10th Indian Division was withdrawn into Corps reserve after arriving on the River Reno. All the Engineer units of the Eighth Army excelled themselves in the advance from the Senio to the Po, building altogether more than 400 bridges and other crossings. The 56th and 78th Divisions were also soon on the Po having broken through the Argenta Gap on April 18th and 19th. On the 23rd, they had by-passed Ferrara which was occupied on the following day by other troops. The enemy was now showing signs of disorganization though still prepared apparently to offer some opposition to a crossing of the Po by the 5th Corps near the east coast.

At this season of the year, the Po had a sluggish current running in a sandy bed between lofty flood banks about 400 to 1,500 feet apart. The 5th Corps was to attempt a crossing on a two-divisional front, the 56th British Division on the right and the 8th Indian Division on the left where a floating bridge was to be built, north of Ferrara, by the Corps Troops, followed by another, further to the east, when more equipment was available. Meanwhile, the divisions would have to cross by rafting. Each was allowed six rafts, some light, others heavy. The 8th Divisional Engineers began their ferrying operations north of Ferrara on the night of April 25th/26th. On the left, 7 Field Company built and operated a Class 9 Close Support raft from equipment which was quite novel to them, while on the right 66 Field Company operated two rafts. 69 Field Company produced a Class 40 raft for tanks. On the 13th Corps front to the left, the 6th Armoured Division and the 2nd New Zealand Division also crossed the Po without much trouble. At all the crossing sites the infantry were ferried over in advance in amphibious tanks and other motorized craft. They rushed onwards to traverse the Bianco Canal and arrived on the banks of the River Adige, 15 miles away, while the Sappers were still rafting and bridging far behind them. The pursuit was developing into a rout. The end was obviously in sight.

7 Field Company was the first unit of the 8th Divisional Engineers to reach the Adige. It arrived there on April 28th and immediately began to improvise rafts for jeeps. 66 and 69 Field Companies followed and built a 460 feet folding boat bridge which they called the "Roorkee Bridge". This was on April 29th, but on the same day, when the Companies were due to cross to the far bank, they were ordered to remain where they were. There were rumours that a German surrender was imminent and that Mussolini had been executed by partisans. Padua fell on April 30th. A number of bridges now spanned the Adige and all organized resistance had ceased. The 13th Corps, headed by the New Zealanders, chased some of the remnants of Kesselring's Fourteenth German Army across the Piave and Isonzo Rivers and entered Trieste on May 2nd while the 6th Armoured Division rushed northwards to prevent any escape into the Alps. Venice had already been occupied by the 5th Corps. Thus the war in Italy came to a glorious end on May 2nd, 1945, the day on which Berlin surrendered to the Russians and just a week before the final capitulation in Europe. Complete victory had been secured in the Italian theatre, but at what a cost in life and material! Could these sacrifices have been avoided by adopting a less ambitious policy? The verdict may be left to posterity who will be able to view the entire World War in better perspective.

So many officers and other ranks of the Indian Engineers gained awards for bravery in the Italian field that it is impossible to record all their names in this narrative. The outstanding award was, of course, the George Cross given posthumously to Subedar Subramaniam of 11 Field Park Company for his heroic act near Cassino in February 1944. Several British officers of the Sapper units won the D.S.O. and a much greater number the M.C. or the M.B.E. The names of many Viceroy's Commissioned Indian Officers appeared in the lists of awards as recipients of the Order of British India

Indian and British Engineers of the Eighth Army spanning the River Po with a 1,370 feet pontoon bridge, the longest military bridge in Italy

(O.B.I.), Indian Order of Merit (I.O.M.) and Indian Distinguished Service Medal (I.D.S.M.). The 10th Divisional Engineers alone secured no less than 13 Military Crosses. The other ranks in all three Indian Divisions could show a fine array of I.D.S.Ms. and M.Ms. (Military Medals), and the names of those mentioned in despatches would fill several pages. A point which may strike a student of the campaign is the absence from the Honours List of the names of any King's Commissioned Indian Officers (K.C.I.Os.) or Indian Commissioned officers (I.C.Os.) of the Engineer units. This is easily explained. Hardly any of these officers were present.[1] The Company Commanders and Company Officers of the units were almost entirely British. Their Indian counterparts could be more usefully employed nearer to their own country in the fight against Japan, but the experiences of a K.C.I.O. who was in Italy as a prisoner-of-war throw so much light on the Italian character that they should not be omitted.

As recorded in Chapter II, Lieut. Shamsher Singh of 61 Field Company set out in June 1942 to do demolition work west of Mersa Matruh during Rommel's breakthrough. He was not seen again, for he was captured and sent to Italy.[2] When the Italians surrendered in September 1944, the Italian Commandant of the Indian P.O.W. Camp at Avezzano, in the Abruzzi Mountains east of Rome, told the prisoners that he was to hand them over to the Allies; but on September 14th, after the Italian sentries had left their posts and no action had been taken, most of the prisoners dispersed over a countryside thick with Germans. As Shamsher and two other Indian officers had been promised a safe conduct to the British lines by an Italian doctor, they decided to await his appearance next morning. This was unfortunate because German paratroops arrived instead and the officers were obliged to hide for three days in the roof of a hospital building. One of them managed to walk out of the camp dressed as an Italian workman. Shamsher and the other arranged a *rendezvous* with the doctor in some woods and were just about to start out with an Italian guide when they heard a prolonged burst

---

[1] No K.C.I.Os. of the Madras, Bengal or Bombay Groups served during the war in Italy, though the following I.C.Os. were present: (i) Lieut. A. L. Talwar, 301 Field Park Company (Bombay). (ii) Lieut. P. K. Ramakrishnan, 61 Field Company (Madras). (iii) Lieut. K. M. Somana, 10 Field Company (Madras). After the war, Lieut.-Colonel R. E. Aserappa, R.I.E., commanded the 7th Engineer Battalion in Italy from September 1945 to February 1946.

[2] Notes by Colonel Shamsher Singh, Commandant Madras Group, Engineers, dated January 14th, 1953.

of machine-gun fire. A party of V.C.Os. had tried to rush the wire after dark and all had been killed. Nevertheless, Shamsher and his companion crept out later and headed for the small village of Luco, north of Avezzano, where the doctor lived. Their guide had vanished at the sound of the firing and they soon stumbled into a Panzer laager, but fortunately all the Germans were asleep and after four hours' marching they took cover in a haystack. At daylight they found they were close to the village whose inhabitants, including the doctor, gave them a most friendly welcome. There they stayed for some time, living in small stone huts among vineyards and climbing a near-by mountain by day to watch the British air-attacks below or to shelter in caves if the weather was bad. They fetched their food from the village—a daily dish of beans and macaroni and a lunch consisting of two potatoes and a slice of bread.

From the middle of October, the Germans started to hunt the prisoners-of-war with troops armed with mortars and machine guns, though without success. On November 5th, after snow had fallen, the fugitives managed to find shelter in Luco in a friendly farmer's house, but not for long because the man was terrified at the prospect of reprisals. Sure enough, a party of Germans arrived one morning before dawn, captured two of Shamsher's friends and asked "Where is the third man?" The farmer and his family refused to answer and were brutally beaten up. Shamsher was hiding under a bed. A German soldier removed the blankets, but when his electric torch went out he cleared off. The farmer's wife then reappeared, sobbing, and gave Shamsher some clothes in which he escaped alone into the hills. On December 8th, with two others, he started to try to reach the British front near Cassino. They ran into a cordon of Italian Fascists and had to turn back. At Luco once more, they were given shelter by a young Italian smuggler. This man was quite willing to take them in provided that they would agree that between his smuggling trips he and his wife should occupy the only double bed in the house! Of course, they agreed gladly, and during the long winter months they spent most of their time in bed while the smuggler was absent. Food was scarce and they were weak. On March 6th, 1945, as the weather had improved, they decided to start out once more. They climbed into the hills and immediately were engulfed in a storm. At 2. a.m. while sheltering in some caves, they were roughly awakened by a party of Germans. A Fascist had sold them for 5,000 lire apiece. And so, back they went to Luco and then to a P.O.W. camp after six months of comparative freedom in the Abruzzi Mountains.

No doubt, many other Allied prisoners-of-war had similar experiences in Italy. They had been advised by their Governments not to attempt to escape after the Italian armistice but to stay in their camps until liberated. This proved to be most unfortunate, for the Germans took charge at once. Yet many officers and men were hidden and shielded by the Italians until the Germans were thrown out of the country. Shamsher Singh records that his chief problems were cold, lice and Germans, in that order. The Italians themselves seemed to be simple, honest country folk, kind and hospitable. They gave of their best, and the services of some of them were duly recognized after the war. The Italian doctor, for instance, was awarded a M.B.E.

After the German capitulation on May 2nd, 1945, there was much work for the Indian Engineer units in the way of dismantling some bridges, completing others, building prisoner-of-war camps to hold thousands of the enemy, collecting stores and packing up. The 8th Divisional Engineers dismantled several bridges on the River Adige, including the 'Roorkee' Bridge, and 7 Field Company completed a 510 feet high-level Bailey bridge at Badia on the same river. Afterwards, the Division was withdrawn to a rest camp at Foligno, south of Perugia, whence it moved down to Taranto where 7, 66 and 69 Field Companies and 47 Field Park Company embarked for India on June 20th. They had a great welcome when they reached their headquarters at Roorkee in July. They were followed by other units of the Bengal Group. 1 Field Company embarked at Taranto on July 15th, but 5 Field Company and 41 Field Park Company of the 10th Divisional Engineers did not get away until November, as also the other two units of that formation, 10 and 61 Field Companies of the Madras Group. There was much reconstruction work to be done, and huge camps for prisoners-of-war were required at Rimini where 52 Army Troops Company was employed until it left for India in July. 97 Field Company (Bombay) and 14 Field Company (Madras) were kept in Italy until the autumn of 1945. 14 Field Company reached Taranto from the north in the middle of May and began to build P.O.W. cages for 50,000 men; but on July 18th, when it was actually on the quayside waiting to embark for India, the order were cancelled and it was sent far northwards to the region of Venice to build bridges, erect huts and demolish dangerous buildings. 97 Field Company suffered a like disappointment, and it was not until October 19th that both units were able to sail from Taranto.

By the middle of November, not a single Field unit of the Indian Engineers remained on Italian soil.

At the conclusion of the campaign Field-Marshal Alexander sent the following message to all the Allied Engineer units in Italy. "Seldom have Engineers been faced with a more difficult task than in the Italian campaign. By surmounting every obstacle which has confronted you, from the beaches of Sicily across the mountains and rivers of Italy to the Alps, and by developing with such success the local production of equipment and material, you have in no small measure contributed to our victory. Feats of engineering without parallel in any other campaign have been performed. You may be proud of your achievements and I congratulate you on your magnificent work". Thus the Indian Engineers, together with their British, American, French, Italian, Brazilian, Polish, Jewish, Greek and Algerian comrades, received a fitting recognition of their work in a long and exacting struggle.

The story of the Indian Engineers in Africa, the Middle East, Italy and Greece ends with their departure from Taranto after the defeat of Germany in all theatres. It is a remarkable one, but a still greater remains to be recorded—that of the war against Japan. This was an ordeal much nearer the home of every Indian soldier and consequently of more intimate concern to the gallant Indian Army.

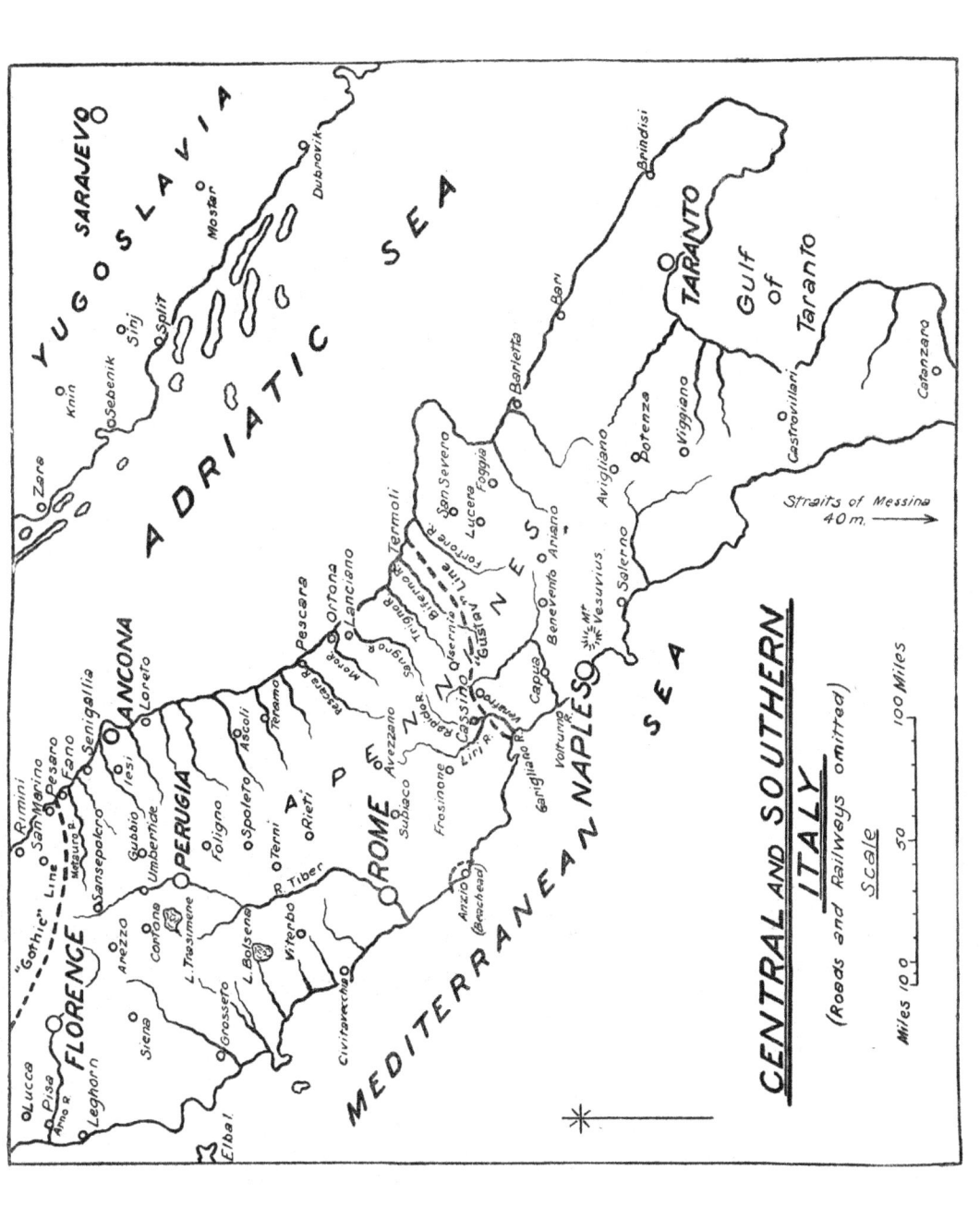

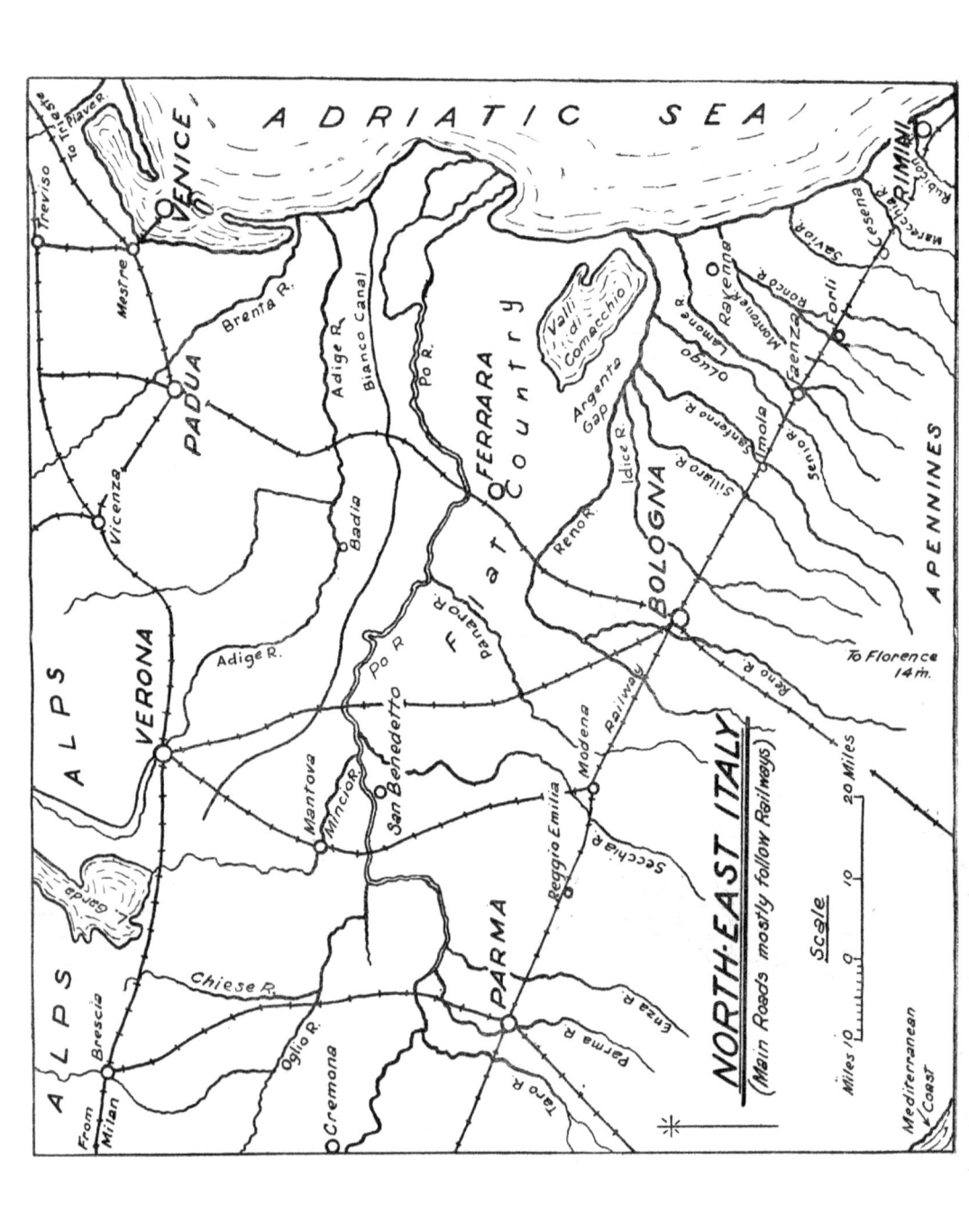

CHAPTER VII

MALAYA, 1941 - 1942

EARLY in 1942 the Bombay Sappers and Miners suffered the greatest disaster in their long record of distinguished service, for when Singapore surrendered to the Japanese they lost two-thirds of their Regular units. At Kut-al-Amara in the First World War they had lost two Field Companies[1], but at Singapore they were deprived of no fewer than four Field Companies, a Field Park Company and an Army Troops Company. Thereafter only by the most strenuous efforts could they recruit and train men to take the place of those who had become prisoners of war, for there were few old soldiers left in the headquarters at Kirkee to form a nucleus for an expansion which had to reach almost ten times the pre-war strength. Yet the seemingly impossible was accomplished, and with such speed that units were able to take a conspicuous part in the campaigns in Burma. The Madras and Bengal Sappers also suffered at Singapore though much more lightly. The former lost two Field Companies, an Army Troops Company and two Bridging Sections; the latter, a Field Company and a Field Park Company. The price exacted by a vacillating pre-war policy in Malaya was indeed a heavy one.

A fortress incapable of all-round defence belies its title. Such was Singapore in 1941. As in the cases of Sebastopol in the Crimean War and Port Arthur in the Russo-Japanese War it fell to an assault from land. So also did Hong Kong; but Hong Kong like Gibraltar was at least designed by Nature for defence. Singapore, on the other hand, had no such advantages. Deep shelters could not be dug in its flat expanses of reclaimed mangrove swamp. To seaward it was immensely strong. Two batteries of huge 15-inch guns, and many others of smaller calibres, could sweep the sea approaches for miles, but to landward it was wide open to attack. Under the conditions obtaining in 1941, it could no longer be considered defensible against a major assault unless we held command of both the sea and air. It was the site of an important naval base; but the base was located on the northern side of Singapore Island and separated from the mainland only by a very narrow stretch of water.

---

[1] See *In Kut and Captivity*, by Major E. W. C. Sandes, M.C., R.E., (the present author).

The Malayan Peninsula is about 450 miles in length from the border of Thailand (Siam) in the north to the narrow Strait of Johore which separates the mainland from the Island of Singapore. The Island itself is about 28 miles from east to west and 14 miles from north to south. Its only link with the mainland is the Johore Causeway, a wide and massive structure, about 1,200 yards in length, which carries two lines of railway, a road and some large water mains. A range of mountains forms a backbone to most of the peninsula. To east and west, there are coastal plains. The eastern coastline has many sandy beaches suitable for landings, but the western littoral is composed largely of mangrove swamps. Three-quarters of the peninsula is covered with dense jungle—huge tropical trees laced with strong creepers, impenetrable bamboo thickets, exquisite flowers and gigantic ferns. It is all remarkably beautiful and all equally deadly to human life. Malaria stalks the unwary. The humid atmosphere saps the strength of the intruder. Wild animals and poisonous snakes infest the forest depths, and the perpetual twilight beneath the canopy of tall trees induces a feeling of melancholia and malaise. Hundreds of small rivers and streams afford means of inland travel, but otherwise the communications in the interior are primitive, or were so in 1939. In those days a single line of railway followed the west coast northwards from Singapore to the Thailand border beyond Alor Star, with a loop line from Gemas to Kota Bahru at the eastern end of the border. The loop line continued onwards into Thailand, rejoining the main line near the port of Singora (Songkhla) on the east coast.[1] A good tarred road followed the west coast, but road communications on the east coast were often very defective or even non-existent. In many places, the jungle had been cleared to form rubber estates or mining areas, each of which had a network of small but excellent metalled roads. Out of a total population of 5,300,000 no less than 2,200,000 were Chinese. Indeed, they slightly outnumbered the Malays themselves, the remainder being composed of 740,000 Indians, 47,000 Europeans and Eurasians, 30,000 Aboriginals, 8,000 Japanese and some thousands of Jews, Arabs and other nationalities. The Chinese, mostly capitalists and traders, were pro-British in that they hated and feared Japan. The Malays disliked the Chinese because the latter had exploited their country; their attitude to the British was therefore doubtful. Some of the Indians were traders, but most were coolies

---

[1] See the map of Malaya included in this chapter.

from the Madras area. The Europeans and Eurasians were in Government service or employed in mining areas, rubber estates or business concerns. The Japanese were mostly spies disguised as photographers, fisherman, traders, or what not. In Singapore itself, three-quarters of the population of 700,000 were Chinese. It is obvious that Malaya afforded ideal opportunities for 'Fifth Column' activities, a fact which the Japanese were not slow to recognise. They surveyed the country, and its resources and peoples, with the greatest care.

In order to explain the nature of the employment of the Indian Sappers and Miners in the Malayan Campaign, it is necessary to examine the situation in the Far East after the First World War in which Japan had been our ally. Soon after the 1914-18 War it became apparent that an over-populated and ambitious Nippon might become inimical to our interests and that therefore we needed a naval base in Far Eastern waters to supplement Hong Kong. Singapore was selected as the site. It lay on the main shipping route between Europe and the Far East, and the Strait of Johore, separating the island from the mainland, afforded a fine natural harbour. Therefore it was decided in 1921 that we should establish a naval base on Singapore Island to counter any threat by Japan against Hong Kong, Malaya, British Borneo, New Guinea, Australia, New Zealand and perhaps Burma and India. Various schemes were considered, but when a Labour Government came into power in 1924 all preliminary work was suspended though it was resumed under a Conservative Government at the end of the year. This break in continuity was not only unfortunate but expensive. The defences of Singapore were designed on the presumption that the security of the base would depend on the ability of the British Fleet to retain control of the sea communications leading to it. The seemingly remote possibility of a landward assault on the island was, of course, considered; but with a British Fleet in full control of the seas, Japan's only hope of capturing Singapore appeared to be by a surprise landing of a small expedition near Mersing on the east coast of Malaya from which shore-based aircraft could operate. The expedition could not be large because the nearest Japanese base was at Formosa, 1,520 miles away, and the range of aircraft at that time was strictly limited. The defence of the entire Malayan peninsula seemed unnecessary. The problem was confined to the defence of Singapore Island and the adjacent waters, for which only a small military garrison would be needed. Therefore, as the landward side appeared to be secure, the naval base and other important installations on the island were placed on that side, contiguous to the anchorages in the Johore Strait. The seaward side was made impregnable by massing heavy guns capable of repelling any surprise attack by hostile ships which might evade our fleet.

The rapid development of air power soon began to affect the problem and it became possible that Singapore might be exposed to attack by carrier-borne and shore-based aircraft operating from much greater distances. By 1925, the question of the best means of closing the 'back door' to the fortress had become pressing. The Cabinet decided that it should be closed by air, operating from aerodromes as near the Thailand frontier as possible. Four years later, following on another change of Government in England, the work at Singapore suffered a further interruption and was not resumed until April 1933, when Japan announced her withdrawal from the League of Nations. It was then decided that work on the defences should be accelerated and completed within $3\frac{1}{2}$ years. Colonel A. C. Dobson arrived as the first Chief Engineer, bringing with him a large staff of R.E. Officers, and the armaments and defences on the seaward side grew rapidly.

The question of the best locations for additional aerodromes to protect Singapore from the north was already under discussion. At the moment, only one aerodrome was available, situated on Singapore Island. To obtain the greatest air-range in the direction of the potential enemy, Japan, it was decided that some aerodromes should be constructed on the east coast which had purposely been left without good communications in order to present an invading force with transport difficulties. The Army stipulated that these aerodromes should not be made unless they could be occupied and operated to full capacity by the Royal Air Force and properly defended by ground troops. An alternative plan for locating them on the west coast was abandoned because our aircraft would have to cross a range of mountains before coming into action eastwards. Army dispositions had to conform to Air dispositions, and the latter were dependent on suitable ground for aerodromes for heavy bombers. The only suitable areas on the east coast happened to be close to beaches which were, in fine weather, ideal for enemy landings, and accordingly the Army problem was extended from the defence of the naval base at Singapore to the defence of these exposed aerodromes. Eventually three such aerodromes were built. They were completed in 1941 just in time to be a priceless gift to the Japanese.

In November 1935, Major-General W. G. S. Dobbie (late R.E.) was appointed G.O.C. Malaya, and two years later, Colonel (afterwards Lieut.-General) A. E. Percival, who was General Dobbie's G.S.O.1., prepared an appreciation, from the Japanese point of view, for an attack on Singapore. The situation in Europe having deteriorated, Percival remarked that it was unlikely that the British Fleet could reach Singapore within 70 days, which was then estimated as the time during which the garrison might be able to hold out unaided, and that therefore the Japanese might be able to land powerful forces on the east coast, seize the aerodromes on that side, move across the peninsula to capture Penang Island, and finally attempt to take Singapore. They might even try to occupy Southern Thailand and establish bases there. Air and ground reinforcements were therefore urgently needed. It will be seen that the future Wartime Commander of the forces in Malaya was under no illusions as to the increasing danger of the situation. In May 1938, General Dobbie himself wrote that the greatest potential danger to Singapore was an attack from the north, and that such an attack could be carried out during the period of the north-east monsoon. He added that, contrary to previous ideas, the Malayan jungle was *not* impassable for infantry and that he was reconnoitring for further defensive positions across the peninsula some 25 miles north of Singapore Island. A line of concrete pill-boxes was started along the eastern half of this defensive zone and was being extended westwards when General Dobbie was succeeded in 1939 by Major-General L. V. Bond, (late R.E.), an ex-Bengal Sapper and Miner. The work had to be done mostly by contract labour so that secrecy was impossible. It is evident therefore that a serious attack on Singapore from the north was envisaged at least two years before it actually occurred even though, for various reasons, the measures taken to resist that attack were inadequate. Meanwhile, £60,000,000 had been spent on making Singapore the strongest naval base in the world. To seaward it merited that description, but only to seaward.

As already indicated, the defence policy up to the summer of 1939 was founded on the assumption that the arrival of the British fleet might be expected within 70 days of the outbreak of war against Japan, but the period was then extended to 180 days because of the critical situation in Europe. This extension immediately changed the defence requirements in Malaya. Given a longer respite from naval attack, the Japanese could afford to establish their main bases at a greater distance from Singapore, probably in Southern Thailand, with or without the consent of the Thais. It might therefore be necessary to hold the northern frontier of Malaya for several months against a powerful army, and it was estimated that, even if our Air Force could deal effectively with any sea-borne expeditions, we should require about 2½ divisions, with supporting arms, to hold our own. The problem, in fact, had developed into a defence of the entire peninsula and not merely of Singapore Island and a strip of the adjacent mainland. Full reliance was still placed, of course, on the ability of the French forces in French Indo-China to prevent an enemy advance overland towards Thailand and Malaya. The French were reinforcing their garrisons and seemed to be full of fight.

Such was the general situation shortly before war was declared on Germany on September 3rd, 1939. The garrison of Malaya then amounted to considerably less than the equivalent of one division, though afterwards it was reinforced from time to time as the political horizon darkened in the Far East. Malaya ranked low in order of priority for reinforcement because Japan was still neutral. However, the first nucleus of a Field Force was despatched as soon as possible from India. It consisted of the 12th Indian Infantry Brigade ("Emu" Brigade) under Brigadier A. C. M. Paris with some Mountain Artillery and 15 Field Company, Q.V's O. Madras Sappers and Miners, the latter being commanded by Major J. F. Godwin, R.E. Pending the arrival of more troops, the primary duty of the 12th Brigade was to defend the naval base on Singapore Island. 15 Field Company, together with 5 Field Company (Bengal) and 22 Field Company (Bombay), had been selected in 1934 for "Indianization,"[1] and all four subalterns of the unit were now Indians. They were Lieuts. Partap Narain, R. K. Kochhar, M. G. Bewoor and A. N. Kashyap. The Company disembarked at Singapore on August 8th, 1939, and for some months was employed chiefly on improving the accommodation on the island and building a light railway. "On August 10th", writes Brigadier Partap Narain[2], "I was ordered to take my Section to Penang. It was the only Engineer Unit in Northern Malaya so I spent the next few days in reconnaissances along the border. We reconnoitred all the roads and bridges, and particularly the railway lines, leading into Thailand. On a peaceful Sunday, September

---

[1] See *The Indian Sappers and Miners*, by Lieut.-Colonel E. W. C. Sandes, D.S.O., M.C., p. 657.

[2] "With the Madras Sappers", by 'Kashmiri', appearing in *The Journal of the Institution of Military Engineers*, October 1950, pp. 341-347.

3rd, as we sat in the Mess, we heard the news of the declaration of war against Germany. We started repairing the fixed defence lights and got the engines at Batu Maung working by the 13th, but otherwise life went on much as usual with parties, lunches and bathes on the beautiful beaches. On October 23rd I took the Section out to camp at Alor Star for a week. We lived in the drill hall of the Malaya Volunteers, a force composed mainly of European planters who, like everyone else in Malaya, took life very easily. One of our major tasks was to prepare the railway line from Thailand for demolition. All the bridges were prepared with charges in the abutments and steel plates on the girders for placing charges. My Section had not only to prepare the railway bridges for demolition but also all the other bridges on the routes into Malaya—a really stupendous undertaking as I had no other officers or N.C.Os to help me and only two havildars. After nearly six months in Penang we were relieved by another Section under Bewoor and moved to Kuala Lumpur to construct a brigade camp, and later, on completion of this work, we went back to Singapore and rejoined the Company in Tyersell Park Camp which housed our famous "Emu" Brigade under Brigadier Paris. From Singapore I went on various reconnaissances including those to the east coast where the Japanese finally decided to land in spite of the fact that it was believed at that time to be too treacherous for such operations."

The collapse of France in June 1940 radically altered the situation in the Far East. French Indo-China, under Vichy control, now no longer provided a buffer State north and east of Thailand. In September 1940, the Vichy authorities allowed Japanese forces to occupy the northern portion of their territory and thus to concentrate within striking distance of Malaya. The Japanese were then well placed to launch amphibious attacks, supported by shore-based aircraft, across a comparatively short sea-gap. Nevertheless, Japan was still nominally neutral, as also was Thailand whose inhabitants, it was hoped, would resist a Japanese incursion if we were careful to respect their neutrality and keep to our side of the border. It was obvious, of course, that Japan intended to invade Malaya at some future date, and from the summer of 1940 onwards, every effort was made to reinforce the garrison. Two British battalions arrived in August from Shanghai, which had been evacuated, and in October and November the 6th and 8th Brigades of the 11th Indian Division (Major-General Murray-Lyon) landed from India. In February 1941 came the first contingent of Australian troops belonging to the 8th

Australian Division (Major-General Gordon Bennett), and in March, the 15th Brigade of the 9th Indian Division (Major-General A. E. Barstow), followed in April by the 22nd Brigade. The 15th Brigade then joined the 6th Brigade to form the 11th Division which was to hold the frontier in Kedah State in the north-west while the 22nd Brigade, with the 8th Brigade, formed the 9th Division guarding the east coast.

In May 1941, Lieut.-General Sir Lewis Heath assumed command of the 3rd Indian Corps in Malaya which comprised the 9th and 11th Indian Divisions, the Singapore and Penang garrisons, and the Federated Malay States and Straits Settlements Volunteers. Roughly speaking, the two Indian divisions held the northern frontier and east coast and the 12th Brigade supplied the garrisons for the two islands. In the Malacca and Johore States, the 8th Australian Division blocked the road southwards to Singapore. But every division was under strength. Most of the men were practically untrained in jungle warfare, for which their equipment was also unsuitable. They were supported by inadequate air strength and artillery, they had hardly any anti-aircraft guns, *and they had no tanks*. This last was the fatal deficiency which eventually proved their undoing. Yet they did their utmost to prepare for the coming storm. Several anti-invasion defence schemes were launched in which the Engineer units took a prominent part. These included the preparation of defences at probable landing places near Kota Bahru and Mersing on the east coast and on Singapore Island itself, and also fortifying a 'Jitra Defence Line' in Northern Kedah, some 10 miles short of the nearest part of the Thailand border.

A number of Sapper and Miner Units arrived in Malaya during 1940 and 1941 to reinforce 15 Field Company of the Madras Corps, which, from December 1940 onwards, was under the command of Major R. B. Muir, R.E. Of the Bengal Corps, 3 Field Company (Major A. R. Beattie, R.E.), together with 43 Field Park Company and 54 Field Stores Section, disembarked in November 1940. During 1941, with various brigades, many Bombay Sapper Units made their appearance in Malaya. These were 17 Field Company (Major N. S. Bhagat, I.E.), 19 Field Company (Major M. Delmé Radcliffe, R.E.), 22 Field Company (Major H. T. Heard, R.E.), 23 Field Company (Major J. E. Bate, R.E.), 42 Field Park Company (Major T. W. Nash, R.E.), and 45 Army Troops Company (Major R. Dinwiddie, R.E.). 1 Artisan Works Company (Major J. H. Heep, R.E.), also landed. The Madras Sapper units which arrived during 1941 were

Jungle training in Malaya

46 Army Troops Company (Major J. R. S. W. Elkington, R.E.) and 6 and 14 Bridging Sections (later called Platoons). Neither of the Bridging Sections had their full equipment so they were employed mostly on defence work and 'ferrying' troops and stores from place to place. 13 Field Company (Major B. E. Whitman, R.E.), the last Sapper and Miner reinforcement sent to Malaya, did not reach the country until January 3rd, 1942.

When war was declared against Japan, Brigadier I. Simson was Chief Engineer, Malaya Command, having succeeded Brigadier J. A. C. Pennycuick in that appointment. Colonel H. A. Urquhart was Deputy Chief Engineer. The Chief Engineer, 3rd Corps, was Brigadier K. B. S. Crawford, an ex-Bombay Sapper and Miner of Kut-al-Amara days who, having been a prisoner of war for $2\frac{1}{2}$ years with the Turks, was destined to spend a still longer period in Japanese prison camps. The 9th Divisional Engineers (C.R.E. Lieut.-Colonel T. H. Lindesay, R.E.) comprised 19 Field Company (8th Brigade), 22 Field Company (22nd Brigade) and 42 Field Park Company. The 11th Divisional Engineers (C.R.E. Lieut.-Colonel J. F. D. Steedman, R.E.) comprised 3 Field Company (6th Brigade), 17 Field Company (28th Brigade), 23 Field Company (15th Brigade) and 43 Field Park Company. As Corps Troops, there were 45 and 46 Army Troops Companies and 1 Artisan Works Company. These, with the two Bridging Sections, complete the list of Indian Engineer units. In addition there were two Australian Engineer Field Companies with the 22nd and 27th Australian Brigades of the 8th Division and also an Australian Field Park Company. The Singapore Fortress Engineers, under Lieut.-Colonel H. M. Taylor, R.E., included 35, 36 and 41 Fortress Companies, R.E., and there was an R.E. Works organization under Colonel W. H. Treays, late R.E. An Engineer Section of the Federated Malay States Volunteers operated as Corps Troops, and another belonging to the Straits Settlements Volunteers helped the Singapore Fortress Engineers. Altogether, there was quite an imposing array of Engineer talent, but it came too late to save Malaya and it arrived in driblets. The Chief Engineer and his Deputy were saddled with much detailed work in connection with accommodation and other matters on the lines of communication and on Singapore Island from which they should have been relieved by the formation of L. of C. and Base Areas. Yet they never ceased to press for more defences at the front and on the island and to endeavour to improve those already in existence.

Based on the idea that attack is the best method of defence, a scheme had been evolved to counter a possible pre-war Japanese move into Thailand. This was to advance to and occupy the Thai port of Singora on the east coast which the enemy would probably use for an invasion of the Kedah State preparatory to a thrust down the west coast towards Singapore. At Singora, in the event of war, we should be able to meet the enemy on the beaches and make use of additional aerodromes, but unfortunately our forces in the Alor Star district of Kedah were 30 miles from the Thailand border and amounted to only two weak brigades of the 11th Division. A still more ambitious plan to advance to the narrowest neck of Thailand—the Kra Isthmus, 200 miles beyond Singora and adjacent to Port Victoria at the southernmost tip of Burma—was also considered but was abandoned as impracticable. A decision was reached that "Operation Matador", the occupation of Singora, should be launched when opportunity offered, and as this scheme involved an advance from an inland frontier village called Kroh in order to capture a commanding position called "The Ledge" on the road to Patani, which lay far beyond the frontier, some Sapper officers disguised as planters or mining engineers were sent to make the necessary reconnaissances. As a safeguard against the failure of "Operation Matador", the construction of a defence line was begun in Kedah itself. This was known as the "Jitra Line." Strenuous efforts were made to complete the undertaking in the limited time available; but labour was scarce, and without the necessary excavators and pumps, little could be accomplished. Much of the Jitra Line existed only on paper when the Japanese attack developed.

Meanwhile, on the east coast of Malaya, the 9th Divisional Engineers were busily engaged on beach defences. Again, there was not sufficient time, labour or materials. At Kota Bahru, the 8th Brigade had to defend no less than 26 miles of beach and 3 aerodromes. Additional pill-boxes were built hurriedly on the beaches by 19 Field Company while the infantry put up defensive wiring. Attempts were made also to extemporise anti-boat obstacles with timber in the absence of tubular scaffolding, but they were not very successful. There was only one way in which the brigade could hope to defend the beaches and that was by the use of mobile columns. These needed good roads; but most of the road-making machinery and transport had been allotted for the construction of seventeen airfields in various parts of the country. There was no road southwards from Kota Bahru. Communication was maintained along the railway line through Kuala Lipis and Jerantut. At Kuantan, further south, the problems of the 22nd Brigade and 22 Field Company were very similar except that communication was entirely by road as there was no railway connection. The river mouth at Kuantan presented a bottle-neck to any withdrawal as it had not been bridged. The construction of a floating bridge made of local boats was therefore put in hand. The boats had to be towed from Singapore since no road transport could be obtained. Many foundered *en route*, and those which arrived needed extensive repairs. Thus in spite of every effort, the Kuantan bridge could not be completed in time.

Some of the tribulations of the Sapper Companies with the 11th Division in the north may be gathered from an account by Lieut.-Colonel J. R. S. W. Elkington, R.E., who was then in command of 46 Army Troops Company.[1] This unit landed at Port Swettenham, near Kuala Lumpur, on June 4th, 1941, and moved northwards by rail to Sungei Patani, some 40 miles south of Alor Star.[2] It camped in a rubber plantation which the Madras Sappers, accustomed to brilliant sunshine, found most depressing. . "Even the birds and monkeys fight shy of rubber plantations" writes Elkington. "They are no places for men to live in." It seems that the prevailing habit was to locate camps on rubber estates. Good local communications were thus secured and also concealment from the air, but at a considerable price in comfort and happiness. Perhaps the Malayan campaign might have ended differently if some of the pre-war labour devoted to camp sites had been used instead on additional defence works. But ·it is easy to be wise after the event. The policy was laid down by Government and the Engineers had to carry it into effect.

The defence area allotted to the 11th Division extended from the Thailand border back to the mouth of the Muda River at Sungei Patani and was divided into a series of demolition belts. Of these, 46 Army Troops Company was responsible for three—Belt "A" on and immediately south of the border, Belt "B" centred on Alor Star, and Belt "C" centred on Sungei Patani and the Muda River. It was appreciated that in the humid conditions in Malaya the waterproofing of demolition charges would be very important, and 46 Company was the first unit to use a well-known rubber article,

---

[1] Notes entitled "46 Army Troops Company in the Malayan Campaign, 1941 to February 1942", by Lieut.-Colonel J. R. S. W. Elkington, R.E., dated March 5th, 1951.

[2] See the map of Kedah and Perak States included in this chapter.

obtainable from chemists' shops, to protect its detonators and primers. This soon became the standard practice with all Engineer units, and during the months that followed, every chemist's shop in the country was denuded. Malthusian principles were applied to warlike operations, and with remarkable success. Had this not been done, hundreds of demolitions would have failed while our troops were withdrawing before the enemy.

It soon became apparent that, if the Japanese attacked, 46 Army Troops Company might have to assist in the destruction of airfields. Some gelignite which the Royal Air Force had stored for this purpose had deteriorated, and the Company was detailed to remove and destroy it. A brown fluid was already oozing from the canisters so the task was highly dangerous and unpleasant, but it was performed without any casualties. During November 1941 the tension in the Far East increased, and on November 30th one Section of the unit was sent northwards to a railway station in Belt "A" on the frontier to demolish the station and a number of bridges while the remainder of the men worked in the Jitra position. The unit had been allotted its part in "Operation Matador." It was to move to Hat Yai Railway Junction, south of Singora in Thailand, for road maintenance, but it was likely that it might have to act also as a Field Company. For such a role it lacked the necessary equipment. Improvisation therefore became the order of the day. Bamboo was used to make Bangalore torpedoes and booby traps, and igniters for demolitions were manufactured from rifle cartridges, using a nail as a firing pin.

A Bengal Sapper unit which did good work near the Thailand border before hostilities began was 3 Field Company under Major A. R. Beattie, R.E. With 43 Field Park Company, it had landed in Malaya on November 1st, 1940, and had spent nearly a year with the 11th Division in the Jitra region engaged on the construction of concrete pill-boxes and other field defences, bridging, well-sinking and providing booms across the mouths of rivers. Meanwhile 43 Field Park Company, established first at Kuala Lumpur, operated workshops which produced sets of shuttering for the pill-box work and many other useful articles. In May 1941, it moved up to Sungei Patani to join the 11th Division and established a forward dump for the supply of materials to the Jitra Line, including sets of mobile timber bridging to accelerate the work. The Jitra Line, however, already extended some 18 miles inland from the west coast and it could not be properly fortified and prepared for demolition before the storm broke. The troops had been taught to think 'offensively.' They were eager to advance into Thailand and were confident that the position would never be used. This, no doubt, had some effect in slowing down the pace of construction although the infantry working parties and civilian labour gangs were busy from sunrise to sunset under very trying conditions. The truth is that the Jitra Line was located too far forward to stop a really serious invasion from the north combined with threats from the east.

At 7.50 a.m. on December 7th, 1941, 360 Japanese planes, operating from carriers below the horizon, made a surprise attack on the American fleet and installations at Pearl Harbour in the Hawaii Islands of the Pacific while Japanese envoys were in peaceful discussion with the American Government in Washington. No declaration of war preceded this unique act of treachery. The attacking planes came on in three waves directed against the American warships, moored closely in harbour, the troops in barracks and the airfields. Of eight battleships, one was wrecked, another capsized and three others were submerged. No less than nineteen ships were hit, though fortunately the aircraft carriers escaped damage as they happened to be at sea. Three-quarters of the aircraft at Pearl Harbour were destroyed on the ground, and a total of 2,800 officers and men were killed and 900 wounded. This dastardly act brought the United States automatically into the war against Japan, and with her, Great Britain. Italy and Germany promptly declared war against the United States. By a *coup de main* the Japanese Navy had gained complete command of the Far Eastern seas. In the Pacific, Guam and Wake Islands fell to the enemy; only Midway Island survived to form an American outpost. Hordes of Japanese invaded the Philippine Islands, north of Borneo, where the American General MacArthur put up a desperate defence. Hong Kong, the only remaining British foothold in China was besieged.

No Indian Sappers and Miners were in Hong Kong when it was attacked, but as the C.R.E., Lieut.-Colonel J. B. Wilson, R.E., was an ex-Bengal Sapper and Miner, a brief description may be given of the course of events. The small garrison fought with great determination though under hopeless conditions. They could expect no reinforcement by land, sea or air. As the defence plans pre-supposed a friendly China and envisaged only a sea-borne attack, the coastal artillery had been sited accordingly. The garrison took up battle stations two days before the Japanese crossed the land frontier at Kowloon at dawn on December 7th, 1941. Demolition charges were then blown and the forward troops fell back to a defended line across the Kowloon isthmus, but as the line was 11 miles in length there were insufficient men to hold it. A further withdrawal to the Hong Kong peninsula was unavoidable. There, a few days later, the enemy succeeded in making a landing and cutting the defence in two. Gradually, the garrison was worn down. Under continuous bombardment and assault, the defenders reached a state of complete exhaustion and on Christmas Day they were obliged to lay down their arms. Thus a natural fortress which was expected to hold out for 6 months fell in the short space of 18 days.

"The Japanese forces were well-trained troops who had served in China" writes Lieut.-Colonel Wilson.[1] "They were supported by ample artillery and the infantry had small quick-firing guns. For close support they relied on mortars which had a range of about 2,000 yards. Their artillery fire was accurate, but the shells were of poor quality. The infantry fought well with the bayonet. Air action took the form of frequent light raids with small bombs. After the surrender, the Japanese adopted their usual custom of giving complete licence to their victorious troops. There was much looting, rape and murder. The inhabitants were forced to pay elaborate signs of respect to the conquerors. The attitude towards prisoners-of-war was very uncertain. If you met an educated Japanese officer who was not responsible for you he might be quite friendly; but those charged with your custody were expected to treat you as something lower than a coolie. The rank and file of the P. of W. guards were Formosans. Only the officers and senior N.C.Os were Japanese. The real power was held by the Colonel—fat, elusive and repulsive—and by the N.C.Os and interpreters. The N.C.Os managed the Formosans and awarded punishments for most derelictions of duty. They dealt with minor cases with a slap, and more serious cases with a regular 'beat-up.' One got the impression that the enemy was desperately short of the real officer class." There can be no doubt that the Japanese habitually treated the rank and file of their prisoners-of-war with the utmost brutality. Hundreds died during a cruel march from Hong Kong after the surrender, and hundreds more during the ensuing years of captivity. To the Japanese soldier, surrender is an unspeakable degradation and he treats his captives accordingly. Simultaneously with the attack on Hong Kong, Japanese columns crossed into French Indo-China. Troops from enemy warships were landed near Bangkok and the Thai capital was

---

[1] Notes of Lieut.-Colonel J. B. Wilson, R.E., dated November 7th, 1951.

was occupied on December 8th. Within the next fortnight, the Thais signed a treaty of alliance with the enemy. Thus, except for such resistance as might be offered by three weak divisions, Malaya was immediately thrown wide open to invasion, not only by land, but by sea and air.

On December 6th, before Pearl Harbour, our air reconnaissance had reported two Japanese convoys, comprising both warships and transports, south-east of Cape Cambodia in Indo-China, and on the 7th an enemy aircraft, flying very high, was detected over Alor Star airfield. This was probably the first hostile machine to cross the Thailand border. The feasibility of launching "Operation Matador" now receded into the dim distance as the Thais had not agreed to allow our troops to enter their territory unopposed. The uncertainty of the situation was dispelled after midnight on December 7th/8th when the enemy landed on the beaches at Kota Bahru against stiff resistance, and without opposition at Singora and Patani in Thailand. At Kota Bahru they captured our most advanced aerodrome, and Singapore Island suffered its first air raids. "Operation Matador" was then cancelled and orders were issued for the occupation of the Jitra Line. The offensive, however, was not abandoned tamely to the enemy. Small raids were organized to cross the Thai border and delay the Japanese advance. A road column from the 6th Brigade, including two Sections of 17 Field Company, reached Sadao on December 8th and the Sappers prepared three bridges for demolition. Two of these were successfully blown before the column withdrew. An armoured train set out also, keeping in touch with the road column by wireless. With it went a Section of 3 Field Company under Lieut. S. V. Poyser, R.E. To guard against derailing and booby traps, Poyser lay on the front of the leading truck inspecting the line as the train proceeded and signalling back to the driver. After the train had travelled about ten miles beyond the border it came to a very large girder bridge which Posyer decided to prepare for demolition; but before the work had been completed to his satisfaction, firing was heard far in rear and the bridge had to be blown at once. The first attempt failed; but the next succeeded and the bridge was left with two halves precariously interlocked. The train returned safely and Poyser's Section then rejoined 3 Field Company which moved at once to support the 6th Brigade in the western portion of the Jitra Line.

Another raid into Thailand was carried out from Kroh by a column known as "Krohcol." 45 Army Troops Company operated with this column which soon met with considerable resistance from Thai troops and police. "The object of Krohcol was to reach a position called 'The Ledge', some 22 miles beyond the frontier" writes Lieut.-Colonel Dinwiddie who was then O.C. 45 Company.[1] "It was a place where the road from Kroh to Patani ran along a steep jungle-clad slope for about six miles affording a secondary route by which the Japanese could come in at the rear of the main British positions held by the 11th Indian Division in Northern Kedah. On December 9th, slow advances were made against the Thais opposing Krohcol, but in the evening their resistance broke and, early on the 10th, the 3/16th Punjab Regiment, supported by the Company, reached the southern extremity of 'The Ledge'. Two miles further on, the first Japanese troops were encountered and the remainder of Krohcol were ordered to occupy a lay-back position half way between 'The Ledge' and the frontier. Severe fighting lasted until the morning of the 12th, and eventually, as a result of enemy infiltration in rear and casualties estimated at 350, the order was given to withdraw to a prepared position just west of Kroh. The Company had to demolish six bridges *en route*. The first, a bamboo structure, was destroyed with axes, crowbars and saws as there had been no time to lay demolition charges. Shells and bullets from a Japanese tank flew over the heads of the Sappers for the tank crew could not depress their weapons sufficiently to bear on the bridge itself. The second bridge failed to go up (the only failure by the unit throughout the campaign). This was because the guncotton primers had become sodden through being exposed to heavy rain for several hours. Thereafter, all primers and detonators were protected by rubber sheaths obtained from chemists' shops. The other four demolitions were successful, and interference by Japanese tanks was thus effectively stopped on this route. On December 12th, Krohcol broke off contact with the enemy who nevertheless were quick to follow up as many of their troops were provided with bicycles. On the 13th, Krohcol was merged into the 11th Indian Division".

Meanwhile, the 9th Division was faring badly on the east coast. According to Lieut.-Colonel Muir,[2] heavy fighting took place against

---

[1] Notes by Lieut.-Colonel R. Dinwiddie, R.E., entitled "The Story of the 45th Army Troops Company, Royal Bombay Sappers and Miners, in the Malayan Campaign 1941-42", dated September 26th, 1951.

[2] "Sappers in the Malayan Campaign, 8th December 1941-15th February 1942", by Lieut.-Colonel R. B. Muir, R.E., appearing in *The R.E. Journal*, December 1950, pp. 433-454.

Japanese invasion forces supported by land-based fighter aircraft operating from airfields in Thailand. By the evening of December 9th, the enemy had forced our troops away from the Kota Bahru aerodrome. With unimpeded landings elsewhere, the situation deteriorated steadily until, on December 16th, a general withdrawal from Kelantan State was ordered along the railway which formed the sole and very precarious line of communication. It was completed successfully during the next six days. The 9th Divisional Engineers carried out much demolition work in the face of the advancing enemy, including the destruction of the longest railway bridge in Malaya. 19 and 22 Field Companies and 42 Field Park Company, all of the Bombay Corps, were responsible for most of the work, but 1 Artisan Works Company took its share. The War Diary of this unit throws some light on the confused conditions under which the fighting on the east coast took place. "*Peringat. 7th December*, 0100 *hrs*. Sound of heavy shelling 20 miles to north-east. O.C. Unit advised that Japanese naval forces were bombarding beach north-east of Kota Bahru. 0500 *hrs*. O.C. advised that Japanese forces had landed and were attacking Kota Bahru aerodrome. 2100 *hrs*. Telephone orders from Brigade Major, 8th Infantry Brigade, for unit to retire to Milestone 19 on Kota Bahru - Kuala Krai road. No transport available. *8th December*, 0100 *hrs*. Personnel commenced to march on foot from Peringat. Arrived Keteren 0330 hrs and embussed in lorries. Arrived Pulia Chondong Village at Milestone 19 . 0400 *hrs*. Peringat now in front line fighting...... *13th December*. Arranged to work with 19 Field Company...... *16th December*. Marched on foot to Kuala Krai for evacuation. Train departed 0930 hrs. Arrived Jerantut 1600 hrs. Camped in rubber. No shelter. No water. 19 Field Company arrived."

The methods by which the Japanese gained their rapid successes in Malaya should be considered. For years they had studied jungle warfare, no doubt with Malaya in view, and for years they had practised amphibious landings in all weathers. "They wore the lightest of uniforms" writes Ian Morrison,[1] "a singlet, cotton shorts, rubber-soled shoes, and sometimes Malay *sarongs*. Two prisoners captured near Batu Pahat were disguised as Chinese coolies. Our men could never be certain that the young Malay lolling on the far side of the road, or the Tamil coolie just disappearing into a rubber plantation, was not a Japanese in disguise. Undoubtedly,

---

[1] *Malayan Postscript*, by Ian Morrison, pp. 78, 79.

there was a native element working actively with the enemy, but there were many more who helped us, and native co-operation with the Japanese in Malaya never assumed the proportions which it did, for example, in Burma." The Japanese being mainly rice-eaters, were able to live off the country, while our soldiers were dependent on elaborate and diverse catering arrangements for which motor transport was needed. A Japanese soldier could set off alone into the jungle with a bottle of water and a ball of rice and subsist quite well on these for several days. Most of the enemy infantry were armed with tommy-guns or other light automatic weapons ideal for close-range jungle fighting. They had a plentiful supply of small hand-grenades and were supported by light 2-inch mortars. Mobility was secured by the use of bicycles, mostly commandeered from the inhabitants. They made full use of rivers, creeks or swamps which they navigated in collapsible rubber boats or native craft. Infiltration was the keynote of their tactics. Small groups were told to *rendezvous* at some point miles ahead in the jungle. There they would assemble and await their opportunity, keeping in touch with the main body by wireless. They might proceed to assault a small outpost frontally, but if they met with any considerable opposition they would always creep round to attack from the flank or rear. The tactics adopted by the Japanese in their advance down the west coast were largely amphibious. Launches towing barges filled with soldiers would move down by night, land the men and return for more. Parties so landed would strike deep into the jungle and lie quiet for perhaps two days before ambushing one of our convoys many miles behind the front. But the major advantage held by the Japanese was in the matter of tanks, of which, as already stated, we had none whatever. Our infantry also had very few anti-tank guns. The widely spaced trees of the rubber plantations offered no obstacle to the enemy's medium tanks which could accordingly bypass any position astride a main road and attack it from the rear.

Regarding the situation on the outbreak of hostilities, Lieut.-General A. E. Percival, G.O.C. Malaya Command, wrote as follows in 1946 after his release from captivity. "The Navy no longer controlled the sea approaches and there was a shortage of craft for coastal defences. The Air Force, in place of the 566 first-line aircraft asked for by the Air Officer Commanding, or the 366 approved by the Chiefs of Staff, had a force of only 141 operationally serviceable machines, very few of which were of the most modern type. There were no modern torpedo-bombers, no dive-bombers and no transport aircraft. There were also comparatively few trained pilots and a great shortage of spare parts. As regards the Land forces, the dispositions on the mainland had been designed primarily to afford protection to the aerodromes. Had it not been for these, better and more concentrated dispositions could have been adopted. As soon as the threat to Malaya developed in the summer of 1940, everything possible was done to strengthen the land defences; but time proved too short to put a country almost the size of England and Wales into a satisfactory state of defence...... I estimate that the Japanese employed a minimum of 150,000 men, with 300 tanks, in the Malayan campaign. Against this we had, on the outbreak of hostilities, the equivalent of 3½ divisions with fixed and anti-aircraft defences but no tanks. On the British side, the total number who took part in the campaign was a little over 125,000, though the strength in Malaya at any one time was considerably less than this and the number included a high proportion of Command, Base and Line of Communication troops."

By the afternoon of December 11th, the Japanese were engaging the outposts of the Jitra Line in Kedah and had established complete supremacy in the air where our old Buffalo fighters were no match for their "Navy O" machines. The Jitra Line was at that time the only obstacle between the enemy in the north and the Johore State, 450 miles to the south. The uncompleted eastern sector tailed away into the jungle. The western sector ran for 8 miles south of a large mangrove swamp, with pill-boxes and trenches sited in paddy fields and rubber plantations. As the enemy advanced, 3, 17, and 23 Field Companies, 43 Field Park Company and 46 Army Troops Company started their demolitions. About dusk, the Jitra Line began to crumble. News reached 17 Field Company before dawn on December 12th that the demolition of a bridge some miles north of Alor Star had not been effected. "This demolition was considered important" writes Major N. S. Bhagat,[1] "because the bridge was immediately in front of our forward defence localities and it was feared that the enemy might rush tanks and carriers over it. 23 Field Company had already tried to demolish it but had not succeeded. O.C. 17 Field Company then went up and reached the forward Section post. As our own guns were shelling the bridge, he asked Battalion H.Q. to have the shelling stopped to enable him to go forward, but the Battalion Commander advised him to wait as he

---

[1] War Diary, 17 Field Company, December 12th, 1941.

felt certain the bridge was held by the enemy. Shortly afterwards his words were confirmed. The enemy launched an attack but were held up. O.C. and party returned to camp after four or five hours in the forward posts. O.C's truck was riddled with bullets and had to be abandoned."

Up to 3 p.m. on December 12th, our troops continued to offer stiff resistance to increasing enemy pressure, but a portion of the Jitra Line along the Bata River was only thinly held. "A call for Sappers was made" continues Bhagat, "and 'A' and 'B' Sections were led straight to this sector. It was not realized till later that they would have to hold the line for the night. There was no food or water. Towards dusk, the O.C. contacted the infantry on the left and pointed out the extent of the position, and at about 8.0 p.m. fire was exchanged with the enemy". After midnight, the enemy began to infiltrate on both flanks. Orders for a withdrawal had already been issued, and 17 Field Company leapfrogged back with 3 Field Company, which was in position behind it. The two units then marched to Alor Star. This employment of Sappers as infantry prevented the proper demolition of the Alor Star road and railway bridges. The latter fell almost undamaged into enemy hands. It was hoped that by running an armoured train across it a slightly weakened section might be made to collapse. The train was set in motion and the driver jumped off; but the bridge did not collapse, and the driverless train was found eventually some fifty miles to the south.

Disaster on the sea had already been added to misfortune on land. The battleship H.M.S. *Prince of Wales* and the battle cruiser H.M.S. *Repulse*, which had reached Singapore on December 2nd, had sailed northwards on the 9th with escorting destroyers. As darkness fell, the squadron, under the command of Admiral Tom Phillips, R.N., was spotted by a Japanese reconnaissance plane and shadowed by more planes from dawn onwards. Being without air-cover it turned back and headed first towards Kuantan owing to an incorrect report of a Japanese landing. It then steamed southwards, but at 11.0 a.m. on December 10th a formation of enemy bombers approached and scored direct hits on both capital ships. Torpedo-carrying aircraft followed and the *Prince of Wales* was hit by a torpedo. More bombers and torpedo-carrying aircraft appeared and attacked continuously until first the *Repulse* and then the *Prince of Wales* disappeared beneath the waves with their guns firing to the last. The destroyers picked up survivors and made for Singapore. Our fighters arrived on the scene from a distant aerodrome too late to interfere. The loss of these two fine ships, combined with the crippling of the American Pacific Fleet, gave the enemy temporary command of the sea. Japan's long lines of sea communication were now safe. She could land troops wherever she wished on the Malayan coast. Singapore could be bombed at will by carrier-borne aircraft. Thailand became her ally, and waverers in Malaya began to go over to her side.

In order to break the morale of the Malayan population and at the same time to secure a good harbour and suitable aerodromes for an advance down the west coast, the enemy launched a violent air attack on Penang Island and the adjacent mainland. On December 11th, squadrons of dive-bombers wrecked the crowded native quarters of Georgetown on the island, killing hundreds of men, women and children. The population fled to the hills on the mainland. Further bombing followed, and within the next few days the Japanese occupied Penang after our small garrison had been withdrawn. No Sappers and Miners were present, though a Fortress Company, R.E., was there and demolished most of the installations before it left with the other troops.

By the evening of December 12th, the Japanese were in full possession of the Jitra Line and the 11th Division was withdrawing southwards to a position in the Gurun area which had been reconnoitred but not yet prepared for defence. The main road between Alor Star and Gurun traversed a vast paddy area, and from Gurun onwards to the River Muda it led through rubber plantations intersected in all directions by small roads. 3 and 17 Field Companies had already lost so heavily that 45 Army Troops Company was merged into the 11th Division to act as a Field Company. "From now onwards it was a tale of continuous retreat" writes Lieut.-Colonel Dinwiddie who commanded 45 Company at that time.[1] "There were many demolitions as well as the destruction of water-supplies and sometimes of machinery in rubber factories and tin dredges. The ordinary rules for demolitions went by the board. There were never enough infantry to protect final demolitions until the last troops had passed through. The Sappers protected them themselves and blew on the order of the rearguard Commander."

---

[1] "The Story of the 45th Army Troops Company, Royal Bombay Sappers and Miners, in the Malayan Campaign", by Lieut.-Colonel R. Dinwiddie, R.E., dated September 26th, 1951.

When the 6th Brigade of the 11th Division reached Gurun on December 14th, the men were so exhausted that little digging was possible. Within the next 24 hours the enemy had burst through and the retreat was resumed. Our rearguards did their best to check the flood, and 3 Field Company, in a chaos of traffic and an atmosphere of overpowering uneasiness, fell back with the main body and blew demolitions whenever opportunity offered. The usual procedure was to take up a position in front of a demolition belt, and when the enemy attacked, to withdraw through the demolitions which were then blown to give the tired infantry time to get back to the next selected position. The 12th Brigade was now brought up to the front from the south, and with it came 15 Field Company. Its task was to protect the right flank of the 11th Division from encirclement by Japanese forces moving down from Patani on the east coast. Contact with the enemy was established north of Grik on the night of December 16th/17th and during the next five days a fierce battle raged down the Grik road as far as its junction with the main road at Kuala Kangsar. Our troops counter-attacked repeatedly, and thus the 11th Division escaped encirclement. 15 Field Company and 46 Army Troops Company carried out many demolitions, and 6 Bridging Section did excellent work in ferrying back engineer stores and men. The destruction of the main road bridge over the Muda River near Sungei Patani fell to 46 Army Troops Company. The bridge had large reinforced-concrete bowstring girders, and two Sections worked on it for nearly three days, often under machine-gun fire from enemy planes. The demolition was fairly successful in the end although a hitch occurred when someone was found to have inadvertently connected the electric leads wrongly.[1] Two of the three spans were brought down and the back of one of them was shattered.

The hard pressed 11th Division was soon across the Muda River. While 46 Army Troops Company was demolishing the concrete bridge, "A" Section of 17 Field Company had been trying to destroy a wooden bridge. This type was particularly difficult to deal with as the wood would not burn and the beams seemed to hang together by their fibres even when cut individually. Meanwhile, "C" Section was sinking all boats on the river. "B" Section could do little as 33 men were missing. On December 17th, "A" Section was busy at Butterworth opposite Penang Island destroying cranes, petrol tanks,

---

[1] *A Short History of the Q.V's O. Madras Sappers and Miners during World War II*, 1939-1945, by Lieut-Colonel R. A. Lindsell, R.E., p. 25.

rice stores and boats, while the survivors of "B" Section set fire to aircraft and cratered the runways of the aerodrome. "C" Section sank large tugs and boats but had to leave intact a plentiful supply of Engineer stores. Only a few hours were available for the work which, according to the War Diary, could have occupied the Company fully for four days. Before dark, the unit concentrated in Taiping near Kuala Kangsar.

The next obstacle to the enemy's advance was the Perak River which flows southwards through swamps and then turns to reach the sea 60 miles below Taiping. On December 19th, 17 Field Company was at a place called Parit on this river preparing to destroy the important Blanjar Pontoon Bridge. This bridge was in three portions, a ramp on the right bank, a pontoon section in the middle, and a ramp on the left bank. The maximum depth of water was about 8 feet. Major N. S. Bhagat decided to swing the floating portion across the river to the left or near bank before destroying it in order to prevent the enemy from using the grounded pontoons to effect a passage. By the afternoon of the 22nd, the near end had been anchored and cutting charges placed in position. The 28th Brigade was expected to cross that evening, but it did not appear as it had taken another route. It was learned on the 23rd that only one battalion and some armoured cars would cross. From morning till evening the enemy bombed the bridge and its approaches, hitting it in three places and severing all detonation circuits. Not until after dark could work be resumed, the first task being to make the bridge usable once more. This was accomplished by 10 p.m. and the {waiting column began to cross, the last vehicles being some 6-ton armoured cars although the bridge was designed for only half that load. All having crossed, the demolition and swinging of the bridge were begun. The right bank portion was first destroyed; then the central floating portion was swung round to the near bank by releasing all anchors, the end arriving to within 50 yards of the bank where the pontoons grounded. These were promptly sunk and the superstructure smashed. All this was done under incessant bombing and machine-gunning from the air.[1] Two other bridges over the Perak River were destroyed by other Sapper units. These were the 'Iskander' Bridge, the longest in Malaya, situated south of Kuala Kangsar, and an adjacent through-girder railway bridge. Thus the Engineer units did their best to hold

---

[1] A detailed account appears in notes by Lieut.-Colonel N. S. Bhagat, Engineers, entitled "An Unusual Bridge Demolition in Malaya", dated February 1951.

up the rapid Japanese advance, but conventional rearguard actions proved of little avail against the bold outflanking and infiltration tactics of the enemy.

"With our troops across the Perak River", writes Lieut.-Colonel R. B. Muir,[1] "a determined effort to stem the invasion tide was to be made at Kampar, about 30 miles south of Ipoh, one of the strongest natural defence positions in Malaya. Only two Brigade Groups, the 6/15th[2] and 28th, were available to man the position and only 48 hours could be spent on its preparation. The Battle of Kampar began on December 29th when our delaying troops were forced back through the outposts. Two main demolition belts were organized around the Kampar area, and all demolitions were executed successfully in the face of heavy enemy opposition. In the midst of the battle, the Japanese made an amphibious landing on January 1st, 1942, on the west coast near the Perak estuary, and on the 2nd a force came down the Perak River in boats to attack Telok Anson. The build-up proved too strong for the opposing troops (12th Brigade) and endangered the security of Kampar. Accordingly, when further landings developed to the south and armoured thrusts made inroads on the main position, we were forced to evacuate Kampar on January 3rd. On the following night the Japanese succeeded in landing near Kuala Selangor. The 6/15th Brigade was able to localize the effect of this threat up to the night of January 10th/11th when it was obliged to withdraw through Kuala Lumpur".

Regarding the Kampar position, Major A. R. Beattie, R.E., O.C. 3 Field Company, writes as follows[3]:— "The Dipang Bridge was the only one which crossed a small river in front of the position. It carried the main road from Ipoh. Behind the river were the 28th Brigade on the right and the 6th/15th Brigade on the left. 23 Field Company, in support of the 28th Brigade, had become responsible for the demolition of the bridge, but on December 29th the unit was ordered to remove the charges. This was done, though without taking serious note of how the charges had been laid. 3 Field Company, in support of the 12th Brigade which was then fighting

---

[1] "Sappers in the Malayan Campaign; 8th December 1941-15th February 1942", by Lieut.-Colonel R. B. Muir, R.E., appearing in *The R.E. Journal*, December 1950, pp. 433-454.

[2] The 6th and 15th Brigades had been amalgamated about December 19th owing to heavy casualties.

[3] Notes by Major A. R. Beattie, R.E., dated June 25th, 1947.

a rearguard action north of the bridge, had to be ready to repair the bridge if it was damaged by bombing. During the afternoon, it became apparent that a hurried withdrawal would take place, and Lieut. Poyser, R.E., at 12th Brigade H.Q., twice warned the Brigade Commander that the bridge was unprepared for demolition. A message sent back to 28th Brigade H.Q. failed to arrive and the whereabouts of 23 Field Company H.Q. was unknown. The Commander, 12th Brigade, became increasingly worried about the bridge as its destruction was to cover his withdrawal, and finally, at about 5.0 p.m. he asked Poyser if 3 Field Company could prepare it for demolition in half an hour. A Jemadar and a Havildar of 23 Field Company then appeared who knew where the explosives were but did not know where the charges were to be fitted into position on the bridge. It started to rain. Infantry, carriers and armoured cars were pouring over the bridge in frightful confusion, making work very difficult. The charges could only be tied on roughly and there was no time for proper tamping. After about three-quarters of an hour the charges were ready and the circuits wired up. The last infantry withdrew and the demolitions were fired. The detonators exploded, dislodging the charges and blowing some of them into the river, but they failed to ignite the primers which had got wet and would not explode. No rubber protectors were available. Some enemy tanks were 300 yards away round a bend in the road and there was cover for enemy infantry within 200 yards of the bridge. A Gurkha battalion, guarding the bridge, said they could not protect us by overhead fire while we were at work on it though they could place a couple of Sections on the bank on either side of it. A small quantity of explosive being still available, circuits were fitted up under intermittent mortar and small arms fire and three more attempts were made at demolition before the bridge had to be abandoned an hour later. It had dropped at one end but was not a good obstacle".

This was one of the very few demolition failures during the retreat and it can hardly be said that 3 Field Company was to blame. Explosives in large quantities, and time in which to lay them in position, were needed by all the Engineer units, and in the confusion of a rapid withdrawal a regular and sufficient issue of gelignite, guncotton, primers and detonators was often impossible. Those responsible for the supply did their best to expedite despatch to the front. The War Diary of 42 Field Park Company shows that on December 1st no less than 7,500 lbs of gelignite and 600 electric detonators were sent to Jerantut by that unit for the use of 22 Field Company.

On the east coast, patrols of the advanced 22nd Brigade, in contact with the enemy moving down from Kota Bahru, had been pushed back on December 26th into Pahang State. On the 30th, the Japanese were approaching the Kuantan airfield in strength, and during the early hours of January 1st a ferry west of Kuantan was destroyed by 22 Field Company. A swinging boat bridge had been under construction but could not be completed because sufficient boats in good condition were not available. Owing to the serious reverses sustained by the 11th Division on the west coast, the 22nd Brigade was forced to abandon the Kuantan airfield during the night of January 3rd/4th and after very heavy fighting reached Jerantut in the early hours of January 7th. Its escape was due largely to the delaying demolitions of the Sapper units. A 'scorched earth' policy was now in full swing. It had been in operation on the west coast since December 20th when 3 Field Company, in the Taiping area, had flooded some square miles of low-lying country by breaching canal banks. From December 31st to January 5th, 45 Army Troops Company was attached to the 9th Division and helped the 22nd Brigade to extricate itself from the area east of the Pahang River by establishing a duplicate ferry near Jerantut where 54 Field Stores Section was at work.

The exploits of 22 Field Company before and during the withdrawal from Kuantan deserve some notice. A boom had been constructed across the mouth of the Kuantan River and was operated by the Company. This was a difficult task for it had to be opened and closed frequently for the passage of ships. Pill-boxes had already been built along the beaches and in the tidal mangrove swamps flanking the river. These were two storeyed structures because the tide level varied by 20 feet. The Sappers and infantry working parties laboured cheerfully from sunrise to sunset, often in deep mud and bitten to pieces by mosquitoes. Communications were improved, large areas mined and many bridges and cuttings prepared for demolition. When the fighting started, the boom gave much trouble, for it had to be opened hurriedly at midnight to allow a coasting steamer to escape. According to an officer who was with 22 Field Company[1] the oil from some petroleum tanks which had been blown up had spread over the water and was giving off powerful fumes. The weight of the couplings which joined the two portions of the boom having caused the connecting link to sink about 8 feet below the surface,

---

[1] Notes by Captain A. W. Haley, R.E., dated April 11th, 1951.

some Sappers had to dive into the oil-coated water to uncouple it, getting more and more sick with the fumes and wondering when the oil would catch fire. However, the boom was finally opened and the ship departed. The Sapper party then tackled their next task, the demolition of the ferry already mentioned. Throughout the day it was under accurate mortar fire. Towards evening, charges were prepared to demolish the wireless controlling it and the troops crowded aboard. Excitement reached a new level when it was found that the ferry had grounded under the abnormal load. However, it was rocked free and shot across to the far side. By the time all the men had disembarked and moved away, the charges placed in the wireless set had done their work and the ferry was then sunk. Meanwhile, a Section of 22 Field Company had been drawn into the defence of the airfield. This detachment suffered very severely, losing 27 men including the Section Commander, 2nd Lieut. J. R. Hannington, R.E., and an Indian officer who were over-run while still firing at the enemy. Further demolitions were carried out during the withdrawal from Kuantan. The unit then moved to Bentong, north-east of Kuala Lumpur. Afterwards, it concentrated on demolishing every road and rail bridge, and cratering the road at intervals, all the way back to Singapore, accomplishing nearly one hundred successful demolitions during January. Another Indian officer and some men were killed by mortar fire while awaiting orders to blow, and several parties had miraculous escapes. Infantry cover was rarely available. One party was actually sent back unescorted into enemy held territory to rebuild a crossing over a river and only two men survived to tell the tale. In the end, after the enemy had landed north of Mersing, the unfortunate 22nd Brigade was completely cut off and Major-General Barstow, the 9th Divisional Commander, was killed; but 22 Field Company was not involved in that catastrophe.

3 Field Company continued to do fine work on the west coast and lost heavily in the process. Assisted by coolie labour, it began to dig and wire a position for the 11th Division at Bidor and then sent a Section to start work at yet another at Trolak, where the road and railway ran close together through a bottle-neck in dense jungle. Given the necessary respite, the Trolak position might have been strongly fortified; but there was no respite, and when the enemy advanced to the attack, they found only a few dozen booby-traps laid near the road and railway and some hastily erected wire. Behind the position, the country opened out into rubber and oil-palm areas ideal for the Japanese tanks. The 11th Division then fell back to

the Slim River. Concrete road-blocks and concertina barbed wire did little to delay the enemy, who, on January 7th, attacked the position in strength with tank support. Our demolition detachments were over-run and almost wiped out. They could get no orders as all communications had been interrupted. Some of the Japanese tanks were eventually stopped by a 25-pounder gun near 3 Field Company H.Q. about 15 miles beyond the Slim River where they were stalked and driven off by a party of Sappers under C.S.M. Topham, R.E. The Slim River Battle saw practically the end of the 11th Indian Division as a fighting force. All its guns and most of its equipment were lost and hundreds of officers and men were taken prisoner. The enemy next advanced rapidly through the capital, Kuala Lumpur, towards the northern border of Johore State where the 8th Australian Division was preparing to give battle to save Singapore. On January 9th, General Wavell visited the front and decided that the 9th Division and the remnants of the 11th Division should fall back a distance of 125 miles to Singapore, covered by the Australians. The great exodus began on January 10th in every imaginable sort of vehicle. This was the beginning of the end.

The Australians, under Major-General Gordon Bennett, fought as they had always fought, expecting no quarter and giving none. On January 15th, a few miles north of Gemas, they laid an ambush on a bridge and the Japanese came marching across, many of them wheeling bicycles. Up went the bridge, and hundreds of Japs with it, and the 'Aussies' attacked with the bayonet. Then they fell back south of Segamat on the railway. The brigade in question, with part of the 9th Division, held a line along the Muar River between Segamat and the sea where the newly arrived 45th Indian Brigade had recently met with a serious reverse. A few days of intense battle followed, with heavy losses on both sides. Only 800 of our men, out of 4,000 engaged, emerged from the Muar battle.

At about this time, the 53rd British Brigade, which had landed recently in Singapore, was rushed up to the front and brought into action while the other two brigades of the 18th British Division were still at sea. This attempt to relieve a critical situation failed and the 53rd Brigade was badly mauled. 45 Army Troops Company was in support and suffered accordingly. One Section, under 2nd Lieut. M. M. Pillai had to find its way back for four days through dense jungle in order to rejoin our forces.

The Muar River Battle saw also the virtual end of 13 Field Company, under Major B. E. Whitman, R.E., which was attached to the

Australians. On January 14th, the Company had successfully demolished a large bridge, but on the 15th it lost 28 officers and men in a severe action. Three days later, an enemy attack with tanks was repulsed by the Australians and nine tanks were destroyed, six of which were close to 13 Field Company; but once again heavy casualties were sustained and still more when enemy detachments infiltrated during the night of January 18th/19th. On the afternoon of the 19th, 13 Field Company was shelled with devastating effect and 25% of the unit, including three officers, were killed or wounded. Every escape route being already blocked when the Company was ordered to withdraw, it became necessary to abandon all transport and proceed in small parties through the jungle. This was done, but not many managed to rejoin our retreating forces. Whitman himself was captured on January 28th. The casualties sustained by 13 Field Company were estimated at 4 officers and 60 men killed and 2 officers and 60 men wounded.

Many of the wounded fell into Japanese hands. Here is the story of Havildar John Benedict of 13 Field Company who was afterwards awarded the Military Medal.[1] He was wounded in the leg on January 19th, and on the following day, with some of his comrades, was captured by the Japanese. The prisoners were placed under guard in a bungalow and during the evening were taken in small batches to the bank of a stream where their captors proceeded to behead them in cold blood. Benedict and another man were escorted to the stream by three Japs, but when they came to the place of execution, the Havildar knocked one of the escort aside and both prisoners dived into the water. Benedict himself managed to swim under water till he could hide under some fallen trees. There he remained concealed until after dark when, hearing cries for help, he swam back to rescue two Sappers one of whom had a sword cut which seemed to have half severed his head from his body. He assisted these men across, rendered first aid and then accompanied them in an attempt to rejoin our forces, but all three were recaptured a fortnight later. It is marvellous to record that the desperately wounded Sapper survived his injury and returned three years later to Bangalore, but unfortunately he died in January 1946, perhaps as a result of his experiences.[2] This is no isolated example of Japanese barbarity.

---

[1] Jemadar Chinnadurai was awarded the Military Cross for gallantry in the same action.

[2] *A Short History of the Q.V's O. Madras Sappers and Miners during World War II, 1939-1945*, by Lieut.-Colonel R. A. Lindsell, R.E., pp. 27, 28.

Many prisoners were murdered in similar fashion elsewhere, and particularly captured airmen.

On the night of January 25th/26th, in spite of successful delaying tactics and demolitions, our troops were forced out of Batu Pahat on the west coast and Mersing on the east coast, and the enemy, now strongly reinforced, captured Kluang airfield, the last remaining air base on the mainland. We had insufficient strength to hold the 90-mile front from coast to coast in Central Johore. Then followed the final withdrawal to Singapore Island. The Sappers had excelled themselves in hasty demolitions during the retreat from Muar and in the collection and repair of damaged transport, but now their duty lay further south. Orders to withdraw to the island were received on January 27th, and 15 Field Company was detailed to destroy the Johore Causeway after the other troops had passed over it. During the long retreat down Malaya, the six Sapper units operating with the 11th Division had accounted for 600 bridges and culverts, and of these, 3 Field Company had demolished 150 and 43 Field Park Company nearly as many. The units with the 9th Division had done equally well. In a campaign of consistent adversity and hardship, the Sappers maintained their high reputation.

The last troops to traverse the Johore Causeway into Singapore Island were the Argyll and Sutherland Highlanders who marched across early on January 31st, 1942, to the accompaniment of their bagpipes. At about 8.0 a.m., charges placed by 15 Field Company were detonated, and with four tremendous explosions the long causeway was cut. The water mains which carried most of Singapore's supply from two large reservoirs in Johore perished with it, but there was, for the moment, a sufficient reserve stored in two reservoirs in the centre of the island. The food supply gave no anxiety. There was enough to last the population for six months. Shortly after the destruction of the causeway, General Percival issued a stirring appeal to the garrison. "Our task is to hold this fortress until help can come, as assuredly it will come" he wrote. "Our duty is clear. With firm resolve and fixed determination we shall win through. For nearly two months our troops have fought an enemy on the mainland who has had the advantage of great air superiority and considerable freedom of movement by sea. Our task has been to impose losses on the enemy and gain time to enable the forces of the Allies to be concentrated for this struggle in the Far East. Today we stand beleaguered in our island fortress". The appeal, no doubt, helped to revive the flagging spirits of many weary soldiers, but most must have asked themselves the question as to whence any help could reach them before their strength failed.

The truth is that the defences of Singapore Island against an attack from the mainland were still woefully inadequate when the Japanese appeared from the north. Early in January, Brigadier A. C. M. Paris had been appointed to organize the defences; but by that time the civilian labour, by means of which much of the work had to be executed, was beginning to vanish under increasing enemy air attack. An idea seems to have been held that if large defensive works were started on the northern coast of the island while our troops were locked in battle with the Japanese north of Kuala Lumpur, it would be bad for their morale. More probably they would have been buoyed up by the knowledge that they were supported by a powerful defensive position in rear to which they could retire, if need be, for reorganization before resuming the offensive. But the fact that Singapore was indefensible at the end of January 1942 was in no way the fault of the Engineer Commanders and formations. The policy to be followed was dictated to them. The Engineers had started defence preparations long before the troops withdrew across the Johore Causeway. Additional pill-boxes and wire, the manufacture of under-water and contact electric mines, and of petrol drums for water-surface fires, had kept them very busy; but they were ordered to devote their attention first to the defence of the north-east coast of the island, where the naval base lay, rather than to that of the north-west coast which was the more probable line of enemy attack. Thus there were few defences to the west of the causeway, either in the water or on land, to stop the Japanese.

The Singapore Island defences were organized in three areas. The northern coast, east of the causeway, was held by the 18th British Division and some remnants of the 11th Indian Division. From the causeway westwards and then southwards, the coast was held by the 8th Australian Division and a newly arrived 44th Indian Brigade. Singapore Town and the remainder of the coast was defended by two Malayan Brigades, Volunteer formations and certain Fortress troops. The garrison totalled about 85,000 men, but many were allotted to administrative duties. During the first week of the investment there was heavy artillery action by both sides. The enemy's fire, however, was so intense that work on our forward defences could be done only at night. Officer patrols crossed the Johore Strait frequently under cover of darkness to obtain information regarding the Japanese preparations. The Engineer units supervized infantry working parties, laid anti-tank minefields, placed naval mines across water approaches, built gun emplacements for the close defence of the few airfields and arranged for water-supply. The Works Services in Singapore under Colonel W. H. Treays, late R.E., afforded the greatest assistance to the Engineer field units, and 41 and 45 Fortress Companies, R.E., did trojan work. Treays records that he received much help from the Straits Settlements Volunteers in demolishing buildings along the south coast to open up lines for machine gun fire.[1] The Works Services converted private houses into hospitals, built camps, provided water-supplies and ran a couple of saw mills and, later in the siege, assembled patrols for front line duties.

The final Japanese offensive against Singapore Island was launched during the night of February 8th/9th, 1942, after a very heavy artillery barrage lasting several hours. The fire was concentrated on the north-west sector where the Australians and the 44th Brigade had only had time to dig the most meagre defences. Guns and mortars of all calibres swept the ground from the shore inland, and then back again to the shore. At 11 p.m. the enemy sent up a green flare as a signal for the assault. The night was black as pitch and our men were dependent on a few searchlights—some of them car headlights—to see anything coming across the narrow Johore Strait. The searchlights were switched on, but one by one they were extinguished by machine-gun fire. Two enemy divisions set out from the mainland in successive waves of motor driven craft, each carrying about 40 men with their mortars and machine guns. The Australians on the shore took a heavy toll; yet they could not prevent large numbers of Japanese from obtaining a foothold while the assault craft returned to bring more across. The main attack developed against the 22nd Australian Brigade west of the Kranji creek and the Johore Causeway, the chief objective being the Tengah airfield which lay about four miles inland.[2] Confused fighting followed. The Australians put up a bitter resistance but were gradually pushed back. No less than 13,000 Japanese landed during the night and a further 10,000 followed. By 8.0 a.m. on the 9th, the invading troops had captured the airfield. The same evening, the enemy made a second crossing just west of the causeway. Command reserves were rushed up and some ground was regained by a counter-attack, but this was only a flash in the pan and by February

---

[1] Notes by Colonel W. H. Treays, dated February 23rd, 1951.

[2] See the inset map of Singapore Island included in this chapter.

10th the Japanese threat had reached Bukit Timah in the centre of the island. The vital water reservoirs were now in imminent danger. Our last few aeroplanes—seven in all—had already departed to Sumatra. Enemy machines roamed the skies unhindered, bombing and machine-gunning all points of resistance. Heavy fighting raged throughout the 11th and 12th, and on the morning of February 13th we evacuated Changi at the eastern tip of the island after the defences had been demolished. All General Percival's troops were then grouped in a wide perimeter around Singapore Town.

While the Japanese were advancing across the island to Bukit Timah the Engineer units had been engaged entirely on mining avenues of approach and destroying stores, plant and munitions, but from February 10th, in view of the critical situation, some of them assumed a new role. A composite Battalion was formed under the command of Lieut.-Colonel H. M. Taylor, R.E., comprising a Fortress Company, R.E., and three Sapper and Miner Companies including 45 and 46 Army Troops Companies. The R.E. Battalion was detailed to assist a Malayan Infantry Brigade and took up its position on a road outside Singapore Town. On February 13th it was ordered to withdraw to another position in a Chinese cemetery near a biscuit factory. Desperate fighting began on the 14th, and at 2.0 p.m. on the 15th, the Battalion position was violently attacked, 45 Army Troops Company alone sustaining 40 casualties.[1] Lieut. T.D. Hyamson, R.E., was killed, 2nd Lieut. A. Gilmour, R.E., was mortally wounded, and Lieut. R. M. Lindley, R.E., and Jemadar Bhaginji More were also wounded. A few days earlier, General Yamashita, the Japanese Commander, had invited the garrison to surrender and had met with a curt refusal; but by the afternoon of Sunday, February 15th, it had become obvious that capitulation was inevitable. The enemy now controlled the reservoirs, the only source of water-supply. Gun ammunition and petrol were running short and the defenders were completely exhausted. The surrender was authorized by Government and was carried into effect by General Percival at 8.0 p.m. Thus, at the end of one of the most tragic episodes in British history, 70,000 soldiers passed into cruel captivity. Many were destined to perish miserably through starvation and disease while working like slaves on a railway which the Japanese were building through the dense jungles separating Thailand from Lower Burma, and the

---

[1] 45 Army Troops Company had already lost 60 officers and men in previous actions.

remainder will bear to their graves the mark of the hardships and humiliations they endured as prisoners.

Yet a few soldiers, a very few, managed to get away from Singapore, and among them 2nd Lieut. M. M. Pillai of 45 Army Troops Company. Pillai, a Tamil from Southern India, escaped from his prisoner-of-war camp outside the town, and suitably disguised, mingled with the local population. He made his way to Penang where, claiming to be a merchant, he obtained a passport from Japanese Headquarters to leave Malaya. Though his attempts to enter China proved fruitless, he managed to get a *visa* to enter Burma from the Japanese Consul at Renong, a Siamese port. He made his way slowly to Prome via Mergui, Pegu and Rangoon. His efforts to get to Akyab did not succeed. He therefore worked his way up the Irrawaddy as a cook in a boat carrying a number of the enemy, and when they reached Northern Burma he took to the jungle. There he marched alone for three weeks, sick and starving, until finally he gained the British line near Fort White. For this remarkable exploit he was awarded the Military Cross.

Another fortunate officer was Colonel W. H. Treays. Two days before the surrender, he was detailed to select a party of officers and men to go to Java to build camps. The last ships of any considerable size to leave Singapore sailed early on February 12th. These were the *Empire Star*, 11,000 tons, and an Australian vessel of about 3,000 tons. The *Empire Star* carried more than 2,000 civilians, key officers and men, invalids and nurses, and though savagely bombed and hit four times, landed her passengers safely in Sumatra and Java. Treays, with 22 men, left Singapore after midnight on February 13th/14th in a small oil-tanker at the tail end of the evacuation. They were lucky, for very few of the smaller ships got throguh. The oil-tanker was bombed and sunk so they transferred to another ship which landed them at Tembilihan in Sumatra. Thence they moved to Padang and voyaged in a cruiser to the southern coast of Java. On February 27th they left Java in a Yangtse river-boat in a convoy bound for Colombo, but as the boat could not keep up with the other ships she was soon left far behind. Fortunately, her draught was very shallow, for two torpedoes from a Japanese submarine passed close beneath her and another ahead. So Treays and his party reached Ceylon and lived to fight again.

The effect of the loss of Singapore was world-wide. The whole internal defence scheme of Australia was based on this fortress and the presence there of a powerful Allied fleet. Singapore was the core

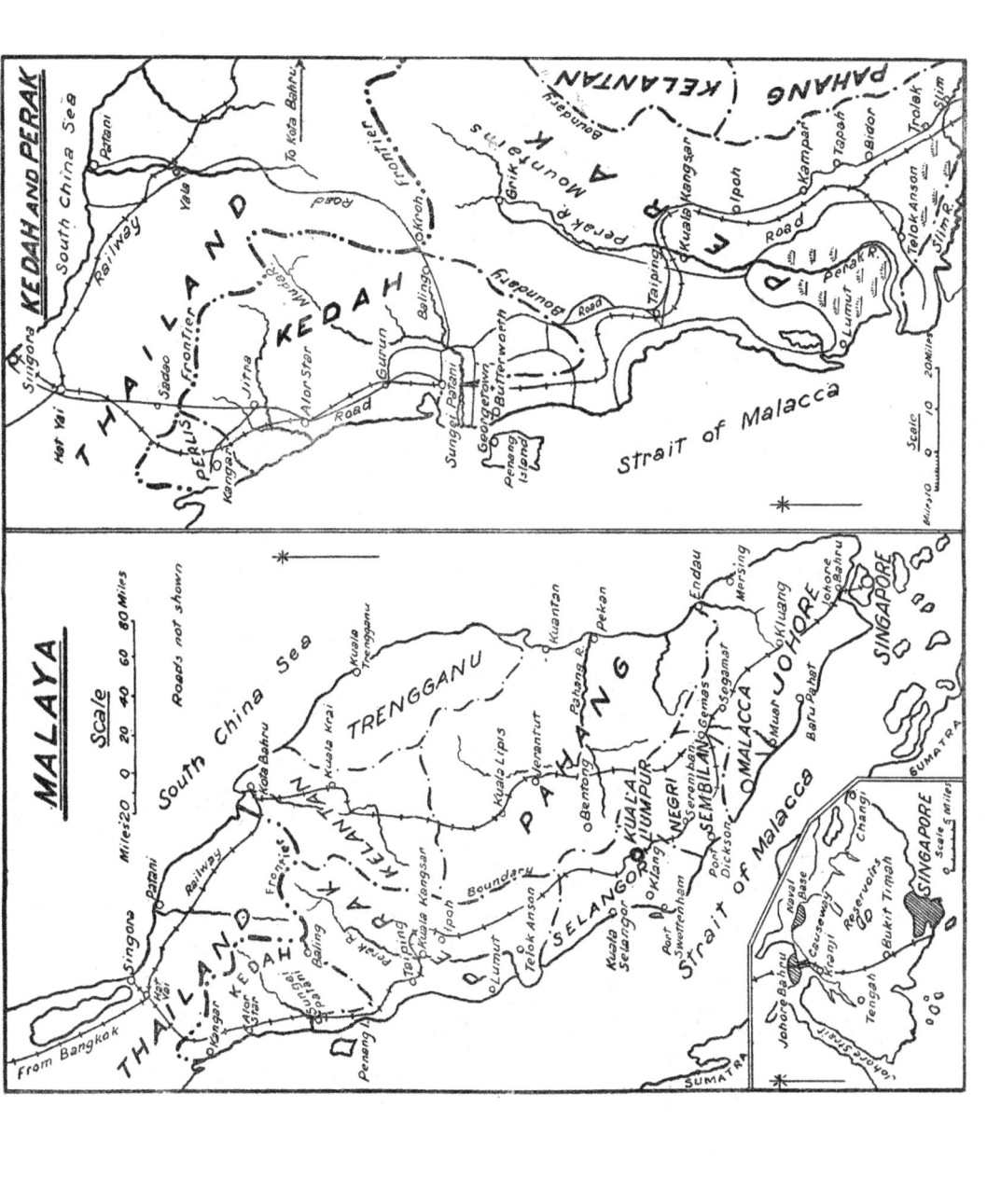

of British power in the Far East. It was the gateway to Burma, India, and the Middle East. It guarded the riches of the Netherland East Indies. Its loss was a shattering blow to British prestige throughout Asia and seemed to confirm the invincibility of Japan. Yet this can be said of the Malayan campaign as a whole. Whatever the errors in advance planning, training, equipment and strategy, those who actually fought in the jungles showed the greatest stubbornness and bravery under appalling conditions and the Engineer units rarely failed in their main task of delaying the enemy's advance.

CHAPTER VIII

RETREAT FROM BURMA, DECEMBER 1941 - MAY 1942

ALTHOUGH the Japanese must have been fully aware that the conquest of Burma should precede any attempt to invade India, they could hardly have hoped to launch that operation as early as the end of 1941. Yet their easy occupation of Thailand and their surprising successes in Malaya encouraged them to do so, and as a first step they took possession of Victoria Point at the southernmost tip of the Tenasserim strip, whence our small garrison had been withdrawn. This occured on December 14th within a week of their first landings in Malaya and only four days after the sinking of the *Prince of Wales* and *Repulse* which had given them local command of the seas. To ensure early success in Burma it was necessary to seize and occupy Rangoon. There was no rail connection between Burma and India, nor even a good road, and there was no railway between Burma and Thailand. The communications in Burma, by rail, river or road, ran north and south. The country was in fact an isolated buffer State between China and Thailand to the east and India to the west, but its occupation was necessary to Japan to safeguard her projected conquests in the East Indies. The invasion of India was to follow when the means were at hand and she had secured safe entry to the Bay of Bengal. Therefore, her first operations against Burma were of a tentative nature and conducted very carefully in the extreme south.

At the beginning of December 1941 our forces in Burma, as in Malaya, were not only inadequate but totally unfitted for war against a major military Power, and in India there was not one single fully trained division. Burma had not been organized to face a massive invasion, but a decision had been reached that in such an event the line of the Salween River should be held at all costs.[1] The operations in Malaya soon showed that Japanese mobility had been greatly underestimated and that therefore the enemy should be checked if possible in Southern Tenasserim, preferably at Tavoy which is more than 200 miles from the Salween estuary. The garrison of

---

[1] See the map of Lower Burma included in Chapter XIII.

Mergui, a further 100 miles southwards, was to be evacuated by sea to Rangoon. On December 11th, the Japanese opened their offensive by bombing Tavoy. On the 13th, they launched air attacks on Mergui and Victoria Point, and having occupied the latter outpost, spread 90 miles up the coast. Rangoon was bombed by 80 Japanese aircraft on December 23rd. Two thousand people were killed and the rest stampeded to the open country. The enemy planes tried to repeat the assault on Christmas Day but were driven off by our meagre air forces and lost heavily. Responsibility for Burma had recently been transferred from the Far Eastern Command to that of the Commander-in-Chief, India (General Sir Archibald Wavell). The G.O.C., Army in Burma, was Lieut.-General T. J. Hutton.

Negotiations were already in progress between General Wavell, the Chinese General Chiang Kai-Shek and the Americans for the reinforcement of Burma by Chinese troops. Chiang Kai-Shek was vitally interested because the 'Burma Road' from Chungking through Yunnan to Bhamo in the far north[1] was his sole link with the Allies and the only route along which he could receive Lease-Lend supplies from America. He had the men, but not the equipment, for modern warfare, and he offered no less than twelve divisions. This offer was declined for political reasons, but in the end it was agreed that two Chinese Armies, the Fifth and Sixth, should march into Burma from Yunnan to defend the Toungoo region if the British were forced to abandon Rangoon. For some reason it had been anticipated that the Japanese would invade Upper Burma by striking at Toungoo from Northern Thailand. The Chinese came in slowly like a swarm of locusts, living on the country as they went. They were jovial comrades and good fighters but no match for the highly trained Japanese, and they arrived too late to save Lower Burma. They would not submit to British control although Chiang Kai-Shek had agreed that the American General Joseph Stilwell, otherwise 'Vinegar Joe', should command the Chinese forces in Burma. Co-operation with the British was therefore exceedingly difficult, and 'Vinegar Joe' himself, though brave as a lion, was no boon companion and was usually to be found only in some remote northern area.

Up to the end of 1941, the defence of the eastern frontier of Burma devolved mainly on the 1st Burma Division, under Major-General J. Bruce-Scott, strung out over a distance of 800 miles from beyond Mandalay southwards to Victoria Point and providing also a garrison

---

[1] See the map of Upper Burma included in Chapter XIII.

for Rangoon. The division was under-strength and lacked supporting arms, anti-aircraft guns and wireless. It had little mechanical transport and no air cover. A reinforcement was therefore ordered in the shape of the 17th Indian Division, whose Commander, Major-General J. G. Smyth, v.c., arrived in Rangoon, ahead of his troops, on January 9th, 1942. Two of his brigades had been diverted to Malaya, and the third, the 46th Brigade under Brigadier R. Ekin, could not be expected before the end of the month. Smyth established his headquarters at Moulmein and assumed command of all the troops between Papun, 100 miles to the north, and Mergui, 300 miles to the south. These amounted to the equivalent of only two weak brigades. During the first half of January, Moulmein, Martaban and Tavoy were bombed by the Japanese and an enemy force was reported to be advancing westwards on Tavoy from Thailand. The 17th Division was therefore ordered to concentrate in Moulmein, Tavoy and Kawkareik, 40 miles east of Moulmein. Mergui was attacked by the Japanese 55th Division on January 19th and the garrison was withdrawn by sea after the airfield and all stores had been destroyed. About the same time, another enemy force crossed into Tenasserim from Thailand through the Kawkareik Pass to threaten Moulmein and Martaban at the mouth of the Salween. Tavoy was then evacuated and all efforts were directed towards holding the line of the Salween River northwards from Moulmein.

Moulmein was to be defended by the 2nd Burma Brigade. Part of the 16th Indian Infantry Brigade was in Martaban across the Salween estuary, and the 46th Indian Infantry Brigade was assembling in Bilin, 60 miles further north, but without its transport. No proper defences existed at Moulmein, and the perimeter was far too large to be held by one brigade. The enemy landed and attacked on January 30th, and on the following day the 2nd Burma Brigade was ferried across to Martaban and withdrawn northwards along the coast through Thaton and Bilin to Kyaikto on the Sittang estuary. It had lost 617 men in the fighting and was badly mauled. Yet the 17th Division was still expected to hold the Salween line for a length of 60 miles above Martaban and also the country between it and the sea. It had to cover the Bilin and Sittang rivers and in particular the Sittang railway bridge near Mokpalin.[1] Apart from ferrying, this structure afforded the only means of transit across the river south of Toungoo, which lay nearly 110 miles upstream, and it was therefore

---

[1] See the map of the Waw Area included in this chapter.

a vital link with Rangoon. According to General Smyth, his forces were disposed so as to cover that port from a distance and thus to gain time for the Chinese to arrive.[1] The final arrangement was that the Salween line to Kamamaung (60 miles) should be held by the 16th Brigade with headquarters at Thaton. The 46th Brigade was to prolong the line northwards for another 50 miles to Papun, and in support was the 2nd Burma Brigade, shortly to be reinforced by the 48th Brigade of Gurkhas from India. The Japanese lost no time in pushing up the Salween from Moulmein. On February 9th, the 16th Brigade had to evacuate Martaban. On the 10th, the enemy crossed the river at a point east of Thaton, which was abandoned two days later. The 46th Brigade then withdrew to Kyaikto and the 16th Brigade to a defensive line behind the Bilin River.

General Smyth was not to withdraw from the Bilin line without permission from General Wavell who was still confident that help would arrive from Australia. Yet, with a threat further north against his left flank and possible enemy landings behind his right flank, Smyth realized that he could hardly hope to hold the Bilin line without adequate reserves. A withdrawal to the stronger Sittang line was obviously unavoidable and this was approved by Wavell on February 19th. The 48th Brigade was to cover the movement, while all the remaining troops, including the 46th Brigade, were to guard the approaches to Kyaikto. It was intended that the 17th Division should cross the Sittang Bridge on February 22nd; but the withdrawal to the bridge promised to be very slow and laborious because the metalled road from the south ended beyond Kyaikto and was replaced by an earthen track through dense jungle. Then it was learned that no assistance could be expected from Australia. This matter is discussed fully by Sir Winston Churchill in Volume IV of *The Second World War*. The Australian Government, fearing an invasion of their country, had decided to refuse a request by the British Prime Minister that an Australian Division, returning from the Middle East, should be diverted to Burma although they had been promised reinforcements from America. This refusal is quite understandable because the Australians wished not only to safeguard their country from the horrors of invasion but also to preserve a firm base from

---

[1] "The Campaign in Burma", by Brigadier J. G. Smyth, V.C., M.C., appearing in *The Journal of the Royal United Service Institution*, August 1943, pp. 188-197. This article is a condensed version of another published in July 1942 in *The Journal of the United Service Institution of India*.

which to launch a counter-offensive in the East Indies. Nevertheless, the refusal sealed the fate of Burma.

It is time now to describe the part played by units of the Indian Engineers in these stirring events. Before the outbreak of hostilities the only regular Engineer field unit in Burma was 1 Field Company, Burma Sappers and Miners, with headquarters at Mandalay, but shortly afterwards, other units began to appear on the scene. The first to land in Rangoon were 50 Field Park Company (Capt. R. Kent, R.E.) and 60 Field Company (Major R. K. Kochhar, I.E.) both of which arrived during the third week of December 1941 as part of the 17th Divisional Engineers under Lieut.-Colonel R. S. B. Ward, R.E. The Malerkotla State Sapper Company (Major R. C. Orgill, R.E.) also arrived and was posted to the 1st Burma Divisional Engineers under Lieut.-Colonel D. C. T. Swan, R.E. Several weeks then elapsed before the next Sapper reinforcements appeared, for it was not until January 31st, 1942, that 18 Artisan Works Company (Capt. W. Crockwell, I.E.) disembarked at Rangoon to join the 17th Divisional Engineers. 24 Field Company (Major J. McC. Smith, R.E.) and 56 Field Company (Major M. P. R. Sloot, R.E.) landed on February 6th. Thus it is clear that while the Japanese were advancing up Lower Tenasserim our troops had little Engineer assistance. This was unavoidable because the rapidity of the advance was wholly unexpected. 70 Field Company (Major I. H. Lyall-Grant, R.E.) did not arrive until March 3rd, long after the Sittang Battle had been fought.

50 Field Park Company moved up-country and during January and and February arranged water-supplies and operated workshops at Taunggyi, east of Meiktila. Early in March it was in Toungoo, and not until March 24th did it enter the battle zone which had shifted by that time to the Irrawaddy. The Malerkotlas also went to Taunggyi to build bridges and improve communications for the 1st Burma Brigade and the 13th Indian Infantry Brigade of the 1st Burma Division which were defending that front. The 2nd Burma Brigade in Tenasserim, and the 16th Indian Infantry Brigade from Mandalay, joined the 46th Indian Infantry Brigade in the south before the end of January to complete the 17th Indian Division. The Malerkotla Company, ordered southwards, arrived in Kyaikto by rail on January 29th. 24 Field Company detrained on February 7th at Hninpale, beyond Bilin. 60 Field Company had already moved down to Thaton, where the railway station had been heavily bombed and much repair work was needed. Then, continuing to Moulmein, it found itself in the thick of the fighting.

A Section of 60 Field Company, under Capt. A. R. Jardine, R.E., was at work on demolitions while our troops were withdrawing across the Salween estuary to Martaban during the night of January 30th/31st.[1] After finishing the demolitions, Jardine embarked his men on a steam launch for transit to Martaban, nearly three miles across the water. The Japs were getting very close, and just as the launch was about to leave, a party of stragglers arrived for embarkation. The Brigade Major of the 48th Brigade ordered Jardine to unload his men and defend the jetty until the stragglers could be evacuated; so Jardine, Jemadar Malligarjunan and their detachment of Madras Sappers disembarked, made a breastwork out of rolls of bedding, and covered the departure of the crowded launch. Soon afterwards, Jardine was wounded and Malligarjunan assumed command. He was joined by Lieut.-Colonel Taylor, O.C. 8th Burma Rifles, and as it was now obvious that no ferry boats were coming back, the whole party took refuge under the jetty while the enemy arrived, set up mortars on top of it, and opened fire towards Martaban. Darkness fell and the party still remained undetected. Colonel Taylor takes up the story. "A little later", he writes, "I heard odd sounds coming from an adjacent yard and found that the Sappers had disappeared. The sounds persisted so I decided to investigate. Peeping round a wall, I was staggered to find the Sappers industriously building a petrol-barrel raft with their Jemadar giving instructions in loud whispers. Having completed the raft, they launched it; but the Jemadar, apparently not being satisfied, had the raft pulled ashore and taken to pieces to replace a leaking barrel. It was then re-launched; but still the Jemadar was not happy about it and had it rebuilt a second time. Then he smiled his satisfaction, came up to me, and saluting smartly said "*Raft tayar hai Sahib*". We climbed aboard, but as we dared not use paddles, the Jemadar and his men stripped and gently slid the raft into the water and guided it to safety. By keeping calm and cool in the face of the enemy, and by thinking clearly and setting a fine example, he saved me, two other officers and all his men from capture". One would imagine that Jemadar Malligarjunan would at least have been mentioned in despatches, but it was not so. Hardly any honours were bestowed on the Sappers who fought in the First Burma Campaign. Records are liable to be lost during a retreat

---

[1] *A Short History of Q.V's O. Madras Sappers and Miners during World War II. 1939-45*, by Lieut.-Colonel R. A. Lindsell, R.E., pp. 29-31.

and there are few reliable eye-witnesses. The spotlights are on the winning side, not the losers.

Leaving the Martaban area, 60 Field Company demolished a number of road bridges near Thaton and on February 1st arrived by train in Kyaikto whence it moved to join the 46th Brigade at Hninpale. Afterwards, it prepared for demolition some bridges in the Bilin area until it handed over charge to 24 Field Company on February 7th. Then it returned to Thaton for a few days to repair the damage caused by persistent enemy bombing.

Another Sapper unit which did good work in Tenasserim was 18 Artisan Works Company[1] in which Lieut. L. S. Dubashi, I.E., was a Company Officer. "When fighting was going on at Moulmein", writes Dubashi[2], "I was ordered to embark with half the Company and all the kit at Calcutta on January 27th, 1942. We reached Rangoon on the 30th, but as the city was being bombed we did not disembark till the following day. On February 3rd, as no labour was available, we loaded our kit into railway wagons and moved by rail to Hninpale where we arrived on the 6th. Fighting was in progress nearby. We worked there in conjunction with 24 Field Company, and later with 60 Field Company, preparing a bridge on the road to Thaton for demolition and operating the railway service between Thaton and Pegu. Fortunately, we had a British N.C.O. who was experienced in railway work, and with his help we managed very well. We had to work day and night, and one Sapper who had had no sleep for three days was killed while shunting was in progress. He was our first casualty. About February 10th, as the 17th Division was retreating, we moved back towards Kyaikto. Leaving Hninpale by train after dark on February 15th, we were joined at Kyaikto by the other half-Company which had come from Rangoon. We took over some installations from a Burma Company and began to load stores for despatch to Pegu. On February 20th, we moved by rail to the Sittang River Bridge. Almost immediately after our arrival before dawn on the 21st we were ordered to build a large stone jetty for a ferry service across the river in case the bridge had to be blown up. Some 300 men, including Pioneers, were collected and work started at once. We laboured all day at this job and finished it after dark. There was frequent bombing to which our anti-aircraft guns replied. The early hours of the 22nd were spent in guiding mechanical transport along the

---

[1] Later known as 518 Artisan Works Company, I.E.

[2] Notes by Major L. S. Dubashi, Engineers

approach to the bridge. Troops were coming over incessantly from the Mokpalin side. The bridge had no railings, though it was decked to take road vehicles, and many mules fell off into the river. Enemy snipers, firing from trees, caused some confusion and a temporary withdrawal; but later we marched forward again to the bank where 300 native boats were moored. We had been ordered to destroy them so that the enemy might not use them. Only pickaxes were available, but under intermittent fire we sank the boats. At 1.30 p.m. the order came to retire so we marched about 15 miles to Waw, collecting 102 rifles *en route* and arrived there at 10.0 p.m. On the 24th we went by rail to Pegu, and on the 25th to Rangoon. The city had been evacuated and looting was going on everywhere. We operated sawmills and worked on the railway, but we managed also to assemble two 30-cwt lorries from hundreds of packages of lorries and jeeps lying on the wharves. We left Rangoon for Prome by train on February 28th".

At the end of January, the Malerkotla Sapper Company, under Major R. C. Orgill, R.E., was engaged on water-supply at Kyaikto for the 2nd Burma Brigade which, as already related, had been withdrawn while the 16th and 46th Brigades tried to hold the Japanese further south. Early in February, the unit was erecting obstacles and repairing bridges near Bilin. The 17th Division was now reinforced by the 48th (Gurkha) Brigade from India, together with 24 Field Company, but it was still too weak to hold the extensive Thaton salient and by February 15th had retired to the Bilin River. On the 21st, after the Malerkotlas had prepared the bridges around Kyaikto for demolition, they blew a large road-bridge at Thebyugyaung on the Bilin road. By this time, the enemy had occupied a village on the coast within four miles of Kyaikto. There was heavy machine-gun fire during the night, and before dawn the enemy cheered and shouted and showered red tracer bullets on our men in an effort to spread panic. However, the 48th Brigade crossed the road-bridge at Kyaikto—a difficult bottle-neck—in good order and 24 Field Company prepared the village for demolition. The road and railway bridges were then blown on the order of the rear-guard commander, and Kyaikto was left in flames. Major Orgill, with Lieuts. Hudson and Bashir Ahmed, subsequently made their way back to Mokpalin with firing parties of the Malerkotlas. "The journey was unforgettable", writes Major B. A. Khan,[1] "as we and the retiring troops of the 46th and 16th Brigades

---

[1] *Regimental History of Malerkotla Sappers and Miners*, by Major B. A. Khan, Engineers, p. 35.

were subjected to intermittent dive-bombing and machine-gunning from the air for three hours before darkness put an end to the activities of the day." Many of the enemy planes had British markings on wings and fuselage. Mokpalin was reached at dusk and the Malerkotlas crossed the Sittang Bridge to the west bank.

Some extracts fron the Official History may help to explain the course of events near Mokpalin. During the night of February 21st/22nd, the 17th Divisional transport began to cross the Sittang Bridge, but before dawn it was held up by an overturned lorry. From the bridge, right back to Mokpalin, the bomb-pitted road soon became choked with vehicles in two lines, and, to add to the congestion, the transport of the 16th and 46th Brigades began to arrive. Fortunately a Gurkha battalion of the 48th Brigade had already crossed. At 8.30 a.m. the enemy attacked from the jungle to the north-east of the bridge and almost reached it before being repelled by a counter-attack. Brigadier N. Hugh-Jones (48th Brigade) then assumed local command and ordered the destruction of the 300 native boats collected near the right bank. Such was the situation when Brigadier J. K. Jones brought his 16th Brigade, and 300 survivors of Brigadier Ekin's 46th Brigade, into Mokpalin after the confused fighting along the road from Kyaikto. At dusk on the 22nd, attacks on Mokpalin from three directions were repelled and a perimeter defence was organized. Japanese machine-guns, established on the railway line, swept the whole length of the Sittang Bridge. The bridge presented a difficult problem. If it fell intact into Japanese hands, the road to Rangoon would lie open. If, on the other hand, it was blown up, all the troops and transport remaining on the left bank might be lost. Hugh-Jones therefore consulted General Smyth and was ordered to blow the bridge before daylight. Accordingly, at 5.30 a.m. on February 23rd, 1942, after the covering troops had been withdrawn, the bridge was destroyed. No avenue of retreat then remained for the thousands of men still waiting to cross.

While detachments of the 16th and 46th Brigades held off repeated enemy assaults on Mokpalin, large numbers of men set to work to build bamboo or timber rafts with petrol tins or water-bottles to give extra flotation. Some of the slightly wounded tried to swim the river, but the case of the seriously wounded was almost hopeless. At 11.15 a.m., 27 enemy bombers attacked the bridgehead and the mass of transport blocking the approaches. Gun ammunition exploded. Vehicles burned. The jungle blazed and casualties mounted rapidly under heavy mortar fire. At 2.0 p.m., Brigadier Hugh-Jones ordered a general withdrawal across the river. Guns, machine guns and mortars were rendered unserviceable. Most of the men threw their rifles into the Sittang. Mokpalin village was set on fire so that the smoke should give some concealment to the swimmers and those on rafts. The river was soon a mass of bobbing heads. Though sniped from the bank and attacked from the air, parties of men egged each other on to swim faster. They laughed. They made jokes about 'the Boat Race' even in the face of death. Swimmers assisted non-swimmers. Some swam back across nearly a mile of water to bring over more of the wounded. February 23rd was marked by deeds of heroism worthy of the highest traditions of the British and Indian Armies. But the 17th Division had ceased to exist, for the time being, as a fighting force. It could muster only 3,350 men and 149 officers with 1,420 rifles. General Wavell now stated that he was doubtful whether he could hold Burma.

Major B. A. Khan gives a good description of the part played by the Malerkotla Company in the destruction of the Sittang Bridge. "Immediately on our arrival in the Mokpalin area", he writes, "firing parties set out to destroy a dozen factories, mills, power stations and waterworks' plants. The vital parts of the machinery were blasted and the remainder set on fire after drenching with oil. At 7.30 p.m. on February 21st, the Company was given the task of preparing the Sittang Railway Bridge for demolition. Major Orgill and a party of officers and N.C.Os. were employed on this job throughout most of the 22nd under continuous enemy fire. The bridge was the second largest in Burma, consisting of eleven spans of through-girder, each 150 feet long. It had been adapted for use by mechanical transport by filling in sleepers in the rail gaps. The approaches were difficult, and the width of roadway dangerously narrow. Throughout the night preceding the demolition, 2nd Lieut. Macklin was loading charges into boxes. An enemy attack on the bridgehead took place but was held by the Gurkhas. The Malerkotlas then started placing charges on the upper and lower booms and cross-stiffeners of the three central spans. Major Orgill, Lieut. B. A. Khan and 2nd Lieut. Macklin were in charge of the three spans. Explosive stores were brought to the site by two parties under Capt. Corfield and Lieut. Hudson. Shortage of stores meant that the spans had to be dealt with separately and differently. Bullets hit the girders while the Sappers worked, but the preparations for demolition were finished by 3.0 p.m. Brigadier Hugh-Jones, Commander, 48th Brigade, was made responsible for ordering the demolition. After the bridge had been shelled and mortared rather accurately, orders were given to withdraw from the east bank. This left only the Sapper firing party and a Vickers gun crew on the bridge. However, as there were still two brigades south of the Sittang, no orders for demolition were issued and about 5.0 p.m. a bridgehead was re-established on the east bank by the Gurkhas as it had been decided to wait and see whether the 16th Brigade, which was ahead of the 46th Brigade, could reach the bridgehead before dark. The 16th Brigade, however, failed to reach it. At 2.30 a.m. on the 23rd, the enemy put in a fairly strong attack and it was decided that the bridge could not be held for another hour and must be blown up. The demolition was quite successful although the stores provided were insufficient for the task. The firing party under Lieut. B. A. Khan rejoined the Company next morning at Abya, half-way to Waw, and on the 25th the unit moved to Waw where it prepared further demolitions which were executed by 60 Field Company. Among the troops picked up by a train coming from Mokpalin were Jemadar Khalil Ur Rahman and his firing party from the Sittang Bridge who had managed to cross the river on improvised rafts."

Lieut-Colonel Orgill writes as follows[1]:— "There were enough stores to demolish one span with instantaneous fuze, another on an electric circuit, and a third with lots of explosive and safety fuse which we hoped would go up by sympathetic detonation; but when the bridge was blown, the third span, though damaged, did not drop, although the other two spans went. Owing to shortage of electric cable, my exploder had to be on the bridge itself, about three spans back from the one electrically prepared. We thought that the bridge would be blown soon after the demolitions were ready, and at about 3.0 p.m. the troops holding the bridgehead were withdrawn and we prepared to fire. This, however, proved to be a false alarm and the bridgehead was re-occupied before dusk. On the east bank, a battle went on throughout the night. We had men on all three spans, guarding the charges. About 2.0 a.m. on the 23rd, the Brigade Commander asked me whether I could guarantee that the bridge would go up if the bridgehead was overwhelmed after daylight, and I replied that I could not give any such assurance though we should have a good try. About two hours later, the decision was made to withdraw and blow the bridge. The Brigade Commander then told me to blow, and after seeing the bridgehead troops across,

---

[1] Notes by Lieut.-Colonel R. C. Orgill, O.B.E., R.E., dated February 16th, 1951.

we lit the safety fuzes and then touched off the instantaneous fuse, and also the electric circuit with the exploder, while the battle raged practically on the bridge itself."

Few commanders in the field have been faced with a more terrible problem than that which confronted Major-General Smyth in the early hours of February 23rd, 1942. "At 4.0 a.m.", writes Smyth himself,[1] "the Brigadier in charge of the bridge defences reported that he could not guarantee to hold the bridge for more than another hour. I had then to decide whether or not to blow the bridge knowing that three-quarters of my troops were on the wrong side of it. However, there was no doubt as to the right course. If the enemy gained the bridge, not only could he push over a whole division straight towards Rangoon, but, with both banks of the Sittang in his possession, the chance of getting more troops across the river was remote. I told the Brigadier to blow, and this was most gallantly done by the Sappers under close fire. The effect on the Japanese was immediate. Having failed in their object, they drew off. Parties of our men started in broad daylight to swim and float themselves over, first discarding their clothes and boots. On the far bank they had some distance to walk on stony ground, and the feet of the British soldiers were soon in an appalling state. The enemy, however, had had enough. His casualties had undoubtedly been heavy for it was estimated that there were 2,000 Japanese dead in the vicinity of the bridge alone."

Baulked at Mokpalin, the Japanese did not attempt for several days to cross the Sittang higher up. The Chinese approached from the north and it became possible to save some of the stores in Rangoon and to prepare for a fighting withdrawal towards Prome on the Irrawaddy. Early in March, Major-General Smyth handed over command of the 17th Indian Division to Major-General D. T. ("Punch") Cowan who thereafter led the Division with great success during the retreat northwards and later in the defence of Imphal. It is interesting to note that General Smyth entered Parliament after the war and held a prominent post in the Conservative Party under Mr. Winston Churchill in 1953.

On March 4th, 1942, General Sir Harold Alexander, who had conducted the final evacuation from Dunkirk, arrived by air in

---

[1] "The Campaign in Burma, 1942", by Brig. J. G. Smyth, V.C., M.C., appearing in *The Journal of the Royal United Service Institution*, August 1943, pp. 188-197. This is a condensed version of an article entitled "The Start of the War in Burma" by Brig. Smyth which appeared in *The Journal of the United Service Institution of India* in July 1942.

Calcutta to relieve Lieut.-General T. J. Hutton in command of the Army in Burma. There he met General Wavell and was instructed to hold Rangoon as long as he could as the retention of that port was vital to the whole situation in the Far East. Yet he must not risk the destruction of his Army but should withdraw if necessary to defend Upper Burma and particularly the large oil-fields at Yenangyaung and Chauk on the Irrawaddy. He should maintain contact with the Chinese and manoeuvre so as to cover the construction of a line of road communication between India and Burma. Alexander reached Rangoon on March 5th. He found the 17th Division holding the area between Pegu and Hlegu, the 48th Brigade and the newly arrived 7th Armoured Brigade being at Pegu and the 16th Brigade at Hlegu. Another new arrival, the 63rd Brigade, was in position 16 miles north of Rangoon though without its transport. The 1st Burma Division, having handed over the defence of the Southern Shan States to the Chinese Sixth Army, had the 13th Brigade at Mawchi, 50 miles east of Toungoo, the 1st Burma Brigade at Pyu, 30 miles south of Toungoo, and the 2nd Burma Brigade at Nyaunglebin, 50 miles north of Pegu. There was thus a dangerous gap of 40 miles between the two divisions. Japanese forces were already in Waw and close to Pegu, and others were crossing the Sittang at night and infiltrating through the gap north of Pegu into the Pegu Yomas, the hilly jungle country north-west of that place. Alexander at once ordered a combined offensive to close the gap between the divisions, but while it was in progress the enemy captured part of Pegu and held it firmly against all assaults. On March 6th, the enemy blocked the road between Pegu and Rangoon. Alexander then decided to abandon Rangoon. At midnight on March 6th/7th he ordered the destruction of the great oil refineries at Syriam, the final evacuation of the city by all troops, and the re-grouping of his Army in the Irrawaddy Valley to the north. A detachment of 60 Field Company had been in Rangoon since March 1st trying to salvage as much as possible of the material lying around. The place was like a city of the dead. Not a soul was to be seen. An officer who was sent to an Ordnance dump 16 miles to the north to prepare it for demolition reported that explosives and ammunition were stacked in an area covering nearly one square mile. He tried to arrange transport for some of these munitions towards Tharrawaddy but could do little in the time available. Accordingly, everything that could be destroyed was destroyed. Nevertheless, the Japanese could have fitted out an Army Corps with the stores they secured in and about Rangoon.

General Alexander's plan was to withdraw the 17th Division, under Major-General Cowan, northward by the road through Prome on the Irrawaddy until he could link up with the 1st Burma Division under Major-General Bruce-Scott which was concentrated south of Toungoo on the Sittang. He hoped to make a stand on the Prome-Toungoo line as the Chinese 55th Division was converging from the north on the same line. In the Rangoon area the situation was obviously hopeless as the enemy was already threatening the road to Prome and had cut the road to Toungoo. At Taukkyan, a road junction 21 miles north of Rangoon, the enemy established a road-block and held it almost long enough to capture Alexander himself. Then the race for Prome was resumed.

Among the retreating troops was 70 Field Company, under Major I. H. Lyall-Grant, R.E. This unit had landed in Rangoon on March 3rd and moved northwards on the 7th while the battle at Taukkyan was in progress.[1] Mobility being essential, it abandoned or burnt most of its tents, private clothing and stores on the way to Tharrawaddy, retaining, however, its arms, ammunition, engineer tools and explosives. On March 9th, it harboured beyond Tharrawaddy, where the 17th Division was reorganizing, and during the next few days carried out many demolitions in the neighbourhood. For instance, on the 10th it demolished two large bridges near Okkan, south of Tharrawaddy. As the unit was to be lightly motorized, all non-essential Engineer equipment was then sent forward to Prome. On the 13th, it moved to Okpo, between Letpadan and Zigon, while detachments left behind demolished a large railway bridge near Tharrawaddy and another on a branch line to Henzada. The railway station at Okpo was then demolished. March 20th saw the unit at Natalin, between Zigon and Paungde, building defences and improving communications, and there it remained until it arrived in Prome on March 30th. There was much work to be done in and around Prome and little time in which to do it. Jetties were needed on the river bank, a new road had to be made to link with the main highway from Mandalay, shipping had to be sunk, and power stations and petrol tanks blown up. Road-blocks also were required to the south of Prome. In these and many other ways, 70 Field Company helped to check the Japanese advance.

---

[1] *Brief History of the K.G.V's O. Bengal Sappers and Miners Group, R.I.E., August 1939-July* 1946, by Lieut. G. Pearson, R.E., p. 28.

Lyall-Grant records some interesting details about the equipment and transport of his unit.[1] The inadequate supply of explosives, secured here or there from dumps, was supplemented by judicious private enterprise. For instance, he acquired 600 lbs. of guncotton from a warehouse in Rangoon docks and discovered a store of gelignite in a cave at Prome. Commando troops gave him plastic explosives and the Chinese some gelignite. Explosives were obtained also from mining and commercial concerns. Each Section carried 200 lbs. and the Company Headquarters, 2,000 lbs. Yet these amounts barely sufficed because about 400 lbs. were needed for every bridge demolition. When the supply of guncotton was exhausted, gelignite had to be used entirely. Few tools were required, and the only stores carried were explosives, spikes, dogs and binding wire. After the unit was motorized, each Sub-Section of 12 men travelled in a 15-cwt truck together with its kit and tools. Fortunately, Lyall-Grant was able to augment his normal transport by a 5-ton Studebaker and a 40-seater bus found in Rangoon and a couple of fire-engines discovered in Prome. These, with a 3-ton Chevrolet bestowed on him by the Chinese and a number of abandoned lorries and cars retrieved on the road, solved the problem of mobility.

When the first Japanese patrols moved into Rangoon on March 8th, a sorry sight must have met their eyes. The wreckage of Government buildings, post offices, power houses and factories strewed the streets. To the east, billowing clouds of smoke showed where the Burma Oil Company's refineries had been destroyed. The flicker of flames was reflected from the clouds. But the enemy had undoubtedly gained a prize of untold value from a strategical aspect. Alexander could now expect no reinforcements because there was no port where they could be landed. His aircraft had already had to fly up-country to hastily prepared landing grounds, and thus the enemy was able to add local command of the air to their supremacy on land and sea. On March 23rd, the Japanese occupied the Andaman Islands, thereby obtaining adequate cover for their sea approaches to Rangoon.

In order to secure the necessary unity between the 17th Indian Division and the 1st Burma Division it was arranged that a Corps Headquarters should be set up at Prome, and on March 19th, 1942, Lieut.-General W. J. Slim, formerly Commander, 10th Indian Division, was appointed as Commander, 1st Burma Corps, otherwise known

---

[1] Notes by Major I. H. Lyall-Grant, R.E., dated February 1st., 1948.

as "Burcorps" but shortly to be renamed the "4th Indian Corps". General "Bill" Slim, who has already appeared in these pages, was a happy choice in every respect. A fine strategist and tactician and a strict disciplinarian, he inspired "Burcorps" with the confidence and endurance necessary to conduct a fighting withdrawal under adverse conditions. It is not surprising that his rise was meteoric, and that after commanding successively the 4th Indian Corps and the 15th Indian Corps, he became, on October 15th, 1943, the Commander of the Fourteenth Army which smashed the last Japanese resistance in Burma. His career, after the war, was varied and notable. During the latter half of 1945, he was Commander-in-Chief, South East Asia Land Forces, and then, for two years, Commandant of the Imperial Defence College in England. He retired from the Army in May 1948 to become Deputy Chairman of the Railway Executive but was recalled in November to succeed Field-Marshal Viscount Montgomery as Chief of the Imperial General Staff. Finally, in 1953, Field-Marshal Sir William Slim was appointed Governor-General of Australia. Such was the man who was destined to retrieve a lost Burma in the fateful years which followed the retreat from Rangoon so ably planned by General Alexander.

While the 17th Division was withdrawing up the road to Prome, the 1st Burma Division was concentrating south of Toungoo to complete, with the help of the Chinese Fifth Army from the north, the Prome-Toungoo line of resistance. But that line could not be held. Japanese reinforcements were pouring into Rangoon, and on March 21st disaster overtook the Allied Air Force. Reduced to two British fighter squadrons and a miscellaneous assortment of out-of-date British and American machines, it was caught on the ground at Magwe, far north of Prome, by a powerful Japanese air raid and was virtually destroyed. The few surviving R.A.F. planes flew to India: those of the American Volunteer Group made for bases in China. The enemy was then free to bomb such important centres as Mandalay, Thazi and Maymyo unhindered and did so with dire results. To relieve pressure on Toungoo by the Japanese 33rd Division, the 1st Burma Corps was directed to launch a local offensive southwards from Prome, its first objective being Paungde where our rearguard had been overtaken. A striking force moved out on March 28th but had to be diverted to counter a threat against Prome itself. An enemy coulmn had crossed the Irrawaddy, advanced up the west bank, re-crossed at Shwedaung and cut the railway line at Padigon.

Our striking force south of Shwedaung had then to fight its way back to Prome.

The Japanese 55th Division, massed before Toungoo, captured that place from the Chinese Fifth Army on March 29th, thus securing access to a road into the Shan States where the Japanese 56th Division was already operating. This was the signal for the Nationalist Burmese elements to harry our retreating columns and they took the field under the title of the "Burma Independence Army." Consequent upon the loss of Toungoo and the action at Shwedaung, it was decided to regroup the 1st Burma Corps in the Allanmyo area, north of Prome, after evacuating all possible supplies from that town, and accordingly, when the enemy had begun to enter the place after dark on April 1st, our last troops withdrew, carried often on the tanks of the 7th Armoured Brigade. On April 2nd, the 17th Division marched northwards to Dayindabo and established contact with the 1st Burma Division coming from the east. It then passed through that division and reached Allanmyo on April 3rd, the day on which the enemy killed 2,000 people in an air raid on Mandalay. By April 8th, the Burma Corps was holding the general line Minhla-Taungdwingyi, east of the Irrawaddy and covering the important oil-fields at Yenangyaung. On April 12th, it repulsed an enemy assault; but the Japanese were not to be denied, and moving round our left flank they struck straight at the oil-fields where there were no less than 4,000 wells.[1]

The Engineer units with the 1st Burma Division had been very busy during March 1942. Under Lieut.-Colonel D. C. T. Swan, R.E., as C.R.E., they comprised 50 Field Park Company (Capt. R. Kent, R.E.) 56 Field Company (Major M. P. R. Sloot, R.E.) and the Malerkotla Field Company (Major R. C. Orgill, R.E.). All three took part in active operations against the invaders, and the Malerkotlas excelled themselves in rafting during an offensive on the Nyaunglebin front.[2] Another Engineer unit, 1 Company, Burma Sappers and Miners, was present but had practically ceased to be of any value. While in Toungoo, 50 Field Park Company built bamboo bridges and ramps for loading trains and provided men to run power-houses, operate rail-yards and even to drive trains as most of the civilian railway employees had vanished. Leaving Toungoo on March 24th, the

---

[1] *From Pyramid to Pagoda*, by Lieut.-Colonel E. W. C. Sandes, D.S.O., M.C., p. 29.

[2] *Regimental History of Malerkotla Sappers and Miners*, by Major B. A. Khan, Engineers, p. 42.

unit acted as infantry during a battle at Kyundon airfield, south of Meiktila, where Captain Kent was wounded by a bomb. Then it moved to the Irrawaddy at Allanmyo which it reached on March 30th. 56 Field Company was also in action and suffered many casualties. Major M. P. R. Sloot, R.E. was mortally wounded. His successor, Major G. M. Eccles, R.E., was captured a few weeks later and finally Major P. F. Garthwaite, R.E., took command. This occurred on the Irrawaddy when the Burma Division was withdrawing northwards with the 17th Division.

The War Diary of 60 Field Company throws some light on the conditions during the retreat. "*Prome. 1st April*. Diversion for bridge north of Prome all day. M.T. sent back to Allanmyo as Divisional Commander fears road block. *2nd April*. Battle went on all night. After 0600 hrs., moved two miles north to Divisional Area. At 0800 hrs., ordered to march north to crossroads. Our two bullock carts were very slow. Ordered to keep moving to Allanmyo. Four lorries gone on ahead, leaving only two. Late in the afternoon we got a lift on tanks about 8 miles to Divisional Camp. *Allanmyo. 3rd April*. Started marching this morning to Allanmyo. Discarded our bullock carts. Company marched 16 miles and was then lifted by M.T. to a camp 5 miles north of Allanmyo. *Nyaungbintha*.[1] *4th April*. Company left by M.T. for north. *5th April*. 2nd Lieut. Yarrow demolished a bridge, 100 yards long, 20 miles to the north. *Taungdwingyi. 6th April*. Arrived 1900 hrs. *8th April*. Talk by General Slim, Corps Commander. He explained that we had reached a stage when victory hung in the balance and that it was 'the last ten minutes' that counted. Taungdwingyi was to serve as the pivot on which the Corps worked, so the latter had to be mobile. The whole 17th Division started digging in and building defence works. *9th April*. Lieut. Park started a 'controlled' fire of half the town. Fire itself took control for some time but was brought under control later. *10th April*. Controlled firing of rest of town. *12th April*. Eight enemy bombers over the town. Third salvo fell around our lines but just missed us. Slit trenches saved us from shrapnel. *19th April*. The 'Bangalore Tank'[2] was evolved. Burdiv, on our right, has already withdrawn from Magwe and Yenangyaung to Kyaukpadaung.[3]

---

[1] Nyaungbintha is 26 miles N.N.E. of Allanmyo on the road to Taungdwingyi.

[2] A canvas tank, with 4 bib-cocks, supported by rope tied to the corners of a wooden framework. Carried, folded, on a lorry. When unfolded and filled on arrival, it could be used to replenish water-containers direct from the lorry.

[3] Kyaukpadaung is 30 miles north of Yenangyaung.

On learning this, the Chinese on our left started to withdraw towards Meiktila. Thus we formed a 'spear-head'. Hence the 17th Division began to withdraw. *20th April.* Company started moving from Taungdwingyi to Natmauk, 30 miles. Arrived 1800 hrs. The road had been developed from a track by 24 and 70 Field Companies as we had been cut off at Magwe. Mahlaing[1]. *23rd April.* Arrived midnight 22nd/23rd. Met Chinese in large numbers *en route*. They stopped our overcrowded vehicles, at the point of the bayonet, for lifts."

The experiences of 24 Field Company were very similar. After being severely bombed at Prome on April 1st, the unit was ordered to move to Allanmyo. It lost most of its mechanical transport in a road-block and then adopted pack transport. At Taungdwingyi, which it reached on April 8th, it prepared defences such as anti-tank ditches and road-blocks and also helped to wire infantry positions. Enemy air attacks were frequent. On April 14th it repaired the road to Myothit (15 miles) as an alternative route in case the Magwe—Yenangyaung road was cut by the enemy. Early on the 15th it started for Natmauk, but within a few hours it was delayed at a nullah called the Pinchaung, a scene of heavy fighting. The entire Company started at once to improvise a track over the Pinchaung and continued throughout the night while transport floundered across. The *chaung* was about 600 yards wide and had a bed of loose sand. The brushwood track required constant renewal, but on April 18th a more durable track was begun. Part of this was made with 5,000 sleepers lifted from the railway line, and although only 80 men were available the track was ready for use by the 17th Division and 7th Armoured Brigade at dusk on the 20th. On April 23rd, the unit arrived in Mahlaing and reached Ondaw, west of Mandalay, on April 26th.

Major L. S. Dubashi relates some of the experiences of 18 Artisan Works Company over the same period. "After a week or so at Prome, we moved to Allanmyo and made diversions to bridges on the road to Magwe in case the bridges had to be demolished. Early in April we went to the Yenangyaung airfield and parties of Sappers were trained in running the power-houses, water-supply plant, synthetic petrol plant and other essential services. Arrangements had been made to build a low wall round the installations so that the latter could be flooded with oil from pipes and then set on fire. A detachment at Magwe had to load coal into river steamers, day and night,

---

[1] Mahlaing is 20 miles north of Meiktila.

for local labour was no longer available. As the Japanese advanced, our forces had to retreat from the Magwe and Yenangyaung airfields, but the Magwe detachment was kept there for a time to prevent the enemy from crossing the river. On April 14th this detachment and other troops were encircled by Japanese infiltration forces, but with the help of tanks a road-block was removed and the detachment escaped in a 30-cwt lorry. Later on, there was heavy fighting and some of our men went astray and were reported as missing. Firing started during the night. A motor-cycle which we possessed was carried tied down on to the bumper of our lorry with somebody's turban as the noise of its engine might give away the direction of our withdrawal. On April 16th we moved to a camp on the Meiktila road, and later to Meiktila itself. There we strengthened nine bridges. Afterwards, we moved to Sagaing, south of Mandalay, and a party was sent to the Myitnge River where a 100-feet railway bridge had to be decked. We started work at 5.0. p.m. and continued with only half an hour's rest until the job was finished at 3.30 p.m. on the following day, and in addition we maintained a ferry service some miles upstream. During the last week of April, we marched to Shwebo, which was burning. Though it was difficult to find a way through the town at night, we managed to discover the road to Ye-U."

Allanmyo, and Thayetmyo across the Irrawaddy, were both evacuated by "Burcorps" on April 6th and left in flames after all possible stores and ammunition had been removed, and by April 8th the Corps was on the general line Minhla-Taungdwingyi, which, however, it could not hope to hold in depth. A reinforcement promised by the Chinese failed to arrive. The Japanese ignored the Taungdwingyi defences, brushed aside the right flank of the Chinese Fifth Army north of Toungoo and made for Yenangyaung which they began to attack in force on April 11th during a violent thunderstorm. Space does not permit a description of the confused fighting which ensued during the next few days except to remark that General Slim brought the enemy almost to a standstill. The operations are described in some detail by Sir Compton Mackenzie in his excellent history of the war entitled *Eastern Epic*.[1] There was desperate fighting on two nullahs, the Yinchaung and, to the north of Yenangyaung, the Pinchaung where 24 Field Company laboured for so many days. The 1st Burma Division was cut off and in danger of annihilation, but it won through in the nick of time. Then followed the destruction

---

[1] *Eastern Epic*, by Compton Mackenzie, Vol. I, pp. 470-477.

of the Yenangyaung and Chauk oilfields, a heartrending though unavoidable undertaking.

The task of denying the oilfields had been entrusted to the officials of the Burma Oil Company who carried out their dangerous work with commendable thoroughness. On April 15th, a sheet of flame from millions of gallons of crude oil rose to the sky. Explosions rent the air in all directions. Dense clouds of smoke swirled over the forest of derricks and turned day into night, and thus the work of years was ruined in a few hours and some of the finest oilfields in the world became an abomination of desolation. On April 21st, the Burma Division having been extricated, all the British and Chinese forces withdrew successfully north of the Pinchaung, though they had to abandon most of their transport. The Chinese were losing heart, and little reliance could be placed on them. General Alexander had now no option but to withdraw further northwards as quickly as possible and the only route was by way of Kalewa on the Chindwin River, up the dreaded Kabaw Valley to Tamu, and over the Naga Hills to Imphal in Manipur. But could he accomplish this feat before his troops were bogged down by the approaching monsoon? It seemed hardly likely. In the Shan States, the Japanese were victorious everywhere. They had thrown the Chinese back towards the Salween and opened the way to Lashio which they soon occupied and thus cut the famous 'Burma Road' to China. While the British and Indian forces moved up the Chindwin, the Chinese withdrew to Bhamo. A wedge had been driven between the Allies. On April 28th, the British fought a brilliant action at Kyaukse, south of Mandalay, to cover the passage of their artillery and armour across the great Ava Bridge over the Irrawaddy, and then, on the 30th, blew up two spans of the bridge after the guns and tanks had crossed. The Chinese armies dispersed gradually towards Yunnan or wandered by a circuitous northern route to a refuge in India. The Japanese occupied Mandalay and on May 7th reached Myitkyina, the northern terminus of the railway. So much for the general course of events which must form a prelude to the narrative of Engineer exploits in the later stages of the campaign.

70 Field Company, with the 48th Brigade of the 17th Division, arrived at Kyaukse on April 27th and proceeded to provide demolition parties for the two bridges at that place. The enemy had to be delayed at all costs so that the Ava Bridge might be used without congestion. Kyaukse was in flames, but its bridges were intact. Preparations to blow the bridges were begun on April 28th as the enemy patrols approached. "The battle at Kyaukse shows the difficulties besetting

demolition parties", writes Lyall-Grant.[1] "We had four bridges to demolish in less than 24 hours in addition to the railway station and other targets. One of these bridges, at Dwehla, was 7 miles away to the west, so a detachment, under an R.E. subaltern, was sent out there with a covering party of a few tanks commanded by another subaltern. In the middle of the night, while the battle for Kyaukse was at its height, I was informed by the Brigadier that the Dwehla Bridge had been blown without orders and that my R.E. subaltern had been put under arrest. The procedure was supposed to have been that the Tank subaltern was to receive from Divisional or Brigade Headquarters a wireless order to blow the bridge, but he now admitted that he had given the order himself. Consequently, I took my subaltern to the Brigadier who promptly cancelled the order of arrest. The withdrawal from Kyaukse started at 5.30 p.m. on April 29th with the enemy in close contact. Just after 6.0 p.m. the bridge on the main road south of the town was blown. The noise was terrific and the whole battle stopped for about two minutes. There was complete silence everywhere. Two of our tanks, which had been left deliberately on the far side, then drove round and entered the town by another bridge. As they came over, the crews shouted cheerfully "The whole Jap Army seems to be behind us" and promptly disappeared up the main road. The order to blow this bridge was then given by the Brigade Major and we began to insert detonators in the charges, a difficult business underneath the structure. However, by 6. 22 p.m. all was ready, and within another minute the bridge went up. The Sapper party, in a truck and a car, had then to drive right into the middle of the town to gain the main road, expecting every minute to meet the leading enemy infantry. They were lucky to get away, for the last of our own troops were already nearly a mile down the road."

24 Field Company, now under Major G. V. C. Darley, R.E., had a very busy time when ordered to demolish some of the most important bridges in Northern Burma. While the unit was resting at Ondaw on April 27th the order came that the Pawlaung Railway Bridge, the Myitnge Road and Railway Bridges and the huge Ava combined Road and Railway Bridge were to be destroyed. The Pawlaung bridge was to be blown at Darley's discretion, the Myitnge bridges on the order of the Commander, 63rd Brigade, and the Ava structure on that of Major-General Cowan, Commander, 17th Division. At 7.0 p.m. three Sections of Bombay Sappers left Ondaw and assembled

---

[1] Notes by Major I. H. Lyall-Grant, R.E., dated February 1st, 1949.

at the northern end of the Ava Bridge to move explosives up from dumps. Preparations were made at noon to blow the Myitnge bridges. The charges were fixed after dark by Major Darley and 2nd Lieut. Rhodes, R.E., and both bridges were demolished at 10.30 p.m. The charges were fired simultaneouly with Cordex. Two spans of of the road bridge fell, but only one span of the railway bridge which was an iron structure with 180-feet girders. It is believed that the Japanese managed later to jack up this span and support it on a crib pier, but the demolition must have delayed their rail traffic for at least six weeks.

After blowing up the Myitnge bridges, Major Darley went to the Ava Bridge to assist 2nd Lieut. Mackay, R.E., in fixing the charges. Work proceeded throughout the night of April 29th/30th and the circuit was completed before daylight. During the day, enemy planes dropped about 60 bombs close to the bridge but none of the Bombay Sappers was injured. At 10.0 p.m. on April 30th, General Cowan arrived and gave orders for the demolition to be prepared immediately, so Darley and Mackay fixed the electric detonators and primers and checked the circuit. Two safety fuses were also arranged to fire in ten minutes, and one in two minutes in case the bridge was rushed by the enemy. The rearguard had passed over the bridge some hours before, and no troops now held the southern bridgehead though Chinese troops and transport were still going across. No time was to be lost as it was reported that the Japanese were advancing rapidly. Therefore, the order to fire was given by General Cowan as soon as the bridge could be cleared. Mackay lighted the safety fuses and rejoined General Cowan, Lieut.-Colonel Ward (C.R.E.) and Major Darley in their dug-out where, at 11.21 p.m., he fired the charges on the electric circuit. Two spans fell with a resounding crash and the Ava Bridge was wrecked. 24 Field Company then moved to Ye-U, north-west of Shwebo, where it arrived on May 2nd with 70 Field Company. All packs, respirators and surplus stores were destroyed prior to resuming the retreat.

Meanwhile, on the Chindwin, there had been heavy fighting at Monywa to the west of Mandalay. The town was held by only a small detachment of the 1st Burma Division. Suddenly, at 7.0 p.m. on April 30th, fire was opened on the place from the west bank and enemy troops began to cross the river further north to establish a roadblock. The Monywa detachment was withdrawn to protect the road to Ye-U and two brigades of the Burma Division advanced on May 2nd to recover Monywa. They had little success and had to be recalled.

The Malerkotla Sappers were involved in these operations, as also were 50 Field Park Company and 56 Field Company of the Madras Corps. During the night of April 30th/31st the Malerkotlas were defending a sector of the river bank. Sounds of motor-boats had been heard, and at dawn the enemy could be seen crossing the wide river. The Japanese landed and opened a destructive fire from behind some deserted houses, and although the Malerkotlas returned the fire with good effect they had to withdraw after suffering a number of casualties. Here may be told the story of 'Gemma', a dog owned by 56 Field Company.[1] As the C.R.E. and his Adjutant, with Major Garthwaite and a handful of men of 56 Company, were moving back from their headquarters in Monywa which had been over-run by the enemy, Japanese machine-gun bullets were throwing up spurts of dust in the paddy fields around. The small party found some cover from which fire could be returned, but not so 'Gemma' who ran around in the open, busily investigating the bullet marks. Tail up, frantically happy, she scampered here and there, drawing Japanese fire which might have been directed on the men, and she was last seen surrounded by a hail of bullets from a machine-gun firing from within fifty yards. Later in the day, some British tanks and infantry arrived and the Sapper party was able to return to its headquarters which were then burning fiercely. Garthwaite recovered what he could from the wreck of his office and, as an afterthought, looked inside an abandoned Staff car which the Japs had destroyed before they left. The engine had been smashed, the seat-cushions ripped up and the windscreen and windows broken. But there, inside, was 'Gemma', looking entirely unconcerned. How she got back to the car from where she was last seen, more than a mile away, and how she had faced the Japs, only she could tell. This was not the first time she had been a prisoner-of-war. In the battle of the oilfields, a fortnight earlier, she had been in Japanese hands for no less than three days when the Burma Division had been cut off. On that occasion, she was discovered sitting calmly in the wreck of Garthwaite's car. A battle had been raging over the area for more than two days, but except that she was rather thin and tired she seemed none the worse.

The 1st Burma Division having been extricated from Monywa, Alexander set out by road for Kalewa on the Chindwin, for the

---

[1] *A Short History of Q.V's O. Madras Sappers and Miners during World War II, 1939-1945*, by Lieut.-Colonel R. A. Lindsell, pp. 32, 33.

enemy had closed the Irrawaddy route. Movement along the route from Ye-U was most difficult, yet the utmost rapidity was essential to win the race against both the pursuing enemy and the monsoon rains. The metalled road ended abruptly a few miles beyond Ye-U, after which a hurriedly prepared track had to carry all the traffic, much of which was still mechanized. The track crossed and re-crossed dry *chaungs* full of soft sand in which many vehicles foundered. Broken down transport littered the track, and hordes of wretched refugees obstructed progress. For more than 80 miles the scene was one of dire confusion. The troops had been on half rations for some time, and water could be obtained only by digging in the *chaungs*. Yet the fighting units maintained their cohesion and morale and plodded doggedly onwards in clouds of choking dust. The War Diary of 60 Field Company throws some light on the employment of the Engineer units. "*Ye-U. 2nd May*. Took over maintenance of bridge from 18 Artisan Works Company. "Burdiv" having lost most of its M.T. and equipment is returning along the Monywa-Ye-U Road. Sent out our M.T. to collect stragglers of 50 Field Park and 56 Field Companies and 123 Inland Water Transport Company. Picked up and fed 150 stragglers and 75 civilian refugees. *3rd May*. Sent 3 lorries to pick up remainder of 50 and 56 Companies. Fed and housed them till they left next day. Firing broke out at night near our harbour. We stood-to. All quiet after an hour. Next morning we heard that the affair was caused by a Burmese who had objected to his wife being raped by another Burmese! *4th May*. Company ordered to move to Pyingaing, 63 miles. Convoy very slow but arrived 0530 hrs. on the 5th."

70 Field Company, traversing the same route, was delayed repeatedly by ditched lorries whose drivers had fallen asleep through exhaustion. It was seventeen hours on the road to Pyingaing for it had to stop at many places to improve *chaung* crossings or dig for water. During the afternoon of May 8th, it started on an arduous night march to Shwegyin on the east bank of the Chindwin. Its transport negotiated many sandy crossings with success, but other units were less fortunate and the Sappers had to destroy dozens of abandoned vehicles. Before dawn on the 9th, the Company bivouacked two miles east of Shwegyin. Its vehicles were then dispersed in paddy fields and the unit harboured on the river bank near a jetty. The Chindwin was half a mile wide and flowing fast between hilly and forest-clad banks. On the far bank, but six miles upstream, was Kalewa with which communication was maintained during the day

by five paddle-steamers. 70 Field Company began at once to build a proper pier and to deck boats for use as rafts. It still possessed some mechanical transport. In this it was more happily placed than some other units, for when many miles short of Shwegyin most of the infantry had been told that there was little hope of getting any of their trucks across the river and they had burned most of them together with their surplus kit and the bulk of their ammunition. They kept only what they could carry on their backs, and before they reached their destination they were ordered to destroy their last few vehicles.[1] These they drove into ravines, and then, draining off the water and oil, ran the engines at full throttle till they seized up. The vehicles were finally soaked with petrol and set on fire. Shwegyin became a cemetery of derelict transport. It was a horrid sight.

The Japanese did their utmost to prevent the crossing to Kalewa. After dark on May 9th, they landed a force downstream on the east bank, and taking a circuitous route, attacked towards the river on the 10th. This put a stop to all ferrying, but General Cowan fought back and began to march his troops upstream along a winding jungle track to a point immediately opposite Kalewa. All his remaining tanks, artillery and vehicles had to be sacrificed in the effort to escape. Stores were destroyed wholesale. Guns and mortars fired off their last ammunition. The tanks were stripped of their guns which were then buried as deeply as possible, after which the tanks themselves were set on fire. In any case, they had become almost useless as their tracks and engines were worn out. Eventually, our troops won through to the Kalewa ferry and crossed the Chindwin before the Japanese could interfere. With the river between them and the enemy, there was now every prospect that they would succeed in reaching Imphal though the way promised to be long and hard.

According to Lyall-Grant, the men of 70 Field Company at Shwegyin heard some rifle fire soon after dawn on May 10th, this being their first intimation of the Japanese attack, but it was not until 4.0 p.m. that they knew that a withdrawal was being planned. Work was continued on the jetty until 5.30 p.m. when Lyall-Grant asked for permission to destroy the last of his vehicles and was told that he could do what he could with sledge-hammers but must not use explosives or fire because these might reveal to the enemy the imminence of a withdrawal. Sledge-hammers, however, were useless,

---

[1] *From Pyramid to Pagoda*, by Lieut.-Colonel E. W. C. Sandes, D.S.O., M.C., p. 33.

and the vehicles were therefore rendered unserviceable by seizing up the engines. At about 6.15 p.m., orders arrived that the Company was to march by the jungle path to the Kalewa ferry and the unit set off. Each Section carried only 3 picks, 3 shovels and their cooking pots and *pakhals* slung on bamboo poles. The Japanese were on some cliffs overlooking part of the route, but the ferry was reached, after a nightmare march, at 9.30 a.m. on May 11th and soon afterwards the unit crossed to the west bank and moved to a bivouac some 4 miles from the river.

On May 12th, while our troops were beginning their arduous journey through the malarial country and over the rugged heights which still separated them from Imphal, the Japanese entered Kalewa. Fortunately, they were now too exhausted to follow up quickly. The end of the retreat from Burma was in sight and the enemy had been cheated of his prey. But we had still to traverse the unhealthy Kabaw Valley to reach Tamu on the Indian frontier, and then to surmount a range in order to arrive at Palel, whence a motor road led to Imphal. Every yard of the 132 miles to Palel was a purgatory to the weary troops. Sometimes, motor transport was available; more often it was not. Tens of thousands of refugees blocked the road. "Months latter", writes Roy Mc.Kelvie,[1] "when the first British returned to Tamu, they found skeletons sitting, lying or propped up, just as they had been before dying. In the Post Office, twenty skeletons were around the counter and one hung round the broken telephone. It is not difficult to imagine the agony and desolation of the exodus from Burma. Disease, under-nourishment and weariness had broken down the will to live. The prospect of one last drag over the cold, rain-soaked mountains was more than they could stand. Only the strong survived. Yet nearly 200,000 refugees crossed from Tamu to Imphal, some to die of strain, others to die in hospitals so crowded that the staffs were incapable of handling the patients. Over ninety per cent of the army and civilians who tried to cope with this mass trek suffered from malaria."

The War Diary of 24 Field Company describes the difficulties and hardships of the move to Imphal. "*Kalewa. 11th May.* Company crossed the Chindwin by the last boat at 1300 hrs. and at 1800 hrs. moved to transit area at Milestone 4. Slept by roadside. Ordered to be ready to move at 0900 hrs. by M.T. *12th May.* M.T. not available. Marched to Milestone 18. Troops hot and tired. M.T. to Inbaung

---

[1] *The War in Burma*, by Roy Mc.Kelvie, pp. 44, 45.

Transport on the Tamu-Palel Road

(north of Kalemyo) not available until very late in day. Last party arrived in camp at 0100 hrs. *Yazagyo*. 13*th May*. At 0300 hrs, orders came to move. Waited for transport at 0830 hrs. None available by 1100 hrs. Ordered to march and arrived Yazagyo 1700 hrs. *Khampat* (north of Yazagyo). 14*th May*. Ordered to leave by march route to await M.T. after 12 miles. Lifted by M.T. at 0800 hrs and arrived Khampat Camp 0930 hrs. Site too filthy for occupation, so O.C. moved camp 1 mile. All men marched happily." On May 15th, the unit marched 10 miles before getting a lift in some lorries to Tamu, where the last party came in long after dark. On the 16th, although the men had to march over a height of 5,000 feet to reach Lokchao, only one fell out through exhaustion. Motor transport was then promised for the 20 miles to Tengnoupal. None came, so the men plodded on through hilly country on May 17th and reached camp before dark. Here, General Slim complimented the unit on its marching which, he said, was the best he had yet seen. The 12 miles to Palel were covered on foot during the morning of May 18th, but that was the end of 'foot-slogging' as the Company was then lifted 45 miles by motor transport to a camp site at Kanglatongbi, a few miles north of Imphal on the road to Kohima. The rain was streaming down. There were no tents, and few of the men had ground sheets. They bivouacked in the mud. Three tents arrived on May 21st. Malaria began to take its toll. Dysentery was always with them. Now, after being parched and enfeebled by heat, they were to suffer from cold and want. There was no air supply, and adequate rationing was impossible along a single road often blocked by landslides. But at least they were still alive and had escaped the graves in Burma, or the years of slavery under the brutal Japanese, which fell to the lot of their less fortunate comrades.

The other Sapper units fared no better than 24 Field Company. 70 Field Company arrived in Kanglatongbi after dark on May 18th. In pouring rain, it was allotted an area of scrub jungle as a camping site. Again, there were no tents. Each man had a mosquito net but neither ground sheet nor blanket. "It was indeed a cold and miserable reception to India", writes Lyall-Grant. During the next three days, some shelters were built with tarpaulins and brushwood, but it was impossible to dry any clothes, and not until May 22nd, when the unit moved to Imphal, was there any relief or comfort. By that time, one man in every five was in hospital. 50 Field Park Company, 56 and 60 Field Companies, the Malerkotlas and 18 Artisan Works Company had similar experiences. The same hardships were borne, and borne stoically, by every officer and man in Alexander's Army. The time had been too short for proper arrangements to be made to receive them. Worn out by their exertions and weakened by malaria, many succumbed in the hospitals at Imphal.

But although the facilities for accommodating and feeding the Burma Army were inadequate, every effort had been made to help it on its tragic journey to Imphal, and in this task 59 Field Company, under Major J. D. H. Hibbert, R.E., played a notable part, as also did the Tehri-Garhwal Field Company under Major A. G. Hellicar, R.E., and an Excavating Company and some Pioneers. A formation called 114 Works Battalion, under Lieut.-Colonel Pritchard, R.E., had been engaged for many weeks on the repair or construction of the road to Kalewa by way of Wangjing, Palel and Tamu. Major O'Callaghan, R.E., who served under Pritchard, remarks that, early in May 1942, refugees from Burma began to arrive in thousands—men, women and children, all struggling to get to safety before it was too late.[1] The route was difficult and its perils many. Palel, and the highway to Imphal, became strewn with decomposing bodies which the survivors had no time nor energy to bury. Vultures might have helped, but there were none in that area. However, some excellent relief organizations were set up by Government and private communities such as the tea planters of Assam, and relief camps were established after a time at Palel and Wangjing as well as in Imphal. The death rate amongst the refugees was thus reduced, and food, shelter and medical aid were given. The largest camp, that at Imphal, was managed by an elderly English lady assisted by the wife of a local Superintendent of Police.

59 Field Company had arrived in Dimapur (Manipur Road) from Assam on April 12th, with other troops of the 23rd Indian Division, and had then moved through Imphal and Tamu towards Kalewa. Early in May all its efforts were being concentrated on improving the Kalewa road for use by the retreating Burma Army. The men worked from dawn till dusk on road repairs and the provision of nullah crossings, but on May 11th they began to go down with malaria. The unit had a Section at Htinzin, north of Khampat, and it also maintained at Tamu a bridge built by 'Elephant Bill' (Lieut.-Colonel J. H. Williams). Later, a Section of the Tehri-Garhwal Company began to replace this structure with a more permanent one on concrete piers, but the work had to cease when the Japanese

---

[1] Notes by Major O'Callaghan, R.E., dated February, 1951.

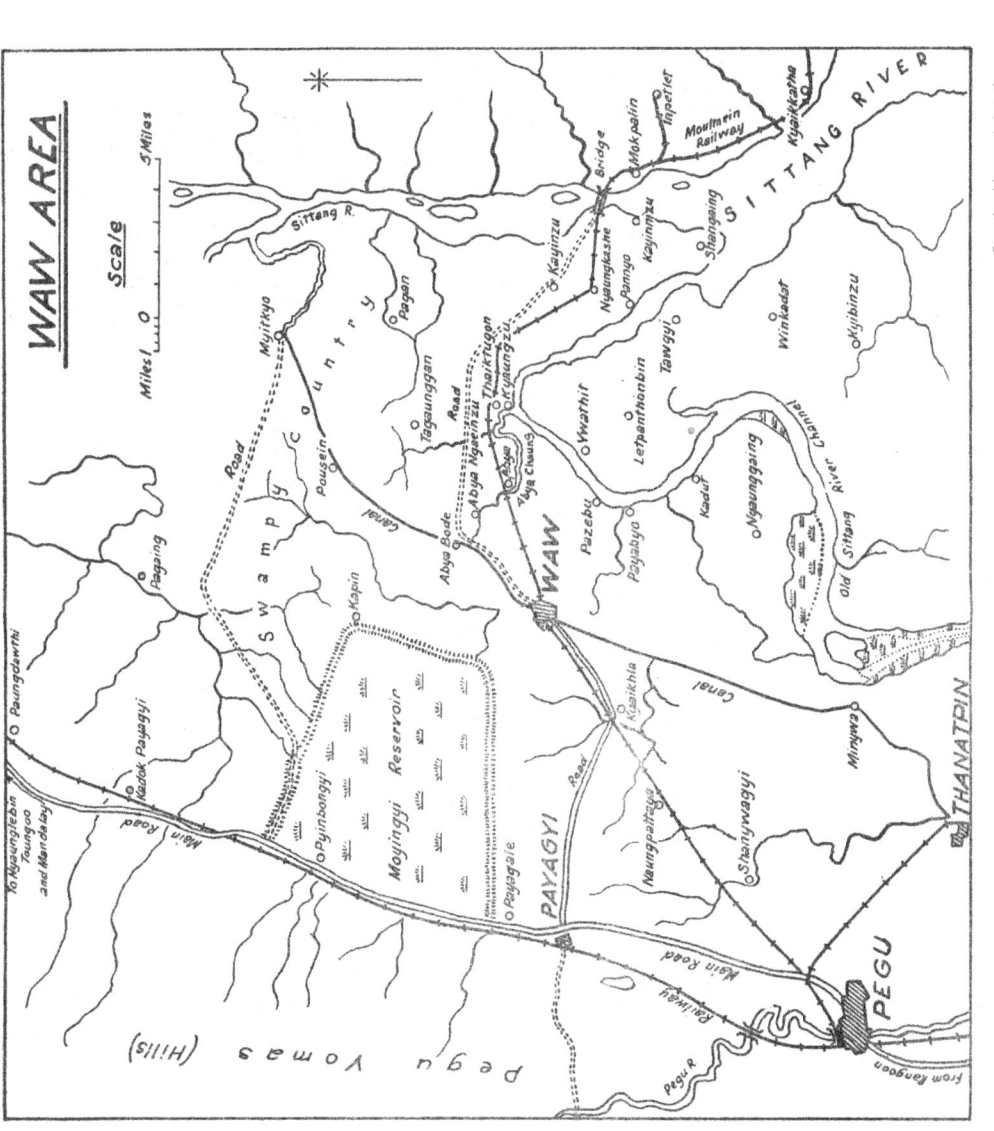

advanced. On May 17th, when the Burma Army was able to take over some road maintenance, 59 Field Company moved back to Lokchao and thence towards Palel to dig trenches and lay mines for a Brigade position at Shenam. The Tehri-Garhwals were there also. Half the men in 59 Field Company were now incapacitated with malaria. The steady stream of refugees interfered with their work. Heavy rain, early in June, caused many falls of rock and earth and added to their labours. By the end of that month, 59 Field Company could muster only 64 officers and men. Those evacuated on account of sickness never returned, and no reinforcements were received. Other Sapper units on the Palel Road during May 1942 were 71 Field Company (Major T. A. C. Brownlie, I.E.) and 414 Bridge Construction Section (Capt. R. Blagden, R.E.). A Section of 71 Company reached Palel on May 7th and helped to bury dead refugees. During April, 414 Section had spanned the Lokchao River with a fine Inglis bridge, but this was dismantled in May and brought back to Palel where 71 Company was preparing a defensive position.

The Burma Army under General Alexander ceased to exist on May 20th, 1942. The 4th Indian Corps, under General Slim, then assumed control and new formations were assembled gradually in and around Imphal to meet the Japanese threat to India. The building up of this new Army must form the subject of another chapter. For the moment, India was saved. It remained to General Slim to consolidate his position, to collect sufficient forces to repel any assault, and finally to burst through in overwhelming strength to sweep the invaders from Burma. All these tasks he accomplished and thus established his reputation as one of the greatest commanders in the Second World War.

CHAPTER IX

THE BUILD-UP IN ASSAM, JUNE 1942 - MARCH 1944

LESS than half of the original 25,000 combat troops of the Burma Army reached Imphal in May 1942, and of these, hardly any were fit to fight. A grim situation confronted General Wavell, the Commander-in-Chief, India. A few weeks earlier, he had informed the Secretary of State for War that if the Japanese pressed boldly westwards without pause, India would be in grave danger. The crucial months were likely to be May and June, and Wavell was much disturbed to find that the proposed occupation of Madagascar and the provisioning of Malta would cause the diversion of reinforcements intended for India. It was fortunate that the Japanese in Burma were too exhausted to press their advantage in the face of steadily increasing resistance in the air, and thus a catastrophe was avoided. But whence could reinforcements be obtained? India had been treated as an emergency reservoir for the supply of troops to many theatres. Divisions, hastily formed, had been rushed to Africa and the Middle East. After Germany invaded Russia, others had been sent to Iraq to open a line of supply through Persia. Rommel's advance to El Alamein, and the German progress towards the Caucasus, caused fresh demands on men and material. The cupboard was swept almost bare. The Eastern Army, under General Sir C. Broad, had to defend a frontier zone 800 miles in length, embracing Bengal, Arakan and Assam, an area larger than Great Britain. The desperately weak 4th Indian Corps, now under Lieut.-General N. M. S. Irwin, was responsible for the defence of Assam. The 15th Indian Corps, under Lieut.-General Sir N. Beresford-Peirse, guarded Bengal, and the greater part of the 70th British Division was held in reserve at Ranchi to counter any Japanese landing on the coast of Orissa.

General Irwin had to hold 500 miles of the Burma frontier and in particular to guard the Imphal Plain behind it and, further in rear, the village of Kohima on the main road leading back to the only rail-head at Dimapur (Manipur Road Station). His most pressing tasks were to rebuild the Dimapur-Imphal Road, 136 miles in length, and to make a new road from Imphal southwards at least as far as Tiddim, a further distance of 163 miles.[1] Yet it should not be imagined that a passive resistance was ever contemplated. The reconquest of Burma was being planned even while General Alexander was withdrawing from Rangoon in 1942, and, after he had reached Imphal, a plan of operations was cabled to England; but fate stepped in and the demands of other fronts prevented the launching of any large offensive. Thus a stale-mate developed on the Burma front during the latter half of the year and the sole event of much interest was the transportation by air of 13,000 Chinese troops over the "Hump" Route from China to increase the Chinese strength in India to two divisions. But although there was little fighting, there was much engineering. The possibility of launching an offensive rested not only on the arrival of reinforcements but on the effort of the engineers to provide the necessary roads, airfields and other facilities, and thus the 'build-up' period in Assam from 1942 to 1944 gave unlimited opportunities to units of the Indian Engineers to show the results of much intensive training. At the outset, however, those units which had taken part in the retreat from Rangoon were in a deplorable condition. For instance, when 50 Field Park Company was moved back to Shillong in July 1942 it could muster only 3 British and 27 Indian ranks. Some of the remainder were on leave, but most were in hospital. By the middle of September, the strength had dwindled to 1 British officer, 2 V.C.Os., 5 N.C.Os. and 2 Sappers and no work whatever was possible other than the supervision of infantry working parties.

General Wavell's original plans for the post-monsoon period of 1942 were for an advance by General Stilwell's forces from Ledo into Upper Burma and the reoccupation of Upper Arakan by General Christison's 15th Corps combined with the capture of Akyab from the sea. At the same time, General Scoones' 4th Corps, advancing from Manipur, was to occupy Kalewa and Sittaung on the Chindwin and raid the enemy's lines of communication beyond that river.[2] Before November, however, these plans had to be modified and the operations in Arakan were restricted to an overland advance. The resulting campaign in that region, which will be described in the next chapter, was a strategical failure though it taught many useful lessons. We are concerned at present only with the operations in the north.

The first Indian Engineer units to work on the Imphal-Tamu Road were the Tehri-Garhwal Field Company, under Major

---
[1] See the map of Upper Burma included in Chapter XIII.
[2] See the map of the Tiddim Road, Chindwin River Area, included in this chapter.

A. G. Hellicar, R.E., and 414 Bridge Construction Section. When the Tehri-Garhwals reached that line of communication in March 1942, the road extended only about three miles beyond Palel. "Later, I sent a Section to Tamu", writes Hellicar,[1] "and it stayed there until just before the evacuation of the Burma Army in May. Another Section, at Lokchao, remained until after the Burma Army had passed through and helped to dismantle the Inglis bridge at that place.[2] This bridge had a remarkable career. It had been sent originally from Roorkee and after being dismantled was used in our monsoon camp on the Imphal-Palel Road for training. Later, we rebuilt it at a river crossing near the camp, and thence it went to another crossing on the Tiddim Road. I think it was blown up when the Japs attacked in March 1944."

An Engineer formation which did good work on the Tamu Road in the early days was 114 Works Battalion under Lieut.-Colonel G. A. T. Pritchard, R.E. It was made responsible for the route from Imphal through Wangjing and Palel to Tamu and for an extension finally to Kalewa on the Chindwin. "When the road was started in the spring of 1942", writes Major O'Callaghan,[3] "there were no Military Engineer personnel in the Imphal Plain other than one M.E. Company and the officers of 114 Works Battalion, but a passable route was completed in time to evacuate the greater part of the Burma Army. With the resources available in India, it was impossible to allot any equipment to the troops at Imphal. We had no defences whatever against air attack although, from May onwards, Japanese reconnaissance planes flew over us daily. Suddenly one morning, two formations of bombers appeared heading for Imphal. Their bombs rained down on the town and resulted in a heavy loss of life and the complete breakdown of all water and electric installations. Colonel Pritchard sent me to Imphal from Palel to do what I could; but without materials, tools or labour it was difficult to restore the water supply. I tried to discover someone who could give me the lay-out of the pipe-lines and found a man called Gopal through whom I was able to locate a few of the original native staff of the Public Works Department, most of whom had fled. Together we repaired the main line and headworks, and next morning a part of Imphal had a supply. Later, we were joined

---

[1] Notes by Major A. G. Hellicar, R.E., dated July 21st, 1953.

[2] The bridge had been built in April 1942 by 414 Bridge Construction Section.

[3] Notes by Major O'Callaghan, R.E., compiled in 1950.

by a Field Company and most of the water-supply system was reinstated, though our work was hampered by a second air raid which caused even more damage than the first. Owing to the disappearance of the P.W.D. employees, 114 Works had to take over all their duties, but with the help of the Field Company the electric supply to Imphal was also restored quickly. During the months which followed, Gopal became universally popular with soldiers and civilians alike and it was tragic that he should afterwards have met his end while trying to repair a high-tension line that was inadvertently switched on while he was at work."

A very early arrival from India was 91 Field Company (Bombay), under Major J. R. G. Finch, R.E., which reached Imphal on June 8th, 1942, and began to repair roads and bridges in the Litan area towards Ukhrul, which lies to the north-east of the Imphal Plain. The unit was sadly ravaged by malaria, but in addition to its road work it managed to build a number of boats with the help of local tradesmen.[1] A small party under 2nd Lieut. Chambers was detailed to accompany some Gurkhas to Fort Hertz, the distant outpost far north of Myitkyina, which General Wavell wished to reoccupy in order to protect its landing strip and encourage the local Kachins. Chambers took his party to Dimapur and arrived at Dinjan aerodrome about June 15th. He was ordered to form a fortified base at Fort Hertz from which levies of Kachins could be raised to operate in the surrounding districts. The orders emanated from a senior Staff Officer stationed more than 1,000 miles away in Delhi. Chambers was told that he could expect to be at Fort Hertz for six months and that there were only two land routes between it and India, one leading into Tibet at 11,000 feet and the other into Assam at 14,000 feet. He was warned that he would find no Engineer stores at the fort, no quinine, no clothing and no boots. It was a dreary prospect. The Sappers and Gurkhas were to go by air and therefore with the minimum of kit. They drew two months' rations and waited at Dinjan for a week, mostly prostrated by malaria. Then, happily, a Deputy Commissioner arrived who had recently walked over the mountains from Fort Hertz. He told Chambers that the place had already been looted by 5,000 Chinese, that it was no more than a bamboo and mud affair surrounded by swamps, that the local Kachins would not fight, and that the detachment might expect to be almost

---

[1] *The Fighting Cock* (History of the 23rd Indian Division), by Lieut.-Colonel A. J. F. Doulton, O.B.E., p. 34.

obliterated by black-water fever and beri-beri unless withdrawn in the rains. He wound up by dubbing the whole project as "The Seven Pillars of Folly". In this he had the keenest support from the Royal Air Force who stated that the landing ground at the fort was merely a football field bordered by jungle grass. These matters having been represented to the senior officer at Delhi, a welcome order arrived on June 30th directing the Sappers to rejoin their headquarters at Imphal, which they did after being held up for three days by a landslide. The episode furnishes a striking example of the evils of remote control and insufficient information.

Another Sapper unit which was early in the field was 71 Field Company (Bengal) under Major F. W. Pritchard, R.E. It arrived in Manipur in June 1942 with the 49th Brigade to join the 23rd Indian Division which was guarding Imphal. Employed chiefly on defence works and water-supply, it also kept open the first six miles of the Palel-Tamu Road. In addition, it reconnoitred many hill-tracks, one reconnaissance extending as far down the Manipur River as Tonzang. The return journey through the mountainous tracts to the west of the river constituted the earliest reconnaissance of part of the route adopted later for the Imphal-Tiddim Road. A half Section of the Company succeeded in reaching Fort Hertz by air, complete with picks, shovels and tommy-guns, and set to work at once on improving communications. In December, when the Americans took charge, the detachment assisted them in cutting a track through the Naga Hills which was developed later into part of the famous Ledo Road. Two months earlier, the remainder of the unit, under Major T. A. C. Brownlie, I.E., had moved down the Tamu Road to the Shenam Saddle for road and defence work.

After the monsoon of 1942 had ceased, 70 Field Company (Major I. H. Lyall-Grant, R.E.), together with 71 Field Company and the newly arrived 68 Field Company (Major J. R. Rawlence, R.E.), was employed on the Tamu Road. The casualties from malaria were terrible at this period. 71 Field Company, for instance, could provide only 30 men fit for duty. Nevertheless, it was able to begin the conversion of a bridle path from Tengnoupal to Mombi into a track passable for jeeps. The two places, though less than 30 miles apart, needed 50 miles of track to connect them. The route traversed steep hill-sides and swung crazily round rocky precipices; but after four or five months, jeeps were able to crawl along it. Meanwhile, on the main Tamu Road, the outstanding achievement was the bridging of the Lokchao River. Part of the old Inglis Bridge erected by 414

Bridge Construction Section was launched on a new site. "The Sappers indulged in a fair imitation of 'hunt the slipper' over the Imphal Plain", writes Lieut.-Colonel Doulton.[1] "Dismantled in haste at a time of crisis, its bits and pieces were everywhere. Eventually, they were collected, but their return home was not easy as the transoms were 17 feet long. 71 Field Company assembled the bridge at the gap and meditated how to hoist the finished article into position. The answer was to use one bulldozer as a counterweight while a second provided the propulsive power."

By the end of November 1942, the road-makers were near Sibong, 10 miles short of Tamu, and on December 20th, the Palel-Tamu Road was declared open to 3-ton lorries. 71 Field Company was then camped at Moreh, 4 miles short of Tamu and close to the Indo-Burma frontier. Reconnaissances were made along a rough track leading southwards along the frontier towards Witok. These were then extended as far as Kalewa, 100 miles down the Chindwin, and the track was gradually improved. In January 1943, 68 Field Company, which had been working on the road to Shuganu at the southern end of the Imphal Plain, moved to the Yu River beyond Tamu to make a jeep track towards Sittaung, and in the following month 71 Field Company moved to a village called Sunle, bulldozing the way ahead and maintaining the track in rear. Bridges of teak logs, cut by coolie labour, were built along the route, the interstices being filled with gravel after the logs had been placed in position by elephants. The Sappers learnt to appreciate the value of these powerful animals and to agree with the American versifier who wrote:— "Elephants are useful friends, equipped with handles at both ends." The work had often to be done far in advance of infantry protection so the Sappers had to provide their own covering parties.

As already stated, General Wavell had planned that during the winter of 1942/43 the 4th Indian Corps (17th and 23rd Divisions) should advance into Burma and establish itself on the Chindwin River between Kalewa and Sittaung. This was in order to lessen the enemy's resistance to General Stilwell's progress from Ledo towards Myitkyina and that of other Chinese forces from Yunnan. There were two possible routes by which the 4th Corps could reach the Chindwin. One was through Palel and Tamu. This was a single-way mountain road liable to be washed away in the rains. The distance from Imphal to Palel was 28 miles and Tamu lay 36 miles beyond.

---

[1] *The Fighting Cock*, by Lieut.-Colonel A. J. F. Doulton, O.B.E., p. 42.

Thence to Sittaung on the river bank was another 25 miles or so. The total distance from Imphal was therefore under 90 miles by road. The other route lay through Bishenpur southwards to Tiddim (163 miles) and thence eastwards to Fort White and down into the Kabaw Valley at Kalemyo, a further 40 miles, making a total distance of over 200 miles.[1] This route, however, was screened by hills to the east until it approached Kalemyo, whereas the Tamu route was exposed throughout to enemy attacks from across the Chindwin. It was decided at first that most of the roadmaking resources should be devoted to the Tiddim route, but soon after the New Year the decision was reversed because there was not sufficient time to develop that route properly and because of its extraordinary engineering difficulties. Therefore, the main roadmaking effort was switched to the shorter and easier, though more exposed, Tamu route. Later, owing to a shortage of transport and material for road construction the advance of the 4th Corps to Sittaung and Kalewa was postponed, and when it was discovered that the Chinese in Yunnan had no immediate intention of co-operating with General Stilwell, the operations of the Corps were limited to offensive patrolling. This restriction, though unfortunate from a strategical point of view, was not altogether unwelcome to the hard-worked Engineer units for it gave them more time in which to improve the routes to the Chindwin. The Tiddim route was incredibly difficult. For the first forty miles from Imphal there was a fairly good and level road which was passable for jeeps in all weathers and for lorries except in heavy rain, but beyond that point there was only a track suitable perhaps for jeeps in good weather, though not as far as the Manipur River crossing at Milestone 126. After leaving the Imphal Plain the route crossed hills rising to 7,000 feet and traversed slopes of 70 degrees before plunging down 1,800 feet to the river, and some distance beyond the crossing it climbed rapidly for 2,000 feet to Tiddim. Most of the road alignment had to be hacked through dense jungle. Innumerable streams had to be crossed and every stream was liable to sudden spates, and when the monsoon came, the entire country was blanketed in mist and drenching rain.

While the 4th Corps Engineers were trying to cope with the extension of the alternative routes to the Chindwin, other formations were developing the meagre line of communication far behind the Manipur

---

[1] See the two maps of the Tiddim Road, Milestones 32 to 83, and Milestone 109 to Kalemyo, included in Chapter XII.

front. Assam is cut off from the rest of India by the great Brahmaputra River, unbridged throughout its length and with a waterlevel which is liable to rise 25 feet in the rains and a course which may change several miles either way. In 1942, the railway system east of the river was limited to a single metre-gauge line with very few resources in locomotives and rolling stock. To connect it with the west bank system, wagon-ferries were maintained at two places. There was no all-weather road up the west bank, and on the east bank only a narrow road extending eastwards from the ferry at Gauhati. Consequently, the railway deficiencies could not be relieved appreciably by additional road transport. Nor could river transport solve the problem because many steamships had been sent to Iraq. The transportation difficulties had a considerable effect on the military operations. For many months, the troops at the front had to live on reduced rations and therefore suffered in health and became less able to fight. Between October and December 1942, no fewer than 20,000 sick had to be evacuated from the Eastern Army, quite apart from the 15,000 evacuated after the Burma Army reached Imphal. It was obviously necessary to supplement ground transportation by a vast system of air supply which entailed also air defence. At the beginning of the year, the air strength in India had been almost negligible and the few operational airfields that existed were situated near the North-West Frontier. A programme for the construction of 200 new airfields was therefore launched, and by the end of November 1942 about 150 were ready for use. There had also been a great increase in the number of air squadrons, and the Indian Air Force alone had 10 squadrons equipped with modern aircraft. Offensive operations were undertaken against the Japanese airfields and communications in Burma, and command of the air passed to the Allies. Over and over again, our supremacy in the air saved a critical situation. Isolated detachments were supplied. Sick and wounded were flown to hospital. Morale was raised. Aerial reconnaissance revealed the enemy's positions, and the whole aspect of the fighting underwent a radical change for the better.

The task of building airfields in Assam and Bengal for the air forces supporting the troops defending India from invasion, and for the American transport aircraft carrying supplies over the "Hump" route to China, was undertaken in 1942 by the Military Engineer Services assisted by any Field Engineer units which happened to be available. This organization was replaced in the spring of 1943 by a General Reserve Engineer Force (G.R.E.F.) working under the direction of the Engineer-in-Chief, India (Lieut.-General H. E. Roome). Though much of the actual labour was undertaken by the Public Works Department, military engineer units of all kinds were also employed. Stone and cement were scarce, and as about 200 tons of stone were needed daily for each airfield under construction, dozens of quarries had to be opened and crushing plants installed. The transport of stone threw a heavy additional strain on the already overworked railways and river craft, and consequently the engineers often tried to supplement the stone supply with locally-burnt bricks. This, in turn, necessitated vast quantities of fuel for burning clay and the transport of that fuel to the site, and so the full cycle of obstacles was completed. The construction of an airfield is roughly equivalent to that of 60 miles of concrete road, a fact which gives some idea of the magnitude of the requirements. G.R.E.F., however, was not concerned solely with airfields. Its activities extended far and wide and included the laying of 140 miles of petrol pipe line to Dimapur to relieve the railway.

Many units of the Indian Engineers helped to build airfields in Assam, but it must suffice here to record some of the experiences of 362 Field Company of the Madras Corps under Major J. W. Bossard, R.E. When a decision was reached in March 1942 that the 1st Indian Chemical Warfare Group should be assembled, 362 Field Company was one of the units formed for that purpose, with bridging as a subsidiary role; and when the C.W. Group was abolished in May 1943, the Company was posted to a Forward Airfield Construction Group to build an airfield at Dergaon in Assam under the auspices of G.R.E.F. Its journey from Deolali to Dergaon was one to be remembered. To begin with, owing to some miscalculation, the men sat for 24 hours in the train in Deolali Station, and when they had covered only 30 miles from Deolali, the locomotive gave up the ghost and they had to wait a further 8 hours for a relief engine. Although halts of three hours for meals had been carefully arranged, the train invariably stopped a mile or two from the selected spots and remained there for a few hours. Then it would pull slowly into the station and the official meal halt would begin. At Calcutta, a reversing station, the locomotive had to be shifted to the other end of the train, whereupon the guard insisted that his van must go also. The driver did not agree, so they sat down and argued the point for an hour, after which the driver walked to a signal box and got a special shunting order. Three telegrams were received *en route*, each changing the unit's destination, and to crown everything, some

Oil tank under construction by General Reserve Engineer Force at Dibrugarh

sparks from the locomotive set fire to the unit's transport. Yet 362 Company arrived safely on June 15th in North-East Assam and began to build the Dergaon airfield.

A runway 2,600 yards long and 50 yards wide was needed and also 5,000 feet of taxi strip and 45 hardstandings of Pressed Steel Planking (P.S.P.), which was here used for the first time in India.[1] An American Engineer Officer who had laid a runway at Dakar in Africa was brought in to advise. His men, he said, had been Pennsylvanian miners, whom he described as "Purty tough and mighty mean", and he looked askance at the Madras Sappers. 362 Field Company soon showed what they could do and he changed his opinion At first there were many casualties from malaria, but these were reduced by rigid anti-malaria discipline. Work then proceeded very rapidly with the help of mechanical equipment, and some weeks before the unit left Dergaon in October 1943 for employment on the Tamu Road, the airfield was in full use by aircraft of all types.

We revert now to the situation early in 1943 on the Manipur front where the greater part of the 4th Corps Engineer effort was being directed to the development of the Tamu Road while the 17th Divisional Engineers carried on as best they could with the longer Tiddim Road. The Tamu Road had to be extended not only to Sittaung on the Chindwin but also southwards down the malarial Kabaw Valley. Many streams had to be crossed, so it was fortunate that a new type of bridge, the Bailey, had recently arrived in India and that bulldozers were becoming plentiful. One of the reasons for the rapid extension of the Tamu Road was a feint attack on the Japanese forces at Kalewa which the 23rd Indian Division was to carry out in order to cover the advance of Brigadier Orde Wingate's "Chindits" (known officially as the 77th Infantry Brigade) who were to cross the Chindwin at points north of that place and penetrate deep into Burma. Although no Indian Engineer units accompanied this first Chindit Expedition, one or two Royal Engineer Officers were included, among them being Major J. M. Calvert who commanded one of the four columns. The force comprised some 3,000 British, Burmese and Gurkha troops and was designed to operate without any kind of land communication. Each column was entirely self-contained, with pack transport, machine-guns and mortars but no artillery, and every officer and man carried a 70-lb pack holding 5 days' rations and an

---

[1] "A Sapper and Miner Field Company from 1942 to 1945", by Major J. W. Bossard, M.B.E., R.E., appearing in *The R.E. Journal*, June 1950, pp. 149-161.

elaborate jungle kit. The Chindits proposed to reach and sever the railway line running northwards from Mandalay to the Myitkyina terminus, to harass the enemy in the Shwebo region, and then, if possible, to cut the Maymyo-Lashio branch line towards the Chinese frontier. Covered by the 23rd Division's diversionary operations, in which 71 Field Company was concerned in the Kabaw Valley, Orde Wingate's columns crossed the Chindwin in February 1943 and plunged into the jungle, although the scheme was nearly cancelled at the last moment because the Chinese forces in Yunnan had refused to co-operate. The Myitkyina railway was cut in many places, but the Lashio line could not be reached, and in June 2,000 exhausted Chindits trickled back to Manipur in small parties. In general it must be admitted that the expedition was a strategic failure for it did not take the enemy by surprise nor did it disorganize his offensive plans; but the experience gained was put to good use a year later when Wingate's Long Range Penetration Group of six brigades (camouflaged as the "3rd Indian Division") was transported into Northern Burma, mostly by air. One of the brigades of that force was commanded by a Royal Engineer, Brigadier L. E. C. M. Perowne.

Lieut. G. Pearson describes the work of some of the Bengal Sapper units in the Tamu area in 1943.[1] In March, 71 Field Company and other Divisional Engineers provided a ferry over the Yu River at Minthami, south of Tamu, which was subsequently used by the Chindits returning from the Burma jungles. In addition, a road along the Indo-Burma frontier was maintained as far south as Htinzin, 35 miles from Tamu. In the Sittaung direction there was some fighting against enemy patrols. Here, 68 Field Company was making a fair-weather road for 15-cwt. vehicles, and blasting, bulldozing and cutting of timber for bridges were in full swing. The blasting and timber-cutting parties went ahead while behind them came the bulldozers clearing a track which could be widened later. Elephants helped to haul into position the logs needed for the timber bridges. Based on Moreh, 71 Field Company maintained many stretches of road, much of which was corduroy. Cutting and collecting wood was exhausting work, so the men were glad when the unit was ordered to make two flying ferries over the Lokchao River and to repair a number of timber bridges. Afterwards, the Company was employed in putting down shingle on the Sittaung Road and, early in June,

---

[1] *Brief History of the K.G.V's O. Bengal Sappers and Miners Group, R.I.E., (August 1939-July 1946)*, by Lieut. G. Pearson R.E., pp. 53-55.

began to open a track towards Mintha. Both 68 and 71 Companies then left the front, 68 Company to practice watermanship on the Waithou Lake near Imphal and 71 Company to undergo training at Wangjing in attacking bunkers with pole-charges. Meanwhile, a tremendous amount of work was in progress on the Dimapur-Imphal Road as well as on the Tamu Road. 75 Field Company, under Major J. S. Dhillon, I.E.,[1] was engaged on the Tamu Road. Since November 1942, this unit had been working on communications in the Imphal Plain and on the road from Imphal to Bishenpur, whence a track led westwards to Silchar. Shingling and metalling of the Tamu Road was continued steadily during the monsoon with the help of 2,000 coolies and the surface was thus kept suitable for motor traffic, the necessary road-metal being obtained from local quarries.

The Madras Sappers were strongly represented in 1943 in the Tamu area. 59 Field Company (Major J. D. Hibbert, R.E.) helped to prepare the track to Sittaung and worked later on the Palel-Tamu Road, where 428 Field Company (Major Partap Narain, I.E.) was already engaged. 429 Field Company (Major J. H. F. H. Jolly, R.E.) was on the Tamu Road during the autumn, employed under G.R.E.F. 422 Field Company (Major I. B. C. Taylor, R.E.) began to work on the Sittaung track in October, and 424 Field Company (Major J. E. Barnes, R.E.) in December. The latter unit had moved to the Tamu Road from the Tiddim Road in March. Several Bombay Sapper units were also in the Tamu region. 24 Field Company (Major G. V. C. Darley, R.E.) arrived there early in April 1943 and erected a triple-truss double-storey Bailey Bridge of 160 feet span—the first of this kind to be built east of Suez. In October, the unit was transferred to the Tiddim Road. 91 Field Company (Major J. R. G. Finch, R.E.) was engaged from February to April on tracks from Moreh to Mintha and Sunle and in May erected a Bailey Bridge of 120 feet span over the Lokchao River at Moreh. Then it went to Shenam. 92 Field Company (Major A. C. Lewis, R.E.) arrived on the Tamu-Sittaung track in November and worked there for several months, as also did 481 Field Company (Major M. I. Pritchard, R.E.). Field Park Companies of all three Corps were in support, but space does not allow a record of their employment. Sufficient has been written to show the magnitude of the Engineer concentration in the Tamu sector of the Chindwin River front.

---

[1] In July 1943, Major J. S. Dhillon handed over command of 75 Field Company to Major L. G. Kirton, R.E.

The War Diary of 59 Field Company contains a copy of the instructions issued in March 1943 by the Chief Engineer, 4th Corps (Brigadier L. D. Grand),[1] regarding the Tamu Road Project.[2] The object was to provide a two-way all-weather road from Palel by November 1st. Two main factors had to be considered — malaria and the monsoon, which might be expected to arrive together. Work in malarial areas was therefore to be finished quickly and the troops moved to safer areas; but if possible, all work should be completed before the rains. The difficult nature of the country and the interference caused by constant traffic might make it advisable sometimes to cut a second one-way road rather than widen the existing road for two-way traffic. Every effort should be made to complete the Lokchao-Tamu section before the onset of the rains. The next in priority was the Palel-Shenam section, since two-way traffic was urgently needed to Shenam. For about half the distance from Palel, the existing road was fairly wide and could be converted easily for two-way traffic. The remainder would have two one-way thoroughfares, as also would the section between Shenam and Lokchao. And finally, in order that the work should proceed quickly, the existing road would be closed periodically for three days and then opened for two days to traffic. The orders give a good idea of the problems confronting the 4th Corps and other Engineer units employed in the spring of 1943.

Some extracts from an article by Brigadier Partap Narain will show the conditions under which most of the Sapper units worked.[3] The story begins in India. "In August 1942", he writes, "I took 428 Field Company for a month to the newly established Jungle Training Camp at Shimoga. Colonel J. F. D. Steedman, then Commandant, had just returned from Malaya. The rain hardly ever stopped. There were no camp structures and we lived in tents and trained on the banks of a large river in spate. None of the men had ever lived under such conditions — dense jungle, leeches and over two inches of rain per day—but after the first few days of cursing,

---

[1] Brigadier L. D. Grand was succeeded in June 1943 by Brigadier H. Williams.

[2] The Order of Battle shows that in March 1943 the following units were detailed to work on the Tamu Road Project. Between Milestones 29 and 42 (under C.R.E. 4th Corps Troops) 24, 75 and 424 Field Companies and 22, 33 and 36 Artisan Works Pioneer Battalions. Between Milestones 42 and 71 (under C.R.E. 107 Works) 59 and 428 Field Companies, 25 Artisan Works Company, 6 and 16 Engineer Battalions and 17, 39, 40 and 51 Auxiliary Pioneer Battalions. Three Gurkha Battalions were attached to provide infantry working parties.

[3] "With the Madras Sappers". by "Kashmiri", appearing in *The Journal of the Institution of Military Engineers*, October 1950, pp. 341-348.

we settled down. After the camp, most of the men went on a month's leave before proceeding to Burma on active service with barely six weeks' training. The final order to move, however, did not come till November. Capt. D. I. Perdue was posted as my second-in-command, and I got Jepson, Kochhar, Pringle and Crabtree as Company Officers. Our vehicles had balloon tyres and we were really equipped for the desert. Realizing that malaria was to be our main enemy rather than the Japs, we began to enforce a ruthless anti-malaria discipline and avoided a long stay at Manipur Road. After a few weeks at Kanglatongbi, north of Imphal, we went forward to Palel for work on the Tamu Road. We came under command of C.R.E. 107 Works—a very nice civilian put straight into a Lieut.-Colonel's uniform—who took me to Tamu for a reconnaissance. I believe our jeep was the first to travel along the road since the retreat of the Burma Army in the preceding summer. The road was littered with skeletons and abandoned equipment. We soon moved forward and took over the task of opening the route from Shenam to the Lokchao River, a stretch of about 40 miles. Our camp was on the famous Khongkhang Ridge where we were to stay through the next monsoon. The bulldozers began to improve the road surface while we started a factory for the manufacture of box-frames for culverts. Each Section of the unit was allotted its own sector where it established its camp. Six months of hard work made the road passable. Detachments went forward to help the Engineer Battalion, ahead of us, in the more technical work and bridge construction. More Engineer units arrived and our task became more concentrated, though two of the three Sections had still to live in detached camps. In the middle of June, the monsoon broke. It was hell working on the road—just clearing mud along with Pioneer and other labour. The 23rd Division had to be withdrawn after the first Wingate expedition had returned, and we were left as a forward unit and had to act as infantry in addition to our normal tasks. For nearly six months we never saw fresh meat and the men started getting 'browned off' with shovelling mud. So much so that one day I had a heart-to-heart talk with Brigadier H. Williams, who was then Chief Engineer, 4th Corps, and asked that the unit should be employed on soldiering for a change. This request bore fruit and in September we got orders to move to Tiddim in support of the 17th Light Division.[1] This division had

---

[1] The 17th Indian Division and the 39th Indian Division (formerly the 1st Burma Division) were reorganized in January 1943 as Indian "Light" Divisions and their engineer field units became "Light" Engineer Companies.

only two brigades and had therefore been allotted only two Field Companies, 60 (Madras) and 70 (Bengal). Both these units were now being rested as they had had a tough time when they came out of Burma with the 17th Division in 1942, and we thus got an ideal opportunity of proving our worth with the famous "Black Cats". We established our headquarters at Tiddim, in advance of which the 63rd Brigade was holding Kennedy Peak and the country right up to Fort White and beyond."

Important changes in the higher commands in India took place during the summer of 1943. On June 20th, General Sir Claude Auchinleck became Commander-in-Chief in place of General Sir Archibald Wavell who was appointed Viceroy. Since the outbreak of war, Wavell had directed some fourteen campaigns—the Western Desert, British Somaliland, Eritrea, Italian Somaliland, Abyssinia, Greece, Crete, Iraq, Syria, Persia, Malaya, the Dutch East Indies, Burma and Arakan. The fighting forces were sorry to lose a Commander of such exceptional ability, but they had every confidence in Auchinleck who was a product of the Army in India and had shown his prowess by defeating the German and Italian attack on Egypt in July 1941 after he had succeeded Wavell in the chief command in the Middle East. Although Auchinleck was well fitted to shoulder the burden of the war in Burma, the struggle was soon to develop such proportions that it became advisable to relieve him of some of his responsibilities and this was secured by the creation of a separate South East Asia Command (S.E.A.C.) which included Burma, and the appointment of Admiral Lord Louis Mountbatten as its Supreme Commander. Meanwhile, the war in Burma was controlled from Delhi and the 'build-up' in Manipur proceeded as rapidly as circumstances would allow.

Although most of the Engineer formations were engaged in improving the route to the Chindwin through Tamu, General Irwin, the Eastern Army Commander, now decided that the Tiddim route should be given priority in spite of its mountainous character. He wished to forestall any possible enemy advance to Tiddim, and to secure this object he had to arrange for the provisioning of the 17th Division in this forward area where there was a serious shortage of supplies such as rice. By March 1943, the Tehri-Garhwal Field Company had improved the first 100 miles of the Tiddim route to such an extent that it could carry light motor traffic; but beyond that point, through the indescribably rugged country extending down to the Manipur River crossing at Milestone 126, there was nothing which could be called a road. The shortage of Engineer formations had to be made good by infantry labour and consequently the entire 17th Division was thrown into the scheme known as "Exercise Navvy." The Tehri-Garhwals had already built a great number of temporary wooden bridges along the route so that the roadmaking equipment should not be held up. These bridges were supposed to last only a few weeks under lorry traffic, but actually many of them were still standing a year later.

The *magnum opus* of the Tehri-Garhwal Field Company was the building of the piers and abutments of a new bridge at the Manipur River crossing to supplement an old 300-feet suspension bridge. "We decided to build an abutment on a rock foundation on the near side", writes Hellicar,[1] "and by using a 180-feet span, we could place the central pier on the far edge of the boulder-strewn river at low water. During the rains this pier would be in the centre of a roaring torrent moving at perhaps 20 miles per hour, so it was obvious that the foundation would have to be very deep. We used sheet-iron caissons for the first six feet, and then, by grubbing out boulders from beneath them and replacing quickly with sandbags filled with cement, we got down to 14 feet below bed level. The hole was filled with concrete, and on this base we raised a stone pier 25 feet high. Although we finished the piers before the road-makers reached the river, it was decided that it was then too late in the dry season to bring up a Bailey bridge and that mule and jeep transport must be used to supply Tiddim, so we strengthened the existing suspension bridge by building another around it and joining the two together, and we also built and operated a flying ferry to carry bulldozers singly or jeeps three at a time. The raft was made from local timber and empty oil-drums, and when fully loaded, the decking was under water. The piers and abutments for the Bailey bridge were finished about two months before we left the site in August 1943. The bridge itself was completed later by 60 Field Company, and I believe that it was opened by the Maharajah in January 1944."

The real effort on the Tiddim Road began early in March 1943 when the 17th Division undertook the rapid construction of 26 miles of roadway from Milestone 100 down to the Manipur River crossing. In this "Exercise Navvy" every unit was allotted a stretch of alignment for digging and blasting and worked under Sapper supervision. The Engineer units were concerned mostly with bridges and culverts.

---

[1] Notes by Lieut.-Colonel A. G. Hellicar, R.E., dated October 2nd, 1951.

70 Field Company built no less than 47 of these in a length of 8 miles, all being of timber and spike design, and 60 Field Company was similarly employed. Brigadier H. E. Horsfield, at that time Chief Engineer, Fourteenth Army, gives the following description of the tribulations experienced on the Tiddim Road[1]:— "The road was the main artery for the forward troops and it had always been as incomprehensible and fickle as any member of the fair sex. At one time, mud slid over it at Milestone 42. At another time, a driver left his car on it overnight and in the morning found that that bit of road had slipped down and there was his car, still on the road, but 30 feet below the normal level. Life was never dull on this 135-mile stretch when it was pouring with rain and the ditches were overflowing."

Serving with 70 Field Company was Lieut. R. T. Urwin, R.E., who writes as follows[2]:— "Equipment was always in short supply and much improvisation was necessary. Our transport was often limited to a jeep and about thirty mules per platoon. The Sappers had to be prepared to attack and defend. The terrain called for toughness, and the work was exhausting. I remember one section of the road when it was no more than a line of wooden pegs in the jungle. Then a mule track was cut and this was widened to take jeeps, and still later, 15-cwt. trucks. At this stage the Divisional Field Companies moved ahead and left to others the task of developing the track into a road for 3-ton lorries. Most of the work was done with axe, pick and crowbar, assisted where possible by little 15-cwt. compressor trucks. The road was cut into the mountain side, and every re-entrant had to have a bridge or a culvert. Local timber was used for the forward bridges. The road surface was always a problem. During the monsoon, only 4-wheel-drive vehicles could be sure of getting through. In the summer, the dust rose in choking clouds. Although there was always water in the deep valleys, the supply to the troops on the ridges was a difficult problem, and it was a familiar sight to see mule-drivers taking their animals down as much as 1,000 feet to bring up water." On May 1st, 1943, the Tiddim Road was declared open for lorry traffic as far as the Manipur River crossing at Milestone 126 from Imphal, but beyond that point there was still only a precarious jeep track to Tiddim. A few weeks later,

---

[1] "Engineer Operations with the Fourteenth Army in 1943-44", by Brig. H. E. Horsfield, C.B.E., M.C., appearing in *The R.E. Journal*, December 1945, pp. 241-243.

[2] Notes by the Revd. R. T. Urwin (formerly Major R.E.) dated November 7th, 1951.

as the Japanese were reported to be moving towards Tiddim from Kalemyo, a party of 70 Field Company was sent forward to improve the track beyond Tiddim while another was detailed to attend to a boat bridge at the crossing as the water-level showed signs of rising. Sure enough, a sudden flood came down one night and the bridge was saved only through a rapid decision by Jemadar Dharam Singh to dismantle it forthwith. The river continued to rise, but on June 12th 70 Field Company managed to build a flying ferry across the raging waters and thus maintained some sort of supply to the forward troops.

Meanwhile, the bulk of the labour on "Exercise Navvy" had fallen naturally to the infantry of the 17th Division, so perhaps some of the experiences of the 1st Battalion, The West Yorkshire Regiment, will not be out of place. On March 20th, the battalion was moved to Milestone 108 when the road was open only as far as Milestone 82. The track was then being widened on a steep ascent to the crest at Milestone 100 which was nearly 6,000 feet above sea-level. Beyond that point, all seemed to be virgin jungle. The completed portion to Milestone 82 bore little resemblance to a proper motor road. It was merely a rough passage, hacked through the forest, without any surfacing other than a coating of reddish-brown dust. The following description of the infantry at work comes from the pen of a Lance-Corporal.[1] "When we moved forward, each man carried either a large pick, a shovel or a crowbar in addition to his normal equipment. The trip in jeeps to Milestone 100 was pleasant enough though most of us did it with one leg over the side because the sight of a sheer drop of 3,000 feet to left or right was not conducive to steady nerves. At Milestone 100 we made the acquaintance of our invaluable friend, the mule. The units assembled and marched to Milestone 108 which was to be our first bivouac area. The march was gruelling because it led steeply downwards the whole way and we could discover no track of any description. We had to cling to the hillside like flies. Arrived at Milestone 108, we settled in for the night and made ourselves as comfortable as we could with only one blanket and a ground sheet per man. Morning dawned, and with it the start of many weeks of hard work. Each man had to shift about 60 cubic feet of earth a day and this often entailed the blasting of trees and boulders weighing many tons. Every officer and man, from the C.O. downwards, had the same task and the same rations.

From Pyramid to Pagoda, by Lieut.-Colonel E. W. C. Sandes, D.S.O., M.C., pp. 44, 45.

Each morning we had to march some three miles before we reached our stretch of road. The alignment seemed to twist and turn without apparent reason; but it was, in fact, a remarkable engineering feat, ably supervised by Major R. K. Kochhar, O.C. 60 Field Company, Indian Engineers. The road was first dug out of the mountain side by hand to a width of 11 feet to enable the Sappers to bring up their bulldozers and make it capable of taking two-way traffic.[1] We worked in shorts and boots alone, day in, day out, until 5.30 p.m., with short breaks for 'elevenses' and 'tiffin'. At last our task was completed, and when Major Kochhar came along the new road in a jeep we downed tools and gave him a right royal reception."

The day's routine on "Exercise Navvy" was ordered by the sun, for at 6.00 a.m., as the first rays appeared over the mountains, the men were awakened by the unholy din of the Cicada insects in the trees and bushes. Arrived at the road face, everyone hacked away the undergrowth and shovelled the soil over the *khud*. It might be loose dust, heavy clay or shale. Rocks were blasted with gelignite after holes had been jumped laboriously with crowbars. Progress was slow at first, but when the track was a few feet in width a pneumatic drill team from 60 Field Company arrived in a truck and made the holes more rapidly. The Sappers found willing helpers and advisers among the West Yorkshires, many of whom had been coalminers in civil life. After the end of the day's work, the infantry marched back to camp for a wash and a meal, and as the light faded they were treated to another serenade by the indefatigable Cicadas. "Exercise Navvy" was a race against the monsoon which was expected to break about May 15th. The 17th Division won that race, thanks to the energy of the infantry and the expert supervision of the working parties by the Indian Engineers.

The extension of the motor road to Tiddim itself was planned by the C.R.E. 17th Division but executed by civilian labour under the Public Works Department. Many thousands of Chin coolies were employed on an alignment which ran, for the most part, halfway up the mountain side. The scenery was indescribably beautiful. Range upon range of forest-clad hills stretched to the horizon. Some of the higher peaks, south-east of Tonzang, rose to 8,000 feet, and in the dim distance beyond Tiddim, Kennedy Peak soared to nearly

---

[1] The actual tasks were first to widen the track to 4 feet for mule traffic and then to 11 feet for 15-cwt. trucks. After the infantry had moved on, the bulldozers widened the road for two-way traffic.

9,000 feet. The final stretch of the road involved a climb of 2,000 feet in 4 miles and had 30 hairpin bends. This was known as "The Chocolate Staircase", so called because, viewed from below, it appeared as a series of golden-brown steps hewn out of the purple jungle. The original track had been built by Chin labour in 1942 to supply our forward troops in the Chin Hills. Tiddim was a straggling village, 5,600 feet above the sea and overlooking the deep gorge of the Beltang Lui. Beyond it, the track meandered past Kennedy Peak, Fort White and the old British outposts known as the "Bamboo Stockades", and passing through Kalemyo on the Myittha River, ended at Kalewa on the Chindwin. This was the only passable route in the entire region, but it traversed appallingly difficult country. Outposts on adjacent ridges might be almost within shouting distance, and yet an attempt to move from one to the other would involve a descent and ascent of thousands of feet through dense jungle and would occupy the greater part of a day.

In due course, the 17th Division moved forward to Tiddim and beyond though it could be supplied only with the greatest difficulty owing to the crippling of the Manipur River bridges by the spate in June. As already related, although preparations had been made by the Tehri-Garhwal Field Company to erect a Class 18 Bailey Bridge to meet such an eventuality, the parts could not be brought forward until the road from Imphal had been further improved. Therefore, the existing suspension bridge was strengthened for jeep traffic, a project which presented many transport problems because the cables, each weighing 1,300-lbs, had to be carried for 126 miles on trains of three jeeps coupled together. However, after the suspension bridge had been finished in August, jeep traffic poured across it until the end of the year. The low water-level then permitted the reconstruction of a floating bridge to take lorry traffic, and the Imphal Road having been further improved with stone secured by 442 Indian Quarrying Company from quarries excavated at Milestones 109 and 127, the stores for the Bailey Bridge arrived and the structure was erected.

The creation of the South East Asia Command was a very wise measure. The formation of this Command had been decided in Washington as early as May 1943 when it was agreed that it should include not only Burma but also Ceylon, Malaya, Sumatra, Thailand and French Indo-China and that Admiral Lord Louis Mountbatten should be appointed Supreme Commander of all the Allied land, sea and air forces operating therein. Mountbatten arrived in Delhi on October

7th, flew to China to contact his Amercan Deputy, General Stilwell, visited the headquarters at both Imphal and Chittagong, and was back in Delhi on October 22nd. The former Eastern Army, now under Lieut.-General Sir George Giffard, was split into the Eastern Command, India, under Lieut.-General A. G. O. M. Mayne and the Fourteenth Army in Burma under Lieut.-General W. J. Slim who assumed command on October 15th after commanding of the 15th Corps for four months. General Giffard became Commander, 11th Army Group, which comprised the Fourteenth Army, the forces in Ceylon and certain outlying garrisons. The Fourteenth Army, under General Slim, consisted of the 4th Indian Corps (Lieut.-General G. A. P. Scoones) based on Imphal and the 15th Indian Corps (Lieut.-General A. F. P. Christison) based on Chittagong. Mountbatten, being a sailor, planned at first to retake Burma by an amphibious operation using a large number of landing craft to seize the Andaman Islands as a prelude to an attack on Rangoon; but when, a few months later, most of the craft were withdrawn for operations in Europe, he was obliged to concentrate on a purely land attack. Undeterred by previous custom, he resolved to fight as hard in the monsoon as in dry weather and to make the fullest possible use of air supply to overcome the difficulties of road transport in the rainy season. He resolved also to select the most unhealthy areas for his operations because his troops were adequately safeguarded from malaria by the use of Mepacrine while the Japanese had no such advantage.[1]

In November 1943, we were in contact with the Japanese on three major land fronts: in Arakan (including the Chin Hills), in the Manipur region of Assam, and in Northern Burma. On the Arakan front, the 5th and 7th Indian Divisions of the 15th Corps were in the process of relieving the 26th Indian Division, and the 81st West African Division was arriving. On the Assam front, the 4th Corps, now comprising the 17th, 20th and 23rd Indian Divisions, guarded the approaches south and east of Manipur and was preparing to assume the offensive. On this front also there was an independent brigade operating in the Lushai Hills.[2] The Northern Burma front (known as the Northern Combat Area Command or N.C.A.C.) was

---

[1] Before the introduction of Mepacrine, 120 malaria cases were admitted to hospital for every admission on account of wounds. At the end of the war, the proportion had fallen to 6 to 1.

[2] 432 Independent Platoon, formed from 63 Field Company in January 1942, was attached to this brigade until early in 1943.

held by General Stilwell's force of two Chinese divisions based on Ledo, with a third division in reserve. A small garrison, mainly of Kachin levies, held Fort Hertz. Wingate's "Chindits" had not yet reappeared at the front. Expanded into six Long Range Penetration Brigades and camouflaged as the "Special Force" or "3rd Indian Division", they were undergoing further training in Central India. It may be interesting to note that although Wingate's L.R.P. Force was now composed mainly of British troops together with some Gurkhas and West Africans, six "Special Sections" of the Indian Engineers had been formed by the Bengal Corps in August 1943 to accompany some Gurkha reinforcements for the force. These Sections moved into Assam in December, so it is possible that some of them accompanied Wingate into Burma in March 1944. An attempt was made to form two mixed British and Indian Field Companies (89 and 90), but the system proved unsatisfactory and the units were re-formed with entirely British personnel. Eventually, 89 Field Company reverted to being an Indian Engineer unit.

In the autumn of 1943, the Japanese had only five infantry divisions in Burma though a sixth was on its way. The 55th Japanese Division was in Arakan while the other four composed the Fifteenth Japanese Army, under Lieut.-General Mutagachi, with headquarters near Mandalay. Of this Army, the 31st and 33rd Japanese Divisions faced the 4th Indian Corps along the Chindwin, the 18th Japanese Division opposed Stilwell in Northern Burma, and the 56th Japanese Division held the Chinese forces along the Yunnan border. The total enemy fighting strength was about 135,000 men. But already a railway link was being forged between Bangkok in Thailand and Moulmein in Tenasserim which would, when completed, greatly facilitate the arrival of enemy reinforcements. This was the infamous "Railroad of Death", 260 miles in length, on which thousands of British and Indian prisoners-of-war from Singapore perished miserably in the jungles from exhaustion, starvation and disease. The line was not fully opened until 1945, yet even without its aid the enemy strength in Burma increased with considerable rapidity so that by January 1944 it amounted to no less than 16 divisions comprising more than 200,000 men. These were the flower of the Japanese Army—hardy, specially trained and incredibly fanatical. It was fortunate for India that she was able to reinforce her frontiers with soldiers equally good, and in the end even better, and by superior leadership and greater strength to roll back the tide of invasion. The Japanese planned to split open the Allied front, sealing off the two halves and cutting all lines of communication. Each half was then to be destroyed separately, after which the victorious armies of Nippon would push forward into Bengal and Assam through Chittagong and Dimapur. The conquest of Arakan was to come first, Chittagong being seized and the Fourteenth Army reserves attracted southwards to help the 15th Indian Corps. Then, our northern sector having been thus weakened, the main thrust would be made towards Imphal and Dimapur, and if successful, would be followed by the severance of the Assam line of communication to China *via* the "Hump" and the invasion of the remainder of Assam and most of the rest of North-East India. The enemy still assumed that, if he out-flanked our forward positions by marching through dense jungle, we should retire to protect our lines of communication as we had done in Malaya, and he counted on replenishing his supplies from captured dumps as he advanced. He did not realize that air supply had changed the whole nature of the fighting. Detachments threatened with encirclement need no longer be withdrawn. Supplied and even reinforced by air, they could hold their ground. This miscalculation was fatal to the Japanese plans, and particularly so in Arakan as we shall see later.

Towards the end of 1943 the dispositions of General Scoones' 4th Corps on the Manipur front were as follows. The newly arrived 20th Indian Division, under Major-General D. D. Gracey, had its headquarters at Shenam on the Tamu Road and was engaged in patrolling across the Chindwin. The 23rd Indian Division, under Major-General O. L. Roberts (an ex-Bengal Sapper and Miner), was in the Tamu area; and the 17th Indian (Light) Division, under Major-General D. T. Cowan, was on the Tiddim Road with its headquarters about Milestone 102. Soon afterwards, the 20th Division relieved the 23rd Division which was withdrawn to the Imphal Plain. In the far north, General Stilwell's troops had made fair progress along the Ledo Road. They were established at Shingbwiyang and had completed the road up to that point. A petrol pipe line was also under construction for their supply. But in the dense forests of the Hukawng Valley Stilwell was now meeting stiffening opposition and it became clear that unless the Chinese co-operated effectively from Yunnan there was little prospect of opening the land route to China in 1944 by a junction of the Ledo Road with the old Burma Road. Stilwell's operations, however, are outside the scope of this narrative since no units of the Indian Engineers took part in them.

The 33rd Japanese Division, facing the 17th Indian Division in the Tiddim region, had launched attacks in October against Falam, to the south, and had pushed towards Kennedy Peak; but before this, 428 Field Company had received orders to move to Tiddim to support the Division which at the moment had only two brigades, the 48th and 63rd, and two Engineer units, 60 and 70 Field Companies. At Tiddim, 428 Field Company joined the 63rd Brigade which was holding Kennedy Peak and the road up to Fort White. Brigadier Partap Narain gives the following description of the experiences of the unit which he then commanded.[1] "Our first interesting job was to support the Gurkhas in an attack on the 'Bashas' (hill features) beyond Fort White, held by the Japanese. We spent a few days in planning reconnaissance routes and watersupply points and experimenting with bulk charges for the demolition of bunkers. Pole charges and bulk charges were made up in sealed tins of sizes which could be carried by a man. We tried them on our own bunkers and they proved most effective. I detailed Kochhar's Section to support the attack. Our troops surprised the Japs in their pyjamas; but unfortunately, just as we were going into position, our planes bombed us by mistake and there were a number of casualties. Young Kochhar was lucky enough to be pulled into a nullah by a Gurkha and thus escaped being written off. As soon as the monsoon was over, the Brigade Commander started getting worried about the water-supply at Kennedy Peak and the surrounding areas, and the Divisional Commander about the supply at Tiddim. The supply to small garrisons was an easy matter; but for Tiddim, with its population of nearly a brigade and some Divisional troops, we had to instal a proper water-supply. To get sufficient water we had to go right down to a stream more than 2,000 feet below the town, make a *bund* in the bed and instal twelve large Waluska pumps, pumping up in stages. More than 4,000 yards of 4" pipe had to be laid, and to get the engines to the various stages we had to make a jeep track. It is a great pity that the installation had later to be blown up when we were forced to evacuate the place."

The Tiddim water-supply scheme is described in detail in an article by Major J. V. Corbet, R.E.[2] The town, perched on a lofty ridge, was served before the war by a small gravity system which yielded

---

[1] "With the Madras Sappers", by 'Kashmiri' (Brig. Partap Narain), appearing in *The Journal of the Institution of Military Engineers*, October 1950, pp. 341-348.

[2] "Tiddim Water Supply Scheme", by Major J. V. Corbet, R.E., appearing in *The R.E. Journal*, June 1945, pp. 79-82.

little during the dry season. This supply was quite insufficient for the needs of the 17th Division and accordingly the C.R.E. (Lieut. Colonel R. S. B. Ward) had to produce a better system at very short notice. He entrusted the work to 428 Field Company. The final stretches of the Imphal-Tiddim Road were hurriedly made suitable for 15-cwt. trucks, but it was still necessary to transport the heavy pumping plant piece-meal. As a 50 h.p. pump could supply only 10,000 gallons per hour at 350 feet head, pumping had to be arranged in stages. The idea was to have five stages, four of which would have two pumping sets. At each stage there would be a 10,000 gallon reservoir and at the top some main reservoirs to hold a total of 50,000 gallons. Preliminary work began with marking the pipe-line and making a jeep track with the help of Chin labour, but the slope was so precipitous that the track was never really negotiable by wheels and visiting officers usually refused to descend to the bottom of the gorge. This was not surprising as the gradient on some of the lower hair-pin bends was 1 in 2. The system subsequently needed some alteration, but on the whole it yielded a good supply of water to the troops. 414 Field Park Company,[1] under Major R. Blagden, R.E., assisted 428 Field Company in some stages of the construction and then maintained the system until it had to be destroyed in March 1944.

Some mention has already been made of the experiences of a Section of 428 Field Company in action beyond Fort White as related by Brigadier Partap Narain. 70 Field Company shared also in the fighting beyond Tiddim which began in August 1943. A Section of that unit took part in an attack on 'Basha East', the highest part of a bare ridge in jungle-covered country to the south-east of Tiddim. The Sapper party reached the forming-up point after a night march in heavy rain and darkness so complete that the men had to stick phosphorescent leaves into their packs to keep contact with each other. Unfortunately, on this occasion they never came into action because the infantry attack failed. But elsewhere they had sometimes to act as actual assault troops. The enemy's bunkers, made of timber and earth, were very elaborate and had interior blast-walls so that a grenade thrown through a firing slit would probably fail to dislodge the defenders. This was where the Sapper 'bunker-busting' parties came into their own. A party usually consisted of

---

[1] 414 Field Park Company had been formed from 414 Bridge Construction Section.

an N.C.O. and 3 men, each man carrying an explosive charge of 20-lbs. made up in tins. The N.C.O. carried the firing mechanism, with detonator and primer connected up. If the infantry were checked they called for a Sapper Assault Party of this nature and indicated the target. The Sappers then crawled forward, rushed up to the bunker and piled their charges one on top of the other, and the N.C.O. having fixed the firing mechanism and pulled out the pin, they dived for the nearest cover. But things did not always pan out so well. Urwin gives an instance in his account of the assault on 'Basha East'. "As soon as the barrage stopped", he writes, "we began to move forward though not fast enough to satisfy the infantry Company Commander who started to encourage his men in no uncertain terms. We were only a few yards away, so I began to add my encouragements to his. Naturally, the Sappers thought I was addressing them, and, with a Moslem war-cry, they began to advance much faster than the rest. In fact, we got well in front as the infantry had slowed down because the Japs were not where they had expected them to be. The enemy were in a strong position to one flank and firing straight across the bare summit, so our troops went to ground and tried to adjust themselves to this new development. Suddenly, both sides ceased fire and we could hear the Jap commander exhorting his men. Having finished his speech, he shouted "Charge" in English, and both sides let loose at once. Neither could see the other and both thought the other was charging. When the firing died down, we found that we were in the front line with the infantry and there we dug in. After an hour or so, the Battalion Commander sent for me and said he thought there was a bunker we could deal with and that he would get some Gurkha scouts to pin-point the position for us; but when I brought up a Sapper party, both sides resumed firing and we had to wait. After another hour, all was silent again, but by this time the moonlight was so bright that the C.O. said we should get picked off if we attempted to deal with the bunker. Accordingly, we stayed in position on the perimeter and remained there for 48 hours while the infantry infiltrated round behind the Japs and, by cutting their water-supply, forced them to withdraw. Only after our Company Commander had protested that if we were not going to be used as Sappers he would like to have us back were we allowed to leave our sector of the defence and rejoin the unit. Such co-operation with infantry was common in the days when we held Tiddim."

A further account of Sapper activities on the Tiddim front is given by Brigadier Partap Narain who writes as follows:—[1] "In November 1943, after an unsuccessful attack by us, the Japs started attacking Fort White. A Battalion Group (of the 63rd Brigade) was therefore put in between Kennedy Peak and Fort White and 428 Field Company had a Sub-Section with it for water-supply duties. During the night of November 13th, our position was heavily shelled by the enemy and was over-run at dawn next day. I went up to Kennedy Peak to see the stragglers coming in. There were Punjabis, Gunners, Signallers, Service Corps, all and sundry, returning with awful tales, but I could see no sign of my Sappers. In fact, there was no sign of them for two days and I felt sure I had lost them. Then suddenly they marched into camp, properly dressed and complete with arms and ammunition. They had had a hard time marching in and out of the Jap lines without food or water. This is what had happened. Naik Dorairaj Nadar, having received no orders to withdraw the Sub-Section, had taken up an alternative position from which, after reconnaissance, he returned later to his original post. Here he organized a meal for his men and sent out patrols. He held his post till 4.0 p.m. on November 14th, eight hours after the Battalion had been withdrawn, and only left it when the evening patrol reported a large concentration of the enemy. Then he burnt all maps and papers and withdrew the Sub-Section. After marching over devious routes for about 22 miles through dense jungle, he reported at Section H.Q. at 3.0 p.m. on the 15th. He was helped by Lance-Naik Pandiayan who had led the evening patrol on the 14th. While on this patrol, Pandiayan was captured by the enemy and deprived of his rifle and helmet. A Japanese officer threatened him with a revolver and asked him for information. This he refused to give, and hitting the officer with the spare barrel of a light machine gun, knocked the revolver out of his hand and escaped under heavy fire to give the alarm to his men. He reported that he had seen the Japs driving up and down in our abandoned jeeps and throwing *atta* about merrily. The Divisional Commander was very pleased and told me he had recommended both N.C.Os. for the Indian Distinguished Service Medal and the men for mentions".[2]

---

[1] "With the Madras Sappers", by 'Kashmiri' (Brig. Partap Narain), appearing in *The Journal of the Institution of Military Engineers*, October 1950, pp. 341-348.

[2] The I.D.S.M. was awarded, however, only to Naik Dorairaj Nadar, and none of the others was mentioned in despatches. Another account of this action appears in the Bangalore News Letter dated December 1946.

By the end of 1943, the Engineer 'build-up' in Assam and Arakan had assumed vast proportions and included a great number of field units of the Indian Engineers in addition to other Engineer formations of all descriptions. Among the Madras Group units were 56, 60, 62, 362, 365, 421, 424, 428, 429, 430, 431 and 432 Field Companies and 44, 303, 323, 326, 327 and 330 Field Park Companies, as well as 1 and 10 Bridging Sections and 101 Railway Construction Company. The Bombay Group was represented by 20, 24, 28, 30, 91, 92, 98, 328, 363, 402, 403, 481 and 483 Field Companies, several Field Park Companies and 9 and 889 Bridging Sections. The Bengal Group had 2, 68, 70, 71, 73, 75, 77, and 94 (Faridkot) Field Companies and 322, 332 and 414 Field Park Companies. The list may be incomplete, but it is evident that at least 33 Field Companies of the Indian Engineers were present. Accordingly, it is impossible to deal with them individually. The experiences of a few, as given in this narrative, must be taken as typical of those of the remainder. Most of the work was hard, exacting and often monotonous, but not a minute was wasted and it was due in no small measure to the labours of the Engineers in 1943 that the Japanese onslaughts in 1944 in both Arakan and Manipur were defeated with great slaughter and the way opened for a decisive counter-offensive.

As early as the end of January 1944, evidence had begun to accumulate of the enemy's intention to launch a general offensive against the 4th Corps in Manipur. Our air reconnaissance had reported troop movements, road building and the construction of rafts on the Chindwin River. It was therefore decided that, when the attack came, the Corps should concentrate in the Imphal area and fight the decisive battle on ground of its own choosing. Imphal was the nodal point on which hinged the defence of Assam. With the Imphal Plain in their hands, the Japanese would be able to build forward airfields from which to attack our air bases in Assam and Bengal and to interrupt our land communications with General Stilwell and our air route to China. The enemy's offensive was expected to take the form of an advance on Tiddim to cut off the 17th Division with the help of encircling thrusts northwards towards Imphal on either side of the Tiddim Road. Other enemy columns would push towards Imphal up the Tamu Road and towards Ukhrul, north-east of Imphal. Still further north, a smaller force would strike at the Imphal-Dimapur Road as a prelude to attacking Kohima and the rail-head, airfields and dumps at Manipur Road Station. The forecast proved remarkably accurate and was followed almost exactly by the enemy. The dispositions of the 4th Corps were based on it. But General Scoones was placed in the unenviable position of having at first to defend long stretches of the Tiddim-Imphal Road which ran roughly parallel to the enemy's front along the Chindwin. His main lines of communication were therefore terribly vulnerable. Still, he knew that a successful concentration on Imphal would lengthen the enemy's line of communication, already stretched to breaking point. On the Manipur front, January 1944 passed quietly enough with constant patrolling and intensive preparation for the coming storm. It was far otherwise in Arakan where General Christison's 15th Corps was already taking the offensive in order to disorganize the enemy's obvious preparations for the first phase of his invasion of India. The patrols in Manipur were often accompanied by parties of Indian Engineers, particularly those sent out from Tiddim towards Yazagyo. Here the jungle was so dense that the men had either to use elephant tracks or follow the dry beds of streams. In bivouac at night, the stillness was so deadly that even the sound of a falling leaf was startling. The enemy seemed to lurk in every shadow. Nerves were strained to the limit, and never was the rising sun more welcome.

The 'build-up' in Manipur had now reached such proportions that it was decided that Major-General Orde Wingate's Second Chindit Expedition should be launched into Upper Burma to co-operate in the offensive which we had planned for 1944. Six Long Range Penetration Brigades were to be despatched, mostly by air. They were intended to help the advance of Stilwell's forces down the Ledo Road, to reduce the opposition offered to a Chinese advance from Yunnan and to disorganize the enemy's rear areas in the north. The movement began on February 5th, 1944, when one of the brigades set out on foot from Ledo. A month later, "Operation Thursday" was launched by flying 10,000 men and 1,000 pack animals over the mountains and jungles by night and setting them down far behind the enemy's lines. Wingate proposed to establish strongholds deep in the enemy zone and thence to start large-scale operations in several directions. To use his own words, he would "insert himself in the guts of the enemy", and go, not where the enemy was, but where he was not. Five brigades were set down on two clearings—"Broadway" and "Chowringhee"—situated about 150 miles east of the Chindwin in the triangle formed by Mogaung, Indaw and Bhamo. The first waves came in gliders, towed in pairs over an 8,000 feet mountain barrier; but out of 67 gliders that took the air, only 32 landed at "Broadway". Some had crashed on the way; others had been forced to turn back. One glider, loaded with a bulldozer, plunged into the surrounding wall of jungle at 60 miles an hour. Its wings were torn off, and when the fuselage stopped, the bulldozer continued to smash its way through the trees. But luckily, as the bulldozer left the fuselage, it had operated a hinge by which the two pilots' seats could be swung upwards to give more room. Pilot and co-pilot were consequently thrown into the air while the bulldozer made its exit beneath them, and they landed back in the wrecked fuselage, unhurt, after the machine had left. "I planned it just that way" said the American pilot.

Four hundred troops and a mass of equipment were soon delivered at "Broadway" though not without scores of casualties. The infantry fanned out and the engineers worked desperately to make an airstrip. This was completed in 24 hours and dozens of Dakotas landed with more troops of the first two brigades and heavier equipment and stores. The same procedure was followed at "Chowringhee", further south, where another brigade came in. Yet another brigade arrived on March 23rd on an alternative air-strip called "Aberdeen". This was Wingate's last exploit. Flying back to India on March 24th, his plane crashed in the jungle and he was killed. The leadership of the "Chindits" then fell to Major-General W. D. A. Lentaigne. The Second "Chindit" Expedition undoubtedly disorganized some of the Japanese rear communications and therefore must have affected the strength of the enemy's onslaught in March, but, as already stated, there is no evidence that any Indian Engineers were concerned in it.

The first ripples of the Japanese offensive against Imphal and Kohima began to lap round our forward positions on March 6th, 1944. General Mutagachi told his Fifteenth Army that the fate of the Empire depended on the result and that Imphal must be taken, whatever the cost. The order was passed on by the Commander of the 33rd Japanese Division, a man of few illusions. "You will take Imphal", he wrote, "but the Division will be annihilated". He was wrong in his first prognostication: right in his second. The 17th Indian Division was to be the chief executioner though it escaped disaster in the early stages only by a narrow margin. The enemy offensive opened on March 8th, a week earlier than had been expected. It took the form of two thrusts by the 33rd Japanese Division, one up the west bank of the Manipur River and the other northwards up the Kabaw Valley in the Tamu region. Early in the month it had been decided that, if there was a risk of the 17th Indian Division being cut off, it should be withdrawn at once towards Imphal; but General Cowan was reluctant to abandon his ground and was determined to see his wounded, transport and stores safely on the way before his fighting troops withdrew. The date was left to him and he chose March 14th, by which time the route to Imphal had already been cut. In consequence, the 23rd Indian Division had to send two brigades down the Tiddim Road to help the 17th Division in the later stages of its withdrawal, and the 4th Corps reserves were thus depleted. Lord Mountbatten, the Supreme Commander, then summoned the 5th Indian Division from Arakan by air, taking the responsibility himself of diverting 30 Dakotas from the 'Hump' route for that purpose. It was a bold decision though well justified in such an emergency. The 15th Corps could spare the troops: the 4th Corps had not a man to spare.

When the 17th Divisional Engineers began to withdraw with the other troops from the Kennedy Peak area on March 14th they left delayed demolitions and booby-traps all along the Tiddim Road. At Tiddim, they destroyed all installations and stores and set fire to the houses. On the 20th Division front, where the centre of the Japanese offensive had to be met, 309 Field Park Company and 422 Field Company were both engaged, the latter being heavily attacked on several occasions while the Division was withdrawing up the Tamu Road to Shenam. The G.R.E.F. organization handed over its available field units to the Chief Engineer, 4th Corps, who thus gained the services of 428, 429 and 362 Field Companies. The two latter were sent afterwards to work on the Bishenpur-Silchar track where they were isolated for six weeks and were engaged in hand-to-hand fighting with the enemy. 424 Field Company carried out demolitions on the Sittaung track as the 20th Division withdrew and then worked on strengthening the defences at the Shenam Saddle, where a determined stand was to be made. Thus the Madras Sappers took a prominent part in delaying the Japanese advance on Imphal in its early stages, as did also the units of the other two Corps which were in the forward areas.

Precautionary measures had been taken to guard against a direct thrust at Kohima. Two battallions of the 50th Parachute Brigade had arrived to reinforce the few troops in the wild and mountainous country east of that place, and as soon as it was seen that an attack was probable between it and the head of the Kabaw Valley, the Engineers began to make a jeep track running eastwards to Jessami, then southwards towards Ukhrul, and finally south-eastwards to the Kabaw Valley. This track was completed in the nick of time and proved a most useful line of lateral communication.

A few more personal experiences at the front may serve to round off this chapter on the 'build-up' period. Major Bossard writes as follows about 362 Field Company on the Tamu Road.[1] "From the lessons learnt during a 'flap' in December when all civilian labour had been withdrawn towards Palel, a new scheme for evacuation had been evolved. It was in three phases, "A", "B" and "C", and in Phase "C" all Engineer troops were to drop everything, wire themselves in, and prepare to stay to the last round. In February we knew that the enemy was concentrating and that he outnumbered us by about three to one. Then suddenly, on March 17th at about 11.0 a.m., the unit received the code-word for Phase "C", never having been given "A" or "B". The Japs had crossed the Chindwin and were already in Laiching, only 17 miles to the east. The scenes that followed were reminiscent of France in 1940. The civilian labour was just told to go. No transport was available. We dug in and wired our perimeter and took a 25 pr. battery under our wing, coming under command of the 80th Brigade which established itself on the next hill, about 600 yards away. The 32nd Brigade was forward in Tamu and Moreh. Two nights later, the first Jap patrol came in, about 30 strong, and fired red tracer into the camp from a hill 900 yards away. The enemy tried to tear open the perimeter wire and scale a cliff from the road, using bamboo ladders. This was too much for the Sappers who opened up with everything they had. The battle went on through most of the night, and the Company lost two killed and two wounded. Then it settled down to an infantry role. By now, pressure was increasing all round. The Japs had cut in behind Nippon Hill. They were pushing up the Mombi and Sita tracks and were hammering at Tamu which the 32nd Brigade had begun to evacuate. The Company's lines were continually peppered. When the 32nd Brigade began to withdraw, we were switched on to the road, and it was then that we lost Wright, a Platoon commander. About April 2nd, the 80th Brigade also began to withdraw and 362 Field Company pulled out and marched to Shenam."

The Revd. R. T. Urwin gives the following impressions of the withdrawal along the Tiddim Road when he was a subaltern with

---

[1] "A Sapper and Miner Field Company from 1942 to 1945", by Major J. W. Bossard, M.B.E., R.E., appearing in *The R.E. Journal*, June 1950, pp. 149-161.

70 Field Company.[1] "It was a sad business blowing up the road and the bridges that had been made with such labour. We didn't really know what was happening. Nerves were taut and we had to grow accustomed to the idea of being surrounded. It was three months before we could feel that the Japs were only in front and not everywhere else as well. Certain things stand out in my mind. The slowness of the convoy as we moved away from Tiddim; a piece of rock falling on my tin helmet after a demolition; being badly 'jittered' by the Jap in camp at night; a reconnaissance at a ruined camp at Milestone 109; finding a tin of milk and drinking it straight off; marching a very long way one night, and finally being shelled when we reached the Imphal Plain." A vivid word-picture, typical of the blurred recollections of those who have had the misfortune, like the author, to take part in that most exhausting of military operations, a long and hurried retreat before a victorious enemy.

The defence of Imphal, which will form the subject of another chapter, may be said to have begun on March 12th, 1944, when the full weight of the Japanese offensive was developing and the enemy's intentions were clear. The attacks by the 31st, 15th and 33rd Japanese Divisions, ranged in that order from north to south, were closely co-ordinated and had as their primary object the capture of Imphal. Having already failed in Arakan, the enemy now staked all on his operations against the 4th Corps in Manipur. While the 33rd Japanese Division tried to trap and annihilate our 17th Division, the 31st and 15th Divisions joined in the fray to the north-east. Columns of the 31st Division crossed the Chindwin between Thaungdut and Homalin in a thrust towards Kohima, and others, of the 15th Division, advanced against our 20th Division which was withdrawing slowly along the Tamu-Palel Road. The Japanese, in their usual grandiloquent fashion, soon claimed to have obliterated the 17th Division with the exception of a detachment surrounded at Tonzang. Their radio described the scene at Tiddim, where the Division was said to have made a last stand. "In that picture of desolation", said the announcer, "one can read the panic which must have reigned in the hearts of the soldiers in their last moments". But there were no last moments except for those few brave soldiers who gave their lives to check the yellow flood. The 17th Division was by no means destroyed and had the satisfaction later of destroying

---

[1] "Recollections of the Tiddim Road", by the Revd. R. T. Urwin, dated November 7th, 1951.

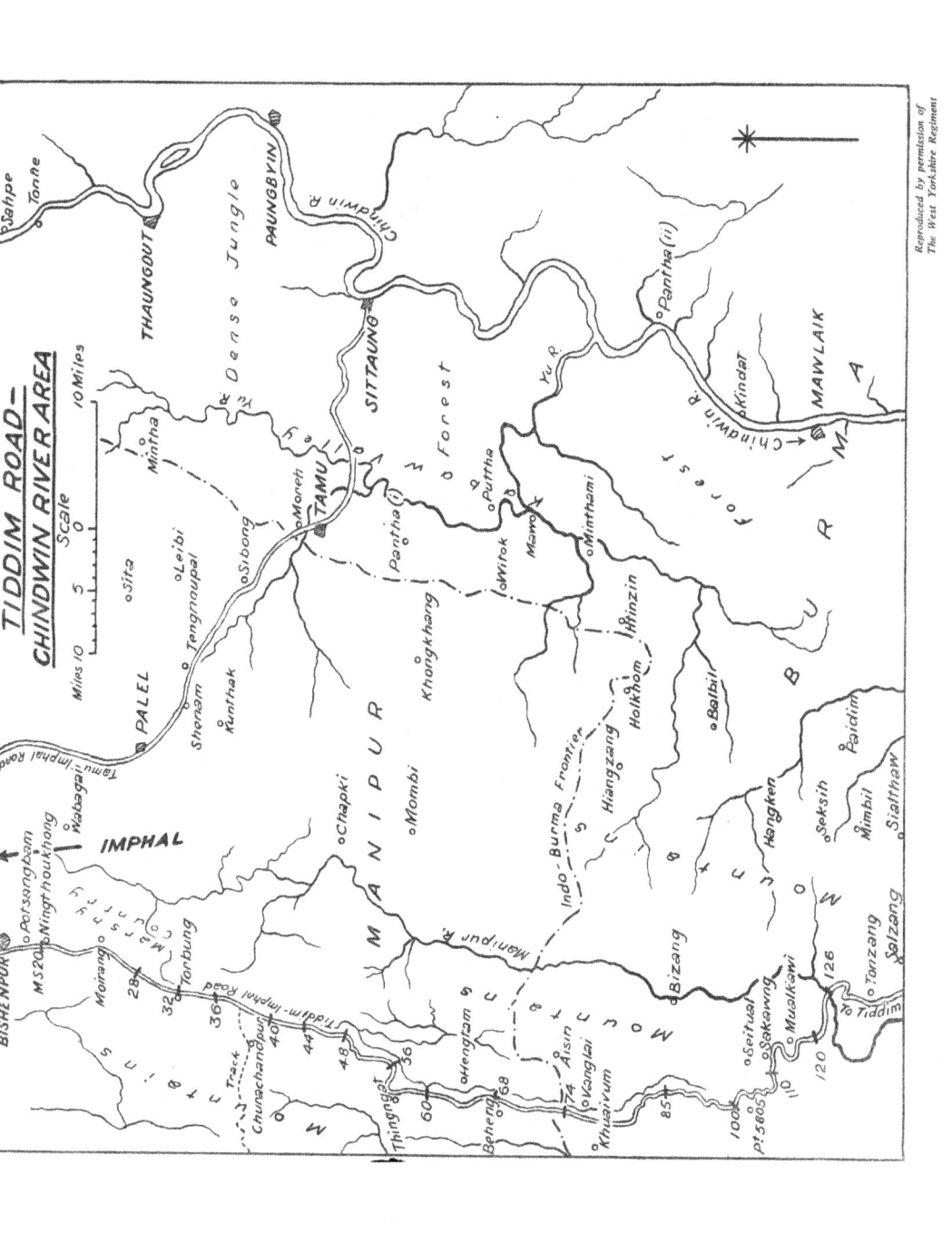

their opponents. Nevertheless, the general situation on the Manipur front in the middle of March was undoubtedly serious. The 33rd Japanese Division was trying to break the hold of the 17th Division on the Manipur River bridge at Milestone 126. The 15th Japanese Division, across the Chindwin and overlooking part of the Kabaw Valley, was fanning out south-westwards to co-operate with the 33rd Division in an assault on Tamu. Further to the north, the 31st Japanese Division was crossing the Chindwin as a prelude to an advance on Kohima through Ukhrul where the 50th Parachute Brigade lay in wait. Five days after passing the Chindwin, many thousands of Japanese crossed the frontier of India and the flag of the Rising Sun was hoisted for the first time on Indian soil. The 'March on Delhi' seemed really to have begun. The 4th Corps fought for time. The 20th Division retreated slowly and stubbornly along the Tamu Road, holding every defensible position as long as possible. The 17th Division withdrew rapidly, bursting all barriers and repelling all attempts at encirclement. The 23rd Division, in reserve, defended the Imphal Plain. Large reinforcements were on the way, but it was doubtful whether they could reach the battle zone before the monsoon washed away our slender line of communication with Assam. Every aircraft, every train and every road-vehicle was pressed into service, and on every road the Engineers redoubled their efforts to keep the traffic moving forward to the hard pressed front in Manipur.

CHAPTER X

ARAKAN, 1942 - 45

THE First Arakan Campaign was a gamble, pure and simple. This was admitted later by General Wavell, the Commander-in-Chief, India, who took the risk of ordering an advance from Chittagong to Akyab when he had no longer the necessary sea and air support. Chittagong, 250 miles east of Calcutta, had a good harbour and was connected by rail with Comilla, Dacca and the remainder of Assam, but southwards the railway extended no further than Dohazari, about 25 miles. From Dohazari to Bawli Bazar there was a single fair-weather road, but thence through Maungdaw and down the Mayu Peninsula to Foul Point facing Akyab Island there was nothing which deserved the name of road. In fact, it was hardly feasible to take Akyab by a land advance unless the resistance offered by the enemy was very small. The formation detailed for this almost impossible task was the 14th Indian Division under Major-General W. L. Lloyd, reinforced later by other brigades. The troops had been trained for the defence of India against invasion. Of jungle warfare they knew practically nothing, nor were they equipped for it. They never possessed the numerical superiority necessary for the assault of skilfully entrenched positions. Success depended on a rapid advance; but bad weather hindered the start and gave the Japanese time to pour troops into Akyab and the adjacent country. It is not surprising, therefore, that the campaign resulted in a costly failure, and that although much experience was gained, an exorbitant price in life and loss of morale had to be paid for it. Was the venture justified? Some would say it was not. Yet it should be borne in mind that the acceptance of considerable risk was perhaps permissible in order to offset the dire political effects of the fall of Singapore and the retreat from Rangoon, and also to dispel the myth of the invincibility of the Japanese. Wars are rarely won by leaders who play invariably for safety, and it must be remembered that Wavell had already routed the Italians in North Africa by a very bold and even hazardous offensive.

The coastal tract of Arakan is ideal for delaying tactics—a jungle-covered country with steep hills, deep ravines and, near the sea, muddy creeks or *chaungs* fringed with mangrove swamps. From a narrow coastal strip, dotted with paddy-fields and villages, rises the Mayu Range, sheer, rocky and thickly wooded. Some miles to the east lies the wide Kalapanzin Valley, more open and cultivated, down which flows the river of the same name which is known in its lower reaches as the Mayu. Beyond this valley rises a more formidable range, the Arakan Yomas, anything up to 25 miles in width and 2,000 feet in height. Like the Mayu Range, this barrier is a wilderness of jungle, intersected by ravines and with knife-edged ridges ideal for defensive positions. East of the Yomas, the Kaladan River runs southwards to debouch into the Bay of Bengal below Akyab Island while the Mayu River comes in north of the island. During the dry season, the innumerable *chaungs* in the valleys are passable anywhere for wheeled or tracked vehicles; but as soon as the monsoon starts, all traffic is tied to the recognized roads, if such exist. The valleys are dotted with hillocks covered with scrub which make excellent defensive positions. Three factors hamper road communication—heavy rain, water crossings and lack of stone for road repairs. These were the chief natural obstacles confronting the Engineer units of the 14th Division in 1942.

From the railhead at Dohazari, all traffic had to move southwards through Chiringa, Ramu, Taungbro and Bawli Bazar to reach the small port of Maungdaw opposite the southern end of the narrow Teknaf Peninsula.[1] From Maungdaw to Foul Point, the southern tip of the Mayu Peninsula, there was only a rough track passable for jeeps in dry weather but involving the crossing of many unbridged coastal *chaungs*. There was no other direct land route towards Akyab Island, the northern shore of which was 15 miles from Foul Point. Troops and supplies sent by sea from Chittagong, could be disembarked at Cox's Bazar, a small port near Ramu, or further down the coast at Maungdaw, but the latter could not be used during the monsoon. Elsewhere, the heavy surf prohibited a landing. When supplies had been unloaded, they could often be sent inland in local boats, known as *sampans*, plying along tidal *chaungs*, and this relieved to some extent the congestion of road traffic. The heat and dust in Arakan during April and May are very trying, and during the monsoon period from the middle of May to the end of September life becomes almost unbearable. The jungle sprouts visibly in the humid atmosphere. Deluges of rain fill every ravine with a roaring torrent. Roads are obliterated

---

[1] See the map of Arakan included in this chapter.

in mud. Mosquitos and leeches abound. In 1942-43, sickness decimated the troops. The only relief was afforded by the winter months from December to March when the sun shone on a wonderfully beautiful scene and the nights were cold. This was ideal campaigning weather.

In October 1942, the 14th Indian Division moved southwards from Chittagong and occupied Maungdaw and Buthidaung without much difficulty, thereby securing temporarily a valuable line of transverse communication behind its front, but it soon had to withdraw to Bawli Bazar owing to Japanese landings on the coast. The Divisional Engineers under Lieut.-Colonel R. H. Muirhead, R.E., comprised 26 and 28 Field Companies (Bombay), 73 and 74 Field Companies (Bengal), a Sirmur State Field Company and 305 Field Park Company, quite an impressive array of talent. Other Engineer formations followed, including the 8th and 10th Engineer Battalions, the 15th, 17th, 42nd and 55th Auxiliary Pioneer Battalions and 9 and 11 Bridging Sections in addition to a Field Company and a Field Park Company, R.E., a Forestry Company and an Army Troops Company.[1] It is clear that the engineering difficulties in Arakan were fully appreciated.

26 Field Company, under Major L. A. Thorpe, R.E., which disembarked at Cox's Bazar on October 6th with the 123rd Brigade, was employed in improving the main road north and south of Ramu and afterwards made a track for pack transport to Bawli Bazar where it established a ferry across the Purma *chaung*. Meanwhile, 73 Field Company, under Major C. G. Figgins, R.E., was working on the main road further north, converting it from a mere cart-track with many water gaps into a route fit for light military traffic. Temporary bridges were built with felled trees, and if the gaps were too wide for bridging, they were made fordable or provided with ferries of country boats. The Company was still equipped for operating in North Africa and had no mule transport for bringing up stores. Heavy rain at the beginning of November caused much disorganization. The War Diary of 26 Field Company has the following entries. "Major Thorpe returned to the unit having had to walk from Cox's Bazar to Ramu through water 3 feet deep on the main road and swirling across it at 4 knots. All roads quite impassable. Diversions have either been washed away or have sat down like hot blancmanges. Small bridges have mostly disappeared. All timber

---

[1] Notes by Brigadier R. H. Muirhead, O.B.E., dated February 1st, 1954.

collected for the unit by the Forest Officer has been lost. This had been intended for new piers at Cox's Bazar and had taken ten days to prepare." 73 Field Company had similar tribulations, but happily the deluge was brief and both units soon made good the damage so that on November 17th the road was re-opened for traffic. 73 Field Company then moved to Bawli Bazar and built a 400-feet bridge across the Purma *chaung*. Here it was joined by 74 Field Company, under Major D. C. S. David, R.E. This unit had been properly trained and equipped for jungle warfare and was the first of its kind to reach the front. By November 20th it had completed a 'Class 5' road between Ukhia and Bawli Bazar. The Divisional Engineers also made a track from Bawli over the hills to Goppe Bazar on the Kalapanzin River, a distance of seven miles.

When the First Arakan Campaign opened in December 1942, two battalions of the enemy held Maungdaw and Buthidaung. Our plan for the capture of Akyab envisaged an advance down the Mayu Peninsula by the 47th, 55th, 88th and 123rd Brigades of the 14th Indian Division, after which the 6th Brigade of the 2nd British Division would make a landing on the island. The Japanese, however, must have had news of our intentions, for on December 16th, just as our advance was beginning, they abandoned Maungdaw and Buthidaung and retreated southwards. The 14th Divisional Engineers, who had been working on the roads and mule-tracks forward of Bawli Bazar and Goppe Bazar, were then able to extend the tracks towards the Maungdaw-Buthidaung Road. 74 Field Company completed a track from Goppe Bazar through Taung Bazar to Buthidaung and then, with 73 Field Company, set to work on the Maungdaw-Buthidaung Road. 26 Field Company and 28 Field Company (Major M. E. F. Bell, R.E.) improved the main road from Bawli Bazar towards Maungdaw or built jetties on the Teknaf peninsula for a sea-borne entry into Maungdaw across the narrow Naf estuary. By December 23rd, both these Bombay Sapper units were in Maungdaw, building jetties for landing supplies or working on the road towards Buthidaung.

The Maungdaw-Buthidaung Road, the scene of so much bitter fighting, deserves some description.[1] For the first few miles from Maungdaw it traversed a coastal strip of broken and jungle-covered country before mounting the Mayu Range, twisting its way through the hills and descending to Buthidaung, 16 miles away. It was too

---

[1] See the map of the Maungdaw Area included in this chapter.

narrow for two-way traffic, though the surface was roughly metalled. In one section it burrowed through a couple of spurs by means of tunnels. The west tunnel, about 300 yards in length, was roughly half-way between Maungdaw and Buthidaung, and a mile beyond it lay the east tunnel, made in two short lengths with an intervening gap. The road had been developed from a projected railway line, the tunnels having been built in 1918 by a Rangoon firm; but shortly afterwards a steamship company, fearing railway competition, had purchased the whole concern and the permanent way was then used as a road. The Japanese stored ammunition and supplies in the tunnels and surrounded them with a maze of defensive positions extending from the Razabil Fortress, 4½ miles from Maungdaw, to a smaller fortress at Letwedet near Buthidaung. Razabil grew in time to be a veritable rabbit-warren of gun positions, bunkers, deep shelters and tunnels covering a very wide area, though in the early days of the advance southwards it was in its infancy.

So well did our advance progress that by December 27th the 14th Division, moving down the coastal road and the Mayu Valley in two columns, had reached Indin and almost to Rathedaung and had consolidated on a line 25 miles south of the Maungdaw-Buthidaung Road. The 47th Brigade was preparing to move to Foul Point, and a patrol had actually reached it and could look across the straits to Akyab Island. The 123rd Brigade was outside Rathedaung beyond the Mayu estuary. But the two brigades were now 150 miles from the railhead at Dohazari and bad weather intervened to upset their supply by road. A delay of ten days ensued, and when the advance was resumed on January 6th, 1943, it was found that the enemy had fortified Donbaik, a coastal village 12 miles south of Indin, as well as the town of Rathedaung across the Mayu River. Nevertheless. with Akyab almost in his grasp, General Lloyd was prepared to make a desperate attempt to reach his goal before his supplies ran out. On January 18th, and again on the 19th, the 47th Brigade attacked the Donbaik position and failed. On February 1st, the 55th Brigade failed also though supported by tanks of the 26th Indian Division which was now coming up. The 123rd Brigade could make no headway against Rathedaung and was repulsed on February 3rd. Again, on the 17th, the 55th Brigade tried to pierce the Donbaik defences but without success and was then relieved by the 71st Brigade of the 26th Division. The enemy now had the equivalent of a complete division at the front and it seemed improbable that the Mayu Peninsula could be cleared before the onset of the monsoon made any attempt to land on Akyab Island very hazardous. Yet General Wavell directed that another assault should be made on Donbaik and this time in great strength and depth. The 6th (British) Brigade was to be brought forward from Chittagong for the purpose, with the 71st Brigade in support. But before the assault could be launched, the enemy began a counter-offensive in the Kaladan Valley. A brigade under a certain Colonel Tanahashi, infiltrating through the hills, attacked the communications of the 123rd Brigade facing Rathedaung. The 123rd Brigade withdrew and was relieved by the 55th Brigade. The latter was attacked in turn and forced to withdraw, but with the help of the 71st Brigade it succeeded in reaching a position covering Buthidaung. Tanahashi continued his offensive. He crossed the Mayu River by night, and climbing the Mayu Range, threatened to cut off our forces on either side of it. Meanwhile, on March 18th, the 6th Brigade had made the final assault on the Donbaik position. The initial onrush had pierced the Japanese defences, only to be broken up among the dozens of bunkers whose defenders remained in action behind the leading waves of our infantry. While trying to get at the enemy deep underground, our men were machine-gunned and mortared off the tops of the bunkers. The losses were very heavy and the remnants of the gallant 6th Brigade had to be withdrawn.

By the end of the month, the 26th Indian Division, under Major-General C. E. N. Lomax, had taken over the greater part of the front. General Wavell still hoped to regain the initiative and accordingly instructions were issued that positions covering the Maungdaw-Buthidaung Road and the mouth of the Naf Estuary should be held during the monsoon while offensive action was resumed on both sides of the Mayu River. But the plans could not be carried out. The troops had already suffered 2,500 battle casualties, and malaria had accounted for a far greater number. "I set a small part of the Army a task beyond their training and capacity," wrote Wavell, "and the main responsibility for the failure is mine." By the middle of April 1943, we were back on a line covering the Maungdaw-Buthidaung Road. The enemy followed up and pierced the line. Buthidaung was then evacuated, and, on May 13th, our advanced base at Maungdaw was abandoned. The troops fell back slowly and sullenly to the positions covering Bawli Bazar whence they had started out so full of hope nearly six months earlier. The victorious Japanese consolidated for the monsoon period in the Maungdaw-Buthidaung area, for they also had suffered severely. Some consolation for our failure was derived later from captured Japanese documents which showed that the launching of the offensive had upset the enemy's plans for an invasion of India during the winter of 1942-43.

The Indian Engineer units involved in the First Arakan Campaign acquitted themselves well under great handicaps. In December, 74 Field Company repaired a large steel bridge at Letwedet and then pushed a mule-track forward to Hwitze, 20 miles south of Buthidaung. This involved four ferries and much bridging. Then, after the 123rd Brigade had failed to take Rathedaung, the Company began to convert the track into a road for jeep traffic. On March 10th, 1943, when enemy forces threatened to cut off the brigade, 74 Field Company was ordered to complete the road so that relief battalions could come forward and also to defend a vital bridge to the last man. The Sappers were soon committed to battle as infantry. The Japanese had to be evicted from a knoll two miles north of Hwitze. This was done chiefly by the 55th Brigade on March 14th, and the 123rd Brigade was extricated successfully although all its animals and heavy equipment had to be abandoned before it could be ferried across to the right bank of the Mayu. 74 Field Company provided and operated these ferries and afterwards carried out demolitions behind the retreating infantry. The Japanese, under Colonel Tanahashi, followed across the river and over the hills beyond until, as already stated, they were in a position to interrupt the communications of the brigades attacking Donbaik on the coast. 74 Field Company went to Maungdaw, but on March 26th it was ordered back to act again as infantry in checking Tanahashi. It moved as far southwards as Indin, where it remained until April 9th when it returned to Maungdaw and left soon afterwards for India.

Meanwhile, 73 Field Company had improved the harbour facilities at Maungdaw and at Teknaf across the Naf estuary and had worked also on the coastal road south of Maungdaw. During March and April it made an all-weather road as far south as Indin. The 26th Divisional Engineers then took over all commitments, and 73 Field Company, having handed over to 72 Field Company under Major J. W. Snape, R.E., returned to India with other units of the 14th Divisional Engineers. 72 Field Company settled down for the monsoon in the Bawli Area. There was much to learn—the need for concealment, track discipline, absolute quiet in camp after dark and a host of other things—and there was also plenty of employment in supporting patrols, building jetties and repairing tracks. Thirteen inches of rain fell in six days, but the men remained cheerful in spite of being constantly wet and often shivering with malaria.

The Bombay Sapper units vied with their comrades of the Bengal Corps in road repair and bridging. Early in January 1943, 26 Field Company was employed near Indin on hacking a mule-track through dense forest to connect the forward troops on either side of the Mayu Range. Four days after the abortive attack by the 47th Brigade on Donbaik on January 18th, when the unit was at Kodingauk midway between Donbaik and Indin, the following entry appears in its War Diary:— "Enemy dropped a good bunch of bombs but cleared off in a hurry. It was disappointing not to see any of the planes shot down, though it was stated later that some fell on the other side of the hills. This has since become a regular statement as no planes have ever been seen to fall, for the Gunners always say that they fell on the other side. This may be true, but we should like to see them fall on *our* side sometimes!" At the beginning of March, the Company was still in Kodingauk and mention is made of the Sirmur Sapper Company which was then with the 71st Brigade and had been involved in considerable fighting in the Donbaik region. Subsequent entries run as follows:— "*Kodingauk. 28th March.* Rush order received to make a pack route over the hills between Indin and Sinoh (near Kanyingyaung) as the enemy has captured the other end of the only other route for getting supplies to the 47th Brigade. Two Sections of 73 Field Company came under command. *30th March.* Track opened and the 47th Brigade traffic poured through. *3rd-6th April.* Heavy Jap attacks and withdrawal to defensive positions. Indin occupied by enemy. 6th Brigade withdrew and 47th Brigade had to fight its way through and assemble 7 miles in rear. Three Sections of 26 Field Company were with 47th Brigade. *18th April.* Relieved by 72 Field Company and returned to Maungdaw. *24th April.* Company being reformed at Chittagong."

28 Field Company remained even later in the field. On May 3rd it was still in Buthidaung operating a ferry across the Kalapanzin River for the 55th Brigade. The town was bombed on the following day and the brigade was ordered to move into the hills. This move was completed on May 6th when 28 Field Company was the last unit to leave Buthidaung. While proceeding along the road to Maungdaw on May 7th with the 26th Brigade it lost most of its transport and equipment in forcing a passage through a road-block, but it arrived in Maungdaw on the 8th and reached Bawli Bazar on the 11th. There was little Sapper work during this precarious

withdrawal. As so often when in tight corners, the Sappers fought as infantry.

The state of the main line of communication during the monsoon may be judged from the experiences of Captain J. H. Clark, R.E., who joined 28 Field Company at Bawli Bazar at the end of May 1943. This is what he writes.[1] "The dry-weather road from Chittagong to Cox's Bazar being unusable, one had to transfer to a small coastal vessel for the journey by sea. From Cox's Bazar to Tumbru Ghat on the Naf River estuary, one could travel in a vehicle; but owing to the continuous repair work as the surface sank in the mud, the road was only open for one-way traffic at certain hours and was sometimes completely closed. The only materials available for road-making were timber and bricks, the latter being baked in kilns alongside the road. Gangs of coolies worked all along the route. From Tumbru to Bawli Bazar the road was also unusable, so a ferry service of steamers with barges was maintained down the Naf River and up the Purma *Chaung*. All movement from Bawli Bazar towards Maungdaw, or from Goppe Bazar towards Buthidaung, had to be made with animal transport, and the latter route was sometimes impassable even for mules. The 36th Brigade Group at Bawli lived in *bashas* (bamboo huts on stilts) on high ground around the flooded paddy-fields. Here I found 28 Field Company. Everyone and everything was permanently wet. Skin troubles were common, and malaria also because the first issue of Mepacrine was not made until June." The building of the Arakan Road from Chittagong to Bawli was a remarkable engineering achievement. According to Brigadier Horsfield[2] nearly 5 miles of bridging had to be provided in a total length of some 200 miles, and as the country was mostly under water from June to December, the roadway had to be raised on an embankment 6 feet high and 30 feet wide. Yet the task was finished in six months by manual labour alone. No less than 80 million bricks were burnt and laid on the road in 1943, and this stupendous total was far exceeded in 1944 when the figure rose to 180 million.

Generally speaking, the Arakan front remained quiet between June and November 1943 except for occasional patrol actions. One brigade of the 26th Division held a sector extending from Nhila on the Teknaf Peninsula eastwards to Bawli Bazar, while another,

---

[1] Notes by Major J. H. Clark, M.C., R.E., dated February 2nd, 1954.

[2] "Engineer Operations with the Fourteenth Army in 1943-44", by Brigadier H.E. Horsfield, C.B.E., M.C., appearing in *The R.E. Journal*, December 1945, pp. 241-243.

beyond the Mayu Range, held the area between Goppe Bazar and Taung Bazar. The headquarters of the 15th Corps, then under Lieut.-General W. J. Slim, were at Chittagong. A few raids were attempted. Early in July 1943, two companies of The Lincolnshire Regiment penetrated to Maungdaw and occupied it for some hours, and in the middle of the month a small detachment of The North Staffordshire Regiment raided the Maungdaw-Buthidaung Road. A party from 28 Field Company was concerned in this affair. The object was to ambush enemy transport, and if possible to secure a prisoner for identification. Anyone performing this rare feat was granted automatically a month's leave. The raid showed that our troops, however brave, could not cope at this period with the highly trained enemy, for Jungle Warfare Training Divisions were not formed in India until late in the year. The party supplied by 28 Field Company comprised a British Officer, an Indian Officer and 12 Indian other ranks. The road towards Maungdaw was so bad that the Sappers had to be left behind for a time to see the mules through while the infantry went ahead to Zeganbyin where the Sappers rejoined them before dawn. Unfortunately, the whole of July 16th was spent in Zeganbyin and enemy agents reported the presence of the force. After dark, the raiders struck south-eastwards in brilliant moonlight towards the 'Tunnels' area of the Maungdaw-Buthidaung Road. The track petered out in a *chaung* and the local guides announced that they were lost. The troops then took up a position in dense jungle. At daylight, the enemy opened fire and the infantry attempted to withdraw to a better position. One of the two platoons suffered heavily in the process. The other, with the Sappers, got clear and climbed down into the bed of a *chaung*. There it was ambushed and after fighting hard for an hour had to disperse in small parties into the jungle. On July 18th and 19th the survivors trickled back in twos and threes to Zeganbyin, and so ended a disastrous venture from which much was learned, the chief lesson being that jungle warfare is an art in itself.

The 26th Indian Division held the forward areas throughout the monsoon until it was relieved by the 7th Indian Division under Major-General F. W. Messervy. Opposing it were two regiments of the 55th Japanese Division with headquarters at Akyab. Both sides were exhausted and neither wished to resume the struggle in deluges of rain and a welter of mud. The procedure of fighting throughout the monsoon had not yet been adopted, and Mepacrine had not yet appeared to combat malaria. "Custom and military opinion", writes Earl Mountbatten,[1] "regarded the south-west monsoon as a close season. No operations had yet been undertaken in this period since the Allied (and evidently the Japanese) commanders considered that the drain on resources would place the side which attempted them at a grave disadvantage when the dry season returned. I determined that we must fight on as hard in the monsoon as in the dry weather and thus gain the advantage which comes to the side that perseveres when the other is expecting that both sides will stop." It is not too much to say that this decision, promulgated soon after Mountbatten's arrival in October 1943, altered the whole conception of the conduct of the war in Burma.

When the 26th Indian Division was relieved on September 19th, 1943, by the 7th Indian Division, several Field Companies of the Indian Engineers made their first appearance in Arakan. These were 62 Field Company (Major H. C. Lee, R.E.), 77 Field Company (Major H. F. Kelly, R.E.), 421 Field Company (Major M. G. Bewoor, I.E.) and 331 Field Park Company (Major J. H. Moss, R.E.), the whole being under Lieut.-Colonel P. J. Cator, R.E. General Messervy was told that as soon as the 15th Corps had concentrated for an offensive his task would be to seize the Maungdaw-Buthidaung Road, cut in behind the Letwedet stronghold and occupy Buthidaung. The 7th Indian Division—the famous "Golden Arrows"—had earned a high reputation in North Africa though it had still to learn the technique of the Arakan jungles. In anticipation of the arrival of the 5th Indian Division (the "Fighting Fifth") under Major-General H. R. Briggs, Messervy began to move his 33rd Brigade into the Kalapanzin Valley to take over from the 26th Division in Goppe Bazar and Taung Bazar and to patrol eastwards. The 114th Brigade was to advance southwards to the line of the Ngakyedauk *chaung*, and the 89th Brigade was to move over the Ngakyedauk Pass and form up on the right of the 114th. These dispositions would protect the start of Sapper work in the Pass to convert the existing rough track into a road suitable for mechanical transport. The 5th Division arrived in due course, and General Briggs was ordered to capture Maungdaw and the adjacent Razabil Fortress. General Slim had now been appointed Commander, Fourteenth Army, and Lieut.-General A. P. F. Christison was in command of the 15th Corps. Christison proposed to seize both ends of the Maungdaw-Buthidaung

---

[1] *Report to the Combined Chiefs of Staff*, by the Supreme Commander, South-East Asia, 1943-45, p. 15.

Road, locking up the Japanese garrison in the central tunnels for subsequent destruction. The 5th Division, advancing along the coastal strip, was to be careful to include the western slopes and crest of the Mayu Range and so to maintain close contact with the 7th Division advancing down the Kalapanzin Valley. The importance of the Ngakyedauk Pass route was evident. So long as the enemy held the Maungdaw-Buthidaung Road he could switch his troops rapidly from one side of the range to the other, and therefore we should be able to do likewise. The 15th Corps, however, comprised not only the 5th and 7th Indian Divisions but also the 81st West African Division, and, in reserve, the 25th and 26th Indian Divisions. The 36th British Division at Chittagong was also available for a sea-borne landing on Akyab Island. In the previous campaign, the enemy had slipped round the eastern end of our front. This was not to be permitted again, and consequently the West Africans were to march down the Kaladan Valley, far inland, in step with the progress southwards of the 5th and 7th Divisions on either side of the Mayu Range.

The improvement of the Ngakyedauk Pass track to make it fit for jeeps was begun in October 1943. In the First Arakan Campaign it had been considered waste of time to make it suitable even for mule traffic, but the strategical requirements had altered. A mule track, however, was the first requirement, and in ten days 62 and 77 Field Companies, assisted by large gangs of coolies, cut a track 5 miles in length through the most difficult part. The result was so successful that a jeep road was put in hand at once. A new alignment in the first two miles involved much rock blasting, but the work of widening, re-grading and bridging proceeded so rapidly that the road was finished on November 13th and two days later Admiral Mountbatten drove a jeep over the Pass. The jeep road was then widened and improved, and by the end of December the road could be negotiated by tanks. Meanwhile, steps were taken to ensure due care in driving. At the foot of the Pass on the western side was a sign "A Happy Christmas to you. Peace on Earth and Goodwill to All Men—*and* 15 m.p.h. if you please." Again, further on, another which read "A Jeep can go anywhere", together with an illustration of a vehicle falling over a precipice. These examples of humour were matched by a notice on the main coastal road in the direction of the Razabil Fortress which ran "Stop. If you drive past this point you probably won't come back. *They didn't.*"[1]

---

[1] *Ball of Fire* (History of the 5th Indian Division), by Antony Brett-James, p. 259.

With the 5th Indian Division from the Middle East came 2 Field Company (Major A. E. Scott, R.E.), 20 Field Company (Major P. G. Hatch, R.E.), 74 Field Company (Major D. C. S. David, R.E.) and 44 Field Park Company (Major M. J. P. Keating, R.E.). While the 7th Indian Division side-stepped to the east of the Mayu Range, the 123rd Brigade of the 5th Division took over the front between the Naf River and the crest. 74 Field Company, which was with this brigade, reached Bawli Bazar and began to work on the Maungdaw Road. Unlike the other Sapper companies, it had had previous experience of Arakan as it had taken part in the first campaign. The Ngakyedauk Pass having been opened for jeep traffic, all was ready for the offensive by the 15th Corps. In the middle of December 1943 the 5th Division moved southwards along the western side of the Mayu Range while the 7th Division, keeping in close touch, advanced down the Kalapanzin Valley on the eastern side. On January 9th, 1944, Maungdaw was occupied by the 5th Division which then proceeded to clear the enemy from most of the adjacent country although the defenders of the Razabil Fortress refused to budge. 74 Field Company was involved in much fighting at Razabil. Detachments accompanied the leading infantry, carrying Bangalore torpedos, pole charges, bee-hive charges and 14 lb. bulk charges to deal with any posts which were holding up the advance. The Sappers lifted mines, disarmed booby-traps and blew gaps in the enemy's wire provided that the infantry could get sufficiently close to the positions, which was not always the case. Once, when the infantry were held up fairly close to a bunker, a Sapper N.C.O. dashed forward alone with a pole charge and thrust it into the entrance. The explosion killed a number of the defenders, but still the infantry could not dislodge the rest. The Japanese soldier was matchless in his determination to fight to the last. Invariably, unless prostrated by wounds or disease, he died where he stood, and often by his own hand rather than surrender.

By the end of January 1944, enough of Razabil had fallen to allow General Christison to transfer the bulk of his armour over the Ngakyedauk Pass to help the 7th Division in its operations against Buthidaung and the Letwedet strong point. Far out to the east, the 81st West African Division had reached Daletme, about 25 miles north of Paletwa in the Kaladan Valley, thus beginning to fulfil its role as left flank guard. Its engineers had built a fine jeep track, 73 miles in length, along which it was supplied from Chiringa. The Africans continued to move down the Kaladan through dense bamboo forest and, supplied chiefly by air, captured Kyauktaw. They were then in a position to guard effectively against any outflanking attempt. In the meantime, the 7th Division, reinforced from the 5th Division, was approaching Buthidaung. It was unable, however, to turn the enemy out of the Letwedet stronghold in spite of determined attacks in which the Sapper companies did a lot of 'bunker-busting.' Thus, at the beginning of February, the situation was as follows. The 15th Corps was holding the Mayu Peninsula as far south as, but not including, the Maungdaw-Buthidaung Road. The 5th Division, mostly west of the range, was in Maungdaw and had possession of a small part of the Razabil Fortress, and the 7th Division was hammering at the outlying defences of Letwedet and maintaining careful contact with the 5th Division through the Ngakyedauk Pass. Along the remainder of the Maungdaw-Buthidaung Road the 55th Japanese Division, with some attached troops and elements of a so-called 'Indian National Army', occupied a series of deeply fortified strong-points, particularly in the central 'Tunnels' area, and thus prevented us from using the road as a forward line of transverse communication.

The tide now turned in favour of the enemy who proceeded to embark on the first phase of an invasion of India. This vast offensive was designed to start with the annihilation of the 5th and 7th Indian Divisions in Arakan and the capture of Chittagong. The 55th Japanese Division, under Major-General Sakurai, was reorganized into three Task Forces, the most important of which was "Tanahashi Force" under the redoubtable Colonel Tanahashi. This force, of two battalions, was to skirt Buthidaung by night, move up the east bank of the Kalapanzin River between the 7th Indian Division and the 81st West African Division in the Kaladan Valley, take Taung Bazar from the rear, and then, swinging gradually south-westwards, cut across the rear of the 7th Division, climb the Mayu Range and block the Ngakyedauk Pass, thus trapping the 7th Division on the eastern side of the range. Meanwhile, "Kubo Force", of one battalion, was to follow a parallel route further northwards to Goppe Bazar before pushing westwards over the Goppe Pass and down the western slope till it cut the coastal road and thus severed the communications of the 5th Division. "Doi Force", of two battalions, was to make a holding attack in the Maungdaw-Buthidaung sector in order to pin down our troops in that area while "Tanahashi" and "Kubo" Forces prevented their withdrawal, reinforcement or inter-communication. General Sakurai assumed that the 7th Division would try to escape across the Mayu Range. It could then be cut to pieces and all three Task Forces could combine to crush the 5th Division. So confident was he of early victory that his men were allowed to carry only 7 days' rations. Afterwards, they would live on captured supplies. The plan was bold, some might say foolhardy, for it pre-supposed a state of panic among our troops and it neglected altogether the advantages of our abundant air supply. These foolish miscalculations had their inevitable result. They brought defeat and destruction in their train.

General Christison was not taken altogether by surprise for his intelligence service had given some warning of a possible Japanese counter-offensive and dispositions were being made to deal with such an eventuality though time was very short. In order to serve his own offensive on the eastern side of the Mayu Range, Christison had already prepared a forward maintenance base near the village of Sinzweya at the eastern foot of the Ngakyedauk Pass and about four miles south-west of the 7th Division Headquarters which were located at a village called Laungtaung. Although this administrative enclosure was designed primarily to support an offensive by the 7th Division it was organized also to resist raids, and steps were taken immediately to strengthen its meagre defences. The area became known as "The Admin. Box", and as such it is now famous in military history. At the beginning of February, the enemy had already begun to infiltrate slowly up the Kalapanzin Valley from Buthidaung, and some of our first casualties were those sustained by 303 Field Park Company, under Major W. S. D. Cooper, R.E., stationed in the lee of a large hill (Point 315) to the north-east of the Admin. Box.[1] "On the night of February 2nd/3rd", writes Captain Goodall,[2] "the O.C. and the Field Platoon Officer went out with a small reconnaissance party of officers and men to plan a tank approach to Buthidaung. They were ambushed while returning, and Lieut.-Colonel P. J. Cator (C.R.E. 7th Division) and Major Cooper were killed and another officer wounded. This was the first sign of Japanese activity."

Soon afterwards, disaster overtook the 7th Division Headquarters. In the early hours of February 4th, the 114th Brigade, east of the Kalapanzin River, reported to Major-General F. W. Messervy that

---

[1] See the map of the 7th Indian Division Admin. Box., Sinzweya, included in this chapter.

[2] Notes by Captain S. E. M. Goodall, R.E., dated October 1953.

many refugees and some Japanese troops had passed across the front and that the enemy was being engaged by administrative troops about five miles south-east of Taung Bazar. Further reports confirmed that the Japanese were closing in on Taung Bazar from several directions. "Tanahashi" and "Kubo" Forces were on the move. Messervy at once sent his 89th Brigade into action, but Tanahashi could not be stopped. On the 5th, Messervy prepared to move his headquarters to the shelter of the Admin. Box but decided to remain where he was until the situation was clearer. Before dawn on February 6th, Tanahashi fell upon him. In waist-high mist, shouting "Banzai", the enemy rushed towards the camp while their mortars poured in a heavy fire. The only defenders, a Signals Company and another of the 24th Engineer Battalion, replied as best they could and beat off assault after assault. But this could not continue for long, and before midday Messervy ordered a general withdrawal to the Admin. Box. The remnants of the Headquarters troops, including the General and his Staff, succeeded in reaching Sinzweya by wading in small bodies through *chaungs* and hacking their way through the enemy-infested jungle. Desultory fighting then spread over the countryside and casualties mounted. On February 7th, 421 Field Company lost its able and popular commander, Major M. G. Bewoor, I.E., while serving with the 114th Brigade.

"At Sinzweya", writes Goodall, "none of us knew what was happening till just before dawn on the 6th we heard a tremendous din from beyond Point 315. It was evident that the enemy were attacking Divisional H.Q. and we could hear their "Banzais." Unfortunately the order to withdraw to Sinzweya never reached the Engineer Battalion Company and most of the men died in their fox-holes. The Divisional Signals Company did not retire until two hours after the main H.Q. and lost more than half its strength. We listened to the noise and waited anxiously, for we were the next in line between Laungtaung and Sinzweya, with Point 315 between. Nothing had happened by 7.0 a.m. so the men were ordered to breakfast in shifts. At about 10.0 a.m., Brigadier G. C. Evans, to whom the command of the Sinzweya area had been delegated, came round and told us the plan of defence. We were to hold a portion of Point 315, but when the Brigadier was told our small strength he ordered us to withdraw about 100 yards to a nullah. Dawn on the 7th was very welcome. Good liaison was established and the perimeter of the Box was strengthened. Sapper work in the Box seemed to be finished apart from that of a single bulldozer which was making gun emplacements. Our other two bulldozers had been lost. Our task was merely to hold our own portion of the perimeter. On the evening of February 7th, the Japs opened up with mortars and medium machine-guns. It was a very disturbed night. If one part of the perimeter started firing, the fusillade spread rapidly all the way round. The jungle was full of weird noises. Jackals and gekkos added to the din and often the Japs imitated them. By dawn on the 8th, the expected attacks had not materialized, though at 10.0 a.m. there was firing within our own perimeter. It appeared that the enemy had infiltrated up a nullah during the night and had overrun the makeshift Main Dressing Station, killing most of the doctors and orderlies. They were also at the back of our Company position, hidden in thick jungle. We were moved later to the south side of the perimeter where we dug in. Night fell, on the 8th, with the perimeter complete and it did not vary much until we were relieved. The noises when the Japs attacked after dark were calculated to try the best of nerves. Many times they shouted in English, and amongst the devices they used were explosive bullets which burst on impact with a crack that gave the effect of fire from behind."

Tanahashi Force cut the Ngakyedauk Pass road on February 10th and thus accomplished its main task. Kubo Force was not so successful. While still a mile short of Goppe Bazar it ran into an Indian Mule Company whose men stood their ground and fought like highly trained infantry. The Japanese commander, suspecting the presence of a larger force, swung left and by astonishing efforts surmounted the Mayu Range further south and descended onto the coastal road where he interrupted the supply of the 5th Division until he and his men were liquidated. Doi Force, in the Maungdaw-Buthidaung region, fulfilled its role but could make no headway. Meanwhile, the 7th Indian Division was standing firm in the Kalapanzin Valley, and the 26th Indian Division had already retaken Taung Bazar and was making steady progress southwards.

The only Indian Engineer units in the garrison of the Administrative Box at Sinzweya were 62 Field Company, 303 Field Park Company and 17 Bridging Section. With the 33rd Brigade, a few miles to the south, was 77 Field Company, and with the 114th Brigade, 421 Field Company. These units formed the 7th Divisional Engineers. After the death of Lieut.-Colonel Cator, they were commanded by Major H. C. Lee, R.E. (O.C. 62 Company) until the arrival of Lieut.-Colonel T. Wright, R.E., at the end of the siege. Also present in the Admin. Box area was a Heavy Bridging Platoon equipped with pontoons intended for bridging the Kalapanzin at Buthidaung during our projected offensive. The pontoons, on their lorries, were parked outside the south-eastern perimeter of the Box and, incredible as it may appear, they were never damaged by the enemy. It seems that the Japanese had strict orders not to destroy our transport because it was to be used later for their victorious advance on Chittagong. At night, some of the enemy slept in the pontoons, and parties of our engineers occasionally visited the pontoon park to draw tools and stores. Within the perimeter was a mass of other transport which General Messervy called his "Ascot Car Park", and as these vehicles were liable to be damaged by badly aimed shells and bombs intended for the troops, they were transferred piece-meal, as occasion offered, to the pontoon park where they would be safe from Japanese fire and ready for our own use when the enemy had been driven off. In the matter of transport the Japanese therefore gave us every assistance.

Engineer work inside the Box was mostly of a routine nature though it sometimes called for considerable ingenuity. For instance, 303 Field Park Company was required to fit our tanks with some form of protection against the Japanese magnetic limpet mine. By experimenting on a damaged British tank it was found that a limpet mine shattered $\frac{3}{4}''$ armour but could not pierce 2" plate. Accordingly, the thinner armour was covered with rabbit-netting raised clear of the surface, and in two days the Company produced adequate protection for two squadrons of tanks. Life was never dull in the Box. One morning, a gunner seated beside his 5.5" gun gave a shout of surprise and drew attention to an amazing sight. The bamboo jungle on the far slope of a ridge in front of Point 315 seemed to be moving bodily forward. Our guns promptly opened fire, and then it appeared that the bamboos were carried by a Japanese assaulting party. The attackers wilted and fell under the storm of steel and the attempt was not repeated.

Before the Admin. Box was invested, the 9th Brigade of the 5th Division had been sent from the Maungdaw front over the Ngakyedauk Pass to reinforce the 7th Division in the operations against Buthidaung, and the brigade was south of Sinzweya when the Japanese counter-offensive was launched. This was most fortunate because three companies of The West Yorkshire Regiment were able to reach Sinzweya shortly before the Box was surrounded and thus to provide a stiffening of first-class infantry. They found there a medley of some 8,000 administrative troops with only a few regular tank, artillery and sapper units. No more than two days' rations were in store, and had it not been for the 60 tons of supplies dropped daily by American planes the garrison would have starved. The Admin. Box occupied a cup-shaped area of wooded hillocks, dry paddy fields and *chaungs*, roughly a mile square and surrounded by higher hills covered with trees and undergrowth of incredible density. Nature had not designed the place for defence, yet it had to be defended. The Japanese seized most of the surrounding heights and from there plastered the confined area with shells and bombs. Guns of heavy calibre joined in from Buthidaung. Every movement by day, every glimmer of light by night, attracted fire. Enemy snipers, tied to trees, took a constant toll. General Messervy now sent orders to the 89th Brigade to reinforce the garrison, but the leading battalion of Gurkhas, moving towards it from the north-east, was ambushed and severely handled. Two companies, however, reached "Gurkha Hill", near Point 315, and the remainder of the battalion arrived after a company of the West Yorkshires had driven the enemy back. The Japanese suffered heavily in an attempt to penetrate the southern perimeter by marching up a dry *chaung*. So many were killed here that the *chaung* became known as "Blood Nullah",[1] but still the little yellow men continued to use this route because they had been ordered to do so.

On February 11th, the enemy occupied the crest of "Artillery Hill", just outside the southern perimeter, and were driven off by the West Yorkshires and some tanks. A difficult problem now arose. This was to evacuate our wounded which was possible only by carrying them through the jungle by night to the 114th Brigade Box to the north-east, whence they could be flown out. For this and other reasons it was imperative that the Ngakyedauk Pass route should be re-opened as quickly as possible and the task was allotted to the 123rd Brigade of the 5th Division operating from the coastal road on the other side of the range. The sounds of battle reached the Box daily. Two brigades of the 26th Division were moving down the Kalapanzin Valley while another was clearing the enemy from the crest of the Mayu Range and the western slopes. The situation of the Japanese around Sinzweya was becoming desperate, yet they fought on with the courage of despair. On February 15th they attacked an outpost on "C Company Hill" at the exit of the Pass, gained a footing, and were then driven off. The first sign of relief

---

[1] See the map of the 7th Ind. Div. Admin Box, Sinzweya.

occurred on the 16th when the leading battalion of the 123rd Brigade marched in after ten days' fighting in the Mayu Range. There had been a particularly bloody struggle for a certain Hill 1010 overlooking the top of the Pass. The enemy had now almost shot his bolt. His troops were starving. A prisoner taken later said that he and his comrades had lived on roots for ten days. Yet on the night of February 21st/22nd a party of Japanese made a desperate assault as a final act of "Bushido." All were killed. On the 22nd, more troops of the 5th Indian Division, preceded by a bulldozer of 44 Field Park Company, debouched from the Ngakyedauk Pass and entered the perimeter. Supplies poured in. General Briggs arrived in a tank, bearing some bottles of whisky and kegs of rum, to congratulate General Messervy, Brigadier Evans and Brigadier D. Crowther of the 89th Brigade who had recently assumed charge of the defence. The Japanese had sustained their first major defeat. It had been proved to all the world that they had met their match. As Compton Mackenzie remarks,[1] the victory of the Admin. Box had a decisive effect on the course of human history and might be compared with that at Marathon where the Greeks defeated the Persian invaders long before the Christian era.

Some of the Sapper units with the relieving forces had had a very busy time. With the 26th Division on the Goppe Pass, 72 and 73 Field Companies had worked on a new alignment for mechanical transport to allow the Division to pass through. The first jeep surmounted the crest on February 18th and the troops then began to move southwards towards the Admin. Box. 2 Field Company was concerned chiefly with water supply as the weather was very dry. Meanwhile, 74 Field Company, with the 5th Division, was struggling with the problems of the Ngakyedauk Pass. Until February 11th it made mule-tracks for battalions assaulting the various hill features overlooking the road. Then a concentrated effort began to open up the Pass. Slowly but surely the infantry blasted and winkled the enemy from their positions so that on February 18th, 74 Company was able to begin work on the road itself. Clearing away obstacles, filling craters, cutting diversions and repairing culverts, it pushed forward under fire with tanks in close support, and through its exertions, and those of other Sapper units, the tanks of the 5th Division were able to link up with those of the 26th Division at Sinzweya on February 26th. In support of the 26th Division, 72 Field Company

---

[1] *All Over the Place*, by Compton Mackenzie, p. 143.

had already converted the jeep track from Taung Bazar into a passable road. After the relief of the Admin. Box, 77 Field Company returned with the 33rd Brigade to the Buthidaung front, sweeping for mines *en route*. One night, a Section was building a trestle bridge over the Letwedet *chaung* while, 20 yards away, the C.R.E. and another officer were reconnoitring an existing iron bridge. Nearby, another Section was constructing tank ramps. Measuring up the iron bridge took some time, and just as the two officers left the bridge it blew up! It appears that despite the presence of the Indian Sappers and an infantry covering party, some Japanese Sappers had been preparing the bridge for demolition. The enemy certainly did not lack courage.

After all Japanese resistance east of the Ngakyedauk Pass had been overcome, General Christison was able to resume his offensive southwards. This he did on March 5th, 1944, encouraged by the fact that the 36th British Division, under Major-General F. W. Festing, was arriving in Cox's Bazar from Calcutta in support. His first objective was naturally the Maungdaw-Buthidaung Road. The mouth of the Naf River was also to be seized so that supplies could reach Maungdaw safely by sea. The advance made slow headway, for the enemy resisted strongly and the coastal road was in a shocking state. However, on March 11th the 7th Division was in Buthidaung and then proceeded to assault the hill positions to the south and west. On the following day, the 5th Division was in possession of Maungdaw and the Razabil Fortress. After a fine attack by the 161st Brigade the enemy had vacated the Fortress, and the brigade then fought its way along the Buthidaung road towards the central 'tunnels' sector.

Towards the end of March, the 25th Indian Division, under Major-General H. L. Davies, began to arrive in replacement of the 5th Indian Division which was to be flown northwards to the front in Manipur. The 7th Indian Division followed later to Manipur, and with the approach of the monsoon the Second Arakan Campaign came gradually to an end although sporadic fighting continued around parts of the Maungdaw-Buthidaung Road. The 25th Division comprised the 51st, 53rd and 74th Brigades, and its Divisional Engineers, under Lieut.-Colonel I. G. Loch, R.E., included 63 Field Company (Major V. Panch, I.E.) 93 Field Company (Major R. B. Johnson, R.E.), 425 Field Company (Major P. M. Bennett, R.E.) and 325 Field Park Company (Major P. V. Subramanyam, I.E.). Unfortunately, Major Panch died in April 1944 when he was succeeded by Major W. G. Tollworthy, R.E. The 25th and 26th

Divisions now held the front in Arakan. The Engineer units of the 26th Division had much strenuous work and a considerable amount of fighting along the eastern portion of the Maungdaw-Buthidaung Road where the enemy still held the eastern tunnel and some surrounding positions. Early in April, 72 Field Company distinguished itself during the capture of two hill features near Buthidaung. Afterwards, it swept mines in that neighbourhood and joined in May in a final and bitter struggle around the tunnels by which the two divisions wrested the road from the Japanese. During the monsoon, Buthidaung was evacuated and attention was devoted chiefly to improving the port facilities at Maundgaw and making a new road over the Goppe Pass further north. These tasks kept the 26th Divisional Engineers very busy. The Malerkotla Field Company had already done excellent work at Maungdaw in rebuilding a 225-feet bridge in 24 days and strengthening a steel girder bridge.

August 1944 found the 26th Division in reserve at Cox's Bazar, leaving the 25th Division to consolidate the Maungdaw-Buthidaung line until the offensive could be resumed after the monsoon. The 25th Division had already seen much fighting while the last Japanese were being evicted during May. Major Bennett records that 425 Field Company, operating with the 53rd Brigade at that time, was made responsible for a hill section of the road where the enemy held several key features, including a knife-edged one called Point 551.[1] This was captured and handed over to the brigade. The Company had to defend Brigade Headquarters, and the strain of working hard all day and mounting perimeter picquets at night was very heavy. The work consisted mainly of cutting tracks forward to infantry posts and usually without any infantry protection. Each Sapper Section therefore kept two look-out men on duty, and every man had his rifle and a couple of grenades close at hand. Each morning the infantry re-opened their particular sections of the tracks by patrolling in carriers, accompanied by a few Sappers to remove the road-mines placed overnight by enemy patrols. 425 Field Company had also to maintain a water-point in a gorge 800-feet deep to supply a battalion perched on the summit of the Mayu Range. Soon after Point 551 was captured, the enemy re-took the crest and held on to it for another month. Our infantry occupied very exposed positions lower down, and the Sappers had to cut mule-tracks towards them

---

[1] "The History of a Wartime Field Company of the Q.V's O. Madras Sappers and Miners", by Major P. M. Bennett, R.E., appearing in *The R.E. Journal*, September 1949, pp. 273-290.

under constant sniping and mortar fire. They also built a bridge across a *chaung* at the foot of the hill and erected and operated an aerial ropeway to facilitate the supply of stores and ammunition to the troops far above. Building this ropeway was a very dangerous proceeding, for it had to be done in full view of the enemy and the men at the upper terminal were exposed to mortar and machine-gun fire as they lashed the blocks and guys to trees. Towards the end of May, the enemy tried to drive our infantry off the hill, but the position was restored by a counter-attack and, early in June 1944, the Japanese withdrew from Point 551 and from the entire spine of the Mayu Range.

This mention of an aerial ropeway recalls another and larger installation in Arakan erected in the Goppe Pass between high peaks and over deep ravines. The Goppe ropeway, $2\frac{1}{2}$ miles in length and operated by an engine at the summit, was built before the monsoon of 1944 to supplement road transport in bad weather and was the first to be constructed entirely by Indian Engineer units. From the end of August 1944 it was operated by 403 Field Park Company under Major W. G. Carter, R.E., and it was not dismantled until April 1945 when a platoon of 96 Field Company removed the cable and other gear.

Throughout the 1944 monsoon, 425 Field Company remained with the 53rd Brigade which was deployed along the 'Tunnels' section of the Maungdaw-Buthidaung Road. The remainder of the 25th Division was installed in bamboo *basha* camps in the Maungdaw Plain. Two inches of rain fell daily for over three months, so the Sappers had their hands full in dealing with landslides, improving shelters and repairing mule tracks. The most serious problem, however, was the road itself where 425 Field Company was in charge of an 8-mile stretch. It had little soling and was surfaced only with soft local stone. The enemy remained passive. The fight against disease never ceased, and particularly against jaundice and skin complaints. Everyone was soaked by the unceasing downpour, but a generous issue of rum helped to restore flagging spirits.

Early in September 1944 there was some fighting south of Maungdaw when an attempt was made to surprise the enemy before he had further strengthened his positions. The objective was a couple of positions on Hill 1433 which overlooked the plain, and a Section of 425 Field Company was allotted to each of the attacking companies of Gurkhas. The infantry broke into both positions but were driven out again and reformed about 70 yards down the hill-side. Havildar Sankaranarayana Nair, who commanded a Sapper Section in the first attack, was ordered forward again after dark to ascertain whether the Jap bunkers could be demolished with explosives. With Naik Subbiah and Sapper Ramasamy carrying made-up charges, he worked his way through the undergrowth and pin-pointed some enemy posts. The party then crawled round to a *basha* a few yards behind and, covered by the tommy guns of the other two, the Havildar entered it, placed his charge in the centre, piled some Japanese ammunition and other articles around it, lit the fuse and withdrew his party under point-blank fire. On the following morning, with one companion, he again entered the position and placed and lit charges in a *basha* and a dug-out before escaping under a shower of grenades. For these gallant exploits he received the Indian Distinguished Service Medal and his companions the Military Medal.

The initial attacks on Hill 1433 having failed, the Gurkhas were told to hold on as close as possible to the enemy and accordingly 63 and 425 Companies had to cut tracks forward. They hacked and dug furiously all day in pelting rain and at night concentrated in 'boxes' alongside the tracks. The nights were miserable. Each man had only a ground-sheet and a jersey, and when morning came the sole means of lighting a fire was to burn some guncotton. By the end of the third day the Sappers were completely exhausted, but fortunately by that time paths for porters were ready and blankets and rations arrived. Two days later it was found that the enemy had vanished, so their positions were occupied and the tracks extended along a ridge thick with Japanese corpses. It was an unpleasant scene, but two young Lance-Naiks of 425 Company found it inspiring. "Sahib", they remarked to their O.C., "the next time our unit helps in an attack, we want to be in the assault parties."

At the end of September 1944, General Christison was directed to resume the offensive in Arakan in order to contain enemy forces which might otherwise interfere with the offensive by the 4th and 33rd Corps across the Chindwin River into Central Burma which was planned to begin in December. During October, the 26th Division repelled a Japanese attack on Taung Bazar. Meanwhile, the 25th Division drove the enemy from his remaining positions south of the Maungdaw-Buthidaung Road. The 81st West African Division, which had withdrawn from Paletwa for the monsoon, re-occupied that place and prepared to advance down both banks of the Kaladan River to act as a flank guard. The 82nd West African Division now made its first appearance in Arakan. The 15th Corps was to undertake a land advance down the Mayu Peninsula and the Kalapanzin and Kaladan Valleys in order to clear the enemy from the whole of Arakan north of Akyab and then to provide troops for an amphibious assault on Akyab Island. With these orders, Christison launched the Third Arakan Campaign on December 12th, 1944. The offensive was opened by the 25th Indian Division moving along the coastal area and the 81st West African Division down the Kaladan River, while the 82nd West African Division advanced down the Kalapanzin Valley where it had relieved the 26th Indian Division. On December 15th, the 82nd Division captured Buthidaung while the 25th Division, under Major-General G. N. Wood, was pushing southwards astride the Mayu Range, supplied chiefly by sea. On Christmas Day, the 51st Brigade was at Foul Point, looking across at Akyab Island, and the 81st West African Division had seized the ferry across the Kaladan at Kyauktaw. It is interesting to note that the 51st Brigade of the 25th Division was the first all-Indian brigade to fight in the front line in the Second World War. It was commanded by Brigadier K. S. Thimayya and its three battalions were officered solely by Indians. The 74th Brigade followed the 51st Brigade down the coast while the 53rd Brigade moved down the Kalapanzin Valley.

The coastal advance to Foul Point encountered many natural obstacles though little enemy resistance. The beaches made excellent roads but the transport became bogged periodically at the mouths of muddy and unbridged *chaungs* and much time had to be spent in unloading and extricating vehicles.[1] The 51st Brigade was maintained by means of small steamers plying from Maungdaw, with *sampans* to land stores. On the Kalapanzin River, the maintenance of the 53rd Brigade was more difficult. At Buthidaung the river was about 200 yards wide with a rapid tidal current, and lower down, where known as the Mayu River, it broadened into an estuary between one and two miles in width. Road supply being out of the question, everything depended on the collection of a satisfactory fleet of river craft. There was only sufficient folding boat equipment (F.B.E.) for a single troop of 25 pr. guns. A few locally manufactured pontoons were available for rafting, but unit transport consisted chiefly of *sampans* and assault boats, some of which had outboard motors. 425 Field Company assembled and repaired the craft, while 325 Field Park Company provided the superstructure and anchors.

---

[1] "Water Lines of Communication along the Arakan Coast", by Colonel Arjan Singh, appearing in *The Journal of the Institution of Military Engineers*, April 1950, pp. 123-126.

Vehicles were discarded because land transport in future would be by mules or porters. After Buthidaung had been occupied by the West Africans, 63 and 425 Field Companies set to work to prepare launching sites on the Kalapanzin for the hundreds of craft expected by road from Maungdaw.[1] Buthidaung being now almost hidden in tall elephant grass and scrub jungle, the two companies had first to clear half a mile of the river bank with bulldozers before they could cut slipways and prepare parking areas in rear. The pontoons and boats soon began to arrive on lorries from Maungdaw and the work of repairing damaged craft was taken in hand. Outboard motors were fitted whenever possible. Gradually, the fleet was launched, loaded and despatched downstream to the forward troops, and finally the Sappers themselves embarked on rafts and boats and followed. "*Sampans* replaced jeeps", writes Colonel Arjan Singh, "and rafts replaced gun tractors and ammunition trailers. The 2-pounders, mounted on rafts, led the columns, with infantry moving on foot on either bank." Christmas Day and Boxing Day were spent in ferrying the troops and guns across the Mayu River near Rathedaung, and on January 3rd, a platoon of 425 Company, with the leading infantry, reached the northern end of Akyab Island, 50 miles by water from Buthidaung, shortly after the island had been captured from the sea. The careful training of the Indian Engineers in watermanship had already paid a good dividend.

Akyab, though valuable as a port, was far more so as an air-base. Lieut.-General Sir Oliver Leese, the 11th Army Group Commander, had been ordered to capture both Akyab and Ramree Islands by seaborne landings, the primary object being to secure airfields from which the Fourteenth Army could be supplied during its long advance southwards to Rangoon. That army was already approaching Mandalay and its tenuous line of land communication with Imphal was near breaking point though supplies could be brought by air. At Meiktila, 80 miles beyond, it could be supplied by air from Chittagong, but from Meiktila to Rangoon the supply would have to be from airfields further south. The most important task of the 15th Corps in its offensive down the Arakan Coast in 1945 was therefore to secure air-base after air-base and this could best be achieved by a series of sea-borne landings designed to force the Japanese either to evacuate their positions or to face encirclement

---

[1] "The History of a Wartime Field Company of the Q.V's O. Madras Sappers and Miners", by Major P. M. Bennett, R.E., appearing in *The R.E. Journal*, September 1949, pp. 273-290.

and destruction. Fortunately, the enemy chose to evacuate Akyab, and when the 3rd Commando Brigade landed on the island on January 3rd, 1945, they met no opposition. They bicycled across the island quite happily and were soon in Akyab Town at the southern end. The island was eminently suitable for development as an air-base and thus the uninterrupted advance of the victorious Fourteenth Army beyond Meiktila could be assured.

The 'Beach Group' now makes its appearance in this narrative. Five Beach Groups had come into existence in the summer of 1943, shortly after an Indian Expeditionary Force was formed in India for amphibious operations, and each Group was then about 1,900 strong. The first to appear was 41 Indian Beach Group, formed north of Bombay in July under Colonel A. W. Edwards. In October, the Expeditionary Force became the 33rd Indian Corps, and as such, moved to the Manipur front and therefore left behind it the Beach Groups intended for amphibious assaults. These continued their specialized training. In April 1944, 41 Beach Group was transferred across India to Cocanada on the east coast for combined training, and a few months later 42, 43 and 44 Beach Groups were disbanded, leaving only 41 and 45 Groups which were then expanded gradually till they each attained a strength of more than 3,000 officers and men. A Field Company of Indian Engineers formed part of a Beach Group. The five Field Companies required for the Groups needed elaborate training in watermanship, but the training was seriously interrupted in the middle of April by a demand for engineer assistance to cope with the widespread damage caused by a great explosion in the Bombay Docks. For instance, 361 Field Company, belonging to 43 Beach Group, was employed until September on clearing debris, demolishing damaged buildings and erecting temporary structures in Bombay, and by that time its services with a Beach Group were no longer needed.

Towards the end of 1944, 41 Indian Beach Group had become a very complicated organization. In addition to the 14th Indian Engineer Battalion it included 78 Field Company of the Bengal Group, a Pioneer Company, an amphibious Transport Company, a Beach Hospital, Supply, Ordnance, Provost, Signals, R.A.F., R.E.M.E. and Mechanical Equipment Sections and a couple of small Naval Commando units. Attached to it was a Special Movement Control unit to supervize the landing arrangements for troops and stores and the discharge of ships. The Group was designed to operate in the following manner. It would arrive after the leading infantry had

Landing at Akyab

secured a foothold on the beach and would prepare for landing reinforcements, guns, tanks, vehicles and stores brought by the Navy. The best exits must be found to the nearest roads and cleared of mines, first for tracked vehicles and then for wheeled vehicles using Sommerfeld track if necessary. Bulldozers would bring the track ashore on sledges and then go ahead to level exits to the roads. Wave after wave of guns and lorries would finally pour down the ramps of the landing craft, involving unceasing repair work to the exits. Such, very briefly, were the tasks of the Field Company of a Beach Group. If the landing were opposed the Sappers were certain to suffer severe casualties, and it was therefore most fortunate that few of the landings on the Arakan Coast had to be made under fire.

78 Field Company was commanded by Major T. Beaumont, R.E., with Captain W. Byrde, R.E., as second-in-command and Lieuts. A. H. W. Sandes, R.E. (son of the author), Naresh Prasad, I.E., P. R. Francis, R.E., and I. A. A. Clark, R.E., as subalterns. After a summer spent in the sweltering heat of Cocanada, the unit was glad to embark at Vizagapatam on December 28th and to reach Chittagong on January 3rd, 1945, though all ranks were greatly disappointed to miss the landing on Akyab Island, the first large-scale amphibious operation in Burma. Beaumont had gone ahead and was in Akyab when the Company disembarked on January 9th. "The 25th Division", he writes,[1] "were boasting that by the time the Commandos landed, the Divisional troops had had tea and biscuits waiting for them on the beach! When I approached the mansion allotted to 78 Field Company I found that it had been burnt to the ground and there was a dead dog in the well. I toured the looted and desolate town which had been abandoned by the inhabitants for at least two years to escape Allied bombing. In the main street the vegetation had grown up between the road and the buildings so that it seemed as if one were walking along a jungle path. As soon as the ships were in harbour the various units of the Beach Group started to disembark into landing craft, and at this point the Japs decided to remind us that this was not the pleasure cruise it had seemed. Just as the unit commanders were assembling at a crossroads for orders, we heard violent machine-gunning from the harbour and anti-aircraft fire from the ships and airfield. We could see a

---

[1] Notes by Major T. Beaumont, R.E., dated January 1947, and entitled "Whom We Salute."

few small planes swerving and diving high up in the sky and then a large Dakota came in low over the trees with bits of its tail dropping off. Soon afterwards, Adrian Sandes came up the road from the beach, at the head of his platoon, with a broad grin on his face. It appeared that they had been disembarking down scramble-nets into a landing craft when suddenly a Jap "Zero" had dived at them with machine-guns blazing. Miraculously, no one was hurt. That evening, the enemy radio at Saigon announced that Jap aircraft had carried out an intrepid raid on a British Naval Force at Akyab and had sunk one cruiser and severely damaged another!"

Adrian Sandes' own account of his adventure was as follows.[1] "We were practically all aboard the "Z" landing craft when I saw an aeroplane diving straight at us. A small black object dropped from it and hit the water about a hundred yards to starboard. Realising immediately that this was a Jap air attack, the Subedar and I lay down on deck, vaguely aware of machine-guns firing and the splash of bullets around. We heard no sound of the bomb. As soon as the plane had gone, we got up and were astounded to see all the 150 men standing upright in the "Z" craft, goggling and saying that it had indeed been an exceptionally fine demonstration by the R.A.F. such as they had been accustomed to see at Cocanada! By dint of hard yelling, I got them to lie down, and soon the plane was back again followed by another. They concentrated on our ship but failed to do any damage although one bomb fell very close. Our anti-aircraft guns opened an ear-splitting barrage and the Spitfires joined in, and we heard later that six Jap planes had been shot down. After this little excitement we made an uneventful trip across the harbour and landed on the beach to be welcomed by our O.C."

78 Field Company was soon installed in a camp near the derelict aerodrome outside the jungle-covered town. "Jap bunkers were everywhere", continues Sandes, "and so thick was the undergrowth that one literally could not see them even when standing on them. Their average field of fire was only a few yards. The town seemed deserted, and we settled down in our field and built corrugated iron shelters and pitched tents in some aircraft dispersal bays. After Cocanada, Akyab was delightful. So beautiful with its fine trees, European houses and tarred roads, and from an engineering point of view quite wonderful. In the miles of derelict rice-factories one could find anything from furniture to water-pipes. Our jobs were chiefly

---

[1] Letter from Captain A. H. W. Sandes, R.E., dated May 18th, 1945.

water-supply and road repair. The bathing was excellent—off vast sandy beaches in clear water with rolling breakers. So here we stayed for a month while one platoon went off to Myebon and thence to Kangaw with the Commandos. Akyab was coming to life before we left. We had cinemas and Ensa shows, and I even met a few nurses from a nearby hospital. Our only lack was cigarettes which were always scarce."

To avoid the delay involved in awaiting the arrival of 41 Beach Group, the 25th Division had improvised a Beach Battalion of its own for the landing at Akyab. A platoon of 63 Field Company was with the Commandos while the remainder of the Company, together with 93 Field Company, prepared embarkation points at Foul Point to await the return of the first flights of landing craft. The other platoons then embarked in support of the 51st Brigade, followed by the Beach Battalion, and thus 63 Company was the first Sapper unit to reach the island. It remained there until the middle of January engaged in clearing a fair-weather fighter strip and working on communications. 78 Field Company made exit roads for amphibious landing craft (Dukws), using sandwich layers of Sommerfeld track, coir matting, iron sheeting and logs, and about 200 Dukws negotiated the exits daily for more than a fortnight. 73 Field Company crossed from Foul Point on January 18th and started building huts and *bashas*. Akyab became a hive of engineering industry as other units flocked in, and so it remained until the end of the campaign.

The air raid on January 9th had added to the chaos in Akyab harbour, but nevertheless a further advance down the Arakan coast was started on the 12th when the 3rd Commando Brigade set out for Myebon, 32 miles to the south-east, and after a heavy bombardment, made a successful landing. A brigade of the 25th Division followed, and then most of the remainder of the Division after a bridge-head had been consolidated. The enemy counter-attacked and a week of severe fighting ensued while our forces pushed northwards up the Myebon Peninsula.[1] By January 21st, 1945, this had been effectively secured. In the meantime, plans had been made to capture Ramree Island and in particular the port and airfield site of Kyaukpyu, at the northern tip, which lies about 45 miles south of Myebon. Kyaukpyu was known to have a good anchorage for ships bringing supplies from India, but its chief asset was that it could provide

---

[1] See the map of Lower Arakan included in this chapter.

another forward air-base for the supply of the Fourteenth Army. In addition a naval detachment was to be landed on Cheduba Island, south-west of Ramree. On January 21st, a brigade of the 26th Division, sailing from Akyab, captured Kyaukpyu and began to clear Ramree Island, and five days later, Cheduba Island was taken; but the mopping up of the final pockets of enemy resistance on Ramree was not completed until February 22nd by which time most of the Japanese garrison had been liquidated while trying to escape to the mainland.

With the Commandos in the initial landing at Myebon was a detachment of 41 Beach Group, under Major Norman Hunter, which included a platoon of 78 Field Company under Lieut. P. R. Francis, R.E. The Sappers helped the Commandos to consolidate and afterwards lifted a number of 120 lb. Japanese mines of a new type. They were hemispherical in shape and each had a couple of horns, made of lead, which projected above the sand when the mine was buried in a beach. Francis sent some of these mines back to Akyab, where Adrian Sandes spent many hours in experimenting on them. "There were two methods of disarming the mines", writes the latter. "The first was to remove the horns which unscrewed with a left-hand thread. The second was to lift a small brass plunger, thereby breaking an electric circuit by which the mine would be detonated if the horns were crushed. The plunger had a little tapped hole in the centre and I found that it could be raised easily by screwing into the hole a piece of soft copper wire which engaged the threads. Francis, I believe, had raised a plunger by hooking it with a piece of bent wire inserted through one of the horn sockets." The experiments were carried out in a corner of the camp where it is said that Sandes' friends seldom cared to visit him. However, all went well and a regular disarming drill was evolved for future use. In the middle of January, 63 Field Company joined the platoon of 78 Field Company at Myebon, and 93 (Mandi) Field Company arrived at the end of the month. There were then sufficient engineer units for maintaining beach roads, establishing water-points and supplying engineer stores.

On Ramree Island, one of the Sapper units with the 71st Brigade Assault Group of the 26th Division at Kyaukpyu was 28 Field Company (Bombay) under Major C. H. Cowan, R.E. This unit performed Beach Group duties when the landing took place and then accompanied the brigade southwards towards Ramree Town at the other end of the island, losing *en route* Captain F. E. Henson,

R.E., who was unfortunately killed in action on January 23rd. Another early arrival at Ramree was 72 Field Company (Bengal), under Major J. R. Macdonald, R.E., which followed the leading troops on "D" Day. Its first task was to construct fighter and Dakota air-strips. Usually, it was considered advisable to provide new airstrips rapidly rather than spend time on clearing existing aerodromes, but in this case the aerodrome site was tackled. Though it was studded with sharpened stakes and intersected by deep ditches, 72 Field Company was not deterred. The ditches were filled in by bulldozers, the stakes extracted by coolies; trees were cut down, and bricks for metalling brought from derelict houses. Sommerfeld track was laid in the worst places, and in five days part of the aerodrome was ready for use. The final touch was a wind-sock made from the white-washed *pagris* of one of the platoons! 98 Field Company (Bombay), under Major L. Lubert, R.E., reached Kyaukpyu on January 21st, and most of 78 Field Company (Bengal), under Major T. Beaumont, R.E., landed on February 9th and took over the aerodrome which had been aptly named "Ditchfield." On the same day, the 71st Brigade entered Ramree Town. 78 Field Company found Ramree Island not nearly so pleasant as Akyab. The climate was getting steadily hotter, and blowing up endless trees was monotonous work. Yet there it had to remain for nearly three months, living in a small sandy area and working hard on the aerodroms or on roads and beaches. Another Sapper unit in Ramree was 423 Field Company, under Major J. F. Butlin, R.E., which disembarked there on February 11th. It began to erect petrol storage tanks and a ship-to-shore pipeline, 600 yards long, for discharging tankers, a difficult job which was not completed until May 3rd. Other units in Ramree during the spring of 1945 were 93 (Mandi) Field Company, 404 and 405 Field Companies and 326 Field Park Company.

While Ramree Island was being cleared of the last Japanese there had been heavy fighting on the mainland not far from the Myebon Peninsula where we had been trying to cut off the escape southwards of enemy forces retreating before the advance of the 81st West African Division down the west bank of the Kaladan. The key point on the escape route was the village of Kangaw on the coastal road and accordingly an amphibious assault on it was planned to take place on January 22nd. The assault was to be made by the 3rd Commando Brigade, supported by the 51st Brigade under Brigadier K. S. Thimayya, while the other two brigades of the 25th Division drove northwards up the Myebon Peninsula to capture

Minbya and the 82nd West African Division[1] occupied Myohaung on the Kaladan. Myohaung was not to be occupied until the enemy's escape route had first been effectively blocked at Kangaw. It was anticipated that a landing near Kangaw would be heavily opposed. The coast was intersected with mangrove-covered *chaungs*, beyond which were paddy fields with a background of densely wooded hills. However, the Japanese were taken by surprise and the Commandos landed on the 22nd and secured a tiny bridgehead on the bank of a narrow tidal *chaung* about a couple of miles from the village. During the night of January 23rd/24th they were reinforced by the 51st Brigade which landed under fire and then began to fight its way forward towards the road through swampy country. The enemy had rushed up reinforcements and offered powerful resistance. Day by day the battle continued while the bridgehead was steadily enlarged. On the 28th, the enemy deluged the area with shells and after dark made a series of desperate counter-attacks which were repulsed. Two days later, our troops went over to the offensive. They took Kangaw and blocked the road. The Japanese made their final counter-attack on January 31st, directing it chiefly against a wooded ridge which we had occupied. A party carrying explosive charges on long poles rushed at our tanks, one man hurling himself under a Sherman and dying as he demolished it. But the 82nd Division was fast approaching, having occupied Myohaung on the 25th. Caught between the West Africans and the 25th Division, the enemy broke and tried to escape over the hills towards the Irrawaddy. They left 2,000 dead and 16 guns around Kangaw and only a few managed to by-pass the village. Our casualties numbered 600. Parties of Japanese who got away southwards made for the village of An, whence a track led over the Arakan Yomas to the Irrawaddy; but on the whole it may be said that the victory at Kangaw was complete and comparable with those at Sinzweya and at Kohima in the north.

A reconnaissance party from the platoon of 78 Field Company under Lieut. P. R. Francis, R.E., disembarked at Kangaw with the leading Commandos. According to Major Beaumont, the Commandos first tried to land on the banks of the main stream and found that the mud was over their knees, so they then reconnoitred with Francis to discover a better place. They went in boats up a *chaung* so narrow that the branches of trees met overhead and, meeting no enemy, landed and explored inland towards the ridge

---

[1] The 81st West African Division was now being withdrawn to Africa.

already mentioned and in the direction of Kangaw Village. Then they returned to report, and the main body of the Commandos came up the *chaung*, disembarked and occupied the ridge. They were soon discovered by the enemy who opened fire with guns and mortars but fortunately could not see the crowded beach where the Sappers were hard at work. 63 Field Company arrived from Myebon and helped the platoon of 78 Field Company to land tanks and stores, and to extend the beach-head and make exits from it, a difficult task as no bulldozers were available. Major Norman Hunter, commanding the 41 Beach Group detachment, was killed and Francis had to take charge as the next in seniority. 63 Field Company was involved in much heavy fighting. It provided 'bunker-busting' parties for the infantry and made jeep tracks across the paddy fields from the *chaung* to the ridge; and as it happened to be encamped there when the Japs made one of their fiercest assaults, it was engaged in hand-to-hand combat and suffered a dozen casualties.

After Kangaw, operations were resumed to clear the enemy from the coast to the south in order to prevent the remnants of the 54th and 55th Japanese Divisions from reinforcing the enemy opposing the advance of the Fourteenth Army, and also to secure fair-weather airstrips pending the completion of all-weather airfields at Akyab and Kyaukpyu. A bridgehead was to be established at Taungup, 100 miles south of Kangaw, and the track leading from Taungup across the hills to Prome on the Irrawaddy was to be seized. Early in February 1945, the 25th Division and the 82nd West African Division were still mopping up in the Myebon-Kangaw area, while the 26th Division was busy clearing Ramree Island. General Christison's plan was now to complete the destruction of the 54th Japanese Division in the Tamandu-An area, south of Kangaw, and to block the escape route from Taungup to Prome. The 82nd West African Division was to move southwards while the 25th Division made an amphibious landing at Ru-ywa, west of An. When An had been captured, Taungup would be the next objective so that the coastal road would be cut behind the enemy. Everything went according to plan. The 53rd Brigade of the 25th Division landed at Ru-ywa on February 16th, taking the enemy by surprise. Indeed, it was not till three days later that the bridgehead was heavily attacked, and then unsuccessfully. The remainder of the division followed and the An area was cleared. This exploit may be said to mark the end of the Third Arakan Campaign. Thenceforward, the operations of the 15th Corps had to be curtailed in the interests of the Fourteenth

Army, which was to have priority in air supply for its advance on Rangoon.

The experiences of 425 Field Company in the landing at Ru-ywa are related by Major P. M. Bennett.[1] The first flight of the assault, comprising a British battalion and a platoon of the Company, touched down on the beaches at 10.30 a.m. on February 16th. As each landing craft arrived, a few Sappers leapt ashore and began to cut a way through mine-fields and dense and prickly jungle for the assaulting infantry, and then, with Hessian or wire netting, to improve it as far as high-water level, 300 yards away. When the remainder of the Company appeared with bulldozers and other equipment, the path was converted into a jeep track of corduroy logs. Two days later, an alternative beach-head was developed for landing guns and lorries, after which the unit returned to the original one and began digging for water and making airstrips. The enemy shelled the beach-heads and their exits whenever a landing craft was seen approaching, but the Sappers suffered few casualties although the Pioneers unloading the craft were less fortunate. On February 26th, guns and tanks were landed and passed successfully over the corduroy exit road. Early in March, the unit moved southwards to repair a ford overlooked by the enemy and on March 14th embarked for Akyab *en route* to India. The other Field Companies with the 25th Division were employed also at Ru-ywa, chiefly in making wells by blasting with explosives as there were no streams and the hot weather was approaching. They moved to Tamandu to prepare an area for the occupation of the 82nd West African Division after the 25th Division had gone. The last to leave was 93 Field Company (Bombay), under Major J. K. Wren, R.E., which sailed on March 22nd.

After Ru-ywa, the next operation was a landing at Letpan, 36 miles to the south, which was accomplished by the 4th Brigade of the 26th Division from Ramree Island on March 13th. This was the last of its kind in Arakan. From Letpan the brigade turned southwards, and after some fierce fighting, captured Taungup on April 14th. 72 Field Company was the only Engineer unit present. It sent forward a few officers and men with the fighting patrols of a reconnaissance formation, known as "D" Force, which preceded the brigade. It was during the advance of this force that Lieut. C. Raymond, R.E., gained a posthumous Victoria Cross for extreme

---

[1] "The History of a Wartime Field Company of the Q.V's O. Madras Sappers and Miners", by Major P. M. Bennett, R.E., appearing in *The R.E. Journal*, September 1949, pp. 273-290.

gallantry. 72 Company moved down the coastal road to Taungup, making it fit for tanks, preparing air-strips, clearing mines and ferrying infantry across *chaungs*. The West Africans were approaching down the coast. On April 28th they were in Taungup and on May 9th in Sandoway, and by May 13th, after they had spread further southwards to Gwa, the liberation of Arakan was complete. The 15th Corps had suffered more than 5,000 battle casualties including 1,155 killed, but it had inflicted far heavier losses on the enemy and the main objectives had been achieved.

Although Arakan had been cleared, it was doubtful whether the Fourteenth Army, coming down from the north, could reach Rangoon before its line of land communication was wrecked by the monsoon. On April 25th, the mechanized 4th Corps, under Lieut.-General F. W. Messervy of 'Admin Box' fame, began its final dash along the last 144 miles to the city. Lord Mountbatten, however, had already taken precautions against a failure to beat the rains by preparing Operation "Dracula" which involved the capture of Rangoon from the sea by the 26th Division voyaging from Ramree Island. The monsoon might break at any moment and Messervy's tanks were showing signs of wear, so the odds were in favour of the sea-borne expedition. Six convoys of troopships and a host of landing craft and mine-sweepers were ready to sail from Ramree under the protection of a powerful fleet and overwhelming air cover. Little was known of the perpetually shifting channels of the Rangoon River or the location of the minefields encumbering them, so the final ascent to the City of Golden Pagodas promised to be slow and laborious; but it was arranged that the 26th Division's attack should start with the dropping of parachutists on the defences at Elephant Point at the mouth of the river, followed by the landing of a brigade on each bank.

Operation "Dracula" does not properly belong to the story of Arakan; but it would be unfair to the 26th Indian Division and its engineer formations to omit some mention of their crowning exploit which was rendered possible only by their previous victories on the Arakan Coast. The first ships carrying the 26th Division, now under Major-General H. M. Chambers, sailed from Ramree on April 27th, 1945, and the main convoys a few days later. The Rangoon estuary was reached without incident, and very early on May 1st the 50th Parachute Brigade of Gurkhas was dropped on the enemy position at Elephant Point after a heavy bombardment. The parachutists soon obliterated the small garrison. On May 2nd, in pouring rain and through rough seas, the troops were put ashore in landing craft but were subsequently re-embarked and sent forward up the river to land again within a few miles of Rangoon, and by the evening of May 3rd, the brigade on the east bank was in the city. As the 17th Indian Division, leading the 4th Corps' advance from the north, was then on the Pegu Road, 32 miles away, the 26th Indian Division had won the race to Rangoon; but had it not been for the pressure exerted by the 4th Corps, the sea-borne expedition might have fared badly. General Chambers had expected little opposition after May 1st because an aircraft flying over the city early on that day had reported that the words "Japs Gone" were painted on the roof of the gaol in which our prisoners-of-war were known to be confined. Nevertheless, the bombing of Rangoon was continued, though great care was taken to avoid hitting the gaol. During the afternoon of May 2nd, the pilot of a Mosquito aircraft, seeing no signs of the enemy, decided to land on the Mingaladon airfield to the north. He and his navigator then walked into Rangoon, visited the gaol and saw the prisoners who confirmed that the Japs had gone, and finally they sailed down the river in a *sampan* and informed the vanguard of the assaulting troops. By May 4th, 1945, the 26th Division was firmly installed in Rangoon, and three days later it linked up with the Fourteenth Army.

To return now to the experiences of some of the Indian Engineer units which sailed from Ramree for the assault. 28 and 98 Field Companies embarked on April 28th and both were in Rangoon by the evening of May 3rd after helping the other troops to land, re-embark and land again. Once in the city, they were faced by the stupendous task of rehabilitating a huge port, neglected by the Japanese, bombed by the R.A.F., and ravaged by looters. Their Field Park Company had not arrived; they had little equipment and no vehicles; and their C.R.E., Lieut.-Colonel R. S. B. Ward, had been killed when his landing craft struck a mine off Elephant Point. Nevertheless, they set to work with a will, concentrating first on the Mingaladon airfield. 72 and 73 Field Companies soon came up the river. Other engineer units followed, and the work of restoring the water and electricity systems, repairing docks, wharves and roads, and demolishing wrecked buildings, was accelerated. The Sappers even operated railway trains, the first of which left the docks early on May 8th and reached Mingaladon safely an hour later.

78 Field Company, now under Major W. Byrde, R.E., with Captain A. H. W. Sandes, R.E., as second-in-command, did not leave Ramree until May 4th. Once again, in common with most of 41 Beach

Group, it missed the initial landings, but by May 6th it was in Rangoon. "As we sailed up the river", writes Sandes, "the city presented a picture of the most complete desolation it is possible to conceive. Miles of riverside wharves were deserted and lined with sunken boats. Some of the jetties were mere masses of wreckage and many of the houses just rubble. On landing, we walked straight into our allotted area near the Mayo Club, and you may imagine our delight on seeing great sheds, with roofs on, for the men and a fine house for our Mess. Of course, the whole place was in a disgusting state owing to the looters. Exploration revealed miles of dumps of every conceivable kind. There were vast engineering workshops and shipyards, timber mills, rice mills, piles of steel joists and stacks of piping, but almost everything was rotten, rusty and broken. The streets were covered with litter and strewn with worthless Japanese currency notes. I have never seen so much money in my life. The cranes were out of order, the railways overgrown with vegetation, and the stations masses of twisted metal and debris. There were no trains, water-supply, or electric light. Here and there lay dead bodies, and the stench of rotting rice was abominable. Exploring the place was an eerie experience. Doors hanging open, creaking in the wind: piles of ashes stirring in the breeze: smashed furniture lying about: everywhere, deserted and derelict houses. The Japs had placed fire-bombs in some buildings, but these had already been extinguished. Wherever you went you could see Jap money, abandoned motor cars, lorries by the hundred stripped of their parts, wrecked bulldozers, rusty steel helmets. I entered the Secretariat, looking for mines. The Japs, in their inexplicable way, had used this beautiful building as a warehouse. There were great halls full of rice, rooms filled with broken packing cases, others piled with rotting State archives, and others again full of old boots. Never have I seen such confusion. And the smell! It made one realize, as never before, the meaning of so-called Japanese co-Prosperity."

The 'War of the Chaungs', a long and bloody struggle, is now but a memory, but it takes its place in military history as an ideal example of the co-operation of all arms. Transported and landed by the Royal and Indian Navies, and covered by the Royal, Indian and American Air Forces, the Army reached its zenith in jungle warfare. The troops in Arakan, as in the rest of Burma, turned initial defeat into overwhelming victory. Inexperienced at first in jungle warfare, they improved month by month and year by year till finally they could outdo the Japanese in every artifice and manoeuvre. They were better led, better supplied, better armed. Only in physical courage were the two sides evenly matched. Heat, rain, sickness, mountains, rivers, jungles and swamps were often greater obstacles to success than the enemy; but the Indian Engineers triumphed over all and, time and again, fought with rifle and bayonet alongside the infantry.

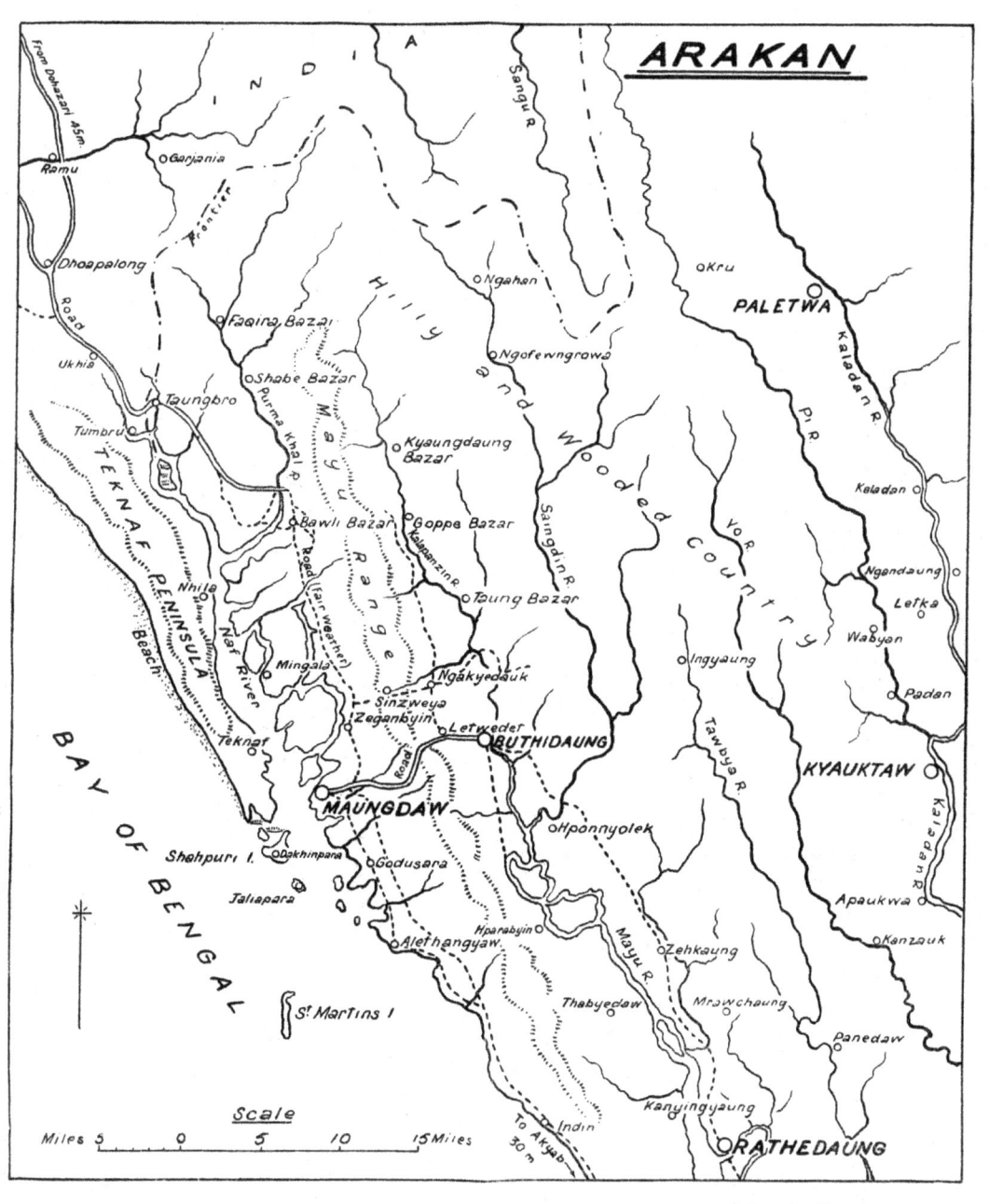

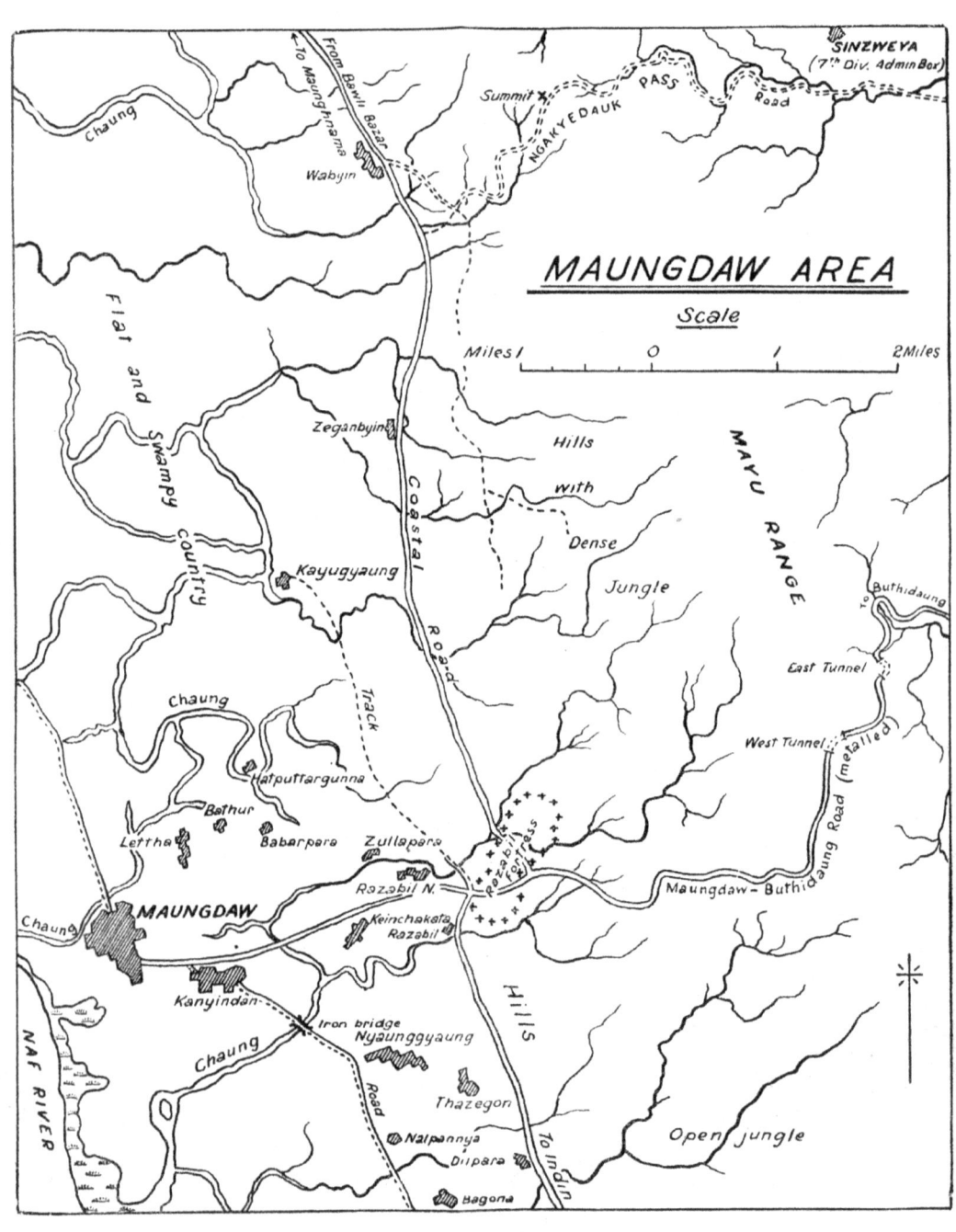

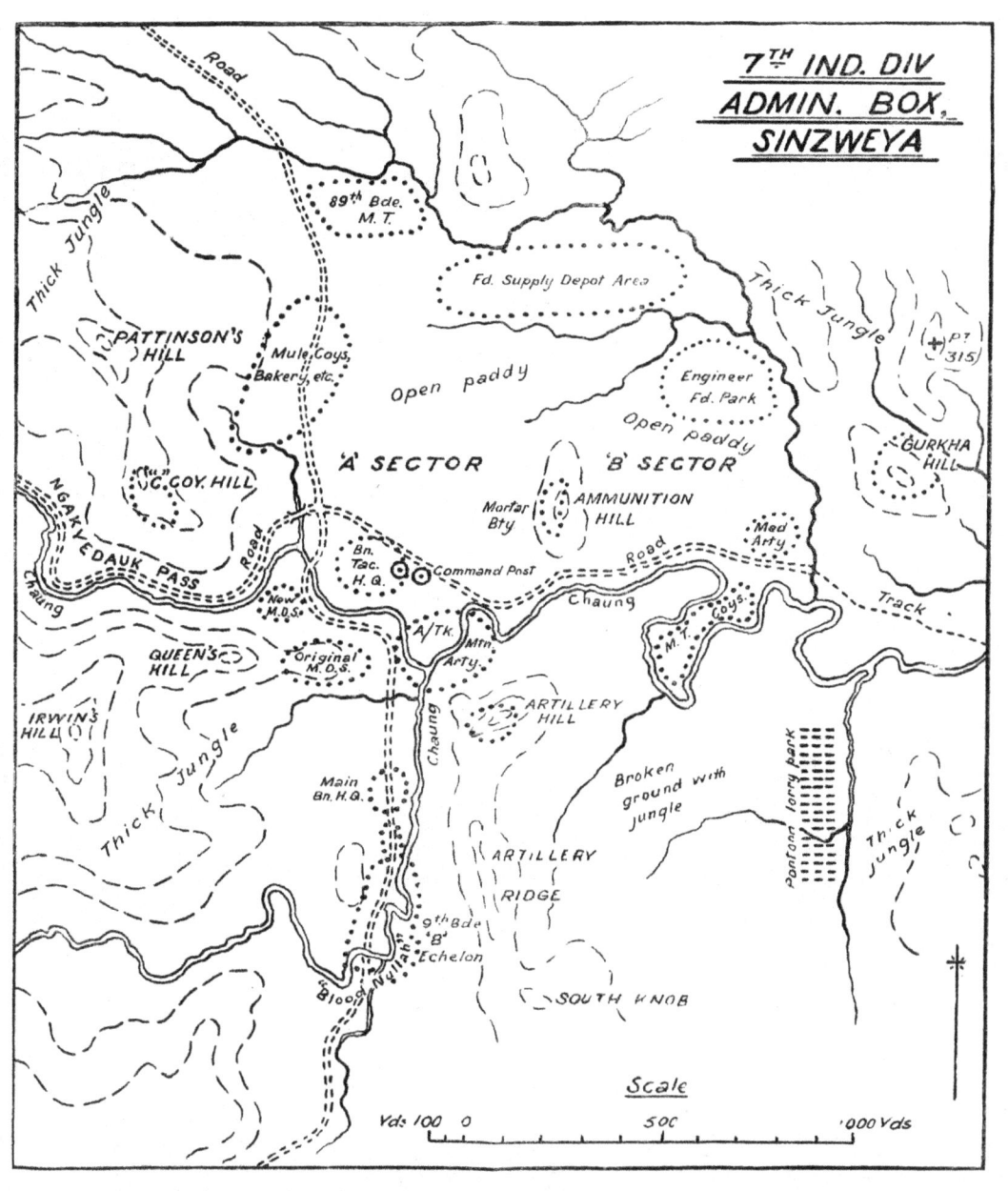

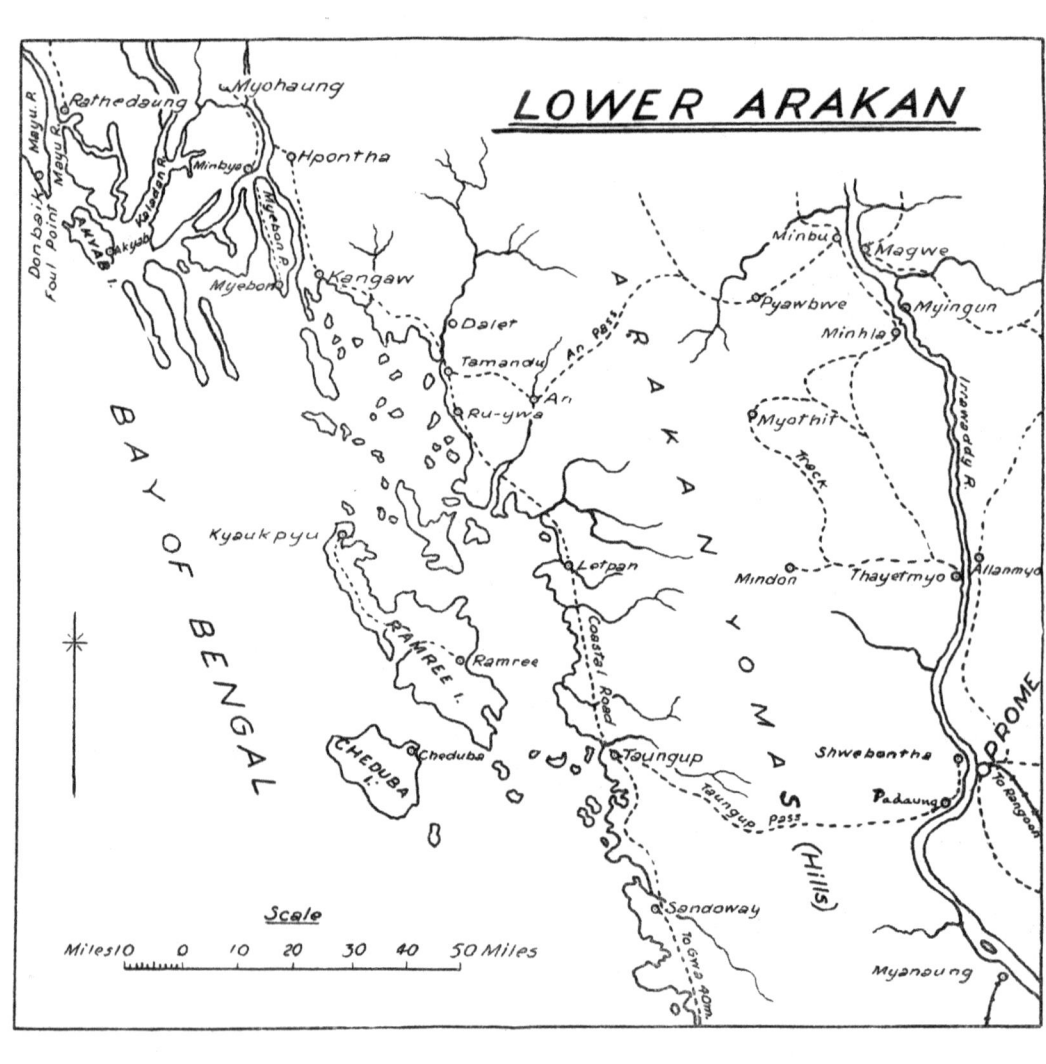

CHAPTER XI

THE DEFENCE OF IMPHAL, MARCH-JULY 1944

A LITTLE over a month after the Japanese had launched their offensive in Arakan they proceeded to set in motion their main effort in Manipur on a scale three times as large. This was their final bid for entry into the wide plains of India, and for it they employed their very best troops. As described in Chapter IX, the Fifteenth Japanese Army under General Mutagachi crossed the Chindwin River at several points in the middle of March 1944 in an attempt to destroy the 17th Indian Division on the Tiddim Road, to drive back the 20th Indian Division on the Tamu Road, and to capture Imphal itself, which was defended by the 23rd Indian Division. One Japanese division was to by-pass Imphal to the north, strike at Kohima and occupy the rail-head beyond it at Dimapur (Manipur Road Station). Success in this venture would prevent the arrival of reinforcements for the 4th Indian Corps in the Imphal region. It would also halt General Stilwell's offensive in Northern Burma, directed on Myitkyina, and would isolate China by closing the "Hump" air-supply route to that country. With the Assam air bases in their hands, the enemy would have taken the first step towards the domination of all India and final victory in the Far East. Thus the importance of Imphal can hardly be exaggerated.

Just as the defence of the Imphal Plain may be said to have begun when the Japanese columns crossed the Chindwin in March 1944, it may be deemed to have ended when they were rolled back towards, or beyond, that river in the following July and August, for the operations immediately preceding and following a siege are part and parcel of it. On March 12th the 33rd Japanese Division advanced up the Tiddim Road against the 17th Indian Division under Major-General D. T. Cowan and, by a series of hooks, tried to isolate it in its exposed position far south of Imphal and to seize the Manipur River crossing at Milestone 126, where lay the most forward supply base of several which the 4th Corps had established along the Tiddim Road.[1] Further north, the 15th Japanese Division crossed the

---

[1] See the map of the Tiddim Road, Milestone 109 to Kalemyo, included in Chapter XII.

Chindwin and fanned out south-westwards to co-operate with the 33rd Division in an attack on the 20th Indian Division, under Major-General D. D. Gracey, in the Tamu region;[1] and still further north, the 31st Japanese Division also crossed the river to advance through Ukhrul and Jessami towards Kohima and Dimapur.[2] The 23rd Indian Division, under Major-General O. L. Roberts, an ex-Bengal Sapper and Miner, was in reserve in the Imphal Plain. Roberts had many commitments. He might be called upon at short notice to stop any gap in the defensive screen in any direction. He might have to help to extricate the 17th Division from its predicament on the Tiddim Road, or to reinforce the 20th Division on the Tamu Road, or to assist the 50th Parachute Brigade at Ukhrul to the north-east in order to interfere with the enemy thrust towards Kohima, or even to deal with Japanese columns attacking Imphal from west of the Tiddim Road after moving far round that flank. It was an onerous burden for the Commander of a formation which had been long in the area and was depleted by sickness.

General W. J. Slim, the Fourteenth Army Commander, was very wise to order the concentration on Imphal of the 4th Corps under Lieut.-General G. A. P. Scoones in the event of a massive enemy offensive and thus to give battle on ground of his own choosing where supplies were available and aircraft could land; but the date of the withdrawal of the 17th Division was left to Major-General Cowan who did not start until March 14th when it was almost too late. The 33rd Japanese Division moved with great rapidity to cut the Tiddim Road at several places between the Manipur River crossing and Bishenpur, and part of Roberts' 23rd Division had to come to the rescue from Imphal. Yet Cowan's bold decision hindered the first onrush of the invading columns and gave us time to evacuate to Imphal quantities of supplies which would otherwise have been lost. As in Arakan, the enemy relied largely on captured supplies to maintain the impetus of his attack. Nevertheless, the retreat of the 17th Division along a road parallel to the front was a dangerous undertaking, and it succeeded only through the stubborn fighting of all units and the assistance afforded by the 23rd Division from Imphal in opening the way.

The Imphal Plain lies 3,000 feet up in the heart of the Manipur mountains. It is formed by a widening in the course of the Manipur

---

[1] See the map of the Tiddim Road, Chindwin River Area, included in Chapter IX.

[2] See the general map of Upper Burma included in Chapter XIII. Jessami is about 30 miles east of Kohima.

River on its way to the Chindwin at Kalewa. This green plateau, largely water-logged in the monsoon, is many square miles in area and was recognized as the only suitable site for a large base from which aircraft could operate close to the front. The town itself, the capital of Manipur, could easily be surrounded with the necessary depots, dumps, hospitals, workshops and camps needed for an army. Yet it had some serious drawbacks. It lay many miles from the railhead at Dimapur with which it was connected only by a single narrow hill-road often blocked by land-slides, and that road was parallel to the probable front of attack and therefore under constant threat. It is true that another line of communication existed between Bishenpur, south of the town, and Silchar in Assam; but this was merely a rough track through impossibly difficult terrain and quite unsuitable for heavy traffic. For offensive purposes there were two roads leading southwards into Burma, the Tiddim Road and the Tamu Road, and another north-eastwards towards Ukhrul.[1] The strategic importance of Imphal was that in our hands it could maintain large forces in the Chin Hills or along the west bank of the Chindwin. To the Japanese it would have been a prize of untold value as a main base for the invasion of India. Hence the bitter struggle for its possession.

With the 17th Division in its hazardous withdrawal up the Tiddim Road were 60 Field Company (Madras) under Major P. A. Walker, R.E., 70 Field Company (Bengal) under Major I. H. Lyall-Grant, R.E., and 414 Field Park Company (Bengal) under Major R. Blagden, R.E., the whole being under Lieut.-Colonel R. S. B. Ward, R.E., as C.R.E. Moving back from the Kennedy Peak and Tiddim areas, the Field Companies cratered the road and booby-trapped all possible diversions. Every installation of the slightest value to the enemy was destroyed, and Tiddim was left in flames. At Milestone 124, beyond the Manipur River, was the Tehri-Garhwal Field Company under Major K. Tylden-Pattenson, R.E. This unit had already placed demolition charges on the bridges across the river at Milestone 126, a sad business because one of them, a fine Bailey structure, had been built by the unit not long before and the men were proud of their work. 70 Field Company crossed the river on March 18th. The withdrawal had been subject to constant interruption by small parties of the enemy firing down from ridges or lurking in long grass near the road. A continuous rearguard action was fought by the

---

[1] See the map of Imphal included in this chapter.

infantry among whom 70 Field Company was scattered in small detachments to demolish road-blocks, make diversions and clear mines. During the first day the 17th Division covered 40 miles, every officer and man, even General Cowan himself, marching on foot. When the 63rd Brigade reached the Manipur River bridge on March 18th, it halted and established a defence "Box". The 48th Brigade continued along the road and on March 20th arrived at Milestone 111, where it encountered the encircling enemy. The Japanese had already sent a column up the west bank of the river to attack a large supply base at Milestone 109 which was located in a depression in the hills and defended only by administrative troops. They descended upon it from all sides and the garrison had to abandon it. Further north, at Milestone 82, there was another large supply base. This also was threatened by the enemy who set up a road-block between it and Milestone 109 and caused some confusion within the perimeter by sending out "jitter" parties every night.

The 63rd Brigade had placed two companies of Gurkhas to cover a defile in the road where it passed over a spur before dropping down towards the Manipur River crossing at Milestone 126, 3,000 feet below. Here, the Sappers laid a small minefield by collecting a few mines and placing them in rows in the defile. The same evening, the Japanese attacked with tanks whose presence had not been expected. On came the leading tank and entered the defile. Not a mine was touched until the tank reached the last row, but there it was blown up. A second tank came through and disintegrated also at the last row. A third followed and was destroyed before it reached the wreckage of its predecessors. Nevertheless, a fourth tank came roaring onwards, only to perish alongside the third. Seven mines had accounted for all four, and the Sappers were delighted with their work, for these tanks might have caused great damage if they had got through to attack the mass of men and vehicles in the valley below. The episode shows the gallantry usually displayed by the enemy, and at the same time his stupidity and inability to alter his plans once they had been made.

Some Engineer units, mostly of 465 Army Troops Engineers, were working at this time on the Tiddim Road near Milestone 109 under Lieut.-Colonel A. J. R. Hill, R.E., previously O.C. 8th Engineer Battalion,[1] who, as the senior officer in the vicinity, was ordered to

---

[1] Lieut.-Colonel A. J. R. Hill had been appointed C.R.E., 465 Army Troops Engineers, on February 25th, 1944.

undertake the defence of the Forward Supply Depot at that spot. The units were 24 Field Company (Bombay), 428 Field Company (Madras), 414 Field Park Company (Bengal) of the 17th Divisional Engineers, and 442 Quarrying Company. When the position became untenable, the troops were ordered to destroy and abandon their vehicles and stores and make their way back through the jungle. The Sapper Headquarters were almost the last to leave. Hill ordered his Adjutant and a few men to retire a couple of miles and await his arrival while he himself stayed behind with three companies of Jats which were to form the rearguard. The enemy followed up closely and eventually the Jats withdrew. The Adjutant waited at the rendezvous for some time, and then, assuming that Hill had gone back by another path, resumed his march and rejoined the nearest troops 25 miles in rear. There, to his surprise, he was told that Hill had not arrived. He waited for some days but could get no news of his Commanding Officer, and it was obviously impossible to return to the depot area to search for him. Until April 1st it was hoped that Hill might re-appear; but after that date he was shown as missing at Milestone 109 on March 18th. So perished an able and gallant officer.

414 Field Park Company had a very unpleasant journey to the rear after the order was received to abandon the depot at Milestone 109, for it had to help in the evacuation of a large number of wounded men over the roughest of jungle tracks. No less than fifty crossings of a stream were involved, and after nine miles of stretcher bearing the Sappers were so exhausted that many of them had to be sent to Imphal in motor transport. The remainder reached the town on foot, but most of their equipment had been lost.

The serious plight of the 17th Division had been realized in Imphal as early as March 13th when the 37th Brigade of the 23rd Division—the only formation available in the plain—received a warning order at 9.30 a.m. to go to the rescue. The next evening it was 82 miles down the Tiddim Road, and on the 15th it was engaged in a tense battle at Milestone 100, the highest point. Most of the 49th Brigade followed from the Ukhrul area and moved to Milestone 82, while the 1st Brigade returned to Imphal from the Kabaw Valley to garrison the town. The 37th Brigade was ordered to prevent the enemy from cutting the Tiddim Road between Milestones 82 and 100 and to contact the leading troops of the approaching 17th Division, while the 49th Brigade was to guard the road between Milestones 70 and 82. By the evening of March 17th, General Roberts had no less than five brigades under his command. His responsibilities stretched from Milestone 100 back to Imphal, where the 1st Brigade had concentrated with the 254th Tank Brigade, and thence to Ukhrul and Jessami, 40 miles further north, where the 1st Assam Rifles were in position to cover Kohima. As Lieut.-Colonel Doulton remarks,[1] the 23rd Division front was little short of 200 miles in length. Fierce battles soon raged at both extremities and at Ukhrul. The 50th Parachute Brigade had been sent from Kohima to fill the gap at Ukhrul and, with a battalion of the 49th Brigade, had taken up a defensive position at Sangshak, 8 miles south-west of the village. Such were the dispositions made to assist the withdrawal of the 17th Division up the Tiddim Road and to safeguard Imphal and Kohima. It would be incorrect to imagine that the 17th Division would never have reached Imphal without the help of the two brigades of the 23rd Division, but it would probably have lost many guns and much equipment in the process. The "Battle of the Road Blocks" between Milestones 100 and 82, which lasted from March 15th to March 28th when a battalion of the 37th Brigade met the forward troops of the 17th Division at Milestone 102, was a desperate and bloody affair in which the 37th Brigade acted as an anvil for the hammer of the 17th Division. Between them, they cut a way through all obstructions and so the Division was able to reach Imphal in good shape to play a leading part in the defence.

The experiences of 428 Field Company (Madras) under Major J. V. Corbet, R.E., before and during the withdrawal up the Tiddim Road, afford a good example of those of some other Engineer units. On March 4th the Company was visited at Milestone 100 by Brigadier H. E. Horsfield, Chief Engineer, Fourteenth Army, and Brigadier H. Williams, Chief Engineer, 4th Corps,[2] and three days later it was visited again by Williams in company with Brigadier E. F. E. Armstrong. It was then fairly clear that great events were impending. On March 13th the unit was ordered to move into a "Box" at Milestone 109, and there, on the 16th, it came under artillery fire. Early on the 17th, the position was machine-gunned. Captain D. I. Perdue, R.E., was shot through the head and evacuated, and the same afternoon the unit was ordered to retire up the bed of a nullah. It

---

[1] *The Fighting Cock* (History of the 23rd Indian Division), by Lieut.-Colonel A. J. F. Doulton, O.B.E., p. 80.

[2] Brigadier H. Williams was C.E., 4th Corps, from June 20th, 1943, to August 24th, 1944. On January 1st, 1948, he was appointed Engineer-in-Chief, India, with the temporary rank of Major-General and held that appointment until October 16th, 1955.

assembled on the following day in a camp at Milestone 82, whence it moved on the 19th in lorries to another camp at Milestone 35 and finally came to rest in Imphal on March 20th. But the brunt of the delaying operations fell naturally on the 17th Divisional Engineers. 60 Field Company, 70 Field Company and the Tehri-Garhwal Field Company were involved in almost continuous fighting though they found time also to accomplish most valuable engineer work in the way of destroying communications, bridges and dumps of petrol and stores, and laying mines and booby traps to hinder the enemy's advance. Except for the last 40 miles to Imphal, which they reached early in April, they covered the entire distance on foot. "A large road-block had been established by the enemy between Milestones 110 and 100", writes Pearson.[1] "The 48th Brigade distinguished itself on the night of March 23rd/24th in attacks on the high ground overlooking Milestone 110. Not a little of its success was due to 70 Field Company which continued to dig the mule path on which the Brigade was dependant for supplies while the battle raged around it. The Japanese were pinned to the ridge and the road was cleared to Milestone 109. 70 Field Company then salvaged a quantity of vehicles and stores from the old Administrative base before going on. Another battle was fought by the 48th Brigade on April 1st to break a road-block at Milestone 72. Here, 70 Field Company cut mule tracks for each of the assaulting battalions, cleared mines in front of the tanks, and by evening had started to remove the block. At midnight, the way was clear again. The Sappers had often to march and work all day, and then dig in and act as infantry all night."

Some allusion has already been made to the demolition of the bridges at the Manipur River crossing at Milestone 126 by the Tehri-Garhwal Field Company under Major K. Tylden-Pattenson, R.E. The charges had been placed in position on March 13th, and at 11.30 a.m. on March 26th the order was received to blow. The east abutment and central pier of the fine Bailey structure were completely destroyed. The bridge was cut in ten places and most of the panels buckled. The pier of the suspension bridge was set alight with petrol and oil, and the cables and pylons were cut. At noon, the firing parties left to prepare another bridge at Milestone 117 for demolition. This was blown after dark, and then another at Milestone

---

[1] *Brief History of the K.G.V's O. Bengal Sappers and Miners Group, R.I.E.* (*August* 1939-*July* 1946), by Lieut. G. Pearson, R.E., pp. 79, 80.

113, leaving only an old bridge to take the traffic. At midnight the firing parties rejoined the rest of the Company at Milestone 109 in support of the 63rd Brigade. The old bridge at Milestone 113 was demolished on March 27th and the road heavily mined, and on the following day the road and the cliff face at Milestone 111 were dealt with and further mines laid. The Tehri-Garhwals marched on the 29th to Milestone 91 and afterwards to the 17th Division Headquarters at Milestone 82, which they helped to defend. They reached the "Catfish" Box at Imphal on April 25th and soon afterwards Major J. Lindsay, R.E., took over command of the unit.

The final stages of the withdrawal of the 17th Division to Imphal began early on April 2nd, 1944, after the breaking of the road-block at Milestone 72 with the help of the 37th and 49th Brigades of the 23rd Division. The 37th Brigade formed the rearguard and effectively checked the Japanese at Milestone 82; but during some heavy shelling of the area by long-range enemy guns on April 3rd it suffered a number of casualties, among them being Major F. W. Pritchard, R.E., O.C. 71 Field Company, and Captain R. A. Dedman, R.E., his second-in-command. Major J. S. Beddows, R.E., O.C. 91 Field Company, then took command temporarily until the arrival of Major T. W. I. Hedley, R.E., from 323 Field Park Company on April 9th at Imphal.

When the 31st Japanese Division advanced towards Kohima and Dimapur and blocked the Kohima Road north of Imphal, the importance of the only other line of communication with Assam was greatly enhanced. This was the Silchar track starting from the Tiddim Road near Bishenpur. Every effort had to be made to open it for motor traffic, for there was a rail-head at Silchar which might conceivably be used if Dimapur were lost. Accordingly, work was started at once on the development of the track. On April 2nd, 1944, 24 Field Company (Bombay) under Major J. F. W. Rusted, R.E., arrived in Bishenpur for that purpose. The track was about 109 miles in length and wound its way through dense jungle over five mountain ranges. There were often a dozen hair-pin bends in a mile, and suspension bridges up to 400 feet in length carried the track over streams which became raging torrents after heavy rain. Extracts from the War Diary of 24 Field Company make illuminating reading. "*9th April.* Parties of Japs moving along track to destroy suspension bridges at Milestones 31 and 51.[1] *12th April.* Japs

---

[1] The mileages were measured from Imphal, Bishenpur being at Milestone 18.

destroyed bridge at Milestone 51. Ordered by C.R.E. to defend bridge at Milestone 31. 13*th April*. Enemy established road-block between Milestones 23 and 24. No communication possible with Bishenpur. 14*th*-18*th April*. Enemy in force at Tairenpokpi (Milestone 26) and in contact with our forces moving up from Bishenpur. Road-block at Milestone 27. Enemy in village 5 miles south of bridge at Milestone 31. 19*th April*. O.C. decides to withdraw Company to Milestone 51 to contact 362 Field Company. 22*nd*-30*th April*. Several small actions against enemy and frequent patrolling. 1*st*-4*th May*. Enemy in strong positions across track at Milestone 27. 17*th May*. Company moved to Milestone 64 *en route* to Silchar. 19*th May*. Arrived Base Camp at Milestone 98. 14*th June*. Unit moved by rail from Silchar to Dimapur (Manipur Road)."

The other Engineer units engaged with 24 Field Company on the improvement of the Silchar track were 362 and 429 Field Companies. The 8th Engineer Battalion was there also. 362 and 429 Field Companies arrived in Bishenpur early in May and were ordered to make the track passable for 15 cwt. lorries within three weeks—an obvious impossibility. However, all three Field Companies set to work with a will. 362 Field Company was employed at first at Milestone 36 but was soon ordered to Milestone 51 as a party of Japanese was reported to be moving thither to blow up the 330-feet suspension bridge at that point. So close were the pylons of this bridge to the cliff face at either end that jeeps had to reverse twice in order to get on to the bridge, and consequently the first task of the Sappers was to dig into both cliffs. The Japanese were only half a mile away, and early next morning enemy planes dive-bombed the site. After dark, there was a devastating roar and the bridge collapsed, though no bomb had hit it. It seems that a few intrepid Japs had managed to crawl unseen on to it and had escaped after placing a pressure charge in position. One of them, indeed, was seen to jump 80 feet into the water below. The enemy next succeeded in cutting the track completely at Milestone 27, thus isolating all the Sapper units. These had then to be supplied entirely by air and to remain on half-rations until they could establish road communication with Silchar. 362 Field Company built a timber trestle bridge at Milestone 51 under observation by the enemy on the heights above. As soon as it had been completed, the Japanese attacked it but were beaten off. The Company then set to work to repair the suspension bridge. Much improvisation was needed because the necessary stores could not be obtained from Bishenpur. The men found an old disused suspension bridge in the jungle, dismantled it and spliced lengths of its cables into those of the wrecked structure. The damaged slings were replaced, the roadway repaired, and on June 10th the suspension bridge was re-opened to traffic. Five days later, 362 Field Company began the long march to Silchar where it arrived safely, though without its vehicles and most of its stores. Meanwhile, 429 Field Company, which had been working for a few days between Milestones 63 and 75, had returned on May 14th to help 362 Field Company at Milestone 51 before resuming its movement westwards. Altogether, the three Sapper companies were isolated on the Silchar track for no less than six weeks and were fortunate to reach Silchar in a fit state for further work. Thence they moved northwards by rail to Dimapur, where their services were very urgently needed.

Fighting of vital importance had been in progress, meanwhile, around Kohima, south-east of Dimapur; but before dealing with the events in that area it may be well to turn to the central front where, in March 1944, the 20th Indian Division, under Major-General D. D. Gracey, was trying to stop the Japanese advance through Tamu and Palel. The Division comprised the 32nd, 80th and 100th Brigades, and the Divisional Engineers, under Lieut.-Colonel A. R. S. Lucas, R.E., included 75 Field Company (Bengal), 362 and 422 Field Companies (Madras) and 309 Field Park Company (Madras). Some of the experiences of 362 Field Company with the 80th Brigade have been given already in Chapter IX and may be said to resemble those of the other Sapper units. Before the end of the third week in March, the enemy's intentions were fully apparent. While two regiments of the 33rd Japanese Division harassed the 17th Indian Division on the Tiddim Road, the third, with medium artillery and light tanks in support, advanced northwards through, and to the west of, the Kabaw Valley. Between March 12th and 14th, the enemy attacked in the Htinzin and Witok areas, forcing our outposts to withdraw northwards, and on the 15th, enemy forces occupied Holkhom, 7 miles west of Htinzin.[1] By March 18th, other forces, advancing on Tamu, were within 8 miles of their objective. After occupying the northern part of the Kabaw Valley around Mintha, a regiment of the 15th Japanese Division turned south-westwards to co-operate with the 33rd Japanese Division in assaulting Tamu, and at the same time other enemy troops, pushing westwards through the hills from Mintha, reached Sita, 12 miles east of Palel, and

---

[1] See the map of the Tiddim Road, Chindwin River Area, included in Chapter IX.

threatened the road to Imphal. The 1st Brigade of the 23rd Indian Division was now ordered to operate against any enemy forces attempting to infiltrate into the Imphal Plain through these hills and did so with good effect.

On March 22nd, elements of the 15th and 33rd Japanese Divisions made an unsuccessful attack on the 20th Indian Division's positions at Tamu; but meanwhile some enemy detachments had almost reached Sibong on the road to Palel and were reported also at Leibi further north. After dark on the 22nd, others were only 7 miles south-east of Palel itself. The Tamu-Palel Road was cut temporarily at Tengnoupal, and with the enemy astride the road, the maintenance of the troops in the Moreh region was hardly possible, so General Gracey was ordered to evacuate Moreh, Sibong and Khongkhang and to concentrate in Sita, Tengnoupal, Shenam, Chapki and Mombi in a wide arc covering Palel and the Tiddim Road to the west. He evacuated Moreh on April 1st, transferring his 32nd Brigade to the Imphal Plain as a reserve for the 4th Corps and preparing to hold a group of strong positions in the Sita-Tengnoupal-Shenam area with his 80th and 100th Brigades. At the end of the first week of April, the general situation on the Manipur front was as follows. The 17th Indian Division, having completed its fighting withdrawal to the Imphal Plain, had the 63rd Brigade at Sengmai, 12 miles north of Imphal, with the 48th Brigade close behind it. The 20th Indian Division was in battle positions centred on Shenam. The 23rd Indian Division held the Imphal Plain, and the newly arrived 5th Indian Division, of which more anon, covered the approaches from the northeast in the hilly country between the Ukhrul and Kohima Roads. The 20th Division continued to block the Japanese advance at the Shenam Saddle until May 11th when Lieut.-General G. A. P. Scoones, the 4th Corps Commander, ordered it to change places with the 23rd Division which at that time was operating chiefly on the Ukhrul Road. Thus the task of defeating the final Japanese attempt to reach Imphal by the Tamu Road fell to Major-General O. L. Roberts.

The evacuation of Moreh is well described by Major J. H. Clark, R.E., O.C. 92 Field Company. "Moreh", he writes,[1] "is some three miles north of Tamu in the Kabaw Valley where the road to Imphal starts to climb into the hills. A forward base was being built there, and towards the end of March frantic efforts were being made to

---

Notes by Major J. H. Clark, R.E., dated February 2nd, 1954.

evacuate masses of stores of every description. Little progress, however, was possible in the few days available for the place was under constant shell fire, so 92 Field Company was made responsible for destroying all the dumps and installations on the withdrawal of the 32nd Brigade on April 1st. No sounds of demolition were to be made until 9.30 a.m., one hour after the last troops had gone, in order that no warning should be given to the enemy. The use of the normal delay fuses was forbidden because they had proved unreliable in that climate, so the interval of one hour was arranged for by joining lengths of safety fuse to the 120-feet lengths of instantaneous fuse. The dumps were scattered on both sides of the road through Moreh. The Engineer Stores Dump was a massive collection of timber and steel covering a wide area, so that little could be done in the way of 'back-loading' or demolition. The Petrol and Oil Dump, however, was divided into sixteen smaller dumps, so these were connected to a prima-cord ring main and the prima-cord was given several turns round petrol drums in each dump. The Supply Dump was an awkward problem. This depot was stacked with solid walls of tins and mountains of sacks of *atta*, *dhal*, mule fodder, etc. It was obvious that explosives would merely scatter the tins without breaking them, and accordingly Sherman tanks were used to knock down the walls and squash the tins and also to scatter the sacks. The whole area was then sprayed with petrol and oil. The Ordnance Dump held both clothing and ammunition. The stacks of clothing were connected by a prima-cord ring main, and in each stack some prima-cord was wound round petrol drums to set the clothing alight. This also was successful. The only unsatisfactory item was the destruction of the heavy ammunition for the guns. Every alternate shell was de-fused and gelignite on prima-cord inserted; but when we returned to Moreh a year later, we found that, although the shells had been scattered far and wide, a large number were still intact. We also destroyed three water-points by wrecking the plant. Finally, we had to deal with the Bailey bridge over the Lokchao River, a high-level structure across a deep gorge. It had been prepared for demolition, but on the day before the withdrawal we were ordered to leave it intact, so I asked the battalion holding the covering positions to ensure that the explosive charges were removed and dropped into the river below. This was done, but shortly afterwards our planes bombed the bridge and demolished it. I was greatly disgusted to learn later that it had been suggested that 92 Field Company had blown the bridge against orders! The withdrawal started early on

April 1st, the last troops to leave being the 4th/10th Gurkha Rifles with the Sapper firing party. By that time, the exit from Moreh was under shell fire. We had an exciting ride back to Palel as the enemy had reached the road at several places and the 32nd Brigade and its transport suffered a number of casualties. An hour after the fuses had been lit, the demolitions in Moreh exploded. Two huge clouds of smoke mounted slowly into the air, one black, the other white. The former came from the Oil Dump, the latter from the Ordnance Dump. They were a source of great satisfaction to us, for we had foiled the enemy on April Fool's Day." 92 Field Company left Palel with the 32nd Brigade on April 5th and moved to Wangjing, 13 miles towards Imphal. Nine days later it accompanied the brigade to the Bishenpur area on the Tiddim Road where on April 18th it distinguished itself by making a track for heavy tanks to attack an enemy position on a hill.

424 Field Company (Madras), under Major J. G. Mitchell, R.E., was another unit involved in the withdrawal from Moreh. On March 15th, while engaged in building a bridge over the Lokchao River, it received a warning order to move and was detailed to defend the Divisional Headquarters when established at Moreh. Two days later a detachment was sent out to blow all demolitions along the track to Sittaung. Early on March 20th, when fighting had started in the vicinity, the Company was ordered to move in fifteen minutes. All that could be done was to pile some equipment into the four jeeps with the unit and set out for Moreh forthwith. There it dug in alongside 92 Field Company and was detailed to guard the Petrol and Oil Dump. On the 22nd, after burying much of its remaining equipment, it prepared to move again at short notice. A fierce battle started after dark to the north-east, and another to the south, and Japanese artillery shelled Moreh. However, the infantry clung to their positions and the Sappers continued to wire the perimeters. It was not until March 29th that 424 Field Company quitted Moreh and withdrew to a position in a Supply Dump at Shenam to work on the defences of various dumps. On April 2nd, 94 (Faridkot) Field Company under Major R. M. Willis, R.E., took over this duty and 424 Field Company began to dig gun positions. A Company Battle Cry was evolved —"*Manju Eli Kollu*" meaning "Kill the Yellow Rats". Afterwards, the unit laboured mostly on communications until, on May 20th, it moved to "Prawn" Box in Imphal.

Also at Shenam was 481 Field Company (Bombay), under Major M. I. Pritchard, R.E. This unit was employed during April chiefly in an infantry role, holding perimeter posts on the Saddle, and it continued to act as infantry throughout May. Some extracts from the War Diary in June may be given. "10*th*/11*th June*. Enemy attack on No. 1 Platoon and Company H. Q. position at Bastion Point at 18.20 hrs. Enemy shelled position and at 20.15 hrs attacked from east and south-west having blown or dismantled booby-traps and cut perimeter wire with Bangalore torpedoes. At 00.15 hrs. on 11th, No. 1 Platoon withdrawn to Brigade Hill as enemy had occupied a large part of Platoon position. Our casualties on withdrawal were 5 killed, 8 wounded and 8 missing. Enemy casualties, inflicted by the Platoon, were approximately 40 killed. Wounded unknown. Office, Mess and M.I. Room equipment, Platoon Store, bedding, cookhouse equipment, 3 Bren guns and the rifles of killed or wounded had to be abandoned. All three Bren gunners among the killed. Most of the equipment was destroyed later by shelling. Further casualties were suffered, as the Platoon withdrew, from enemy grenade discharge and mortar fire from Bastion Point. Captain A. P. Smith, R.E., Lieut. W. M. Colvin, R.E., Subedar Bhadra, I.A.M.C. and one Sapper were wounded and one Sapper killed as they were approaching No. 3 Platoon position on Brigade Hill. Major M. I. Pritchard, R.E., and Captain R. C. H. Greet, R.E., arrived there from "B" Echelon and reported to the 100th Brigade Commander. They were ordered to counter-attack Bastion with the remnants of No. 1 Platoon supported by a troop of Stuart tanks and a platoon of Frontier Force Rifles. Three tanks were to start at 08.45 hrs., assisted by a Section of F.F. Rifles, and No. 1 Platoon was to assault and mop up when the tanks had got into the position. The tanks were to advance to within 175 yards and then blast the forward bunkers from hull-down position; then to move forward, in line ahead, to a point due west of the position and 40 yards outside the perimeter trench; and finally, to turn into line abreast and advance on the position, one tank engaging either side of the perimeter trench and the centre tank advancing through the position to hold the reverse slope against any counter-attack. Personnel of No. 1 Platoon and one Section of No. 3 Platoon were divided into three parties to assault left, right and through the centre, but unfortunately the tanks approached the enemy position direct without halting to give covering fire from the hull-down position. The Sapper parties were therefore held up, but all combined to reach a point 75 yards from the trenches. Meanwhile, the tanks had also been held up and two had been knocked out. As the Sappers could not assault without tank support, Major

Pritchard then decided to withdraw the three parties to 150 yards from the position. At 11.30 hrs., Bastion was again counter-attacked by fresh troops with tanks and this succeeded. The eight wounded Sappers left in the position the previous night had all been killed by the enemy, so the total casualties of 481 Field Company in the Bastion battle were 16 killed and 24 wounded. Lieut. W. M. Colvin later died of wounds."

Throughout June 1944, 481 Field Company was still employed largely on infantry duties at the Shenam Saddle and it was not until July 21st that, under Major C. H. Cowan, R.E., the unit was moved to a rest area. The foregoing extracts from the War Diary emphasize the unfortunate results of the employment of Sappers as infantry, a course which can only be justified in a highly critical situation. Many other Sapper units were so employed and acquitted themselves well in their unaccustomed role; but the principle remains unaltered that the duty of Engineer troops should be to open the way for the infantry assault, to clear the captured position and to facilitate the arrival of reinforcements, and not to attack or defend with rifle and bayonet.

Among other Sapper units engaged in the operations on the Tamu Road were 402 Field Company (Bombay) under Major I. G. Maclaurin, R.E., and 429 Field Company (Madras) under Major J. H. F. H. Jolly, R.E. 402 Field Company took a conspicuous part in the fighting during April around "Nippon Peak" at the Shenam Saddle. 429 Field Company took up a defensive position on March 16th in the Sibong area and then moved northwards to defend a Supply Depot until the brigades of the 20th Division began to leap-frog back to the Shenam-Palel area in April. After being often under shell fire it reached Shenam on May 4th and moved to Bishenpur on the Tiddim Road to work on the Silchar track as already described.

The experiences of the Bengal Sapper units on the Tamu Road are given by Lieut. G. Pearson.[1] "One night in March", he writes, "75 Field Company, under Major L. G. Kirton, R.E., discovered that it had become the garrison of Shenam and that the Japs were on their way *via* the Mombi Track. The camp was soon filled, however, as other troops came back from Moreh. At this stage, morale was excellent and everyone seemed imbued with the idea of becoming infantry. It was therefore with mixed feelings that the Company quitted Shenam for Imphal and occupied part of

---

[1] *Brief History of the K.G.V's O. Bengal Sappers and Miners, R.I.E., (August* 1939–*July* 1946), by Lieut. G. Pearson, R.E., p. 80.

"Prawn" Box just outside the town." Pearson mentions also 332 Field Park Company which was part of the General Reserve Engineer Force (G.R.E.F.) engaged in making a new Tamu Road through to the Chindwin. This unit withdrew to Shenam when the Japanese flood broke through and did much valuable patrol work before being transferred to Imphal. 68 and 71 Field Companies also took part in the defence of Shenam. From the day that the 37th Brigade of the 23rd Division took over, the troops occupying the "Scraggy", "Malta" and "Gibraltar" boxes along the road had little respite from shelling by day and jitter raids or assaults by nights. On one day in March, 250 shells fell on "Malta"; and on another, 100 shells crashed onto "Gibraltar" in the space of an hour. The trenches were inadequate and casualties heavy. It is recorded that nearly fifty casualties were carried out of the battle each day until 68 and 71 Field Companies revetted and improved the defences. On July 24th, when the tide had turned and "Nippon" fell to the Seaforth Highlanders, a Lance-Naik of 68 Field Company coolly reconnoitered six Jap bunkers on the reverse slope from a distance of 15 yards. He then placed his charges and blew in all six. "It was such episodes", remarks Lieut.-Colonel Doulton,[1] "that built up the mutual respect between the British and Indian troops of the 23rd Division." Again, on July 26th, after an attack by a Mahratta battalion had failed, a detachment of 71 Field Company showed great gallantry. The Japs had a machine-gun only fifty yards away and were spraying the Sappers with bullets. Yet the men persisted in their efforts to form a roadblock of tar barrels and anti-tank mines. These are but two of the many instances of the gallantry shown by the Sapper companies.

The story of 422 Field Company on the Tamu Road is worthy of record. This unit of the Madras Sappers, under Major J. E. Ralph, R.E., was engaged, early in 1944, on the conversion of the jeep track to Sittaung into a road for heavier transport. When the enemy advanced in March, the unit was ordered to lay ambushes, carry out patrols and act generally as infantry. Accordingly, it moved back to the Mombi track and took up a position in some hills together with a company of Patiala Sikhs. One day a patrol under Jemadar Appa Rao noticed an enemy position in the jungle. The Jemadar halted his men 200 yards further along the track and concealed them on both sides of it. The Japs had seen the patrol and a platoon of them came rushing along, shouting "Banzai". Five of

---

[1] *The Fighting Cock*, by Lieut.-Colonel A. J. F. Doulton, o.b.e., p. 198.

them were killed and a number wounded; but the remainder rallied and began to spray the jungle with bullets as they advanced, so Appa Rao withdrew his men, covered by a Bren gun. 422 Field Company soon moved to another position on a small hill overlooking the track. Other hills were occupied by our infantry and the Japs wandered along the valleys between them, frequently interrupting our supply lines. Rations and water were brought forward in jeeps and finally man-handled to the tops of the hills, a very exhausting process. At night the enemy always sent jitter parties close up to our positions and frequently launched small attacks. On one occasion, a Sapper sentry, suspecting the presence of some Japs, threw grenade after grenade into the jungle till he had emptied two whole boxes. He was lucky, for next morning his friends found sixteen bodies and took one wounded prisoner. During April, the enemy's shelling increased in volume and his attacks became more vehement. Major Ralph was awarded the Military Cross, and Jemadar Appa Rao gained a Military Medal for gallantry in repelling an assault. The rumble of enemy tanks could be heard every night. It was decided that the Brigade should withdraw to the Shenam Saddle. This was accomplished successfully and all the small hills above the road were soon thick with troops. 422 Field Company was located on "Water Tank Hill" about half way along the defended stretch of road. The most advanced position in the Tamu direction was "Scraggy". Then came "Malta" and Gibraltar", and, 2 miles behind "Scraggy", the lofty "Recce Hill", encircled by the road and forming the heart of the defence. In rear were "Water Tank Hill" and "Brigade Hill", with "Patiala Ridge" and "Signal Hill" to the north and "Sapper Hill", "Punjab Hill", "Seaforth Hill" and "Gurkha Ridge" to the south. Altogether, a most elaborate lay-out. The defence of the Saddle was a 'dog-fight' from beginning to end. The roar of artillery was incessant, and little sleep was possible in the forward positions. But although, during May, the Japanese succeeded in occupying several of the more exposed localities, their hopes of reaching Imphal by the Tamu Road were shattered before the middle of June. By that time, however, 422 Field Company was no longer at Shenam, for it had left the Tamu Road before the end of May and was working on the road to Ukhrul.

Meanwhile, the 23rd Division, based on Imphal, had been filling the unenviable role of the old-time maid of all work, ready to help anyone, anywhere, in any emergency and at short notice. The Indian Engineer units under Lieut.-Colonel A. G. P. Leahy, R.E., were 68

Field Company (Bengal) under Major W. F. Towell, R.E., 71 Field Company (Bengal) under Major F. W. Pritchard, R.E., 91 Field Company (Bombay) under Major J. S. Beddows, R.E., and 323 Field Park Company (Madras) under Major T. W. I. Hedley, R.E. 68 Field Company had been working near Wangjing on tank crossings for the road to Shuganu and over the Thoubal River, and when the enemy began to advance, it dug in at Thoubal. 71 Field Company was on the Imphal-Ukhrul Road beyond Litan, 15 miles from Ukhrul, and proceeded with the 49th Brigade down the Tiddim Road to help the 17th Division. 91 Field Company, having moved from Shuganu to Waithou on March 3rd, began to make a defensive position at that spot. 323 Field Park Company, stationed in Imphal, was exceptionally busy. When the men of that unit first surveyed the area allotted to them their hearts must have sunk for it consisted mostly of two hillsides so steep that they could be climbed only by clinging to bushes. The rest was a stretch of paddy about 30 yards wide. However, they did not despair and by digging night and day they excavated a maze of dug-outs and galleries so intricate that visitors often got lost in it. Indeed, it is said that one guest, who had come to dinner, re-appeared an hour later at another entrance bewildered, earthy, perspiring and very hungry. The Company had to improvise almost everything. Among other jobs it was ordered to produce an explosive charge sufficiently powerful to demolish a Japanese bunker yet light enough to be carried by an assault party. The bunkers were known to be very formidable. Usually, they were roofed with two layers of heavy logs covered by six feet of earth. After long experiment, a suitable charge was produced from sheet iron, old tins and some explosive which was supposed to be plastic but required much kneading to make it so. The Sappers employed on this job were not to be envied. They suffered severely from headaches as they worked like bakers day after day in an atmosphere of nitroglycerine fumes.

The Ukhrul region was the scene of heavy fighting during March 1944 after General Roberts had been obliged to send two of his brigades to the Tiddim Road. The 49th Brigade left Ukhrul on March 16th on relief by a battalion of the 50th Parachute Brigade which had been summoned from Kohima with all speed. A column of the 31st Japanese Division was advancing rapidly on Ukhrul, and on March 22nd the Parachute Brigade and a Mahratta Battalion were surrounded at Sangshak, 8 miles to the south. The task allotted to this brigade was to hinder the enemy advance on Kohima from

Homalin on the Chindwin, but the initiative rested with the Japanese. The Sangshak 'Box' was so small that supply by air was hardly possible, and consequently on March 26th, the brigade was ordered to break out in small parties and make for Imphal. This it did, and the remnants reached their destination by devious ways through the jungle. The brigade had certainly caused the enemy considerable delay, but its withdrawal exposed the Imphal-Kohima Road. The 31st Japanese Division, having occupied Ukhrul, Sangshak and Litan, handed them over to the 15th Japanese Division and made for Kohima, its main objective. Happily, no units of the 23rd Divisional Engineers were involved in the disaster at Sangshak.

The time has now come to deal briefly with the desperate struggle north of Imphal while the 4th Corps was defending the southern and eastern approaches to the town. Early in March it had become obvious that the 4th Corps would need reinforcement if seriously attacked and that consequently another division should be transferred at once to the Manipur front. The choice fell on the 5th Indian Division, under Major-General H. R. Briggs, then in Arakan, and the move of this formation, mostly by air, began on March 19th and finished in the beginning of April. The fly-in of the Division was undoubtedly one of the greatest achievements of the war. Thousands of men, hundreds of jeeps and mules and tons of equipment were transported in a few days some 400 miles over the most impassable country in the world. An Indian officer and his platoon from Arakan found themselves, in less than 24 hours, fighting the Japanese north of Imphal. The 123rd Brigade led the way, being flown straight to Imphal. The 9th Brigade followed to Dimapur, and the 161st Brigade, the last to go, reached Kohima from Dimapur in the nick of time to reinforce the hard pressed garrison before all the exits were cut by the 31st Japanese Division. Heavy equipment and supplies went by road; but if the whole Division had been sent by this means it would have taken at least a month to reach the northern front. The collection of the necessary aircraft at short notice was sanctioned by Lord Mountbatten on his own responsibility. The process of emplaning was a triumph of organization. Many of the mules objected most strongly to entering a plane. A British sergeant at the Dohazari airfield was heard to remark to an Indian comrade " 'Ere, you *puckero* 'is *topee* while I *gurm* 'is *peachee*" (intended to mean "you hold his head while I warm his behind") and thus a particularly obstinate animal was coaxed up the gangway.

Once aboard, the mules gave little trouble and were landed in Manipur in fine fettle.

The 161st Brigade joined the first arrivals of the 33rd Indian Corps under Lieut.-General M. Stopford at Dimapur. Most of this Corps had to be brought from the far side of India, and General Auchinleck, the Commander-in-Chief in India, had arranged to rush forward the Corps Headquarters, the 2nd British Division under Major-General J. M. L. Grover, the 26th Indian Infantry Brigade, two regiments of tanks and some other troops. The 2nd British Division started on March 24th, but its two leading battalions did not reach Dimapur until April 5th. Fortunately, the 7th Indian Division, under Major-General F. W. Messervy, was available from Arakan and followed the 5th Indian Division northwards by air from April 6th onwards. Its 33rd and 114th Brigades were allotted to the 33rd Corps at Dimapur while the 89th Brigade went to the 4th Corps at Imphal. The 33rd Corps was given three tasks—to prevent the enemy from entering the Brahmaputra and Surma Valleys, to keep open the Dimapur-Kohima-Imphal Road, and to move to the assistance of the 4th Corps in the region west of the Chindwin River. The situation, however, was daily becoming more discouraging. The road to Imphal and the Silchar track had already been cut. The 4th Corps was, in fact, completely isolated by land. On April 4th, before the leading troops of the 2nd British Division could arrive, the Japanese opened their attack on Kohima with two regiments and gradually pushed back the weak garrison from the outer defences. The situation in the north now became critical, for the enemy was rapidly bringing against Kohima his entire 31st Division. The rail-head at Dimapur was therefore in imminent danger, and not only the rail-head but all our lines of communication in Assam. It was estimated that if the enemy maintained the speed of his advance he might reach Dimapur by April 11th. This would have spelt disaster of the first magnitude.

Kohima was a straggling town of timber huts with corrugated iron roofs, perched on the highest part of a sharp ridge five thousand feet above the sea and surrounded by patches of cultivation on terraced slopes. The wooded hills around were beautiful, the climate invigorating. But by June 1944, the place was unrecognizable. It had become a waste of rubble, bare ridges and blasted trees, and more than a thousand graves dotted the slopes. Overlooking it were the remains of the Deputy Commissioner's bungalow and his tennis court which had been a No Man's Land. It is happy to record that the town has now been restored and that the dead are buried in a fine cemetery. The Reverend R. M. Bennett, who commanded the 1st Battalion of the Indian Engineers during the war, revisited Kohima in 1952. This is what he writes. "The hills are the same cloud-covered heights, the Nagas the same friendly people with the same imperishable smile. Their flimsy houses, destroyed by gun-fire, have been rebuilt. The old telegraph and electric light poles are seen here and there, some bent and twisted by shrapnel, others riddled with rifle fire. New poles have been made from the chassis of old military vehicles, welded together to give the necessary height, and the military-installed electric plant works spasmodically, as does the water-pumping plant. Kohima has benefited a good deal by the 'left-overs' of the war. The old military hospital is now a smart and clean civil hospital, staffed with Indian and Naga doctors and Naga and Khasi nurses, and across the valley is a bright new high-school with about 900 Naga boys and girls in attendance." Thus good has come out of the evil which obliterated the settlement in 1944.

Before the Japanese attack, Kohima was defended only by some units of the Burma and Assam Regiments and certain formations of administrative troops—perhaps 3,500 men in all. Dimapur was held only by administrative and railway troops. Covering positions at Jessami and other places to the east and south-east were garrisoned by the Assam Rifles. On these fell the first onslaught of the 31st Japanese Division and they were soon overwhelmed. Afterwards, the Japanese Commander made a mistake that probably affected the whole course of the war in Assam and Burma. Instead of containing Kohima and pushing on to seize the rail-head at Dimapur, he sat down to reduce the garrison of Kohima. With the rail-head in his hands he could have starved the 4th Corps into surrender or forced it to attempt to cut its way out after abandoning all the stores and munitions in Imphal. The leading troops of the 33rd Corps were still some distance away, but fortunately the Japanese General missed his opportunity.

On April 5th, after the attack on Kohima had begun, the two leading battalions of the 2nd British Division de-trained at Dimapur. A battalion of the 161st Brigade of the 5th Indian Division, flown from Arakan, reached Kohima on the 6th though too late to prevent the enemy from occupying the greater part of the town and its vicinity. The other two battalions were halted by enemy opposition three miles short of the place. On the 7th, the Japanese captured the water-supply, and on the 8th they began a general attack from every direction on the main position where the garrison held out grimly until finally driven on to "Garrison Hill", a height which dominated the main road. Here our men, supplied by air, resisted assault after assault. Brigadier D. F. W. Warren, who commanded the 161st Brigade,[1] had decided not to attempt to put the whole brigade into Kohima and had established a defensive box some two miles away to give support by fire. It is impossible in this brief narrative to give a detailed account of the gallant defence. The names of "Garrison Hill", "Picket Hill", "Hospital Ridge", "Summerhouse Hill", "Naga Village", "Church Knoll", "Kuki Picket", "Jail Hill", "G.P.T. Ridge" and "Aradura Spur" are prominent in military history. "Unforgettable to those who endured the siege was the District Commissioner, Mr. Charles Pawsey" writes Brett-James.[2] "He lived mostly with Colonel Richards, the garrison commander, in a large bunker on Summerhouse Hill and was to be seen, wandering through the fighting, dressed in grey flannels and an old trilby hat. Day by day he watched his bungalow being shelled and mined. Its terraced garden had been gay with flowers. His private tennis court became the No Man's Land of a battle. The Royal West Kents held trenches along its upper edge, and before long the Japanese had burrowed their way into fox-holes on the lower side. Almost hourly, grenade and rifle duels were fought across the width of this court. The position on the slopes of Summerhouse Hill was terribly exposed. The wounded could watch the Japanese loading shells into their mortars. Many died of gangrene and a few of despair. Burial of the dead was almost impossible, and towards the end the stench of the corpses became hideous."

The garrison was reinforced on April 18th when an Indian battalion, supported by tanks, cleared the road from Dimapur and entered the defences. "We must have presented a strange spectacle", writes a survivor. "Bearded, filthy men, with glazed eyes. Wounded, with filthy bandages and pale, grey faces and weak but cheerful grins. The entire hill-side was pock-marked with trenches and the trees battered by shell-fire and festooned with parachutes." Some desultory fighting took place on the 19th, but on April 20th the 6th Brigade of the 2nd British Division, coming down the road from Dimapur, broke through the last Japanese road-block west of the town and

---

[1] In September 1944, Brigadier D. F. W. Warren succeeded Major-General H. R. Briggs in command of the 5th Indian Division.

[2] *Ball of Fire*, by Antony Brett-James, pp. 311-315.

Reinforcements and equipment arriving in Kohima

relieved the garrison. Nevertheless, fighting still continued at various points. Two brigades of the 7th Indian Division entered the fray and distinguished themselves on "Jail Hill", and later in capturing the final enemy stronghold at "Naga Village". During the first half of May, the 2nd British Division, with the 33rd and 161st Brigades under command and aided by tanks, proceeded steadily with the reduction of the outlying enemy positions. The fighting was bitter in the extreme and the Division lost 2,500 men. On "Jail Hill" there now stands a monument with the inscription "For your tomorrow, they gave their today". It is a fitting epitaph for every soldier who died at Kohima.

The 31st Japanese Division, recoiling gradually from Kohima, clung stubbornly to many points along the road to Imphal, including a large supply depot which we had established at Kanglatongbi, and the 4th Corps therefore remained entirely dependent on air supply. Around Kohima, the Engineer units continued to make tracks through precipitous and jungle-covered country to enable our tanks to reach and demolish enemy machine-gun nests, and thus they saved the infantry hundreds of casualties. The 7th Indian Division, released from Kohima, began to carry out an outflanking movement to the east along the Jessami track and early in June was pressing on towards Ukhrul in heavy rain across mountains 4,000 feet high and through roaring torrents. Meanwhile, the 2nd British Division had begun to move down the Kohima-Imphal Road. The thrust by the 7th Division against the Japanese communications, and the operations of the 23rd Long Range Penetration Brigade further to the east, soon began to tell, and June 5th saw the 31st Japanese Division retiring southwards down the road to Imphal with the 2nd Division close behind it. The assault on Kohima had cost the enemy 4,000 dead, and the "March on Delhi" had failed. But the progress of the 2nd Division towards Imphal was slow and laborious. The Japanese defended every defile, and the passage of each obstruction on the road necessitated a small battle before the advance could be resumed. Thus the link-up of the 2nd Division with the 5th Division north of Imphal did not take place for more than a fortnight later.

As stated in Chapter X, the 5th Divisional Engineers under Lieut.-Colonel E. C. R. Stileman, R.E., comprised 2 Field Company (Bengal) under Major A. E. Scott, R.E., 20 Field Company (Bombay) under Major P. G. Hatch, R.E., 74 Field Company (Bengal) under Major D. C. S. David, R.E., and 44 Field Park Company (Madras) under Major M. J. P. Keating, R.E. On arrival from Arakan, 44 Field

Park Company remained in Dimapur. 2 and 20 Field Companies helped the R.E. Field Companies of the 2nd British Division at Kohima and 74 Field Company went on to Imphal. "There were many new tasks for the Engineers at Kohima" writes Brigadier H. E. Horsfield, the Chief Engineer, Fourteenth Army.[1] "The hills were so steep that tanks could not get up them to deal with the Japanese resistance points, normally at the top. The Engineers were therefore repeatedly called upon to make tracks and haul tanks up the steep slopes with bulldozers and tackles. Perhaps the most famous of these tasks was getting a tank up "Summerhouse Hill" as this was the deciding point in the battle for the Deputy Commissioner's bungalow and Kohima itself. Many heroic deeds were performed also in blowing in Jap bunkers and clearing road-blocks during the advance." It is recorded that 2 Field Company distinguished itself on several occasions. On April 7th, a detachment under Lieut. J. W. Wright, R.E., was engaged in a successful counter-attack on "Jail Hill". The Sappers demolished the walls of some buildings in which the Japanese were hiding and after a fierce hand-to-hand encounter the enemy fled. No less than 44 Japs were shot as they plunged down the hillside. Again, on the 9th, a small party under Lance-Naik Abdul Majid attacked with explosives a bakery building in the Forward Supply Depot in which a large number of the enemy were concealed. The demolition wrecked the building, killing many of the occupants outright. The Japanese lost 120 men in this affair and the Lance-Naik was awarded the Indian Distinguished Service Medal. A Section of 44 Field Park Company, equipped with bulldozers, worked at Kohima in support of the 2nd British Divisional Engineers whose bulldozers had not yet arrived. This Section made a road up "Gun Spur" to enable our tanks to attack "Church Knoll", almost the last Japanese stronghold, and the bulldozers were employed to tow medium tanks into positions from which they could fire on the enemy at close range.

The Engineer units of the 2nd and 5th Divisions were glad indeed to welcome their comrades of the 7th Divisional Engineers under Lieut.-Colonel T. Wright, R.E., when these arrived in the Kohima area in May. The units were 62 Field Company (Madras) under Major H. C. Lee, R.E., 77 Field Company (Bengal) under Major R. R. L. Harradine, R.E., 421 Field Company (Madras) under Major

---

[1] "Engineer Operations with the Fourteenth Army, 1943-44", by Brigadier H. E. Horsfield, c.b.e., m.c., appearing in *The R.E. Journal*, December 1945, pp. 241-243.

A. Dexson, R.E., and 331 Field Park Company (Madras) under Major J. H. Moss, R.E. 62 Field Company was flown straight to Imphal; the others operated in the Dimapur-Kohima area. A Section of 77 Field Company entered the Kohima perimeter with the 33rd Brigade and distinguished itself on May 10th in destroying a dominant bunker in an attack on a strong position. Together with 2 Field Company, 77 Field Company afterwards screened the roads out of Kohima against enemy air-raids and lifted mines from the Jessami track. On May 29th, two days before the Kohima area was finally cleared, the unit again attacked some Japanese bunkers. On this occasion the Brigade Commander wrote that, in his opinion, troops of such calibre had every right to consider themselves among the finest in the world. No higher tribute to the Corps of Indian Engineers could be desired.

After Kohima, some of the Sapper units followed the disheartened enemy down the Imphal Road, lifting mines, removing road-blocks, bridging streams, clearing land-slides and arranging diversions for the passage of transport, while others accompanied the 7th Indian Division towards Jessami. 421 Field Company found the Jessami track a sea of mud. "The break-out from Kohima was impressive", writes Lieut.-Colonel Frank Owen.[1] "The road to Imphal is carved out of a cliff and can be commanded from a hundred positions. The difficulty of fighting across this terrain was multiplied by the arrival of the monsoon. From the end of April onwards, it rained hard every day. For every two steps a man climbed up a hillside he slipped back one. The mud and the monsoon, however, increased the strain on the weak Japanese supply organization. The Japs still got their rations, but their ammunition began to run short. Not that their resistance failed. At Viswema, a five days' delaying battle took place. At Maram, the dash of the Worcesters captured in 36 hours a Jap position designed to hold for ten days. Meanwhile, the 7th Division, having severed all enemy communications between the enemy's bases along the Chindwin River and his troops on the Imphal Road, turned westwards and rejoined the 2nd British Division. General Briggs' 5th Indian Division and General Gracey's 20th Indian Division were already fighting their way northward from the Imphal Plain to meet the relieving forces, and the enemy was now everywhere on the defensive. His greatly reduced forces were streaming along the Imphal Road, though their grip at either end of it was being broken.

---

[1] *The Campaign in Burma*, by Lieut.-Colonel Frank Owen, O.B.E., p. 106.

What would happen next? The British leaders planned to destroy the crack Japanese divisions so that the reconquest of Burma might begin, and the annihilation operation was based upon a plan agreed between the 4th and 33rd Corps Commanders. Neither had overlooked the importance of Ukhrul, the enemy's great mountain base, and already Brigadier Perowne's 23rd L. R. P. Brigade was moving upon Ukhrul's line of communication in a wide hook. At noon on June 22nd, the jaws of the Fourteenth Army snapped together on the Imphal-Kohima Road when the leading echelons of both Corps met at Milestone 100, a few miles north of Imphal. From there, the two Corps Commanders set in motion the second operation. Brigades of the 7th Division drove eastwards to Ukhrul while units of the 20th Division pressed on north-eastwards along the Imphal-Ukhrul axis. Perowne's columns had already closed in from the north. Ukhrul's fate was sealed and it became in due course the biggest burial ground for Japanese in the length and breadth of Manipur."

The junction of the 4th and 33rd Corps north of Imphal on June 22nd, 1944, was not effected without heavy fighting. At Kanglatongbi, 15 miles from Imphal, there was a 'Box' in which, on April 7th, the only combatant troops happened to be two Field Companies of Indian Engineers and a company of Assam Rifles. The other occupants—some 10,000 men in all—consisted of administrative troops and camp followers. The enemy advanced rapidly to seize this depot, but in co-operation with three companies of the West Yorkshires from Imphal, the Sappers and Assam Rifles evacuated all the non-combatants and stores and made a successful withdrawal. Operations were soon in progress along the Iril Valley to the northeast where the 9th and 123rd Brigades of the 5th Division, and the 89th Brigade of the 7th Division, fought at Nungshigum, Molvom, Mapao and elsewhere. 20, 62 and 422 Field Companies were concerned in these battles. On May 28th, 62 Field Company erected an aerial ropeway over the Imphal *Turel* (stream), and three days later, constructed a mule track, 4,000 yards long, to a height above Mapao. Next, it built a 210-feet suspension bridge over the stream before moving in the middle of June to the Kohima Road shortly before the junction of the 4th and 33rd Corps. Afterwards, it assisted the 23rd L.R.P. Brigade. 422 Field Company provided a Double Bailey bridge, 160 feet in length, across the Iril River at Sawambong. This was a remarkable achievement as the men had had no previous experience of Bailey bridging; but every part of the structure was found to fit perfectly and it was soon in use by tanks. In the middle of July, the Company built a fine timber trestle bridge of 15 spans across the Thoubal River, and later on it bridged the flooded Iril River several times. When the supply of explosives was exhausted, the Sappers used Japanese shells for demolition work on roads.

We must hark back now to the beginning of April 1944 to describe the struggle on the Tiddim Road which followed the safe arrival of the 17th Indian Division in Imphal. The situation at that time was menacing. In the north, the enemy held Kanglatongbi on the Kohima Road, a spur east of Molvom, some high ground towards Mapao and an area further to the west. North-eastwards, the enemy had overrun most of the Iril Valley and the country between Nungshigum and Ukhrul. To the south-east and south, he was established at Tengnoupal on the Tamu Road and at Ningthoukhong on the Tiddim Road and was patrolling the tracks to the west of the latter. To counter these threats to Imphal, the greater part of the 5th Indian Division was disposed north-east of the town along the Iril Valley, the 23rd Indian Division was on the Tiddim Road, most of the 20th Indian Division held the Shenam Saddle facing Tengnoupal on the Tamu Road, and the 17th Indian Division, based on Imphal, patrolled westwards and blocked the Kohima Road north of Sengmai. On April 17th, the 17th Division took over from the 23rd Division the defence of the Tiddim Road, having under command the 32nd Brigade of the 20th Division which was ordered to prevent the enemy from pushing northwards across the Silchar track.

The 33rd Japanese Division under Major-General Tanaka—perhaps the best division in the Japanese Army—had followed boldly from Tiddim. Tanaka planned to move northwards through Tairenpokpi on the Silchar track and strike at Imphal from the west. But to accomplish this manoeuvre safely, he had first to capture Bishenpur. On the 17th, one of his regiments dug in south of Tairenpokpi, and a few days later another approached Buri Bazar only 10 miles from Imphal. By April 26th, the Japanese were around Bishenpur in considerable strength. They attacked strongly at Milestone 21 for several days but were repulsed by the 32nd Brigade and the road to Imphal was then re-opened for transport. Heavy fighting developed on May 8th at Potsangbam, south of Bishenpur, where the 63rd Brigade held all attacks in a welter of rain and mud. However, by the end of the month there were definite signs that the tide was turning. The Japanese were short of food, although they still hoped apparently that starvation on the British side might yet bring them the prize of Imphal; but General Scoones had taken the precaution of evacuating more than 50,000 non-combatants from the beleaguered town to guard against such a catastrophe. Nevertheless, while the road to Kohima remained closed and all supplies had to be brought by air, a crisis developed in Imphal at the beginning of June. The 4th Corps needed 16,000 tons of food, ammunition and petrol monthly, and during May, owing to bad weather, only 5,000 tons were delivered. Reserve stocks had fallen to two weeks' supply of food on a reduced scale and only one week's supply of petrol, and the reserve of ammunition was perilously low. And at this critical juncture, Mountbatten was ordered to release six Dakota squadrons for the invasion of Europe! He protested vigorously, and fortunately the order was countermanded. The Dakotas continued to operate, the weather improved, and so the crisis passed.

Stiff fighting followed around Ningthoukhong on the Tiddim Road. Both sides used their armour and the enemy increased his artillery fire. Towards the end of June, when the Kohima Road had been opened, the 5th Division was freed for action on the Tiddim Road in co-operation with the 17th Division. While the latter attacked southwards, the 5th Division cleared the area north of the Silchar track. For weeks the Japanese had been feeding almost entirely on small quantities of rice. They were dying by hundreds from the ravages of beri-beri, dysentery and malaria. Every day, scores committed suicide. In some places, the ground was carpeted with rotting bodies which had to be pushed into mass graves by our bulldozers. Yet the men of the 33rd Japanese Division continued to sit till the last moment in their water-logged trenches and withdrew only to occupy other positions in rear. No one will ever know how many Japanese perished in the battles of the Imphal Plain; but as a conservative estimate the figure may be put at 30,000 men between the middle of March and the middle of June 1944 while our losses amounted to less than 13,000 killed, wounded and missing. About 10,000 dead Japanese were actually counted by the 4th Corps.

Fighting stubbornly, the Japanese were not ejected from Ningthoukhong and Kha Khunou until July 16th and then only after a terrific concentration of artillery fire followed by a massive infantry assault. Kha Khunou was utterly destroyed. Pursued now by the 5th Division, the enemy retreated towards the Manipur River and Tiddim. At first, the withdrawal was very slow. Then, repeated air-strikes and tank attacks had their effect and the pace increased. Our guns were hauled up precipitous hillsides to bear on the Japanese positions, and the Sappers cut paths through the jungle. Huge craters in the road were encountered at awkward bends. Every bridge had been blown. Enormous landslides had to be cleared. In one stretch of six miles there were fourteen landslips. Felled trees blocked the road. Vehicles sank to their axles in the mud. Beyond the Manipur River crossing at Milestone 126 the road was hardly passable even for jeeps until the Sapper companies set to work on it. Their labours along the Tiddim Road were stupendous, and no account of the defence of Imphal would be complete without a proper recognition of their contribution towards the defeat of the enemy.

Among the 17th Divisional Engineer units on the Tiddim Road was 92 Field Company (Bombay) under Major J. H. Clark, R.E., which had arrived at Bishenpur with the 32nd Brigade from Wangjing on April 18th. The brigade had been detailed to hold the approaches to Imphal for a time while the 17th Division withdrew to re-organize. A "Brigade Box" was therefore established on a steep jungle-covered hill between the enemy and the junction of the Silchar track with the Tiddim Road, while behind the junction was a "Gunner Box". For two months, during which battles raged unceasingly around Ningthoukhong and Potsangbam, 92 Field Company held part of the perimeter of the Brigade Box in addition to searching for mines, patrolling and supporting tanks in assaults. The chief task, however, was to keep the communications open by minor bridging and making diversions where necessary. When the Japanese began to infiltrate past Bishenpur along a high ridge to the west, two battalions were sent up to a pass, where the Silchar track crossed the ridge, to occupy "Wireless Hill" and "Hampton Hill" overlooking the pass. The locality between these peaks was known as "Road Head" because the track beyond it had been destroyed. "Wireless Hill" was commanded by another peak to the south which was held by the enemy, and this area became the scene of many attacks and counter-attacks. Eventually, one of the battalions called for tanks. Grant tanks had climbed with great difficulty to "Road Head", but there appeared to be no feasible route up the steep and jungle-covered sides of "Wireless Hill". Nevertheless, 92 Field Company set to work on April 18th and before dusk a whole troop of heavy tanks reached the summit while the noise of their engines was drowned by air craft flying overhead. The track was made as follows. From an adjacent hill, Clark chose the most likely spur for an alignment and then made a rapid reconnaissance of it with an Abney level. Next, having ascertained the steepest slope which the weakest tank could climb, he placed his men along the selected spur to demolish the jungle to a width of

15 feet. All went well except that one stretch of 40 yards proved too steep and required intensive pick and shovel work by relays of men so that it was late in the afternoon before the weakest tank could be coaxed up it. When the Japs attacked that night, they were blinded by the headlights of the tanks and slaughtered by machine-guns. They were taken completely by surprise and the battle was quickly over. This is quoted as one of the many instances in which units of the Indian Engineers helped to bring tanks into action in seemingly impossible positions. Improvization and more improvization was the order of the day. There was an apt saying "The difficult can be done at once: the impossible will take a little longer". The Sappers set out to prove its truth.

On the Tiddim Road, in May 1944, the 48th Brigade of the 17th Division was sent round behind the enemy's positions at Potsangbam to make road-blocks at Milestone 33, south of Torbung, and to occupy some commanding features from which it could harry the enemy's communications. It was then to fight its way back up the road to meet another brigade. 70 Field Company was engaged in this affair. "We were behind the Jap lines for a little over two weeks" writes the Revd. R. T. Urwin, then a subaltern in the Company.[1] "We were supplied by air, but sometimes it seemed as though most of our food fell among the Japs and we were left only with mule fodder. After the road-blocks had been held for a week and we had inflicted severe casualties on the enemy, we began to force our way back towards Imphal. It had become clear that the other brigade would be unable to meet us and so we withdrew towards the remainder of the Division, clearing the Japs out of each village as we came to it. On one occasion, some of our tanks were expected from the Imphal direction, but at dusk we were surprised to hear enemy tanks approaching from the Tiddim side. Three of them came to within 70 yards of our position and for a time kept up a heavy fire on us. At dawn, however, only one withdrew as the others had been destroyed by the Japs after they had struck mines. The monsoon had now started and water was creeping into our slit trenches. We occupied that position for only two nights, but by the end of the second night the trenches were completely flooded."

Throughout most of June, the 17th Division held the enemy on the Tiddim Road and 70 Field Company had many skirmishes. On June 28th, the 5th Division came up to clear the enemy from the

---

[1] Notes of the Revd. R. T. Urwin, dated November 7th, 1951.

Silchar track and 2 Field Company made mule tracks and swept mines. 70 Field Company took part in the final battles for Bishenpur and frequently assaulted bunkers under heavy shell fire. The battle for Kha Khunou was won on July 16th, leaving the place nothing but a wilderness of water-logged craters, shell holes and sticky mud with not a house nor tree standing. Afterwards, the Engineer units moved down the Tiddim Road as far as the fork to Moirang and then returned to Imphal with the 17th Division, and later to Ranchi in Assam, while the 5th Division took the lead. The 5th Divisional Engineers had a sticky job in every sense of the word. In front of the advancing troops were huge craters, mile upon mile of mud, steep ascents and descents, and the Manipur River swollen by rain into a roaring torrent. The enemy disputed every inch of the way. Narrow paths had to be cut to enable our tanks and artillery to climb the thickly wooded slopes so that their guns could be brought to bear on the Japanese positions, and, as the road became more precipitous, both tanks and artillery had to be winched up the hill-sides. Already the 5th Division had to be supplied largely by air, and the time was not far distant when all supplies had to be sent by plane and dropped by parachute. The Sappers set the pace of the advance. Across the larger craters they built Bailey bridges. Huge landslides, with the consistency of porridge, blocked the road. Again and again, with explosives and bulldozers and followed by labour gangs with picks and shovels, the Sapper units remade the surface so that the transport could flounder ahead. After Milestone 100, the number of land-slides increased. At Milestone 112 a bulldozer of 2 Field Company began to slip down a land-slide towards a precipice below; but the Company officers, following it down, managed to attach a rope to it and make the rope fast to a tree just as the machine was on the point of toppling over into the abyss.

By the end of July 1944, the Imphal Plain had been completely cleared and General Slim had re-grouped the formations of the Fourteenth Army. The 4th Corps now consisted of the 5th and 17th Indian Divisions, while the 33rd Corps comprised the 2nd British Division, the 7th, 20th and 23rd Indian Divisions, the 50th Parachute Brigade, 23rd L.R.P. Brigade, 254th Indian Tank Brigade and 3rd Commando Brigade. Under the Army Command was a Lushai Brigade which was doing good work around Tiddim in disorganizing the communications of the retreating 33rd Japanese Division. The 4th and 33rd Corps were under orders to pursue the enemy without respite in two main thrusts southwards which were to unite at

Kalemyo, the 4th Corps advancing along the Tiddim Road to break the 33rd Japanese Division while the 33rd Corps pushed through Tamu and down the Kabaw Valley and drove the remnants of the 15th and 31st Japanese Divisions across the Chindwin. Ukhrul had fallen to the 7th Indian Division and the 23rd L.R.P. Brigade early in the month. But the plan of campaign was not merely to drive the enemy back across the Chindwin; he was to be followed without pause into the Mandalay Plain and there brought to decisive battle before he could reorganize. It seems that General Kimura, the Commander of the Fifteenth Japanese Army, still thought that fighting on a large scale would not be attempted in the frontier mountains during the rains and expected to be able to retain control of the Mandalay Plain until the next monsoon. Then, when the Fourteenth Army had wasted away sufficiently through being bogged down in the wet zone at the end of a 400-mile supply route, he would launch another massive counter-offensive, supplied from large dumps which he had established around Mandalay. He needed time to complete his strategic dispositions, but he was allowed none. His two fatal mistakes were to imagine that General Slim would desist from operations during the monsoon and to underestimate the enormous advantages conferred on the Fourteenth Army by domination of the air.

After the fall of Ukhrul, a strong Japanese force held out for a time on the Imphal-Ukhrul Road, but by July 14th it had been encircled and wiped out. While the 33rd Japanese Division retreated before the 4th Corps down the Tiddim Road towards the Manipur River crossing, the 33rd Corps made steady progress down the Tamu Road and a brigade of the 2nd British Division entered Tamu on August 2nd. The scene there was indescribable. Unburied corpses lay among abandoned guns, tanks and vehicles. Skeletons sat at the wheels of burnt-out wagons. The wounded had been left to die of starvation unless able to commit suicide in the usual Japanese manner. Tamu was a charnel house, but its possession gave us great advantages. It afforded an entrance to the Kabaw Valley and access to the tracks leading eastwards to Sittaung and southwards to Kalemyo. In fact, it opened the door to the banks of the Upper Chindwin.

The 23rd Divisional Engineers excelled themselves in the advance from Shenam. For instance, on July 26th they found that 200 yards of the road near Lokchao had vanished down the hillside; but by midday on the 27th they had excavated, on the Shenam side of the break, a 1 in $2\frac{1}{2}$ incline down which vehicles were lowered by winches to a track leading up to the road beyond the gap. *Facilis descensus*

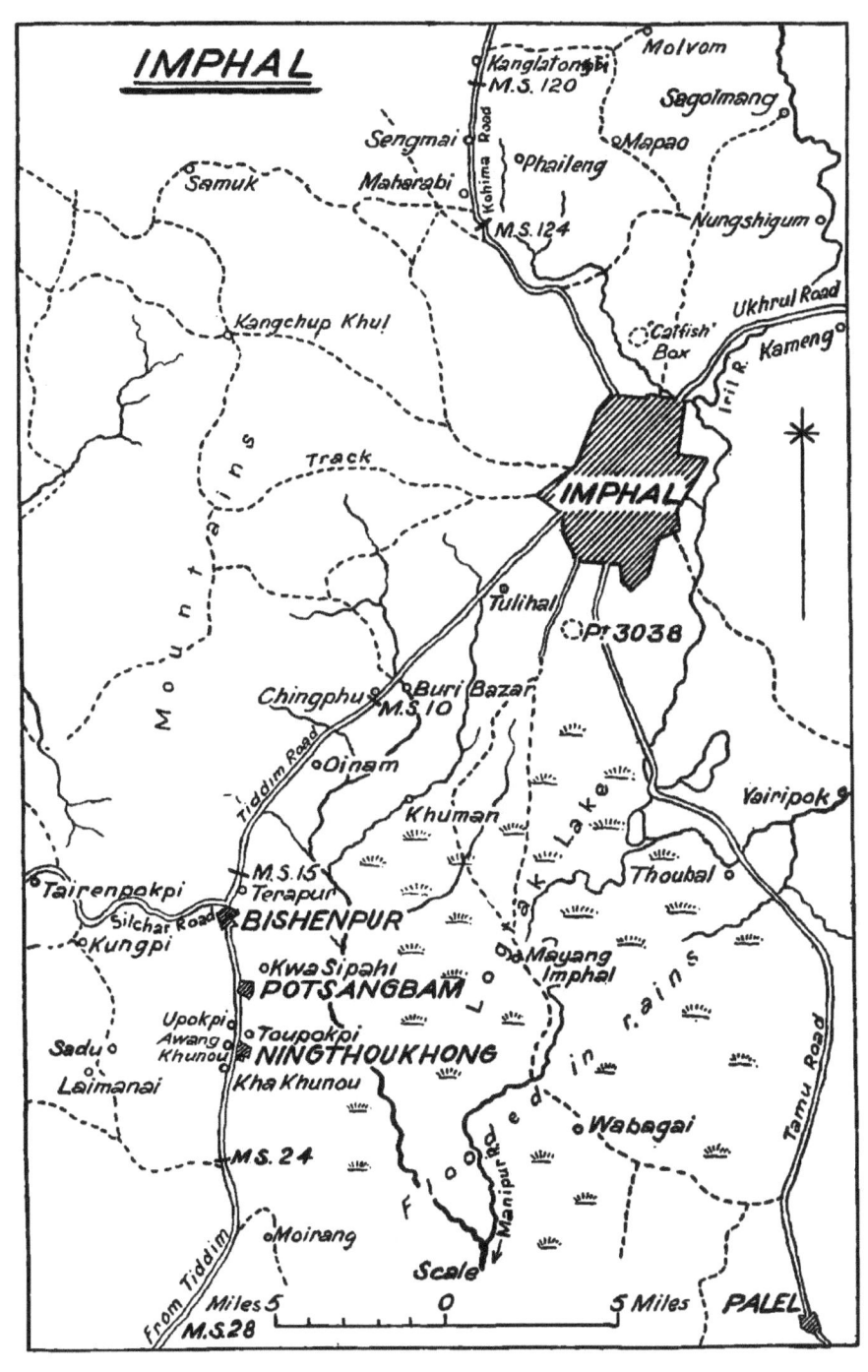

Averno. It was easy to go down to the muddy bottom, but there was no return that way. Ammunition and stores were slid down a chute. Petrol drums were rolled down. By dint of working night and day in pouring rain and a howling gale, the Sappers kept the road open and supplies moving forward. On July 31st, a battalion of Mahrattas crossed the swirling waters of the Lokchao by using as a footway the two remaining cables of the suspension bridge, and after it had gone forward to attack the enemy, 94 Field Company provided an aerial ropeway and then a Bailey bridge for the passage of the 5th Brigade to Moreh and Tamu.

The Reverend R. M. Bennett gives a picture of the Imphal region as he saw it in 1951, seven years later. "Imphal itself is the same straggling town of many villages and is said to be the largest in Assam; but you would never know it because the hamlets are tucked away in bamboo groves as they always were. As at Dimapur, nature has overtaken the sites. Bamboo and jungle vine have worked their way through every camp site and across many of the roads. There is little left to indicate what was once an enormous tented city. As for Kanglatongbi, you would recognize it only if someone told you it was there. Of the camps and installations, not a vestige remains. The Imphal-Silchar track is no longer 'jeepable', though the Tamu-Palel Road still exists, as do the bridges we built at Lokchao and Tamu. The military cemetery at Kohima is the most beautiful I have ever seen. A whole hillside has been set aside for it and terraced step by step. When I was there, the slope was covered with *poinsetta* trees in full bloom and the cemetery with wild roses, *cannas* and *lantana*. Above the acres of British dead were still further acres of Indian dead, comrades in death as in war. The Imphal military cemetery was also beautifully kept, with cultivated flowers in a sea of green lawns. It is comforting to know that the resting-places of our dead, so far from their native lands, are so well cared for."

So, as the tide of battle ebbed away in the autumn of 1944, peace returned gradually to war-torn Imphal; but only gradually because the town remained for some months an all-important forward base for the vast counter-offensive into Burma. The victorious Fourteenth Army had yet to cross the Manipur River, the Chindwin and the great Irrawaddy before it could give the *coup-de-grace* to Japanese aggression, and with it went those many units of the Indian Engineers without whose help it could never have attained its goal.

CHAPTER XII

THE ADVANCE TO MEIKTILA AND MANDALAY,
AUGUST 1944 - MARCH 1945

BY August 1944, the end of the war in Burma was in sight. Outfought, out-manoeuvred and out-numbered on land and sea and overwhelmed in the air, the Japanese were everywhere on the retreat. Their Fifteenth Army, the invaders of Manipur, was disintegrating. The remnants of their 18th Division, opposed to General Stilwell's American-Chinese troops in the north, had fallen back towards Bhamo, and Stilwell had occupied the railway terminus at Myitkyina and was approaching Mogaung on the "Railway Corridor" between Myitkyina and Katha.[1] Further eastwards, the main Chinese forces had crossed the Salween River in May and were advancing slowly through the mountains of Yunnan towards the Burma frontier. On the Manipur front, the 20th Indian Division and the 23rd L.R.P. Brigade had recaptured Ukhrul and straddled the escape route of the 31st Japanese Division. The 23rd Indian Division, and the 2nd British Division from Kohima, had pursued the 15th Japanese Division from Palel to the Chindwin. The newly arrived 11th East African Division was pushing down the Kabaw Valley towards Kalewa and eastwards towards Sittaung, and the 17th Indian Division was forcing the redoubtable 33rd Japanese Division to withdraw step by step down the Tiddim Road where the last Japanese crossed the Indo-Burma frontier at Milestone 75 on August 25th.[2] Reinforcements of men and material were now reaching the Fourteenth Army in considerable numbers. On the other hand, General Kimura, the Japanese Commander-in-Chief, had been informed by Tokyo that he could expect no outside help. His position was almost desperate. Strafed from the air, harried on the ground, reduced by starvation and disease and with casualties mounting daily, the Japanese armies faced annihilation. Beri-beri, malaria and dysentery were rampant among them. Our doctors reported the discovery of groups of dead,

---

[1] See the map of Upper Burma included in Chapter XIII.

[2] See the maps of the Tiddim Road, Chindwin River Area, in Chapter IX, and the Tiddim Road, Milestones 32 to 83, in this chapter.

each man with a little bag of rice which he could not digest. Many of the living were too weak to carry out the normal Japanese practice of killing their seriously wounded or sick comrades, and few of the latter were strong enough to commit suicide. The country reeked with the stench of decomposing bodies. Hundreds polluted the streams and rivers. And so, through a welter of rain, mud and filth, the liberation of Burma was begun.

The assistance afforded by Stilwell in the far north was a notable feature in the general scheme, and Stilwell himself a notable character. Early in August 1944, during the operations following the capture of Myitkyina and Mogaung, the 36th British Division had been sent to reinforce him in an advance southwards down the "Railway Corridor" from Mogaung to open the line for traffic. When Major-General F. W. Festing, the Divisional Commander, contacted Stilwell he found him pondering over some maps in a tent. The British General saluted smartly and said "Festing reporting for duty, Sir". The American, without looking up, replied "Take Taungui". So Festing saluted again, turned about, marched out and in due course took Taungui, a small railway station on the line leading southwards to Hopin. Such was Stilwell. Few could have co-operated with him so well as Festing who was a man of deeds rather than words. It may be added that the Indian Engineers who came under Festing's command at a later date had the greatest confidence in his ability and showed it by their achievements.

The 4th Corps having been withdrawn to India at the end of July 1944 for rest and training, the conduct of the general offensive from Manipur devolved on the 33rd Corps under Lieut.-General Sir Montagu Stopford whose instructions were to pursue the enemy along the Tamu and Tiddim Roads, to occupy Sittaung in order to deny him the use of the Chindwin River, and to capture Kalewa and establish a bridgehead over the Chindwin at that place. Throughout September and October, the 11th East African Division made steady progress in appalling weather down the Kabaw Valley where every *chaung* had overflowed and inundated large areas. This "Valley of Death" was rampant with malaria and scrub typhus, a disease about which little was known at that time, but casualties were reduced by spraying the road and camp sites with D.D.T. Behind the advancing infantry, the road was made passable for wheeled traffic by the unceasing labours of many Engineer formations. On September 4th, a brigade occupied Sittaung and established a small bridgehead across the Chindwin, and on October 4th the main body captured Yazagyo, half-way down the valley,[1] and secured several tracks leading eastwards to the river. The rain ceased after the middle of October, and the 11th East African Division occupied Kalemyo on November 15th. That it was able to do so was due in no small measure to the labours of a gradually expanding Engineer organization called 145 D.C.E. Works (Indian), under Lieut.-Colonel P. O. G. Wakeham, R.E., which comprised at the outset three Field Companies of Indian Engineers, an Indian Engineer Battalion and some Indian Pioneer Companies.

The story of the Tamu-Kalewa Road is told by Brigadier Wakeham in *The R.E. Journal*.[2] In mid-October the single fair-weather track south of Tamu was a morass, and the East Africans had to be supplied by air. As the monsoon ceased, another fair-weather road was cut through the jungle at the rate of four miles a day to carry the supporting 2nd British Division. This rapidly became the sole line of communication for the Fourteenth Army and was used by about 3,000 vehicles daily. The construction of an all-weather road was begun later. The northern section from Tamu to the neighbourhood of Kalemyo led down the Kabaw Valley for 76 miles through heavy teak forest and dense undergrowth, finishing with tall bamboo. Then came the final section eastwards to Kalewa through the rugged Myittha Gorge. Work was started in the Kabaw Valley in December but was postponed in the Myittha Gorge until April 1945 to permit the quarrying and transportation of 75,000 tons of stone required for surfacing this 18-mile stretch of mountain road. The new line of communication was finished in June 1945 and was undoubtedly one of the most remarkable engineering achievements of the war in Burma. The field units of the Indian Engineers, though not employed on the road during the later stages, had the satisfaction of having started the great project.

The most spectacular and important employment of the Indian Engineer units during the advance into Central Burma was the ferrying or bridging of rivers, often in the face of enemy opposition. These waterways were the greatest natural obstacles which they encountered although the lack of roads presented them also with unending problems. Mines and booby-traps had to be cleared, airstrips were required to keep pace with the advance; but nothing

---

[1] See the map of Central Burma included in this chapter.

[2] "The Tamu-Kalewa Road", by Brigadier P. O. G. Wakeham, O.B.E., appearing in *The R.E. Journal*, September 1946, pp. 161-188.

could exceed in urgency the provision of means for crossing the Manipur tributary of the Chindwin, the Chindwin and other tributaries of the Irrawaddy, and finally the great river itself at several places. Here the Sappers filled their true role, and here they showed the results of months of careful training in watermanship and displayed those qualities of cool courage under fire for which they were and are renowned. It is proposed, therefore, to concentrate chiefly on the river crossings during the offensive.

While the East Africans were progressing down the Kabaw Valley, the 5th Indian Division was making a parallel advance southwards down the Tiddim Road. By the end of August 1944, it appeared likely that the 33rd Japanese Division, opposing the 161st Brigade, would withdraw across the Manipur River at Milestone 126 which the brigade might hope to reach in the middle of September. Major-General G. C. Evans, the Divisional Commander, had foreseen that the flooded river would be a serious obstacle and had therefore decided to turn the enemy's flank in order to avoid an opposed crossing. With this end in view he sent the 123rd Brigade back to Imphal by motor transport and thence down the east bank to Shuganu, whence the brigade marched through mountainous country to some heights beyond the Manipur River crossing and thus caused the enemy rearguards to withdraw without serious fighting. The 5th Divisional Engineers, under Lieut.-Colonel E. C. R. Stileman, R.E., comprised 2, 20 and 74 Field Companies and 44 Field Park Company, and it fell to 74 Field Company to supply the Engineer element with the detached 123rd Brigade. The Sappers cut mule tracks, bridged streams, and helped the infantry to establish and hold a road-block on the Tiddim Road some distance beyond the river crossing. 2 Field Company, under Major C. W. Williams, R.E., was then called upon to span the raging torrent at Milestone 126 with ferries or bridges to transport the 161st and 48th Brigades to the far bank. The first infantry patrols arrived at the site on September 14th. The river was 110 yards wide and running at 12 feet per second with a deafening roar. It seemed that no boat could attempt to cross without being smashed to pieces on the jagged rocks around which the seething waters swirled. A British officer and eleven men tried to cross by boat on September 16th and failed. Then 2 Field Company attempted to provide an aerial ropeway and this also met with no success. A Sapper set out to swim the river. He was swept away and would have been drowned had it not been for the gallantry of Jemadar Jahan Dad who jumped in and hauled him to the bank and thus earned the George Medal. Some time afterwards, a line was thrown across by attaching it to a 3-inch mortar shell. This was hauled in by a few men who had reached the far bank in a folding boat. A single cable and a double cable followed, and finally a 3-inch wire hawser which had been discovered on the spot. On September 19th, a folding boat ferry was installed by 2 Field Company, and then another by 20 Field Company under Major P. G. Hatch, R.E., and thereafter the ferries averaged ten to twelve crossings per hour. On the 20th, 2 Field Company took over both ferries. The men had an unenviable task. The river was still rising and the current had increased to 17 feet per second. The wire hawsers could hardly stand the strain. In one boat, the bollards to which the traveller leads were made fast were torn completely out, leaving gaping holes in the side through which the water poured. A boat capsized and five men were drowned. Five more were drowned later. By this time, however, the folding boats were being replaced by rafts capable of carrying 9 tons. On September 21st, the river rose another 3 feet, but ferrying by raft was now well established and a few days afterwards some rafts were coupled together to give sufficient deck space for mules, guns and vehicles. Later still, three rafts were fastened together and carried four medium tanks across in an hour. Ferrying continued at night in the glare of the headlamps of a number of vehicles, and by October 4th not only had the 161st Brigade and a number of tanks been carried across but also two field hospitals and a mass of equipment of all kinds. The 48th Brigade followed. As Antony Brett-James remarks,[1] the 5th Division could not have crossed the Manipur River without the rapid work, ingenuity and untiring energies of 2 and 20 Field Companies. The Bengal Sappers of 2 Field Company and the Bombay Sappers of 20 Field Company vied with each other in this notable feat of engineering.

Major-General Evans having been stricken with scrub typhus on September 23rd, the 5th Division was now commanded by Major-General D. F. W. Warren. Supplied by air, it made good progress along the road to Tiddim. 74 Field Company spanned the raging Beltang Lui with a cable-way and then built a Bailey bridge. In an attack up the famous "Chocolate Staircase", a mass of hairpin bends, the unit was with the leading troops, clearing the road of mines, and when Tiddim was captured on October 18th it began to restore the damaged water-supply system. 2 Field Company arrived on the

---

[1] *Ball of Fire*, by Antony Brett-James, p. 370.

26th and both units set to work on the repair of the road to Kennedy Peak and Fort White.[1] The enemy positions at "Vital Corner" were captured on November 2nd, and those on Kennedy Peak (8,871 feet) on November 4th. Meanwhile, the independent Lushai Brigade was harassing the enemy south of Fort White. On November 13th, the leading troops met those of the 11th East African Division at Kalemyo. The task of the 5th Division had been completed. It was flown out of Burma for a rest and with it went its Engineer units. The main body of the 33rd Corps, led by the East Africans, then pushed eastwards through the narrow defile of the Myittha River and reached its confluence with the Chindwin at Kalewa on December 2nd.

A new formation had recently appeared at the front. This was the 19th Indian Division, under Major-General T. W. Rees, consisting of the 62nd, 64th and 98th Brigades. The 4th Corps, under Lieut.-General Sir Geoffrey Scoones, had returned from India at the end of October and had re-opened its headquarters near Imphal with the 19th Indian Division and 268th Indian Infantry Brigade under command. The 19th Division was to lead the way across the Chindwin. Its Divisional Engineers, under Lieut.-Colonel F. M. Hill, R.E., comprised 29 Field Company (Bombay), 64 and 65 Field Companies (Madras) and 327 Field Park Company (Madras). The Division moved to Tamu and, early in November 1944, set out along the track to Sittaung on the Chindwin, all three Field Companies being employed on road repair and bridging. 65 Field Company reached Sittaung on November 13th and began to build bamboo rafts for jeeps, and folding-boat rafts for men and animals, while a 3-inch rope was being put across the river. The 62nd Brigade had been detailed to push forward beyond the Chindwin towards Pinlebu and at 7.30 a.m. on November 18th it began to cross in two folding-boat rafts. Much trouble was experienced with the 9.8 and 22 h.p. outboard motors and it was difficult to get the mules aboard; but during the day, 65 Field Company managed to carry 170 mules across on rafts while the remainder swam. Two platoons went ahead with the 62nd Brigade, and the third, gathering experience, rafted 700 men, 350 mules and 20 jeeps and trailers to the far bank on the 19th. Two days later, 64 Field Company took over the rafting. The motors still gave trouble and the Sappers often had to row the rafts.

---

[1] See the map of the Tiddim Road, Milestone 109 to Kalemyo, appearing in this chapter.

The 62nd Brigade having passed through, it was decided to divert the remainder of the 19th Division northwards and accordingly 64 Field Company joined 29 Field Company at Nanthanyit, upstream of Thaungdut. 29 Field Company took the 64th Brigade across at this point on December 10th, and on the 11th, 64 Field Company began crossing the 98th Brigade and its transport, an operation which lasted a week. A Ramped Cargo Lighter (R.C.L.) proved a most useful addition to the rafts. This peculiar craft was made of wood. It was 52 feet long and drew only 2½ feet of water when loaded with 25 tons of stores. Power was supplied by two 85 h.p. engines. Its components had been transported by road from Dimapur and assembled on the banks of the Yu River, south of Tamu, where it was launched with the aid of elephants. Thence it had been floated down to the Chindwin. It was obvious that the Chindwin would become increasingly important as a line of communication southwards, and therefore an Inland Water Transport Service was organized and a site for building craft of various sorts was selected at Kalewa. Here, in addition to R.C.Ls., steel Unicraft barges and tugs, wooden Higgins barges and Eastern Army Boats were produced. The latter were pontoon-shaped and 40 feet long, and three of them, formed into a raft and decked with Pierced Steel Planking (P.S.P.), could carry a load of 30 tons. Hundreds of boats were built during the winter of 1944-45 by 536 Artisan Works Company, assisted by Forestry Companies, a Workshop Company and native tradesmen. The story of the development of the Chindwin fleet is told by Lieut.-Colonel D. C. Merry, R.E., in *The R.E. Journal*.[1] The fleet served to relieve the traffic on the many miles of track which the Indian Engineers had to maintain, and its work was therefore of the greatest assistance during the advance of the Fourteenth Army. It may be interesting to remark that two gunboats, mounting Bofors and Oerlikon guns, were eventually built and launched on the Chindwin. They were probably the first warships ever constructed by the Army for the Royal or Royal Indian Navies.

Although the ferrying of the 19th Division across the Chindwin was a fine achievement, the outstanding exploit on that river was the construction of a floating bridge at Kalewa by the 33rd Corps Troops Engineers under Lieut.-Colonel F. Seymour-Williams, R.E. The units employed on the work were 67, 76 and 361 Field Companies

---

[1] "Development of I.W.T. on the River Chindwin, 1945", by Lieut.-Colonel D. C. Merry, R.E., appearing in *The R.E. Journal*, September 1947, pp. 235-240.

(Bengal), 322 Field Park Company (Bengal), two Bridging Companies and some other technical formations. The water-way at Kalewa was more than 1,000 feet in width, and equipment was scarce because it had to be transported along 310 miles of difficult road from the rail-head at Dimapur. The longest floating bridge that had till then been built in any theatre of the war was needed to reach the far bank. This had been foreseen as early as October when Seymour-Williams had begun his planning while at Imphal.[1] At that time a site could be selected only by examining a few inferior aerial photographs taken when the river had been in flood in August. These showed a 30-feet bank on the near shore and a stretch of soft sand, 500 yards wide, on the far shore, beyond which there was a road on a high embankment. As there was no space for building rafts on the near shore, a site for this purpose was chosen 800 yards up the Myittha confluent. The 11th East African Division was given some folding boats with which to carry out the first assault crossing.

Unquestionably, the most difficult phase of the scheme was to transport the available bridging material from Dimapur to Indainggale, a village near Indainggyi a few miles north of Kalemyo. Thence it had to be carried a further 21 miles by road to reach the selected site at Kalewa. This narrow thoroughfare, cut into the cliffs of the Myittha Gorge and damaged by previous heavy traffic, required the building of 9 Bailey bridges and 22 timber bridges before it could be used with even moderate safety. All the equipment and the Engineer troops were marshalled at Indainggale on December 1st, and the first Field Company moved off on the 4th. Progress was slow because the East Africans had been given priority of traffic. On December 5th, Seymour-Williams reconnoitred the Kalewa site under enemy artillery fire and designed his bridge which was to have 22 floating bays, mostly 42 feet long, in addition to landing bays and ramps. The overall length amounted to 1,153 feet. Work was begun early on December 6th, and on the morning of the 9th the first floating bays were ferried down from the Myittha to the Chindwin and taken across to the far bank. Both landing bays were completed the same evening. The approach road across the 500 yards width of sand on the far bank was covered with sandwich layers of coir matting and Sommerfeld track. It was finished by mid-day on the 10th while the last floating bay was being rafted into the bridge. Three

---

[1] "Bridging the Chindwin at Kalewa, December 1944", by Colonel F. Seymour-Williams, D.S.O., O.B.E., appearing in *The R.E. Journal*, June 1946, pp. 139-142.

hours later, "Grub Bridge", as it was called, was opened to traffic and Lieut.-Colonel Seymour-Williams and Major-General C. C. Fowkes, the 11th East African Divisional Commander, drove across in a jeep, the first to cross since 1942. "Grub" Bridge remained in use until replaced a few months later by the "Falls Bridge", two miles further upstream, which had to span no less than 2,000 feet of the river when in flood and to allow for a rise of 40 feet in the water-level.

An amusing incident during the Chindwin crossing is described by Lieut.-Colonel N. B. Grant, R.E. A 3-ton lorry had broken down, bringing a convoy of 100 lorries to a standstill, so a Sapper party was sent forward to help. Suddenly, a British officer appeared and ordered the Sappers to throw the offending vehicle into the river. The driver objected violently and wanted to know how he was going to explain the loss of his lorry to his Commanding Officer. Whereupon the officer gave the man a note for his O.C. and told him not to worry. The note read "With the compliments of General Slim".

Lieut.-Colonel G. A. Clayton, R.E., who was acting at the time as C.R.E. 33rd Corps Troops Engineers, records that there were only four spare pontoons when the far bank was reached, and that had the bridge (a Class 30) been damaged by floating mines it could only have been re-assembled as a Class 18 structure and the traffic would consequently have been much restricted.[1] A cable boom was therefore provided upstream and Bofors guns were mounted to destroy mines. Happily, no mines were released by the enemy, though floating logs of heavy teak caused some anxiety. A solitary enemy bomb damaged two pontoons, but these were quickly replaced. The bulldozer drivers of 322 Field Park Company worked continuously for 54 hours on the east bank approaches. "Grub" Bridge, however, would have been next to useless had it not been for the numerous bridges built in the Myittha Gorge. "I have particularly in mind a Bailey Bridge opened on Christmas Day" writes Clayton. This was built round a cliff a few miles south of "Grub" Bridge by 67 Field Company and had to be launched uphill and into space. It was lowered on to a pier built out from the sheer face of the cliff and was then cut in the middle and the interval filled with concrete. It was not only bent in the middle but rose to an apex on the middle pier. The bridge had to be constructed beneath an existing Japanese wooden walk-way around the cliff face. This "Christmas Bridge"

---

[1] Notes by Lieut.-Colonel G. A. Clayton, R.E., dated June 1953.

was probably the most vital one on the line of communication, for there was no alternative route except through virgin jungle."

An exploit by a platoon of 361 Field Company during the advance down the Kabaw and Chindwin valleys in December 1944 should not be overlooked. Twelve jeeps with trailers had to be delivered at a place on the Chindwin River about 30 miles north of Kalewa, and enemy opposition might be expected *en route*. The only method was to raft the jeeps downstream from Tamu, and this was difficult because suitable material was scarce. Accordingly it was decided to wrap each jeep and trailer in a huge tarpaulin and strap these watertight packages together to form rafts. Each raft was then fitted with an outboard motor, and under the command of Lieut. J. A. Palfrey, R.E., the expedition set out downstream. It must have been a curious sight. Many of the tarpaulins were torn on rocks and the rafts had to be beached for repairs; but no jeeps or trailers were lost, the enemy did not interfere, and the whole consignment was delivered safely. For this remarkable feat, Palfrey was awarded the Military Cross.

The mastery which the Allies achieved on the Chindwin is shown by the manner in which 75 Field Company joined the 4th Corps at Kalewa. The unit travelled 139 miles down the river in 8 days in a convoy of rafts bringing ferrying equipment which had been used at Tonhe. On five folding-boat rafts and a Japanese boat, each fitted with an outboard motor and towing a raft made of bamboo, were piled masses of bridging stores, Sommerfeld track and petrol containers. A motor boat accompanied the flotilla which passed Sittaung and Mawlaik and negotiated successfully the whirlpools above Kalewa, where it arrived on January 4th, 1945, and moored near the "Grub" Bridge.

By November 1944, many changes had taken place in the higher commands in Burma. The American General Stilwell (nicknamed "Vinegar Joe") being unable to collaborate with the Chinese General Chiang Kai Shek, had been recalled to Washington and replaced by Lieut.-General D. I. Sultan. Lieut.-General Sir Oliver Leese had arrived to relieve General Sir George Giffard in supreme command of the land forces in Burma which comprised General Slim's Fourteenth Army on the Chindwin front, Lieut.-General Sultan's American-Chinese command on the Ledo Road and about Myitkyina, and Lieut.-General Christison's 15th Indian Corps in Arakan. Slim's Corps Commanders were Lieut.-General M. M. Stopford (33rd Corps) and Lieut.-General G. A. P. Scoones (4th Corps), but on December 8th, Lieut.-General F. W. Messervy, previously commanding the 7th Indian Division, took over the command of the 4th Corps from General Scoones.

Lord Mountbatten's plans for the reconquest of Burma envisaged the completion of the Ledo Road, the protection of the "Hump" air-route to China, the capture of Mandalay, the destruction of the Japanese forces in Central Burma, the clearance of the whole of of Arakan, and finally the occupation of Rangoon. Of these, the most important was the destruction of the Japanese forces in Central Burma, and next, the capture of Mandalay. Both tasks were assigned to the Fourteenth Army. After the bulk of the 11th East African and 20th Indian Divisions had been ferried across the Chindwin in the Mawlaik region, the 2nd British Division crossed at Kalewa while the 5th Indian Division was flown out of Burma for a well-earned rest. The 19th Indian Division, having crossed the Chindwin, then pushed eastwards from Sittaung towards Pinlebu so as to link up with the 2nd British Division at Shwebo. General Slim had now at his disposal the 2nd British and the 5th, 7th, 17th, 19th and 20th Indian Divisions, in addition to two tank brigades and two independent infantry brigades, and he was supported by a very powerful air force. He decided to fight the main Japanese concentrations in the Shwebo Plain, north of the loop of the Irrawaddy which runs from east to west between Mandalay and Pakokku. Therefore, the Fourteenth Army was ordered to mass with all speed in the Shwebo Plain. On December 8th, the 4th Corps headquarters were moved from Imphal to Tamu, and on the Corps front, which lay north of that of the 33rd Corps, the 19th Indian Division and the 268th Indian Infantry Brigade proceeded to thrust eastwards, according to plan, over exceptionally difficult and almost trackless country. On December 16th, the 19th Division took Pinlebu and Banmauk and made contact at Indaw with the 36th British Division of General Sultan's N.C.A.C. Group. It occupied Wuntho on the 19th, Kawlin on the 20th and Kokoggon on the 23rd. It seems that the Japanese Commander, Lieut.-General Kimura, had ordered his 31st Division to hold the Shwebo Plain long enough to enable the remainder of his Fifteenth Army to cross the Irrawaddy, after which it would establish itself south-west of Mandalay. However, as soon as these intentions became apparent, General Slim changed his plans and decided to cross the Irrawaddy, even if opposed strongly, and to fight the decisive battles on the further side, before the end of February, in the plains around Mandalay and the low hills around Meiktila; and since he did not possess enough equipment to make a single crossing in overwhelming strength against heavy opposition, he proposed to deceive the enemy by crossing, or feinting at crossing, at several places. He would first cross in considerable strength north of Mandalay in order to entice the enemy in that direction, and would then make his main crossings *south* of the enemy forces guarding the Irrawaddy below Mandalay.

The most ambitious crossing was to be made by the 4th Corps after it had been switched with the utmost speed and secrecy from the left or northern flank of the Fourteenth Army to the right or southern flank. Thus, instead of pushing eastwards from Kalewa, this Corps would turn southwards down the Gangaw Valley, moving across the rear of the 33rd Corps and seizing a bridge-head over the Irrawaddy near Pakokku. Then, with mechanized, armoured and partly air-borne forces, it would strike south-eastwards at Meiktila and Thazi. These places were key points on the enemy's communications by road and rail from Mandalay to the south. They had five good airfields and their capture would isolate most of the Japanese forces in Central Burma. Afterwards, when the enemy had been defeated, the Fourteenth Army would make a lightning thrust to Rangoon. It was hoped that, as the Mandalay battle developed, the Japanese defenders of Meiktila might be drawn away in that direction and thus simplify the task of the 4th Corps. This seemed probable because the 33rd Corps was to secure a bridgehead across the Irrawaddy north of Mandalay before the 4th Corps attacked Meiktila. General Slim's chief difficulty was to deploy two complete Corps along a single axis of advance—the Imphal-Tamu-Kalewa Road—and to disguise adequately his intention to move against Meiktila. From Tamu to Pakokku the 4th Corps had to cover 238 miles of rough road, two feet deep in dust and liable to become impassable if rain fell. The distance from rail-head at Dimapur to Meiktila was no less than 573 miles. Fortunately, it was possible to supplement road and air transport by water transport on the Chindwin between Kalewa and Myingyan, a distance of 200 miles. From Myingyan to Meiktila, a further 55 miles, there was an all-weather road and a railway. The plan evolved by the Fourteenth Army Commander met with the success it deserved. The enemy was completely deceived and a mortal blow was struck. Everything depended, however, on the ability of the Engineers to get the troops rapidly to the banks of the Irrawaddy at several places, and having got them there, to ferry them across.

Let us examine first the operations upstream of Mandalay. As early as August 1944, two brigades of the 36th British Division, under Major-General F. W. Festing, had begun to march down the "Railway Corridor" from Mogaung to Naba Junction, near Katha, on the western flank of General Stilwell's forces to which they were attached. On December 16th, as already stated, they made contact with the leading troops of the 19th Indian Division coming from the west, and shortly afterwards, another brigade arrived from the north to complete the establishment at Katha. The 36th Divisional Engineers, under Lieut.-Colonel P. A. Easton, R.E., comprised 236 Field Company, R.E., 30 Field Company (Bombay), 324 Field Park Company (Bombay) and the 15th Indian Engineer Battalion. These units were joined, early in January 1945, by 58 Field Company (Madras).[1] Owing to the state of the Ledo Road, unit transport was severely restricted. A Field Company had to be content with a single jeep and a trailer, and as all Engineer equipment came by air from a dump 190 miles away in Assam, it also was very scarce. Personal equipment consisted of what each man could carry on his back. The troops marched along earthen tracks which often became watercourses under heavy rain. The only method of road repair was to make a rough corduroy surface with small logs and brushwood and hope for the best. It was fortunate that some transportation could be organized along the single line of metre-gauge railway from Myitkyina through Mogaung to Naba Junction, a distance of 140 miles. A short branch line led from Naba to the Irrawaddy at Katha while the main line continued southwards through Indaw, Wuntho and Shwebo and across the Irrawaddy to Mandalay.[2]

The railway between Myitkyina and Katha had been badly damaged by our air forces and by the retreating enemy. All the larger bridges were down, and long stretches of the track had been torn up. Nothing heavier than a fish-plate could be flown in for repair work; yet the Sapper units managed to restore the track and build 28 timber bridges, and the line was re-opened for traffic in the middle of December. The lack of locomotives was met by the employment of jeeps fitted with flanged railway wheels. A normal jeep-train consisted of two 10-ton box-cars coupled to a jeep, the car-load being limited to

---

[1] "Improvisation in North Burma", by Lieut.-Colonel P. A. Easton, O.B.E., R.E., appearing in *The R.E. Journal*, September 1948, pp. 210-216.

[2] See the map of Central Burma included in this chapter and also the map of Upper Burma in Chapter XIII.

THE ADVANCE TO MEIKTILA AND MANDALAY

7 tons. These jeep-trains were not easy to drive. Starting was accomplished by engaging low gear, stamping on the throttle and letting in the clutch with a bang.[1] This made the wheels spin madly but usually resulted in starting the train. If not, the train had to be pushed by gangs of sweating men until it began to move. Stopping was even more difficult. The jeep's brakes being far too weak for the job, the train had to be allowed to roll to a standstill against the jeep's engine compression, a process which normally required 500 yards. It can be imagined, therefore, that a speed limit of 25 m.p.h. was most necessary and that driving a jeep-train was very exhausting. Later, two locomotives were built by the R.E.M.E. from salvaged wagons, British engines and Japanese gear-boxes. These contraptions could haul ten loaded wagons, and if going downhill with a following wind, could attain a speed of 40 m.p.h. provided the driver was sufficiently daring; but in the early days in the "Railway Corridor", the jeep ruled the roost.

The 36th British Division, having cleared the "Corridor" and reached Katha on December 11th, 1944, was ordered to cross the Irrawaddy and advance south-eastwards through Mongmit towards the old Burma Road in order to threaten Maymyo and Mandalay. The Division was split temporarily into two brigade groups. The 29th Brigade moved downstream and crossed at Tigyaing, some 30 miles below Katha, while the 72nd Brigade, followed by the 26th Brigade, crossed at Katha itself and advanced through forest country into the Shan States in the loop of the Shweli River. Both prongs made rapid progress against slight opposition. The crossings of the Irrawaddy were accomplished easily with the help of rafts made from discarded Japanese pontoons or country boats. The Division also had a number of American "Ranger" boats. Both rafts and boats were fitted with outboard motors. The crossing of mules was a difficult matter, but some were persuaded to swim by dangling from the stern of a Ranger boat a tempting nose-bag full of corn.

The main Japanese stand against the 36th Division was made at Myitson on the Shweli River, 30 miles beyond the Irrawaddy and about half-way between Katha and Shwebo. This occurred on February 1st. The Indian Engineer unit chiefly concerned was 58 Field Company, under Major H. R. Gregson, R.E., which was attached to the 26th Brigade. Forty Ranger boats having been

---

[1] "Jeep Railway in Burma", by Lieut.-Colonel P. A. Easton, O.B.E., R.E., appearing in *The R.E. Journal*, December 1946, pp. 329-332.

allotted to the leading battalion, the Sappers inflated them and took them to the point of embarkation. Each boat had to carry five infantrymen, with their arms and equipment, and three Sappers for paddling. The first wave set out at mid-day, and with it went Lieut. M. R. Rajwade, I.E. The boats came under fire when half-way across and an unsuccessful attempt was made to recall them. The crossing was therefore continued, though under increasingly heavy fire, until nearly half the battalion was committed. Men and boats were now being hit repeatedly. Many boats, out of control, drifted downstream with their loads of dead and wounded. Some grounded on sandbanks where the last of the wounded met their fate.

Meanwhile, those of the infantry who had succeeded in landing were engaged in a hand-to-hand fight with the Japanese in Myitson Village. Lieut. Rajwade remained all day, and during the following night, in the small bridgehead, collecting the survivors of 58 Field Company and arranging for the return of undamaged boats when this should become possible. Most of the boats, however, had been lost and ammunition was running low. Consequently, at 5.30 a.m. on February 2nd, it was decided to evacuate the bridgehead under cover of the morning mist and a smoke screen. Rajwade was one of the last to return. This he accomplished by swimming the wide river. He was rightly awarded the Military Cross, and several of his men received Military Medals. The following extract from *The Historical Records of The Buffs*, 1919-1948, regarding the first attempt to cross the Shweli River is worthy of note. "For the armed soldier, who has a chance to retaliate, the crossing of the river under such conditions was, to say the least of it, an extremely unpleasant experience; but for the Indian crews it was a cold-blooded task of sitting to be shot at, paddling, pushing and shoving off sandbanks, without the opportunity to shoot back. The conduct of these Madras Sappers was magnificent, and the survivors returned unflinchingly to make a second or even a third journey." 58 Field Company lost 9 men killed, 16 wounded and 13 missing, believed killed. The operation had been a failure, though redeemed by the heroism shown by all ranks. But the 36th Division was not to be denied, and a week later, a bridgehead was established successfully further downstream where 58 Field Company started a ferry service on February 10th. 30 Field Company (Bombay), under Major D. S. Wilson, R.E., was also present and ferried 2,000 men and 50 tons of stores and vehicles across in a single day. 58 Field Company was transferred to the further bank on February 15th. On March 1st, the Division resumed its advance towards Maymyo, and by April 10th, 58 Field Company was installed in that picturesque little hill station.

Although the 36th Division's task was important in the general scheme, the spearhead of the advance into Central Burma was undoubtedly the 19th Indian Division, under Major-General T. W. Rees, which we left on the far bank of the Chindwin after the crossings at Sittaung and Nanthanyit in mid-December. The role of the 19th Division was to cross the Irrawaddy north of Mandalay in order to draw on itself Japanese pressure which might otherwise be employed against us in a more vital area—an unenviable task as anyone will admit. The Division was to operate in the region south of the 36th Division which was coming down from the north to replace the withdrawing contingents of the Second Chindit Expedition. An Indian Sapper detachment had done fine work for the Chindits during the summer of 1944 on the great Indawgyi Lake to the west of Mogaung. It was concerned chiefly with building and operating a fleet of most peculiar craft to further the evacuation of sick and wounded by flying boats. The "Indawgyi Grand Fleet" boasted three squadrons, each of three "Dreadnoughts." These were large bamboo rafts composed of rubber Ranger boats encased in enormous tarpaulins and powered by 22 h.p. outboard motors at the stern. The Ranger boats were delivered by air, and each "Dreadnought" could carry 6 mules, 35 men and a couple of jeeps.[1]

On the 33rd Corps front, at the beginning of January 1945, the 19th Indian and 2nd British Divisions were racing towards Shwebo. The contest was won by the former which entered Shwebo on January 7th, one day ahead of its rival. The 2nd Division had crossed the Chindwin at Kalewa in the wake of the 11th East African Division, now resting in Assam. The rapid advance of the 19th Division was secured largely by the labours of its Engineer units. By December 20th, 29 Field Company had opened 76 miles of road to Pinbon, while 64 Field Company repaired bridges in rear. 64 Field Company then moved southwards to Pinlebu on the Mu River and built an "Elephant Bridge" (a causeway of logs) over a *chaung*. Christmas Day found the unit working on a Dakota airstrip at Kawlin, south of Wuntho. The main axis of the advance on Shwebo lay almost parallel to the Irrawaddy, and 64 Field Company was soon employed on building airstrips behind the leading brigades at

---

[1] "Indawgyi", by Major K. M. Robertson, R.E., appearing in *The R.E. Journal,* September 1948, pp. 217-230.

Tantabin, using the bulldozers of 327 Field Park Company. And here a story may be inserted of a derelict steam-roller discovered, lying on its side, between Pyingaing and Ye-u on the way to Shwebo. One of the Field Companies had two 4th Grade Engine Drivers who were left behind to get the roller upright and bring it to Ye-u where there was difficult bridging to be done. Three weeks later, the roller came puffing slowly in. When asked why they were so late, the drivers said that they had righted the roller and started it working in a few days but had been obliged to fire the boiler with brushwood gathered from the local jungle and for the first part of the trip they could not maintain sufficient steam pressure to move more than twenty yards at a time! Later, however, they had found some cut logs and were able to proceed at a steady speed of one mile an hour, which they thought was very creditable under the circumstances. Such persistance deserved its reward, and both men were immediately up-graded.

During the passage of the 33rd Corps across the dry belt of Central Burma, the Engineer units were often faced with problems of water-supply and an Army Order was published calling for any men who had had experience as water-diviners. The order caused some amusement, but several amateur "dowsers" came forward and sometimes gave useful help. For instance, a Field Engineer at 33rd Corps Headquarters, who said that he was a "dowser", advised the sinking of a Norton tube well at a certain spot in a dry *chaung* where a number of Sappers had already dug unsuccessfully, and within an hour the well yielded a plentiful supply of pure water. Against this happy result may be set the fact that Australian "dowsers" operating in the Sinai Desert during the First World War rarely found any subterranean supply. Was the success in Burma therefore merely a matter of chance, or did the Field Engineer possess a sixth sense? Who can say? In any case, fresh water was most welcome in Central Burma for many of the streams were useless for drinking purposes as the liquid was impregnated with purgative salts.

The Corps of Engineers had also to deal frequently with bomb disposal. A slab of guncotton detonated against the side of the bomb was the normal method of destruction. Between Shwebo and Sagaing there were a number of 500 lb. bombs buried in the slopes of road embankments. In a fox-hole close to each bomb squatted a Jap suicide-man whose job it was to detonate the bomb with a stone when a vehicle passed overhead. Fortunately, the presence of these bombs was usually detected before the transport came along and the Japanese suiciders were shot before they could blow up the vehicles and themselves.

The Divisional Engineers had often to prepare airstrips, though the greater part of such work was undertaken by 459 Forward Airfield Engineers which included the 21st Engineer Battalion and some Field Companies. As soon as a new airstrip was required, one or more Companies of the Engineer Battalion marked it out, preferably in open paddy fields, and then set to work to level the strip and clear away all obstructions with the help of native labour. The surface was disturbed as little as possible, and frequently the only levelling needed was the removal of the small earthen embankments marking the boundaries of fields. A strip 375 yards long and 30 yards wide could sometimes be made ready for use by light aircraft in a single day. On the other hand, a Dakota airstrip, 1,200 yards long and 50 yards wide, might require six days' work. After the landing ground had been levelled, the sides of the run-way were marked with wicker frames covered with parachute cloth, and a large white reversible "T" was placed in position to serve as a landing guide. These and other elaborations might occupy a week or more; but the pilots often did not wait for the finished article and as many as 300 landings and take-offs might be expected in 24 hours as soon as a light airstrip was usable with moderate safety. As the 33rd Corps progressed towards the Irrawaddy, more and more supplies were sent by air until finally it may be said that the very existence of the troops, let alone the success of the offensive, depended on air supply.

In the advance across Central Burma the Fourteenth Army had to adapt itself to a war of mobility in open country. Here, the tank came into its own. The 19th Division covered 140 miles in 28 days, and having taken Shwebo, pushed forward to cross the Irrawaddy. A diversionary crossing by the 98th Brigade, with 65 Field Company attached, was planned at Thabeikkyin, a few miles north-east of Shwebo, and assault boats and country craft for rafting were assembled there. A successful crossing was then made in spite of considerable shelling and bombing, and the 98th Brigade was installed in a small bridgehead on the east bank. The main crossing took place at Kyaukmyaung, east of Shwebo. Nobody was allowed down to the beach in daylight. During the night of January 15th/16th, with the help of 29 and 64 Field Companies, a battalion was paddled across, and after dark on the 17th, and again on the 18th, reinforcements and animals were ferried over on folding-boat rafts. An early reconnaissance at Yedaw, above Kyaukmyaung, had proved very difficult

owing to lack of boats. Only four were available at the moment, and these were leaking badly. An officer of 64 Field Company writes:—
"I remember that night quite well. It seemed much too light and the river had a horrible shimmering sheen. Two men went across first to reconnoitre and came back to report that there were Japs on the opposite bank. Two more boats were then sent and nothing more was heard for some time. Then, firing broke out immediately opposite to us and the attempt to cross there was postponed. The two boats returned about four hours later with exciting stories of Jap bunker positions. Three nights afterwards, everything was ready. Two Field Companies and the Assault Platoon of a Bridging Company were available. Another crossing site was selected above Yedaw. No one had ever seen this site by daylight, and after dark the boats were carried there for two miles by parties of Gurkhas. The first man to cross was an Infantry officer and I was to follow in another boat, each of us with two men. We were to flash a light back to say that all was clear and then the leading wave of the assault would come over. I remember feeling very frightened as I stepped into the three-men boat with two Sappers, but we reached the other side, 700 yards away, safely. About 9.0 p.m. the first wave crossed and we soon had a Company with us on the far bank. The second wave was half-way across when a light machine-gun and some rifles opened on them. However, firing soon stopped and by 7.0 a.m., before dawn, the whole battalion was across and the boats hidden." By a miracle, the enemy had been taken by surprise. Another battalion crossed during the following night and the bridgehead was made secure.

On January 19th, the first daylight crossing of the 19th Division took place, and with it went a platoon of 29 Field Company. After that, with the help of an increasing number of floating boats fitted with outboard motors, there was little difficulty and the crossing of more troops and stores proceeded steadily day by day. 429 Field Company (Madras), under Major G. W. Pinto, I.E., arrived from the 268th Brigade to assist in the ferrying. On the 24th, the bridgehead was moved down to Singu and then at last the enemy realized the position and bombarded the bridgehead with 70 guns. But he was too late. Ferrying by raft went on without intermission. On February 6th, 29 Field Company took across 8 Lee tanks and on the following day 16 Stuart tanks, and by February 16th, when it handed over the rafting to 431 Field Company of 459 Forward Airfield Engineers, the crossing of the 19th Indian Division at Singu may be said to have been completed. About ten days later, the Division broke out of the bridgehead in a triumphant progress southwards towards Mandalay. Major-General Rees had acted with great boldness and had accepted considerable risks; but he had succeeded in attracting enemy forces away from the region west of Mandalay where the main battles were to be fought.

Meanwhile, moving simultaneously across the Central Burma plains to the south of the line of advance of the 19th Indian Division, was the 2nd British Division which had relieved the 11th East African Division at Kalewa and had received orders to make for Ye-u. By January 9th, the Division was in Shwebo and then advanced towards the Irrawaddy south of Mandalay. It reached the river at Nzagun, about 10 miles east of the 20th Indian Division, and on February 23rd began its attempt to cross in the face of fierce opposition. The leading waves of men had their boats sunk under them, but others established a footing on the far bank, and after 72 hours of sustained effort, Major-General C. G. G. Nicholson had 6,000 men and 200 vehicles across the river. Thence the Division advanced towards Ava Fort, downstream of Mandalay, and captured it on March 17th before swinging south-westwards to clear the country in the direction of Myingyan and Meiktila. The operations of the 2nd British Division, however, do not really concern this narrative as no units of the Indian Engineers were present.

Parallel to the line taken by the 2nd British Division, and still further to the south, moved the 20th Indian Division under Major-General D. D. Gracey. The Divisional Engineers, under Lieut.-Colonel A. R. S. Lucas, R.E., comprised 92 Field Company (Bombay), 422 Field Company (Madras), 481 Field Company (Bombay) and 309 Field Park Company (Madras). The 32nd Brigade had begun to cross the Chindwin by ferry at Mawlaik early in December 1944 in order to contact the 2nd British Division southeast of Kalewa and capture Budalin. The remainder of the 20th Division followed the 2nd Division across the "Grub" Bridge at Kalewa and met the 32nd Brigade at Budalin, which was taken on January 10th after three weeks of bitter fighting. The Division then split into three brigade columns, the 32nd Brigade taking Monywa on January 22nd while the 100th Brigade occupied Myinmu and the 80th Brigade cleared the area around the confluence of the Chindwin and Irrawaddy. The whole Division then concentrated for a crossing of the Irrawaddy at Myinmu, a few miles downstream of the crossing point allotted to the 2nd British Division.

Major J. H. Clark, R.E., gives the following account of the experiences of 92 Field Company with the 32nd Brigade.[1] "November saw the Brigade setting out on a pack basis into the hills south of Imphal along the Mombi track. We debouched into the Kabaw Valley and proceeded south-eastwards to Mawlaik which had recently been cleared of the enemy by the East Africans. On December 1st I reconnoitred for a crossing of the Chindwin. We had only thirteen outboard motors in our equipment, but a dozen Ranger boats were soon dropped to us by parachute. Downstream of Mawlaik, the river ran in several channels, so a site was selected upstream of the place where the river was 600 yards wide and clear of sandbanks. The current ran at 5 knots. The Brigade Group normally comprised about 5,000 men with 1,500 animals and 30 tons of stores, but it was now increased by the arrival of an additional battalion of Gurkhas. Two rafts were improvised with empty oil-drums and palm trees, each with several motors attached. Other motors were fixed to native craft, and a workshop was started to keep the motors repaired. On December 2nd, the 1st Northants established a bridgehead and pushed out patrols, and by December 4th the whole battalion was across and on its way into the hills to the east. The remainder of the Brigade was across by December 7th, and 92 Field Company followed on the 8th. To get the mules across, each animal was led to the rear of a Ranger boat containing two Sappers and eight infantrymen. Its load and harness had already been dumped on a raft. The inflated boat was then paddled out from the bank at a steeply sloping place until the mule's head could be hauled up on to the rear bulwark and held there securely so that it could breathe freely. The swimming of the mule helped the boat forward, though some skill was needed to steer the animal in the right direction. After we had put the 32nd Brigade across, the Company marched up the bed of a *chaung* for a week. The country was very dry and arid and there was much difficulty with water supply. We debouched into the plains near Budalin, captured the place and moved on to take Alon and Monywa and force a crossing of the Irrawaddy. The 32nd Brigade Group had marched 230 miles in 6 weeks on a pack basis from Imphal to Budalin where it met its transport which had come down the Chindwin on rafts.

Meanwhile, 422 Field Company, under Major R. T. Gerrard, R.E., and 481 Field Company, under Major M. I. Pritchard, R.E., had

---

[1] Notes by Major J. H. Clark, R.E., dated February 2nd, 1954.

been assisting the main body of the 20th Division at the Kalewa crossing. Previously, 422 Company had been employed on the Kabaw Valley road and cutting a track through virgin jungle towards Mawlaik. While one of the platoons was bridging a *chaung*, the famous "Elephant Bill" (Lieut.-Colonel J. H. Williams) arrived and provided six elephants to speed up the work.[1] The bridge, which was 180 feet in length, soon took shape. A Danaram saw was used for felling trees and cutting the timber into lengths, while the elephants pulled the logs to the water's edge and placed the road-bearers neatly in their correct places.

422 Field Company built rafts at Kalewa and loaded them with stores to be taken downstream to Maukkadaw, three days' journey. The first fleet of five rafts started at the end of December with a flag, consisting of a Sapper's pair of pants, waving proudly in the breeze from the top of a boat-hook erected as a mast on the leading craft. As the fleet neared Maukkadaw in a fast current, the commander saw an officer waving frantically on the bank, so he pulled in to the shore to get berthing instructions. He was annoyed to find, however, that the officer, who was a keen fisherman, merely wished to warn the fleet to keep clear of his lines! For the next six weeks, the Company continued river transport and ferrying work at Maukkadaw and then moved to Alon, where it arrived on January 21st while the battle for Monywa was raging four miles away. Great was its disappointment when told that the arrangements for crossing the Irrawaddy would devolve on the other two Field Companies of the 20th Division. 422 Field Company was detailed to make airstrips and send out "bunker-busting" parties with the infantry and tanks. During one of these expeditions it lost Lieut. E. J. Wright, R.E., who was mortally wounded in a gallant attack on February 12th. The infantry had been unable to subdue the enemy snipers and consequently the Sappers could not get on to the bunker which was being attacked. Wright then seized a bee-hive charge and rushed forward alone. He reached the top, but as he was placing the charge, a sniper shot him through the head and he died a few hours later in hospital. Both 92 and 481 Field Companies had been engaged since December in ferrying at Maukkadaw after their stores and jeeps had come down by river from Kalewa, and they were very busy also with training and with preparations for the great task which lay ahead.

---

[1] *History of* 422 *Q.V's O. Madras Indian Field Company, R.I.E.,* by Major D. W. McGrath, R.E. Lieut.-Colonel J. H. Williams is the author of *Elephant Bill* (1950) and *Bandoola* (1953).

The crossing of the Irrawaddy at Myinmu by the 20th Indian Division was a fine achievement. In order to distract attention from the main bridgehead, the 32nd Brigade made a subsidiary crossing near Myaung, a few miles to the west. 92 Field Company was responsible for the ferrying which had been rehearsed at Monywa on the Chindwin. On February 9th, Major Clark reconnoitred the near bank after dark. It was high and covered with elephant grass, but there were good lines of approach along some dry watercourses. On the 10th the approaches were prepared for vehicle traffic, and on the 11th the floating equipment and stores were moved up to the assault area after dark. As most of the available boats were required for the main crossing at Myinmu, 92 Company improvised a raft to carry mules, anti-tank guns, jeeps and signal cable. The raft had five piers, each of two Jap timber pontoons found at Monywa, with old rails as road-bearers and a decking of planks. At 7.0 p.m. on February 12th, the available equipment was launched and building started. The light equipment consisted of three tows, each of a Jap steel boat with two 22 h.p. motors attached to the stern, behind which were towed ten Ranger or Assault boats in two files. Each of the tugs was manned by five Sappers. Soon after 11.0 p.m. the first flight crossed almost unopposed, and by dawn on the 13th, the greater part of the 1st Northants were on the far bank despite considerable trouble with the motors. Then the enemy began to re-act with artillery fire and it was arranged that a smoke-screen should be laid down before dawn. The first flight by daylight started well, but the engines failed in mid-stream and the boats began to drift down the river helpless. The smoke cleared quickly and left them in full view of the enemy. Lieut. H. R. Balston, R.E., immediately volunteered to take another tow across to rescue them; but by the time he reached them, they were under heavy fire and he was shot through the arm and one of his engines was put out of action. He continued, however, to the far bank where the men took cover while a mortar detachment tried to silence the enemy's fire. The battle continued throughout the day, but after dark the isolated troops were able to move upstream into the main bridgehead. Four more flights came across in boats and the raft made several trips. By the morning of February 14th, the Northants and a wing of another battalion were across, and also guns, jeeps, mules and stores; and on the following night, while a violent battle raged on the far bank, two rafts and three tows of boats were in constant use. One of the

Ferrying armour and transport across the Irrawaddy

tows unfortunately came right into the battle and was sunk. Attempts to ferry by daylight were then abandoned, though night ferrying continued. On the 16th, the beaches were under accurate shell fire all day, and another big battle commenced on the far bank. Rafting ceased altogether and the Sappers manned the perimeter on the near bank. February 17th was spent by them in repairing damaged boats. On the 18th, however, rafting was resumed by daylight and was continued during the 19th in spite of shell fire which caused a number of casualties. Among these was Major J. H. Clark who was wounded in the leg and evacuated. Crossings continued on a decreasing scale until February 27th when the entire 32nd Brigade was able to leave the bridgehead for the advance towards Kyaukse, south of Mandalay.

481 Field Company (Bombay) was the Engineer unit chiefly responsible for ferrying the bulk of the 20th Division across the Irrawaddy during the main crossing at Myinmu. Due, probably, to the diversion afforded by the 32nd Brigade, this operation was very successful, though made under considerable difficulties. The date of the crossing had been fixed for the night of February 12th/13th. 422 Field Company, under Major D. W. McGrath, R.E., worked on the approaches through long elephant grass and laid tapes to the beaches. The bulldozer drivers of 309 Field Park Company assisted by making ramps down to the beaches. 481 Field Company then began the ferrying using Ranger boats at first and, later on, rafts of folding boats for the infantry and others of country boats for the jeeps and stores. The crossing continued steadily during the 13th and 14th while the small bridgehead was gradually expanded. 422 Field Company went over to lay Sommerfeld track across the wide belt of sand on the far shore. The 100th Brigade was holding on grimly in the bridgehead though losing rather heavily from shelling and bombing. Slowly but steadily the bridgehead was expanded, and with this expansion the Sappers of 422 Field Company were called upon to make many tracks through elephant grass to the forward positions. Snipers lurked in the grass, and direction could be maintained only by compass bearings. Bulldozers were useless for making these tracks because they would raise dust and bring down enemy artillery fire. Consequently, the grass was cut by hand and laid flat on the dusty surface. After 481 Field Company had ferried across some Stuart tanks, the expansion of the Myinmu bridgehead was accelerated. Neighbouring villages were cleared of the enemy; and on February 27th, when the main bridgehead was 8 miles long and $2\frac{1}{2}$ miles deep, the 80th Brigade broke out and made for Kyaukse

in company with the 32nd Brigade from Myaung. On March 2nd, the 20th Division established contact with the 2nd British Division on its left and thereafter advanced rapidly, mopping up Japanese remnants and playing havoc with the enemy's lines of communication. Myotha was taken on March 12th; Wundwin and its large dumps on the 21st. Two days later, a brigade turned northwards and destroyed a large Japanese force at Kume, thus cutting the main enemy escape route from Mandalay to the south. On March 30th, the other two brigades took Kyaukse after a week of severe fighting. The road and railway line of communication from Mandalay to Rangoon was thus severed at yet another point. The 20th Divisional Engineers were fortunate to share in these victorious operations towards which they had contributed much in blood and sweat.

The time has now arrived to deal with the most important and decisive operations undertaken during the invasion of Central Burma. These were to be carried out by the 4th Indian Corps under Lieut.-General F. W. Messervy. At the outset the Corps comprised the 7th and 17th Indian Divisions and the 255th Tank Brigade. With the 7th Division, under Major-General G. C. Evans, were 62 Field Company (Madras), 77 Field Company (Bengal), 421 Field Company (Madras), and 331 Field Park Company (Madras), the C.R.E. being Lieut.-Colonel T. Wright, R.E. With the 17th Division, under Major-General D. T. Cowan, were 60 Field Company (Madras), 70 Field Company (Bengal), the Tehri-Garhwal Field Company and 414 Field Park Company (Bengal), and the C.R.E. was Lieut.-Colonel T. H. F. Foulkes, R.E. 36 Field Squadron (Madras) was attached to the 255th Tank Brigade. The role assigned to the 4th Corps was to make a surprise crossing of the Irrawaddy and to strike directly at the nodal point of the Japanese road, rail and air communications and supply organization at Meiktila in rear of their forces guarding Mandalay or opposing the 2nd, 19th, 20th and 36th Divisions. The enemy would thus be caught between the anvil of the 4th Corps and the hammer of the 33rd Corps descending from the north. The plan was daring because, as already explained, it involved the secret transfer of the 4th Corps across the rear of the 33rd Corps. Elaborate deception was necessary and wireless silence. The movement of the 4th Corps was headed by the 28th East African Brigade, which did not belong to the 11th East African Division. By employing this brigade south of Mandalay it was hoped to deceive the enemy into believing that he was still fighting the 33rd Corps and that the 4th Corps was still operating in the north. The fact also that the 19th Division, formerly with the 4th Corps, was now pushing towards the Irrawaddy well to the north of Mandalay, might help to confirm this belief. Parachutists were dropped across the Irrawaddy where no offensive was intended, and many such areas were also bombed. Yet had it not been for the Chindwin River line of supply it is doubtful whether the transfer of the 4th Corps across the rear of the 33rd Corps would have been feasible in spite of the benefits of air supply, nor its rapid advance to the Irrawaddy. The 4th Corps was to cross the river at Nyaungu, near the ancient city of Pagan, while feints were made at Pakokku upstream and Chauk downstream. There was to be no preliminary bombardment nor air-strike. Surprise was the essence of the whole undertaking. The 7th Indian Division would cross first. Then, two mechanized brigades of the 17th Division would follow and rush upon Meiktila where the 5th Division, coming mostly by air from Imphal, would take a hand.[1]

At the end of January 1945, the 4th Corps was moving down the Gangaw Valley faced with the problem of traversing a narrow hill-road into the Irrawaddy Valley. From Kalemyo to Pakokku, some 230 miles, the road was quite unsuitable for the passage of scores of tanks and hundreds of bridging lorries, and for the first 140 miles to Tilin it was deep in dust. In the hill section from Tilin to Pauk, the gradients were severe and the corners designed only for jeeps. Any bridging lorries which broke down had to be pushed over the side or halted for several days at a passing place. The traffic was so dense that the Sappers working on the road had often to be supplied with rations by air because they could not fetch them themselves. The units available for the work were the 7th Divisional Engineers, 4th Corps Troops Engineers (2 Faridkot, 75 and 424 Field Companies and 305 Field Park Company), 36 Field Squadron, the 12th Engineer Battalion and an East African Field Company. This was a strong cadre, yet it was insufficient to bring the road up to the necessary standard when little assistance could be given by other arms. The problems of the advance to the Irrawaddy were greater than those of the actual crossing because the current at Nyaungu was sluggish, and the river, though wide, could be crossed easily by loaded rafts without fear of grounding. The allotment of

---

[1] The 5th Indian Division was commanded by Major-General D. F. W. Warren until February 11th, 1945, when he was killed in a plane accident. He was succeeded by Major-General E. C. Mansergh.

Engineer duties was that the 7th Divisional Engineers, with 36 Field Squadron and the East African unit, made the road passable for 3-ton lorries, while behind them came the Corps Engineers and the Engineer Battalion improving it so as to take tank-transporters and repairing or by-passing any weak bridges. Although the crossing site had its advantages, it was by no means ideal. On the near side there was a stretch of soft sand, 600 yards wide, ending with a vertical drop of 4 feet to the water-level. On the far side there was a slope of hard clay with deep water close in shore, but beyond the slope was a vertical rise of considerable height. These conditions applied only to a length of about half a mile along the banks, beyond which the river ran in many channels with intervening sandbanks. Landing stages and equipment had therefore to be concentrated in a small area and offered a perfect target for air attack.[1]

Several airstrips were needed urgently down the Gangaw Valley for the maintenance of the 4th Corps. One was completed at Kan during the first half of January and another at Tilin. On February 1st, an air-head was started at Sinthe, a few miles below Pauk on the Yaw tributary, and the Forward Airfield Engineers built a strip there in four days. Others followed quickly. The completion of the Sinthe air-head was vital to the success of the whole operation and into it was flown the Sommerfeld track and additional folding boat equipment needed for the crossing as well as supplies and ammunition. Within a few days, 500 tons of stores were being delivered in 24 hours. An advanced airstrip was provided on February 16th at Myitche to complete the chain of air supply.[2] Our mastery of the air prevented any serious interference with these activities.

Major D. De Souza describes some of the experiences of 421 Field Company of the 7th Divisional Engineers during the approach to the Irrawaddy. "Six days before D-Day", he writes, "motors and serviceable boats were loaded onto very ancient bridging lorries. The convoy was large and heavy and it had 140 miles to cover. It set off with a Sapper escort and fervent prayers for its safe arrival. The journey was to take several days along a narrow and tortuous road and the traffic already moving forward was prodigious. Two days later, the Field Companies were briefed as to their tasks and a composite Assault Company was formed from all Engineer units.

---

[1] "The Crossing of the Irrawaddy by 4 Corps, February 1945", by Colonel A. Murray, appearing in *The R.E. Journal*, March 1947, pp. 19-28.

[2] "Engineer Aspect of 4 Corps Operations, Imphal to Rangoon", by Major W. W. Boggs, R.E.

The Companies then moved forward to the assembly area. The Divisional Engineer convoy arrived there in fine style but found it only partially cleared of Japs, so a new area was allotted and the Engineer units assembled there. Equipment was off-loaded, checked, repaired and loaded again. After dark, two days before D-Day, the enormous convoy moved forward again along a narrow, sandy track to the forward assembly area near the beaches. It was a sleepless night for everyone. The sand did its evil job only too well and some of the heavy lorries failed to arrive before dawn. They remained camouflaged throughout the day, ready to move to the beaches the next night. The final briefings and study of air photos were carried out by the Assault Company, and reconnaissances of the beaches and approach roads were made."

The responsibility for the Engineer arrangements for the actual crossing of the 7th Indian Division at Nyaungu on February 14th, 1945, devolved on Lieut.-Colonel T. Wright as C.R.E. Topographically, Nyaungu was an unlikely crossing place, and it was therefore only weakly held by the enemy although the approaches were under close observation from cliffs beyond it. It appears that the Japanese imagined that only one division was advancing down the Gangaw Valley and that it would exploit southwards towards the Chauk and Yenangyaung oilfields instead of crossing the river. This belief was fostered by the despatch of the East African Brigade to Pauk and onwards to a point opposite Chauk, and from the heavy resistance offered by the enemy in this region it is evident that he swallowed the bait. The Irrawaddy crossing was to be made in three stages. First, the capture of Pakokku and the concentration of the 4th Corps in the crossing area. Next, the establishment of a bridgehead on the far bank; and finally, the massing of the Corps on that bank. The crossing would be followed by a lightning thrust to the Meiktila-Thazi area with the help of air-borne reinforcements and supplies and all available armour. The enemy forces in Central Burma could then be destroyed between the 4th and 33rd Corps. The 7th Division was to establish a bridgehead through which the 17th Division and armoured forces would pour for the advance on Meiktila. The 5th Division, previously held in reserve, would be brought forward rapidly to help in the capture of Meiktila.

By the evening of February 13th, Lieut.-Colonel Wright had succeeded in concentrating his Engineer units and equipment as close to the selected beaches as he was allowed to go. There were three beaches. "A" Beach opposite Nyaungu with a watergap of 1,200 yards; "B" Beach, further upstream, with a gap of 1,800 yards; and "C" Beach, still further upstream, where the width was 3,700 yards owing to a wide area of sand in the middle. The approach to the river at "B" was fairly good, but at "C" there was 500 yards of sand on which no preparatory work could be done until the far bank was cleared of the enemy. Although "A" Beach was the most attractive since it had the shortest water-gap, it was decided that it should not be used for the initial crossing. The choice fell on "C" where a company of infantry was to be paddled across by night in assault boats. Once established, it was to be followed, under cover of darkness, by two more companies carried in folding or assault boats equipped with outboard motors. These craft would make for a point on the far side opposite "B" Beach and then return to that beach to pick up the rest of the battalion.

The Sapper companies had a prodigious task during the night to coax the bridging lorries along the 1½ miles of track leading towards the river. It took five hours of unremitting toil. At one moment, Wright almost despaired of reaching the bank before daybreak. And this was by no means the end of the story, for as he approached the bank he was confronted with a final obstacle of more than a quarter of a mile of the softest sand in Asia, across which the assault craft had to be man-handled to the launching points at "C" Beach because no preparatory work had been permitted. "The Engineers of both the 7th and 17th Divisions combined to support the 7th Division in the initial task of crossing the river" writes Pearson.[1] "Work on the approaches had not been heavy although the sandy soil was soon cut up by the bridging lorries. On February 13th, 77 Field Company started work on "C" Beach, assembling folding and assault boats, while 70 Field Company improved the route to "B" and "C" Beaches with bamboo matting and timber. The lorries were strung out along the narrow Kanhla-Myitche road, slowly bringing their loads to "C" Beach which the last vehicle reached at 1.0 a.m. on February 14th."

The first assault troops—a Company of South Lancashires— embarked in folding boats at "C" Beach and were paddled by Sapper crews across the dark waters under a moonless sky. They landed unobserved and took up a position to cover the arrival of reinforcements. The next flight, of two more Companies, followed in assault boats fitted with outboard motors, while our planes roared overhead

---

[1] *Brief History of the K.G.V's Own Bengal Sappers and Miners Group, R.I.E. (August 1939 - July 1946)*, by Lieut. G. Pearson, R.E., p. 123.

to drown the noise of the engines. Dawn, however, was already breaking and the boats were still 200 yards from the far bank when they were revealed to the enemy in the pearly light stealing across the water. There had been some delay because many of the outboard motors had refused to start and others had failed in mid-stream. Japanese machine-gunners opened fire from caves in the face of the cliffs and the men in the boats suffered a number of casualties. Several boats were sunk and all on board killed, wounded or drowned. A few crippled boats managed to struggle slowly back to their starting point, where the wounded were landed and the engines re-fuelled for a second attempt. This was made, a few hours later, by the 4/15th Punjabis. The enemy was now fully aware that a major crossing was intended. With maddening sluggishness the boats nosed their way forward. It was a long trip—4,300 yards in all owing to the diagonal nature of the crossing from "C" Beach to a point downstream on the opposite bank. The enemy's fire increased in volume and intensity from both front and flank. Two boats grounded on a sandbank near the far shore, but the infantry waded to the bank. Other boats arrived and soon the men were swarming up the cliffs to join the South Lancashires holding out bravely in their small position. More and more boats followed, all heavily laden with assault troops, until boats were going both ways in continuous streams. By nightfall, three battalions had crossed and the rafting of vehicles and ammunition was in hand. Then came the tanks. 36 Field Squadron had built three Class 40 Bailey rafts, and with these the unit ferried across six Sherman tanks of the 255th Tank Brigade. Smaller rafts and landing stages were now being built at "B" Beach, but a landing stage on the far shore was not ready when the Shermans appeared there. Nothing daunted, the drivers drove the tanks straight off the rafts on to the bank to save time, fortunately without damage to the rafts or themselves, and within the next few minutes the tanks roared into action.

A few extracts from the War Diary of 62 Field Company, under Major R. S. A. Pryde, R.E., may be quoted to show the strenuous nature of the work on D-Day. "Lieut. S. E. M. Goodall, R.E., and one Sapper were in the first wave which came under heavy fire. It succeeded, though with severe casualties. 62 Company was delayed until the Punjab Battalion was across. Major Pryde and Lieut. W. Milton, R.E., accompanied the Punjabis to reconnoitre the far beach. On arrival there at 11.00 hrs, the Company began to build landing stages for rafts, search for mines and make exit roads. By evening everything was well organized, and men, stores, tanks and transport were pouring across and being cleared quickly. The gallantry shown by our two representatives in the assault wave makes thrilling reading. Lieut. Goodall piloted his boat towards the shore under a hail of fire which followed him as he tried frantically to dodge it. A burst caught his boat, killing all but three of his sixteen passengers, smashing his left arm and wrecking the engine. He tried to paddle the boat to the shore but could not manage it, so the few survivors left the boat and began to swim back a mile to their own shore. How Goodall did so with a stump of a left arm and weak from loss of blood is beyond comprehension. The Sapper with him had been wounded in the head and had not sufficient strength to continue after swimming about a hundred yards, so he turned back towards the enemy shore and made for a boat that was drifting downstream with its driver dead and the others dead or wounded. He boarded the boat and, though close to the enemy positions, tried for half an hour to start the engine. In the end, he succeeded, and, four miles down the river, brought his boat and the dead and wounded to the near shore. His action was described by the Commanding Officer of a British Battalion who witnessed it as one of the bravest he had ever seen."

On February 15th (D+1 Day) the splutter and roar of engines started again at daylight. Heavy rafts with more Sherman tanks crossed safely, and a steady stream of smaller rafts brought men, ammunition and mules from "B" Beach which was now coming into use. Meanwhile, some of the Sapper units were hard at work on the approach roads to "A" Beach which was to operate when the enemy had been driven from the vicinity. The Nyaungu bridgehead was already securely held, thanks to the gallantry of the assault troops and the feints at crossing which had been made at Pakokku on February 13th by the 7th Division and at Chauk by the 28th East African Brigade. A reconnaissance of the river banks on the 15th confirmed the plan to conduct further crossings at "A" Beach and to transfer all equipment gradually downstream to that point. Early on the 16th, the C.A.G.R.E. assumed responsibility for the crossings at "A" Beach, having under his command the 7th Divisional Engineers (62, 77 and 421 Field Companies and 331 Field Park Company), 60 and 70 Field Companies of the 17th Divisional Engineers, the 4th Corps Troops Engineers (2 Faridkot, 75 and 424 Field Companies and 305 Field Park Company), 36 Field Squadron, and 854 Bridging Company of Army Troops Engineers. These units were joined later by the 12th Engineer Battalion and a

Indian Troops in action at Seywa during the advance to Meiktila

Mechanical Equipment Platoon. All were not present on February 15th but the cadre was soon completed.

February 16th and 17th were somewhat disappointing days at "A" Beach. Sommerfeld track for the approaches should have arrived on D-Day, but although Dakotas and Commandos landed continuously on the forward airstrips, no track appeared for some time, and when eventually it began to arrive it was found to be deficient in pickets and other stores required for laying it. Infantry working parties scoured the adjacent villages for materials while bulldozers and teams of men hauled the bridging vehicles across the sand to the water's edge. By nightfall on the 18th, there were sufficient landing stages and rafts at "A" Beach for ferrying to begin on the following day with the help of the rafts previously operating from "B" and "C" Beaches. A supply of Sommerfeld track had come also and was being laid on the approach roads. Some impatience had been shown because of the delays which had occurred, although these could not be attributed to any lack of energy or foresight on the part of the Engineer units. This was nothing new, and to illustrate the point one may quote a story related by Major-General E. H. W. Cobb who was then B.G.S. 4th Corps.[1] Cobb writes that before the Corps reached the Irrawaddy there was a shortage of Bailey bridging and perforated steel planking for rafting and approaches, and that Lieut.-General F. W. Messervy, the Corps Commander, was continually asking Brigadier W. W. Boggs, his Chief Engineer, when it was going to arrive. At last, to Boggs' delight, news came that plentiful supplies were on the way by air, so he went to the airfield to watch the unloading of fifty Dakotas. The doors were opened and unloading began. Alas, there was no Engineer equipment whatever! Nothing was visible except hundreds of drums of crude oil which had been substituted at the last moment in order to lay the dust on airstrips. "Useful, no doubt, to pour on troubled waters" remarked the disconsolate Boggs as he pictured his next interview with the impatient Corps Commander!

However, the delays and difficulties of the first few days at Nyaungu were soon over, and while the Sapper units were therè, more than

---

[1] Notes by Major-General E. H. W. Cobb, c.b., c.b.e., dated February 20th, 1954. Brigadier Cobb was B.G.S. 4th Corps from December 1944 to November 1945. Afterwards, he commanded the 33rd Brigade of the 7th Indian Division in Bangkok and Malaya until December 1946. As a junior officer he had served for many years with the Bengal Sappers and Miners.

20,000 vehicles were ferried across. Night work was abandoned, but a 12-hour day was the rule, and woe betide those responsible if the first flight of rafts had not set out by 6.15 a.m. Eight landing stages were in use on each bank, and 1,000 vehicles often made the trip in a single day. And what vehicles they were! As a truck or lorry broke down it was converted into a trailer to be towed behind a stronger specimen. There were literally hundreds of such lame ducks to fill most of the limited deck space on the rafts. The competition among the Sapper units engaged in ferrying soon became terrific. Each raft flew its Company "House Flag", and each Company established its "Shipping Office" on the beach. Notices appeared such as "Don't waste time. Travel by the Red Line", or "Quickest and safest by the Blue Line". Another notice extolled the virtues of "The Irrawaddy Steamship and Transport Company", and a large board, labelled "Form at a Glance", showed the progress day by day in what was known as "The Irrawaddy Regatta". The scene resembled Margate on a Bank Holiday, but with this difference that work and not pleasure filled every hour. During the month that followed D-Day, the entire 4th Corps was ferried across the Irrawaddy —three divisions, the Corps troops, and all their transport and supplies. It is said that the record number of crossings in a single day was held by 62 Field Company; but if so, the other units could not have been far behind.

Once across the Irrawaddy, the nature of the engineer problems changed. The 4th Corps was now in a dry belt and the roads were good. Sufficient water could be secured by digging in the beds of *chaungs*, though the issue had to be carefully supervized. The *chaungs* themselves were crossed on causeways made with brushwood and toddy palms because Sommerfeld track was scarce owing to lack of transport. There were few enemy obstacles. The Japanese seemed to rely chiefly on buried bombs and shells, which were easily detected and disarmed. Thus the leading troops of the victorious 4th Corps rushed almost unhindered towards Meiktila, led by the mechanized 48th and 63rd Brigades of the 17th Division and the 255th Tank Brigade. These brigades were ordered to capture Taungtha and Mahlaing, seize an airstrip north-west of Meiktila for the fly-in of the 99th Brigade, isolate, and if possible capture, Meiktila, and finally occupy Thazi beyond it. On February 24th, they took Taungtha, and on the following day, Mahlaing, and on the 26th they seized an airstrip at Thabutkon, 15 miles north-west of Meiktila where the 99th Brigade began to arrive by air on the 27th. The main body of the 4th Corps was then driving on towards Meiktila where some of the most important Japanese airfields in Burma were situated. If these were lost, the whole structure of the enemy's defence of Central Burma would probably collapse.

About 13,000 Japanese soldiers had been hurriedly assembled in and about Meiktila, of whom 4,000 were inside the town. The approaches to it from the west and south were very difficult, being narrowed by large lakes which, with numerous irrigation channels, hampered the use of tanks. Nevertheless, at dawn on February 28th, 1945, the assault on Meiktila was begun from all points of the compass, and by nightfall, after very heavy fighting, the town was surrounded. Three days of hand-to-hand combat ensued, the Japanese fighting to the death in the narrow streets and alleys; but by March 4th, the greater part of the town, and the main airfield on its eastern side, were in our hands. A few days later, when the battle was over, 2,000 enemy dead were counted. Only 47 prisoners were taken, most of them wounded. A story about General Slim, who was present at Meiktila, may be included here. The General was most particular about wireless security, and so, when calling up a certain battalion during the attack, he began by saying "Hullo, hullo! This is Number Nine, the very big Number Nine". The C.O. was mistified, so Slim continued "Hullo, hullo! This is Bill, the Thin Man, speaking". To the horror of those around him, the irate C.O. shouted back "And who the Hell *is* the Thin Man?" No one was more amused than the Army Commander himself, for he had the keenest sense of humour.

The enemy reacted strongly to the loss of Meiktila. A Japanese division advanced from the north and north-west and a regiment moved up from the south, while all available artillery was massed in the area. The enemy re-occupied Taungtha, thus blocking the arrival of 5,000 vehicles, and fought hard also to regain control of the main airfield at Meiktila. General Slim's nearest reserve was the 5th Indian Division, far away in Assam, and so the 9th Brigade was ordered forthwith to Meiktila. It came by air from Palel and landed between March 15th and 18th in time to resist a strong enemy counter-attack. The struggle at Meiktila did not end until March 28th when the last Japanese were killed or driven off. As General Slim once remarked, they were indeed "the most formidable fighting insects on earth". The loss of Meiktila was a devastating blow to General Kimura. He had diverted troops too late to save the situation and in so doing had laid open to the 19th Indian Division the road to Mandalay.

Engineer duties at Meiktila were prosaic though useful. The Field Companies were involved occasionally in street fighting, but normally they were employed on defence work, lifting mines, providing water supplies and sending out parties with mobile columns. Work on the defences included the improvement of communications, minor bridging, the construction of command posts and shelters, and the provision of protection for guns. They levelled many enemy bunkers and buried the enemy dead with their bulldozers. Last, but not least, they completed four additional airstrips, and when the infantry were called away they took their share in manning the perimeters of the various 'Boxes'.

The capture of Mandalay followed close on the heels of the first entry into Meiktila. It was the privilege of the 19th Indian Division, which we left on the far side of the Irrawaddy after the crossing at Singu in January 1945. On February 26th, the Division began to push southwards, demoralising the enemy by the speed of its advance which was made with powerful air support. By March 5th, a bridgehead had been established over the Magyi Chaung, the last natural barrier before Mandalay. Japanese positions about Madaya were assaulted and captured, and on March 9th the forward elements entered Mandalay City. Siege was laid immediately to Mandalay Hill, a rocky eminence, about 800 feet high and covered with pagodas and temples, which dominates the north-east sector of the city. South-west of the hill lay Fort Dufferin. This was a large area enclosed by solid masonry walls 20 feet high, backed by 60 feet of earth and encircled by a moat about 70 yards wide. Mandalay Hill was captured on March 11th after severe fighting. The city was then cleared, and three days later, Fort Dufferin was invested. On the 16th, several air attacks were made on the massive walls with little effect. Medium artillery also failed to breach them. However, another air-strike having made a small opening, an infantry assault was attempted by night. It was repulsed, and three more assaults on March 18th met with a similar fate. An attempt to cross the moat early on March 19th failed because the water was choked with weeds. Later that day, three planes carrying 2,000 lb. bombs managed to blow a 15-feet hole in the wall by using a special technique. The bombs were released at a low level, ricochetted off the water, and exploded against the masonry. At last, on March 20th, our assault troops forced an entry, only to find that the bulk of the defenders had vanished. A few suicide squads remained, but these were gradually eliminated. On March 21st, 1945, Mandalay was officially declared to be clear of

65 Field Company opening the gates of Fort Dufferin at Mandalay, March 20th, 1945

the enemy. The 19th ("Dagger") Division had delivered the *coup de grace* to Japanese prestige in Burma. The ancient Burmese capital had fallen. The battle of annihilation in the Mandalay Plain was in its closing stages, and the 33rd Corps was driving the remnants of three enemy divisions eastwards into the Shan States or southwards down the Rangoon road.

The 19th Divisional Engineers did trojan work in the advance to Mandalay and the siege operations which followed. At the Magyi Chaung, 64 and 65 Field Companies laid a corduroy road and bridged a deep channel to maintain the speed of the advance. North of Madaya, a platoon of 29 Field Company branched off eastwards with the 62nd Brigade to occupy the hill-station of Maymyo while another accompanied the 98th Brigade in the main advance. This platoon sent a party forward to reconnoitre Fort Dufferin. The men cut through barbed wire fences and crawled through long grass between the moat and the wall and afterwards returned to make a second reconnaissance to ascertain, if possible, the actual thickness of the wall, but heavy fire necessitated their withdrawal. On March 10th, when 64 Field Company had reached the outskirts of the city, a demolition party was sent to the top of Mandalay Hill to assist in its capture. They used bee-hive charges to blast holes through the concrete roofs of strong-points so that the infantry could finish off the enemy inside with grenades. The fight for Mandalay Hill was a bloody one and 64 Field Company took part in several assaults.

During the eight-day siege of Fort Dufferin, most of the Engineer work was done at night. 29 Field Company moved into the city to build a light airstrip on the Race Course. 327 Field Park Company, with the help of 29 and 64 Field Companies, prepared scaling ladders in case the walls had to be surmounted in the old-fashioned style. 65 Field Company was as usual well to the fore, and on March 18th a small detachment from the unit carried out a daring reconnaissance. On the northern side of Fort Dufferin there was a sewerage tunnel which ran under the moat and the wall and emerged among some trees inside the enclosure. Captain R. W. T. Britten, R.E., and Subedar Pappala Yakub went forward to find out whether troops could enter the Fort through this tunnel. They waded through two feet of filth, dragging behind them a tracing tape as a communication cord with their men outside, and actually penetrated into the Fort, but it was decided that the sewer was not suitable for assaulting infantry and the project was abandoned. Britten was awarded the Military Cross and Yakub the M.B.E.

When news was received at 1.0 p.m. on March 20th that the Japanese had gone, the Sappers cleared the rubble away from the gates of battered Fort Dufferin, and their C.R.E., Lieut.-Colonel F. M. Hill, made a triumphant entry in his jeep, the first vehicle to arrive. The troops streamed in amid general rejoicings, and the Sappers built a platform of Bailey bridging equipment with a silver-painted telegraph pole as a flagstaff for the hoisting of the Union Jack by General Slim. Then they set to work to repair railway lines, clear away debris and lift enemy mines. Mandalay was a sorry sight—a travesty of the picturesque city of King Thebaw's day—and the Field Companies were glad to leave it in rotation for a short rest at Maymyo. Before transfer to Meiktila, 327 Field Park Company had the satisfaction of bringing in the first railway train since the evacuation in 1942. The locomotive, though riddled with bullet holes, had been successfully repaired and drew the train in fine style.

The flag was now about to fall for the race to Rangoon. It was realized fully that this was a gamble, and that if the fates were against us and we could not reach the city before the monsoon burst in full force, we might have to withdraw towards Imphal and throw away much if not all that had been won. But every officer and man in the Fourteenth Army was determined that the gamble should succeed and was ready to put his last ounce into the effort to clear Burma of the Japanese. Never was morale higher than in the spring of 1945 on the banks of the mighty Irrawaddy.

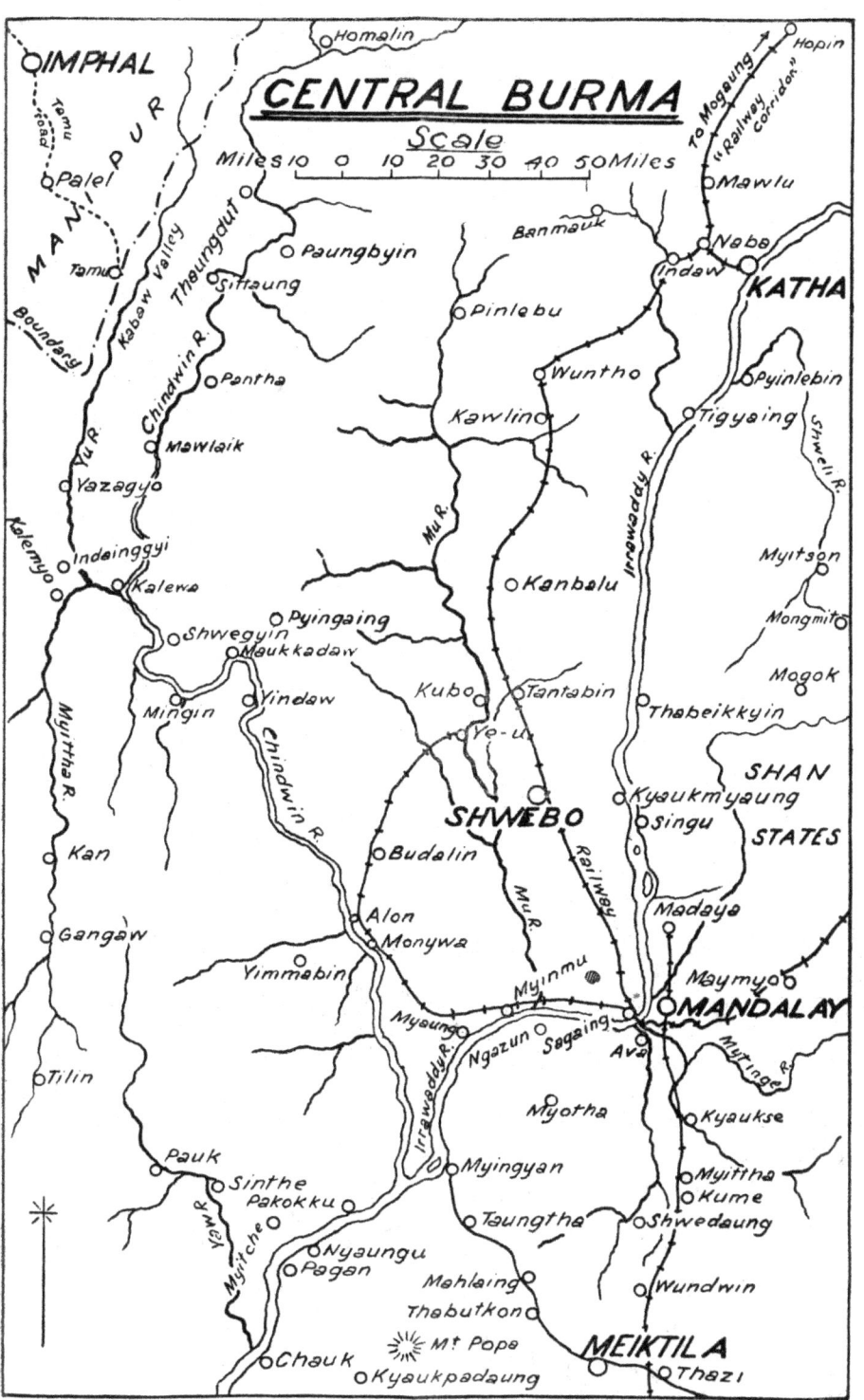

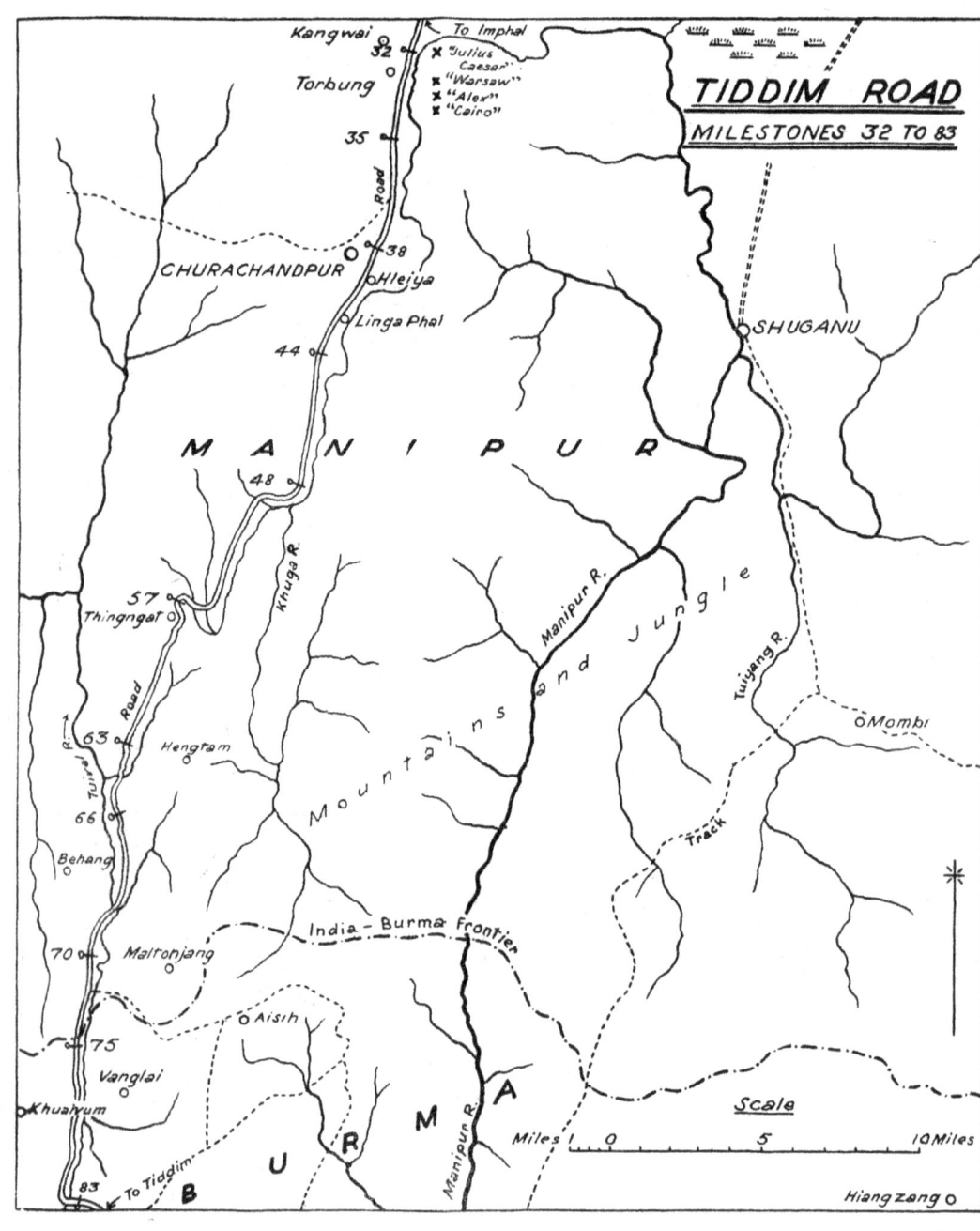

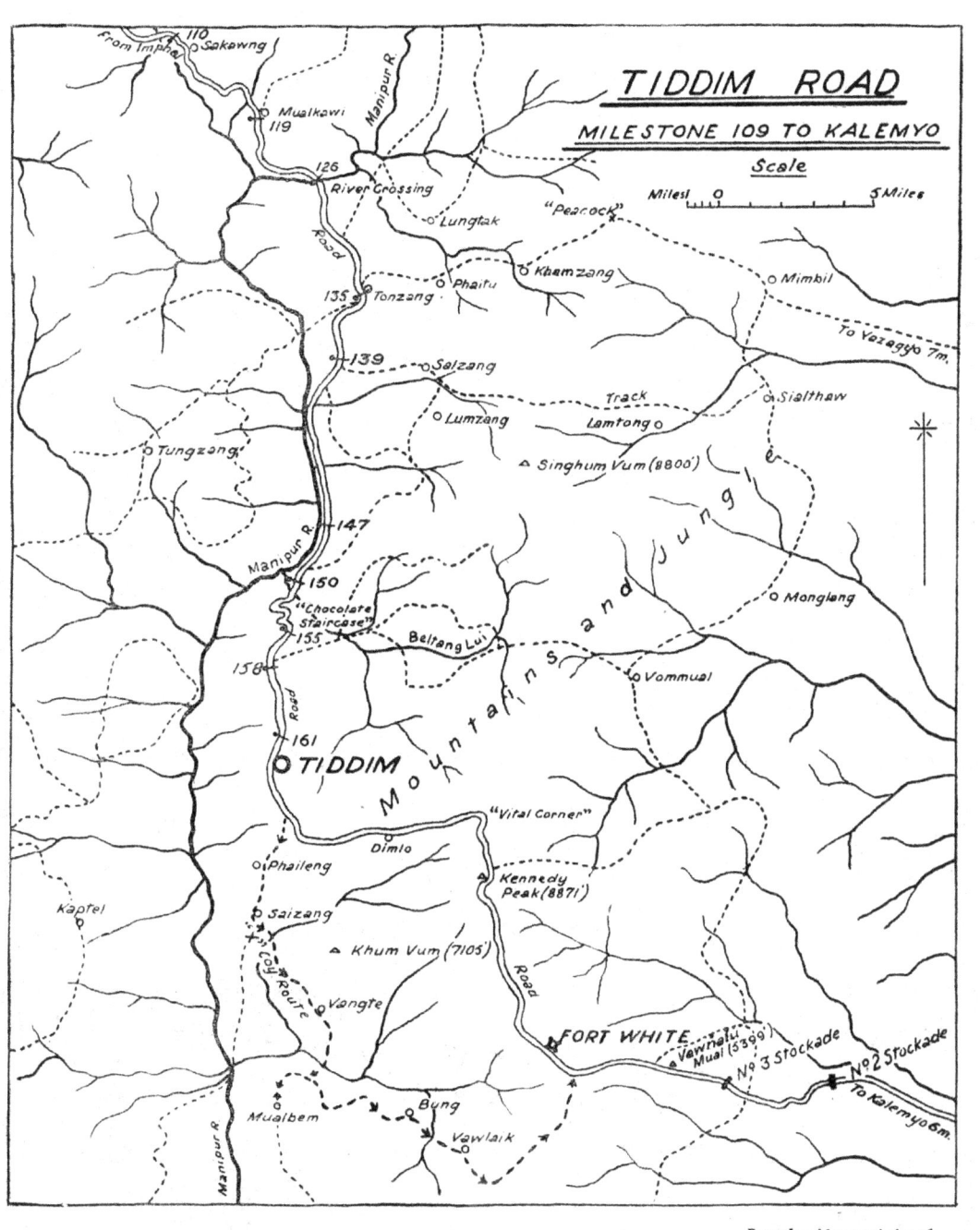

CHAPTER XIII

THE RECONQUEST AND RESTORATION OF LOWER BURMA, APRIL 1945 - OCTOBER 1947

EARLY in 1945, the Fourteenth Army began to re-group for the thrust to Rangoon. It seemed, at that period, that even if the adventure were completely successful it would be necessary afterwards to clear the country by a long process of annihilation because the Japanese would never surrender. There remained the possibility that their Government might be forced to sue for peace and consequently order its armies in Burma to cease hostilities. At the moment, this appeared improbable, though it was actually brought about later by the use of the atom bomb which was approved at the Potsdam Conference in Berlin on July 24th. The secret of this new weapon, however, was closely guarded, and the commanders in the field were unaware of the Potsdam decision. Rangoon was their immediate goal, and they had to reach it before the monsoon wrecked their communications. The laborious process of clearing the country would follow, as it did in the South African War.

General Slim had planned originally to send the 4th Corps, under Lieut.-General Messervy, down the Irrawaddy, and the 33rd Corps, under Lieut.-General Stopford, down the Mandalay-Rangoon road; but as a swift advance down the road would cut off large enemy forces in the Pegu Yomas and prevent their escape eastwards towards the Sittang, he decided instead to send the largely mechanized and mobile 4th Corps down the road and the adjacent railway and to despatch the 33rd Corps down the Irrawaddy. The 4th Corps was in a better position than the 33rd Corps for a rapid advance on Rangoon as it was concentrated in the Meiktila area, some 50 miles south of its rival. The new plan involved a complicated manoeuvre since the bulk of the 33rd Corps, consisting of the 2nd British Division, 20th Indian Division and 268th Indian Infantry Brigade, would have to move from north-east to south-west across the lines of communication of the 4th Corps which comprised the 5th and 17th Indian Divisions and the 255th Tank Brigade. After arriving in the Irrawaddy Valley, the 33rd Corps would be reinforced by the 7th Indian Division which had previously belonged to the 4th Corps. During the regrouping stage, the 4th Corps would occupy Pyawbwe, 25 miles south-east of Meiktila, and use it as a springboard for a further advance when ready, while behind it the 19th Indian Division (now under Army Command) cleared the country between Mandalay, Thazi and Chauk.[1]

Undoubtedly the most spectacular feature of the last phase of the war in Burma was the advance of the 4th Corps on Rangoon, so it is proposed to deal now with that operation and the experiences of the Indian Engineers engaged in it. The advance began on March 30th, 1945, when the 17th Division moved southwards from Meiktila to threaten Pyawbwe from the north and west while the 255th Tank Brigade dealt a decisive blow from the south-west. Fierce opposition was encountered. Almost every village was defended by suicide squads. Yindaw was found to be so strongly held that the 17th Division was ordered to by-pass it and leave its clearance to the 5th Division which was following on its heels. Yindaw resisted for three days and was not taken until the garrison had been wiped out. Pyawbwe fell to the 17th Division on April 10th, and the way then lay open for a thrust towards Pyinmana and Toungoo. The latter was particularly important because it had airfields which could be used not only to support a further advance on Pegu but to provide air cover for the sea-borne attack on Rangoon from Arakan by the 26th Indian Division. The 17th Division had done very well while in the lead. In a fortnight it had killed 2,900 Japanese and captured or destroyed 44 guns, 6 tanks and 70 vehicles. The Tank Brigade had also taken a heavy toll of the enemy.

The 5th Division now took over the lead, and preceded by an armoured column, two mechanized brigades passed through the 17th Division. By the evening of April 10th, the armour was beyond Yamethin. The infantry and transport, following more slowly, were held up temporarily by enemy forces which had returned to Yamethin under cover of darkness; but these Japanese were liquidated after a couple of days' fighting and the advance was resumed. Shwemyo, 30 miles beyond Yamethin, fell to the 5th Division on April 16th. The armoured column, and a mechanized infantry brigade which followed it, were checked for a time at the Shwemyo Bluff, a ridge dominating the main road and railway for several miles. However, another mechanized brigade arrived on the scene, and by outflanking

---

[1] See the maps of Upper and Lower Burma included in this chapter.

the defenders, forced their withdrawal on April 18th. The Division then advanced towards Pyinmana,[1] which the armoured column reached on the 19th. By-passing the town, the Division seized the important airfield at Lewe and prepared it to receive light planes and gliders. Pyinmana having been captured on April 21st, the troops pressed on towards Toungoo which was already under heavy air attack. This town was valuable strategically not only as a forward air base but because a road ran eastwards from it to the Salween River near Mawchi along which the enemy might escape into Northern Thailand. On April 22nd, the armoured column, closely followed by a brigade of the 5th Division, swept into the place. It took the enemy so completely by surprise that a Japanese traffic policeman, on point duty, signalled to the tanks to stop. Those were the last signals he ever made. By April 24th, Toungoo had been cleared and from one of its three airfields our fighters were able to cover Rangoon, 160 miles away to the south. Meanwhile, the armoured column and the leading infantry brigade had gone far ahead towards Pyu which they captured on the 25th in spite of a serious check at the Pyu Chaung where, as related later, a bridge had been destroyed. The 17th Division now passed through the 5th Division to resume the lead in the thrust towards Pegu.

During the three weeks which had elapsed since General Messervy's 4th Corps had burst out of Meiktila it had advanced 170 miles and killed 4,800 Japanese. Its progress had been so rapid that at times the Forward Airfield Engineers had been unable to keep pace with it. In order, therefore, to ensure the least possible delay in making or repairing airstrips, a reconnaissance party of engineers travelled with the armoured spearhead. The Field Companies of Indian Engineers followed as closely as they could and managed to open no less than 9 airstrips in 11 days over a distance of 200 miles. The Japanese were rushed off their feet and were rapidly losing heart. General Kimura, recognizing that the situation in Southern Burma was hopeless and that his last chance of saving Rangoon had gone, ordered the evacuation of the city and transferred his headquarters to Moulmein on the Tenasserim Coast. He had lost effective control of his armies and had few reserves. Yet he was still determined to fight for Pegu which controlled the road and rail route to Moulmein,

---

[1] Pyinmana is a railway junction, north of Toungoo, from which a branch line runs to Taungdwingyi and Chauk.

and therefore he scraped the bottom of the pot to find men to hold that town and garrison Moulmein.

The 17th Division, preceded by an armoured column of the 255th Tank Brigade, left Pyu on April 25th for the final dash towards Pegu and Rangoon. It was fitting that this Division should have the honour of leading the victorious 4th Corps during the last stage of the advance because it had borne the burden of the dogged retreat in 1942 and had since established an unrivalled reputation in bitter fighting on the Tiddim Road. The axis of the 4th Corps' final advance to the south has been described as "the longest and narrowest salient known in warfare", for it was seldom wider than 200 yards on either side of the road and railway. Our tank crews, racing down the road could see Japanese infantry trudging along parallel to them in the hills to right and left. These men belonged to a Japanese division moving southwards from the Shan States. Stragglers were picked up by the 19th Division in the Toungoo region or fell victims to Karen guerillas hiding in the jungles. Many were killed by detachments of the "Burma National Army", 7,000 strong, under Major-General Aung San, which had come over to our side when an Allied victory seemed assured.[1]

The distance by road from Pyu to Rangoon is only about 140 miles, so there still seemed to be a chance that the 17th Division and 255th Tank Brigade, followed by the 5th Division, could reach the city before the 26th Division arrived by sea from its advanced base on Ramree Island. The leading troops of the 4th Corps were now on reduced rations. Food supplies had to be sacrificed to meet the voracious demands of the armoured vehicles for petrol and oil. Yet there were no complaints. "Sorry you've got to do all this on half rations" remarked General Slim to some toiling and sweating Gunners. "Never mind, Sir", they replied. "Give us quarter rations and enough ammunition and we'll get you to Rangoon". While the 19th Division in rear was pushing slowly eastwards from Toungoo up the Mawchi Road, the 17th Division arrived on April 26th in Daik-u, within 85 miles of Rangoon, and was held up for a time near the Moyingyi

---

[1] The Burma National Army had various names at different times. Early in 1942, when fighting for the Japanese, it was known as the "Burma Independence Army". In August 1942 it became the "Burma Defence Army". In March 1945 it was renamed the "Burma National Army"; and finally, in July 1945, it was called the "Patriotic Burmese Forces".

Reservoir by suicide squads, mines and swamps.[1] Nevertheless, advanced elements of the 255th Tank Brigade penetrated into the outskirts of Pegu early on April 28th while others struck south-eastwards to cut the escape route towards Waw and the Sittang.[2] On the same day, the 17th Division recovered 400 British, Indian and American prisoners-of-war who had marched from the Rangoon Gaol. Then the monsoon descended in full force. All the airstrips were put out of action. Tanks and vehicles could not leave the main roads, and the Pegu River rose in flood and barred all forward movement. There were three bridges over the river, a main road bridge in Pegu itself, a railway bridge about a mile to the north, and three miles further upstream, a second railway bridge. All were held by the enemy and prepared for demolition. On April 30th, despite fierce resistance, a brigade and some armour gained a foothold in part of Pegu on the east bank and another brigade crossed under fire over the remains of the northernmost bridge after the enemy had demolished most of it. One brigade was then left in Pegu while the other two and the armour set out on May 2nd for Rangoon; but when still 32 miles short of their goal they received news that the city had already been occupied from the sea. Thus the Fourteenth Army was beaten on the post. It was a bitter disappointment to all ranks though they had the satisfaction of knowing that without their great efforts, and the support given by their planes, the 26th Division could not have taken Rangoon with so little loss. That the 4th Corps so nearly won the race was due in no small measure to the energy and enterprise of its commander, Lieut.-General F. W. Messervy, who had led the "Gazelle Force" of armoured cars successfully in the operations against the Italians in the Sudan and Eritrea in 1940-41 and also the famous 7th Armoured Division ("The Desert Rats") in the struggle against the Germans in the Western Desert in 1942.[3]

This brief account of the operations of the 4th Corps as a whole may be supplemented by some details of the achievements of the Engineer formations, under Brigadier W. W. Boggs, which enabled the advance to proceed with such astonishing speed. In a rapid offensive of this description the problem of moving the Engineer

---

[1] See the map of the Toungoo-Rangoon Area included in this chapter.
[2] See the map of the Waw Area included in Chapter VIII.
[3] See Chapters II and IV.

units forward from job to job is most intricate. Some detachments of the 4th Corps Engineers were still only 50 miles south of Yamethin when the armour reached Pegu. About 1,900 tons of Bailey bridge material were used during the advance. The Engineer units with the leading Division had to get it forward by hook or crook, so they were given a Bailey Platoon from a Bridge Company to help them. The Engineers with the supporting Division, though expected to bridge gaps as rapidly as possible or to improve bridges already made, had no such expert assistance. With the leading Division were also the Forward Airfield Engineers and a Mechanical Equipment Company. The Japanese airfields were vital objectives, and the Forward Airfield Engineers were usually flown in to develop an airfield directly it had been taken. Behind them and the 4th Corps Engineer units came the Army Engineer formations to build large bridges, repair the railway and improve and maintain the line of communication. At the outset, when the 17th Division was in the lead, the most urgent work, with the exception of airstrip construction, devolved naturally on the 17th Divisional Engineer units under Lieut.-Colonel T. H. F. Foulkes, R.E. These comprised 60 Field Company (Madras) under Major P. A. Walker, R.E., 70 Field Company (Bengal) under Major W. A. Livings, R.E., the Tehri-Garhwal Field Company under Major T. D. Badhani, I.E., and 414 Field Park Company (Bengal) under Major I. R. Ireland, R.E. Most of the work consisted of rapid Bailey bridging, at first over dry *chaungs* and then, as soon as the rains had begun, over flooded *chaungs*. The units were involved in occasional skirmishes with the enemy. Between Meiktila and Pyawbwe, 70 Field Company accounted for a number of Japanese, particularly in bayonet attack ahead of 414 Field Park Company's bulldozers which were making a diversion. Near Pyawbwe, the Company eliminated a party of Japanese snipers, bringing the total bag to 30 killed. Experiments were made with a jeep train at Pyawbwe, and the railway line to Yamethin was repaired when clear of the enemy. 60 Field Company had some fighting after it left Meiktila on April 4th with the 63rd Brigade. It gave close support to the infantry and tanks and destroyed many enemy dumps. In the assault on Pyawbwe on April 10th, it was in the forefront of the battle and assisted the infantry in clearing the village on the following day.

After the 5th Division had assumed the lead at Pyawbwe, the 5th Divisional Engineers, under Lieut.-Colonel R. C. Orgill, R.E., moved up in support. The units concerned were 2 Field Company (Bengal) under Major C. W. Williams, R.E., 20 Field Company (Bombay) under Major J. D. Holland, R.E., 74 Field Company (Bengal) under Major D. Brunt, R.E., and 44 Field Park Company (Madras) under Major H. F. Thompson, R.E. At the Shwemyo Bluff, 74 Field Company helped the leading brigade to clear the enemy position while 2 Field Company crossed the Sinthe Chaung and went forward to make a diversion to by-pass Pyinmana. Bulldozers and motor graders were used to provide a route across paddy fields and sandy ground, and the Company joined the infantry in a battle against snipers hidden in fox-holes and trees. Williams was somewhat shaken when the bodies of two snipers, shot down from trees, landed within a few yards of him! Further crossings of the Sinthe Chaung were made under heavy shell fire. At one time the shells were dropping all round the Sappers as they laboured on a tank crossing. Following closely behind the leading tanks, the 5th Divisional Engineers also provided numerous crossings over smaller *chaungs* by bridging or by laying Army track, and by April 22nd most of them were well beyond Pyinmana. The 17th Divisional Engineers came hard on their heels. Major T. D. Badhani, O.C. Tehri-Garhwal Field Company, records that two diversions were made near the Shweymyo Bluff, two more at Pyinmana and another at the Yonbin Chaung near the Lewe Airfield.[1] Occasional showers of rain had begun to fall and the diversions were deteriorating rapidly. The greater part of the 99th Brigade was carried in huge transporters which could not negotiate the curves and gradients which had sufficed for the 5th Division's traffic under better conditions, and the bridges could not take such heavy loads. These were some of the problems encountered by the 17th Divisional Engineers while following the rapidly moving 5th Divisional Engineers towards Toungoo.

At Pyinmana, as a very large bridge had been demolished by the enemy, the 4th Corps had to cross by fords or temporary bridges. The repair of this bridge was undertaken later by 362 Field Company (Madras) of the Command Army Group Engineers (C.A.G.E.). The trusses which were still standing were blown up and the pieces dragged away by recovery vehicles. Bailey crib piers were then built on the existing foundations, and over these was launched a continuous Triple-Single Bailey structure to take Class 40 loads. This bridge is

---

[1] "Engineer Operations of the 17th Indian Division, February-June 1945," by Major T. D. Badhani, R.I.E.

said to have been the first of its kind in Burma. It was a good example of Sapper ingenuity.

Although the Field Companies of the 4th Corps Troops Engineers had to work desperately hard to maintain the impetus of the advance, the most exciting experiences fell naturally to 36 Field Squadron (Madras), under Major W. B. J. Armstrong, R.E., which operated with the spearhead provided by the 255th Tank Brigade. On April 11th, the unit was in Pyawbwe, and a week later, after Yamethin and Tatkon had been captured, it reached a village called Kanhla, about 40 miles south of Yamethin, where a bridge over a deep *chaung* had been demolished and was well covered by enemy fire. The *chaung* made an effective anti-tank obstacle and the advance was halted. Lieut. D. A. Orr, R.E., then went forward in a Scissors Bridge tank and superintended the laying of a bridge across the 30-feet gap under heavy rifle and mortar fire. It was laid straight and evenly although it was impossible for anyone to direct the operation from outside. The fighting tanks crossed quickly, and under cover of their fire, the infantry followed to clear the far bank. The scissors bridge was then adapted for jeep traffic, and vehicles of all sorts began to use it. Some of the drivers did not like the height above the water and had to be guided very carefully across. The main body of the Brigade being now well beyond the *chaung*, Lieut. G. C. Hodgson, R.E., reconnoitred the banks to find a place where a bulldozer could be got across. He discovered a suitable spot, but while returning to report, his jeep ran over a mine. Fortunately, it was exploded by a rear wheel, and Hodgson and the driver escaped injury though covered with picric acid and dust. The last vehicle crossed before dusk. A Valentine tank was then brought forward to lift the bridge; but just as the lifting gear was being adjusted, a party of Japs came down the *chaung* and attacked the infantry covering detachment, so the work had to cease while the tank withdrew into the perimeter defences. More Japs appeared and a brisk exchange of fire lasted throughout the night. The next morning, however, the enemy had gone and "B" Troop of 36 Field Squadron was able to go out and remove the bridge.

After the 5th Division had passed Pyinmana, the Forward Airfield Engineers developed the Lewe airfield with the utmost energy while the Divisional Engineers passed on towards Toungoo with the brigades to which they were attached. Ahead of them, as usual, was the 255th Tank Brigade which captured an airstrip at Toungoo on April 22nd. Two days later, 2, 20 and 74 Field Companies were in the town. They were followed by the Airfield Engineers who included the 23rd Engineer Battalion under Lieut.-Colonel E. E. N. Sandeman, R.E., and 81 Field Company (Bengal) under Major R. S. O. Carter, R.E. These formations then began to repair the main all-weather airfield. Dozens of bomb-craters had to be filled in and acres of Bithess laid on the runways. The 17th Divisional Engineer companies next came through to resume the lead, but always ahead was the 255th Tank Brigade with 36 Field Squadron. Major W. B. J. Armstrong relates an amusing incident which occured in a village near Toungoo. "The place had just been cleared of Japs", he writes,[1] "and "B" Troop was hard at work lifting some aerial bombs, fitted with contact fuses, which had been set in the ground as anti-tank mines. The bombs having been lifted, the fuses were removed and the bombs stacked at the side of the road. A Naik found one fuse which defied his efforts, so he decided, as time was short, to drop the bomb down a near-by well. A violent explosion followed. Water shot up a hundred feet into the air, flooding three Sherman tanks through their open turrets. The Naik himself was lucky to escape with a wetting and a clout on the head from a stone."

The speed of the advance was increasing in spite of numerous obstacles. At Pyu, for instance, a formidable *chaung* barred the way. It was held strongly by the enemy, but the near bank was cleared on April 24th and a small bridgehead established. The *chaung* was 90 feet wide and very deep, and as the bridge across it had been demolished, the progress of the 17th Division, now in the lead, was checked temporarily while a Bailey bridge was being built. It was estimated that this bridge could not be ready before dawn on the 26th, and the 255th Tank Brigade Commander told Major Armstrong that he, at any rate, could not afford to waste a day and that 36 Field Squadron must therefore improvise a crossing for his tanks and transport. Armstrong reconnoitred on the evening of the 24th and found a spot on the far bank where some 15 feet remained of a Japanese trestle bridge. About 30 feet from the near bank, though a little off the centre line of the demolished bridge, was a submerged sandbank, and Armstrong promised the Brigadier that a crossing would be provided there by 10.0 a.m. the next day. Materials were collected, but enemy interference prevented a start until 8.0 a.m. The operation began with building a wooden platform on the sandbank to just above water level. A Valentine Scissors Bridge was

---

[1] Notes by Major W. B. J. Armstrong, R.E., dated May 3rd, 1951.

then laid from the near bank to the platform and a second Scissors Bridge brought forward. With great difficulty, this was laid in prolongation of the remains of the Jap timber bridge, the deck of which was less than five feet above water. A very hump-backed structure resulted, but light vehicles were able to begin crossing only five minutes after the stipulated time. Each was guided across at snail's pace by men stationed at intervals, and lame ducks were hauled over by a winch. Then came the 3-ton lorries. These almost caused the collapse of the old timber bridge, but it was held together somehow by lashings, nails and spikes. By nightfall, 500 vehicles had negotiated the crossing and the Brigade had moved ten miles to the south. The last vehicle crossed after dawn on April 26th. 36 Field Squadron then removed the Scissors Bridge and rejoined the Brigade in a lightning thrust of 40 miles. Such 'Heath Robinson' structures had to be improvised by many Engineer units. No obstacle could be allowed to hinder the advance. Factors of safety lost their meaning. Every reasonable risk was taken. This was no time for text-book methods.

Behind the Divisional Engineer units, the 4th Corps Troops Engineers, Army Troops Engineers and Forward Airfield Engineers flooded into and through Toungoo. It was a mighty influx. The War Diaries of April 1945 indicate the presence of 362, 364 and 365 Field Companies and 327 Field Park Company of the Madras Group, 75, 80 and 81 Field Companies of the Bengal Group, and 29, 363 and 402 Field Companies and 305 Field Park Company of the Bombay Group. There were also many technical Engineer units. The scale on which the communications were being developed will therefore be appreciated. At the Pyu Chaung, for instance, 65 and 424 Field Companies (Madras) were building a Bailey bridge on April 30th. The centre span of a Warren girder bridge had collapsed after heavy rain and the resulting traffic block extended for two miles. Yet the gap was spanned successfully by a Double-Single Bailey after 30 hours' continuous work and the stream of lorries was released to pour southwards towards Nyaunglebin and Pegu.

Stiff battles were fought at Pyinbongyi and Payagale where the main road and railway skirted the western boundary of the Moyingyi Reservoir north of Pegu. A Japanese Engineer Battalion had been at work on demolitions, booby traps and minefields. The booby traps were strewn everywhere, though they caused few casualties unless operated on the spot by suicide men. On April 27th, at Pyinbongyi, 36 Field Squadron encountered for the first time some lone Japs concealed alongside the main road and carrying "Lunge" mines. These weapons consisted of a bee-hive charge on a long bamboo pole which could be jabbed at a passing tank, demolishing it and, of course, killing the operator. Most of these suicidal Japs, however, were discovered and shot before they could do any damage. The armoured attack at Pyinbongyi went in at 10.0 a.m., and Lieut. S. T. Cooper, R.E., was called forward to remove a vehicle placed as a road-block at a demolished bridge. With him in a jeep was Sergeant Pimm of the Bridging Troop, and behind them a small detachment of 36 Field Squadron in a 15-cwt. truck. A Sherman Tank bulldozer, going into action for the first time, brought up the rear. As there was much sniping near the bridge, Cooper halted the tank bulldozer on the road and took his two vehicles off it to some cover afforded by the embankment. He decided that, if the blocking vehicle were pushed aside, a Scissors Bridge could be used, so he sent Sergeant Pimm back to fetch one while he led the Sherman bulldozer forward. He got to within ten yards of the bridge. Then there was a terrific explosion and he disappeared. The tank toppled over, with the bulldozer blade and a sprocket and two bogie wheels smashed, and the sergeant in charge of it jumped out and rushed back to get an ambulance. Armstrong and Pimm came forward alongside the road, but as they approached there were four more explosions and the tank sergeant was blown to pieces before their eyes. Armstrong then went on alone. He decided that some electrically detonated aerial bombs must have been buried near the bridge. The road was already badly cratered and more explosions might be expected unless the concealed Japs operating the mines could be eliminated. Accordingly, a battalion of Gurkhas was sent through Pyinbongyi on either side of the road, accompanied by detachments of 36 Field Squadron. These troops dealt with the enemy snipers around the bridge and discovered and killed the occupants of a fox-hole from which the mines had been detonated. Afterwards, Armstrong and other officers searched in vain for Cooper's body though they found the remains of the tank sergeant about 30 yards off the road.

An unfortunate accident occured during the attack on Payagale on April 28th. A Section of "A" Troop, 36 Field Squadron, was sweeping the road for mines under the direction of Major Armstrong and the Troop Commander, Jemadar Kader Khan. A Naik and a Sapper, moving along 30 yards west of the road, found a Jap hiding in a fox-hole and attacked him with their rifle-butts. The Jemadar, seeing this, rushed across, picked up a Lunge mine lying near the fox-hole, and thrust at the Jap with the pole. The mine immediately exploded, killing the Jap, the Naik and the Sapper and seriously wounding the Jemadar. Armstrong had shouted a warning but it was not heard in time. Though himself wounded by a piece of metal, he was able to walk to an ambulance, with the Jemadar on a stretcher alongside. Further casualties were suffered a few days later. Two Sappers were busily examining an obvious booby-trap when a Jap, hidden in a fox-hole in some near-by bushes, pulled a string laid through loose earth to a switch at the trap. Both Sappers were killed and the Jap immediately shot. Such incidents were by no means uncommon and show the desperate nature of the enemy. A wounded Jap was very dangerous. He might, and probably would, try to kill those who sought to help him. Only the dead could do no harm.

At Pegu, when within 50 miles of Rangoon, the 4th Corps Engineers met their first serious check. On April 29th, four days before a brigade of the 26th Indian Division occupied part of Rangoon, units of the 17th Indian Division were in the outskirts of Pegu, and part of the 48th Brigade, together with 70 Field Company, forded the river to enter the eastern portion before floods prevented an easy passage. As already explained, there were three bridges across the Pegu River—a main road bridge in the town, a railway bridge upstream of it, and another railway bridge on a diversion some miles beyond. The general attack on Pegu began on April 30th. 60 Field Company provided detachments to lift mines while the 63rd Brigade cleared part of the town. The road was dotted with small mounds. These concealed dummy mines intended to delay our mine-sweepers. The Tehri-Garhwal Field Company was detailed to repair the road bridge which, like the other bridges, had already been demolished by the enemy. Major T. D. Badhani states that the 100-feet centre span of this three-span steel girder structure had been cut at one end and that it was difficult to find sufficient space to launch a Bailey span between the trusses. The decking of the other spans was weak, and as the enemy still held the far bank, stores could not be transported to that side. The project was therefore shelved, and instead it was proposed to convert the most distant railway bridge for road traffic. This was a low-level timber pile affair of seven bays which afforded the quickest means of crossing, although the approach road was very long and liable to give trouble under heavy rain. The bridge was repaired and altered by the Tehri-Garhwal Field Company, and the approach road, through paddy fields, improved by 60 Field Company, so that a considerable number of troops and some tanks were able to cross after dark on May 2nd. Then the monsoon started in earnest. 60 Field Company was flooded out and the road became impassable. Attention was transferred, therefore, to the steel road bridge in the town where it was hoped that a Bailey span might be built to replace the fallen span. This scheme, however, was shelved in favour of providing a floating Bailey bridge near at hand although the banks were steep and the equipment hardly suitable. At noon on May 3rd, 60 Field Company and the Tehri-Garhwals started work, and at 9.30 a.m. on the 4th the 63rd Brigade began to cross. Then the water level rose 15 feet. At dawn on May 5th it was found that another span of the adjacent steel bridge had fallen and that the flood, helped by an accumulation of debris, had washed away the floating bridge, parts of which could be seen resting on the far bank some hundreds of yards downstream. 74 Field Company, now in charge of the bridge, began to make preparations for ferrying with motor boats. The river was still rising and the situation seemed almost hopeless. However, by the morning of May 6th the water had subsided six feet and ferrying was started. On the 7th, 60 Field Company began to assist 74 Field Company in the erection of a high-level Bailey bridge to span a wide gap in the steel railway bridge a mile upstream. The remainder of this bridge was decked for road traffic and the rails removed from the approach embankments so that vehicles could reach the bridge. Thus the obstacle of the Pegu River was surmounted at last. The final rehabilitation of the communications fell to the Corps and Army Engineers, but it is evident that the struggle for Pegu was more a fight against the monsoon than against the enemy.

Meanwhile, two brigades of the 17th Division had resumed the advance on Rangoon, only to be held up at the Lagunbyin Chaung at Milestone $32\frac{1}{2}$ just short of Hlegu. Here, a 135-feet brick-arched bridge with high embanked approaches had been demolished. Very little Bailey equipment was available, and more could not be expected at the moment because it had to be brought by air and most of the airfields were flooded. The only solution was to build embanked approaches at the narrowest site so that 110 feet of Bailey would suffice. Bulldozers were employed on the earth work, but they sank or overturned continually in the mud. Nevertheless, the Sappers persisted in their efforts, and within 48 hours 70 Field Company launched a Bailey bridge across which some infantry and armour passed on to Hlegu. The Tehri-Garhwal Field Company afterwards replaced this bridge by a heavier type. At Hlegu itself, the 17th Division was faced with another obstacle. Two spans of a road bridge, destroyed by our planes in 1942, had been replaced by the Japs with timber trestles and these in turn had been burnt down. Bailey equipment was now beginning to arrive again in moderate quantities, so 70 Field Company soon had the bridge in usable condition. Yet the delays at Lagunbyin and Hlegu dashed all hopes that the 17th Division could beat the 26th Division in the race to Rangoon, and nothing could be gained by advancing further.

Some of the airfields in rear were in a sorry state. Their condition may be judged by what happened at Payagyi where there was an airstrip on rough paddy fields. A Commando plane, slightly damaged in a collision, lay there while the rain poured down in an unceasing deluge. An American Colonel came along and, ploughing through the swamp, found a stretch of fairly dry surface only 700 feet in length. "Guess we'll snap her off", said he, and ordered the plane to be dragged into position by a bulldozer. In he got, and after a run of 699 feet, pulled up the wheels and rose into the clouds. Though greatly impressed by his daring, the Sappers exchanged rather sour looks for they had been told that they must always provide a 2,000-yard runway for a Commando and had tried to do so at the expense of much toil and sweat. But then, everyone is not such a care-free and dare-devil flyer as that American.

In all, during the 4th Corps' advance to Pegu and Hlegu, 25 Bailey bridges were built, of which eight were multi-span. Five double-strip and seven single-strip airfields were made or repaired, and 1,900 tons of Bailey equipment were flown in. All this was accomplished in little over a month while the men were on reduced rations. It may be interesting, at this point, to record the overall Engineer achievement during the entire campaign ending in the capture of Rangoon. Lord Mountbatten states that some 2,400 miles of all-weather road were built—a distance as far as from Lisbon to Leningrad.[1] No less than 95 all-weather airfields and 312 fair-weather airstrips were constructed, involving 180 miles of paved runway in addition to aprons, hard standings and taxi tracks of equivalent area. These would be equal to a two-way road from Paris to Moscow. American Engineers laid 2,800 miles of oil pipe line, and Indian Engineers a further 900 miles. During the battles around Mandalay and Meiktila, 20,000 tons of Engineer stores were flown in. And as to the labour employed, 75,000 British, Indian, American, African and Cingalese Engineers

---

[1] *Report to the Combined Chiefs of Staff by the Supreme Allied Commander, South-East Asia,* 1943-1945, pp. 252-53.

were continuously at work, together with 200,000 unskilled labourers. These statistics afford some idea of the vast demands of the final campaign in Burma.

A brief allusion has already been made to the Allied prisoners-of-war recovered near Pegu by the 17th Division. These men had been confined in the Rangoon Gaol, some of them since 1942, and among them were several of the Indian Engineers. Those who were fit enough had been forced by the Japanese to march northwards towards Pegu with a view to evacuating them across the Sittang and down the coast to Moulmein. But after news had arrived that the 4th Corps had taken Payagyi, the Jap escorts decamped and the prisoners were left to make contact with our forces as best they could. They proceeded in small parties, often hiding in Burmese villages to escape roving bands of Japanese. On arrival, they presented a pitiful spectacle. Some were barefooted, and their feet were cut and bleeding after a 50-mile march. They were bearded and emaciated, and many were almost naked, but their joy when they met their comrades was unbounded. They found it difficult to stop talking, even to eat, and afterwards they went on talking till they dropped asleep from sheer exhaustion.

The time has now come to describe as briefly as possible the advance of the 33rd Corps under Lieut.-General Stopford down the Irrawaddy while the 4th Corps was thrusting straight at Rangoon. During the first week of April 1945, the 268th Indian Infantry Brigade and a brigade of the 2nd British Division moved south-westwards from Myingyan, north of Meiktila, and entered the 33rd Corps area on the Irrawaddy, clearing the country as they went. Little opposition was met until the troops reached Mount Popa, an extinct volcano, on which the enemy was strongly entrenched.[1] Here the Japanese held out until April 20th, after which the British brigade was withdrawn and eventually joined the remainder of the 2nd British Division in India. The 7th Indian Division, now in the 33rd Corps, had meanwhile been making steady progress down both banks of the Irrawaddy, encountering little resistance on the west bank but stiffer opposition on the east bank, especially at Kyaukpadaung, the railhead of the branch line from Pyinmana. Kyaukpadaung was captured on April 12th and the advance resumed towards Yenangyaung, a most important oil centre. By April 21st, Yenangyaung was encircled, and in spite of fierce resistance, it was taken on the following day. While

---

[1] See the map of Central Burma appearing in Chapter XII.

these operations were in progress, the 20th Indian Division had not been idle. Two mechanized brigades had begun to push south-westwards towards Taungdwingyi in order to reach the Irrawaddy below Yenangyaung. Taungdwingyi was an important road centre on the Japanese escape route eastwards across the Pegu Yomas. The garrison was taken by surprise, and the town was occupied without much difficulty on April 13th. The 20th Division then swung westwards to the Irrawaddy, capturing Magwe and Myingun on April 19th. It was now well placed to cut off some enemy formations on the east bank which were being driven southwards by the 7th Division. These Japanese managed to cross to the west bank, followed by a brigade of the 7th Division, and for the rest of the month they were driven further and further south down that bank. A brigade of the 20th Division was brought forward and directed straight on Allanmyo while another moved along the river bank. Allanmyo fell on April 28th and Prome on May 2nd. Prome was important because of its port facilities and also because it lay on the only escape route for the enemy forces isolated in Arakan. Having taken Prome, the 20th Division advanced down the main road towards Rangoon after detaching a brigade to follow the river bank and seize any crossing places. Columns were sent westwards along the Taungup Road to meet patrols of the 82nd West African Division coming from Arakan. The task of eliminating a final pocket of resistance established on the east bank of the Irrawaddy a few miles north of Prome was allotted to the 7th Division and 268th Brigade. This proved most difficult and was not completed until early in June when the 7th Division assumed control of the Prome-Shwedaung sector while the 20th Division was located further south in the Shwedaung-Hmawbi sector.[1] But several weeks earlier the campaign on the Irrawaddy had come virtually to an end, for on May 20th a brigade of the 20th Division had met another of the 26th Division coming up the main road 60 miles from Rangoon.

Most of the Engineer work during the advance of the 33rd Corps down the Irrawaddy fell naturally on the 7th and 20th Divisional Engineers. The latter, under Lieut.-Colonel A. R. S. Lucas, R.E., comprised 92 and 481 Field Companies (Bombay) and 422 Field Company and 309 Field Park Company (Madras). The experiences of 422 Field Company, under Major L. S. Henderson, R.E., are described in Major D. W. McGrath's history of that unit,

---

[1] See the map of the Toungoo-Rangoon Area included in this chapter.

some extracts from which will show the general nature of the work, not only of that particular Company, but of others also. "We were to branch westwards from Meiktila into the oilfields districts", writes McGrath, "and then southwards down the road to Prome. The C.R.E. converted his Sappers into an "R.E. Group". One Field Company was with the leading Brigade while the other two followed to tackle the bigger jobs. The leading Company was expected only to do the roughest jobs to get the Brigade forward. Accordingly, on April 14th, 422 Company (less No. 3 Platoon) moved to Meiktila to the concentration of the R.E. Group. The town was absolutely devastated, though the airfields were in good working order. Everything was very bare and dry and our camp was situated among large rocks which radiated heat. We were employed well in front of our infantry on making dry *chaungs* traversable for the whole Division on the road to Kyaukpadaung. One of 481 Company's jeeps blew up on a mine, but we did not even smell a Jap. The 32nd Brigade resumed its advance and we followed closely behind, branching off the main road towards Natmauk which was captured without a fight as the enemy was concentrating around Mount Popa. The Brigade then went on towards Taungdwingyi while we remained at Natmauk. Here, No. 3 Platoon arrived with the 80th Brigade which had been following the 32nd Brigade. The 80th Brigade was to go to Magwe, 30 miles away on the river bank. There were many bad *chaungs* on the road, but Nos. 1 and 2 Platoons made them traversable to within eight miles of Magwe by using Sommerfeld track, brushwood and stones. The Yin Chaung, which kept on cropping up, was our greatest bugbear. The country was covered with stunted jungle, the heat was terrific, and there was practically no water. No. 3 Platoon, with the 80th Brigade, then passed through to clear mines in front of the tanks[1], and Magwe was taken without much opposition. Meanwhile, back at Natmauk, the other Platoons were repairing the road to Taungdwingyi which had been captured by the 32nd Brigade. Once again, the biggest obstacle was the sandy Yin Chaung, here more than half a mile wide. All available Sommerfeld track was soon used up, and for the rest of the distance we laid thousands of bricks and many layers of brushwood. At last we moved forward to Taungdwingyi. The Japs had not realised that

---

[1] The tanks were those of the 254th Tank Brigade to which was attached 401 Field Squadron (Bombay) under Major P. G. Burrell, R.E. 401 Field Squadron reached the Yin Chaung on April 24th. On May 11th it was in Taungdwingyi, on May 12th in Allanmyo, and on the 15th in Tharrawaddy.

our troops had taken the place, and an enemy convoy, coming down the road with its lights blazing, had been promptly wiped out."

"While Nos. 1 and 2 Platoons restored the water-supply in Taungdwingyi", continues McGrath, "No. 3 Platoon was having a rough time at Magwe. A road on the opposite bank, leading to Thayetmyo, was still in enemy hands and our guns opened fire on vehicles moving along it. The Japs replied with such effect that Magwe was known thereafter as the "Shelling Camp". 422 Company now prepared to advance again down the main road *minus* No. 3 Platoon which was given the unenviable job of footslogging with the 80th Brigade along jungle tracks to Allanmyo. All stores and equipment were carried in bullock carts. The rest of the unit moved to Nyaungbintha, half-way between Taungdwingyi and Allanmyo, and No. 2 Platoon pushed on to repair a girder bridge while 481 Field Company, under Major M. I. Pritchard, R.E., made a diversion. Nearing Allanmyo we could see that the battle for the town was still in progress. Each side held half of it. Fighting was fierce all night and the 32nd Brigade was heavily engaged, but by morning we had captured the place. The 100th Brigade now took over the lead, and on April 28th 422 Company camped with it at the Bwetgyi Chaung. As usual, the Japs had destroyed the bridge, so our tanks had to cross elsewhere. The Jap gunners made life very difficult for us until our infantry got among them. Materials for a tank crossing were found in the masses of logs which had collected upstream of the wrecked bridge, and Nos. 1 and 2 Platoons rapidly made a winding staircase down and up the steep banks and filled in depressions in the bed of the *chaung* with stones. It was an alarming sight to see our tanks going down the staircase, for in two places they had to be swivelled round on one track and eased gently down a slope of 1 in 2. The 100th Brigade was moving on towards Prome and we spent another day at the Bwetgyi Chaung maintaining a crossing for 'soft' vehicles made by 481 Company. Rain fell heavily, and winching the vehicles up the slopes was a slow business. Meanwhile, we heard that the 80th Brigade's bullock-cart convoy had arrived in Allanmyo. No. 3 Platoon had marched 70 miles, covering 17 miles on the first day. Foraging had to be done all the way to keep the bullocks fed. It had been a most gruelling journey as the Sappers had not only to march the whole distance and assist at crossings when necessary but also to provide water at every camp."

On May 1st, 422 Field Company (less No. 3 Platoon) moved to the Nawin Chaung, four miles from Prome. The monsoon was now imminent and the 20th Division had been ordered to cover 13 miles a day. The *chaung* was under enemy fire as the unit settled in. Some tanks managed to cross by a ford and it was hoped that others would be able to follow before the flood came down. The Sappers set to work after dark on building a 200-feet folding boat bridge and a Bailey raft and landing stages, but at dawn the monsoon arrived. The water rose at the rate of a foot every 20 minutes. A bridge built further downstream by 481 Field Company was washed away though 422 Company's bridge still held. Next day, the rain ceased temporarily and the water level began to fall. Some tanks were winched across the ford by bulldozers, but the medium artillery failed to make the passage. The approaches had now become absolute quagmires. Splashing through inches of mud, 422 Field Company laid 300 yards of Sommerfeld track on one side while 92 Field Company, under Major J. B. Irving, R.E., surfaced the other side with any materials it could find. Late that night, the Sappers were told that the medium artillery must be got across at all costs for a final attack on Prome. There was nothing for it but to risk taking the 5.5 inch guns over the floating bridge. Swearing gunners were ordered to unload all ammunition and kit from their 'quads'. It was decided that these should cross first, one at a time, and anchor well up the far bank. The guns could then be winched over while the gunners held up the spades and guided the wheels. No. 2 Platoon got four quads and their guns across during the night, though it was a most laborious process. Many times the guns had to be hauled back and another attempt made. The boats almost foundered under the excessive load, while the Sappers baled for dear life. Fortunately, the water level continued to fall, and when daylight came the remainder of the medium artillery could use the ford. On May 5th, after the occupation of Prome, 422 Field Company began to build a Bailey bridge while 92 and 481 Field Companies pushed on. This bridge, 220 feet in length, was opened to traffic on May 12th, the day on which 422 Company captured a Sergeant-Major of the Japanese Sappers dressed as a Burman. On the 13th, the Company moved through Prome to bridge the Inma Chaung, 153 miles from Rangoon, and finished the work in five days. The forward elements of the 20th Division were now beyond Tharrawaddy, 80 miles from Rangoon, and had contacted the 26th Division coming up from the south, so 422 Company moved to Tharrawaddy, building two more bridges on the way, and on May 25th took up monsoon quarters with the 80th Brigade at Hmawbi, within 30 miles of Rangoon.

During the Irrawaddy advance, the 7th Division had co-operated fully with the 20th Division, its first objective being Kyaukpadaung which fell on April 12th. The 7th Divisional Engineers, under Lieut.-Colonel T. Wright, R.E., comprised 77 Field Company (Bengal) and 62 and 421 Field Companies and 331 Field Park Company (Madras). 77 Field Company, under Major T. G. Jamieson, R.E., swept up mines at Kyaukpadaung and took part later in an attack on Chauk, an important oil centre on the river bank. Here, the Sappers used bee-hive charges to help the Gurkhas in dealing with enemy snipers concealed on cliff-tops. The next place to fall to the 7th Division was Singu, a few miles upstream. The Japanese counter-attacked but were repulsed. Some 48 miles south of Chauk lay Yenangyaung, the chief town of the oilfields area and a primary objective of the Division. After its capture on April 22nd, 77 Field Company collected stores for an assault crossing of the Irrawaddy at Kyaukye, just north of the town, and with 60 Field Company, completed the ferrying of the 89th Brigade on the 27th. 421 Field Company had already ferried the 114th Brigade to the west bank from Magwe to Minbu. The 89th Brigade was ordered to cut off the Japs driven southwards by the 114th Brigade, but most of these escaped the net, and in the middle of May 421 Field Company ferried the 114th back to Magwe to resume the advance to Allanmyo. 62 Field Company, with the 89th Brigade on the west bank, then joined in the pursuit southwards along hilly jungle paths, which had to be adapted to carry mechanical transport, until finally the enemy was cornered some 30 miles north-west of Thayetmyo. 77 Field Company, after operating the ferry at Magwe for a time, built a floating bridge over the Yin Chaung and, late in May, a 270-feet Bailey bridge across another *chaung* further down the road. By the end of the month, both 77 and 421 Field Companies were in or near Prome. 331 Field Park Company arrived there early in June, but 62 Field Company did not reach the place until June 20th as it was kept at Allanmyo for ferrying work. There was much to be done in Prome in the way of general rehabilitation and repair of war damage, and 77 Field Company established a ferry to bring some West African troops across from the Taungup Road. Warlike operations on the Irrawaddy were now practically at an end, and late in June all the 7th Divisional Engineers moved down the Rangoon Road through Hmawbi to the Pegu area where the Japanese were making their final stand.

A remarkable feat of navigation was performed by the 33rd Corps Troops Engineers, under Lieut.-Colonel T. G. Morton, R.E., in support of the advance down the Irrawaddy. This was the transport downstream of masses of equipment and material lying on the banks of the river in the Mandalay region. The units involved were 67, 76 and 361 Field Companies and 322 Field Park Company, all of the Bengal Corps. Early in April 1945, 76 Field Company had begun to collect equipment near Mandalay, and on the 15th, in a convoy of rafts known as the "Red Fleet", the unit sailed for Nyaungu where arrangements were to be made to continue the voyage to Chauk and Yenangyaung when possible. At Nyaungu, 361 Field Company was waiting with further equipment and materials, and on April 21st it set out in a convoy called the "White Fleet". Some of the first rafts of this fleet to reach Chauk were sent on at once to help in ferrying the brigade of the 7th Division which crossed the Irrawaddy at Kyaukye, after which they proceeded downstream to Yenangyaung and Magwe. 76 Company's "Red Fleet" followed the "White Fleet". Below Chauk, which both fleets left early in May, the river was very treacherous and navigation extremely difficult. The flotillas of rafts, each towed by a Dukw, could barely negotiate the narrow channels. No time could be lost because Bailey equipment was urgently needed at the front, and by May 4th most of the flotillas had reached Magwe. Here they were unloaded and were joined later by further flotillas brought downstream by 67 Field Company. All three Companies then set to work on bridging *chaungs* on the road to Prome and improving the line of communication. The 33rd Corps would have been sadly handicapped without the good offices of Colonel Morton's Red and White Fleets and the Engineer units which manned them.

Soon after the occupation of Rangoon, the 26th Indian Division received orders to return to India where the whole of Lieut.-General Christison's 15th Indian Corps was to concentrate for the projected invasion of Malaya known as Operation "Zipper". At the same time, sufficient troops were withdrawn from the Irrawaddy Valley to provide a new formation, the 34th Indian Corps, under the command of Lieut.-General O. L. Roberts, an ex-Bengal Sapper and Miner who had till then commanded the 23rd Indian Division. The 15th and 34th Corps made up a re-grouped Fourteenth Army with its headquarters in India, and the command was allotted to General Sir Miles Dempsey who had led the Second Army in the invasion of Germany. In Burma, consequently, there remained only the 4th and 33rd Indian Corps. These were formed into a new Twelfth Army under Lieut.-General Sir Montagu Stopford, previously commanding the 33rd Indian Corps which had been disbanded officially on May 28th, 1945. General Sir William Slim, the former Fourteenth Army Commander, became Commander-in-Chief, Allied Land Forces, South-East Asia, in place of General Sir Oliver Leese, and controlled both the Twelfth and Fourteenth Armies. Lieut.-General Stopford established his Twelfth Army headquarters in Rangoon. He had under his command the 4th Indian Corps (5th, 17th and 19th Divisions and 255th Tank Brigade), the 7th and 20th Divisions and 268th Infantry Brigade, and a brigade of the 2nd British Division. He also controlled the 82nd West African Division in Arakan, the 22nd East African Brigade and the Burma National Army. His task was to destroy the remnants of the Japanese forces in Burma and re-occupy the southern coastal province of Tenasserim. The Twelfth Army, over 300,000 strong, was disposed mostly along the Toungoo-Pegu-Rangoon Road, the largest concentration being in the bend of the Sittang River east of Pegu. The Japanese had little chance against such massive strength and they knew it.

Since it was impossible at first to supply the 4th Corps in the Rangoon area adequately either by sea or air, supplies had to be carried for a time along the land route from the north which was in an appalling condition owing to heavy and continuous rain. The solution of the problem lay in re-opening the port of Rangoon as soon as possible for large ships and building up an air-base in Southern Burma. The Engineers therefore set about the primary task of restoring the badly damaged port facilities, providing railway sidings and airstrips, erecting store-houses, workshops and camps and ensuring proper water and electricity supplies. By May 12th, several berths had been opened for unloading troops, transport and stores from ships, and by the middle of June no less than 3,000 tons of stores were being discharged daily. An enormous programme of airfield construction was initiated at Mingaladon, north of the city, not only to assist the Twelfth Army in Burma but also to provide a main air-base for the invasion of Malaya. In the meantime it was necessary to exploit to the full any advantages which the possession of Rangoon might afford in driving the last Japanese out of the country. The Japanese armies, or what remained of them, were now grouped in four isolated areas. Remnants of the Fifteenth and Thirty-third Armies were in the Shan Hills, between the Mandalay-

Sunset over Rangoon Harbour

Rangoon Road and the Thailand border, covering the escape routes eastwards from Meiktila through Taunggyi and from Toungoo through Mawchi. In the south, at the mouth of the Sittang River and along the Tenasserim Coast between Mokpalin and Moulmein, was the remainder of the Thirty-third Japanese Army. This was the vital area since General Kimura intended to concentrate his disorganized forces in Tenasserim. Elements of the Twenty-eighth Japanese Army were scattered among the Pegu Yomas between the Sittang and the Irrawaddy. And lastly, in the Arakan Yomas to the west of the Irrawaddy, further elements of the same Army were trying to cross the river to join their comrades in the Pegu Yomas and combine with them in a desperate attempt to hack a way through the Twelth Army's cordon along the Mandalay-Rangoon Road.

To deal with this situation, the 4th Corps was ordered to cross the Sittang and, if possible, capture Mokpalin and Kyaikto. It was also to destroy any enemy forces attempting to cross the river further north and to capture Thandaung, 29 miles north-east of Toungoo, which dominated the Mawchi Road. The 19th Division, less one brigade, was deployed along the Mandalay-Rangoon Road from Toungoo southwards to Pyu and was to operate along the Mawchi Road. The detached brigade would advance along the Kalaw Road further north, in the direction of Taunggyi. As there was no serviceable bridge at Pegu owing to the torrential rains, the 17th Division was moved to the north of that town to a sector extending from Pyu southwards to Pyinbongyi, its main task being to prevent any Japanese breakout from the Pegu Yomas. The 5th Division was posted south of Pyinbongyi and was to cross the Sittang to secure Kyaikto if the crossing could be made without incurring casualties. Logistics, however, caused the abandonment of this scheme in favour of a policy of holding the Pegu-Payagyi area strongly in order to prevent a break-out. Thus the general dispositions from north to south along the Mandalay-Pegu Road were the 19th Division, 17th Division and 5th Division in that order. During June, these regular forces began to get an increasing amount of assistance from contingents of the Burma National Army which were becoming skilled in guerilla tactics.

The opening of the "Battle of the Break-out" was not long delayed. The Twenty-eighth Japanese Army, mostly in the Pegu Yomas, was still a fighting force in spite of exhaustion, sickness and lack of equipment and supplies, and towards the end of June it became obvious that an enemy attempt to cross the main road was imminent at various points along a front of 150 miles between Toungoo in the north and Nyaunglebin in the south. The 7th Division was then brought across from the Irrawaddy Valley to the Pegu area to replace the 5th Division which was being withdrawn to train for the invasion of Malaya, and the dispositions from north to south became as follows. A brigade of the 19th Division guarded the main road in Pyinmana district, north of Toungoo; another operated along the Mawchi Road, east of Toungoo; while the third held the line southwards as far as Pyu. In the centre, the 17th Division was deployed between Pyu and Payagyi, and in the south the 7th Division was in contact with the enemy at the mouth of the Sittang River. The Thirty-third Japanese Army counter-attacked violently in the latter region, and early in July the 18th Japanese Division succeeded in recapturing Nyaungkashe. There was bitter fighting also against the 53rd Japanese Division at Myitkyo, a few miles to the north, where the enemy was attempting to reach the line of the Pegu-Sittang Canal. These counter attacks weakened gradually, and the "Battle of the Break-out" ended, late in July, with a general withdrawal of the enemy across the Sittang. Little activity was reported in the central and northern sectors, held by the 17th and 19th Divisions, except on the Mawchi Road and at points on the main road where bands of Japanese had tried to penetrate the cordon. The defeat in the southern sector was disastrous to the enemy, and the Sittang was thick with Japanese corpses. After August 4th, fighting died down everywhere. It is estimated that during the preceding fortnight the enemy lost more than 6,000 killed, half of whom had been shot by guerillas. Only 740 Japanese surrendered. The losses of the entire 4th Corps over the same period amounted to only 95 killed and 322 wounded, a small price to pay for the final liberation of Burma from the Japanese yoke.

The part played by the 5th Indian Division in the Sittang Delta before its withdrawal at the end of June should not be overlooked, nor the support given by its Engineer units, 2, 20 and 74 Field Companies and 44 Field Park Company. The 5th Divisional Engineers had concentrated at Pegu early in May to open and maintain the difficult line of communication between Waw and the Sittang for the projected advance towards Mokpalin. The routes available were the Pegu-Sittang Canal, the badly damaged railway, and a sandy track alongside it. Jeep trains could operate as far as the Abya Chaung, 4 miles beyond Waw, where ferrying was necessary as the bridge had been destroyed; but 74 Field Company, assisted by a platoon of 60 Field Company, soon built a 130-feet Bailey across the gap. 2 Field Company went forward to operate a service of rafts and Dukws on the canal while 20 Field Company replaced a broken span of the railway bridge in Pegu and prepared the bridge to take road traffic.

Engineer units of the 7th Indian Division, 4th Corps Troops and Army Troops carried on the work in the Pegu region begun by the 5th Divisional Engineers. Rafts transported stores along the Pegu-Sittang Canal, rail traffic was increased, and 421 Field Company replaced a floating bridge across the canal at Waw by a high-level 170-feet Bailey structure. In Pegu itself, the most conspicuous achievement was the construction of a 320-feet suspension bridge across the river. This was begun in the middle of August and was completed by 424 Field Company early in September when it was opened by General Messervy and became known as the "Messervy Bridge". It was erected without a hitch although the units concerned had had no previous experience with this type. 62 Field Company operated a jeep train service between Pegu and Nyaungkashe and a Dukw service on the canal. These are a few only of the multifarious duties performed by the Engineer units around Pegu. Airfield construction or repair was in hand not only at Pegu but at several places between it and Rangoon, notably at Mingaladon, north of Rangoon, and at Zayatkwin near Intagaw. Another large airfield was located at Wanetchaung on the Rangoon-Prome Road. 363 and 402 Field Companies worked for several months at Zayatkwin as part of the Forward Airfield Engineers. Small groups of the enemy were often encountered even after the end of the war. For instance, at the Pabst airfield near Hmawbi, 300 Japanese, ensconced in a near-by quarry, refused to believe that hostilities had ceased and continued to raid the airfield by night until they had been obliterated to a man.

During the last phase of the war, very active Engineer operations were undertaken at the northern end of the Sittang line by the 19th Divisional Engineers under Lieut.-Colonel A. G. P. Leahy, R.E. The units were 29 Field Company (Bombay) under Major A. K. Dowse, R.E., 64 and 65 Field Companies (Madras) under Majors C. Hewson and R. W. T. Britten, R.E., and 327 Field Park Company (Madras) under Major D. W. C. McCarthy, R.E. The Field Companies were busily employed on the roads leading eastwards from Thazi and Toungoo along which the enemy hoped to escape. On the Thazi-Kalaw-Taunggyi-Hopong Road, 64 Field Company, assisted by two companies of the 15th Engineer Battalion, worked with the 64th

Brigade after being recalled from Lewe; and at Pyinyaung, between May 10th and 18th, it built two Bailey bridges and put another across the Myittha Chaung. Next, it advanced up the road and built another Bailey at the foot of a difficult stretch known as the "Kalaw Staircase" The tanks came forward and the Sappers cleared the road of mines ahead of them. Often they found themselves cut off in the confusion of a small battle and suffered several casualties. They bridged many gaps and blasted a diversion for a new alignment at one place, using Japanese aircraft bombs lifted from the road. In a single length of two miles of road, 67 mines and 18 aircraft bombs were removed and seven road-blocks cleared. Soon after the Company had reached Kalaw it was ordered southwards to Toungoo to help 29 and 65 Field Companies in a bloody advance along the Mawchi Road, but before leaving the Kalaw Road it got the Thazi-Kalaw Branch railway line into working order for a distance of ten miles from Thazi through level country. The damage in the hilly section beyond that point was too severe to tackle, and the gradients too steep for jeep trains. As will be recorded later, Engineer operations to extend the Kalaw Road through Loilem and across the Salween River towards Kentung and the border of French Indo-China were resumed at the end of June 1945, but meanwhile all activities had to be transferred to the Mawchi Road where most of the 19th Divisional Engineers were already hard at work.

The Mawchi Road, running eastwards from Toungoo, was narrow, winding and only lightly metalled. It crossed and re-crossed dozens of ravines through hilly and jungle-covered country. There was no air supply, and because of the atrocious weather, very little air support, and the enemy contested every yard of the advance. After Toungoo had been cleared during the latter half of April, the 19th Division had been ordered to open the road as far as Milestone 13, where a branch took off north-eastwards to Thandaung. The Japanese had destroyed all means of transit across the Sittang at Toungoo and held strong positions astride the road on the far side. Consequently, the first task of the 19th Divisional Engineers was to restore communication across the river. The main road bridge had consisted originally of six 106-feet spans, four of which had been destroyed by Allied bombing. The Japanese had built a timber pile bridge, 650 feet long, close to it, and when this was threatened, had demolished a length of 60 feet in the centre. 29 Field Company, using trestles, spanned the gap very quickly and re-opened the bridge for light traffic. This structure, known as the "Ramshackle Bridge" was used in the Mawchi Road operations until the beginning of June when some Bailey equipment arrived for the repair of the main bridge. The latter was restored by Army Engineer units and opened to traffic on June 3rd, exactly three days before the "Ramshackle Bridge" was washed away.

But long before this mishap, the 19th Divisional Engineers had had to tackle another problem. A squadron of Sherman tanks was expected to arrive on May 8th, and in the absence of sufficient Bailey equipment for ordinary rafting, a means had to be devised to get the tanks across the river. It was decided, accordingly, to make a tarpaulin raft with Bailey framework. Two huge tarpaulins, with a layer of bitumenized Hessian between them, formed the skin of this extraordinary craft, and pieces of Bailey equipment provided a floor and sides around which the tarpaulins were wrapped. The tanks were ready to cross on May 11th and 65 Field Company put a wire rope across the river to enable the improvised raft to operate, but fortunately it was decided to experiment first with a bulldozer. The raft began to leak, though the bulldozer made the passage, and just as the Sappers were beginning to scratch their heads a consignment of Bailey put in an appearance. "H.M.S. Tarpaulin" was therefore paid off and a Class 40 Bailey raft was soon ferrying the tanks across the wide Sittang. The attempt at improvization had failed, but it was a very laudable effort.

65 Field Company had a hard time on the Mawchi Road where it began by building two Bailey bridges and a diversion at Milestone 3. A platoon working at Milestone 6 on May 12th suffered several casualties while clearing road-blocks under close fire. The tanks pressed forward too rapidly and the Sappers had to make a corduroy road to extricate them from thick mud. Another platoon, arriving to relieve the first, blew up a number of road-blocks of felled trees by using flexible canvas Bangalore Torpedoes. On May 18th so many mines were found that a small party of Sappers had to move ahead of the tanks. Captain K. Mason, R.E., with a couple of men, dashed along, removing the fuses from the shells used as mines, while close in rear of the tanks came mine-detecting parties to sweep the verges of the road. Mason was with some infantry on the following day when they were ambushed at Milestone 10, but he managed to crawl back safely to call up the armoured cars. For this and other exploits he was awarded the Military Cross. On the 24th, when the 98th Brigade took over from the 62nd Brigade, Mason's platoon was relieved by one of 29 Field Company, and soon afterwards another

platoon of 65 Field Company came forward to help the Bombay Sappers in dealing with two huge craters. The Bombay men filled in one crater with the assistance of a bulldozer while the Madrassis bridged the other with a 30-feet Bailey. At Milestone 13½ a platoon of 65 Field Company had to build an 80-feet Bailey bridge. Here the road was so narrow and the turning of vehicles so difficult that bridging lorries were obliged to reverse for nearly three miles to reach the site; and when they eventually arrived there with their radiators boiling, they found a launching space so restricted that an armoured car had to be used as a mobile counterweight. All this took place under the close fire of Japanese snipers hidden in the undergrowth. It can truly be said that the Mawchi operations were no picnic.

The road junction at Milestone 13 having been captured on May 28th it was decided to advance another ten miles to the Thaukygat Chaung although the road was becoming still narrower and the jungle still more dense. No less than 24 Class 40 bridges, averaging 50 feet in span, were needed in this stretch to avoid diversions. The Japs looked on from the heights around, and when bridging was well under way, plastered the Sappers with salvos of shells before moving their guns rapidly to another position. Deep anti-tank ditches were often encountered. These were spanned temporarily with Scissors bridges until they could be filled in. Every road-block was covered by fire from Japanese bunkers; but casualties were reduced by supporting the infantry closely with concentrated fire from the tanks. An infantry platoon usually preceded the leading tank, keeping on the higher side of the road so that the tank could sweep the lower side with fire. Between them, a small party of Sappers moved along in two groups inspecting the road for mines and lifting any which were discovered. An instance is recorded when a tank actually straddled a Sapper engaged in mine-lifting in order to protect him from enemy fire! The Field Companies took the lead in turn during this slow and arduous advance, while behind them, in Toungoo, 80 Field Company (Bengal) and 364 Field Company (Madras) built a fine bridge over the Sittang. This was a 450-feet Class 12 Double-Single Bailey. The work started on May 25th with the demolition of the piers of the old steel bridge, and the structure was opened to traffic on June 3rd.

After Milestone 23 had been reached there was a lull in the Mawchi Road operations because it was considered that the Mandalay-Rangoon line of communication had already been safeguarded sufficiently from enemy interference. Engineer work, however, continued steadily, and in the middle of June, 65 Field Company was ordered to build a pack suspension bridge over the Thaukygat Chaung so that a battalion could be maintained on the far side. The gorge was deep, the river rapid, and the site exposed to enemy shelling. A flying ferry was established first, then an aerial ropeway, and finally, on July 1st, work was started on a 260-feet suspension bridge with a long approach of timber trestles on the near bank. This impressive bridge was completed on July 16th. Three weeks later, the enemy withdrew and the advance was resumed. A serious obstacle was encountered at the Paletwa Bridge over the Thaukygat Chaung near Milestone 26. This bridge had had three long girder spans on masonry piers, but only the piers remained. Beyond it, the road which mounted steeply in a series of zigzags to reach the Mawchi plateau had been breached in 24 places. Covered by some infantry, 65 Field Company began to build a 200-feet Bailey bridge on the piers of the demolished bridge while 29 Field Company went forward to repair the damaged road. The new Paletwa Bridge was opened on August 10th, and five days later both Companies had cleared the route to Mawchi. News arrived on the same day that Japan had surrendered. The announcement was received with much satisfaction; but the War Diary of 29 Field Company runs "Though it is V. J. Day, the unit is still on this *bloody* road and it is still raining." One can sympathize with the writer, buried in the Burma jungles so far from the scenes of enthusiasm which marked the event elsewhere.

There had already been a Victory Parade in Rangoon on June 11th in which the Indian Engineers were represented by small contingents from a number of units; but V. J. Day was a much greater occasion and was celebrated in proper style. The city was taking on a new look. Docks, wharves, buildings of all sorts, electric installations and airfields were being repaired; and last, but not least, the main water-supply. In this, 72 Field Company was intimately concerned. The great pipes which brought water from the Gyobyu reservoirs, 45 miles away to the north, had been shattered by bombing and 72 Company had to restore the supply. Each section of pipe was 25 feet long, 5 feet in diameter, and weighed 5 tons, so it may be imagined that much ingenuity was needed and a liberal use of bulldozers. Yet the damaged sections were replaced in a fortnight and pure water was delivered once more to all parts of the city. If Rangoon presented a busy scene, Mingaladon presented an even busier one.

A host of engineer, pioneer and coolie labour was at work restoring and expanding the pre-war airfield, and when the 23rd Engineer Battalion arrived in August the total number of Engineer and Pioneer troops engaged at Mingaladon rose to 8,000.

Meanwhile, in the Sittang bend and further north, the 7th Divisional Engineers were competing doggedly with the monsoon. Units near the river were often isolated by floods. Maps were reduced to pulp. Patrols went out in boats. Supplies ran short. British formations were being depleted by the repatriation of many men under the "Python" scheme and this threw an additional strain on all units, British and Indian. The climax of the "Battle of the Break-out" came on July 26th, by which time thousands of Japanese had been killed and only 1,200 had managed to escape across the Sittang. The Sapper companies of the 7th and 17th Divisions worked hard and fought hard. Their employment was very varied. In the Pyu area, for instance, 60 Field Company maintained roads, made airstrips, provided a ferry service across the Sittang, operated a jeep railway, arranged for water-supply and worked on perimeter defences around which Japanese jitter parties roamed at night; and when the unit moved southwards to the Waw front early in August, it had to repair the lock gates at the northern end of the Pegu-Sittang Canal.

The end of the war in Burma on August 15th, 1945, followed closely on the dropping of atomic bombs by American planes on Hiroshima and Nagasaki in Japan. The Japanese Government immediately asked for terms, and on August 14th, accepted unconditional surrender. On August 20th, General Stopford ordered General Kimura, the Japanese commander in Burma, to cease hostilities forthwith and make arrangements for the surrender of all his troops. Kimura issued the necessary orders; but many of his formations were out of touch with him and some refused to believe their instructions. Thus sporadic fighting continued till the end of the month and particularly in the Mawchi, Shwegyin and Waw regions. Then, at last, peace and quiet returned to the devastated and water-logged countryside. The "Sons of Heaven" surrendered piece-meal to the nearest British or Indian troops and proved to be quite ordinary mortals and remarkably docile prisoners-of-war; but the process took some time and it was not until September 13th that Major-General Ichida, representing General Kimura, made a formal surrender of all the Japanese in Burma. The surrender was accepted by Brigadier E. F. E. Armstrong, B. G. S. Twelfth Army, acting on behalf of General Stopford. "Effie" Armstrong was a Royal

Engineer who had served for several years with the Bengal Sappers and Miners.[1]

While the mass surrender was in progress, the 17th Division was facing the Japanese in the Mokpalin sector, having replaced the 7th Division at the mouth of the Sittang. The Divisional Engineers under Lieut.-Colonel T. H. F. Foulkes, R.E., comprised 60 and 70 Field Companies, the Tehri-Garhwal Field Company and 414 Field Park Company. In an interesting article in *The R.E. Journal* Foulkes has recorded his impressions of the Japanese in defeat and some of the experiences of his units in the re-occupation of Tenasserim. "I had sometimes flown over the Japanese positions on the railway and in the wooded hills beyond the Sittang", he writes,[2] "but I had never been able to detect a vestige of enemy life. Now that the war was over, there was a sudden change. The Japs emerged from the earth and vegetation by hundreds; stumpy little officers strutting about with big boots and dangling swords, mounted men slouching on shaggy ponies, and marching troops bent double under mountains of awkward kit. For the first few days they were inclined to crouch and run for cover when my little Auster plane zoomed down at them, though some were impudent enough to laugh and wave. From now on, they were at our disposal for work. Divisional H.Q., and a large part of the Division, were to move from Pegu to Moulmein, and as the seaward approaches to that port were still blocked by our mines, we were forced to follow the difficult route by road, rail, canal and ferry through Waw, Kyaikto and Martaban to take the surrender of some 8,000 enemy troops between Mokpalin in the north and Victoria Point, 500 miles further south. As most of the country was still under water it was decided that I and Major R. B. Kean, Brigade Major, 63rd Brigade, should cross the Sittang with an armed Japanese escort to explore the ground. We therefore approached the river bank in a crazy old jeep on rail-wheels, taking with us R.E. Graham, a subaltern of 60 Field Company, who was to start work on the far bank. We also took a Royal Signals officer and a former Jemadar of the Burma Sappers and Miners, hailing from a village near Pegu, who knew every inch of the ground. Standing on the high bank, upstream of the ruined bridge, we watched our Japanese

---

[1] See *The Indian Sappers and Miners*, by Lieut.-Colonel E. W. C. Sandes, D.S.O., M.C., pp. 637, 640.

[2] Extracts from "A 'Close-up' of the Japanese Soldier", by Lieut.-Colonel T. H. F. Foulkes, O.B.E., R.E., appearing in *The R.E. Journal*, September 1950, pp. 293-307.

guide push off from some derelict jetties on the other side in a canoe paddled by two soldiers and cross the 600 yards of brown and swirling water. On stepping ashore he introduced himself in good English as Captain Aoki. He was about half the size of my husky companions and looked like a child dressed up. We were soon crossing the water towards a very peculiar reception committee among whom was an elderly gentleman in the garb of a Second-Lieutenant who seemed well educated and spoke quite good American. All the Jap officers were dressed in khaki tunics and breeches, mackintoshes, boots and leather gaiters. Their soft, peaked, khaki caps had the usual cloth star sewn on in front. For badges of rank they wore little red and gold tabs sewn to chest or collar, with stars according to seniority. They had not yet been relieved of their swords. An armed escort of a dozen soldiers was drawn up in two ranks on the jetty. They were dressed much the same as the officers but wore khaki shirts instead of tunics, puttees instead of gaiters, and inferior canvas shoes. They were armed with a very long bayonet and a long and clumsy rifle, with which they presented arms in British fashion. Of all shapes and sizes, they looked a villainous crew, ranging from the short, sturdy type with spherical head and ruddy cheeks, to the lanky, yellow and cadaverous, and they were badly shaven and dirtier than they need have been. In the course of a long walk in heavy rain we examined the bomb-churned water-front, the sad remains of the railway station, the ruins of Sittang Village and the small Pagoda Hill which commands the great railway bridge. It was from this hill that the Japanese, four years before, had opened small arms' fire on the bridge after working round the flank of the 17th Division, and it was this bridge which had been blown up before a large part of the Division had got across.[1] On the hill were small parties of Japs quartered in shelters and ruined huts. Most of these men saluted smartly as we passed. In accordance with Allied orders, the "Rising Sun" flag was nowhere to be seen. Before we re-crossed the river, a table was set up at which we sat and made notes while the Japs stood by. The unexpected offer of a plate of sweet cakes was rather too fraternal for my liking; but while I hesitated, the elderly Second-Lieutenant exclaimed with a laugh "It's all right. They're not poisoned." In the end we ate some of the cakes and felt none the worse, and the Japs saluted very keenly, with many a courteous bow and smile, as we boarded our launch."

---

[1] See Chapter VIII.

A few days later, with Captain G. N. F. James, R.E., of 60 Field Company, and a Japanese interpreter, Foulkes explored southwards by road for about eighty miles to Martaban, gathering on the way his first impressions of the more senior Japanese officers. With their well-made uniforms, keen and determined expressions and smart bearing, they seemed a race apart from the ordinary regimental officer. They commanded regiments or higher formations and were obviously picked men who had been well trained in Staff duties. The rank and file seemed to be on very easy terms with the local Burmese with whom they fraternized freely in the streets and bazaars. Much had been forgotten or forgiven. As the British Officers went further south beyond Kyaikto they overtook columns of tattered, weary and heavily laden troops on their way to their appointed concentration areas. Martaban had been wrecked by Allied bombing. Only the solid brick pagodas remained standing. A timber jetty, however, was still in existence, so Foulkes ordered the local Japanese Engineer regiment to repair it while he and his following returned in torrential rain to Mokpalin. As soon as the Divisional Engineers had patched up the Sittang Railway and the Pegu Canal, the 17th Division began to cross the river near the wrecked bridge in landing craft; but before the transport could reach Kyaikto, a two-mile stretch of sodden causeway had to be reinforced with stone. The Japanese engineers cooperated by starting at the southern end to meet the Indian engineers in the middle. They showed the utmost zeal, hoping no doubt to propitiate their late enemies. The next obstacles were at the Bilin River where both the road and railway bridges had been demolished by the 17th Division during the retreat in 1942. The flooded river was 700 feet wide, and here the Japanese displayed their remarkable ability in pile-driving which they had practised throughout the war because of their lack of standard bridging equipment. They quickly built a couple of long piers, and with aid of a Bailey raft, the troops and transport were carried across and began to move on towards Thaton and Martaban. The Japs seemed almost tireless in spite of the humid atmosphere. They sang and joked as they worked almost naked in the turgid river. Some months later, a 660-feet high-level Bailey bridge on pile piers was built at Bilin. The Jap prisoners were very keen on the success of this project and quickly learnt to use Bailey equipment. When the approach roads were nearing completion, a shaven-headed interpreter, translating for the Japanese Engineer Captain, bowed, sucked his teeth in the prescribed Japanese manner of showing respect and humility, and delivered himself as follows:—

"This officer has been in charge of many roads in Japan, but of course he has had little experience of tropical conditions. Please excuse him if he suggests that you should use a little more bitumen." Surely the acme of politeness and subservience, and typical of the attitude of the Japanese in defeat.

In due course, the 17th Division moved across the Salween Estuary from Martaban to Moulmein in an extraordinary assortment of old motor craft, manned by Japanese but flying little Union Jacks. At Moulmein, there was the same co-operation. Arms had been stacked, ready for surrender; roads were sign-posted in English, and buildings labelled. Japanese carpenters set to work to build boats in workshops established by 414 Field Park Company. Almost every Japanese soldier bowed or saluted, even when carrying a considerable load, for if he failed to do so he knew he would be hit or kicked by his own officers. One of Foulkes' first actions on reaching Moulmein was to call for a report from the Japanese Railway Regiment which had ill-treated our men so abominably on the new railway between Moulmein and Thailand and was now operating what remained of it under the orders of some of the ex-prisoners. It is said that this 244 miles of line cost the lives of 11,000 Allied soldiers and nearly 100,000 civilian labourers. The largest work undertaken by the 17th Divisional Engineers in Tenasserim was the construction of a coastal road from Moulmein to Ye, 60 miles to the south, whence a road extended a further 100 miles to Tavoy. Moulmein and Ye had been connected by rail, but all the bridges were down. The Tehri-Garhwal Field Company built the new road with the aid of 5,000 Japanese prisoners under a Major-General and finished it in four months although no bulldozers were available. The Major-General, a trim little man in a white cotton shirt, always bowed solemnly on arrival or departure. The Japanese have a motto "Death is lighter than a feather, but Duty is heavier than a mountain". Their Emperor wished them to co-operate with their late enemies and therefore they did so without question. Yet some of these enthusiastic workers had probably been responsible for nameless atrocities during the war. It had been expected that the Japanese prisoners would soon be evacuated from Tenasserim; but this did not happen, and accordingly, early in 1946, the problem of providing monsoon accommodation for them had to be considered. Foulkes sent for the senior Japanese Engineer officer and ordered him to produce a standard design for a bamboo hut, thatched with leaves, to be built by his men. An excellent design was soon submitted, but tools for cutting bamboos were woefully deficient. Thereupon, the Japanese manufactured the necessary cutting implements from the springs of derelict vehicles rotting in a local dump and built the huts at express speed.

The 17th Division was withdrawn gradually from Tenasserim to Meiktila until only the 48th Brigade remained. 60 and 70 Field Companies were ferrying on the Bilin River in September 1945 with a Japanese Engineer Regiment under command, after which 60 Company moved forward to Thaton to make an airstrip and was still there, at the end of the year, collecting timber for the Bilin bridge described by Foulkes. The exodus of the 17th Divisional Engineers began in the spring of 1946. 414 Field Park Company left Moulmein for Meiktila in the middle of March and the Tehri-Garhwal Field Company and 60 Field Company followed in April, the former proceeding direct to Maymyo and the latter by gradual stages to Meiktila where 70 Field Company, the last to leave Tenasserim, arrived on August 20th. The change of scene and climate was very enjoyable. The Sapper camp was on the shore of a large lake and the bathing excellent. Training, and more training, became the order of the day and the time passed quickly. But a sad disappointment was in store for all ranks. This was the announcement of the approaching amalgamation of the 17th Division with the 19th Division by which the former would lose its separate identity as the veteran formation of the Burma War.

A post-war engineer operation of considerable importance had meanwhile been carried out by the 19th Divisional Engineers under Lieut.-Colonel A. G. P. Leahy, R.E., assisted for a time by two Companies of the 3rd Engineer Battalion and a Bridging Platoon of Bombay Sappers. The Thazi-Hopong Road, already mentioned, was to be extended towards and beyond the Salween River in the direction of French Indo-China. On September 7th, 1945, 65 Field Company arrived in Taunggyi, and later, 140 miles further east, established a ferry at Kunhing on the Nampong River where 64 Field Company afterwards built a pile bridge. Ahead lay the mighty Salween, flowing at eight knots and with a stupendous rise and fall. 65 Field Company reached the river after a 32-mile march and provided a flying ferry of folding boats which 64 Field Company converted into a raft ferry. The advance was halted for a time, but early in January 1946, 65 Field Company, now under Major R. C. Gabriel, R.E., was detailed to carry out bridging on the road to Kentung, far beyond the Salween. A small party of Japanese Engineer prisoners arrived in February and became known as No. 4(J) Platoon. A Bailey bridge was first erected near Loilem while equipment was being sent forward for another at Tongta, 88 miles beyond the Salween. Meanwhile, Gabriel went ahead in a jeep to reconnoitre the entire route to Kentung, passing through wild and mountainous country along a very narrow road. Kentung seemed to be a prosperous town, untouched by the war. Its large bazaars were thronged with Thais and Chinese from the border only 60 miles away. The Tongta Bridge was launched on March 12th and was followed by others along the roads leading northwards towards Hsipaw and Lashio. On April 12th, a large bridge was opened to traffic at Namsang, near Loilem. Here, the inhabitants celebrated the arrival of the rains by holding their annual "Water Festival", and Gabriel had to run the gauntlet of laughing people armed with buckets and stirrup-pumps. With all the necessary bridges built, 65 Field Company handed over charge to the Public Works Department and moved to Meiktila and subsequently to Rangoon, where the 19th Divisional Engineers embarked for India at the beginning of June.

The bridging in 1946 of the Myitnge tributary of the Irrawaddy, a few miles below Mandalay, was one of the last, and perhaps the most outstanding, achievement of the Indian Engineers before most of the units were withdrawn from Burma. The road and railway to Rangoon crossed the tributary by two separate bridges about 200 feet apart, both of which had been destroyed. The road bridge had been a continuous lattice girder affair supported on concrete-filled steel columns. The railway bridge had had six spans of Warren trusses resting on brick piers. The remains of the girders and trusses lay in tangled masses in the river bed, but a prodigious Bailey bridge, erected in May and June 1945 by 428 Field Company on the piers of the railway bridge, had served to carry both rail and road traffic across the Myitnge though forming a considerable bottle-neck. The problem was how to reinstate full pre-war road and rail traffic without interfering with the existing traffic. Lieut.-Colonel J. J. D. Groves, R.E., C.R.E. 4th Corps Troops Engineers, was detailed to carry out the work, the units available being 75 Field Company (Bengal), 2 Faridkot Field Company, 305 Field Park Company (Bombay), a Railway Bridging Company, a Plant Troop and a Battalion of Japanese Engineers.[1] It was decided to build a diversion railway bridge, served by a loop line, about 1½ miles upstream of the existing

---

[1] "The Myitnge Project, 1946", by Lieut.-Colonel J. J. D. Groves, M.C., R.E., appearing in *The R.E. Journal*, September 1954, pp. 214-228.

Bailey structure and to provide a Bailey pontoon bridge for road traffic close upstream of the remains of the old road bridge. When these had been completed, the existing Bailey bridge would be removed and the abutments and piers rebuilt to carry new Warren girders. The Field Companies tackled the pontoon bridge, and although the length was 567 feet, they finished their task on January 13th. Meanwhile the Railway Bridging Company was at work on the diversion railway bridge of 40-feet Bailey spans on timber pile piers, and this was completed on February 20th. It was then possible to transfer attention to the main undertaking of dismantling and remodelling the original rail and road bridge. This was begun at once, the Sapper units operating in rotation with Japanese companies; but it was a slow process because the piers required much repair and alteration and new abutments had to be built. In June the river began to rise at the rate of two feet a day. Work on the piers and abutments became increasingly difficult and three officers laboured for several days in improvised gas-mask diving-suits in water more than 20 feet deep. By July 6th, however, the Bailey structure had been removed, the piers repaired and the abutments rebuilt, and all was ready for the erection by civilian engineers of new Warren girders which had already arrived from India.

All Indian Engineer units, whether in Burma or elsewhere, were proud to receive, in February 1946, the notification that the services of their Corps had been recognised by the bestowal of the title "Royal". The "Corps of Indian Engineers" thus became the "Corps of Royal Indian Engineers". The news was received at each Group Headquarters in India with a signal from General Sir Claude Auchinleck, the Commander-in-Chief, which ran as follows:— "Very pleased to be able to tell you that His Majesty the King Emperor has approved the conferment of the title "Royal" on the Corps of Indian Engineers. Please convey to all ranks my heartiest congratulations on this recognition of their magnificent record in the late war and in the many wars and campaigns before it."

By the middle of 1946, there were few Indian Engineer units left in Burma. Most had gone to Malaya, Java or Sumatra. Others had returned to India for disbandment. Those still available had lost many of their most experienced officers, N.C.Os. and men under the repatriation scheme. The effects of repatriation may be judged by the rapid changes in command experienced by 29 Field Company while at Meiktila. In March 1946, the unit was commanded by Major J. Lindsay, R.E.; in May by Major A. D. Arden, R.E.; from the middle of July by Major P. J. Papworth, R.E.; and from the middle of September by Major R. D. Mitchell, R.E. All these officers held Regular Army Emergency Commissions and became due for release in rapid succession. Early in 1947, the process of reduction had run its course and it was decided that three regular post-war Field Companies of the Indian Engineers should be selected to form part of a proposed garrison of Burma. The choice fell on 7 Field Company (Bengal), 19 Field Company (Bombay) and 64 Field Company (Madras). These units landed in Rangoon at the beginning of March 1947. They carried out routine duties in various parts of the country, but occasionally their work was far from normal. For example, while 19 Field Company was at Mingaladon in July, Major-General Aung San, late commander of the Burma National Army, was assassinated by a man called U Saw, and the Rangoon Police suspected that certain incriminating articles had been thrown into the Victoria Lake in front of U Saw's house. Major A. B. Rhodes, R.E., O.C. 19 Field Company, was then asked to get volunteers to dive into the ake to try to find the articles.[1] Eight good Mahratta swimmers volunteered and soon brought up various items including parts of a Sten gun. So important were the articles recovered by Lance-Naik Balkrishna Korde and Sapper Bhimrao Khape that these two soldiers were required to return to Burma in February 1948 to give evidence at the trial of U Saw. They were perhaps the last Indian Engineers to serve in Burma, for 7, 19 and 64 Field Companies had been recalled to India in October 1947.

The connection of the Indian Engineers with Burma had persisted at intervals ever since the 1st Battalion of the Madras Pioneers, the forerunners of the Madras Sappers and Miners, disembarked at Rangoon in May 1824 with the expedition under Major-General Sir Archibald Campbell which advanced up the Irrawaddy to the ancient capital at Ava in the First Burma War. A battalion of Bengal Pioneers fought in Arakan in 1825 as part of an ill-fated expedition from Assam led by Brigadier-General J. W. Morrison. Four companies of Madras Sappers and Miners were engaged in the Second Burma War in 1852-53 and remained in the country until 1856. Another three companies, together with two of the Bengal Corps and one of the Bombay Corps, shared in the Third Burma War which began in 1885; and thereafter one or more units of the Madras Sappers were always stationed in Burma in addition to a Burma Sapper Company

---

[1] Notes by Major A. B. Rhodes, R.E., dated December 2nd, 1954.

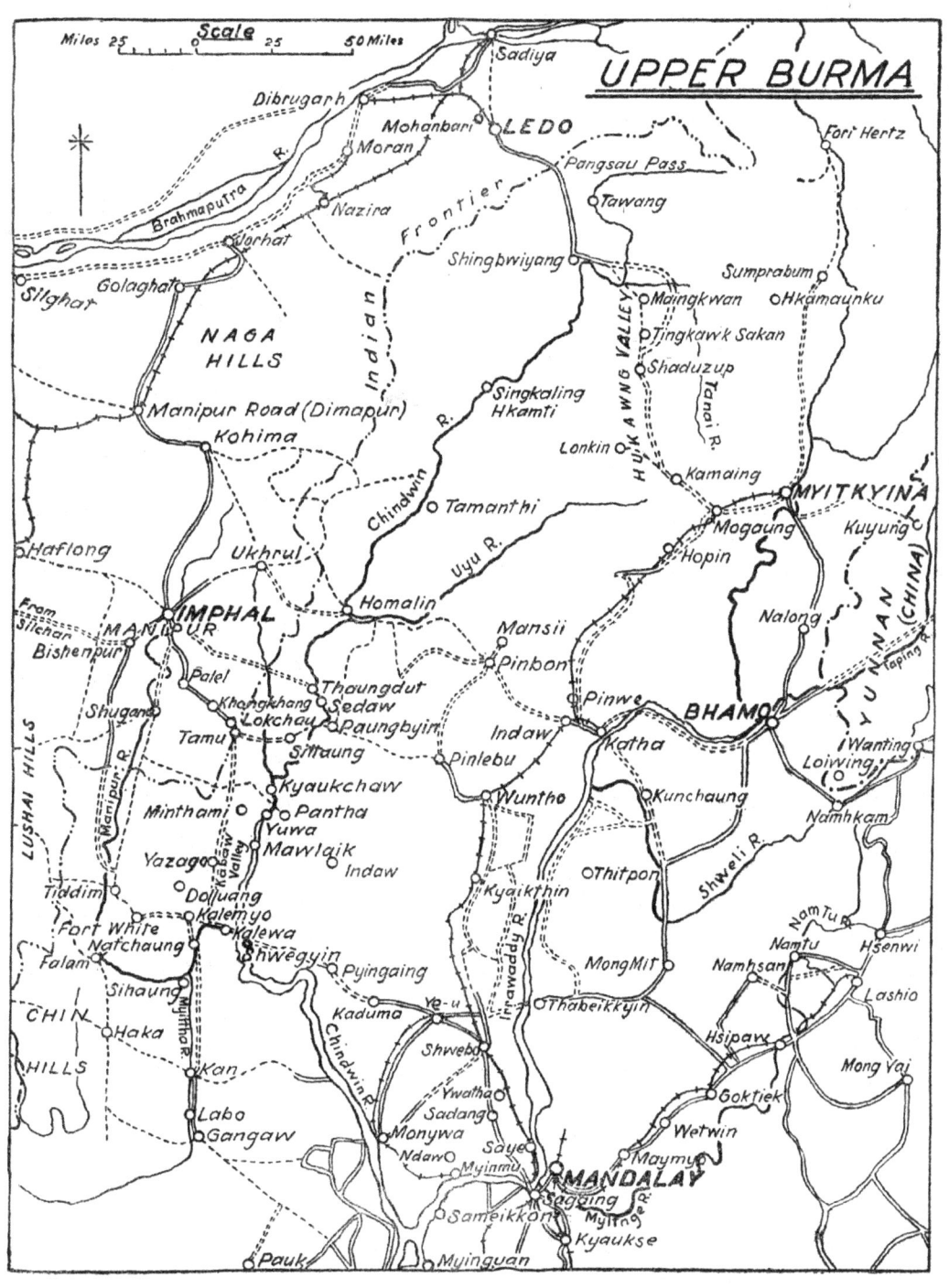

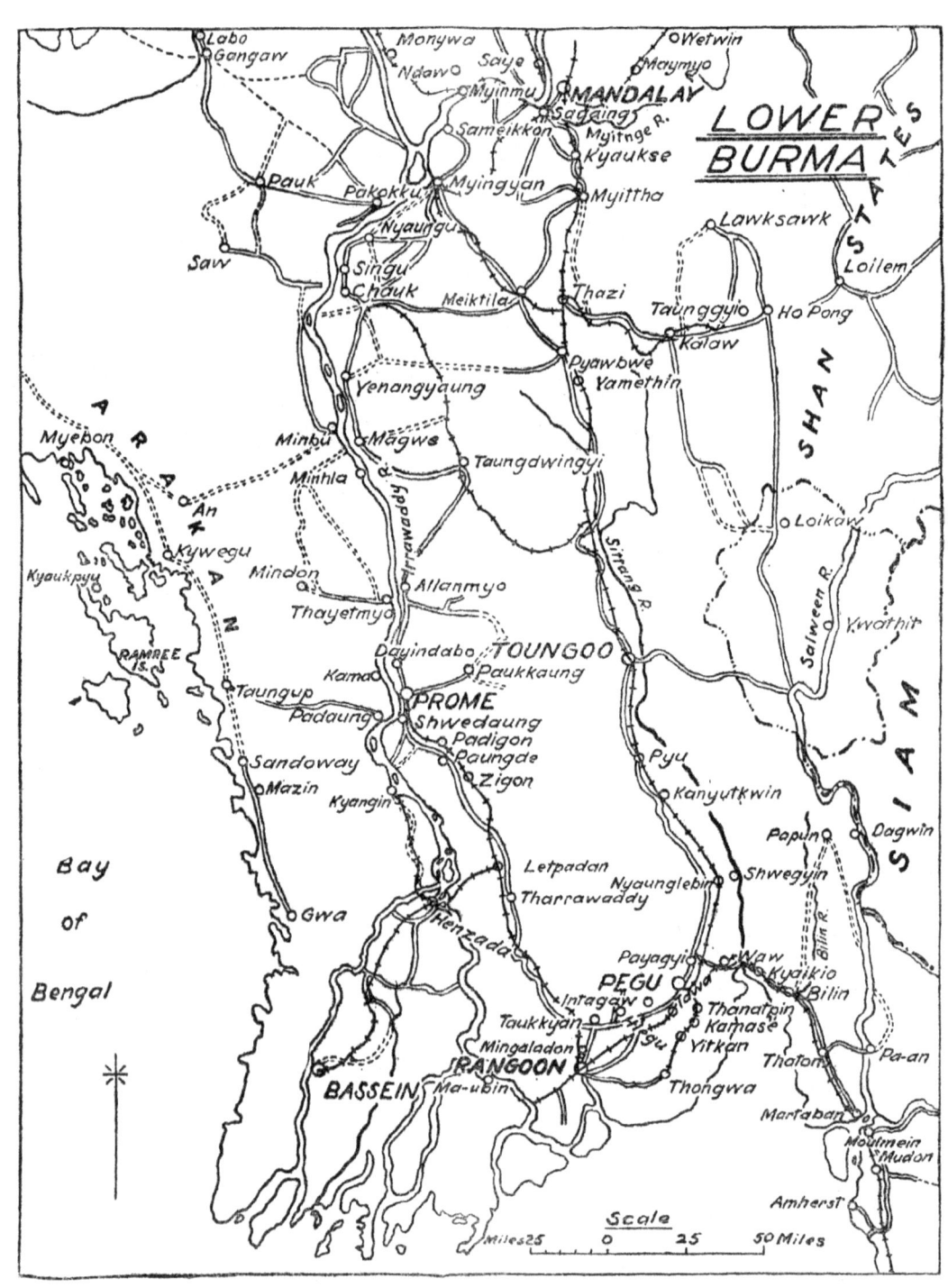

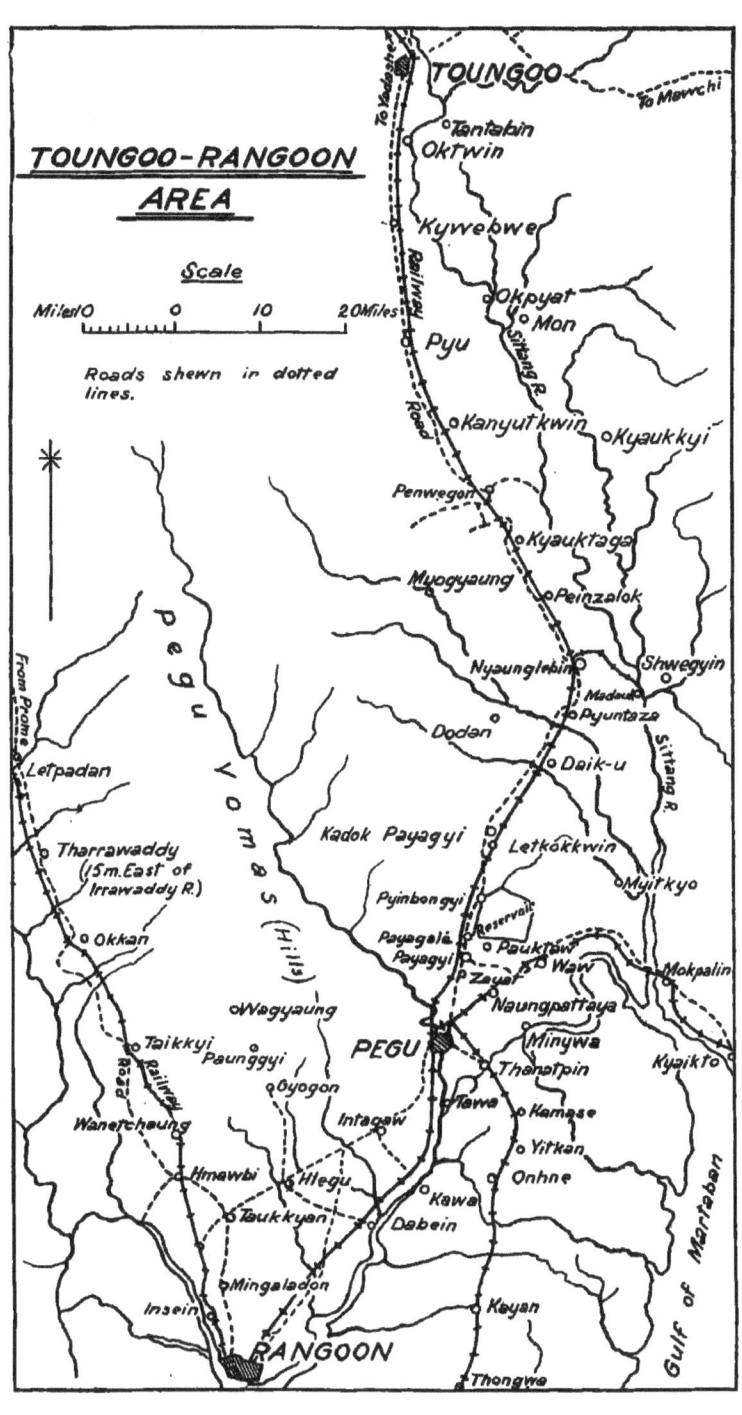

Reproduced by permission of
The West Yorkshire Regiment

raised in 1887. Thus it may be said that the connection of the Indian Engineers with Burma lasted for more than 120 years. After the Third Burma War, the Corps was saddled with the entire responsibility for all engineer work until the Public Works Department took charge, and it had to bear the same burden, for a time, after the Second World War. The modern Republic of Burma, therefore, owes it a debt of gratitude; and although the Indian Engineers may be seen no more in the northern mountains, the dusty central plains, the fertile regions of the south and the jungles of Arakan, they can rest on the laurels so hardly won between 1942 and 1945 against the pick of the Japanese Army.

CHAPTER XIV

POST-WAR OPERATIONS IN MALAYA, THE EAST INDIES
AND THE FAR EAST

LIKE a giant finger pointing southwards from Lower Burma lies the Malay Peninsula, the narrow northern part belonging to Thailand and the wider southern part forming the Federated Malay States with Singapore at the tip. Extending eastwards from Malaya is the world's largest archipelago providing, as it were, a series of stepping stones between Asia and Australia. The Indonesian Archipelago dominates all the gateways between the Indian and Pacific Oceans, but by far the most important maritime passage is the Malacca Strait separating Malaya from Sumatra. The string of islands forming the southern curve of the archipelago—Sumatra, Java and many others—ends at Timor which faces Australia across the Timor Sea. Further north, in a parallel line, lie Borneo, Celebes and New Guinea and clusters of smaller islands, and at the northern apex of the triangle, the Philippines, which face French Indo-China.[1]

After the destruction of the American fleet at Pearl Harbour, the Indonesian Archipelago became a happy hunting ground for the predatory Japanese. It afforded them an almost limitless supply of rubber, oil, minerals and produce of all sorts which they needed for their attempt at world domination, and had it not been for the atom bomb, who knows how long they might not have been able to cling to their ill-gotten possessions. In the autumn of 1945, however, they had to hand over all they had won by an act of treachery unmatched in history. They left Malaya and the archipelago in a sorry state. The industries were wrecked, the rubber plantations dying through neglect, and the inhabitants seething with discontent at facing what they considered to be a mere change of masters. It was into this scene of material and political turmoil that the British and Indian forces were launched after the reconquest of Burma. Victory was already theirs, but the aftermath promised them no easy passage.

Operations "Zipper" and "Mailfist", the plans for the invasion of the mainland of Malaya and the island of Singapore, were prepared

---

[1] See the map of South-East Asia included in this chapter.

while Japan was still a belligerent. The problems were unique. "I always feel", writes a Staff Officer of the 5th Indian Division,[1] "that to give people in Europe an idea of the difficulty of mounting the Malayan invasion one must quote a parallel. Imagine that a number of troops for the invasion of France are in action in Italy two months before "D" Day. Their commanders and staff are summoned to Moscow for planning their part in the invasion. The troops receive new equipment from America and reinforcements from Egypt. The invasion is embarked at points ranging from Marseilles and Gibraltar to Glasgow, and the whole force is to *rendezvous* off a spot on the Malayan coast some days later." The writer was evidently a humorist, but his description is worth quoting. The conditions under which the invasion was to take place changed daily, almost hourly, and it is greatly to the credit of the planners that there was so little confusion and delay.

The Fourteenth Army, now under General Sir Miles Dempsey, bore the responsibility for the operations. A bridge-head was to be formed in the heart of the Malay Peninsula between Singapore and the main enemy forces, which were believed to be in the north. Field-Marshal Terauchi, the Supreme Japanese Commander, had anticipated an Allied advance southwards from Burma down the narrow Kra Isthmus, though he had taken the precaution of reinforcing his garrison on Singapore Island. The initial sea-borne assault on Malaya was to be delivered by the 34th Indian Corps under Lieut.-General O. L. Roberts. Two infantry divisions and a brigade would carry out the first landings, followed by three more divisions and a parachute brigade. Two further divisions would be held in reserve for subsequent operations as necessary. A Japanese counterattack was expected from the north. When this had been defeated and the position consolidated, a thrust would be made southwards to Singapore. These plans, however, had to suffer considerable modification. Man-power was being affected by the extensive repatriation of British ranks under the "Python" Scheme. Orders were received to undertake the responsibility for large areas in the East Indies previously under American control, and American air and sea support was withdrawn. Then came the dropping of the atom bombs on Hiroshima and Nagasaki on August 6th and 9th and the surrender of Japan a few days later. No opposition was expected thereafter in landing on the Malayan coast, but it was decided

---

[1] *Ball of Fire*, by Antony Brett-James, p. 425.

nevertheless that the disembarkation of the 34th Corps should proceed more or less according to plan. The 15th Corps, on the other hand, would be sent direct to Singapore to occupy that island, and Johore State on the adjacent mainland, until it proceeded further overseas.

The plan for the 34th Corps, whose Chief Engineer was Brigadier E. C. R. Stileman, involved two assault landings which, owing to lack of sufficient naval craft, would have to be separated by an interval of three days. On "D" Day, fixed as September 9th, 1945, the 25th Indian Division, under Major-General G. N. Wood, with 46 Beach Group under command, was to land at Morib, 20 miles south of Port Swettenham.[1] Simultaneously, the 27th Brigade of Major-General D. C. Hawthorn's 23rd Indian Division would disembark at two places further south. On "D+3" Day, the 1st and 49th Brigades of the 23rd Division, with the 3rd Commando Brigade and 41 Beach Group, were to land south of Port Dickson to capture the important communications centre of Seremban. The 5th Indian Division, under Major General E.C. Mansergh, was to follow up at Morib, helped by part of 45 Beach Group. The objectives for the "D" Day assault were Port Swettenham, an airfield at Kelanang near Morib, and a crossing of the coastal road over the Sepang River some 10 miles north of Port Dickson. It was hoped that the seizing of this crossing by the 37th Brigade would lead to the occupation of Port Dickson by "D+3" Day. All the assaulting formations belonged to the Indian Army because the only British Division available for the Far East, the 2nd Division, was already committed to sending brigades to Hongkong and Japan while the third brigade was to remain in India.

Towards the end of August 1945, a great armada began to sail from Bombay, Madras, Cochin, Vizagapatam and Rangoon packed with troops who had undergone months of intensive training in preparation for an opposed landing. For most units, the voyage was a pleasant change from the commotion of the last days ashore. Captain A. H. W. Sandes, R.E., of 78 Field Company (Bengal) in 41 Beach Group, writes as follows:—"We left our camp at Bhiwandi outside Bombay on August 30th but did not arrive at the Victoria Docks till sunset, having taken sixteen hours to travel forty miles. There we staggered up the gangway of S.S. *Arawa* laden like pack-horses with equipment and clothing. We remained in dock until September 2nd, loading thousands of bottles of soda-water and

---
[1] See the map of Malaya included in Chapter VII and the map entitled "Landings in Malaya, Sept. 1945" included in this chapter.

detachments of late arrivals, and in the afternoon, amidst general rejoicing, pulled out into the harbour and were able to take stock of the rest of the convoy. Many ships had already gone, but a lot still remained. We sailed that night, and morning found us out of sight of land, steaming southwards over a placid sea. After the first day or two, life settled down to a daily routine of meals, talk, reading, boat drill and sleep. We sailed in undreampt of comfort because there was no black-out. The myriad lights of the convoy looked lovely at night. After about four days we turned east, and so knew that we were south of Ceylon. Then on and on, in perfect formation, until we sighted on the southern horizon some dim hills which we guessed were Sabang, at the northern tip of Sumatra. We overhauled another vast convoy of more than forty ships, and on the following day, passed a lone rock said to be off Penang. We still didn't know definitely that there would be no opposition to a landing, so we were all "briefed" and ready to fight. On the night of September 10th we passed another convoy and moved in single line ahead to get through some minefields. The morning of the 11th was wet and misty, but soon we could see the coast and anchored some ten miles offshore. There was much argument as to where we were, but it finally proved to be Port Swettenham, though the inevitable 'man who had lived there' swore that it was Port Dickson. Masses of ships were anchored for miles along the coast. We lay there all day, ready to disembark, but sailed again during the night and arrived off Port Dickson next morning. Seen from the sea, the place was not impressive except for its green foliage and the blue hills behind in the distance. It lay at the northern end of a long bay, at the southern end of which was a high hill called Cape Rachado, crowned by a lighthouse. Rain fell heavily for a couple of hours while we waited, piled with equipment, for a landing craft to take us ashore, but about noon an L.C.I. came alongside. We boarded it, and the ship's officers entertained some of us to sherry, the first we had tasted for years! As we neared the shore we could see a white sandy beach running up to palm trees and thick vegetation. It did not look very tropical, however, as there were many other trees resembling Scotch firs. A few white houses with red-tiled roofs showed here and there, and on an islet near the shore stood a little temple. Port Dickson reminded us of Akyab, though it was much nicer. Most of the roads were tarred and in good repair, and almost every house had piped water and electricity. The buildings seemed quite palatial, with marble floors, electric fans and all modern conveniences, and appeared to have suffered little from Japanese neglect.

The gardens would have been lovely had they not turned to jungle. The heat during the day was stifling, though the nights were cool, and the people seemed pleased to see us. Along the coastal road outside the town the contrasts in foliage were vivid. On one side, rubber plantations which had been allowed to grow untended and looked exactly like English birch woods. On the other side, mangrove swamps and palms. Rubber seemed to cover most of the countryside. The young trees were only about thirty feet high, with slender trunks quite bare for the first ten feet. Above that height were branches bearing dark green, oval-shaped, leaves which let little light through to the ground. Hence a rubber plantation resembled a vast colonnade of slim pillars under a roof of leaves stretching away into the distance. Apart from rubber, there were palms, giant bamboos, mangrove, eucalyptus and many other types of trees and bushes."

Most officers who were not in the first flights of the landings in Malaya must have gathered similar impressions of the country and had similar experiences, but those who led the way on September 9th and 12th under war conditions, though not under fire, found the problems of rapid disembarkation more formidable. For a distance of 200 miles between Port Swettenham and Singapore, the west coast of Malaya had only two beaches, about a couple of miles apart, which might perhaps be used for landing large bodies of troops and transport, and both were in the shallow bay between Port Dickson and Cape Rachado. Mangrove swamps fringed the remainder of the coast. The two beaches south of Port Dickson had been selected by aerial photography and were called "Dog" and "Charlie". The former was to be used for landing stores on "D+3" Day (September 12th) and the latter for landing vehicles. Both showed sand of an alluring smoothness, though their attractions proved later to be very deceptive. No good word can be said for two other beaches north of Port Dickson on which the actual "D" Day landings on September 9th were to take place. These also had been selected through air reconnaissance. They were called "How" and "Item" and earmarked for the landing of the 37th Brigade. "How" was no more than a flat shelf of mud, half a mile wide, backed by mangrove trees and impossible for vehicles or stores. "Item" looked a little more inviting but flattered only to deceive.

General Roberts' plan envisaged the early capture of Port Swettenham, away to the north, and the development of airfields there and at Kelanang, and consequently, apart from the operation

by the 37th Brigade, the main "D" Day assaults had to be made as
close to Port Swettenham as possible. The only moderately suitable
stretch of coast-line appeared to be a length of seven miles extending
southwards from Morib, some distance south of Port Swettenham.
Here, two beaches "Love" and "King", were chosen as they seemed
to have sandy surfaces. They had, but only as a veneer. The plan for
the main landing near Morib on September 9th, 1945, was as follows.
The 53rd Brigade of the 25th Division would assault on the right
over "King" beach while the greater part of the 51st Brigade assaulted
on the left over "Love" beach. A force of all arms called "Langat-
force", detached from the 51st Brigade, would push inland in amphibious craft to seize crossing places over the Langat River where the
25th Divisional Engineers would establish ferries. The Dukws of
this force were not to go beyond the river; but actually, two
of them, loaded with engineer stores, finished up in Kuala Lumpur
and can be said to have unofficially 'liberated' that city[1]. The first
waves of the brigades and their Beach Groups landed on "D" Day
without opposition, the only hindrance being an enormous traffic
block caused by the arrival of a senior Japanese Officer who wished to
discuss terms of surrender. Support by the 5th Indian Division being
clearly unnecessary, that formation did not disembark but continued its voyage southwards towards Singapore. "Love" beach soon revealed its true nature. It was found to have only a skin of sand, four
inches thick, over a mass of soft mud. A beach roadway for vehicles
was obviously needed, but a senior Naval Officer insisted that all
vehicles should be disembarked forthwith and these immediately
sank over their axles in the mud. Two Dukws and three bulldozers,
sent to the rescue, were also bogged down. Soon the lower part of
the beach was impassable even for a jeep. Sufficient pre-fabricated
roadway sheets (known as "Muckamuck")[2] were not available to cover
all soft patches, and in less than an hour there was a welter of fifty-two
vehicles stuck in the mud up to their frames and doomed to be swamped
by the in-coming tide. However, most of these unfortunates were
recovered and repaired later, and the landings near Morib and further
south proceeded day after day with remarkable steadiness until a

---

[1] "Indian Beach Groups in the Landings in Malaya", by Colonels D. W. Price, C.B.E. and J.R.H. Robertson, appearing in *The R.E. Journal*, Dec. 1947, pp. 288-305.

[2] "Muckamuck" consisted of bamboo panels sandwiched between coir matting and steel mesh which formed the road surface.

total of 42,651 men and nearly 4,000 vehicles had been put ashore. It was a fine achievement by the Royal Navy, the Beach Groups and the Field Companies of the Indian Engineers.

The units of the 25th Divisional Engineers, under Lieut.-Colonel H. R. Greenwood, R.E., which took part in the Morib landings were 63 Field Company (Madras) under Major G. A. P. N. Barlow, R.E., 93 Field Company (Bombay) under Major I. D. Usher, R.E., 425 Field Company (Madras) under Major J. W. L. Row, R.E., and 325 Field Park Company (Madras) under Major J. B. Hooper, R.E. The original landings were consolidated by the arrival of the 23rd Division. The convoys carrying the latter anchored off Port Swettenham on September 11th, and early on the 12th, moved southwards to a new anchorage off the Port Dickson beaches. The 23rd Divisional Engineers, under Lieut.-Colonel R. E. Holloway, R.E., comprised 68 and 71 Field Companies (Bengal) under Majors R. Allen and R. N. B. Holmes, R.E., 91 Field Company (Bombay) under Major J. S. Beddows, R.E., and 323 Field Park Company (Madras) under Major T. W. I. Headley, R.E. Landing craft of all sorts were soon discharging men and vehicles along beach roadways of Sommerfeld track to exits connected by further roads to the main coastal route. The development of such exits, and the preparation and repair of routes inland, were the main tasks of both the 23rd and 25th Divisional Engineers. The traffic was heavy and unceasing, and mud was constantly oozing up through the sandy surface. Major N. H. Bower, R.E., who commanded 227 Docks Operating Company, R.I.E., describes an incident at Morib on September 13th. "I was coming off my ship in a Dukw", he writes, "when I saw a bulldozer stuck in the mud with its Bengal Sapper driver perched on top. The water was already up to the man's waist and the tide was still flooding in. I asked the driver what he intended to do when the tide rose another three feet. He replied calmly that his officer had ordered him to remain till he returned. I told him to get into my Dukw, but he was very loath to leave and was only partially satisfied when I fixed a stick, with a bit of cloth on the end, on top of the bulldozer so that he could locate the machine even when the tide was at its highest. His attitude showed his devotion to duty regardless of his own comfort."

As the 23rd Division flooded into Malaya in the wake of the 25th Division, its Divisional Engineers became widely dispersed. 68 Field Company, with the 1st Brigade, moved to Seremban and then southwards to Segamat on the railway leading from Kuala Lumpur to Singapore. The Company repaired bridges and levelled a site for an airstrip. 71 Field Company remained for a time with the 49th Brigade south of Port Dickson and moved southwards through Kuala Lumpur to Raub, beyond Bentong, to provide ferries at several river crossings along the road to Kuantan on the east coast. 91 Field Company, with the 37th Brigade near Port Dickson, moved to Kuala Pilah, east of Seremban, and afterwards, passing through Segamat, built a 140-feet Double-Single Bailey bridge between Segamat and Kluang on the road leading to Singapore. However, only ten days after the 23rd Division had landed in Malaya, news arrived that it would be transferred shortly to Java, so the 23rd Divisional Engineers had only a very brief experience of the country. Lieut.-Colonel Holloway left Seremban on September 24th with a small advance party to fly from Singapore to Batavia. 68 Field Company sailed from Port Dickson with the 1st Brigade early in October, and 91 Field Company and 323 Field Park Company followed with the 37th Brigade in the middle of the month. 71 Field Company, with the 49th Brigade, was the last to leave Malaya but soon rejoined the other units in Java.

The 25th Divisional Engineers were then left to cope with the work north of Johore State, but by no means alone, for Army, Corps, and Forward Airfield Engineer units were pouring into the country. The chief task was to restore and extend the communications so that prosperity could be revived and troops moved quickly to any point. Jungle tracks had to be made fit for military traffic. This was an arduous and unhealthy business and it became the usual practice for the platoons of Field Companies to relieve each other at intervals of three weeks. Another major requirement was the provision of accommodation for about 50,000 soldiers instead of the 1,000 who had been stationed in Malaya, outside Singapore, before the war. Existing buildings were used as far as possible, but an enormous amount of hutting was needed to protect the troops against the monsoon. Camps surrounded by barbed wire had also to be built to hold Japanese prisoners-of-war. This work was executed mostly by civilian labour under the direction of senior Engineer officers of the Military Engineer Services, though it sometimes entailed supervision by Indian Engineer units.

At least a dozen companies of Army or Corps Troops Engineers, or Forward Airfield Engineers, arrived in Central Malaya during September 1945. The majority were supplied by the Madras Sappers. 430 and 431 Field Companies (458 Forward Airfield Engineers) landed on the Morib beaches on September 9th and 10th with the 21st Engineer Battalion. Soon afterwards 404, 405 and 423 Field

Companies and 326 Field Park Company (Army Troops Engineers) appeared on the scene. On September 12th, 432 Field Company landed at Morib, and on the 25th, 434 Field Company. Four field units of the Bombay Sappers arrived also—24 and 485 Field Companies on September 12th, 324 Field Park Company on the 15th, and 30 Field Company on the 19th. 76 Field Company of the Bengal Sappers was sent direct to Penang Island. Technical and Works units made their apppearance and, with the others, spread over the Malay States north of Johore to complete the work begun by the Divisional Engineers and to initiate more ambitious projects with the aid of civilian or Japanese prisoner-of-war labour. Most of these units passed through Kuala Lumpur, moving along fine roads bordered by rubber plantations in which they remarked a strange absence of animal or bird life. Kuala Lumpur, the capital, had about 140,000 inhabitants and was located on a plain overlooked by hills to the north and east. It had wide streets and many large buildings but was pervaded by an unpleasant odour of dried fish, wafted by the breeze from the Chinese quarter. There was little to buy in the shops, and the prices were exorbitant. Some units, such as 30 Field Company and 434 Field Park Company, moved northwards to the Thailand border or even beyond it; others worked in Penang, Taiping, Ipoh, Telok Anson and Raub, north of Kuala Lumpur; others again at Klang, or at Seremban to the south.

All these units were very busy during the closing months of 1945. A number of bridges along the main west road from Penang southwards had to be rebuilt, often with Bailey equipment. The largest were at Gedong and Juru. They were built by 404, 405 and 423 Field Companies and 326 Field Park Company. The Juru Bridge was the biggest in South-East Asia for it had two 190-feet triple-triple spans and one 110-feet triple-single. When completed in March 1946, it was opened by Lieut.-General Sir Frank Messervy, the G.O.C. Malaya. A great amount of bridging was done on the railways in 1946 by 62 Field Company (Madras) under Major J. H. Hoare, R.E. In March it repaired a 324-feet Japanese timber bridge north of Kuala Lipis on the central line, and in May erected a 120-feet Double-Double Bailey at Bidor near Telok Anson. Early in July it finished its bridging duties near Kuala Lipis and subsequently moved southwards to Kluang for airfield work.

While on the subject of communications in Malaya it may be well to mention the construction of the east coast route from Kuantan northwards to Kota Bahru and the improvement of an extension to the Thailand border at Hat Yai which was begun by Engineer units at the beginning of 1946 with the assistance of civilian and Japanese labour[1]. It was at Kota Bahru that the Japanese made their initial landing in 1942, and since then they had dismantled large sections of the railway line through Kuala Krai, Kuala Lipis and Jerantut which had formed a connection with the southern States. A road was therefore needed to replace the railway. Kuantan was linked with Kuala Lumpur by a good lateral highway which crossed the Pahang River, passed through Bentong and surmounted the central range of hills; but southwards down the east coast towards Mersing there was no road of any description, and northwards, to Kota Bahru, only a rough track. Altogether, about 250 miles of new roadway were needed involving the crossing of eleven rivers or streams.

The first steps in the east coast road project were taken by the 25th Divisional Engineers in October 1945 when 63 Field Company was sent to Kuantan, leaving a Section at Jerantut to assist in operating a 300-yards' ferry across the Pahang. In February 1946, 93 Field Company moved southwards from Alor Star to Kuala Lumpur and thence eastwards to Karak, a few miles beyond Bentong, to commence bridging along the route to Kuantan. Colonel A. E. Anstruthers, commanding 472 A.G.R.E., launched the main undertaking in June 1946, concentrating first on a section of the road from Kuantan northwards to Trengganu, a distance of 128 miles. He had at his disposal 63 and 425 Field Companies and 325 Field Park Company (25th Divisional Engineers) 58, 404, 405 and 423 Field Companies and 326 Field Park Company (Army Troops Engineers), and 430 and and 431 Field Companies and the 21st Engineer Battalion (Forward Airfield Engineers). There were also some technical formations and four battalions of Japanese prisoners-of-war for manual labour. Owing to a shortage of tar and bitumen, only certain sections of the road could be tarred; the rest was merely soled and surfaced. Stone causeways up to half a mile in length were needed in some places, so several quarries were opened to supply the necessary material. Numerous ferries were improved and 16 bridges and 72 culverts built, and in November 1946, when the road was handed over to the Public Works Department, it was nearing completion.

It is advisable at this stage to revert to September 1946 to describe the re-occupation of Singapore and Southern Malaya which was accomplished without opposition while the 34th Corps was landing

---

[1] See the map of Malaya included in Chapter VII.

further north. As already recorded, the 5th Indian Division under Major-General E. C. Mansergh, originally ear-marked as a 'follow-up' formation for the landing by the 25th and 23rd Indian Divisions, was diverted to Singapore in consequence of the enemy's surrender. The Division had sailed from Rangoon on August 27th, 1945, when there was still some uncertainty as to whether the 96,000 Japanese troops on Singapore Island would obey the order from Tokyo to lay down their arms. On September 3rd, the convoy of 32 ships was off Penang where the 9th Brigade was detached in case its services were needed. Some Royal Marines, however, had already disembarked and consequently the 9th Brigade followed the rest of the Division southwards. In the meantime, mine sweepers had been clearing the Malacca Straits and were approaching Singapore, and early on September 4th, H.M.S. *Sussex*, with Admiral Holland, Lieut.-General Christison and Major-General Mansergh aboard, lay some twenty miles off the city awaiting the arrival of Japanese representatives empowered to accept and carry out surrender terms for Malaya. General Itagaki, commanding the Japanese Seventh Area Army, and Vice-Admiral Fukudome, commanding the Tenth Area Fleet, came alongside in a tug and were received aboard the *Sussex* by the British representatives who had assembled in a cabin. The proceedings lasted nearly four hours. Itagaki endeavoured to bargain, but in the end, with tears running down his face, signed the surrender document. He was more to be pitied than Fukudome who had tried to ingratiate himself with the British Commanders by an exhibition of joviality and camaraderie. The terms were harsh. Surrender was to be unconditional. Most of the Japanese garrison of Singapore Island was to march to the mainland, starting that same night. All arms must be handed in, but uniform and badges of rank would still be worn. The Japanese officers would remain responsibible for the discipline of their men, the protection of certain public buildings, the feeding of the civilian population and the maintenance of essential services until relieved of these duties. As a temporary measure, they would provide small guards to prevent damage or looting. No demolition would be permitted. All documents, records, cyphers and lists of available supplies were to be produced. The locations of all Allied prisoner-of-war or internee camps were to be given, and also those of all fortifications, naval installations, tank depots and ammunition dumps. No Japanese aircraft was to leave the ground; no ship was to move. Every Japanese flag must be hauled down before the Allied forces landed. A curfew would be imposed from sunset till sunrise. A

Japanese General must report twice daily to General Mansergh for orders. The other enemy Generals would be confined in Raffles College till evacuated. These were some of the peremptory orders issued, and they were obeyed to the letter. By dawn on September 5th, 35,000 Japanese soldiers had crossed the causeway from Singapore Island to the mainland.

During the night of September 4th/5th, the 5th Divisional convoy, blazing with lights, followed a swept channel through the straits and approached Singapore. H.M.S. *Sussex* was already there with her guns trained on the city. Nothing was left to chance, and when two battalions of the 123rd Brigade landed in the morning they did so fully armed and equipped and ready to fight. However, there was no resistance. The infantry fanned out from the docks and occupied all key positions such as arsenals, airfields, the railway terminus and camps. The 161st Brigade followed and advanced across the island to the naval base on the northern shore and the causeway leading to the mainland. The Japanese were collected in concentration areas pending their removal. They were well treated but were allowed no luxuries, and the British and Indian troops had already been warned that there must be no fraternization. As soon as the 5th Division had begun to disembark, some officers had made straight for the Changi prisoner-of-war camp at the eastern end of the island and the civilian internment camp at Syme Road. In the womens' section of the latter, they were infuriated to find Lady Shenton Thomas, wife of the Governor, clad in ragged clothing and without shoes or stockings, making grass soup in an old bully-beef tin. Supplies were rushed immediately to the Allied prisoners-of-war and internees. There were more than 32,000 prisoners on the island including 16,000 Indians, 6,000 British, 5,000 Australians and 4,000 Dutch. All were emaciated and dressed in rags. They seemed dazed and spoke little of their horrifying experience, but their spirit was not broken. Some of the Indian soldiers, for instance, mounted guards on their camps, armed with only sticks, and when a senior Allied officer approached 'presented arms' in smart fashion. The seriously ill were evacuated to hospitals or hospital ships, and the remainder clothed and fed; but they could eat little after years of semi-starvation and the effects of disease and neglect. The worst cases were those who had slaved on the Japanese railway line from Thailand to Lower Burma. Lieut.-Colonel Lindsell gives a graphic description of the privations suffered by the Indian Engineer prisoners-of-war in Singapore and elsewhere[1]. It is an inspiring tale of fortitude in adversity, but cannot be repeated here. The recovery and welfare of the ex-prisoners and internees was undertaken by an organization known as "R.A.P.W.I." (Recovery of Allied Prisoners-of-War and Internees) and was most efficiently carried out. The Bombay Group of the Indian Engineers had been the chief sufferers in 1942 as regards the number of units lost, and between September and December 1945 no less than 17 British Officers and 1,143 Indian ranks, mostly from Malaya, arrived in Kirkee from prison camps overseas.

The units of the 5th Divisional Engineers which landed at Singapore on September 5th, 1945, or a few days later, were commanded by Lieut.-Colonel R.C. Orgill, R.E. They were 2 Field Company (Bengal) under Major C. W. Williams, R.E., 20 Field Company (Bombay) under Major E. C. Fisher, R.E., 74 Field Company (Bengal) under Major D. Brunt, R.E., and 44 Field Park Company (Madras) under Major H. F. Thompson, R.E. "The Sappers and Miners had many problems to face", writes Antony Brett-James[2]. "The water-supply was improved, public utilities repaired, and reconnaissances made of store dumps. In South Malaya, communications were restored and airfields repaired. Drains were cleared, anti-tank ditches and pot-holes filled in, bridges strengthened or replaced, and road-blocks removed. Classification signs were erected on bridges. Stock lists of Engineer dumps were prepared, and saw-mills and quarries in Southern Johore reconnoitred. All bridges for the first 150 miles from Singapore to Malacca had to be replaced. At night, while the military police closed the road, a platoon or two of Sappers were hastily stripping an old timber bridge and putting up a Bailey bridge by the glare of headlights." The preparation of lists of Japanese engineer stores was difficult because the Japanese had, or seemed to have, little idea of the amount and location of the materials. Their engineer stores were mixed with ammunition, signal and ordnance stores, and at one spot the British discovered a barrack completely filled with new lathes about which the Japanese said they knew nothing whatever.

The greatest hindrance to the early restoration of Singapore was the lack of transport. For some days, the 5th Division had only its unit vehicles. The Japanese had undertaken to produce a number

---

[1] *A Short History of Q.V's O. Madras Sappers and Miners during World War* II, 1939-1945, by Lt. Col. R.A. Lindsell, R.E., pp. 55-58.

[2] *Ball of Fire*, by Antony Brett-James, pp. 438-439.

of lorries and trucks, but they were slow to arrive. A major task for the 5th Divisional Engineers, and for the 15th Corps Troops Engineers who followed them, was the rapid construction of barbed wire enclosures to hold thousands of Japanese prisoners-of-war pending their evacuation to the mainland. Needless to say, having seen the condition of their friends released from captivity, the Sappers derived much satisfaction in thus turning the tables on the enemy. Before the end of the month, 2 Field Company moved northwards to Kluang in Johore State, building eight Bailey bridges along the road. A prisoner-of-war camp was to be prepared close to the Kluang airfield from which all the Japanese in Southern Malaya could be evacuated later to the Riouw archipelago south of Singapore Island. The other Engineer units continued to improve accommodation and communications; but all became aware, at a very early date, that they were mere birds of passage as the 5th Division was already earmarked for service further afield.

September 12th, 1945, was a red letter day in the whole of South-East Asia, for it was the occasion of the official surrender to Lord Mountbatten of all the Japanese forces in that vast area. The surrender took place in the Council Chamber of the Municipal Buildings at Singapore in the presence of senior officers of the British, Indian, United States, Australian, French, Dutch and Chinese forces. Mountbatten arrived in an open car through miles of cheering crowds. He had ordered Field-Marshal Terauchi, the Japanese Supreme Commander, to be present; but as Terauchi was ill, General Itagaki, who had already made the local surrender, was allowed to represent his superior officer at the major ceremony. Terauchi's personal surrender was postponed until Mountbatten could visit the Japanese Headquarters at Saigon[1]. The chief Allied representatives at the ceremony in Singapore were Admiral Sir Arthur Power, Field-Marshal Sir William Slim, Air Chief Marshal Sir Keith Park, Lieut.-General R. A. Wheeler (U.S.), Air Vice-Marshal A. T. Cole (Australia), General Leclerc (France), Major-General Feng Yee (China), Brigadier K.S. Thimayya (India) and Colonel B. van Vreeden (Holland). They sat in line at two long tables between which was a large desk for Lord Mountbatten. On Mountbatten's left was Slim, and on his right, Wheeler, and at the right hand end of the line was Thimayya. Facing them at another table were seven Japanese representatives—General

---

[1] At Saigon, on November 30th, Lord Mountbatten received Field-Marshal Terauchi's sword.

Itagaki, General Kimura, Vice-Admirals Fukudome and Shibata, and Lieut.-Generals Nakamura, Kinoshita and Numata. They had filed in under guard and sat with stony faces, bareheaded and unarmed. In the background, a sentry, grenade in hand, watched the line of little bullet-headed men. The proceedings were brief and formal. Mountbatten announced the terms of surrender. The papers were carried across to Itagaki, and soon after 11.0. a.m. they were signed. Half an hour later, the Japanese were marched away amidst devastating jeers from the watching crowds. The Allied officers emerged and Mountbatten read a proclamation from the steps of the Municipal Buildings. On a parade of Allied troops, a British soldier then hoisted the identical Union Jack that had been lowered in 1942 and hidden ever since, while a salute was fired by an Indian Field Battery. The occasion marked the end of the armed might of Japan, though comparatively few of her armies had been defeated in battle.

To meet the wishes of the Americans, the boundaries of the South-East Asia Command had been extended during August 1945 to include Java and some islands beyond it, in addition to Borneo, Celebes, Dutch New Guinea and part of French Indo-China. This added greatly to Mountbatten's responsibilities. On September 30th the 15th Indian Corps, under Lieut.-General Sir Philip Christison[1], was re-designated "Allied Forces, Netherlands East Indies", or briefly "A.F.N.E.I.", and was ordered to move from Southern Malaya to Java and Sumatra. It comprised the 5th, 23rd and 26th Indian Divisions commanded respectively by Major-Generals E. C. Mansergh, D. C. Hawthorn and H.M. Chambers. At first it had been hoped that the 23rd Division would suffice for the occupation of both Java and Sumatra. Then it became apparent that a single Division could not hold both islands and that the 26th Division must assume responsibility for Sumatra; and finally, when Java proved beyond the unaided powers of the 23rd Division, the 5th Division had to be brought forward to occupy the eastern half of the island while the 23rd Division controlled the western half. Thus, in the end, only the 25th Division, under Major-General G. N. Wood, was left in Malaya; but reinforcements were on their way from India, and on December 8th, 1945, Malaya became a separate Command under

---

[1] On January 30th, 1946, Lieut.-General Sir Philip Christison was succeeded by Lieut.-General Sir Montagu Stopford.

Lieut.-General Sir Frank Messervy, formerly G.O.C., 4th Corps.[1] The A.F.N.E.I. Headquarters were to be established in Batavia, the capital of Java, by October 10th. The Chief Engineer of the new organization was Brigadier D.C. T. Swan[2] who had been C.E., 15th Corps, since April when he had relieved Brigadier L. I. Jacques. Swan had under his orders the 5th Divisional Engineers under Lieut.-Colonel R. C. Orgill, R.E., (later succeeded by Lieut.-Colonel D. W. Price, R.E.,), the 23rd Divisional Engineers under Lieut.-Colonel D. R. Guinness, R.E.,) and the 26th Divisional Engineers under Lieut.-Colonel H. C. G. Richards, R.E., (later succeeded by Lieut.-Colonel D. R. W. Waller, R.E.). There were also certain technical and specialist formations. The Engineer cadre of A.F.N.E.I. was large, but nevertheless barely sufficient to cope with the commitments involved in the occupation of two enormous islands whose inhabitants were seething with discontent afters years of harsh Japanese rule.

On September 25th, 1945, the 1st Brigade of the 23rd Division began to disembark in Batavia, and when the movement was completed on October 4th sporadic fighting against guerilla bands of Indonesians was already in progress in and around the town. The 37th Brigade followed to Batavia in the middle of October, while the 49th Brigade, under Brigadier A.W.S. Mallaby, voyaged further eastwards and reached the Dutch naval base at Sourabaya on October 25th. With the 49th Brigade was 71 Field Company (Bengal) under Major R.N.B. Holmes, R.E. The situation in Java requires some explanation. The sudden capitulation of Japan in the middle of August had left South-East Asia in a turmoil. In Thailand, there were clashes at Bangkok between the Thais and the Chinese. The Annamite National Movement ("Viet-Minh") in French Indo-China, and the Indonesian National Movement in Java and Sumatra, had been encouraged by the Japanese because they were directed against France or Holland, and it fell to Great Britain to restore order until those countries could resume control and decide what action should be taken. This, however, was against the wishes of the inhabitants who were obsessed, perhaps naturally, with the idea of self-determination. A section of the Indonesian movement in Java, under

---

[1] General Messervy held the Malaya Command until he was appointed G.O.C.-in-C., Northern Command, India, on October 15th, 1946. From August 15th, 1947, to February 1st, 1948, he was C-in-C., Pakistan.

[2] Brig. D.C.T. Swan held the appointment of C.E., A.F.N.E.I., until Jan. 20th, 1946, when he was succeeded by Brig. G.A.T. Pritchard.

Dr. Soerkano, seemed willing to collaborate with our forces, but nevertheless Soerkano was resolved that Indonesia should soon become an independent Republic. Before the 23rd Division landed in Batavia and Sourabaya, the Indonesians had received large quantities of arms, ammunition and stores from the Japanese who had withdrawn into concentration areas. Promptly, the Indonesians turned upon the Dutch civilians in their midst and at Sourabaya murdered or imprisoned several hundreds of men, women and children.

On the arrival of the 49th Brigade at Sourabaya, Brigadier Mallaby conferred with Dr. Moestopo, the local Indonesian leader, who had been instructed by Soerkano not to oppose a landing. The Brigade accordingly landed, occupying all key points in the town without bloodshed. On October 27th, some units moved inland to Darmo, a residential area at the southern end where there was a large Dutch civilian internment camp.[1] The Indonesians at once suspected that Mallaby intended to hold them down by force until he could hand over to their previous masters, the Dutch. They had 12,000 ex-Regular soldiers, trained and armed by the Japanese and supported by an armed mob 75,000 strong. On October 28th, this mob poured through the town, murdering isolated parties of British and Indian soldiers and many Dutch women and children. Street fighting began in earnest. Brigadier Mallaby was murdered, and after the 49th Brigade had lost 400 officers and men, it was withdrawn by Colonel L.H.O. Pugh to the dock and airfield area in the north. Shortly afterwards, Major-General E.C. Mansergh arrived by air to examine the situation and it was then decided that the greater part of his 5th Division should be sent from Malaya to reinforce the 49th Brigade of the 23rd Division.

Sourabaya was a large town about six miles in length from north to south and in places nearly two miles wide. Most of its 300,000 inhabitants were Indonesians, but the total included about 38,000 Chinese and some thousands of Europeans. Down the centre of the town ran a canalized river called the Kali Mas and further east a stream known as the Kali Semampir. Near the mouth of the Kali Mas was the Tandjoenperak dock area and an airfield. East of the Kali Mas were miles of squalid suburbs called 'kampongs'. A truce had been arranged with the Indonesians in Sourabaya before the 9th Brigade under Brigadier H.G.L. Brain disembarked as the leading formation

---

[1] See the map of Sourabaya included in this chapter.

of the 5th Division. The landing was unopposed although the troops were obviously unwelcome. An unnatural silence brooded over the town. The 9th Brigade relieved the 49th Brigade in the area east of the Kali Mas and negotiations were begun for the return of a battalion still remaining in Darmo after guarding the evacuation of 6,000 women and children to the dock area. This battalion left Darmo during the night of November 7th/8th and rejoined the 49th Brigade safely. General Mansergh was then able to issue an ultimatum to the insurgents. He did so on November 9th, giving them till next morning to surrender all arms, failing which he would clear the town completely. The ultimatum had little effect, and accordingly, after the 123rd Brigade had landed, a general advance was begun on November 10th. The 161st Brigade was not present as it had been diverted to Batavia. By November 28th, after considerable street fighting, Sourabaya had been cleared of the insurgents; but operations had to be continued throughout December against isolated bands in the surrounding country, and the 5th Division could not be withdrawn to Malaya until the middle of January 1946. The fighting at Sourabaya was the last in which units of the Indian Army were commanded by British officers.

The only Sapper unit at Sourabaya in the earliest days of the disturbance was 71 Field Company (Bengal) under Major R.N.B. Holmes, R.E., Indeed, the first troops to set foot in the town on October 25th, 1945, were some men of the Company's Mechanical Transport party. They had a sullen though not too unfriendly reception. The Company disembarked with most of the 49th Brigade on the following day and a subaltern was sent to reconnoitre the airfield, meeting with much obstruction from the Indonesian officials because they thought he was Dutch. On the 27th, the unit (less one platoon) moved through the town to the Darmo suburb. All was quiet at the moment and the Indonesian soldiers saluted our officers, but serious trouble was evidently brewing. It started on the 28th. There was much fighting in the centre of the town and some of the Company transport in the docks area was ordered to move to Darmo. This it did after dusk under heavy fire. News came that a convoy of nineteen trucks carrying women and children to safety had been ambushed while being escorted by men of the 123rd Company, R.I.A.S.C. Many of these women and children were bayonetted. Others perished when the houses in which they had taken shelter were set on fire. Only thirty survived out of two hundred. The Indian drivers put up a great fight, and all but eight were killed at their posts.

Early on October 29th, fire was opened on 71 Field Company's position in the Darmo barracks. The Indonesians crept up to within fifty yards and casualties began to mount. Holmes then asked for artillery support which was given promptly. Captain D. C. Floyer, R.E., from a very exposed position, directed the fire on to the enemy's trenches, and those Indonesians who tried to escape were mown down by machine guns. At 3.0 p.m. some Thunderbolts came over and fighting ceased, but not before the Company had lost two killed and eleven wounded. October 30th was another exciting day. A detachment of Rajputs in the Darmo Railway Station was short of ammunition, so at 10.0 a.m. Holmes despatched a party to the station in a lorry. Heavy fighting was in progress; but the ammunition was delivered and several wounded Rajputs evacuated to hospital before the party returned to the barracks where the situation was becoming increasingly serious. The Indonesians swarmed on all sides, waving flags, shouting "Don't shoot", and demanding that 71 Company should surrender. Floyer then set out, unarmed, with the Indonesian commmander, to the rebels' headquarters, six miles away, to discuss matters. He returned safely, two hours later, in an armoured vehicle, having been forced to abandon his 15 cwt. truck. Meanwhile, Holmes had waited calmly outside the barracks facing an excited crowd but with four machine-guns placed in convienient positions behind him. Floyer's return fortunately coincided with the arrival of a letter from Dr. Soerkano enjoining moderation. The rebels were sufficiently pacified to disperse to their homes, and soon afterwards Floyer was awarded the Military Cross. Supplìes were dropped by aeroplanes, and for the next three days all was quiet at Darmo. On November 2nd, a convoy transported 1,400 women and children to the docks area. 71 Field Company followed on November 6th and joined in minor offensive operations during the next few weeks. On November 25th it embarked with the 49th Brigade for Batavia, very glad, no doubt, to see the last of Sourabaya.

By that time, the 5th Divisional Engineers were installed in Sourabaya and fully employed. 20 Field Company (Bombay) under Major E. C. Fisher, R.E., had arrived with the 9th Brigade at the beginning of November, and soon afterwards came 44 Field Park Company (Madras) under Major H. F. Thompson, R.E. 2 Field Company (Bengal), now under Major J. S. Dhillon, R.I.E., landed on November 24th and was followed by 74 Field Company (Bengal) under Major D. Brunt, R.E. These units saw no fighting and their work was confined mostly to clearing debris, lifting mines, opening roads and railways, repairing bridges, restoring the sewage system and providing accommodation and water supply—in fact the usual engineer duties in devastated areas. 44 Field Park Company, however, was especially busy for it had to repair and operate most of the public installations in the town in addition to its normal work. It took over the Electric Power Station near the docks and restored the electric lighting of the airfield. It repaired generators and pumps, controlled a plant for pumping oil to the Power Station, supervised cold storage plants, assembled perimeter searchlights, repaired cranes and roadrollers, manufactured coffins, and was even called upon to break open several safes whose owners had vanished with the keys. Anyone who required anything done in the mechanical or electrical line applied to the long-suffering Field Park Company and they were rarely disappointed. 2 Field Company was sent to Batavia in the middle of December but was back in Sourabaya by January 8th, 1946, and there it remained with the other units of the 5th Divisional Engineers, until it sailed for India in April. The first Dutch troops had arrived on February 4th, and by the middle of March a complete Dutch Brigade was present. The transfer of responsibility to the Dutch in Eastern Java was completed at the beginning of May 1946, and June 5th saw the departure of the last British and Indian units.

While the 5th Indian Division was restoring law and order in Eastern Java, the 23rd Indian Division (less, for a time, the 49th Brigade) had been equally busy around Batavia in Western Java. Here, 68 and 91 Field Companies and 323 Field Park Company of the 23rd Divisional Engineers, under Lieut.-Colonel R. E. Holloway, R.E., did excellent work pending the return of 71 Field Company from Sourabaya which took place towards the end of November 1945. 68 Field Company had landed from Port Dickson early in October, and 91 Field Company and 323 Field Park Company had followed in the middle of the month. Other Sapper units reached Batavia during November among them being 433 Field Company (Madras) of the Forward Airfield Engineers, and in December, 78 Field Company (Bengal) of 41 Beach Group, under Major W. Byrde, R.E. The 23rd Division was not involved at first in much fighting although Batavia was the scene of many skirmishes between the Japanese and the Indonesians who wished to secure Japanese arms. At Bandoeng the Japanese retained their arms; at Semarang they handed them over. There were clashes also at Cheribon, Jogjakarta and other places. Jungle law had reigned in Western Java since the collapse of Japan. The

Indonesians wanted freedom, and the Japanese to be absolved from all responsibility, and when the 23rd Division began to arrive the country was already in the throes of a popular uprising. The Indonesians had taken charge of all public utility services. They ran the railways, the post and telegraph services, and the water-supply in Batavia. They commandeered any vehicle they fancied, and seized any building they desired, without interference from the police. The local Press hurled abuse at the Dutch. Ships lay unloaded in the docks. Shooting began in the streets about October 4th, and barricades appeared overnight. A week later, two officers of a Punjab battalion were killed in an ambush and our troops began to fight the Indonesians, so General Hawthorn proclaimed what virtually amounted to martial law. The situation in Batavia improved with the arrival of the 37th Brigade on October 16th, but there still remained the problem of ensuring the safety of 10,000 Dutch internees at Ambarawa and Banjoebiroe, some 20 miles inland from Semarang. This mountainous tract of Central Java was a hot-bed of unrest. On October 31st, fighting started at Magelang, still further south, and it became increasingly difficult to hold Semarang and at the same time to guard the R.A.P.W.I. camps far inland. Semarang and Ambarawa became miniature battlefields, but the situation improved at the end of the November with the arrival of the 49th Brigade from Sourabaya. A fortnight later, Ambarawa was evacuated and our troops fell back on Semarang.

Meanwhile, in Batavia, there had been desultory fighting every night between the Indonesians and the local Dutch, and hostilities now started at Bandoeng, 70 miles to the south-east, where our troops engaged the Indonesians. The first signs of improvement coincided with the arrival of additional forces to reinforce the 23rd Division. These were the 161st Brigade (5th Division) originally earmarked for Sourabaya, the 36th Brigade (26th Division) transferred from Sumatra, and the 5th Parachute Brigade sent from Singapore. The 36th Brigade moved southwards to Buitenzorg, while the Parachute Brigade went eastwards to Semarang after helping to restore order in Batavia. Convoys carrying supplies to Bandoeng had been having a most unpleasant time as the Indonesians, sheltering in fox-holes on the the hill-sides, took every opportunity to lob Molotov cocktails onto passing vehicles. Strong escorts were needed to clear a passage. Early in March 1946, Bandoeng became the scene of the final operations in Western Java. Four Dutch battalions were arriving in Batavia and the 1st Brigade was moving from Buitenzorg to Bandoeng to

Constructing the Kemajaran Airfield near Batavia

replace the 37th Brigade. Aided by mines and road-blocks, the Indonesians launched a heavy attack on a large convoy and a five-day battle ensued in which our troops suffered 115 casualties. The fighting ceased, however, on March 15th when the last vestiges of insurrection began to die down. As more Dutch troops landed in Western Java our commitments were reduced gradually to Batavia alone, and finally, on November 30th, 1946, the last British and Indian units departed.

The Engineer work in Western Java resembled that carried out in the eastern territory except that there was more to be done in the evacuation of internees and the repair of airfields. The internees had to be collected rapidly in places of safety, and as their camps were often located far inland, whole brigades had sometimes to be maintained in isolated spots for their protection. The roads leading to these distant concentrations needed constant attention in order that they might be kept open for large convoys escorted by armoured cars, and every convoy had to be provided with a detachment from an Engineer Field Company to lift mines and clear road-blocks. Occasionally the Field Companies were also called upon to help the Forward Airfield Engineers in improving airfields, though most of the heavy work was done by civilian labour or by Japanese prisoners-of-war. When Brigadier G.A.T. Pritchard succeeded Brigadier D.C.T. Swan as Chief Engineer, A.L.F.N.E.I., on January 20th, 1946, he found that Batavia itself needed much attention[1]. The main Power House had to be brought into use and maintained, the Flood Control system restored, and the Cold Storage Plant and main Water Supply repaired and operated. The roads were in a shocking condition, and labour was scarce because the Indonesians refused to work under Dutch or Japanese supervision. Another urgent task was the clearance of drainage canals choked with silt and obstructed by a growth of water-hyacinth. The canals also contained many corpses which blocked the sluice gates and had to be removed and buried.

In February 1946, as the greater part of the 23rd Division had already moved inland to the Bandoeng area, the Forward Airfield Engineers and a Works Section took over most of the engineer duties in Batavia. The 23rd Divisional Engineers were widely scattered. One Company remained in Batavia, another was at Buitenzorg, and the Headquraters and the third Company were at Bandoeng. During March, after Brigadier D. R. Guinness had been appointed Chief Engineer, A.F.N.E.I., the Indonesians made so many attacks on

---

[1] Notes by Major-General G.A.T. Pritchard, c.b.e., dated Feby. 11th, 1954.

convoys between Batavia and Bandoeng that the Sappers were constantly required to reconnoitre demolitions and road-blocks and execute rapid repairs or find alternative routes. Courses of instruction for Dutch Engineer units, expected shortly from overseas, had to be arranged. It was known that those coming from Holland would be fully equipped, but that others which were being raised in the Far East would have little or no equipment and all would need training in local methods. The Dutch companies arrived during July 1946 and were duly trained and, when necessary, provided with equipment, and thus the Indian Engineers and Forward Airfield Engineers were able at last to hand over charge and prepare to leave the country.

68 Field Company (Bengal), under Major R. W. Allen, R.E., which was in Batavia until it moved to Buitenzorg early in February 1946, undertook an unusual task while stationed in the capital. This was the printing of *The Fighting Cock*, a 23rd Division newspaper. The first edition appeared on October 23rd, 1945, and was produced, curiously enough, with the full co-operation of both the Indonesians and the Dutch. The title was afterwards adopted for the Divisional History[1]. 68 Field Company moved to Tjandjoer, half way between Buitenzorg and Bandoeng, in March 1946, and to Bandoeng itself in May. It returned to Batavia in July to prepare for evacuation. 91 Field Company (Bombay), under Major H. A. Mavor, R.E., which had reached Bandoeng in the middle of December 1945, was employed until the end of May in clearing obstacles, lifting mines and improving airfields. Then it handed over charge to 68 Field Company and returned to Batavia, leaving a platoon at Buitenzorg until 71 Field Company arrived there on July 1st from Sourabaya. As the Dutch Engineers assumed control in Batavia, opportunities for games and sports became frequent, though the Sappers did not mix freely with either the Dutch or the Indonesians. 91 Field Company was composed of Hindu, Sikh and Punjabi Mahomedan Platoons, and it is noteworthy that during the Muslim period of Ramzan the Sikhs offered to relieve the Mahomedans of most of their guard duties. This is a happy instance of the good feeling which existed in 1946 between men of different creeds and helps to explain why the troubles arising from the separation of Pakistan from India in the following year had so few repercussions among the armed forces.

While Java was in the process of pacification, the adjacent island of Sumatra was being occupied by the 26th Indian Division under

---

[1] *The Fighting Cock*, by Lieut.-Colonel A.J.F. Doulton, O.B.E.

Major-General H.M. Chambers and with much less difficulty than was encountered by the 5th and 23rd Indian Divisions further east. Although Sumatra is more than 1,000 miles in length and three times the size of Java, its population in 1945 did not exceed eight million people, or about one-fifth that of Java. Medan, the capital on the east coast facing Penang Island across the Malacca Straits, had only 77,000 inhabitants of whom 27,000 were Chinese and 4,000 Europeans. Palembang, an oil centre in the south-east had a population of 108,000, while Padang, on the west coast, held 66,000. The communications were poor, vast areas in the interior being either marshy or mountainous and covered with jungle. In Sumatra, as in Java, thousands of released Allied prisoners-of-war and civilian internees had to be collected and evacuated and large numbers of Japanese troops rounded up, and all this had to be done with the least possible interference with the local administration.

The 4th and 71st Brigades of the 26th Division sailed from Madras at the beginning of October 1945 with 28 Field Company under Major C. J. Bewley, R.E., 98 Field Company under Major P. B. Button, R.E., and 328 Field Park Company under Major A. D. M. Dunne, R.E. All these units belonged to the Bombay Group, and with 72 Field Company (Bengal) under Major J. B. H. Knight, R.E., comprised the 26th Divisional Engineers commanded by Lieut.-Colonel H. C. G. Richards, R.E. The 26th Brigade followed at the end of the month with 72 Field Company. Richards had also a couple of Electrical and Mechanical platoons and some Forward Airfield Engineers. General Chambers established his headquarters at Padang, where the 71st Brigade occupied all strategic points, and on October 10th, 28 Field Company reached the town and began to improve the accommodation, water supply and road communications. 72 and 98 Field Companies and 328 Field Park Company were sent to Medan with the 4th Brigade. Palembang was occupied at first by only one battalion, and no Sapper unit was available for the small garrison. At Medan the chief task was to improve the airfield so that the Divisional Headqurters could be transferred from Padang. This work proceeded so well that the transfer was effected in March 1946.

Soon after the arrival of the 26th Division the Indonesians began to give trouble, and particularly at Padang where our troops had to take strong defensive measures. At night, 28 Field Company guarded one of the three defended localities into which Padang was divided. This threw a heavy strain on the men, which became heavier later when it became necessary to detach one platoon to Palembang. Indonesian snipers and grenade throwers ambushed convoys or crept into the town after dark to attack the Dutch. Life at Medan was more orderly, and with the arrival of the 11th Engineer Battalion the work of restoration was accelerated. 328 Field Park Company was especially busy. After providing and operating an Engineer Stores Depot and running a stone-crushing plant, it was moved suddenly ten miles up the coast to Belawan to the site of an old railway workshop overgrown with jungle. It had not only to clear the site and build huts but also to rebuild and re-fit the workshop and organize a large output of metal and woodwork.

By contrast with Medan, life at Palembang was unpleasant, and little engineering could be done by the platoon of 28 Field Company after the departure of the Japanese. The situation both in Palembang and Medan worsened during the summer of 1946 until the evacuation of the 23rd Division from Java provided some reinforcements. 71 Field Company, now under Major M. L. Khetarpal, R.I.E., was sent to Palembang to help the detachment of 28 Field Company. Unrest was widespread. "The Indonesian tactics showed many resemblances to those of the Japanese", writes Major J. S. R. Shave, R.E.,[1] "and it was clear that deserters from the Japanese were encouraging and training the guerillas. Captured arms and equipment were frequently of Jap origin. Our Mahomedan troops were encouraged to desert and promised promotion and good pay if they joined the republican army, but throughout the occupation the discipline and morale of the British and Indian troops was of the highest order. The year 1946 saw a rapid decrease in the strength of our forces in the Far East, yet it was imperative that the eventual hand-over to the Dutch should be well prepared. The C.R.E. accordingly undertook the task of raising a Dutch Engineer platoon in Medan to take over the maintenance and operation of the plant and the port of Belawan from 328 Field Park Company. Some Dutch units arrived during September and October 1946, and a strong force was known to be sailing from Holland and was expected during November. Accordingly, the 26th Divisional Engineers were able to return to India in October, November and December feeling that their contribution towards the restoration of peace and the revival of the island as a productive colony had been considerable". 72 Field Company embarked at Medan on

---

[1] "Sumatra, 1945-46," by Major J. S. R. Shave, M.C., R.E., appearing in *The R.E. Journal*, Sept. 1951, pp. 254-263.

October 27th and the others followed. The O.C. 328 Field Park Company (now renumbered as 42) was disappointed to learn on October 30th that his unit was due for disbandment and wrote in his War Diary "This information comes at a very late date and is considered in a very bad light." The fate of this hard-working unit was to be shared by a number of others. One cannot but sympathize with those who had hoped against hope that they would escape the axe.

The Far-Eastern picture now switches to Thailand and reverts to the autumn of 1945 when it became necessary to land sufficient forces in that country to disarm and concentrate 113,000 Japanese troops, rescue and evacuate 20,000 Allied prisoners-of-war and internees, and secure and repair the Don Muang airfield close to Bangkok, the capital, in order to assist the transport of part of the 20th Indian Division by air to French Indo-China. Thousands of coolies who had been brought from Malaya by the Japanese to labour on the new railway to Burma had also to be repatriated. All this had had to be done while maintaining friendly relations with the Government of Thailand which, though nominally in league with the Japanese, had secretly sided with the Allies. The task was allotted to the 7th Indian Division, under Major-General G. C. Evans, and was subsidiary to the main landing operations in Malaya.

In August 1945, the 5th Division was concentrated in the Pegu district of Southern Burma after being relieved by the 17th Division in the Sittang bend, and in consequence of the decision that it should travel by air it actually provided the first troops in South-East Asia to enter enemy occupied territory, for an advance party, consisting of the tactical Headquarters of the 114th Brigade under Colonel Kalwant Singh and a detachment of 150 infantry, flew to Bangkok from Mingaladon early on September 3rd. It was followed quickly by the remainder of the the Brigade, and then by the greater part of the Division as aircraft became available. The advance party was received by a guard of honour and a number of senior Thailand officers at the Don Muang airfield, and contact was established at once with the Allied prisoners-of-war and internees and with the Japanese. By the end of the first week it was evident that the Japanese would obey all orders transmitted through their own officers, but their methods of achieving efficiency and promptitude were disconcerting. For instance, after it had been pointed out that a junior Japanese officer had failed to complete his allotted task in the proper time, General Evans was informed that the local Japanese commander had sentenced the offender to a month's imprisonment "with bodily torture"![1] The incident reminds one forcibly of Gilbert and Sullivan's opera *The Mikado*.

The 7th Divisional Engineers comprised 62 Field Company (Madras) under Major W. T. Buttrick, R.E., 77 Field Company (Bengal) under Major E. R. B. Hudson, R.E., 421 Field Company (Madras) under Major R. S. A. Pryde, R.E., and 331 Field Park Company (Madras) under Major B. P. Shenoy, R.I.E., the C.R.E. being Lieut.-Colonel P. G. Hatch, R.E. At the outset, owing to the absence of men on leave, a composite unit was formed from 62 and 421 Companies. This composite Company was flown to Bangkok with the 114th Brigade and landed on the Don Muang airfield on September 7th, 1945. It began at once to prepare jetties for small vessels, accommodation for troops, and temporary camps to hold Japanese prisoners-of-war. 77 Field Company followed in October and was soon busy on water-supply and accommodation. 331 Field Park Company arrived on October 24th by sea, and 402 Field Company (Major O. M. R. Arnoll, R.E.), coming also by sea as part of the Forward Airfield Engineers, disembarked late in December.

The employment of these units in and around Bangkok calls for no special remark, but the War Diary of 62 Field Company strikes an unusual note in the way of humour. "*13th September*. Moved into Bangkok itself. Guarding a dump and cutting grass on the Polo ground with Jap labour (with pen-knives). *2nd October*. Officers' latrine floated away on spring tide, but now riding safely at sea-anchor. *4th October*. Japs on Polo ground have cut another two blades of grass, and the goal is well and truly wired in. *5th October*. Polo ground nearly ready, but cannot be used because the only polo pony has died outside the entrance to H.Q., A.L.F., Siam. *9th October*. Trades Havildar has painted a magnificent Madras Sapper crest for our main entrance. Our H.Q. Notice board also is so splendid that twice we have been asked if this is H.Q., A.L.F., Siam, and who actually *is* this "Alfred Siam"? *13th-16th October*. Making landing stages for I.S.Ts at Paknam. *1st November*. Begin work on P.O.W. Camp in Bangkok. *6th November*. Instructed to supply 'bangs' on 11th to denote beginning and end of two minutes' silence. *7th November*. Test 'bang' on Race Course so successful that Divisional H.Q. is said to be digging slit trenches. *11th November*.

---

[1] *Golden Arrow. The Story of The 7th Indian Division*, by Brig. M. R. Roberts, D.S.O., p. 267.

What a day! We got the wrong times for our 'bangs'. The O.C. was simple enough to imagine that the attached Signal Section would have Signal time, and having marched a contingent to church, had to do a quick *chukker* around in a jeep to delay the bangs ten minutes. He just made it in time to lead the Sapper March Past. *1st December*. Move for 89th Brigade Group imminent. *6th-9th December*. Bailey bridging over Menam River. Handed over to 77 Field Company on 9th. *12th December*. Embarked in L.C.I. and transferred to ship. *16th December*. Landed at Port Swettenham, Malaya".

On January 11th, 1946, twenty-two Japanese Generals and Admirals surrendered their swords to Major-General G. C. Evans in Bangkok while similar ceremonies were held at outlying stations. In all, some thousands of swords were received. The troops on parade at the main ceremony included detachments from all Services under Brigadier E. H. W. Cobb, the 33rd Brigade Commander, who was the senior Brigadier in the 7th Division. Cobb had assumed command of the 33rd Brigade on December 10th and remained in this appointment until December 1946 when he went to England to join the Imperial Defence College.[1] The high-ranking Japanese officers arrived on the parade ground under a strong escort of British officers. As each Japanese officer's name was called he stepped forward, handed his sword to General Evans and marched to a flagstaff on which the Union Jack had been hoisted. He saluted the flag, bowed to it, and returned to his place. The effect on a large civilian crowd watching the ceremony was profound, for the proceedings emphasized the utter collapse of Japanese domination in the Far East.

Its task completed, the greater part of the 7th Division began to leave Thailand in February 1946 to undertake internal security duties in Malaya. 62 Field Company had already departed with the 89th Brigade after building a fine Bailey bridge over the Menam River in Bangkok. 77 Field Company and 331 Field Park Company followed later, and 402 Field Company, of the Forward Airfield Engineers, reached Singapore from Thailand on March 30th for airfield work. 62 Field Company was stationed at first near Kuala Lumpur but afterwards opened 81 miles of railway line from Kuala Lipis to Bertam. While in Bangkok, Major E. R. B. Hudson, O.C. 77 Field Company, was interested to meet Captain Hango, a Japanese officer

---

[1] Major-General E. H. W. Cobb, c.b., c.b.e., a most popular ex-Bengal Sapper and Miner, died on May 26th, 1955, as the result of an accident.

who had commanded a Bridging Company of the 33rd Japanese Regiment and had reconnoitred the Sittang Bridge in Burma after our engineers had demolished it in 1942. For some months after the departure of the other units of the 7th Divisional Engineers, 421 Field Company remained in Thailand with the 114th Brigade, but finally it moved in July 1946 to Malaya and was stationed at Kota Bahru on the north-east coast until it returned to India in March 1947.

The occupation of Bangkok in September 1945 provided a re-fuelling base at the Don Muang airfield for aeroplanes flying further eastwards to French Indo-China. Saigon, the capital of that country, was known to be the headquarters of Field-Marshal Terauchi, the Japanese Supreme Commander in South-East Asia, and the task of occupying it and the surrounding territory was allotted to the 20th Indian Division, under Major-General D. D. Gracey, which included the 32nd, 80th and 100th Brigades. The Division was to remain in Indo-China until it was relieved by French troops from Europe, sending out parties to round up scattered Japanese forces and to guard bases, depots, dumps, airfields and ports. The Divisional Engineers, under Lieut.-Colonel R. A. G. Binny, R.E., comprised 92 Field Company (Bombay) under Major J. H. Clark, R.E., 422 Field Company (Madras) under Major L. S. Henderson, R.E., (who was succeeded by Major R. A. Loomba, R.I.E., on October 28th), 481 Field Company (Bombay) under Major J. P. A. Jackson, R.E., and 332 Field Park Company (Bengal) under Major P. B. Nicholls, R.E. When it was known that the Division was destined for Indo-China, many of the Sapper officers had begun to polish up their French, though with no great success, so it was fortunate that Colonel Binny could speak the language fluently. Later, when they met the local French officials, they were surprised to find how little was known about Indian nationalities, castes and creeds. To the French, all Indian troops were "Les Gurkhas" because of the preponderance of Gurkha battalions in the Division. Some of the Sappers were not amused, but nevertheless they accepted the name without protest.

Saigon, 34 miles up the Saigon river, had wide boulevards, a cathedral, fine shops, modern office buildings, public gardens, clubs and several cinemas. In many respects it was quite Parisian, but adjoining it was the densely populated and rather squalid Chinese-Annamite quarter of Cholon which housed most of its 200,000 inhabitants. Waterways and canals, crowded with barges and *sampans*, intersected the place, while a couple of miles to the north was the main airfield which was still usable though it had been heavily bombed by American planes. The first arrivals by air were members of the R.A.P.W.I. organization to contact the Allied prisoners-of-war and internees. After them came General Gracey and some of his Staff; also Colonel Binny and other Engineers and several members of a Control Commission. A battalion of Gurkhas followed. All were welcomed effusively by the French and entertained right royally. The Annamese were cold and distant. As in Java, they had been imbued by the Japanese with a militant spirit of nationalism; but they were more dangerous than the Indonesians because they were a warlike race and better armed and trained. Armed bands were often led by fanatical Japanese officers who had refused to accept the surrender terms. At first, the Japanese, acting under British orders, were able to control the situation; but as the Annamese began to realize that the 20th Division had been sent to Indo-China not only to remove 70,000 Japanese soldiers but also to reinstate the French, they became increasingly restive. The entire Annamite labour force vanished suddenly. All public services ceased to operate. Sniping began in the barricaded streets as Annamite bands attacked the French police. The Japanese, still armed, took no action until made to do so under British orders, and it seemed that Saigon would fare no better than Sourabaya. Anyone might be fired upon at any time. Under such circumstances Sapper work was not too easy and there were several narrow escapes. On one occasion, Major W. L. Lawler, an Australian Engineer who was Colonel Binny's right hand man, was driving with another officer outside the city when the back of his car was suddenly riddled by machine-gun bullets. Though unarmed, Lawler promptly got out, marched back to the firer, and told him in the broadest Australian a few home truths about his antecedents and ultimate destiny. Then he stalked back to the car, turned it round, and drove home past the gaping marksman while his companion removed a couple of bullets from the seat he was sitting on.

It had been intended originally that the greater part of the 20th Division should be carried to Saigon by air; but because of bad weather and a shortage of aircraft, most of the troops and transport had to be sent by sea from Rangoon. However, 422 Field Company, the first Divisional Engineer unit to arrive, was given air transport. It was flown from Hmawbi Aerodrome, north of Rangoon, on September 29th, 1945, while 92 Field Company was embarking with the transport of both units. The next to leave Rangoon by ship was 332 Field Park Company which sailed on October 4th., and 481 Field

Company brought up the rear on October 10th. 92 Field Company landed at Saigon on October 7th, 332 Field Park Company on the 11th, and 481 Field Company on the 17th. 92 Field Company carried out normal duties, mostly in the Cholon suburb, until it was ordered to Borneo on December 19th. 332 Field Park Company took over all Japanese Engineer stores and guarded dumps and camps until it was able to hand over charge to French reinforcements in January 1946 and return to India. 481 Field Company was stationed at first in Cholon but soon moved with the 100th Brigade to Thu Duc, not far from the capital. There, on January 3rd, the Brigade headquarters were subjected to grenade and mortar bombardment by the rebels, so the Company was employed on demolishing a number of houses before it also embarked for India in the following month.

Sapper detachments of 92 Field Company, detailed to guard and operate wells in the Cholon area, were often sniped at night and could never retaliate. Accordingly, permission was obtained to destroy the houses near any well where sniping had occurred. One afternoon, after some thatched huts had been set alight, a strong wind sprang up and part of Cholon quickly became a raging inferno. The panic-striken inhabitants blocked the streets as the conflagration spread, and it seemed that the whole suburb might be gutted and hundreds of lives lost. Attempts to check the fire with water-tank trucks, pumping sets and buckets proved futile; but fortunately the wind dropped suddenly and some rain extinguished the flames, though not before thousands of Annamese and Chinese had been rendered homeless. The incident provided a wholesome lesson to the people, and there was no more sniping near the wells while the Sappers were in charge. Apart from duty at the wells, 92 Field Company repaired roads, billets, and the watersupply and electric installations. It derived much assistance from a Japanese Engineer Regiment formed locally under Japanese officers. A Japanese D.C.R.E. was appointed and four Japanese Garrison Engineers, each with several Assistants who worked well under the direction of British or Indian Engineer officers acting in similar capacities. Colonel R. A. Loomba[1] writes that the Japanese proved obedient and efficient and displayed remarkable energy. Their main task was to repair and maintain the Saigon airfield, but their technicians were always available in an emergency to reinforce the Sapper tradesmen.

---

[1] Notes by Colonel R.A. Loomba, Engineers, dated August 14th, 1953.

Perhaps the best idea of Sapper experiences at Saigon can be obtained from the history of 422 Field Company written by Major D. W. McGrath, R.E. On September 19th, after two false starts, Colonel Binny, Major Lawler and a small party left Hmawbi Aerodrome in a plane carrying a load of watersupply equipment and the Company's pet dog. They refuelled at Bangkok and reached Saigon safely. "At first," writes McGrath, "everything was a shambles because the Annamese had gone on strike and the French were quite unable to handle the lighting and water systems. The Annamese were actively hostile, and the French, to safeguard themselves, had formed a body of armed auxiliary police who were very 'trigger happy' at night. As the French could not run the installations, we had to do so, and the day after our arrival two platoons were sent out to guard and operate various water-pumping stations dotted around Saigon and Cholon in particularly hostile areas. The Annamese were always on the watch to make life difficult, and on most nights parties of them used to creep towards the stations to throw grenades and fire at our men. In addition, they tampered with the electric lights by cutting the cables or firing at the porcelain insulators. The O.C. was appointed Garrison Engineer for the area with Lieuts. Jones and McGrath as A.G.Es. The main electric power stations were fast falling to pieces, so Lieut. Hindmoor was put in charge of repairs with a number of bricklayers and a Section of E & M. Sappers who had been flown in to look after the boilers and dynamos. Major Lawler, who operated the stations, was a brilliant electrical engineer and did wonders with the French, Indians and Japanese working under him although the available fuel consisted mostly of maize. There was abundant coal up-country, but armoured cars would have been needed to guard convoys bringing it to Saigon. The water-supply installation was in an appalling state. American bombing had broken most of the pipes and vast quantites of water were running to waste. At first, we could hardly cope with the work. Our transport had not yet arrived and we had only six Japanese lorries and three Staff cars. On October 12th, however, the transport turned up, and after the C.R.E. had organized a battalion of Jap Sappers to help us, the work was got under control. The Annamese were still hostile and it was impossible to go outside Saigon without a strong escort. The other two Brigades were further up-country. Saigon and Cholon were fairly quiet although some shooting went on at night. French troops had begun to arrive and fired a lot of ammunition. On October 28th, Major R. A. Loomba took over command from Major Henderson.

He was an old friend to many of us who had passed through his hands at one time or another in Bangalore."

It was decided in November that, with the arrival of more French troops, the Japanese should be interned on Cap St. Jacques, a populated and fortified headland at the mouth of the Saigon River.[1] A Sapper officer and a Staff officer went there in a Japanese gunboat to reconnoitre and were met by a Japanese deputation headed by an Admiral. They were bowed ashore, and after much heel-clicking and hissing intakes of breath by their late enemies, were driven in cars to the Grand Hotel where a sumptuous meal was ready. The Annamese had already demolished two reinforced concrete bridges on the road between Saigon and Cap St. Jacques along which the Japanese would have to march for internment, so 92 Field Company was detailed to repair the damage. The men and equipment were carried down the river in barges towed by a Japanese tug, and on arrival, the Sikhs were accommodated near the site of the work. The Mahrattas, however, were housed in the Grand Hotel, where the beds had the finest linen sheets and beautiful coverlets. Curtains shrouded the windows. Embroidered towels hung on brass rails. Never before had the rank and file enjoyed such luxury, and they were most careful to keep their rooms as clean and tidy as possible.

"Early in December", continues McGrath, "warning came that a French operation was about to take place against the Annamese north-west of Saigon for which the assistance of 422 Field Company would be required. Lieut. Hindmoor made an air reconnaissance on the 10th and saw that a 20-feet gap had been blown in the road, so No. 2 Platoon borrowed the Field Park Company's prefabricated bridge of ready-made cribs, road bearers and decking and loaded it up, together with a bay of folding-boat equipment. The column left Saigon at 1.0 a.m. on December 15th. It consisted of armoured cars, armoured jeeps and four 30-cwt. trucks carrying infantry, with Hindmoor and No. 2 Platoon in the lead because the road was very narrow. Rain began to fall, and when the gap was reached at 2.45 a.m. it was found that the Annamese had already widened it to nearly 50 feet. This ruled out the use of the Field Park bridge. A rope was therefore run across, and the infantry waded to the far side through three feet of water. There was some firing but not enough to cause trouble. While the Sappers were building a folding-boat raft, the

---

[1] "Sappers and Miners in Saigon", by Major J. H. Clark, M.C., R.E., appearing in *The R. E. Journal*, Sept. 1950, pp. 279-287.

infantry sent back word that a bridge 300 yards further on had been damaged. The Annamese had ripped up the roadway and had tried to destroy the roadbearers. Here, the decking from the Field Park bridge proved valuable, and the Lance-Naik in charge of the work soon completed the necessary repairs. Seven armoured jeeps were first taken across at the ferry. They pushed on at once, followed in due course by the lorries. The armoured cars used a different route and rejoined the column later. Their work completed, the Sappers were then sent back to Saigon while the French went on to take the objective. This was the first and only time that 422 Field Company co-operated with the French, and as always, the unit gave a good account of itself."

The 20th Divisional Engineers had only a short stay in French Indo-China because their services were urgently needed elsewhere, and the units were soon widely scattered when the Division was split up between Borneo, Celebes, Java and Malaya prior to returning to India for disbandment. As already recorded, 92 Field Company received orders on December 19th, 1945, to proceed to British North Borneo. It landed at Labuan with the 32nd Brigade on the 29th, after a voyage of 700 miles south-eastwards across the China Sea, and relieved 18 Field Company of the Royal Australian Engineers. Its duties in Borneo call for no special remark. On February 3rd, Major J. H. Clark, R.E., handed over command to Major H. E. Allison, R.E., under whom the Company sailed eventually for India on May 28th, 1946, after its embarkation orders had been altered no less than sixteen times! It reached India on June 8th, expecting to be disbanded; but instead its number was changed, and because of its war record, it was retained as one of the post-War units.

The next to leave Saigon was 422 Field Company which embarked with the 80th Brigade on January 21st, 1946. Its destination was Macassar at the southern end of the octopus-shaped island of Celebes, south-east of Borneo. All vehicles were handed over to the French and all duties to 481 Field Company which was to remain in Indo-China for a time with the 100th Brigade. The 80th Brigade was under orders to relieve an Australian brigade in Celebes. An advance party of 422 Field Company started by air on January 11th and refuelled at Labuan. At a farewell parade in Saigon on the 14th, the Madras Sappers marched past the French General Leclerc at the head of the other troops and were much admired in their 'Dupta' fulldress head-gear. The voyage across the China Sea to Singapore was pleasant. After a halt of three days, it was continued until Celebes came in sight on January 31st in a rising gale. Threading a precarious way through a narrow passage in a coral reef, the ship came to anchor near some wharves behind which were clusters of palm trees and a number of buildings.

Macassar was not looking its best under heavy rain, but it improved on acquaintance. The people were friendly, the roads good and the buildings modern. A platoon under Lieut. McGrath was sent at once to an airfield at Mandai, some ten miles inland, and found it in poor condition for it had been heavily bombed by Allied aircraft. Fifty-seven craters on the runway had been filled in roughly by the Australians, but they needed repair with graded stone and bitumen to secure a good surface. The stone was brought in trucks from a quarry seven miles away, and Javanese labour, imported by the Japanese, was employed on the airfield. This was the most important task undertaken by 422 Field Company in Celebes, though much was done also in Macassar itself in the way of repair. Conditions differed from those in Saigon in that the Dutch civilian organizations were in full operation and their engineers were prepared to carry out all major projects unaided. The island had belonged to the Netherlands ever since the Dutch had established trading centres there in the middle of the 17th Century, so its administration was based on sure foundations. The responsibilities of 422 Field Company were therefore confined chiefly to taking over a vast amount of stores from the Australians and issuing them from dumps, duties which would normally have devolved on 332 Field Park Company. The latter, however, was still in Saigon and under orders to return to India. On February 27th, the Mandai airfield was handed over to the Dutch and the detached platoon rejoined the Company in Macassar. The climate gradually became hotter and hotter, so it was fortunate that from April onwards it was possible to send large parties of men on short leave to Malino, a charming hill-station some forty miles inland. On May 22nd, Major Loomba had to be evacuated to Batavia, and afterwards, on account of illness, to India. The command of the unit then fell to Captain McGrath. At a final parade in Macassar on July 1st, 422 Field Company headed the march past and immediately afterwards embarked for India, where it was disbanded. It was the only Madras Sapper unit which had served both in French Indo-China and the Netherlands East Indies. Meanwhile, 481 Field Company and 332 Field Park Company had sailed from Saigon on February 9th with the 100th Brigade. 481 Company arrived in Kirkee on the 19th expecting to be disbanded, but because of its war record it was retained on the establishment under a new number.

Yet another post-War operation in which the Indian Engineers were concerned was the re-occupation of Hongkong, the British base on the southern coast of China about 1,500 miles north of Singapore. The tragic story of the fall of Hongkong on Christmas Day, 1941, has been outlined in Chapter VII, though no units of the Corps were involved in that major disaster. After the collapse of Japan, a mixed force of all arms under Major-General F. W. Festing was detailed for the re-occupation and sailed from Madras at the beginning of November 1945. With it was 96 Field Company (Bombay), under Major G. B. Dawson, R.E. The expedition reached Hongkong about November 19th and the troops relieved some Australians and Royal Navy contingents already ashore. The Sappers began at once to repair the extensive damage to roads, bridges, docks and water and electric installations. On February 11th, 1946, Major K. H. St. C. Pringle, R.E., succeeded Major Dawson in command, and at the end of March, Major-General P. A. Ullman, Chief Engineer, A.L.F.S.E.A. arrived on a visit of inspection. The remainder of 1946 was spent on normal duties including the erection of a hutted camp at San Wai, the Company being stationed in Kam Tsin, a part of the Hongkong Colony. In the middle of January 1947, Major-General G. W. E. J. Erskine succeeded Major-General Festing as G.O.C. Hongkong Garrison. 96 Field Company continued to work at the San Wai site until warned in March that it would shortly leave for India. The actual date proved to be April 6th, when the unit embarked with other troops. Landing at Madras on April 16th it returned to Kirkee, where it was disbanded in July 1947 after a very adventurous career.

The culminating triumph of the Allies in the Far East was the occupation of Japan itself, a task which was allotted to a cosmopolitan force under the American General MacArthur. This representative body of many nationalities had not only to destroy Japan's capacity to make war but also to inculcate democratic principles into a hitherto autocratic regime. Wisely enough, disarmament was facilitated by permitting the Japanese Government to co-operate and by maintaining the prestige of the Emperor. The Government rapidly dissolved its General Headquarters and disarmed and demobilized the naval, military and air forces stationed in the country. Forces outside Japan were dealt with by the local Allied Commanders and the men sent back to Japan as soon as possible to resume civilian life.

The task of abolishing the armed forces was completed within a few months, but the process of instilling democratic ideas was a long one. Although General MacArthur's Occupation Force was chiefly American, it included a British Commonwealth Occupation Force (B.C.O.F.) of 35,000 men, commanded by an Australian, Lieut.-General J. Northcott. Australia supplied 11,000 men, Great Britain nearly 10,000, India about 9,600, and New Zealand about 4,400, Great Britain and India being represented by a British-Indian Division under Major-General D. T. ("Punch") Cowan, famed for his exploits in command of the 17th Indian Division in Burma during the war.

The British-Indian Division destined for Japan was known at first as "Brinjap". It was to have one Indian and one British brigade, with Divisional troops, and was to be formed from selected units of the 36th Indian and 2nd British Divisions. In August 1945, it began to assemble at Nasik. The 268th Indian Infantry Brigade, under Brigadier K. S. Thimayya, was selected to represent the Indian Army, its battalions being the 5/1st Punjabis, 1st Mahrattas and 2/5th Royal Gurkhas. Brigadier Thimayya was well suited by personality and reputation for the responsible post he was called upon to fill in Japan having represented his country at the surrender ceremony at Singapore after leading the Brigade in strenuous fighting during the closing stages of the campaign in Arakan. The British Army was represented by the 5th British Brigade comprising the 2nd Dorsets, 1st Queens Own Cameron Highlanders and 2nd Royal Welch Fusiliers. Among the Divisional troops were the 7th Light Cavalry (Indian Armoured Corps) and 16th Indian and 30th British Field Batteries. The Divisional Engineers, with Lieut.-Colonel H. B. Calvert, R.E., as C.R.E., included 5 Field Company, R.E., 21 Field Park Company, R.E., 429 Field Company, R.I.E., and 907 Indian Works Section.

429 Field Company (Madras), under Major G. W. Pinto, R.E., arrived in camp near Nasik on September 16th, 1945, very happy to rejoin the 268th Brigade with which it had served during the war. The date of departure for Japan was postponed twice; but eventually, on February 9th, 1946, a small advance party left India by air and landed a week later at Kure at the southern end of the Japanese island of Honshu. A contingent of 1,600 men started by sea and reached Kure on March 1st. 429 Field Company was with this party, and disembarking on March 2nd, provided the first Indian guard on Japanese soil. It moved at once into billets at Hiro and began to prepare accommodation for the main body

which was expected shortly. Japanese labour was available, though it was not very satisfactory because the workmen had been treated too generously by the 24th American Division already in occupation. The greater part of the main body arrived in two echelons, the first on April 5th and the second on May 19th. They had been preceded by Major-General Cowan who was received by a Guard of Honour from 5 Field Company, R.E., and 429 Field Company, R.I.E., when he landed from the S.S. *Dunera* on March 25th, a few days before the disembarkation of the 268th Brigade. The scene in Kure was one of extraordinary desolation. Large Japanese warships lay aground, wrecked and abandoned, while all naval structures on Kure Island and along the Inland Sea were mere masses of twisted steel. As Brigadier Thimayya stepped ashore he remarked "We are sorry to have left India at this stage of political change, but the Indian Army has definitely earned a share in the honour of the occupation of Japan and we are looking forward to happy associations with the Empire and other Allied troops." His anticipations were fulfilled. Before they quitted the country, the Indian soldiers stood high in the estimation of all the Allied forces and of the Japanese population.

The designation of the British-Indian Division had now been altered to "Brindiv". Empire Day was celebrated in Tokyo on May 22nd when General Northcott took the salute at a great parade of the Commonwealth Forces. On June 4th, after three months in Hiro, the headquarters of "Brindiv" were transferred to Okayama, 100 miles further east, where arrangements had been made to take over charge from the 24th American Division. General Northcott was under orders to return to Australia to become Governor of New South Wales and was succeeded in the command of the Commonwealth Occupation Force by Lieut.-General H. C. H. Robertson, another Australian. During May and June 1946, additional units of the Royal Indian Engineers set foot in Japan. These were 363 Field Company (Bombay), under Major R. P. Rocke, R.E., which landed at Kure on May 19th, and three Mechanical Equipment units of the Bengal Group.[1] C.R.E. "Brindiv" had charge of all works in the Okayama area, with a D.C.R.E. posted at Shimonoseki at the extreme end of Honshu Island. An Australian C.R.E.

---

[1] 653 Indian Mechanical Equipment Company, and 705 and 709 Indian Mechanical Equipment Platoons.

was in charge of the atom-bombed Hiroshima district some 40 miles north-west of Kure.

Early in July 1946, Lieut.-Colonel H. B. Calvert, R.E., was invalided to India and Lieut.-Colonel H. Carrington Smith, R.E., became C.R.E. "Brindiv". The Sapper units were very busy, and in a workshop at Okayama, 120 Japanese helped the tradesmen of 429 Field Company. Most of the building work was undertaken by Japanese contractors under the supervision of 907 Works Section while the subalterns of the Engineer Field Units acted as Garrison Engineers. 429 Field Company, however, undertook the reconstruction of the Operating Theatre for the Military Hospital and the erection of a number of huts. It also improved an airfield and began to make Squash and Tennis courts for the Officers' Club and six playing fields for other ranks. In October it had to prepare a tented camp and start operations to shift the hospital to a new centre. The Company did well in a number of Athletic Sports Meetings during the autumn, and when wintry conditions set in, took its full share in ceremonial military duties. For instance, on December 2nd, a large party was was sent to Tokyo to join the 5/1st Punjab Regiment in Ceremonial Guard employment and mounted guards on December 6th in the Canadian Legation and the British Embassy. On January 1st, 1947, another detachment mounted a guard at the Imperial Palace itself, and late in March, still another provided a guard at the Palace on no less than three occasions. The "Dupta" head-dress was worn and attracted much interest.

The winter of 1946-47 was marked by an earthquake, no uncommon event in Japan. On December 21st, at 4.0 a.m., there were severe tremors at Okayama, lasting for five minutes. All barracks were evacuated forthwith, and 429 Field Company remained in the open till dawn. Happily, there were no casualties among the troops, though many buildings were damaged and fifty civilians were killed or injured. For the next two days the Company was employed in restoring the electricity and water-supplies; but apart from this interruption, the normal work of the unit continued steadily. On January 23rd, an 80-feet Bailey bridge was launched and completed at Kachimura on the road from Okayama to Imbe. This was the first Bailey to be built in Japan. It was constructed over an existing Japanese bridge which was incapable of carrying tank-transporters.

Early in January 1947, the command of the 268th Brigade passed to Brigadier S. M. Shrinagesh in relief of Brigadier K. S. Thimayya who was under orders to take up another appoinment in India.

"Brindiv" was now dwindling rapidly in strength owing to the departure of men released from service, and in February the entire 5th (British) Brigade sailed for Malaya. It was decided, therefore, that the units of "Brindiv" still in Japan should be formed into a 268th Indian Infantry Brigade Group under the command of an Indian Officer, and on March 12th, 1947, Brigadier S. M. Shrinagesh took over from Major-General D. T. Cowan who left Japan shortly afterwards. "Brindiv" was officially dissolved on May 1st. It had fulfilled its obligations to the letter and had made a lasting impression in the country.

The transfer of 5 Field Company, R.E., to Singapore in the middle of February 1947 threw an additional strain on the depleted 363 and 429 Field Companies of the Royal Indian Engineers. On April 17th, 429 Field Company had to be reorganized on a basis of only three Sections to a Platoon owing to the departure of large drafts to India. Work became increasingly difficult because of a shortage of materials and mechanical equipment. The clock was running down. Yet although all eyes were turned homewards, the standard of accomplishment in work and play was not allowed to suffer. Brigade Sports on July 12th enlivened the proceedings, and on August 15th, Independence Day was celebrated in proper style. It had been decided already that the Indian Contingent in Japan should shortly be withdrawn, and with the departure of Brigadier Shrinagesh to Australia on August 18th to represent India on a Japanese Peace Conference, the command of the 268th Brigade Group devolved on the O.C. 5/1st Punjab Regiment. 363 Field Company embarked for India on September 14th, and 429 Field Company and 653 Mechanical Equipment Company on October 20th. The two Mechanical Equipment Platoons followed early in November. 429 Field Company had the honour of being the last Engineer Field unit to leave Japan just as it had been the first to land. It disembarked at Madras on November 16th and moved to Bangalore for disbandment. As Major-General Shrinagesh afterwards remarked, it had worthily upheld the traditions of the Madras Sappers while serving under his command.

By 1947, the spheres of activity of the Royal Indian Engineers in the Far East were reduced to Japan, Hongkong and Malaya, most of the engineering work being in the Federated Malay States and on Singapore Island. 3 Field Company (Bengal) was sent to Malaya in the spring and returned to India before the end of the year. In March 1947, the Madras Group was represented in Malaya by 62,

63, 421 and 425 Field Companies, 325 and 331 Field Park Companies and 1019 Bridging Platoon. 63 and 421 Field Companies and the Bridging Platoon embarked for India in the summer, leaving 62 Field Company under Major J. H. Trigg, R.E., at Kluang, 425 Field Company under Major G. A. P. N. Barlow, R.E., in the Cameron Highlands, 325 Field Park Company under Major J. R. Radford, R.E., at Taiping, and 331 Field Park Company under Major G. W. Shaw, R.E., at Tampin; and of these units, 425 Field Company and 325 Field Park Company left for disbandment in the middle of September. Thus the exodus from Malaya was fairly general. The Military Works Services and the Public Works Department could cope with most of the work, and the employment of Field units was rarely necessary. The only hostile elements in the country were the bandits who gave so much trouble in later years; but in 1947 they were too poorly armed and organized to cause much harm.

With the declaration of Indian Independence on August 15th, 1947, there could no longer be any justification for the retention of Indian Army units in areas over which the new Republic had no jurisdiction. The Indian Army was being depleted by the departure of thousands of Mahomedan soldiers to Pakistan: thousands more were in the process of demobilization. India itself was in an unsettled condition owing to the sudden nature of the partition. Engineering works and repairs, postponed during the war, demanded urgent attention. Every available pair of hands was needed to restore the country to its pre-War prosperity, and the services of every experienced officer were required to train recruits to replace the soldiers who had fought so well in many campaigns. India possessed no far-flung Empire, though she wisely elected to remain within the British Commonwealth of Nations. She proceeded, therefore, to concentrate her strength and build up her resources, and with such remarkable success that she was soon able to play her full part in world politics as a first class Independent Power.

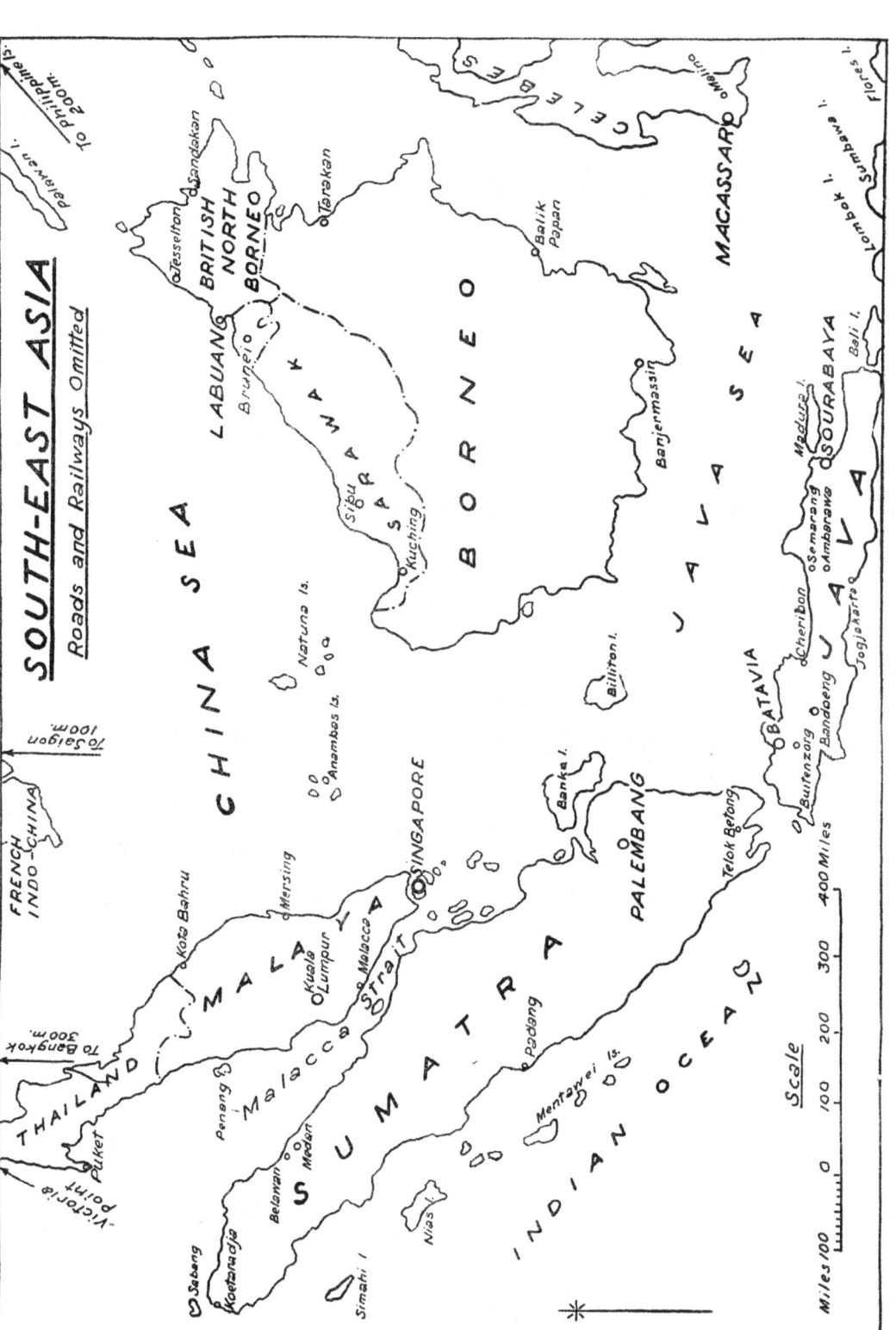

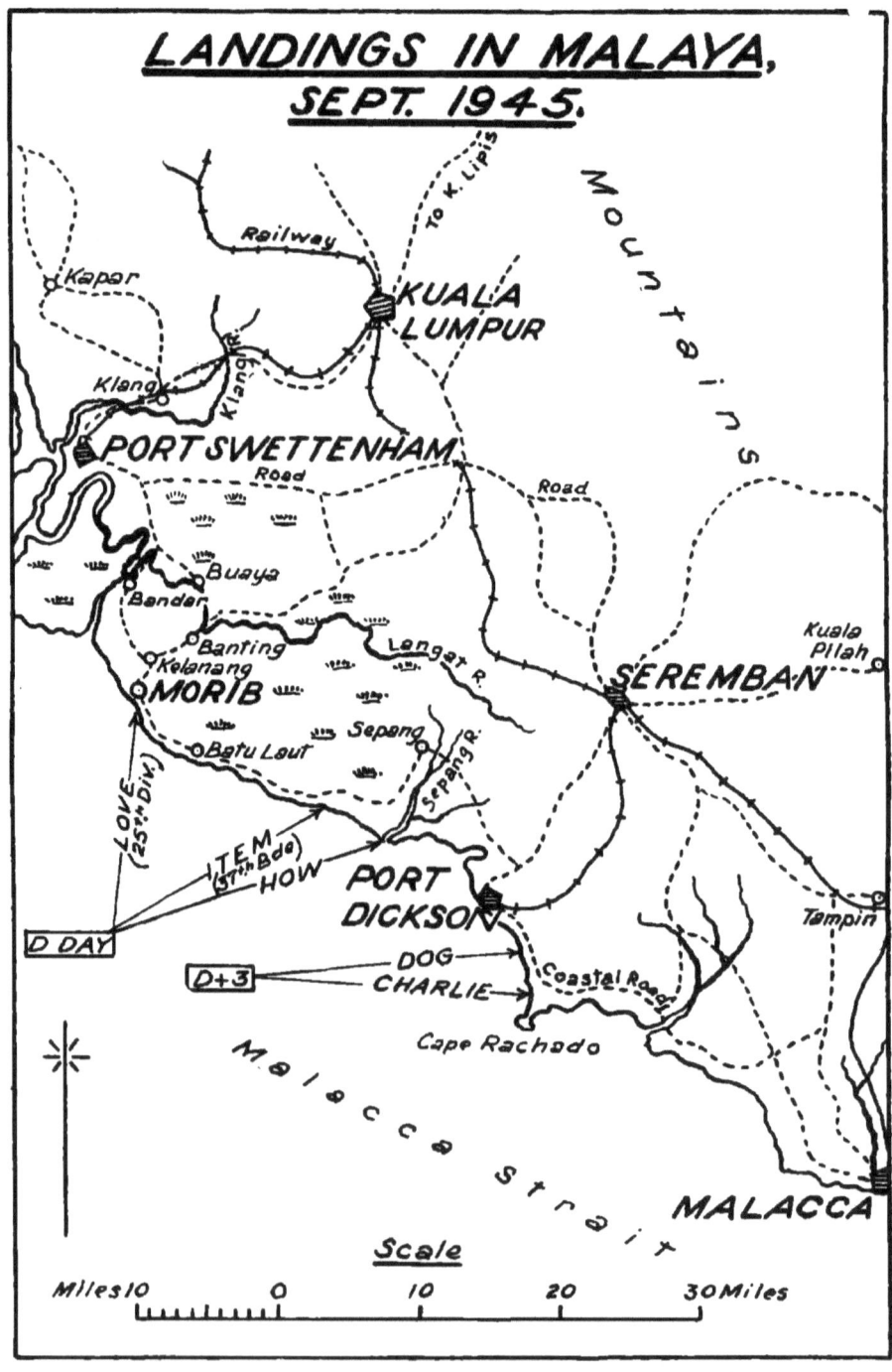

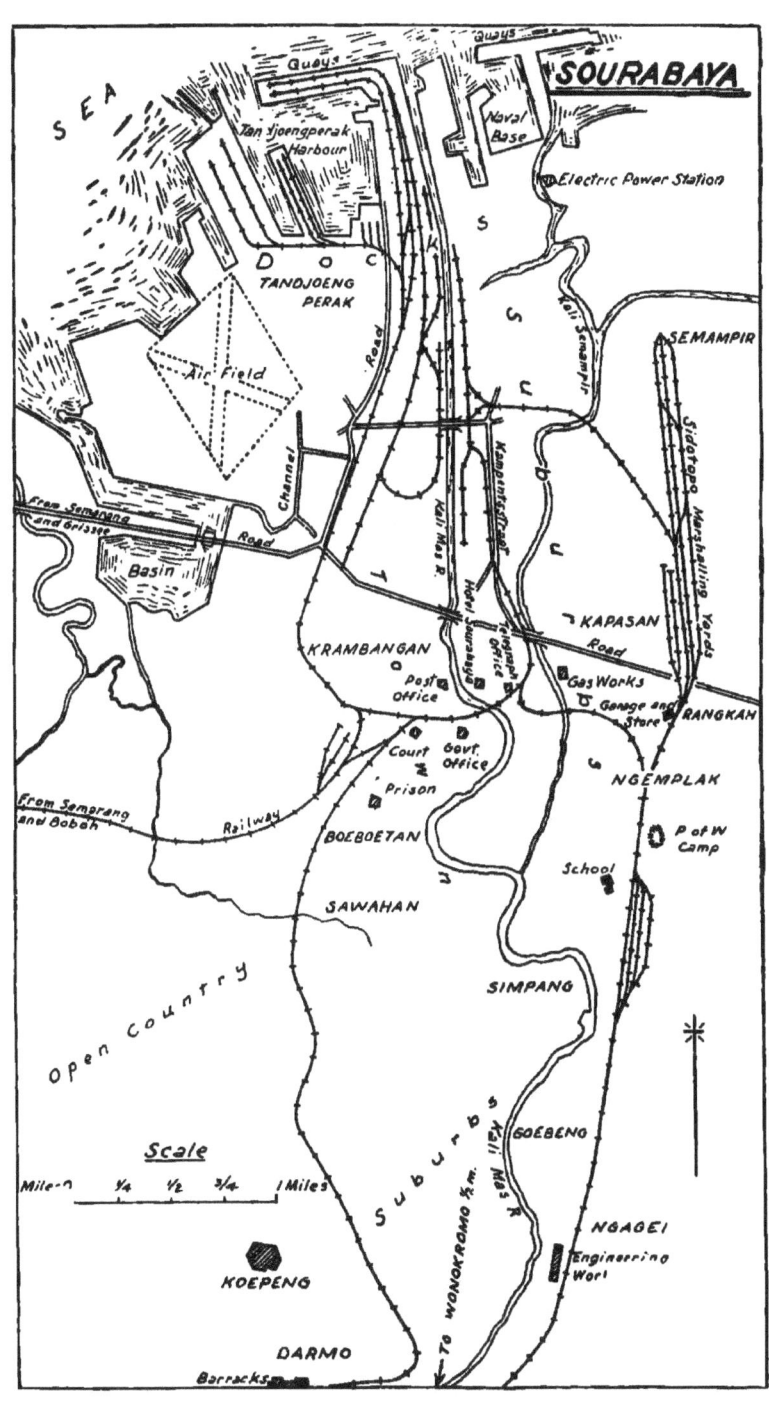

Reproduced by permission of
The West Yorkshire Regiment

CHAPTER XV

INDIA, 1944 - 47

WHILE Indian Engineer units in great numbers were fighting the Germans in Italy and the Japanese in Burma, the work during 1944 at the three Group Headquarters in India, and indeed wherever the training of Engineer troops was being carried out, was heavy and unceasing. The Groups, which in 1939 were of battalion strength, now bore more resemblance to whole divisions. Yet the Commandants were still Colonels, and most of their officers held only temporary commissions. The responsibilities of the few Regular officers at the head of affairs were such that it was a marvel that they could be borne. Nevertheless, trained unit after trained unit was despatched to the battle fronts in a seemingly endless stream by a process of grinding toil which offered few prospects of honour and none of glory.

The complexities of the changes in the organization and administration of the Indian Army during 1944 and 1945 can find no place in this narrative. They are recorded fully in official documents. An outline can, however, be given of particular events and life in general at the headquarters of the Engineer Groups during the later stages of the war, and afterwards up to the partition from Pakistan, in order to supplement the details of earlier happenings included in Chapter I. This outline is based chiefly on letters written by officers who were serving at that time and on the brief histories of the Madras and Bengal Groups compiled by Lieut.-Colonel R. A. Lindsell and Lieutenant G. Pearson. Some light is thrown also on the course of events by entries in War Diaries and by the News Letters of the three Groups, although the letters were necessarily subject to strict censorship while hostilities lasted.

It was fortunate that, from 1944 onwards, the North-West Frontier gave little trouble except in Waziristan. There, the Faqir of Ipi was still actively hostile and disciplinary measures were occasionally needed. Most of these were trivial in comparison with those entailed by the rigid maintenance of the "Forward Policy" of former years, although at one time in 1946 plans were made to send two divisions into the Mahsud country. The Engineer units on the Frontier, together with the Military Engineer Services, had carried out an extensive programme of fortification, and the tribes were heavily subsidized. The powerful fortress of Razmak still dominated Waziristan.[1] Police forces, raised from the tribes, were gaining experience and becoming more reliable. The country had good roads which carried a considerable amount of motor traffic. Provided that Japan was defeated and Russia remained friendly, the tribesmen might hope to attain ultimately some form of self-government. All this should have contributed towards a more peaceful attitude. But the seeds of trouble still remained, and at the end of 1946, when communal tension was rising, a small expedition had to be launched against a gang of Hazaras. This was the last Frontier operation under British command.

The Hazaras had raided Oghi, some 45 miles north-west of Abbotabad, where there were many Hindu traders. They burnt and pillaged the village, and as the ringleaders remained obdurate, it became necessary to despatch the 20th Brigade of the 7th Indian Division, with some medium artillery and tanks, to bring them to book.[2] The Indian Engineer units stationed at Peshawar and Nowshera were 1 Field Company (Bengal), 27 Field Company (Bombay) and 64 Field Company (Madras), but those chiefly employed during the operation belonged to the 7th Divisional Engineers, under Lieut.-Colonel H. C. W. Eking, R.E., located at Rawalpindi and Campbellpore. They comprised 5 Field Company (Bengal), 10 and 13 Field Companies (Madras), and 41 Field Park Company (Bengal). The route between Abbotabad and Oghi was kept open by 1 Field Company, but the weather soon broke and the road and the camp at Oghi became seas of mud. This was serious because the 20th Brigade was dependent almost wholly on wheeled transport. As the weather deteriorated, the truculence of the Hazaras increased, for they imagined that their lair in the hills overlooking Oghi would be beyond the reach of artillery fire. It was decided, therefore, to

---

[1] Razmak was abandoned in December 1947 after 5,000 tons of equipment and stores had been evacuated along 73 miles of road. This was the first major military operation undertaken by the Pakistan Army. The garrison comprised a Brigade Group under Brigadier R. S. Steed and included 31 Assault Field Company and 68 Field Company, Royal Pakistan Engineers. The withdrawal was unopposed, though hampered by bitter cold. (See "Operation Curzon—The Evacuation of Waziristan", by Lieut.-Colonel H. E. M. Cotton, O.B.E., R.E., appearing in *The R.E. Journal*, September 1948, pp. 183-196).

[2] Notes by Major-General C. de L. Gaussen, C.B., M.C., dated May 17th, 1955.

build an approach track for jeeps and guns towards their hide-out, a project involving a length of 10½ miles of track and an ascent of 2,000 feet. Most of the excavation was done by working parties of infantry; but it was the bulldozers of the Divisional Engineers that enabled the track to be finished in less than three weeks. It might have been completed even more rapidly if adequate information about the area and proper large-scale maps had been available. The tribesmen realized that the guns would soon be able to command their positions, so their representatives came into Oghi on January 18th, 1947, to give assurances of good conduct and arrange for the payment of a fine. The expedition affords a good example of the change in Frontier tactics brought about by the mechanization of Engineer equipment.

Although parts of the North-West Frontier remained comparatively undisturbed by the turmoil in Northern India which preceded and followed the partition from Pakistan, the same could hardly be said of Waziristan. On April 15th, 1947, severe rioting broke out in Dera Ismail Khan and large areas of the city were burnt. Fire threatened the wheat market which supplied the whole of Waziristan, and it was only through the energetic action taken by a few Royal Engineer Officers and a small detachment of Indian infantry that order was restored and the conflagration limited by cutting firelanes. The garrison of Tonk reported a shortage of water because tribesmen had seized the headworks of the supply line which lay in tribal territory. This crisis was dealt with by a detachment of 9 Field Company from Razmak, 8 miles of pipe-line being laid from an irrigation channel in 5 days.[1] All energies were then directed to evacuating the Hindu and Sikh employees in Government service. Communications broke down. Every road and every track was covered by armed parties of Mahsuds and Wazirs, and the only safe route was by air. The 1/4th Gurkhas, marching in from Wana, were ambushed in September 1947 in the notorious Shahur Tangi and lost nearly fifty men. Aircraft of all types, however, had been flying for some time from the airfields at Dera Ismail Khan and Bannu, and thus hundreds of non-combatants were saved.

Turning back now to events further south, it may be recorded that during the last two years of the war, the Madras, Bengal and Bombay Groups of the Indian Engineers expanded to enormous dimensions. Then they began to diminish in size as ultimate victory

---

[1] Notes by Lieut.-Colonel A. F. Toogood, R.E., dated August 8th, 1955.

became assured. Training for active service did not, however, account for the whole effort. In the autumn of 1943, for instance, four Companies of the Madras Corps were sent to Bengal to help in coping with a famine. Yet the most important tasks were certainly expansion and training. In August 1943, two Training Divisions had been formed. These were the 14th Indian Division with headquarters at Chindwara in the Central Provinces and the 39th Indian Division located at Saharanpur in the United Provinces. To one or other of these Divisions, the Engineer Groups sent small parties of recruits who had already completed their initial training at headquarters. The men were attached to Indian Engineer units serving with the Divisions and finished their training under the guidance of experienced instructors. Working in conjunction with other arms, they soon became first-class jungle fighters and were able to give a good account of themselves when transferred to the Burma front.

Events in Bangalore during 1943 and 1944 are summarised as follows by Lieut.-Colonel R. A. Lindsell.[1] In October 1943, a Boys Battalion had been formed under Major E. C. Aldous, R.E., while Colonel M. M. Jeakes was Commandant of the Centre. This was an important innovation although Boys had actually been recruited and trained on a small scale since 1941. Towards the end of the year, the training of recruits in the three existing Training Battalions at the Bangalore headquarters was finally standardized. The men received their basic military and field engineering training in Nos. 1 or 2 Training Battalions and were afterwards posted to No. 3 Training Battalion for instruction in trades. Outstanding men were selected as junior N.C.Os. and given special training before being posted to units in the field. The ordinary recruit was sent to one or other of the Training Divisions on leaving No. 3 Battalion. In the Boys Battalion, the lads were given an intensive training in trades for a period of eighteen months, supplemented by some general education. They then joined No. 3 Training Battalion for six or seven months' recruit training before being posted to units. Although this system produced a steady flow of reinforcements it was found to be not altogether satisfactory and was improved at a later date. The Bangalore Centre continued to provide instructional courses for V.C.Os. and N.C.Os., and much attention was devoted to mechanical transport training. All these activities were noted in December

---

[1] *A Short History of Q.V's O. Madras Sappers and Miners during World War II, 1939-1945*, by Lieut.-Colonel R. A. Lindsell, R.E., pp. 75-77.

1943 by Lieut.-General Sir Ronald Charles, the Chief Royal Engineer, during a war-time tour of India where he had served for several years with the Bengal Sappers before the First World War.

The Bangalore News Letter was revived in July 1944 after a lapse of nearly five years. The writer of the first letter mentions with pride the George Cross awarded posthumously to Subedar Subramaniam for his outstanding gallantry in Italy and records that the Subedar's widow had received a personal message from the Governor of Madras and a grant of Rs. 7,500 which was supplemented by another of Rs. 5,000 from the War Fund.[1] "Recruits training goes on as hard as ever", runs the letter, "and the new recruits are still of good physical standard on the whole. The Boys Battalion is full, and it is good to see the keenness displayed by the young entry. The boys (16 to 17½) do about 18 months' training, at the end of which time most of them have got an Artificer trade rating and a 3rd Class School Certificate. They are then mustered as Sappers and do a further seven months in the Young Soldiers Company. In February they had their Annual Sports: also their Boxing Tournament, the results of which were encouraging. Our Colonel, Brigadier R. C. R. Hill, has presented a shield to the Battalion as a boxing trophy, and we are entering a team for the All India Boxing Competition." A new Hindu Temple was opened in the Meeanee Lines on April 7th, 1944, the foundation stone of which had been laid on October 16th, 1942, by Colonel J. F. D. Steedman who was then Commandant. The Madras Centre had received a visit on April 6th from General Sir Claude Auchinleck, Commander-in-Chief, India. In September 1944 the strength of the Madras Group was 616 Officers, 237 British Warrant and N. C. Officers, 466 V.C.Os, 31,710 I.O.Rs and 2,555 Followers, and there were 97 units.[2] The Engineer Officers' Training School (formerly O.C.T.U.) had expanded greatly. There were now 13 Officer Instructors and so many trainees that they had to be accommodated in tents crowded round the Mess. A Jungle Training Camp, started at Shimoga in 1942, provided a splendid testing ground for future officers and N.C.Os. during a four weeks' course. The Indian

---

[1] On October 24th, 1944, the widow was escorted to Delhi by the Commandant and a Guard of Honour to receive the George Cross from the Viceroy.

[2] The maximum strength was attained shortly after the defeat of Japan in 1945 when there were 667 Officers, 217 B.W. & N.C.Os, 607 V.C.Os, 30,630 I.O.Rs. and 2,898 Followers in 101 units. The maximum figure for Indian ranks in the First World War was 7,029. The comparison is worth noting.

Families Hospital was flourishing, and a Womens' Club had been started for the wives of Indian ranks where dressmaking was practised and lectures were given.

In January 1945, the Boys Battalion at Bangalore moved from the Clive Lines into a camp at Jalahalli near a Signals Camp where there was a workshop in which the lads could be trained. A boxing team was sent to Delhi and reached the semi-finals of the All-India Boys Championship. After the defeat of Japan in September, demobilization preparations absorbed the attention of one and all. The Madras Centre was then commanded by Colonel M. M. Jeakes. Lieut.-Colonels G. D. S. Adami and J. A. Cameron, R.E., were Assistant Commandants. Lieut.-Colonel R. A. Lindsell, R.E., was O.C. Training Wing; Lieut.-Colonel I. B. C. Taylor, R.E., commanded the Depot Wing, and other senior appointments were filled by Majors J. R. Henchy, J. H. Partridge, R. L. Forbes and R. N. Edwards, R.E. The first task was to form a Demobilization Centre and evolve an efficient system of working. This was accomplished in a fortnight. Hand in hand with the arrangements for the new Centre went those needed for giving Resettlement training to men about to be thrown on the world without adequate means of earning their living. Many trades and occupations were taught such as weaving, calico printing, lacquer work, basket making and pottery manufacture. Instruction in farming was given in a Group Farm started some time before by Colonel Jeakes. On September 1st, the Centre was visited by Field-Marshal Sir Claude Auchinleck, and eleven days later, a parade was held to celebrate the re-occupation of Singapore, on which occasion the Colonel of the Madras Corps, Brigadier R. C. R. Hill, took the salute at a march past. November 1945 saw the formation of a Madras Sapper Officers' Association and a launching of a Group Memorial Fund. The Boys Boxing Team went to Delhi and reached the finals. No. 3 Training Battalion was abolished before the end of the year, being merged into No. 1 Battalion, and this in turn was combined with No. 2 Battalion to form a single Training Battalion. The war being finished and Malaya re-occupied, large drafts of reinforcements were no longer needed.

While the Madras Centre was engaged in these various activities during 1944-45, the Bengal Centre at Roorkee was equally industrious. Referring to 1944, Lieut. G. Pearson writes:—[1] "With field units

---

[1] *Brief History of the K.G.V s O. Bengal Sappers and Miners Group, R.I.E., August 1939-July 1946*, by Lieut. G. Pearson, R.E., pp. 88-91.

distinguishing themselves in action, Roorkee was busy with great quantities of work necessary to keep so many units supplied with men. Training continued in the light of the experiences of particular Companies, and a constant movement of officers and men in and out of the Centre was some indication of the growth of the Group. In March 1944, a peak of 23,850 men was reached, representing a seven-fold expansion of the pre-War strength. Early in this year, the Bengal Group was able to assist in the establishment of a School of Military Engineering (India) at Roorkee, and many of its courses were subsequently attended by officers of the Group. Within the Group, jungle training had become a fine art, and a Battle School flourished with a great deal of realism. The Bengal Sappers were particularly associated with the activities of the 39th Training Division which by 1944 was settled near-by. Some Field Companies were maintained on the North-West Frontier, and officers were supplied for the various Engineer Training Centres at Jhansi, Meerut and Nowshera. Men of the Group were engaged in operations with the Chindits in Burma; and others, who had long been patient, were encouraged by the prospect of an Airborne Division taking them into action. The Group had two companies with the 39th Training Division. These, originally with the 14th Division, were 367 Field Company and 306 Field Park Company. They were Training Companies. Platoons, complete with V.C.Os and N.C.Os, were sent out from the Reinforcement Battalion at Roorkee and did nine weeks' training. A week was spent in watermanship and improvised jungle rafting on the Ganges, and the last two weeks were devoted to tactical and Engineer schemes in the jungle with platoons of other Field Companies. This system continued until April 1945. 33 Field Squadron and 40 Field Park Squadron were among the units of the 44th Armoured Division detailed in 1943 to defend the east coastal ports in the event of a Japanese invasion of India. By April 1944, however, the danger was past and the 44th Division was broken up, only a skeleton force being left for subsequent expansion into an Airborne Division. Early in 1945, 40 Field Park Squadron returned to Roorkee to re-form for airborne work. There had been rumours in 1944 that 33 Field Squadron was going to become a Parachute Squadron, but in July it was armoured again. In September, however, orders were received for immediate conversion to an airborne role. Intensive physical training was begun, and there was tremendous enthusiasm for jumping. The training was for an actual operation in Burma. Again there was disappointment, as the operation, and another which was planned later, were not required. This was the nearest that the Squadron got to going to the war. It was a tale of hope deferred."

At the beginning of 1944, there were three Training Battalions at Roorkee, and in March a Depot Wing was formed which included Reinforcement, Specialist, Depot and Demobilization Battalions. There was also a flourishing Boys Battalion which had begun its existence early in 1942. So great was the demand for men that the training period for recruits had been reduced in 1943 to only nine months and ended with the completion of a Field Works course. The men underwent a strenuous course in the Battle School before being posted to units. Two O.C.T.Us were located in Roorkee, for which the Bengal Group had to provide Instructors and Staff. In these institutions, cadets were trained for about seven months in engineering subjects before being posted as officers to Engineer Groups. The Roorkee News Letter of January 1944, the last to be issued for two years, describes some events at the Centre. "The S.M.E., India, is now located in part of the Thomason College and has made an interesting addition to the atmosphere of Roorkee. In November last, the Chief Royal Engineer and Colonel of the Corps, Lieut.-General Sir Ronald Charles, visited us for four days and we did our best to entertain him. He saw all stages of our training, met those still in Roorkee who had served with him when he was in the Corps, visited the Sergeants' and V.C.Os' Messes, the Knox Memorial School and the Indian Families Hospital, and dined in the Mess. Our proudest moment was the Ceremonial Parade of the whole Corps on the Corps Parade Ground at which our Colonel was accompanied by Lieut.-General Sir Clarence Bird, a Colonel-Commandant, R.E., and an ex-Bengal Sapper and Miner. The entire ground was covered with troops, and the inspection from a jeep took $9\frac{1}{2}$ minutes along the front ranks only. After nearly $3\frac{1}{2}$ years in Roorkee, Colonel H. N. Obbard has left us for G.H.Q. and Colonel W. L. D. Veitch has returned as Commandant."

The conditions of life at the Bengal Centre during 1945 are described by Lieut.-Colonel J. R. Connor.[1] "In March", he writes, "I returned from Burma to become Assistant Commandant (Training). I had been away three years, during which the face of Roorkee had changed enormously. There were two Messes, each filled almost to overflowing. The hours of work were very long. The hot weather

---

[1] Notes by Lieut.-Colonel J. R. Connor, C.B.E., R.E., dated Jan. 30th, 1955.

programme was 6.30 a.m. to 2.0 p.m. with a break from 8.15 to 9.15 a.m., and then from 4.30 to 6.15 p.m., so there was hardly any time for relaxation. The end of the war in Europe made little difference to us except that a few British officers were allowed to go home as replacements arrived. The main expansion had been completed and the number of recruits was gradually dropping. This eased life a bit; but demobilization plans were in the offing and no one knew what was likely to happen in either the military or political fields. With the end of the war against Japan, and the return of troops from East and West, we had a very busy life and so felt rather guilty when we stopped the evening parade and resumed some peace-time activities such as Athletic Meetings and Games. During the cold weather of 1945-46, I managed to visit the *jheels* fairly frequently. They had changed for the worse since 1942. The Solani was flowing through Panchli Jheel, which had silted up, and later off southwards in one of its old beds, and the *jheels* which remained would take only four or five guns. Polo had died out in 1940-41 and was not resurrected; but a few horses were still in evidence and ran sometimes in small race meetings on parts of the College Maidan which had not been built over."

Brigadier R. E. Holloway, who returned to Roorkee in 1945, corroborates much that Lieut.-Colonel Connor records.[1] He found that the characteristic feature of the years 1945-47 in the Bengal Centre was a feeling of impermanence. In the effort to do their best, everyone worked at the highest pressure. The circumstances were rendered more difficult by the release and repatriation of many British Officers, although most of these held only temporary commissions and could not adapt themselves easily to peace-time conditions. There was a scarcity of almost every commodity—food, drink, clothes and cartridges—and what could be obtained was very expensive. Good servants also were rare. The Commandant and his Assistants were overwhelmed with correspondence and the details of a complex administration. The men, when off duty, had to walk out in uniform because Hindustani clothing was obtainable only at a prohibitive cost. The average Sapper, however, was more intelligent than his pre-War counterpart. He spent more, but in return he expected more in the way of food, recreation and welfare generally. His family was already discarding the *purdah*, and the Commandant was always sure of a warm welcome when touring the family quarters or

---

[1] Notes by Brigadier R. E. Holloway, C.B.E., dated Feb. 7th, 1955.

visiting the Womens' Institute. The Joint Magistrate, though a Muslim, was very popular with the Hindus and Sikhs. Good feeling permeated the countryside. In fact, the Roorkee area was little affected by the disturbances elsewhere. Many of the Sappers had been recruited from the same villages. For instance, in the Jagraon District in Ludhiana there were what may be called 'Sapper' villages in which almost every family had relations serving in the Corps. The V.C.Os., especially the elder ones, were the mainstay of discipline. When it was found in 1945 that few Sikhs were volunteering for service as parachutists with 33 Field Squadron, the fact was mentioned casually to the senior Sikh V.C.O. at the S.M.E. Roorkee. On the very next day, the Commandant was informed that the entire Sikh strength of the Corps were anxious to become parachutists. Could whole-hearted co-operation go further?

In nature and composition, the Bombay Centre at Kirkee in 1944-45 resembled closely the establishments at Bangalore and Roorkee. A Training Wing of three Battalions existed at Dighi, each Battalion having six Companies and a H.Q. Company. The intake for each Battalion was about 120 recruits a month. The Boys Battalion was doing well. Training in general, however, was more difficult than at Bangalore or Roorkee because of the lack of experienced instructors resulting from the loss of so many units when the Japanese overran Malaya in 1942. When Colonel H. P. Cavendish was Commandant in 1943, the system of training, which had catered hitherto for requirements in North Africa or Italy, was switched to those needed for the Burma front and a jungle training site was selected at Supa, near Londa in the Belgaum District. This provided not only for the instruction of Officer Cadets of the Engineer Officers' Training School but also for that of V.C.Os. and N.C.Os. in jungle warfare and engineering. The conditions of life at Kirkee can be gathered from the following description given by Brigadier L. O. Clark who arrived there as Commandant in July 1945.[1] "I had been away from India since 1939 and expected to find the country much changed. But it had changed remarkably little. Servants' wages were higher, as were the prices of most European goods, and nobody, except Anglo-Indian railway guards, ever wore a *topi*. When in uniform, I always wore a beret, hot or cold weather alike, and without any ill effects. Cantonment life went on as before. There was the Western India Club, and also the Poona Gymkhana Club

---

[1] Notes by Brigadier L. O. Clark, o.b.e., dated Jan. 22nd, 1955.

which had as many Indian as British members and provided dances, Bridge, tennis, cricket and hockey. The Royal Connaught Boat Club, commonly knows as the 'Rosherville', still ran its sailing and rowing activities. At the Turf Club, racing was in full swing with its usual magnificent setting of priceless *saris* on green lawns. Outside Cantonments, the country was peaceful, and the Mahrattas the kindliest of village hosts. My wife and I picnicked far and wide and always met with the utmost courtesy. We had two Officers' Messes, one in the original Mess at Kirkee and the other for the Training Battalions at Dighi Camp, some miles away. Both were run on pre-war lines except that officers usually wore Service Dress instead of Mess kit for dinner. The Indian officers conformed to the European style of feeding. Mess entertainments were held at Christmas and on 'gala' or Sports Days. The Corps had a high reputation for Tug-of-War, long-distance swimming and hockey. The work at headquarters was mainly the disbanding of war-time Field Companies, the re-fitting of regular Field Companies, and the demobilization of men, including some thousands of ex-prisoners-of-war of the Japanese. I shall not forget the arrival of the first batch of released prisoners. They were desperately thin and weak, though quite cheerful. They were dressed in any clothes "Welfare" had been able to provide; but every man, throughout three years of captivity in nothing but canvas shorts, had managed to retain his Royal Blue lanyard and displayed it proudly over his right shoulder. After some months, they had recovered sufficiently to dramatize their experiences, and it was wonderful to see a Mahratta, imitating a Jap officer, haranguing a recalcitrant working party of P.Ms. and Sikhs, all in excellent spirits. There were very few Regular British Officers at Kirkee below the rank of Lieut.-Colonel. Most were Short Service Majors, often promoted N.C.Os., and the remainder were young Captains or Lieutenants holding Emergency Commissions, but they were almost uniformly good."

Major P. M. Leslie-Jones, who arrived in Kirkee in October 1945, gives some details of the Boys Battalion.[1] The unit was commanded by a Major and was located at that time in the Westmacott Lines which had been occupied before the war by the Training Battalion. In February 1946, however, it moved to Dighi and came under the command of the Training Wing. When hostilities ended in September 1945 the Boys were being trained rather on 'mass produc-

---

[1] Notes by Major P. M. Leslie-Jones, R.E., dated Jan. 20th, 1955.

tion' lines. Drill, education and physical training were dealt with adequately; but the Workshops' course was very concentrated, and although the Boys emerged nominally as Class II or Class III tradesmen, it was found that they did not come up to the necessary standards because they lacked experience. Thus the original conception of providing a cadre of high-grade tradesmen and potential N.C.Os. was not being fulfilled. The policy was therefore changed and was concentrated on 'leadership' training on the lines of the Boy Scout Movement. The time spent in Workshops was reduced, and as an experiment, the Boys were given an introduction to all trades instead of specializing in one. The inculcation of a capacity for leadership was no simple problem because the Regular N.C.Os. and V.C.Os. who acted as instructors found some difficulty in giving the Boys a free hand. However, the instructors were induced to remain more in the background, and the Boys soon acquired confidence. Scout training had suffered hitherto from being classed under the general title of 'Fieldworks.' Now it came into its own. Another innovation was a Camp of three weeks' duration in the jungle near the hill station of Mahableshwar. This was a great success. Later, a daily compulsory rest period was introduced. Boys were found to be failing to increase properly in height and weight in spite of good food, and the cause was diagnosed as over-work at too young an age. The Recruiting Officer became more selective. Families intimately connected with the Corps were often so eager to enter their sons that they were not too particular about a year or two in age. The general physical standard was much improved also by wrestling and boxing. Although the former still remained the favourite sport, boxing was taken up enthusiastically, and the Bombay lads soon became the chief rivals of those from the Madras Group.

Some mention has been made in Chapter I of the formation of Engineer Groups between 1939 and 1941 in places other than Bangalore, Roorkee and Kirkee in order to cater for the prodigious expansion entailed by the war. An Engineer Depot already existed at Lahore which produced some Artisan or Electrical and Mechanical Companies, but it was utterly inadequate for a World War and accordingly four new Groups of Indian Engineers were raised. These were No. 1 E and M. Group, No. 3 Construction Group and No. 6 Mechanical Equipment Group at Lahore, and No. 4 Engineer Equipment Group at Sialkot. By August 1943, No. 1 Group had raised 60 units, No. 4 had provided 20 Engineer Battalions, and No. 6 had produced 42 units. No. 3 Construction Group, however, should be awarded the palm for it had raised no less than 165 units comprising a total of 15,000 trained men. Brigadier Partap Narain served with this Group as Assistant Commandant (Lieut.-Colonel) from April 1945 to April 1946, first under Colonel D. J. Middleton-Stewart and afterwards under Colonel F. W. L. MacC. Parker. Then he succeeded Parker as Commandant for six weeks. When he arrived in 1945, No. 3 Group consisted of two Training Battalions, a Holding Battalion, a Mechanical Transport Training Centre and a Battle Training School near Pathankot. The Group had been built up from scratch and was nearing its peak of efficiency when orders were received in May 1945 that it was to be disbanded. Training in farming and other useful pursuits was started at once for soldiers who were about to be demobilized. No. 3 Group was a very prosperous concern. It had a fine swimming pool, an excellent cinema, and an Officers' Mess housed in a bungalow owned by Mr. Jinnah. However, the unwelcome orders had to be obeyed and demobilization was begun in November. The three Groups at Lahore had been amalgamated into one under Colonel E. A. E. Bolton and their records sent to the Bengal Group at Roorkee. The end came in January 1946 when it was decided to close the Depot. Even then, the total strength at Lahore exceeded 18,000 men. No. 4 Group at Sialkot provided eventually a nucleus for the Royal Pakistan Engineers after the partition. The standard of the men in these Punjab Groups compared favourably with that of the Madras, Bengal and Bombay Groups. The northern Groups certainly helped in no small degree to meet the voracious demands of the Army, so their foundation was amply justified.

Major-General C. de L. Gaussen, who returned to India in May 1945 after an absence of five years, has much to record about the Indian Engineers and the changes which he noticed. "The Boys Battalions were exceedingly flourishing at all the Corps Headquarters", he writes.[1] "They had been instituted in order to educate lads drawn from the fighting classes to provide suitable material for regular K.C.I.Os. Alternatively, if the Boys did not reach the requisite

---

[1] Notes by Major-General C. de L. Gaussen, C.B., M.C., dated May 17th, 1955.
From May to December 1945, as a Brigadier, General Gaussen was C.E. Central Command which included the Bengal and Punjab Groups. Next, he was Deputy E-in-C. until September 1946, when he became C.E. Northern Command. In July 1947, he was succeeded in that appointment by Brigadier M. R. Jefferis, who later became E-in-C., Pakistan. General Gaussen was then appointed E-in-C., India, under the old regime, and so remained until that post ceased to exist after the Partition as part of the British administration.

standard for commissions, they could receive sufficient education to fit them for the higher technical posts as Warrant Officers for which our previous system did not really provide. Only those who know the intense *esprit de corps* of the Sappers and Miners can fully visualise the keenness and energy that these lads displayed in order to become officers in their family Corps. It was very heartening to see them boxing—a sport foreign to them. The Madras boys were particularly good at boxing and almost swept the championships. It was amazing also to see the very wide use made of mechanical excavating equipment when one remembered that, six years earlier, the Sappers and Miners had only a few mechanical road vehicles. A sign of the times occurred when the Maharajah of Patiala appealed for the help of bulldozers after some disastrous floods. He obtained the use of such a large number that the flood defences of Patiala City were practically remodelled. So far as general training is concerned, the chief innovation was the part the Sappers played in the Training Divisions to which men went after completing their recruits' courses. I visited the 14th Division in the Central Provinces and the 39th Division near Hardwar. The C.R.Es of these Divisions kept in close touch with the Corps Commandants and the training was most practical, unhampered by any restrictions of boundaries or property. If timber was needed, it was felled in the jungle on the spot. Roads could be carved anywhere: demolitions carried out wholesale. Living conditions were hard; but the training made a permanent impression on the young British and Indian officers who went through it, quite apart from its value as a prelude to fighting in the Burmese jungles. The pride of the young British officers in their respective Sapper and Miner Groups was intense. They worked hard at the language and took immense trouble to understand their men as well as mastering technical details. Even more striking were the King's Commissioned Indian Officers. When I left India in 1939 there had been only a handful of such officers who had been through the 'Shop', and they were still subalterns. Now they were Lieut.-Colonels and had, of course, been joined by scores of I.C.Os from the S.M.E. at Roorkee. They modelled themselves in every respect, including their family life, on the pattern set by their comrades, the British officers."

The years 1946 and 1947 were fateful ones for India. Victory had been won, but at a staggering cost. Soldiers were streaming back to a country impoverished by war and permeated by political unrest which culminated eventually in a partition more drastic than any in history. The professional outlook of the Indian Engineers had to be revised almost overnight. Peace-time methods were needed to replace the improvized and often haphazard procedure learnt in war. "Engineering in peace is a matter of careful planning" said Major-General H. Williams when addressing the Institution of Engineers in Calcutta in 1954.[1] "It requires the application of skill and knowledge to produce something to a definite specification. In war, other conditions prevail. Time is always short. Planning is often inadequate and must go on side by side with execution. Events and conditions are never static. Specialization is almost impossible. The Engineer is in competition with others for transport, labour and even space, and the enemy is continually seeking to upset his plans and destroy his work. Engineering in war is only a means to an end, which is victory in battle. The Engineer in the Forces must be a soldier first, well versed in the art of war but at the same time competent, though not necessarily highly specialized, in the engineering which concerns his arm." So the post-War Indian Engineers had not only to reduce their establishments to what the country could afford and the political situation warrant, but also to reach so high a standard of professional attainment that they could match their skill against all competitors in the fields of civil, mechanical and electrical engineering. These tasks were undertaken with much determination. Modernization became the order of the day as India progressed along the thorny road leading to self-government. A heavy burden of responsibility had already rested on the shoulders of Major-General H. E. Roome who was Engineer-in-Chief during the later stages of the war[2], and that which devolved on his successor, Major-General W. F. Hasted, in January 1946 was almost as onerous though different in nature. Roome had had to wield the sword; Hasted to turn it into a ploughshare.

The Sapper units returning from service overseas in 1946 always received a hearty welcome on arrival, but few could have experienced rounds of festivities comparable with those staged in certain Indian States. Take, for instance, the story of the return of the Sirmoor Field Company from Burma in June. To start with, the unit had a

---

[1] Address by Major-General H. Williams, C.B., C.B.E., Engineer-in-Chief, India, as President of the Institution of Engineers, India, delivered in Calcutta on February 13th, 1954, on the subject of the role of the Engineer in the defence of India (See *The Journal of the Institution of Military Engineers*, April 1954, pp. 84-93).

[2] Major-General H. E. Roome had succeeded Major-General R. L. Bond as E-in-C., India, in May 1943.

fine reception in Calcutta, with speeches by Generals and gifts of flowers, cigarettes and sweets. Then, after a month in Roorkee, it left for Nahan, the State capital, which it had not seen since it departed for the North-West Frontier early in the war. "There was a whole month of festivities, *nautches* and parades" writes Captain T. le M. Spring-Smyth, R.E., the Company Commander at the time.[1] "The first parade caught me napping. Much to the mens' amusement, an enormous black charger was led up to me in front of the Company and I was told that it was mine for the month. Hastily remembering how to mount, I had to take over the entire parade for an inspection by the Commander of the Sirmoor State Forces. There were Cavalry, Pipes and Drums, a military Band and a battalion of infantry apart from the Field Company which was itself 300 strong. However, all went well because the charger knew everything about inspections and walked quietly in and out of the platoons and companies without any interference from me! Afterwards, there was a route march through almost every street in Nahan. The Sirmoor State, lying between Dehra Dun and Simla, is extremely hilly, and Nahan itself is built on a series of hills with hardly any level ground between. The streets were cobbled and spotlessly clean but very trying for marching. I had to stop continually to be garlanded, often by pretty girls from first-floor windows which, by virtue of the enormous size of my mount, were nearly level with me. It was not until August that, somewhat the worse for wear after the Maharajah's hospitality, I reported to the Bengal Sappers at Roorkee and was sent to Ranchi to take command of 7 Field Company."

It may be mentioned in parenthesis that when 7 Field Company returned to Roorkee in October 1946 it was re-formed as an all-Sikh unit. It was probably the first Field Company to undergo this change although there was already an all-Sikh Field Park Company. Most of the men were Jat Sikhs and very carefully selected. No man was accepted whose height was less that 5' 11", and in addition he had to have high educational and trade qualifications. The men excelled in all games and sports, particularly hockey in which they never lost a match, even against Battalion teams. In the spring of 1947, as already recorded, the Company was sent to Burma as part of the post-War garrison of that country and did not return to India until October when everything was in a very unsettled state. Yet its discipline remained quite unaffected by political troubles. The second-in-

---

[1] Notes by Captain T. le M. Spring-Smyth, R.E., dated May 14th, 1955.

Command was still a Muslim officer whose relationship with the Sikh officers and other ranks was extremely cordial and whose eventual departure to Pakistan was deeply regretted by them.

A typical welcome home after service overseas was that experienced in 1946 by 65 Field Company (Madras) under Major R. C. Gabriel, R.E. When the transport from Burma docked at Madras, there was music from a loudspeaker and cigarettes and cups of tea were provided by the Womens' Voluntary Services. The Customs authorities turned a blind eye and allowed a score of Japanese swords to pass without hindrance. A hearty reception was anticipated at Bangalore and everyone put on his smartest uniform; but little did Gabriel realize the sort of welcome which awaited the unit. As the troop train entered the Cantonment Station after dark, he found the Madras Sapper Band crashing out "Wings", and a reception committee, headed by the Commandant, waiting on the platform. The officers were soon heavily garlanded and the men lined up for tea and cigarettes handed out by the W.V.S. They were then taken in lorries to the Woodcote Camp to be the guests of a Workshop Company before starting on the long process of reorganization and the release of those who did not wish to stay on.

The process of demobilization is described as follows by Colonel R. A. Loomba.[1] "On return from S.E.A.C. in July 1946 I stayed at Bangalore for a short time. Units were then coming in regularly from overseas for disbandment, and those men who desired release were put through the demobilization machine. The "end of the war" atmosphere was evident throughout except in Group Headquarters where plans were in hand for post-War reorganization of the Centre and of field units. Each disbanding unit held a final parade and a "rich food" before it ceased to exist and passed into the pages of history. A constant stream of officers flowed through the Jalahalli Mess, recounting tales of adventure and praising the "thambi" (Madras Sapper) for his sense of humour and his endless capacity for hard work under the most trying conditions. Some were worried about what the future held for them. The men, on the other hand, were smiling and cheerful as they left the Depot dressed in the best of their newly acquired clothes and with money in their pockets. Their immediate concern was to reach their homes, where they could speak of their experiences to an admiring audience. As to the future, they would see about that after a few months of well earned rest."

---

[1] Notes by Colonel R. A. Loomba, dated August 14th, 1954.

Some events at the Bangalore Headquarters are brought to notice by Lieut.-Colonel R. A. Lindsell in his *Short History*. On January 18th, Colonel M. M. Jeakes handed over charge to Colonel F. W. L. MacC. Parker after having held the post of Commandant for three years, and at the same time Lieut.-Colonel J. A. Cameron, R.E., an Assistant Commandant, was repatriated to the United Kingdom and replaced by Lieut.-Colonel B. E. Whitman R.E.[1] Immediately after Colonel Jeakes' departure came a change in nomenclature when, as mentioned in Chapter I, the title "Sappers and Miners" was relinquished with great regret in all three Groups. The Madras Group nearly lost also the dignified prefix of "Queen Victoria's Own." The News Letter of June 1946 reads:— "A frightful Indian Army Order appeared not long ago which deprived us of our hard won title of 'Q.V's O.' This came as a complete bombshell to us all, including our Colonel. Protests have been innumerable, and we were the first to question the legality of such a revolutionary edict. However, water has passed under the bridge since then, and now, under another I.A.O., we are to be known as the 'Q.V's O. Madras Regimental Centre, R.I.E.' We have thus retained 'Q.V's O.'; but 'Sappers and Miners' was a more difficult problem and we have been voted down. Yet we take heart from the knowledge that you cannot kill 'Sappers and Miners' in under twenty years." Brigadier R. C. R. Hill, who had been Colonel of the Corps since 1942, had no doubt expressed his opinions very forcibly, but unhappily his representations met with no success. With the bestowal of the title "Royal" on the Indian Engineers in February 1946, Hill became the first Colonel Commandant of the Madras Group, as did Major-General Sir Horace Roome of the Bengal Group and Lieut.-General Sir Francis Nosworthy of the Bombay Group. All were well-known ex-Sappers and Miners.

News was received with satisfaction that the first re-union of the newly formed Madras Sapper Officers' Association had been held in London on May 31st. In June, the Madras Group had the honour of providing the main body of a Royal Indian Engineer contingent at the great Victory Parade in London on which it was represented by a V.C.O. and 29 other ranks under the command of Lieut.-Colonel

---

[1] Colonel B. E. Whitman was destined to be the last British Commandant at Bangalore. He held that appointment from October 9th, 1947, to March 11th, 1948, when he was relieved by Colonel R. K. Kochhar, the first Indian Commandant of he Madras Group.

R. K. Kochhar. The contingent was accommodated in Kensington Gardens and was taken on several tours before returning to India. Demobilization continued steadily at Bangalore. In September 1946, the remains of the reinforcement Battalion were absorbed into the Depot Wing in the Meeanee Lines, and the Boys Battalion was moved from Jalahalli to the vacant Institute Camp. The Training Battalion still had 1,650 recruits and the Boys Battalion a strength of 540. The Boys' Boxing team went to Delhi in December and won the All-India Boys' Championship. Enthusiasm for this sport had now begun to spread throughout the Group, and the Bantam Weight All-India Championship at Poona was won by a Madras Sapper Naik.

On September 2nd, 1946, orders were issued abolishing for general use the distinctive Madras Sapper head-gear known as the "*Doopta*" (or "*Dupta*"). An exception was made in the case of the Band, and the Boys Battalion and men of the Depot and Training Wings were allowed to wear the "Doopta" until supplied with berets. It is now worn only by the Band. At a meeting of the Madras Sapper Officers' Association in London in May 1946, Colonel W. D. Robertson, who had served in the Madras Corps from 1894 to 1904, explained how the 'tall hat without a brim' may have originated. He had heard the story from an old Subedar, fifty years before. In the days of the East India Company, many European military adventurers took service under Indian rulers. They trained the armed forces and contracted for the supply of rations and equipment when in the field. Most of these soldiers of fortune were Frenchmen, one being a certain De Boyne who trained the Mysore Army in the days of Haidar Ali and served later under Sindhia in Northern India.[1] After the fall of Seringapatam in May 1799, some Hyderabad units, trained by De Boyne, were incorporated into the East India Company's forces and among these was a regiment of 'Spahis', officered by the Company's Engineers and subsequently called 'Madras Sappers.' The "Doopta", therefore, may have had a French origin for it resembles the old Spahi head-dress without the peak.

At Roorkee, demobilization was planned to be carried out in three phases. The first men to be released were recruits with less than six months' service. The next were those with longer service. This constituted the initial phase of the process. The second phase

---

[1] *The Military Engineer in India*, by Lieut.-Colonel E. W. C. Sandes, D.S.O., M.C., Vol. I, pp. 205-216.

involved the release of trained soldiers, and by the middle of 1946 more than half the men in the Bengal Group had gone. The third phase was intended to secure a reduction to peace-time strength, but it was postponed because of problems arising from the probable partition from Pakistan. No. 2 Training Battalion was converted into a Demobilization Battalion, and in addition to demobilization duties, gave instruction in useful peace-time occupations to men destined for release. The Battalion was commanded by a very shrewd Scot. On one occasion, when a visit of inspection was pending from the G.O.C. Lucknow District whose chief idiosyncracy was known to be a terror of flies, 'D.D.T.' disinfectant was poured into every hole and corner for hours and it was hoped that all would be well. But when the General came to the Demob Battalion Lines he spotted a couple of flies in a Dining Hall and at once started a harangue on his pet subject. A bad report seemed inevitable. The C.O., however, was equal to the occasion. In very broad Scotch he said "You need not worry, Sir. I've noted these particular specimens for demobilization tomorrow", and in the resultant laughter, all was forgiven and forgotten.

Demobilization was carried out as follows. A card was prepared for every man showing his qualifications, details of service and recommendations, and with this he appeared before the Commandant for an interview. The Commandant had two rubber stamps, one marked "Demob" and the other "Retain", and the man's fate was decided according to which stamp went on his card. It so happened that the "Demob" stamp was considerably larger than the "Retain" stamp, and very soon it was noticed that no man ever said whether or not he was being demobilized but whether he had been accorded the *'Bara Mohar'* or the *'Chota Mohar.'* The same expressions are probably in use to this day among ex-Bengal Sappers of the Second World War.

In February 1946, the congratulations of the Commander-in-Chief on the conferment of the title "Royal" on the Corps of Indian Engineers were gratefully acknowledged by the Roorkee Commandant. The post-war composition of the Bengal Group was announced as 50% Mussalmans, 40% Hindus and 10% Sikhs, and it was added that all post-War units were to be of one-class composition. These changes came gradually into force, and by the end of 1946 there were four Mussalman units (2, 4 and 5 Field Companies and 35 Field Squadron) and five Hindu units (1, 3, 67 and 74 Field Companies and 6 Army Troops Company). 7 Field Company had became an all-Sikh unit.

Some interesting impressions of Roorkee in 1946-47 are recorded by a former Bengal Sapper officer, Brigadier C. L. B. Duke, who revisited his old haunts after an absence of about ten years.[1] He found that the traditions of the place remained the same, thanks largely to a few officers who had served almost continuously with the Group. The enormous expansion during the war had necessitated a large constructional programme. Barracks had been built right out to the Rifle Ranges, and two new ranges made beyond them. A Supply Depot, with its own siding, and a new Railway Station called "Dandhera", occupied the area between the railway and the old Range Road. The original Corps Parade Ground, which included Polo, Football and Hockey grounds, remained the same; but barracks filled the area south of the Polo Ground facing the old Training Battalion Office, once the Indian Military Hospital. The Workshops had expanded into all the buildings formerly used as Fieldworks Stores, and new Stores buildings had been built extending up to the Hill Cut. The rest of the Fieldworks Ground showed little alteration. New barracks covered the entire Grass Farm area between the main road and the Ganges Canal as far as Station Road. South of the railway, to a point beyond the Railway Officer's bungalow, were the Boys Battalion lines and a farm. Behind the Corps Orderly Room, now faced by a new block of offices, stood ranks of buildings devoted to Records and Accounts. A billiard room had been added to the Officers' Mess, and the former Commandant's Bungalow served as a second Mess. Married quarters had appeared on the slopes beyond the bungalow. The old Station Parade Ground, and the Polo Ground on the College Maidan, were under crops of wheat. Such was the appearance of post-War Roorkee. It exemplified the Latin quotation *'Tempora mutantur, nos et mutamur in illis.'*

We turn now to Kirkee in 1946. The News Letters had been restarted after a lapse of several years, and we read in the January issue that more than 2,000 men out of a war strength of 24,000 had already passed through the Demobilization Centre to return to civil life. They were mostly pensioners and recruits, but normal releases had begun. No more recrutis were being enrolled although some were still under instruction in the single Training Battalion that remained. British officers and other ranks were arriving and

---

[1] Roorkee News Letter, dated March 1947.

departing at a bewildering rate, and a Transit Camp had been formed for R.E. officers coming from England. The Engineer Officers' Training School was under orders to close down. In April it is recorded that everyone looked askance at the order which dropped the time-honoured title of "Sappers and Miners" and introduced the alien term "Centre." The change, it is said, had been made with the assent of the Group, but by no means with its unqualified approval. The demobilization total had passed 5,000. The tide of repatriation and release flowed on unabated. Many Regular officers were going home to supplementary courses. By July 1946, more than 7,000 men had been demobilized. The Boys Battalion had reached the final of the All-India Boys Boxing Tournament at Delhi. The Group was doing well in Hockey. A Rugby Football team was in the process of formation. By October, 10,000 Indian other ranks had been released and the number of British officers and Warrant and N.C.Os. was diminishing at an alarming rate. No British replacements were being received. December found Kirkee returning to normal peacetime conditions. Bungalows were being re-painted; garden walls rebuilt. The Commander-in-Chief presented new colours to the Boys Battalion on a ceremonial parade. A figure of 15,000 released ranks was reached. The Group was the mainstay of the Poona and Kirkee Hunt and entered two teams in a Point-to-Point Race; but it was remarked that riding might end soon because horses were no longer authorized on the Peace establishments. Yet the Commandant seems to have been in great fettle judging by the following poetic query which he addressed to his Chief Engineer when threatened with a simultaneous visit by the Engineers-in-Chief of both India and the United Kingdom.

> *"When gathered in multitudes, twos and threes,*
> *Are they Es-in-C or E-in-Cs?*
> *The former suggests that they live in clover,*
> *The latter that often they're half-seas over.*
> *Perhaps as a compromise, seeing they're few,*
> *We could leave it at E-in-C (bracketted) two."*

Efforts to secure communal feeding among the men, and life in the Officers' Mess, are described by Major P. M. Leslie-Jones. "Early in 1946", he writes,[1] "attempts were made to break down religious barriers between the three castes in the Bombay Group. This, I

---

[1] Notes by Major P. M. Leslie-Jones, R.E., dated Jan. 20th, 1955.

think, was due to the return to India of units which had been serving in Italy and had mixed freely with European troops. For instance, one Company had all castes messing together even after its return to India. Individuals did not seem to mind much, although their religious leaders and some·of the older V.C.Os. were against such an innovation. In the Boys Battalion we tried to induce all the lads to eat in the same *langar* compound after the food had been prepared in separate caste *langars*, and this system slowly gained acceptance. The Punjabi Mahomedans and Sikhs were the more co-operative though they sat in groups. The Mahrattas at first refused to eat in a communal compound but finally agreed to do so when a flimsy barrier had been put across part of it. When the Boys Battalion moved to Dighi, there was a definite set-back because of the dispersed *langars*. However, one central hut was set aside as a Mess and provided with tables and benches, and the Boys ate in groups in the hut. In the Officers' Mess there had been little change since pre-War days. One was waited upon assiduously by one's bearer. Servant's kit was very expensive, and some of the bearers wore R.I.E. cummerbands. "Dining-in" nights had not been instituted, and Guest Nights were rare. The most important occasion was the farewell 'dining-out' of Subedar-Major and Hon. Captain Taj Din. Three Commandants, Colonels Horsfield, Cavendish and L. O. Clark, were present, and all, including Taj Din, made speeches. Taj Din left Kirkee next morning, literally bowed down with garlands. He was regarded with much awe by the rank and file."

The year 1947 was perhaps the most momentous in the entire history of India. In March 1946 a Cabinet Mission had made far-reaching recommendations to implement the oft-reiterated policy of the British Government regarding the future of India as a self-governing country. The Mission had included Sir Stafford Cripps who, four years earlier, had tried to find a solution to what appeared to be a constitutional deadlock. It had been suggested in 1946 that an Interim Government might be formed; but inter-communal strife in some areas interfered with this solution of the problem. The only alternative seemed to be the division of the country into two separate Dominions. Accordingly, in February 1947, Admiral Earl Mountbatten was sent to India to relieve Field-Marshal Sir Archibald Wavell as Viceroy and to carry the separation into effect.

Lieut.-General Sir Francis Tuker, then G.O.C.-in-Chief, Eastern Command, has much to say about the feelings of the troops regarding the proposal. "At the end of the war in September 1945," he writes,[1] "we soldiers had been plunged at once into the cares of internal security and keeping the peace. We hoped that whatever disturbances there might be would be anti-British and not communal. These would be a smaller danger than a communal outbreak which would be far wider spread, might have its effect on the Army itself, and once started, would break out again and again. We knew that self-Government was imminent and that with it the Army must be nationalized, that is, offered entirely to Indians, before many years were out. We ardently desired that India should be united, strong and friendly to the British Commonwealth, if not a member of it, and that the Indian Army, to which we had devoted the best years of our lives, should remain a solid, efficient and faithful instrument of the new India; but it was apparent that, even in an united India, if the Army were to survive, it would only do so if reorganized into communal classes. So we urged that both officers and men should be grouped into communally homogeneous units and the sooner the process started the better. It was hoped that India would hang together and keep the Army integral; but it was expected that the country would split in half, and that the Army would thus, in any case, be as a consequence divided. That, it would seem, must be the end of our Army; but we saw that there was a chance of saving it if steps could be taken at once to attune everybody's mind before communal feelings became too fierce. Thus our chance lay in handing out to each of the two parts a contingent of its own and keeping a third party under the management of all three parties concerned, British, Hindu and Muslim. If possible, the third contingent should be built round one completely impartial body, the Gurkha Brigade under its British officers. Without this impartially controlled contingent we felt certain that there would soon be a struggle between the two States of Hindustan (India) and Pakistan, and preceding it, a race in armaments among peoples whose standard of living was already too low. There would then be no one left to guard the strategic frontiers. Yet the frontiers were as deep a concern to Hindustan as to Pakistan, for once they were breached, Hindustan would have no natural frontier left to her. If Pakistan could be persuaded to stand beside Hindustan, the latter would have the advantage of this vast cushion of Islam between herself and danger.

---

[1] *While Memory Serves*, by Lieut.-General Sir Francis Tuker, K.C I.E., C.B., D.S.O., O.B.E., pp. 20-28.

Any political solution that made for tranquility within the country would leave India strategically stronger than one which held the country together in a resentful and troubled union. These and other reasons induced us, early in 1946, to anticipate that, whatever the political solution in meeting India's demand for independence, some sort of impartially controlled contingent must be constituted for all-India defence."

Partition having been decided upon, many problems had to be faced. According to Brigadier Partap Narain, one of the most pressing was the retention of British volunteers. Most British officers wished to leave India, though many afterwards regretted their decision. The names of all Muslim officers were listed at Army Headquarters as they would naturally elect for transfer to Pakistan. There were very few senior Engineer Officers amongst them; in fact only two or three commissioned before the war, headed by Lieut.-Colonel Anwar Khan. The posting of replacements had to be arranged by Major-General W. F. Hasted who was Engineer-in-Chief, India, from January 1946 to July 1947 under the British regime. After the Partition the task devolved on Major-General J. F. D. Steedman, the first Engineer-in-Chief under the Indian regime, while General Hasted remained for a time as Engineer-in-Chief, Supreme Headquarters. "It was rather interesting", writes Partap Narain, "to see two Es-in-C. Headquarters, both at Kashmir House." The decision to carry out the Partition was kept secret as long as possible. Some time before the cleavage occurred, Field-Marshal Sir Claude Auchinleck visited Kirkee to present a standard to the Boys Battalion. The Group Commandant, Colonel L. O. Clark, then remarked that it seemed a terrible mistake to return to the policy of "Class" Companies when, after 25 years of hard work, the Bombay Group had at last got all classes in its Field Companies to mess together. Auchinleck replied, rather sadly, that "these things had to be." He knew then, which Clark did not, that Partition had already been decided upon and that therefore it was necessary to divide all prospective Pakistanis from Indians.

It may be said of the British *Raj* in India, as Shakespeare said of the Thane of Cawdor, that 'nothing in his life became him like the leaving it.' Such was Lord Samuel's tribute in the House of Lords to the creation by compromise and mutual consent of two new nations involving one-fifth of the entire human race.[1] In

---

[1] *Mission with Mountbatten*, by Alan Campbell-Johnson, p. 353.

announcing to Parliament on February 20th, 1947, the appointment of Lord Mountbatten as Viceroy, the Prime Minister (Mr. Attlee) stated that he would be entrusted with the task of transferring to Indian hands the responsibility for the government of British India in a manner that would best ensure the future happiness and prosperity of the country. No better selection could have been made. Mountbatten had every attribute—youth, strength of character, a pleasing personality, diplomatic ability and experience in war on both land and sea. He was a natural leader, recognized as such by all the Allied nations. Hindus, Sikhs and Muslims knew him equally well and were aware also that he would be absolutely impartial. Army Headquarters had already begun to arrange for the nationalization of the Army with the exception of a small British Military Mission, and it was anticipated that the undertaking would be completed by June 1948; but the final decision that Partition was not only unavoidable but urgent necessitated drastic modifications in the original plans and an advancement of the date. Partition Committees, representing both sides, were established on June 16th, 1947, and August 15th of that year was fixed as the revised Partition date. There were then barely two months left in which to complete the immense task.

The general basis on which the Army was to be divided was $82\frac{1}{2}\%$ to India and $17\frac{1}{2}\%$ to Pakistan, but this varied in certain instances.[1] India was to be allotted 15 infantry regiments, 12 armoured units, $18\frac{1}{2}$ artillery regiments and 61 engineer units. Pakistan was to receive 8 infantry regiments, 6 armoured units, $8\frac{1}{2}$ artillery regiments and 34 engineer units. A Joint Defence Council was formed to cover both the new countries, and Field-Marshal Sir Claude Auchinleck, the Commander-in-Chief, India, was to keep only administrative control of all existing forces while the division was in progress. After August 15th, he was to become "Supreme Commander" until there was no longer any need for administrative control. Lord Mountbatten gives a striking comparision to show the speed at which the Partition was actually carried out. It had, he said, taken three years to separate Burma from India, two years to separate the province of Bombay from Sind, and two years to separate Orissa from Bihar. The division of India, one of the biggest countries in the world, was accomplished in $2\frac{1}{2}$ months! The Army remained

---

[1] *India since Partition*, by Andrew Mellor, pp. 38, 39.

staunch. Its great traditions, and the ties of brotherhood in war, held all ranks, classes and creeds together until the crisis was past. Blood was certainly spilt—sometimes oceans of blood—but not the blood of serving soldiers. These did their best to minimize the massacres which occurred in the border areas between India and Pakistan, even to the extent of taking action against armed bands of their own kin, and thus they shortened the period of unrest.

There were two factors which simplified the partition of the Corps of Indian Engineers between India and Pakistan. Firstly, all units, except a few of those overseas, had already been re-organized on a one-class basis; and secondly, the disbandment of the Groups at Lahore and Sialkot, and the Training Groups at Jullundur and Deolali, had recently been finished. Briefly, the plan was as follows. The Madras Engineer Centre at Bangalore remained practically unchanged; the Bengal Centre at Roorkee lost its Muslims, or about half its strength; the Bombay Centre at Kirkee suffered a similar loss, amounting in this case to about 40% of its strength. A new Engineer Centre was to be set up at Sialkot by the Pakistan Engineers, now accorded the title of "Royal." As regards the class composition of the reconstituted Royal Indian Engineer Groups, that at Madras was to remain unaltered, the Bengal Group would have Hindus and Jat Sikhs, and the Bombay Group Mahrattas and Mazbhi or Ramdasia Sikhs. The chief sufferer would be the Bengal Group, not only in general strength and in the holders of key appointments, but also in equipment and property. As the Royal Pakistan Engineer Centre would have practically nothing at the start, it had been decided that about one-third of the available engineer equipment should be transferred to it from India, and that, partly because of convenience of transit, it should be drawn mostly from Roorkee. It was fortunate that the Bengal Group had certain equipment in excess of the peace scales which had been left over from the war, for otherwise the cupboard would have been swept almost bare. The Officers' Mess, unlike those at Bangalore and Kirkee, was a Royal Engineer Mess; and although the Commandant was always President, it was not a Sapper and Miner Mess. Some of the Mess silver and other assets might therefore be regarded as the property of all the R.E. officers in the country; but this problem was solved, before the Partition, by the R.E. Corps Committee which had agreed, with the consent of all R.E. officers serving in India, that the Mess silver and assets should be presented to the Engineer

Messes of the two new Dominions. A Sub-Committee in India worked out the details of apportioning funds and assets, including the division of the R.I.E. War Memorial Fund used for benevolent purposes. A further complication at Roorkee was the disposal of the Army equipment installed in the School of Military Engineering accommodated in part of the Thomason College, for the S.M.E. was already due to be transferred to Kirkee.[1] The S.M.E. had been unable to build up any private or Mess funds, so the question of the partition of such assets did not arise; but as the Thomason College had provided the institution with free accommodation during the war, most of the workshop equipment installed there by the military authorities was left for the use of the College, a portion only of the fieldworks equipment being allotted to the Bengal Centre to replace some of that transferred to Pakistan.

The establishment of a School of Military Engineering at Roorkee had been sanctioned as early as September 1943. The technical education of I.E. officers was carried out there until 1945 as well as at the Punjab College of Engineering at Lahore and in certain Engineer O.C.T.Us. However, with the end of the war against Japan, it became apparent that these arrangements were inadequate to cope with the peace-time training of the greatly expanded Corps of Royal Indian Engineers. Early in 1946, the Education Department asked for the return of the Thomason College accommodation lent to the Army, and consequently the S.M.E. had to move elsewhere. In April a site was selected on the Mula River at Kirkee, and planning began at once.[2] The move, however, was delayed by the rapid political changes as Partition approached, so that it was not until June 1947 that preparations could be started in earnest at Roorkee, and August 5th had been reached when the first railway wagons were loaded. The Commandant, Brigadier (now Lieut.-General Sir) H. Williams, was transferred to become C.E. Southern Command. Many of the British Instructors chose to leave India. Disturbances in the Punjab interfered with railway traffic. Floods

---

[1] The Thomason Civil Engineering College was becoming the University of Roorkee. When the S.M.E. was transferred later to Kirkee, the part of the College previously occupied by it was taken over by the Punjab College of Engineering, displaced from Lahore and renamed "The East Punjab College of Engineering."

[2] "The Move of the S.M.E. (India) from Roorkee and its Re-establishment at Kirkee", by Lieut.-Colonel Sir John Forbes, Bt., R.E., appearing in *The R.E. Journal*, March 1949, pp. 52-55.

breached the lines. Yet the transfer was completed by the end of the year, and in February 1948, the instruction of J.C.Os.[1] and N.C.Os. was begun at Kirkee. The first batches of young officers of the R.I.E. and I.E.M.E. commenced their two years' courses at Kirkee during the following summer, and thereafter the new establishment went from strength to strength. It will be seen that the School of Military Engineering, later renamed the College of Military Engineering, survived a very severe transplantation in a time of grave crisis. Much credit is due to those who carried the operation through to a successful conclusion.

As already explained, the Bengal Engineer Centre was the chief sufferer in the Partition. H.Q. 622 Corps Engineer Group, with 31 Assault Field Company, 33 Parachute Field Squadron, 2. 4, 5, 68, 70 and 71 Field Companies, 43 and 322 Field Park Companies and a number of E. & M., Railway and other specialist units were earmarked for Pakistan, leaving only H.Q. 623 Corps Engineer Group, 1,3,7,67 and 74 Field Companies, 40 Airborne Park Company, 41 and 682 Field Park Companies and some specialist units with the Bengal Centre. Almost all the Workshop equipment, and masses of fieldworks equipment and mechanical transport, were transferred to the R.P.E. Centre at Sialkot. On the assumption that the assets at Roorkee included the value of Government buildings and other static property, Pakistan's share involved the transfer of almost everything that was mobile. Early in July 1947, the fateful hour arrived. A letter came from the Engineer-in-Chief, Supreme Headquarters, announcing that the Bengal Engineer Centre would be split in two and would provide the equipment, tools and plant needed for the Royal Pakistan Centre at Sialkot, with the reservation that the requirements of the portion to remain at Roorkee must be kept in mind. Seven British officers chose transfer to Pakistan:[2] six elected to remain in India.[3] Nine Muslim officers departed for Sialkot.[4] The exodus was sudden and crippling. The Workshops

---

[1] Junior Commissioned Officers.

[2] These were Colonel J. R. Connor, Lieut.-Colonel P. F. Hayes, Majors D. R, English, J. G. Wood and G. Black, R.E., and Major J. Davis, I.A.

[3] These were Colonel R. E. Holloway, Lieut.-Colonel W. G. A. Lawrie, Major T. le M. Spring-Smyth, and Lieuts. J. S. Coulson and R. W. S. Biggs, R.E. Most were posted later to the S.M.E. India.

[4] These were Majors J. A. Faruqi, D. M. Khan and M. F. Habib, Captains H. M. Khan, Noor Mohamed and Lehrasap Khan, Lieuts. Mohamed Afzal and Ahmed Din, and 2nd Lieut. K. M. Shah.

were specially hard hit. The printing machinery was removed *en masse* in a single day. The engine sheds and machine shops were soon completely denuded. The Mechanical Transport School had to relinquish its most serviceable vehicles. Training in trades came pratically to a standstill. Instruction in fieldworks had to cease for several months because of lack of equipment and tools. The Scientific Library was emptied. Regimental funds were halved. Roorkee still had a well-equipped Indian Families Hospital, a Women's Institute, the Knox Memorial School and Hostel and a Girls' School, all with some equipment; but as a counter-weight, there had to be a transfer of over 5 *lakhs* of rupees to Pakistan. Practically all the moveable assets of the Roorkee Officers' Mess vanished. Carpets, curtains, furniture, silver, crockery and cutlery went to Sialkot. The V.C.Os.' Messes suffered similarly. The instruments, music scores and funds of the Band also departed so that Roorkee had the players but no instruments and Pakistan the instruments but hardly any players. The movement of men and stores was hindered not only by the tense communal situation in the Punjab but by heavy rain and floods. In July, Roorkee had 14 inches of rain in three days. The country around the Solani River was under water, and the more distant Jumna rose 24 feet. Yet in spite of every handicap and every deprivation, the Bengal Centre survived and struggled slowly back to normal operation, and not only so but launched out later on a process of modernization the results of which can be seen today.

According to Colonel R. A. Loomba, who returned to Bangalore in June 1947 to command the Depot Wing, the Partition effected the Madras group less than either of the others. The disbandment of war-time units was then almost at an end, and the post-war reorganization of the Centre was well in hand. The Boys Battalion had shifted to the Nilsandra Lines in which the Training Battalion had functioned before the war; the three Training Battalions had, by a process of amalgamation, shrunk to one; the Depot Wing was fast dwindling in strength, and the Engineer Officers' Training School was about to close. Great uncertainty prevailed amongst the British officers who were called upon to decide suddenly whether they wished to serve in the new Dominion or not. Some were sceptical as to the future and chose to leave; others, with more faith and confidence, volunteered to remain. Plans were made to grant Regular and Short Term Commissions to deserving V.C.Os. to tide over the period during which there would be a shortage of

·officers. As regards the rank and file, only a handful of very young Muslim Sappers desired transfer to Pakistan, the remainder being unwilling to break away from past traditions to seek their fortunes in a new land which was completely foreign to their customary way of life.

Events at Kirkee during the spring and early summer of 1947 are recorded in the Bombay News Letters of that period. By April, about 2,200 men had been released from service. The rate was falling because most of those who wished to go had already departed. The 'one-classing' of post-war units was nearing completion. The personnel of 17 and 98 Field Companies and 42 Field Park Company were still Punjabi-Mahomedans; those of 20 and 22 Field Companies and 37 Field Squadron were Mahrattas, and 18 and 21 Field Companies and 401 Field Squadron were manned by Sikhs. The composition of 19 Field Company in Burma had not yet been decided.[1] Some units from the disbanded Transportation Training Centres at Deolali and Jullundur were joining at Kirkee, and others from the disbanded Groups at Lahore. The number of applicants to join the post-war units exceeded the vacancies. British officers, and Warrant and N.C.Os., were fast disappearing. Sport continued to play an important part in the daily life though Polo had ceased. The News Letter of July 1947 adds:— "Consequent on the declaration that all British officers will be out of India by June 1948, we are now hurriedly trying to nationalize the Group with Indian officers. This is no easy task as the number of Indians who have been given commissions in the R.I.E. during the war has been small in comparison with other arms. Today we have in the Centre 15 I.C.Os. and in the field units, 20 I.C.Os. The peace establishment of a Field Company authorizes 4 officers, and that of the Engineer Centre is 53 officers. From these figures it can be deduced that we shall be very short of I.C.Os. A scheme is now in operation to grant suitable V.C.Os., who are under 40 and possess certain certificates of education, direct Regular Commissions in the Group. If they are granted commissions, we shall be able to complete nationalization by the due date, not otherwise. The rate of release of men since March has dwindled gradually, and the Demobilization Battalion ceased to exist on March 31st. The total number released from August 15th, 1945, to

---

[1] It should be noted that, in the autumn of 1946, 27, 28, 29 and 92 Field Companies and 328 Field Park Company had been re-numbered 17, 18, 19, 22 and 42 respectively.

June 16th, 1947, is 16,519, *i.e.* V.C.Os. 219, I.O.Rs. 15,571, and B.W. and N.C.Os. 729. The elimination of the last named was practically completed in May. Five only now remain at the Depot. After a lapse of several months, rowing has been revived by a small band of enthusiasts. A race for Junior Fours, organized by the Royal Connaught Boat Club, was held on June 1st and was won by our crew."

The partition from Pakistan was an emergency operation, made at express speed. Almost all the units of the old Indian Army were of mixed composition, and therefore their transfer intact according to their local or territorial names was impossible. The Bengal Sappers and Miners, for instance, had not been recruited from Bengal for more than a century. Hindu squadrons or companies had to be allotted to India while their Mahomedan counterparts went to Pakistan. Officers and men who had lived their lives together found themselves separated as it were overnight. The vacuum caused by the rapid withdrawal of so many British officers holding high appointments resulted in junior Indian officers being raised suddenly to senior ranks. Young blood may be welcome in war: in peace, older and more experienced heads are preferable. In the Indian Army, many Field Officers had to be promoted to Brigadiers, or even Major-Generals, within a few months. Who then could fill their places as Battalion or Company Commanders? It was difficult to find Company Commanders with the necessary experience of peace-time administration, and this affected the Indian Engineers equally with other branches of the forces.

The story of the disturbances along the boundary between India and Pakistan which preceded the actual Partition is a sad one and best forgotten, but some mention may be made of the efforts of certain Indian Engineer formations to minimize communal strife near Sialkot and Lahore in the area destined for inclusion in Pakistan. According to the anonymous writer of an article in *The R.E. Journal*,[1] the trouble in the Sialkot Sub-Area started in February 1947 when two companies of the Frontier Force were deployed along the North-Western Railway in the Gujranwala District. The situation at Gujranwala and Wazirabad remained tense throughout the hot weather while 622 Group, R.I.E., under Lieut.-Colonel D. R. W. Waller, R.E., was forming at Sialkot. This Group comprised 14 and 15 Field Companies (Madras) under Majors P. A. Walker, R. E.

---

[1] "Sappers at Sialkot", appearing in *The R.E. Journal*, June 1948, pp. 89-93.

and R. N. Kumar, R.I.E., and 42 Field Park Company (Bombay) under Major A. D. M. Dunne, R.E. The two Field Companies had to find a mobile column while the Field Park Company guarded vital points. 622 Group was part of a Punjab Boundary Force under Major-General T. W. Rees and was required to co-operate in restoring order. This it did with great effect although 14 and 15 Companies were about to become Dominion of India Troops, and 42 Company, being composed of Punjabi-Mahomedans, was destined for Pakistan. The achievements of these Sapper companies in the Sialkot Sub-Area, both before and after the Partition, are beyond praise. Except for a single company of infantry, they were the only active units in the hands of the local Commander, and they alone had proper transport and means of communication. Their discipline also was immaculate. At Lahore, 474 Engineer Brigade did equally well as part of the Boundary Force. The writer of another anonymous article in *The R.E. Journal*[1] describes some of the nightmare incidents of July and August. Everything was in a ferment. The Muslims blamed the Sikhs for massacres in Bengal in 1946. The Sikhs recalled the massacres of their own people in the Rawalpindi District in the spring of 1947. Lahore was given over to rioting and arson, while the Boundary Force did its best to maintain law and order in the disputed areas on both sides of the new frontier. 474 Engineer Brigade was used almost entirely in an infantry role. Its units tried to maintain order in eighty square miles of country including part of Lahore City. They provided guards for Refugee Evacuation convoys, protected the Lahore Railway Station, and operated with a column sent towards Amritsar. Often they quieted riotous mobs by the simple expedient of making the rioters sit down. The stream of refugees in both directions across the border was prodigious. The number is said to have exceeded the population of Ireland, and far more lost their homes and belongings during the upheaval. As at Sialkot, the Sappers at Lahore did their duty without fear or favour and thus helped to reduce the sum total of death and misery.

On August 15th, 1947, the policy of Partition having been accepted by the leaders of the main political parties of both sides on June 3rd, the sub-continent of India ceased to be a British Dependency, and two new independent Sovereign States—India and Pakistan—

---

[1] "Sappers at Lahore", by "Senator", appearing in *The R.E. Journal*, December 1949, pp. 379-394.

came into being as full members of the British Commonwealth of Nations. Shortly afterwards, Field-Marshal Sir Claude Auchinleck issued the following message to the British forces which had served under him as Commander-in-Chief, India:— "Nearly two hundred years have passed since British soldiers first came to India. The Empire of India under the British Crown has now come to an end and its place has been taken by two new member States of the British Commonwealth of Nations to be known as India and Pakistan. These States will be fully independent and responsible for their own borders. This great change means that there is no longer any need in this country for units of the British Army or the Royal Air Force to form part of the Armed Forces of the two new States. During the long sojourn of the British Army in India, it has always served in peace and fought in war alongside its comrades of the Indian Army. This partnership has been a close and glorious one and has given birth to a great mutual respect and a warm friendship between the two Armies which reached its zenith, perhaps, in the hard school of the last war, the greatest of all wars. You, who are now about to leave these shores, have been worthy representatives of those that have gone before you, and you may go in the knowledge that your comrades of the Indian Army and the Royal Indian Air Force will not forget you or the trials and dangers you have faced together. You, for your part, will, I am sure, remember them as great fighters and staunch friends. You have deserved well of India and its peoples, and in the name of its fighting men, I wish you God speed."

The withdrawal of British forces started at once. On August 17th, a large contingent of the Royal Air Force sailed from Bombay. At the end of November, the Supreme Headquarters were closed and Field-Marshal Auchinleck left by air for the United Kingdom. The Headquarters, British Troops in India, under Major-General L. G. Whistler, moved to Bombay on December 22nd, and on January 1st, 1948, General Whistler assumed responsibility for the final departure of all British troops from India and Pakistan. His burden was eased by the full co-operation of the Armies of both States. Towards the end of February 1948 the only British unit remaining on Indian soil was the 1st Battalion, The Somerset Light Infantry, which had arrived by train in Bombay. At Karachi, in Pakistan, was the 2nd Battalion, The Black Watch. The latter embarked on February 26th, and the Somersets on February 28th. An impressive ceremonial parade was held at Bombay before a vast concourse of people. Guards of honour were provided by the

Royal Indian Navy and regiments of the Indian Army. The parade was attended by H.E. Maharaj Singh, the Governor of Bombay, who took the salute and made a speech of farewell on behalf of al India. The colours of the Somerset Light Infantry were trooped between Indian guards of honour through the famous 'Gateway of India' and afterwards taken by launch to the troopship *Empress of Australia*. This historic departure was marked by a farewell message from General F. R. R. Bucher, C-in-C, Army in India, in reply to one sent by General Whistler. "On behalf of all ranks of the Indian Army", it ran, "I thank you for your message of good wishes. The British soldier's impartiality, good humour and tolerance have given him many friends in this country. His ability to endure hardship, and his capacity for making the best of things wherever he is, have gained him our respect. We hope the comradeship between the Indian and British fighting soldier, which has stood the test of many battles, will long continue."

Many are the tributes to the good feeling which existed in India at the time of the Partition between the Muslim soldiers on the one hand and the Hindus and Sikhs on the other, and also between both and the departing British. Major P. M. Leslie-Jones mentions that when a Bombay Sapper party of Punjabi-Mahomedans, returning from service overseas, was moving across the country on its way to Pakistan, the men insisted on going to say goodbye to their Mahratta and Sikh friends as they passed through Kirkee. Again, when train-loads of Punjabi-Mahomedans left Kirkee for Pakistan a little later, the Sikhs and Mahrattas flocked to the railway station to say farewell. Colonel L. O. Clark, when driving to the station on his departure, noticed teams of combined classes still happily playing football and basket-ball together. Similar scenes might have been witnessed at Roorkee which was much closer to the boundary between India and Pakistan. The ties of brotherhood in war transcended differences of creed, and it was pitiable that they should have to be so rudely severed for political reasons. The British officers encountered on all sides the most profound expressions of regret at their approaching departure. It might have been thought that Independence Day on August 15th, 1947, would have been the occasion of demonstrations against them by the civilian population. In fact, the reverse was the case. The matter having been settled, the people wished to part from the British as friends. The Union Jack which had flown over the Lucknow Residency for ninety years had already been lowered after dark by British hands and the flagstaff itself removed by a party of Bengal Sappers from Roorkee. A new flagstaff was then erected, and the Indian National Flag was hoisted on the 15th in the presence of the Premier of the United Provinces, Pandit Pant. The old flag, and those also from the Delhi Fort and Fort William, Calcutta, were forwarded to Field-Marshal Auchinleck for disposal in England. The last British unit to leave Lucknow was a battalion of the Lancashire Fusiliers, and the last to leave Delhi was the 2nd Battalion, The Duke of Wellington's Regiment which, as the 76th Foot, had been the first to arrive there. Everywhere, the transfer of military control was carried out with due ceremony and the utmost goodwill, and thus the critics of British administration were confounded. On the political side, the Indian Government agreed to the retention of Lord Mountbatten as the first Governor-General of India for a period of seven months after the Partition. Could diplomacy go further?

The history of the Indian Engineers after the Partition will doubtless be recorded later in another volume, but it may be remarked here that 1948 was a year which saw many changes not only in the higher military and political appointments but also in the three Sapper Groups. In January, Lieut.-General Sir Rob Lockhart, who had succeeded General Bucher, handed over the command of the Indian Army to General K. M. Cariappa, and in June Lord Mountbatten, the Governor-General, left the country. The responsibilities of Major-General J. F. D. Steedman as Engineer-in-Chief, India, from the time of the Partition to the end of 1947 had been heavy; but those of his successor, Major-General H. Williams, were certainly no lighter. "Bill" Williams will always be remembered not only as a popular and efficient administrator for a period of eight years but also as a keen mountaineer and the leader of an Indian Engineer expedition which so nearly reached the summit of Kamet (25,447 feet) in June 1952.[1] The last British Commandant at Roorkee was Colonel R. E. Holloway who was succeeded by Colonel J. S. Dhillon in February 1948. At Kirkee, in the same month, Colonel M. R. H. Z. Swinhoe handed over charge to Colonel A. P. Nanda. The latter unfortunately died in November 1948 and was followed by Colonel P. S. Bhagat, the first Indian recipient of the Victoria Cross during the Second World War. At Bangalore, in

---

[1] "Kamet 1952", by Major N. D. Jayal, Engineers, appearing in *The Journal of the Institution of Military Engineers*, January 1953, pp. 19-31.

March 1948, Colonel B. E. Whitman handed over to Colonel R. K. Kochhar. During that year, the Indian Engineers were represented in military operations in the Hyderabad State, and also in Kashmi where 2nd Lieut. R. R. Rane of the Bombay Group was the first officer to be awarded the Param Vir Chakra (the equivalent of the V.C.) for conspicuous gallantry.[1] For several days during April, Rane was in charge of a party engaged in clearing mines and roadblocks so that tanks could get through. He and his men were always under close machine-gun and grenade fire but never rested until the road had been opened. The only British officer serving with the Bombay Sappers after 1948 was Major (later Lieut.-Colonel) A. B. Rhodes, R.E., who remained until the summer of 1954. A couple of months earlier, the Madras Sappers had lost their last two British officers, Lieut.-Colonel J. R. Henchy and Major D. W. Mc Grath, R.E. The Bengal Sappers had already been completely Indianized for several years. Captain J. S. Coulson, R.E., the last British officer to serve regimentally with them, had left Roorkee in April 1948 with two other officers, Captain M. W. Mee and Lieut. R. W. S. Biggs, R.E. By the autumn of 1954, therefore, the exodus of Royal Engineers from India was complete with the exception of the Engineer-in-Chief, Major-General H. Williams, and one or two officers employed as specialists or as instructors at the College of Military Engineering in Kirkee.

"Sarvatra", the motto of the modern Corps of Indian Engineers, means "everywhere." It emphasizes the link with the Corps of Royal Engineers whose motto is "Ubique." The connection is shown also in the wreath appearing on the Indian Engineer badge, although the lotus leaf has been substituted for the laurel. In the centre of the badge is a fort based on the design of the Purana Qila at New Delhi, and around it a Chakra, the quoit-like Sikh weapon of war, on which is inscribed the motto. The name of the Corps appears on a scroll below, and at the top is the three-headed lion of the Asoka Pillar, a symbol of loyalty and integrity. True to its motto, the Corps served and fought over a large part of the globe during the Second World War. The wide tracts of the Sudan, the banks of the Nile, the barren wastes of the Western Desert, the fertile valleys of Tunisia, the rugged terrain of Italy, the deserts of Iraq and Arabia, the uplands of Persia, the jungles of Burma and

---

[1] Other modern Indian Army decorations are the Maha Vir Chakra (D.S.O. or D.C.M.) and the Vir Chakra (M.C. or M.M.).

the swamps of Malaya, in each and all Indian Engineers shed their blood in the cause of freedom. The Corps Day is celebrated annually on January 28th. At a dinner in Delhi on that auspicious occasion in 1951, Major-General S. P. P. Thorat remarked that wherever Indian troops had fought, the Sappers had left behind them footprints for others to follow, recalling to mind scenes of unparalleled determination and devotion to duty, of technical skill and personal bravery. These, said he, would ever remain as living evidence of the achievements of the Corps of Engineers on the field of battle. No epitaph could be more appropriate to those who had fallen, no tribute more inspiring to those who still maintain the great traditions bequeathed to them by past generations.

THE END

APPENDIX 'A'

MADRAS ENGINEER GROUP

STATE OF THE GROUP IN SEPTEMBER 1939

At the outbreak of World War II the Group was distributed as follows:—

At Bangalore
>Group HQ
'A' (Depot) Coy
Training Bn
14 Field Coy
32 Field Troop (later re-designated "Squadron")
44 Divisional HQ Coy (later re-designated "Field Park")

Outside Bangalore
>9 Field Coy and 16 Army Troops Coy at Wana
10 Field Coy at Razmak
13 Field Coy in Mandalay
11 Army Troops Coy, 12 Field Coy and 15 Field Coy which had been despatched to overseas theatres.

Total strength in September 1939

Officers	51
BW and NCOs	55
VCOs	65
IWOs	3
IORs	3,300

REORGANIZATION AND EXPANSION DURING THE WAR

Due to the acute all-India shortage of equipment and the fact that it was not initially anticipated that Indian troops would be required in large numbers, the expansion during the first year of war was only 2,000 men.

In 1940 the Group was responsible for raising three Engineer Training Centres which provided a permanent nucleus with adequate workshop facilities for training engineer units in their areas.

These Centres were:—
No. 12 ETC at Secunderabad
No. 15 ETC at Sialkot
No. 20 ETC at Kohat

The Centres remained in existence for about three years.

In the meanwhile, at Bangalore in November 1940, Group HQ was first reorganized. In 1941 the Forming Troops Bn came into being. Its task was to foster new Engineer formations and to supervise them in the initial stages, their training being co-ordinated and directed by the Forming Troops Bn.

The existing Training Bn was rapidly becoming unwieldy and No. 2 Training Bn was therefore formed, and later, in September 1941, No. 3 Training Bn came into being.

In January 1940 an Officer Cadets Training Unit was formed in Bangalore. It functioned as a GHQ unit and remained affiliated to the Group throughout the war. In June 1941 two separate OCTUs were formed, but they were amalgamated in January 1943. The OCTUs was reorganized in September 1944 and became known thereafter as the EOTS (Engineer Officers' Training School). This reached its maximum strength of 210 cadets in 1946 and was finally disbanded on December 1st, 1947. It is of interest to note that courses were conducted for Officers and NCOs of the West African Div Engineers in November 1943, for Afghan officers in October 1945, and for Burmese officers and cadets in April and December 1946.

In April 1942 the strength of the Group had risen to 17,000 with fifty field units, many of which were serving overseas.

The vast increase in the number of trainees led to a reorganization of the Workshops, when all non-mechanical trades were moved to the Meeanee lines.

Boys first appeared in the Group in November 1941. A small Boys Cadre was formed in No. 1 Training Bn and a Boys Cadre in the Depot Bn, these being grouped together in October 1943 as a Bn. The Boys Bn now took over Clive Lines from No. 1 Training Bn which moved to Jallahalli, replacing the Forming Troops Bn which returned to the Meeanee Lines for disbandment in August 1944. Thus the three Training Bns were co-ordinated under one authority as a Training Wing. In January 1945 the Boys Bn moved to the Institute Camp and was accommodated in the Forming Troops Bn Lines.

THEATRES OF WAR

During the peak period the following numbers of units were based on the Group.

Field Coys	37
Para Fd Coy	1
Workshop and Park Coys	2
Fd Park Coys	12
Army Troops Coy	1
Construction Coy	1
Heavy Bridging Coy	1
E & M Coy	1
Railway Construction and Maintenance Coy	1
Railway Workshop Coy	1
Mechanical Equipment Coy	1
Quarrying Coys	3
M E Platoons	4
Bridge Maintenance Pl	1
Bridging Sections	11
Bridging Coy	1
DCE	1
Div Engineer Groups	6
Army Engineer Groups	3
Army Troops Engineer Groups	2
Forward Airfield Engineer Groups	2
Engineer Training Centres	3
Engineer Bns	2
Southern Army ME School	1

and other minor units.

Units were located in the following theatres:—

M E F
Paiforce
C M F
Italy
Burma
Malaya
Assam
Arakan
Ceylon
Java
India Command

APPENDIX 'A'

UNITS TAKEN PRISONERS-OF-WAR

When Singapore fell on February 15th, 1942, the following units fell into Japanese hands in Malaya.

46 Army Troops Coy
13 Field Coy
15 Field Coy
6 Bridging Section
14 Bridging Section.

HONOURS AND AWARDS

The following decorations were awarded to personnel of the Group during 1939-45.

George Cross	1
Order of Patriotic War (1st class)	1
DSO	8
OBE	6
MC	28
Bar to MC	2
Durand Medal	2
American Silver Star	1
OBI 1st Class	17
OBI 2nd Class	15
MBE	32
IOM	4
DCM	1
George Medal	1
IDSM	18
MM	35
BEM	6

THE DEMOBILIZATION PERIOD, 1945-47

Following the Japanese surrender came orders for the formation of a Demobilization Centre. This was started by the discharge of recruits with less than 16 weeks training in No. 1 Training Bn. The remaining recruits of No. 1 Training Bn were transferred to No. 2 Training Bn, leaving the staff of No. 1 Training Bn available for the new Demob Centre.

The Demob Centre was divided into a HQ Coy, a Release Coy, a Resettlement Training and Trades Training Coy, and a Holding Coy.

Each man spent ten days in the Demob 'machine' during which he was issued with clothing, interviewed for resettlement and given trade tests and an MT driving licence if he so desired.

With the return of units from overseas, the Demob Centre was working to full capacity in 1946. By March 1947, a total of 22,400 men had been demobilized.

The strength of the Group at the time of the Japanese surrender was:—

Officers	667
BW and NCOs	217
VCOs	607
IORs	30,630
NCsE	2,898

There were 101 units in all.

PARTITION

Partition did not affect the Group appreciably. However, considerable changes took place. Indianization set in rapidly, and by December 1947 only three British Service officers remained. The three war-time Training Bns were absorbed into one Training Bn which moved into the Meeanee Lines. The Depot Wing shrank into a Bn commanded by a Major. The Boys Bn was much reduced and moved into the Nilsandra Lines.

CLASS COMPOSITION

The class composition of the Group remained predominantly Madrassi. Only in the Railway Engineer Group was there a sprinkling of other classes.

APPENDIX 'B'

BENGAL ENGINEER GROUP

STATE OF THE GROUP AT THE TIME OF THE OUTBREAK OF WAR

In September 1939 the Group consisted of the following:—

Corps HQ and Depot Units
    Corps Adjutant
    Superintendent of Instruction
    Officer In-charge Workshops
    Corps Quartermaster
    Records and Accounts
    Training Bn
    Detachment "H" Coy RE

Active units

Field Coys	— 1, 2, 3, 4 and 5
Army Troops Coys	— 6 and 8
Field Park Coys	— 41 and 43
Field Troops	— 31 and 35

The total strength of the Group at that time was 3,242 all ranks.

REORGANIZATION AND EXPANSION DURING THE WAR

At the outbreak of hostilities demands for manpower increased immensely. Field units had to be reorganized to make them battleworthy. The immediate operational requirements resulted in the mobilization of the majority of field units then existing and a reserve of manpower had to be maintained by raising new units.

The raising of new units naturally depended on a greater output of men from the Training Bn, Workshops and Field Works, and on drawing manpower from other resources such as the calling up of reservists and re-enrolment of ex-pensioners.

All this resulted in a huge expansion which caused the following major changes:—

Training Bn

Apart from an increase in the holding and output of recruits, the number of Training Bns went up from 1 to 3, the last one being authorized in September 1941.

Depot Wing

The Depot Bn had to be separated from the Training Bn early in 1940. In April 1944 this unit eventually took the shape of a Depot Wing composed as follows:—

Reinforcement Bn

For holding all available man-power as reinforcements.

Specialist Bn

MT Coy	—	For holding MT trainees.
Trades Coy	—	For holding Workshop trainees including clerks.
Staff Coy	—	All Gp HQ instructional and other staff including the permanent staff of the Depot Wing and Depot Bn.
Depot Coy	—	Low medical category personnel, arrivals from units and leave details.
Duty Coy	—	General duties personnel.

Boys Bn

This was originally raised in January 1941 as a part of the Depot Bn. In January 1942 it was reorganized into an independent unit. The intention in raising this Bn was to recruit young boys between the ages of 15 and 16 years and to train them as tradesmen.

OC Troops

This appointment was approved in November 1940. The designation was later changed to OC FTB (Forming Troops Bn).

OCTU

There were two such units in Roorkee which trained officers in all engineering subjects before they were posted to Engineer units.

By March 1944 the Group had expanded to seven times its pre-war strength, the peak effective strength being 23,850. At this stage the number of various types of Field Units was as under:—

Field Coys	—	30
Field Park Coys	—	7
Light Field Park Coy	—	1
Field Sqns	—	2
Para Sqn	—	1
Airborne Fd Sqn	—	1

APPENDIX 'B'

Army Tps Coys	—	5
Engineer Bn	—	1
Bridging Sections	—	5
Bridge Maintenance Pl	—	1
Ind Div Bridging Pls	—	2
Independent Pls	—	3
Road Roller Pls	—	2
Special Section	—	1
Commander Army Group Engineers (473)		1
Corps Tps Engineers	—	2
Divisional Engineers	—	7
Engineer Training Centre	—	3

IMPORTANT THEATRES OF OPERATION

Middle East

Western Desert (Sidi Barrani)	4 Fd Coy (4 Div)
Mount Cochen	— do —
Relief of Tobruk	4 Fd Coy (11 Bde), 1941
El Alamein	2 Fd Coy (4 Div)
	4 Fd Coy
	41 Fd Pk Coy (10 Div)

Italy

Cassino and "Operation Vandal"	7 Fd Coy (8 Div)
	66 Fd Coy (8 Div)
	69 Fd Coy (8 Div)
	47 Fd Pk Coy (8 Div)
	1 Fd Coy (8 Div)
	4 Fd Coy (8 Div)
	5 Fd Coy (8 Div)
	41 Fd Pk Coy (8 Div)
Malaya and Burma	3 Fd Coy (11 Div), 1941
	43 Fd Pk Coy (11 Div), 1941
	70 Fd Coy (17 Div), 1942

Arakan   73 Fd Coy ⎫ 15 Corps, for-
           74 Fd Coy ⎬ merly of 14 Div
           23 Engr Bn (15 Corps)
           77 Fd Coy (7 Div)
           17 Br Sec (7 Div)
            2 Fd Coy (5 Div)
           74 Fd Coy (5 Div)

HONOURS AND AWARDS

The following decorations were awarded to personnel of the Group:—

CBE	— 1
DSO	— 1
OBE	— 8
Bar to MC	— 1
MC	— 39
MBE	— 26
BEM	— 8
IOM 2nd Class	— 7
IDSM	— 22
MM	— 42
GM & Bronze Star (American)	— 4

REORGANIZATION AFTER THE WAR, INCLUDING THE DEMOBILIZATION PERIOD

Demobilization was planned and carried out in three phases as follows:—

Phase I

Demobilization of re-employed pensioners and recruits with less than 6 months' service.

Phase II

Release of trained soldiers to reduce the strength of the Group. This phase lasted from November 15th, 1945, to May 31st, 1946, and the strength of the Group was reduced by more than 50 per cent.

Phase III

Reduction to peace-time strength. Because of partition, this was not actually carried out.

The demobilization was carried out at Group HQ by Records and Accounts and the Demob Bn. All personnel selected for demobilization were posted to the Demob Bn where they were placed in the

Demob chain in batches of 60 to 100. Owing to a very exhaustive and comprehensive system, no major difficulties were experienced in effecting the bulk of the reduction.

Pre-release training was arranged for all men other than recruits with less than 6 months' service and re-employed pensioners. The main subjects in which training was imparted were:—

Education; agricultural subjects; cottage industries; refresher trades; hygiene and sanitation.

CLASS COMPOSITION

The class composition was Hindus (Garhwalis, Purbeas), Muslims and Sikhs. Some units were based on a one-caste system while others were mixed to platoon level. There was no uniform policy, however, and class composition varied from unit to unit.

APPENDIX 'C'

BOMBAY ENGINEER GROUP

STATE OF THE GROUP AT THE OUTBREAK OF WAR

Establishment

Officers	46
BWOs and BNCOs	42
VCOs	63
ORs	2,855

Units

Corps Headquarters
Training Bn composed of:
A Coy — Depot Permanent Staff
B Coy ⎫
C Coy ⎬ Training Coys
D Coy ⎭

Field Units

18, 19, 20, 21 and 22 Field Coys
42 Div HQ Coy
55 Printing Section
CRE 2nd Ind Div, Quetta.

REORGANISATION AND EXPANSION DURING THE WAR

Early stages

Rapid expansion of S & M units had to be catered for during the war. Reservists were called up for colour service by stages beginning from August 1939. By the end of 1940, practically all reservists had been called up. 24 Field Coy was raised in May 1940. Reorganization of the Corps HQ and Depot establishment took place during the same period in addition to the raising of an Army Troops Coy. The Training Bn was also expanded by the addition of F-6 and F-7 Coys at Quetta and Kohat, and 23 Field Coy was raised in September 1940.

The training period for recruits, which was reduced to 50 weeks at the end of 1939, was further reduced to 36 weeks in July 1940, but after a few months it was raised to 52 weeks as it was found that personnel with only 36 weeks' training could not have the full trades training.

The strength of Indian personnel in the Field rose to 10,490 in June 1943, with a monthly intake of 345 recruits and an output of 276. A total of 3,290 men were under training. The strength of the Group was nearly double the above by the end of 1943.

Pioneer Bns were formed in 1941, and Training teams were supplied by the Group. Ex-VCOs on the pension establishment had to be recalled for active service to meet the requirements of the Training teams.

Training teams were also provided for the Engineer Depot, Lahore, to raise Artisan Works Coys (15, 16, 17, 18 and 19) in 1941.

The Peak Period

During the peak period in 1943-45, trained men were required in large numbers to raise the many emergency units of the Group. The Group suffered heavy losses of well-trained pre-war personnel in Malaya, and it was an extremely difficult task to find sufficient men to train recruits. The Training Centre was organized into three Battalions, and a system was built up to turn out Sappers who were fit to serve in field units.

The intake of each of these Training Bns was fixed at 120 men per month, though this varied considerably. The recruiting was originally done by a Group Recruiting Officer. As requirements continued to increase, he was re-designated as the Group Liaison Officer. His task was to act as a link between the Recruiting Officers and the Training Wing in order to maintain a flow of suitable recruits.

Due to the expansion of the Group, the entire Recruit Training Organization was moved to Dighi early in 1942. A Training Wing consisting of 3 Training Bns (Nos. 1, 2 and 3) was formed at Dighi. The recruits were sent to the three Training Bns, each of which was organized as six Training Coys and one HQ Coy. The Training Coys were numbered from F-1 to F-18. There was also a Boys Bn, and all four were controlled by HQ Training Wing. A branch of the Workshops for trades' training was also moved to Dighi under an Assistant Instructor, Workshops, who was responsible to the Chief Instructor, Workshops, at Group HQ.

THEATRES OF WAR IN WHICH UNITS FOUGHT

The Group lost the following units in Malaya in the early stages of the war:—

HQ 9 Divisional Engineers
HQ 11 Divisional Engineers
17 Field Coy
19 Field Coy
22 Field Coy
23 Field Coy
42 Field Park Coy
45 Army Troops Coy

The undermentioned units of the Group took part in major operations during the war, and the men, by their discipline and strong sense of duty, won a good name for the Group. Col. P. S. Bhagat was awarded the Victoria Cross for conspicuous gallantry on active service in the Middle East. He was the first Indian to receive this much coveted award during World War II.

HQ 5 Indian Divisional Engineers
18 Field Coy
20 Field Coy
21 Field Coy
} Middle East and North Africa

HQ 11 Divisional Engineers and units as stated } Malaya

24 Field Coy — Burma

DECORATIONS AND AWARDS

The following is a summary of outstanding decorations and awards won by the Group:—

Award	Count
VC	1
DSO	2
MC	25 (including 2 bars to MC)
IOM	1
Medal of Royal Victorian Order	1
OBE	9
MBE	18
BEM	3
IDSM	12
MM	13 (including 1 bar to MM)

DISBANDMENT

The various types of units disbanded were:—

Field Coys	15
Field Park Coys	4
Field Stores Platoons	4
Army Troops Coy	1
Airfield Engineers	1
Ind Div Engineers	1
Pipe Line Operating Platoons	2
Bridging Platoons	3
Pipe Line Operating Engineers	4
Field Troops	1
Southern Army Bridging Camp	1
Army Troops Engineers	2
Forward Airfield Engineers	1
Engineer Bn	1
Corps Troops Engineers	2
Printing Sections	2

The following numbers were released between August 15th, 1947, and December 31st, 1947.

JCOs	236
ORs	16,055
NCs (E)	818

PARTITION

Move of Personnel

Orders for the move of Punjab Musalmans to the Pakistan Engineer Centre, Sialkot, were received in September 1947. Practically no difficulty was encountered in carrying out the partition of the Group. The move of the troops was accomplished in three phases, as under, by special troop trains:—

1st Phase	—	September 28th, 1947.
2nd phase	—	September 29th, 1947.
3rd phase	—	October 19th, 1947.

All civilians belonging to Pakistan were discharged with effect from September 30th, 1947, and moved in the troop trains.

REORGANIZATION AFTER THE WAR, INCLUDING THE DEMOBILIZATION PERIOD

On the fall of Japan in 1945, the release of the Indian Army started. A Demobilization Centre under the command of a Lieut.-Colonel was established on September 29th, 1945, in the Depot Wing of the Group at Kirkee.

Training in Rural Development and Cottage Industries

Facilities existed in the Rural Development Training Centre for training in the following subjects:—

    Improved methods of farming
    Animal Husbandry
    Village improvement
    Poultry farming
    Weaving
    Sericulture
    Rope-making
    Construction of bamboo screens
    Making of rush mats
    Tailoring
    Dairy farming.

The Demob Bn ceased to exist on March 31st, 1947. Thereafter the Demob Centre consisted of one Demob Coy which had disappeared finally by the end of 1947. The Training Wing moved from Dighi to Kirkee during the month of November 1947. The Reinforcement Bn was merged into the Depot Bn on March 31st, 1948.

RESETTLEMENT

A Resettlement Advice Officer, with staff, was attached to the Demob Centre to give advice and to help men in resettlement.

REORGANIZATION AFTER THE PARTITION

The Peace Establishment of the Centre remained the same after the Partition. In fact, very little reorganization took place after the elimination of the Muslim element. As the Field Coys were already organized on a one-caste system, they were not affected at all.

The Training Bn suffered a loss of trained NCOs which were later replaced gradually from the Field Coys.

A few men had volunteered for training under the Technical Training scheme and were called up for training.

6 Docks Group was badly affected as 40 per cent of its strength chose transfer to Pakistan and moved to Sialkot. The Centre, which was already depleted in strength, was not in a position to reinforce the Training units, especially with important tradesmen such as Serangs and Foremen.

As a result of partition, the Group lost some Field Park and E/M Coys which were manned wholly by Musalmans.

At the end of 1947, British Service officers were asked to volunteer for service with the Indian or Pakistan dominions, but very few did so at that time. The Group was completely nationalized by December 1947, when only two British Service officers were left with the Group.

CLASS COMPOSITION

The class composition of the Group during the War remained as 1/3 Punjabi Musalmans, 1/3 Sikhs and 1/3 Marathas. Amongst the Punjabi Musalmans only Sunnis were enlisted, and amongst the Sikhs only Mazhbis and Ramdasias. A few Shias and Ahmedias who were enrolled in 1940 and 1941 were transferred gradually to other Corps. The amalgamation of Nos. 1 and 2 Transportation Training Centres brought all classes into the Group.

INDEX

Note 1: Abbreviations for countries and theatres of war:—

B	—	Burma (incl. Manipur)
FE	—	Far East (incl. Hong Kong)
Gr	—	Greece (incl. Crete)
Ind	—	India (incl. Pakistan)
Ir	—	Iraq
It	—	Italy (incl. Sicily)
Ma	—	Malaya
Mid E	—	Middle East (incl. Dodecanese Is. and Cyprus)
N Af	—	North Africa (incl. Egypt, Libya, Tripolitania and Tunisia)
NE Af	—	Sudan, Eritrea, Abyssinia and British Somaliland
P	—	Persia
SE A	—	South East Asia (incl. Thailand, Indo-China and the East Indies)
Sy	—	Syria and Palestine.

Note 2: Abbreviations for units and formations:—

Armd	—	Armoured	Pk	—	Park
Bde	—	Brigade	Para	—	Parachute
Bn	—	Battalion	Pl	—	Platoon
Br	—	Bridging	Pnr	—	Pioneer
Const	—	Construction	R	—	Royal
Coy	—	Company	Regt	—	Regiment
Div	—	Division	Rly	—	Railway
Engrs	—	Engineers	S & M	—	Sappers and Miners
Fd	—	Field	Sec	—	Section
Fwd	—	Forward	Sqn	—	Squadron
Gp	—	Group	Tk	—	Tank
HQ	—	Headquarters	Tp	—	Troop
Inf	—	Infantry	Trg	—	Training
IWT	—	Inland Water Transport	TTC	—	Transportation Training Centre
LRP	—	Long Range Penetration			
OCTU	—	Officer Cadet Training Unit	Wks	—	Works.

Note 3: The rank shown against a person's name is usually the highest mentioned in this book, not necessarily the highest attained.

A

Abdul Majid, L/Naik, 336
Adami, Lt-Col G.D.S., 468
Adcock, Maj, 59
"Admin Box", Sinzweya, 288-293
Aerial ropeways, *It*, 164; *B*, 296, 338, 345, 349, 411
Ahmed Din, Lt, 491
Air evacuation of casualties, 247
Airfield construction and repairs, *Ind*, 12, 247-249; *Ir*, 66; *N Af*, 87; *Ma* 178, 428, 429; *B*, 269, 303, 305, 309, 348, 361-363, 367, 372, 380, 381, 385, 388, 390, 391, 396, 404, 407, 411; *SE A*, 443-445, 447, 452, 456; *FE*, 460
Air lifts
  5th Indian Div, *B*, 270, 294, 331, 333, 356, 371, 379; *SE A*, 447
  other units and formations, *Ir*, 53; *B*, 268, 269, 309, 332, 373, 378, 388; *SE A*, 448, 451, 455; *FE*, 458
refugees, 465
Air supplies, *Ir*, 54; *B*, 262, 287, 288, 292, 299, 308, 321, 331, 334, 340, 342, 343, 348, 350, 358, 361, 371, 372, 377, 396, 404, 408
Aizlewood, Brig J. A., 61, 63
Akarit, battle of. 133, 134
Akyab, landing at, 299-303
Alamein, battle of, 108, 113-120
Alam el Halfa, battle of, 108, 110, 111
Alanbrooke, Lord, 108, 150
Aldous, Maj E. C., 466
Alexander, Field-Marshal Viscount, of Tunis, *Mid E*, 108, 123, 134, 135, 138; *It*, 142, 143, 150, 156, 161, 174; *B*, 221-225, 230, 233, 239, 241
Alfrey, Lt-Gen Sir C., 137
Allen, Maj R. W., 444
Allison, Maj H.E., 455

Allied Forces, Netherlands East Indies (AFNEI), **436, 437, 443, 457**
Allied Land Forces, South East Asia (ALFSEA), **404, 457**
Amba Alagi, battle of, **45, 46**
Anant Singh, T/Capt, **4, 72**
Anderson, Lt-Gen K. A. N., **122**
Anstruthers, Col A. E., **431**
Anwar Khan, Lt-Col, **487**
Aosta, Duke of, **20, 44, 45**
Appa Rao, Jemadar, **328, 329**
Arakan campaign, 1st, **274-284**; 2nd, **285-297**; 3rd, **298-307**
Archibald, Lt-Col B. M., **144**
Arden, Maj A. D., **419**
Arjan Singh, Col, **xiii, 2, 30, 32, 299**
"Ark Force", **80**
"Ark" tank, **163, 166, 168**
Armies, American
  5th, **142-144, 150-152, 156, 159, 161-164, 167, 169**
  7th, **140**
Armies, British
  1st, **122, 126, 132, 135**
  8th, originally Western Desert Force, *N Af*, **24, 82, 85, 88, 92, 97, 108, 109, 111, 113, 114, 122, 123, 126, 132, 134-136**; *It*, **140, 141, 143, 144, 146, 149-152, 156, 157, 159, 161-164, 166-169**
  9th, **79**
  10th, **70**
  12th, **404, 405, 412**
  14th, **225, 256, 260, 262, 284, 300, 304, 307-310, 314, 318, 336, 338, 343-346, 348, 352, 355-357, 363, 382, 383, 387, 403, 404, 423**
  Army in Burma, **923**
  Eastern Army, **240, 247, 254, 260**
Armies, "Burma Independence", **226, 386**
  "Burma National", **386, 404, 405, 420**
Armies, Chinese, 5th, **211, 225, 229, 236**
  6th, **211, 222**
Armies, German, 14th, **170**
Armies, "Indian National", **287**
Armies, Japanese, 7th Area, **432**
  15th, **261, 269, 313, 344, 346, 356, 404**
  28th, **405**
  33rd, **405, 406**
Armstrong, Lt-Col A. E., **55**
Armstrong, Brig E. F. E., **318, 412**
Armstrong, Maj W. B. J., **xiii, 68, 390, 391, 393, 394**
Army Groups, British, 11th, **260, 299**
  21st, **150**
Army Groups R.E. (AGRE), 4th Corps, **376**
  16th, **165**
  472nd, **431**
  473rd, **508**
Army Troops Engrs, 7, **503**; *B*, **164, 388, 392, 395, 407, 409**; *Ma*, **429-431**
  465th, **316**
Arnim, Gen von, **135-138**
Arnoll, Maj O. M. R., **448**
Artisan Works Coys, **7, 61, 145**
  1st, **182, 183, 191**
  15th, 16th, *and* 17th, **512**
  18th (later 518th), **214, 216, 228, 234, 237, 512**
  19th, **512**
  25th, **252**
  536th, **352**
Artisan Works Engr Depot No. 3 (later Const Gp), **7, 474, 475, 512**
Artisan Works Pnr Bns, 22nd, 33rd, *and* 36th, **252**
Aserappa, Brig R. E., **4, 72, 171**
Assault landings, *B*, **300-311**; *Ma*, **424**
Assault river crossings, *It*, **146, 147, 154, 155, 166, 168-170**; *B*, **349, 360, 363, 364, 368, 369, 373-376, 389, 402**
Auchinleck, Field-Marshal Sir Claude, *Mid E*, **76, 84-87, 97, 106, 108**; *Ind*, **21, 254, 332, 419, 467, 468, 487, 488, 496, 498**
Aung San, Maj-Gen, **386, 420**

B

Badhani, Maj T. D., **xiii, 388, 389, 394**
Badoglio, Marshal, **141**
"Bagush Box", defence of, **23**
Bailey bridge equipment, *It*, **146, 155**; *B*, **249, 388, 396**
Bailey bridging, *see* Bridging
Balbo, Marshal, **20, 22, 23**
Baldwin, Lt J. R. S., **133**
Balkaran Singh, Havildar, **155**
Balkrishna Korde, Naik, **420**
Balston, Lt H. R., **368**
Bangalore (HQ Madras S & M), **vii, 17, 18, 466-468, 481, 501, 502**
Bannerjee, Lt J. L., **102**
Bardell, Capt D. H., **55**
Barlow, Maj G. A. P. N., **428, 462**
Barnes, Maj J. E., **251**
Barstow, Maj-Gen A. E., **182, 201**
Bashir Ahmed, Lt, **217**
Batavia, fighting in, **437-444**
Bate, Maj J. E., **182**
Bateson, Capt T. C. H., **157**
Battye, Maj S. H. M., **55**
Beach Gps, *Mid E*, **77**; *B*, **300, 303**; *Ma*, **427, 428**
  41st, *B*, **300, 303, 304, 306, 307, 310**; *Ma*, **424**; *SE A*, **441**
  42nd, 43rd, and 44th, **300**
  45th, **300, 424**
  46th, **424**
Beattie, Maj A. R., **182, 186, 198**
Beaumont, Maj T., **xiii, 301, 305, 306**
Beddows, Maj J. S., **320, 330**
Bell, Maj M. E. F., **277**
Benedict, Havildar John, **203**
Bengal Sappers and Miners, re-designated King George V's Own Group, Royal Indian Engineers, and now called Bengal Engineer Group, Corps of Engineers, (*see* Appendix B),
  changes in title, **15, 71, 419, 480, 482**
  class composition, **3, 8, 478, 482, 483, 489, 510**
  Colonels or Colonels-Commandant, **15, 470, 480**

INDEX

Commandants, xi, xii, 2, 4, 9, 15, 133, 470, 471, 482, 489, 498

Companies and other units and sub-units, 507, 508

1 Fd Coy, 1, 6, 506; *Ir*, 55, 67, 68, *Sy*, 74; *Mid E*, 77; *It*, 145, 157, 173, 508; *Ind*, 464, 482, 491

2 Fd Coy, 1, 6, 13, 506; *NE Af*, 29, 31, 36, 37, 41-45; *Mid E*, 76; *N Af*, 89, 94, 95, 100, 109, 112, 118, 120, 123; *B*, 267, 286, 293, 335-337, 343, 349, 350, 388-390, 406, 407, 509; *Ma*, 434, 435; *SE A*, 440, 441; *Ind*, 482, 491

2 Br Sec (formerly 2 Br Train), 13, 29, 31

3 Fd Coy, 2, 6, 506; *Ma*, 182, 183, 186, 189, 193-196, 198-202, 204, 461, 508; *Ind*, 482, 491

4 Fd Coy, 2, 6, 12, 13, 21, 506; *N Af*, 22, 23, 26; *NE Af*, 36, 37, 40, 41, 43; *Gr*, 80, 81; *Sy*, 88, 94; *N Af*, 49, 82-84, 87, 88, 94, 100, 102, 109, 112, 118, 120, 123-125, 127, 129-131, 134, 136-138, 508; *It*, 145, 151, 153, 161, 166, 508; *Ind*, 482, 491

5 Fd Coy, 3, 6, 21, 506; *Ir*, 53, 55, 67, 68, 72; *P*, 61, 62, 73; *Sy*, 74; *Mid E*, 77, 78; *It*, 145 157, 158, 162, 166, 173, 508; *Ma*, 180; *Ind*, 464, 482, 491

5 Br Sec, 151

6 Army Tps Coy, 6, 13, 21, 506; *NE Af*, 29-32, 36, 37; *Ir*,55, 74; *N Af*, 49, 75 82; *Gr*, 80; *Ind*, 483

7 Fd Coy, 13; *Ir*, 55, 61; *P*, 61; *It*, 144-146, 148, 149, 154-157, 163, 166, 168-170, 173, 508; *B*, 420; *Ind*, 478, 483, 491

8 Army Tps Coy, 6, 13, 506; *NE Af*, 29, 32, 45, 46; *Ir*, 74, 75

17 Br Sec, 290, 509

23 Engr Bn, 391, 412, 509

31 Fd Tp (later Fd Sqn; finally Assault Fd Coy), 6, 506; *Sy*, 58, 79; *Ir*, 75; *N Af*, 95, 98, 99; *Ind*, 491

33 Fd Sqn (later Para Fd Sqn), 469, 472, 491

35 Fd Tp (later Fd Sqn), 3, 6, 506; *N Af*, 48, 49; *Ind*, 482

40 Fd Pk Sqn (later Air-borne Pk Coy), 469, 491

41 Fd Pk Coy (formerly Div HQ Coy), 3, 6, 506; *Ir*, 53, 54, 68; *Sy*, 58, 59; *P*, 64; *Mid E*, 76, 77; *N Af*, 95, 100, 101, 508; *It*, 145, 157, 158, 160, 164, 173, 508; *Ind*, 464, 491

43 Fd Pk Coy (formerly Div HQ Coy), 2, 3, 6, 506; *Ma*, 182, 183, 186, 193, 204, 508; *Ind*, 491

47 Fd Pk Coy, 14; *Ir*, 55, 68, 75; *P*, 61; *It*, 144-150, 163, 166, 173, 508

54 Fd Stores Sec, 182, 200

66 Fd Coy, 13; *Ir*, 55, 67; *N Af*, 95, 105-107; *It*, 144-146, 148, 150, 154-156, 168-170, 173, 508

67 Fd Coy, *B*, 352, 354, 403; *Ind*, 482, 491

68 Fd Coy, *B*, 244, 245, 250, 251, 267, 328-330; *Ma*, 428, 429; *SE A*, 441, 444; *Ind*, 491

69 Fd Coy *Ir*, 55, 67, 75; *It*, 144-146, 148-150, 154-156, 163, 166, 168, 170, 173, 508

70 Fd Coy, *B*, 214, 223, 224, 228, 230, 232, 234-237, 244, 254, 256, 257, 263, 264, 267, 272, 315, 316, 319, 342, 343, 370, 374, 376, 388, 394-396, 413, 417, 508; *Ind*, 491

71 Fd Coy, *B*, 239, 244, 245, 250, 251, 267, 320, 328, 330; *Ma*, 428, 429; *SE A*, 437, 439-441, 444, 446; *Ind*, 491

72 Fd Coy, *B*, 280, 281, 293, 295, 305, 308, 309, 310, 411; *SE A*, 445, 446

73 Fd Coy *B*, 267, 276, 277, 280, 281, 293, 303, 310, 509

74 Fd Coy, *Mid E*, 78; *B*, 276, 277, 280, 286, 293, 335, 336, 349, 350, 355, 374, 389, 390, 395, 406, 509; *Ma*, 434; *SE A*, 440; *Ind*, 482, 491

75 Fd Coy, *B*, 251, 252, 267, 322, 327, 355, 371, 376, 392, 418

76 Fd Coy, *B*, 352, 403; *Ma*, 430

77 Fd Coy, *B*, 267, 284, 285, 290, 294, 336, 337, 370, 376, 402, 509; *SE A*, 448, 449

78 Fd Coy, *B*, 300-307, 310; *Ma*, 424; *SE A*, 441

80 Fd Coy, 392, 410

81 Fd Coy, 391, 392

94 (Faridkot) Fd Coy, 3, 267, 325, 345

95 (Mandi) Fd Coy (formerly of Bombay S & M), 16

302 Fd Pk Coy (formerly of Bombay S & M), 55, 75

306 Fd Pk Coy, 469

322 Fd Pk Coy, *Ir*, 76; *B*, 267, 328, 354, 356, 403

332 Fd Pk Coy, *B*, 267, 328; *SE A*, 450, 456

361 Fd Coy, 300, 352, 355, 403

367 Fd Coy, 469

414 Br Const Sec (later Fd Pk Coy), *B*, 239, 242, 244, 245, 264, 267, 315, 317, 370, 388, 413, 416, 417

622 Corps Engr Gp HQ, 491, 494, 495

623 Corps Engr Gp HQ, 491

653 Mechanical Equipment Coy, 459, 461

682 Fd Pk Coy, 491

705 and 709 Mechanical Equipment Pls, 459, 461

A Br Pl, 157

Boys Bn, 8, 475, 476, 507

Forming Tps Bn, 9, 507

HQ and Depot, or Centre, vii, 1, 3, 6, 12-15, 18, 19, 463, 468-471, 475, 489, 491, 506, 507, 509,

OCTUs, 8, 470, 507

Road Roller Pl, 14, 508

Special Secs, 261, 508

Trg Bns, 2, 6, 9, 15, 470, 482, 506, 507
Trg Coys, 469
 demobilization, 419, 420, 470, 481, 482, 509, 510
 expansion, 5-9, 19, 463, 465, 468, 483, 506-508
 honours and awards, 509, *see also* main heading
 Indianization, 3-5, 180, 498, 499
 losses, NE Af, 41; *Mid E* 78; *N Af*, 98-100; *It*, 156, 163; *Ma*, 175
 Partition and reorganization, 488-492, 509, 510
Bennett, Maj C. M., 53, 68, 95, 103
Bennett, Lt, 98
Bennett, Maj-Gen Gordon, 182, 202
Bennett, Maj P. M., xiii, 294, 295, 308
Bennett, Rev R. M., 333, 345
Beresford-Peirse, Lt-Gen Sir N. M., 37-39, 82, 240
Bergonzoli, Gen, 25
Bewley, Maj C. J., 445
Bewoor, Maj M. G., 72, 180, 181, 284, 289
Bhadra, Subedar (IAMC), 326
Bhagat, Lt-Col N. S., 4, 72, 182, 193, 194, 197
Bhagat, Col Premendra Singh, *VC*, 35, 36, 498, 513
Bhaginji More, Jemadar, 207
Bhimrao Khape, Sapper, 420
Biggs, Lt R. W. S., 491, 499
Binny, Lt-Col R. A. G., 450, 451, 453
Bird, Col A. J. G., 4
Bird, Lt-Gen Sir Clarence, 3, 470
Birse, Capt G. M., xiii
Black, Maj G., 491
Black, Lt, 99
Blagden, Maj R., 239, 264, 315
Blundell, Lt-Col J. H., 112, 118, 123, 127, 129-131, 133
Boileau, Brig-Gen G. H.. 15
Boggs, Brig W. W., 372, 377, 387
Bolton, Col E. A. E., 475
Bomb disposal, 120, 362
Bombay Sappers and Miners, re-designated Royal Bombay Group, Royal Indian Engineers, now called Bombay Engineer Group, Corps of Engineers, (*see* Appendix C),
 changes in title, 15, 71, 419, 480, 484
 class composition, 8, 444, 489, 493, 515, 516
 Colonels or Colonels-Commandant, 15, 480
 Commandants, xi, xii, 9, 15, 36, 472, 485, 487, 498
 Companies and other units and sub-units 514
 9 Br Sec, 267, 276
 11 Br Sec, 276
 17 Fd Coy, 14; *Ma*,182, 183, 189, 193-197, 513; *B*, 252; *Ind*, 493
 18 Fd Coy, 6, 12, 21, 26, 511; *NE Af*, 40; *Sy*, 58; *N Af*, 49, 82, 90, 92, 94, 101, 105, 515; *Ind*, 493

 19 Fd Coy, 6, 14, 511; *Ma*, 182-184, 191, 513; *B*, 420, 493
 20 Fd Coy, 6, 511; *NE Af*, 29, 32, 43, 44; *Ir*, 68, 69, 75; *Mid E*, 76; *N Af*, 49, 89, 94, 101, 105, 107, 112, 513; *B*, 267, 286, 335, 336, 338, 349, 350, 389, 390, 406; *Ma*, 434; *SE A*, 440; *Ind*, 493
 21 Fd Coy, 6, 511; *NE Af*, 29, 31, 32, 43; *Mid E*, 76, 77, *Gr*, 80, 81; *N Af*, 49, 89, 94, 105, 124, 134, 136, 138, 513; *It*, 145, 151, 153; *Ind*, 493
 22 Fd Coy, 3, 6, 14, 180, 511; *Ma*, 180, 182, 183, 185, 191, 199-201, 513; *Ind*, 493
 23 Fd Coy, 14, 511; *Ma*, 182, 183, 193, 198, 199, 513
 24 Fd Coy, 511; *B*, 214, 216, 217, 228, 229, 231, 232, 236, 237, 251, 252, 267, 317, 320-322, 513; *Ma*, 430
 24 Engr Bn, 289
 25 Rly Const Coy, 10
 26 Fd Coy, 276, 277, 281
 26 Rly Const Coy, 10
 27 Fd Coy, *Ir*, 55; *P*, 75; *Ind*, 464, 493
 28 Fd Coy, *B*, 267, 276, 277, 281-283, 304, 310; *SE A*, 445, 446; *Ind*, 493
 29 Fd Coy, *B*, 252, 351, 352, 361, 363, 364, 381, 392, 407, 408, 410, 411, 419; *Ind*, 493
 30 Fd Coy, *B*, 267, 358, 360; *Ma*, 430
 37 Fd Sqn, 493
 42 Fd Pk Coy (formerly Div HQ Coy), 6, 14, 511; *Ma*, 182, 183, 191, 199, 513; *B*, 252; *Ind*, 493, 495
 45 Army Tps Coy, 14; *Ma*, 182, 183, 189, 190, 195, 200, 207, 208, 513
 49 Army Tps Coy, 55, 68, 69
 55 Printing Sec, 6, 511
 91 Fd Coy, *B*, 243, 251, 267, 320, 330; *Ma*, 428, 429; *SE A*, 441, 444
 92 Fd Coy, *B*, 251, 267, 323-325, 341, 365-368, 398, 401; *SE A*, 450-452, 454, 455
 93 (Mandi) Fd Coy, *B*, 294, 303-305, 308; *Ma*, 428
 95 (Mandi) Fd Coy (later transferred to Bengal S & M), 16
 96 Fd Coy, *B*, 296; *FE*,457; *Ind*, 457
 97 Fd Coy, *Ir*, 74, 75; *Mid E*, 77; *It*, 145, 157, 158, 165, 173
 98 Fd Coy, *B*, 267, 305, 310; *SE A*, 445; *Ind*, 493
 301 Fd Pk Coy, *Ir*, 55, 67, 68, 75; *It*, 145, 157, 165, 171
 302 Fd Pk Coy, (later transferred to Bengal S & M), 55, 75
 305 Fd Pk Coy, 276, 371, 376, 392, 418
 324 Fd Pk Coy. 358, 430
 328 Fd Pk Coy, (later 42 Fd Pk Coy), 267, 445-447, 493
 362 Fd Coy, 321, 322

363 Fd Coy, *B*, 267, 392, 407; *FE*, 459, 461,
401 Fd Sqn, 399, 493
402 Fd Coy, *B*, 267, 327, 392, 407; *SE A*, 448, 449
403 Fd Pk Coy, 296
481 Fd Coy, *B*, 251, 267, 325-327, 365-367, 369, 398-401; *SE A*, 450-452, 455, 456
483 Fd Coy, 267
485 Fd Coy, 430
889 Br Sec, 267
Boys Bn, 8, 472-476, 484, 485, 512
Br Pl, 417
Forming Tps Bn, 9
HQ and Depot, or Centre, vii, 1, 3, 6, 12-15, 175, 463, 472, 484, 489, 493, 511, 512, 515
OCTU, 8
Pnr Bns, 512
Trg Bns, 6, 9, 15, 472, 473, 511, 512, 515
demobilization, 419, 420, 473, 484, 493, 514, 515
expansion 5-9, 463, 465, 511, 512
honours and awards, 513, 514, see also main heading
Indianization, 3-5, 180, 493, 494, 498, 499, 516
losses, *N Af*, 90, 105; *Ma*, 6, 14, 175, 196, 201, 207, 434, 472, 512, 513
Partition and reorganization, 488-490, 493, 494, 514-516
Bond, Lt-Gen Sir Lionel, xii, 19, 179
Bond, Maj-Gen R. L., 477
Bonetti, Admiral, 44
Bossard, Maj J. W., 248, 271
Bower, Maj N. H., xiii, 428
Boydell, Maj D. H., 157
Brain, Brig H. G. L., 438
"Brick Force", 77, 78
Bridge classifications, 150
Bridging
   "Ark", 163, 166, 168
   Bailey, *Gr*, 81; *It*, 146-150, 154-156, 164-166, 168, 169, 173; *B*, 251, 255, 259, 338, 350, 352-354, 388, 389, 391, 392, 394-396, 401, 402, 407-411, 415, 418, 419; *Ma*, 429, 430, 434, 435; *FE* 460
   floating, excluding Bailey, *Ind*, 2; *Ir*, 58, 69; *P*, 61, 62; *It*, 148, 164, 168-170; *Ma*, 185, 200, 454, 455; *B*, 259, 401, 402
   Hamilton, 74
   Inglis, *Ir*, 74; *B*, 242, 244, 245
   "Scissors", 390-393
   submerged, 63, 164
   suspension, 259, 321, 322, 338, 407-411
   timber, *Ir*, 58; *Gr*, 81; *It*, 164; *B*, 245, 277, 294, 295, 321, 339, 361, 367, 394, 408, 409, 415
Bridging units
   Br Coys, 353, 364, 388;
   854th Coy, 376

Br Pls or Secs, 14, 80, 503, 508, 514, see also Madras, Bengal and Bombay S & M respectively
Engr Depot No. 3, 7
Heavy Br Coy, 503
Heavy Br Pls, 290, 291
Brigades, Australian, 22nd, 183, 185, 206
27th, 183
Brigades, British, 1st Army Tk, 85
3rd Commando, *B*, 300, 303-307, 343; *Ma*, 424
4th Armd, 25, 85, 96
5th 458, 460
5th Para, 442
6th, 277, 279, 281, 334
7th Armd, *N Af*, 83; *B*, 222, 226, 228
8th Armd, 126, 127
16th, 27
22nd Armd, 126
22nd Guards, 83
23rd LRP, 335, 338, 343, 344, 346
26th, 359
32nd Tk, 85
53rd, 202
72nd, 359
74th, 294, 298
201st Guards, 85, 126, 135
255th Tk, *B*, 370, 375, 378, 383, 384, 387, 390, 391, 404
LRP, 250, 261, 268
Brigades, Burma, 1st, 214, 222
2nd, 211-214, 217, 222
Brigades, East African, 22nd, 404
28th, 370, 373, 376
Brigades, Indian
1st, *B*, 317, 318; *Ma*, 424, 428, 429; *SE A*, 437, 442
2nd Armd, 61, 63, 65
3rd Motor, 20, 48, 49, 95, 96, 98
4th, *B*, 308; *SE A*, 445
5th, *NE Af*, 34, 39, 40; *Sy*, 58, 59; *N Af*, 26, 27, 49, 90, 92-94, 101, 102, 107, 118, 128, 133; *B*, 345
6th, 181-183, 189, 196, 198
7th, *NE Af*, 41, 44; *N Af*, 29, 88, 92-94, 127, 131-133, 137
8th, 181-184, 191
9th, Armd, 61, 63, 114
9th, *NE Af*, 29, 31, 35, 41, 42, 44; *N Af*, 94, 97, 105, 107; *B*, 291, 331, 338, 379; *Ma*, 432, 439, 440
10th, *NE Af*, 29, 31, 34, 36, 41, 42, 44; *N Af*, 97
11th, *NE Af*, 34, 39, 40; *N Af*, 22, 27, 82, 83, 92-94
12th (or "Emu"), 180-182, 196, 198, 199
13th, 214, 222
15th, 182, 183, 198
16th, 212-214, 217, 218, 220, 222
17th, *Ir*, 56, 57; *It*, 148
18th, 61
19th, 148
20th, *Ir*, 51, 53, 56, 57; *Ind*, 464

21st, *Ir*, 54, 56, 57; *Sy*, 58; *P*, 63; *N Af*, 95, 102, 103
22nd, 182, 183, 185, 200, 201
24th, 60, 61
25th, *Ir*, 56, 57; *P*, 61 65; *N Af*, 102
26th, 281, 332
27th, 424
28th, *NE Af*, 44; *Ma*, 183, 197-199
29th, *NE Af*, 29, 34, 39, 42, 44, 45; *B*, 359
32nd, *N Af*, 86, 89, 95, 97, 105; *B*, 271, 322-325, 339, 341, 365, 366, 368, 369, 399; *SE A*, 450, 455
33rd, *B*, 284, 290, 294, 332, 335, 337, 377; *SE A*, 449
36th, 282, 442
37th, *B*, 317, 318, 320, 328; *Ma*, 424, 427, 429; *SE A*, 437, 442, 443
44th, 205, 206
45th, 202
46th, 212-214, 216-218, 220
47th, 277, 278, 281
48th (Gurkha), *B*, 213, 215, 217-219, 222, 230, 231, 316, 319, 323, 342, 349, 350, 378, 394, 417
49th, *B*, 244, 317, 318, 320, 330; *Ma*, 424, 429; *SE A*, 437-440
50th, Para, *B*, 270, 273, 309, 314, 318, 330, 331, 343
51st, *B*, 294, 298, 303, 305, 306; *Ma*, 427
53rd, *B*, 294-296, 298, 307; *Ma*, 427
55th, 277-281
62nd, 351, 352, 409
63rd, *B*, 222, 231, 254, 263, 266, 316, 320, 323, 339, 378, 388, 394, 395, 413
64th, 351, 352, 408
71st, *B*, 278, 279, 281, 304, 305; *SE A*, 445
77th, (Chindits), 249
80th, *B*, 271, 322, 323, 365, 369, 399, 400, 402; *SE A*, 450, 455
88th, 277
89th, *B*, 284, 289, 292, 293, 332, 338, 402; *SE A*, 449
98th, 351, 352, 363, 381, 409
99th, 378, 389
100th, *B*, 322, 323, 326, 365, 369, 400; *SE A*, 450, 452, 455, 456
114th, *B*, 284, 288-290, 292, 332, 402; *SE A*, 447, 448
123rd, *B*, 276-280, 286, 292, 293, 331, 338, 349; *Ma*, 433, 439
161st, *B*, 294, 331-335, 349, 350; *Ma*, 433, 439; *SE A*, 442
234th, 77, 78
254th Tk, 318, 343, 379
268th, *B*, 351, 356, 364, 383, 397, 398, 404; *FE*, 458, 460, 461
474th Engr, 495
Gurkha, 486
Lushai, 343, 351
Brigades, Malaya, 205
Brigades, South African, 1st, 45, 46
Briggs, Brig H. R., 41, 93, 284, 293, 331, 334, 337
"Brindiv" or "Brinjap", **459-461**
Britten, Maj R. W. T., **381, 407**
British Commonwealth Occupation Force (BCOF), **458, 459**
Broad, Gen Sir C., 240
Brooke, Gen Sir Alan, later Lord Alanbrooke, **108, 150**
Brown, Maj J. G., 151
Browning, Capt D. C., 165
Brownlie, Maj T. A. C., **239, 244**
Bruce-Scott, Maj-Gen J., **211, 223**
Brunt, Maj D., **389, 434, 440**
Bucher, Gen F. R. R., **447, 498**
"Bunkers", description of, **264, 330**
  demolition of, *see* Demolitions
"Burcorps", **225, 229**
Burma, retreat from, **210-239**
Burma Sappers and Miners, **413**, 1st Fd Coy, **214, 226**
Burrell, Maj P. G., 399
Butlin, Maj J. F., **xiii, 305**
Butterfield, Maj M. C., 151
Button, Maj P. B., 445
Buttrick, Maj W. T., **448**
Byrde, Maj W., **301, 310, 441**

C

C.A.G.E., **389**, 473rd, **508**
C.A.G.R.E., 4th Corps 376
Caffin, Maj C. G., **55, 68**
Callaghan, Maj O, xiii
Calvert, Lt-Col H. B., **144, 458, 460**
Calvert, Maj J. M., 249
Cameron, Maj D. K. S., 55
Cameron, Lt-Col J. A., **112, 118, 123, 133, 136-139, 468, 480**
Campbell, Maj-Gen Sir Archibald, 420
Campbell-Johnson, Alan, 487
Cariappa, Gen K. M., **5, 498**
Carrick, Capt, 118
Carrington-Smith, Col H., 460
Carter, Maj R. S. O., 391
Carter, Maj W. G., 296
Cassino, battle of, **151-156**
Casualties, American, **187**
  British and Indian, *Mid E*, 50, 78; *P*, 64; *N Af*, 94, 97, 104, 117, 138; *Ma*, 201, 202, 207; *B*, 212, 237, 240, 244, 247, 279, 306, 309, 328, 340, 406, 416; *SE A*, 443
  Civilians, *Ma*, 195; *B*, 236, 416
  Engineers, *see under* Madras, Bengal and Bombay S & M, *losses*
  German and Italian, *N Af*, 24-26, 117, 138; *NE Af*, 43-45, 47; *Mid E*, 78
  Japanese, **221, 306, 309, 326, 335, 336, 340, 346, 379, 384, 385, 406**
Cator, Lt-Col P. J., **284, 288, 290**
Cavendish, Col H. P., **9, 21, 48, 84, 472, 485**
Chambers, 2/Lt, 243
Chambers, Maj-Gen H. M., **309, 310, 436, 445**
Chanan Singh, Havildar, 100
Charles, Lt-Gen Sir Ronald, **15, 467, 470**

Chemical Warfare Gp, 1st Indian, 248
Chiang Kai Shek, Gen, 211, 355
Chindits, 249, 250, 261, 268, 269, 361
Chinese tps, 221, 228, 230, 232, 241, 243, 245, 246, 250, 261, 262, 268, 346, 355; *see also* Armies and Divisions
Chinnadurar, Jemadar, 203
Chopra, Brig D. B., xiii, 27, 37, 40, 72
Christison, Lt-Gen Sir Philip, *B*, 241, 260, 268, 284, 286, 288, 294, 297, 298, 307, 355, 403; *Ma*, 432, 436
Churchill, Rt Hon Winston, 10, 13, 28, 108, 126, 140, 150, 213
Clark, Lt-Col G. C., 18
Clark, Lt I. A. A., 282, 301
Clark, Maj J. H., xiii, 282, 323, 341, 366, 368, 369, 450, 455
Clark, Brig L. O., xiii, 472, 485, 487, 497
Clark, Gen Mark, 142, 143, 151, 156, 164
Clayton, Lt-Col G. A., xiii, 354
Cobb, Maj-Gen E. H. W., 377, 449
Cole, Air Vice-Marshal A. T., 435
College of Military Engineering (formerly the S.M.E.), xii, 4, 469, 470, 476, 490, 491, 499
Collins, Brig L. P., 4
Colter, Maj H. C., 80
Colvin, Lt W. M., 326, 327
Commissions, types of, 4, 8, 9, 171, 420, 473, 476, 491-493
Connor, Col J. R., xiii, 470, 471, 491
Construction Gp No. 3, 474, 475
Cooper, Capt A. C., 112, 157
Cooper, Lt S. T., 393
Cooper, Capt W. H., 55, 61, 146
Cooper, Maj W. S. D., 288
Corbet, Maj J. V., 263, 318
Cordery, H. A., xii
Corfield, Capt, 219
Corps, American, 2nd, 132, 135, 151, 152
   6th, 142, 151, 152, 161
Corps, British, 3rd, 67, 74
   9th, 135
   10th, *N Af*, 113, 114, 116, 117, 121, 122, 127, 132; *It*, 142, 143, 151, 152, 159, 162, 169
   13th, *N Af*, 85, 113-116; *It*, 146, 156, 162, 169, 170
   30th, *N Af*, 85, 97, 99, 113-116, 127, 133
Corps, Burma, 1st (originally "Burcorps", finally 4th Indian), 224-226, 229
Corps, Canadian, 1st, 156, 162
Corps, French, 152
Corps, German, Afrika Korps, 47, 86, 137
Corps, Indian, 3rd, 182, 183
   4th, *B*, 58, 225, 229, 239, 240, 241, 245, 246, 249, 252, 260-262, 267, 268, 270, 272, 273, 297, 309, 310, 313, 314, 318, 323, 331-333, 335, 338, 340, 343, 344, 347, 351, 355-357, 370-373, 377-379, 383-387, 389, 396, 397, 404-406, 437
   5th, *N Af*, 137, 138; *It*, 144, 146, 152, 154, 157, 159, 162, 167-170
   15th, *B*, 225,240, 241, 260, 262, 268, 270, 283-287, 297, 299, 307, 309, 355, 403, 509; *Ma*, 424, 436, 437
   33rd, *B*, 297, 300, 332, 333, 338, 343, 344, 347, 351, 352, 354-357, 361-363, 370, 371, 373, 381, 383, 397, 398, 404
   34th *B*, 403; *Ma*, 423, 424, 431
Defence of India, 11
Corps, Polish, 2nd, 156, 159, 167, 169
Corps Engr Gps, 622nd, 491, 494
   623rd, 491
Corps of Engineers, 15, 499, 500
Corps of Indian Engineers, 4-7, 10-12, 15, 36
Corps Tps Engrs, *It*, 155, 164, 168; *Ma*, 429, 508, 514
   3rd, 55, 66, 67
   4th, 246, 249, 252, 253, 267, 268, 270, 371, 376, 388 390, 392, 394, 395, 407, 418
   10th, 159
   15th, 435
   33rd, 403,
   466th, 145, 157, 165
Coulson, Capt J. S., 491, 499
Cowan, Maj C. H., 304, 327
Cowan, Maj-Gen D. T., 221, 223, 231, 232, 235, 267, 270, 313, 314, 316, 370, 458, 459, 461
Cox, Lt E. G., 90
Coxwell-Rogers, Maj-Gen N. A., 147
Crabtree, Lt, 253
Crawford, Brig K. B. S., 183
Creagh, Maj-Gen M. O'M., 25
Crete, battle of, 50, 51
Cripps, Sir Stafford, 485
Crockwell, Capt W.. 214
Crowther, Brig D., 293
"Crusader" campaign, 85
Cunningham, Gen Sir Alan, 29, 45, 46, 85-86
Cutler, Lt-Col R. V., 21
Cyprus, engineer work in, 76, 77

D

Darley, Maj G. V. C., 231, 232, 251
David, Maj D. C. S., 277, 286, 335
Davies, Maj-Gen H. L., 294
Davis, Lt-Col H. A., 71
Davis, Maj J., 491
Dawson, Maj G. B., 457
Dedman, Capt R. A., 320
Defences and fortification, *Ind*, 12, 16; *Ir*, 66-69, 72; *P*, 73; *Mid E*, 76; *N Af*, 23, 82, 84, 85, 89, 94, 126; *Ma*, 175, 178, 179, 184, 186, 200, 205; *B*, 228, 270, 328, 330, 380; *Ind.* 464
De Guingand, Maj-Gen, 134, 142
Demolitions
   Bridges, *NE Af*, 31; *Ma*, 190, 191, 193, 194, 196-200, 202-204; *B*, 216-221, 223, 224, 227, 231, 232, 319, 320
   "Bunkers", *B*, 263-265, 286, 287, 297, 307, 328, 330, 336, 337, 367, 402
   Installations, stores, equipment, *Ir*, 67, 68, 72; *Mid E*, 76; *N Af*, 87-89, 100, 102; *FE*, 187; *Ma*, 185, 186,

195, 201, 202; *B*, 212, 215, 222, 228, 230, 234, 276, 319, 324, 325
strong points and road blocks, 336, 381, 409
Dempsey, Gen Sir Miles, 404, 423
Dentz, Gen, 51, 56, 57
"Desert Rats", 92
De Souza, Maj D., xiii, 372
Devonald, Lt N. S. J., 100
Dexson, Maj A., 337
Dharam Singh, Jemadar, 257
Dhillon, Col J. S., 4, 53, 61, 72, 251, 440, 498
Dinwiddie, Lt-Col R., xiii, 182, 190, 195
Divisional Engineers, *see* Divisions concerned
Divisions, American, 1st Armd, 135
   3rd, 151
   24th, 459
Divisions, Australian, 213
   6th, 24, 47
   7th, 56, 57
   8th, 181-183, 202, 205
   9th, 47, 48, 114-116
Divisions, British
   1st Armd (formerly 31st Armd), *Sy*, 79; *N Af*, 91-93, 96, 97, 114, 115, 121, 127
   1st, 151, 152
   2nd Armd, 47, 48
   2nd, *B*, 277, 332-337, 343, 344, 346, 348, 356, 361, 365, 370, 383, 397, 404; *Ma*, 424; *FE*, 458
   3rd, LRP, 250, 261
   4th, 135, 137
   5th, 146, 151
   6th Armd, 135-137, 170
   7th Armd, *N Af*, 20, 23-25, 90, 96, 114, 115, 117, 120-123, 126, 127, 135-137
   8th Armd, 108
   10th Armd, 108, 114, 115
   18th, 202, 205
   31st Armd, 79
   36th, *B*, 285, 294, 347, 356, 358-361, 370; *FE*, 458
   44th, 108, 114
   50th, *Mid E*, 76; *N Af*, 97, 101, 114, 126-129, 132
   51st (Highland), 108, 114, 115, 117, 120, 126, 132, 133
   56th, 167, 169
   70th, 85
   78th, 141, 142, 144, 146, 148, 152, 167,169
   Airborne, 142, 143
   "Brindiv" or "Brinjap", 458-461
Division Burma, 1st ("Burdiv", later 39th Ind Div), 211, 214, 222, 223, 225-227, 229, 232-234, 253
Divisions, Canadian, 161; 1st, 146, 148, 149
Divisions, Chinese, 55th, 223
Divisions, East African, 11th, 46, 346-349, 351, 353, 354, 356, 361, 365, 370
   12th, 46
Divisions, Free French, 161
Divisions, German, 1st Para, 152

15th Panzer, 86, 95, 111, 117, 121, 127, 129, 134, 140
21st Panzer, 86, 95, 111, 116, 117, 121
90th Light Motor, 47, 86, 111, 127, 134
Hermann Goering, 140
Divisions, Indian, 2nd, 511
   4th, *NE Af*, 28-30, 32, 34, 36-44; *Gr*, 80, 81; *N Af*, 20, 21, 23, 24, 26, 27, 82, 84, 85, 87-90, 92-94, 109, 112, 114, 116-118, 120, 123, 127-138, 144, 508; *It*, 145, 151-154, 157-159, 161, 162, 166
   5th, 13; *NE Af*, 28-32, 34, 36, 39-46, 513; *Ir*, 65; *Mid E*, 76; *N Af*, 20, 49, 89, 91, 93-95, 97, 101, 105, 107, 109, 112, 513; *B*, 260, 270, 284-294, 323, 331-334, 336-340, 342, 343, 349-351, 371, 373, 379, 383-386, 388-390, 404-406, 509; *Ma*, 424, 427, 432-435; *SE A*, 436-442, 445, 447
   6th, 20, 55, 64, 65, 74, 144
   7th, *N Af*, 96; *B*, 260, 283-291, 294, 332, 335-338, 343, 344, 356, 370-374, 376, 377, 383, 385, 397, 398, 402, 404, 406, 407, 412, 413, 509; *SE A*, 447-450; *Ind*, 464
   8th, 13; *Ir*, 55, 65-67; *P*, 60, 61, 64, 73; *Sy*, 74; *N Af*, 105, 144; *It*, 145-149, 154-159, 163, 164, 166, 168-170, 173, 508
   9th, *Ma*, 20, 182-184, 190, 191, 200-202, 204, 513
   10th, *Ir*, 20, 51, 53-57, 65, 66; *Sy*, 58, 59, 79; *N Af*, 95, 100, 101, 103, 104, 508; *Mid E*, 109, 144; *It*, 145, 157-159, 162, 165-167, 169, 171, 173, 224
   11th, *Ma*, 20, 181-186, 190, 195, 196, 200-202, 204, 205, 508, 513
   14th, *B*, 274-278, 280, 509; *Ind*, (Trg Div) 466, 469, 476
   17th, *B*, 20, 212-219, 221-228, 230, 231, 245, 249, 254, (Light Div) 253, 255, 257-260, 262, 264, 267, 272, 273, 310, 313-320, 322, 323, 330, 269, 270, 339-343, 346, 356, 370, 371, 373, 374, 376, 378, 383-389, 391, 394-397, 404-406, 412-417, 447, 458, 508
   19th, *B*, 351, 352, 356, 361, 363-365, 370, 371, 379-381, 384, 386, 404-406, 408, 409, 417
   20th, *B*, 260, 262, 270, 272, 273, 313, 314, 322, 323, 327, 337-339, 343, 346, 356, 365, 367-370, 383, 398, 401, 402, 404; *SE A*, 450, 451, 455
   23rd, *B*, 238, 244, 245, 249, 250, 253, 260, 262, 270, 273, 313, 314, 317, 318, 320, 323, 328, 329, 331, 339, 343, 344, 346, 403; *Ma*, 424, 428, 429, 432; *SE A*, 436-438, 441-446
   25th, *B*, 285, 294-298, 301, 305-308, *Ma*, 424, 427-429, 431, 432, 436

INDEX

26th, *B*, 260, 278-280, 282-285, 290, 292-295, 297, 298, 304, 307-310, 384, 386, 387, 394, 396, 398, 401, 403; *SE A*, 436, 437, 442, 445, 446
39th Light (formerly 1st Burma), 253; *Ind*, (Trg Div), 466, 469, 476
44th Armd, 469
"Brindiv" or "Brinjap", 458-461—Trg, 283
Divisions, Italian, 86, 111
Divisions, Japanese, 261
  15th, 272, 273, 313, 322, 323, 331, 344, 346
  18th, 261, 346, 406
  31st, 261, 272, 273, 314, 320, 330-333, 335, 344, 346, 356
  33rd, 225, 261, 262, 269, 272, 273, 313, 314, 322, 323, 339, 340, 343, 344, 346, 349
  53rd, 406
  54th, 307
  55th, 212, 226, 261, 283, 287, 307, 406
  56th, 226, 261
Divisions, New Zealand, 2nd, *N Af*, 85, 97, 111, 114-116, 120, 126-128, 132; *It*, 152, 167-170
Divisions, South African, 1st, *NE Af*, 46; *N Af*, 85, 97, 114-116
  2nd, 86, 87
Divisions, West African, 81st, 260, 285-287, 297, 298, 305, 306
  82nd, 297, 298, 306-309, 398, 404
Dobbie, Maj-Gen W. G. S., 179
Dobson, Col A. C., 178
Docks, No. 5 Docks and IWT Depot, 7, 10
  No. 6 Docks Group, 516
  Operating Coys, 11; 227th, Coy, 428
Dodecanese Is., operations in the, 51, 76-79
Dorairaj Nadar, Naik, 266
Doulton, Lt-Col A. J. F., 318, 328
Dowse, Maj A. K., 407
Dubashi, Maj L. S., xiii, 216, 228
Dubey, Brig K. N., 72
Duke, Brig C. L. B., 2, 483
Dunne, Maj A. D. M., 445, 495
Dutch Engineers, 444, 446

E

Eagan, Maj R. H., 134, 151
Eason, Maj, W. F., 157, 165
Easton, Lt-Col P. A., 358
Eccles, Maj G. M., 227
Edwards, Col A. W., 300
Edwards, Maj R. N., 468
Eisenhower, Gen, 122, 123, 132, 135, 150
Ekin, Brig R., 212, 218
Eking, Lt-Col H. C. W., 464
El Alamein, battle of, 108, 113-120
Electrical and Mechanical (E & M) units
  No. 1 Depot (later Group), 6, 7, 474
  Madras S & M, 503
  Platoons, 445
Electrical installations, repair and maintenance, *Ind*, 12; *Ir*, 74; *Gr*, 80, *N Af*,

88; *B*, 243, 404; *SE A*, 441, 443, 452, 453; *FE*, 457, 460
"Elephant Bill" (Lt-Col J. H. Williams), 238, 367
"Emu" Brigade, 180-182
Elkington, Lt-Col J. R. S. W., xiii, 183, 185
Elphinstone, Maj H. G. R., 55, 95, 105, 106
Engineer Base Workshops (EBWs), 33, 34
  1st Coy, 59
Engineer Battalions, 7, 66, 145, 253, 348, 474, 503, 508, 514
  1st, 333
  3rd, 417
  6th, 252
  7th, 171
  8th, 276, 316, 321
  10th, 276
  11th, 446
  12th, 371, 372, 376
  14th, 300
  15th, 358, 408
  16th, 252
  21st (Madras), 363, 429, 431
  23rd (Bengal), 391, 412, 509
  24th (Bombay), 289
  No. 4 Engr Depot, 7, 474
Engineer Battalions, Japanese, 392, 418
Engineer Brigade, 474th, 495
Engineer Centre, Pakistan, 475, 489, 491, 514, 516
Engineer Centres, formerly Regtl Centres, 15, 484
Engineer Depots, renamed Groups or Training Centres, vii, 6, 7, 10, 11, 15, 474, 475, 489, 512
Engineer Equipment Group No. 4, 474
Engineer Officers Training School (EOTS), 8, 467, 492, 502
Engineer Stores Base Depots (ESBDs), 33, 34
Engineer Training Centres (ETCs), 9, 469, 501-503, 508
Engineers, Corps of, vii, 15, 499, 500
English, Maj D. R., 491
Erskine, Maj-Gen G. W. E. J., 457
Evans, Maj-Gen G. C., 289, 293, 349, 370, 447, 449
Excavating Machinery units,
  No. 6 Engr Depot (later No. 6 Mechanical Equipment Gp), 7, 474
  Excavating Coy, 238

F

Faqir of Ipi, 463
Faridkot Sappers and Miners, 16
  2 Fd Coy, 371, 376, 418
  94 Fd Coy, 3, 267, 325, 345
Farley, Brig E. L., 19
Faruqi, Maj J. A., 491
Feng Yee, Maj-Gen, 435
Ferrying operations, *P*, 61; *Ir*, 68, 69; *Ma*, 196, 429, 431; *It*, 147, 169, 170; *B*, 212, 215, 229, 235, 250, 255, 257,

280, 298, 299, 309, 348-353, 355, 360, 361, 363, 364, 366-369, 374-378, 395, 402, 403, 409, 411
Festing. Maj-Gen F. W., 294, 347, 358, 457
Field Batteries, British, 30th, **458**
  Indian, 16th, **458**
Field Companies, Australian, 183; 18th, **455**
Field Companies, British, 23
  5th, **458, 459, 461**
  21st Fd Pk, **458**
  236th, **358**
  564th, **168**
Field Companies, Canadian, 155
Field Companies, East African, 371, 372
Field Companies, Indian, *see under* Madras, Bengal, Bombay, Burma, and Indian States S & M respectively
Field Companies, Indian and British mixed, 89th, 90th, 261
Field Companies, New Zealand, 153, **168**
Field Companies, Pakistan, 491
  31 Assault Fd Coy, **464, 491**
  68 Fd Coy, **414**
Field Survey Companies, 11, 12
Figgins, Maj C. G., 276
Finch, Maj J. R. G., 243, 251
Fisher, Maj E. C., 434, 440
Floyer, Capt D. C., 440
Forbes, Lt-Col Sir John, 490
Forbes, Maj R. L., 468
Forestry Companies, 276, 352
Fortress Engineers, Singapore, Companies, 195, 205, 207
  35th, 36th, **183**
  41st, **183, 206**
  45th, **206**
Forward Airfield Engineers, 503, 514; *B*, 248, 372, 385, 390-392, 407; *Ma*, 429, 431; *SE A*, 441, 443-445, 448, 449
  458th, **429**
  459th, **363, 364**
Foulkes, Lt-Col T. H. F., xiii, 370, 388, 413, 415
Fowkes, Maj-Gen C. C., 354
Francis, Havildar-Clerk G , 104
Francis, Lt P. R., 301, 304, 306, 307
Fraser, Lt, 159
Fraser, Maj C. C., 151
Fraser, Maj P. H., 125
Fraser, Maj-Gen W. A. K., 51
Free French, *Sy*, 56, 57; *N Af*, 96, 114; *It*, 152, 161
French, Maj F. H. R., 55, 68
French, Brig J. L., 71
French, Maj J. R. G., 80
Freyberg, Maj-Gen B. C., *VC*, 51
Frusci, Gen, 34, 38, 41, 43, 44
Fukudome, Vice-Admiral, 432, 436

G

Gabriel, Maj R. C., xiii, 417, 418, 479
Gardiner, Capt D., 160
Gardiner, Brig R., 9, 29, 44, 55
Garthwaite, Maj P. F., 227, 233
Gaussen, Maj-Gen, C. de L., xiii, 475
"Gazelle Force", 31, 34, 36-38
General Reserve Engineer Force (GREF), 247, 248, 251, 270, 328
George Cross, awards, 154, 170, 504
Gerrard, Maj R. T., 55, 61, 366
Ghosi Khan, Sapper, 155
Giffard, Lt-Gen Sir George, 260, 355
Gilmour, 2/Lt A., 207
Godwin, Maj J. F., 180
Godwin-Austin, Lt-Gen, 85
Gomes, Col A. L., 72
Goodall, Capt S. E. M., 288, 289, 375, 376
Goodier, Maj B. G., xiii
Gott, Lt-Gen, 97, 108
Gracey, Maj-Gen D. D., 57, 262, 314, 322, 323, 337, 365, 450, 451
Graham, Lt R. E., 413
Grand, Brig L. D., 66, 252
Grant, Lt-Col N. B., 131, 354
Grattan, Maj H., 29, 30, 55
Graziani, Marshal, 23-26, 47
Greece, operations in, 24, 35, 49, 50, 80, 81
Greenwood, Lt-Col H. R., 428
Greet, Capt R. C. H., 326
Gregson, Maj H. R., 359
Griffith, Maj J. M., 95, 98, 99
Grover, Maj-Gen J. M. L., 332
Groves, Lt-Col J. J. D., 418
Guinness, Brig D. R., 437, 443

H

Habib, Maj M. F., 491
Haile Selassie, Emperor, 30, 44
Haley, Capt A. W., 200
Hall, Maj L. C., 80
Hannington, 2/Lt J. R., 201
Harbans Singh, Capt, 55, 72
Hards, Brig F. W. T., 74, 80
Harkirat Singh, Brig, 72
Harradine, Maj R. R. L., 336
Harvey, Maj-Gen, C. O., 60, 66, 73
Hasted, Maj-Gen W. F., 477, 487
Hatch, Lt-Col P. G., 286, 335, 350, 448
Hawthorn, Maj-Gen D. C., 424, 436, 442
Hayes, Lt-Col P. F., 49, 491
"Hazel Force", 63
Heard, Maj H. T., 182
Heath, Lt-Gen Sir Lewis, 29, 31, 182
Hedley, Maj T. W. I., 320, 330, 428
Heep, Maj J. H., 182
Hellicar, Lt-Col A. G., xiii, 49, 238, 242, 255
Henchy, Lt-Col J. R., 468, 499
Henderson, Maj L. S., 398, 450, 453
Henson, Capt F. E., 304
Hewson, Maj C., 407
Hibbert, Maj J. D., 238, 251
Higham, Maj R. G. G., 146
Hill, Lt-Col A. J. R., 71, 316, 317
Hill, Lt-Col F. M., 351, 382
Hill, Brig R. C. R., 15, 17, 467, 468, 480
Hitler, 1, 47, 52, 112, 116

INDEX

Hindmoor, Lt, **453, 454**
Hoare, Maj J. H., **430**
Hodgson, Lt G. C., **390**
Holland, Maj J. D., **389**
Holland, Admiral, **432**
Holloway, Brig R. E., **xiii, 428, 429, 441, 471, 491, 498**
Holmes, Maj R. N. B., **428, 437, 439, 440**
Hong Kong, loss of. **187, 188**; reoccupation, **457**
Honours and awards, *Ind*, **18, 19, 499**; *NE Af*, **35, 37, 41**; *N Af*, **83, 133**; *It*, **153-155, 170, 171, 173, 203, 208, 266, 467**; *B*, **297, 308, 329, 350, 355, 359, 360, 381, 409, 419**; *SE A*, **440** summaries of, **504, 509, 513**
Hooper, Maj J. B., **428**
Horne, Maj G., **xiii, 62**
Horrocks, Lt-Gen B. C., **113, 135**
Horsfield, Brig H. E., **9, 36, 256, 282, 318, 336, 485**
Hospitals, construction of, *Ind*, **12**; *Ir*, **69, 75**; *It*, **158**
How, Maj R. W. W., **29, 89, 94, 105**
Hudson, Lt, **217, 219**
Hudson, Maj E. R. B., **448, 449**
Hugh-Jones, Brig N., **218, 219**
Hull, Brig G. B. G., **62, 63**
Hunter, Maj Norman, **304, 307**
Hutchinson, Col G. F. **xiii, 157, 158, 160**
Hutting, *Ind*, **12**; *Ir*, **74**; *Ma*, **429**; *FE*, **457, 460**
Hutton, Lt-Gen T. J., **211, 222**
Hyamson, Lt T. D., **207**

I

Ichida, Maj-Gen, **412**
Ievers, Maj E. H., **2, 18**
Imphal operations, **267-269, 272, 313-345**
India, Army in, **vii**
India, C-in-C, **36, 84, 211, 240, 254, 274, 332, 419, 467, 482, 484, 488, 496-498**
India, E-in-C, **xii, 3, 6, 7, 10, 248, 318, 477, 487, 491, 499**
Indian Engineer Groups, **vii, 6, 7, 15, 463, 474, 475, 489, 501-516**
Indian Engineers, Corps of, **vii,4-7, 10-12, 15, 36, 71, 419, 499**
Indian Engineers, used as infantry, *NE Af*, **41**; *N Af*, **90, 99, 100**; *Ma* **194**; *B*, **227, 280, 282, 289, 290, 314, 325-327, 388**; *Ind*, **495**
Indianization, **3-5, 180, 488, 493, 494, 498, 499, 505, 516**
Indian Military Academy, **4, 8**
Indian States Sappers and Miners, **3, 16**
Indo-China operations, **450-455**
Inland Water Transport, **7, 10, 11**; *B*, **298, 299, 352, 361, 403, 407**
No. 5 Engr Depot, later No. 1 TTC, **7, 10, 516**
123rd IWT Coy, **234**
Indian Works Sections, **443**
907th, **458, 460**
see also Works Services

Iraq, operations in, **51-60, 65-72, 74-76**
Ireland, Maj I. R., **388**
Irving, Maj J. B., **401**
Irwin, Lt-Gen N. M. S., **240, 254**
Itagaki, Gen, **432, 435**

J

Jackson, Maj J. P. A., **450**
Jacques, Brig L. I., **53, 437**
Jahan Dad, Jemadar, **349**
James. Capt G. N. F., **415**
Jamieson, Maj T. G., **402**
Japanese Engineers, **415-417, 450, 452, 453**
Japan, occupation of, **457-461**
Jardine, Capt A. R., **215**
Jayal, Maj N. D., **498**
Jeakes, Col M. M., **xiii, 16, 17, 466, 468, 480**
Jefferis, Brig M. R., **475**
Jenner, Capt A. C., **xii**
Jepson, Lt, **253**
Jitra, action at, **193-195**
Johnson, Capt, **98**
Johnson, Maj R. B., **294**
Jolly, Maj J. H. F. H., **251, 327**
Jones, Brig J. K., **218**
Jones, Lt, **453**

K

Kader Khan, Jemadar, **393**
Kalwant Singh, Col, **447**
Kashyap, Col A. N., **4, 72, 180**
Kean, Maj R. B., **413**
Keating, Maj M. J. P., **286, 335**
Kelly, Maj H. F., **284**
Kent, Capt R., **214, 226, 227**
Keren, battle of, **34-36, 39-43**
Kesselring, Field-Marshal, **141, 143, 163, 170**
Khalil Ur Rahman, Jemadar, **220**
Khan, Maj B. A., **217, 219, 220**
Khan, Maj D. M., **491**
Khan, Capt H. M., **491**
Khetarpal, Maj M. L., **446**
Kiff, Capt R., **xiii**
Kimura, Gen, **344, 346, 356, 379, 385, 405, 412, 436**
King George VI, **138, 139, 162**
Kinoshita, Lt-Gen, **436**
Kirat Singh, Jemadar, **37**
Kirkee (HQ, Bombay S & M), **vii, 1, 175, 472, 473, 483, 484, 493, 515**
Kirkland, Lt-Col G. W., **71**
Kirton, Maj L. G., **251, 327**
Kirwan, Lt-Col P. L., **144**
Kisch, Brig F. H., **129, 133**
Kitson, Maj H. W., **55, 138**
Knight, Maj J. B. H., **445**
"Knightsbridge", operations at, **95-97**
Kochar, Brig R. K., **72, 180, 214, 253, 258, 263, 480, 499**
Koenig, Gen, **97**
"Krocol", **189, 190**
"Kubo" Force, **287, 289**

Kuldip Singh, Lt-Col, xiii, 123
Kumar, Maj R. N., 495

L

Labour, unskilled, *NE Af,* 32; *Ir*, 66, 67, 72; *Mid E*, 76; *Ma*, 187, 430, 431; *B*, 251-253, 255, 257, 258, 271, 282, 285, 343, 363, 396, 397, 411, 412, 416; *SE A*, 447, 456; *FE*, 459; *Ind*, 465
Lambert, Col J. M., 113
Landon, Maj P. G. O., 78, 95, 102, 120
Lawler, Maj W. L., 451, 453
Lawrie, Lt-Col W. G. A., 55, 491
Leahy, Lt-Col A. G. P., 329, 407, 417
Leclerc, Gen, 435, 455
Lee, Maj H. C., 284, 290, 336
Lee, Col K. J., 2, 9
Leese, Lt-Gen Sir Oliver, 113, 150, 163, 299, 355, 404
Lehrasap Khan, Capt, 491
Lentaigne, Maj-Gen W. D. A., 269
Leslie-Jones, Maj P. M., xiii, 473, 484, 497
Lewis, Maj A. C., 251
Libyan campaigns, 1st, 22
 2nd, 23, 26
 3rd, 26, 47
 4th, 85-87, 89
 5th, 92
 6th, 95-98
 7th, 108, 113
Lillie, Maj W. M. S., 55, 68
Lindesay, Lt-Col T. H., 183
Lindley, Lt R. M., 207
Lindsay, Maj J., 320, 419
Lindsell, Lt-Col R. A., 157, 433, 463, 466, 468, 480
Livings, Maj W. A., 388
Lloyd, Maj-Gen W. L., 274, 278
Loch, Lt-Col I. G., 53, 61, 72, 294
Lockhart, Lt-Gen Sir Rob, 498
Locock, Capt, 103
Lomax, Maj-Gen C. E. N., 279
Long Range Penetration Groups (LRPGs) 250, 261, 268
 23rd Bde, 335, 338, 343, 344, 346
Loomba, Col R. A., xiii, 33, 72, 450, 452, 453, 456, 479, 492
Lubert, Maj L., 305
Lucas, Lt-Col A. R. S., 322, 365, 398
Lumsden, Lt-Gen Sir Herbert, 113
Lyall-Grant, Maj I. H., 214, 223, 224, 231, 235, 237, 244, 315

M

MacArthur, Gen, 187, 457, 458
Mc Carthy, Maj D. W. C., 407
Macdonald, Maj J. R., 305
Mackay, 2/Lt, 232
Macklin, 2/Lt, 219
McGrath, Maj D. W., xiii, 367, 369, 398-400, 453, 454, 456, 499
Maclachlan, Lt-Col C. M., 66, 73, 144
Maclaurin, Maj I. G., 327

McLean, Maj J., 146
Madras Sappers and Miners, re-designated Queen Victoria's Own Group, Royal Indian Engineers, and now called Madras Engineer Group, Corps of Engineers, (*see* Appendix A), *change in title*, 15, 71, 419, 480
class composition, 8, 489, 505
Colonels and Colonels-Commandant, 15, 17, 467, 468, 480
Commandants, xi, xii, 9, 15, 171, 252, 466-468, 479, 480, 499
Companies and other units and sub-units, 503
1 Br Pl (later Br Sec), *Ir*, 55; *P*, 61, 64, 65; *B*, 267
6 Br Sec (later Br Pl), 183, 196, 504
9 Fd Coy, 5, 16, 501; *Ir*, 53, 54, 68; *Sy*, 58, 79; *P*, 61; *Mid E*, 77, 78, 103; *N Af*, 95, 101-103, 120, 121; *Ind*, 465
10 Br Sec, 267
10 Fd Coy, 5, 501; *Ir*, 53, 54, 68; *Mid E*, 77; *N Af*, 95, 103; *It*, 157, 159, 164, 171, 173; *Ind*, 464
11 Army Tps Coy (later Fd Pk Coy), 5, 12, 21, 501; *Mid E*, 76; *Gr*, 80; *N Af*, 22, 26, 49, 82, 112, 118, 120, 123, 124, 127, 129, 133, 136-138; *It*, 145, 151, 154, 170
12 Fd Coy, 5, 12, 21, 501; *NE Af*, 37, 40, 41, 44; *Mid E*, 76, 94; *Gr*, 80; *N Af*, 22, 26, 27, 48, 49, 82, 83, 89, 92-94, 112, 118, 120, 123, 124, 127, 129-131, 133, 134, 136-138; *It*, 145, 151, 153
13 Fd Coy, 5; *B*, 501; *Ma*, 183, 202, 203, 504; *Ind* 464
14 Br Sec (later Br Pl), 183, 504
14 Fd Coy, 5, 501; *Ir*, 55, 67, 69; *Mid E*, 77; *It*, 145, 157, 158, 173; *Ind*, 494, 495
15 Fd Coy, 3, 5, 501; *Ma*, 1, 2, 180, 182, 196, 204, 504; *Ind*, 494, 495
16 Army Tps Coy (later Workshops & Pk Coy), 5, 13, 16; *NE Af*, 29, 32, 33; *Ir*, 76
21 Engr Bn, 363, 429, 431
32 Fd Tp (later Fd Sqn), 5, 501; *Ir*, 55, 68, 75; *P*, 64, 65, 68
36 Fd Sqn, 370-372, 375, 376, 390-393
39 Fd Pk Sqn, *P*, 68, 69; *Ir*, 75 *Sy*, 79, 80
44 Div HQ Coy (later Fd Pk Coy), 5, 13, 501; *NE Af*, 29, 32; *Ir*, 75; *Mid E*, 76; *N Af*, 89, 94, 95; *B*, 267, 286, 293, 335, 336, 349, 389, 406; *Ma*, 434; *SE A*, 440, 441
46 Army Tps Coy (later Fd Pk Coy), 183, 185, 186, 193, 196, 207, 504
50 Fd Pk Coy, 214, 226, 227, 233, 234, 237, 241
51 Printing Sec, 5
52 Army Tps Coy, *Ir*, 55, 68, 69; *P*, 62; *It*, 145, 151, 157, 173
56 Fd Coy, 13; *B*, 214, 226, 227, 233, 234, 237, 267

57 Fd Coy, *Ir*, 55, 68, 75; *P*, 62, 68; *Sy*, 79
58 Fd Coy, *Ir*, 55, 75; *P*, 68; *Sy*, 79; *N Af*, 106; *B*, 358-361; *Ma*, 431
59 Fd Coy, 238, 239, 251, 252
60 Fd Coy, *B*, 214-216, 220, 222, 227, 228, 234, 237, 254-256, 258, 263, 267, 315, 370, 376, 388, 394, 395, 402, 412, 413, 415, 417
61 Fd Coy, *Ir*, 55; *P*, 64, 65; *Mid E*, 76, 77; *N Af*, 95, 102-104; *It*, 145, 157, 159, 164, 171, 173
62 Fd Coy, *B*, 267, 284, 285, 290, 336-338, 370, 375, 376, 378, 402, 407; *Ma*, 430, 461, 462
63 Fd Coy, *B*, 260, 294, 297, 299, 303, 304, 307; *Ma*, 428, 431, 462
64 Fd Coy, *B*, 351, 352, 361, 363, 364, 381, 407, 417, 420; *Ind*, 464
65 Fd Coy, *B*, 351, 381, 392, 407-411, 417, 418; *Ind* 479
101 Rly Const Coy, 10, 503; *NE Af*, 29, 44, 55; *B*, 267
303 Fd Pk Coy, 267, 288, 290, 291
309 Fd Pk Coy, 270, 322, 365, 362, 398
323 Fd Pk Coy, *B*, 267, 320, 330; *Ma*, 428, 429; *SE A*, 441
325 Fd Pk Coy, *B*, 294, 298; *Ma*, 428, 431, 462
326 Fd Pk Coy, *B*, 267, 305; *Ma*, 430, 431
327 Fd PkCoy, *B*, 267, 351, 362, 381, 382, 392, 407
330 Fd Pk Coy, 267
331 Fd Pk Coy, *B*, 284, 337, 370, 376, 402; *SE A*, 448, 449; *Ma*, 462
362 Fd Coy, *B*, 248, 249, 267, 270, 271, 322, 389, 392; *SE A*, 451, 452, 456
364 Fd Coy, 392, 410
365 Fd Coy, 267, 392
404 Fd Coy, *B*, 305; *Ma*, 429-431
405 Fd Coy, *B*, 305; *Ma*, 429-431
421 Fd Coy, *B*, 267, 284, 289, 290, 336, 337, 370, 372, 373, 376, 402, 407; *SE A*, 448, 450; *Ma*, 462
422 Fd Coy, *B*, 251, 270, 322, 328, 329, 338, 365-367, 369, 398-401; *SE A*, 450, 451, 453-456
423 Fd Coy, *B*, 305; *Ma*, 429-431
424 Fd Coy, *B*, 251, 252, 267, 270, 325, 371, 376, 392, 407
425 Fd Coy, *B*, 294-299, 308; *Ma*, 428, 431, 462
428 Fd Coy, *B*, 251, 252, 263, 264, 266, 267, 270, 317, 318, 418
429 Fd Coy, *B*, 251, 267, 270, 321, 322, 327, 364; *FE*, 458-461
430 Fd Coy, *B*, 267; *Ma*, 429, 431
431 Fd Coy, *B*, 267, 364; *Ma*, 429, 431
432 Fd Coy, 267, 430
432 Independent Pl, 260
433 Fd Coy, 441
434 Fd Coy, 430
1019 Br Pl, 462

Boys Bn, 8, 466-468, 475, 476, 481, 492, 502, 505
Forming Tps Bn, 9, 502
HQ and Depot, or Centre, vii, 1, 3, 6, 12-18, 463, 466, 481, 489, 492, 501, 502
OCTUs, later Engr Officers Trg School (EOTS), 8, 9, 467, 492, 502
Training Bns, 5, 9, 15, 466, 468, 481, 492, 501, 502, 504
demobilization, 419, 420, 468, 479, 481, 492, 504, 505
expansion, 5-9, 17, 463, 465-467, 501-503, 505
headdress, 455, 460, 481
honours and awards, 504; see also main heading
Indianization, 3-5, 180, 498, 499, 505
losses, *Mid E*, 77, 78; *N Af*, 94, 102-104; *It*, 154, 159; *Ma*, 175, 203, 504; *B*, 239, 241, 271, 288, 289, 360, 367, 393, 394
Partition and reorganization, 488, 489, 492, 505

Maharaj Singh, H.E., 497
Mahomed Anwar Hussein, T/Capt, 72
Mais, Lt-Col A. R., 71
Malaria, 176, 236-239, 243, 244, 247, 249, 252, 253, 260, 279, 281-283, 340, 346, 347
Malaya Volunteers, 181, 205
Malerkotla Sappers and Miners, 16, Fd Coy, 3; *B*, 214, 217-220, 226, 233, 237, 295
Mallaby, Brig A. W. S., 437, 438
Malligarjunan, Jemadar, 215
Mandalay recaptured, 380-382
Mandi Sappers and Miners, 16; 93 Fd Coy, *B*, 294, 303-305, 308; *Ma*, 428
95 Fd Coy, 16
Mangat Rai, Brig C. R., xiii, 2, 53, 58, 64, 72, 100
Mann, Lt-Col T., 48
Mansergh, Maj-Gen E. C., 371, 424, 432, 433, 436, 438, 439
Mareth, battle of, 126-132
Marriott, Brig J. C. O., 29
Mason, Capt K., 409
Mavor, Maj H. A., 444
Mayne, Lt-Gen A. G. O. M., 29, 45, 73, 74, 76, 89, 260
Mechanical Equipment units, 300, 377, 388, 418, 459, 461, 503
No. 6 Engr Depot or Group, 7, 474
Mee, Capt M. W., 499
Meiktila operations, 378-380
Merry, Lt-Col D. C., 352
Messe, Gen, 128, 134
Messervy, Lt-Gen Sir Frank, *NE Af*, 31, 34, 42; *N Af*, 48, 82, 90, 91, 96; *B*, 283, 284, 288, 289, 291-293, 309, 332, 355, 370, 377, 383, 385, 387; *Ma*, 430; *SE A*, 437
Middleton-Stewart, Col D. J., 55, 68, 475
Miles, Maj P. P., 105

INDEX

Military Engineering Services, **6, 7, 12, 33, 34, 247, 464;** *see also* Works Services
Milton, Lt W., **375**
Mine booby-traps, *N Af,* **102, 103, 119, 122, 125, 159, 163, 270;** *B,* **286, 315, 319, 348, 392, 394**
Mine clearance, *NE Af,* **35, 38, 41, 44,** *N. Af,* **23, 26, 83, 84, 87, 88, 100, 109, 118-121, 125, 131, 137;** *It,* **146-148, 154, 156-160;** *B,* **286, 295, 304, 309, 337, 348, 380, 393, 399, 408, 409;** *SE A,* **441, 443, 444**
Mine clearance drills, **84, 109, 119, 304**
Mine detector, Polish, **109**
Mine laying, *N Af,* **23, 48, 84, 87, 88, 94, 100-103, 105-107, 109, 112, 113;** *B,* **316, 319, 320**
Mines, types of, *N Af,* **23, 83, 107, 122, 125, 147, 159, 160, 163;** *B,* **304, 393**
Mitchell, Lt-Col A. C., **48**
Mitchell, Maj J. G., **325**
Mitchell, Maj R. D., **420**
Moestopo, Dr, **438**
Mohamed Afzal, Lt, **491**
Montgomery, Gen B. L., *N Af,* **108-111, 113, 114, 116, 117, 122, 123, 126, 127, 132, 134, 135;** *It,* **140-142, 147;** to 21st Army Gp, **150, 151**
Moodie, Maj F. K., **29**
Moody, Maj N. M. R., **79**
Moore, Lt-Col P. N. M., **23, 48**
Morris, Capt John, **59**
Morrison, Brig-Gen J. W., **420**
Morton, Lt-Col T. G., **403**
Moss, Maj J. H., **284, 337**
Mountbatten, Admiral Lord Louis, *B,* **254, 259, 260, 270, 284, 285, 309, 331, 340, 356, 396;** *Ma,* **435, 436;** *Ind,* **485, 488, 498**
Muir, Lt-Col R. B., **182, 190, 198**
Muirhead, Brig R. H., **276**
Murray, Col A., **372**
Murray, Lt A., **153**
Murray, Lt-Col J., **18**
Murray, Maj W. J. A., **123-125, 130, 131, 135**
Murray-Lyon, Maj-Gen, **181**
Mussolini, **1, 24, 30, 141**
Mutagachi, Lt-Gen, **269, 313**

N

Nakamura, Lt-Gen, **436**
Nanda, Col A. P., **72, 498**
Napier, Lt-Col A. H. G., **19, 21, 43, 76, 89, 94, 112**
Naresh Prasad, Lt, **301**
Narinder Singh, Subedar, **138**
Nash, Lt, **104**
Nash, Maj T. W., **182**
Neame, Maj B. D., **xiii**
Neame, Lt-Gen Sir Philip, *VC,* **47**
New Zealand Engineers, **153, 168**
Ngakyedauk Pass operations, **284-294**
Nicholls, Maj P. B., **450**
Nicholson, Maj-Gen C. G. C., **365**

Nolte, Col, **137**
Noor Mohamed, Capt, **491**
Norrie, Lt-Gen W., **85, 86**
Northcott, Lt-Gen J., **458, 459**
Northern Combat Area Command (NCAC), **260, 356**
North-West Frontier operations, **1, 15, 16, 464, 465**
Nosworthy, Lt-Gen Sir Francis, **480**
Numata, Lt-Gen, **436**

O

Obbard, Col H. N., **9, 470**
O'Callaghan, Maj, **238, 242**
O'Connor, Lt-Gen R. N., **24-26, 28, 35, 47**
O'Ferrall, Maj J. G. A. J., **87, 100, 112**
Officer Cadet Training Units (OCTUs), **8, 9, 467, 470, 502, 507**
Officers Training School, Engineer (EOTS), **8, 467, 492, 502**
Oghi operations, **464, 465**
Omars, battle of the, **86**
Orgill, Lt-Col R. C., **214, 217, 219, 220, 226, 388, 434, 437**
Orr, Lt D. A., **390**
Owen, Lt-Col Frank, **337**

P

"Paiforce", **59, 70-72, 75**
Paintal, T/Capt J. S., **72**
Pakenham-Walsh, Maj-Gen R. P., **xii**
Pakistan, C-in-C, **437**
Pakistan, E-in-C, **475**
Palfrey, Lt J. A., **355**
Panch, Maj V., **72, 294**
Pandiayan, L/Naik, **266**
Pandit Pant, **498**
Panzer Divisions, *see* Divisions
Pappala Yakub, Subedar, **381**
Papworth, Maj P. J., **420**
Param Vir Chakra award, **499**
Paris, Brig A. C. M., **180, 181, 205**
Park, Air Chief Marshal Sir Keith, **435**
Park, Lt, **227**
Parker, Col F. W. L. McC., **475, 480**
Partap Narain, Brig, **xiii, 72, 180, 251, 261, 263, 264, 266, 475, 487**
Partition of India, and its effects, **462, 486-499, 505, 506, 515, 516**
Partridge, Maj J. H., **95, 468**
Paten, Lt-Col L. A. B., **53, 58, 61, 68, 81**
Patterson, Lt-Col N. E. V., **19**
Patton, Gen, **140**
Paulus, Field-Marshal Von, **71**
Pawsey, Charles, **334**
Pearl Harbour, attack on, **187**
Pearson, Lt G., **74, 463**
Pegler, Lt-Col C. A. N., **165**
Penney, Col T. M. M., **xii**
Penny, Capt R. D., **123**
Pennycuick, Brig J. A. C., **183**
Percival, Lt-Gen A. E., **179, 192, 204, 207**
Perdue, Capt D. I., **253, 318**
Perowne, Brig L. E. C. M., **250, 338**
Persia, operations in, **60-65, 69-71, 73-76**

Philbrick, Maj G. E. H., 29, 32
Phillips, Admiral Tom, 194
Phipps, Brig C. C., xii
Pillai, 2/Lt M. M., 202, 208
Pimm, Sgt, 393
Pinto, Maj G. W., 364, 458
Pioneers, 7, 512; *P*, 61, 73; *Ir*, 66; *B*, 300, 305, 348, 412
    Artisan Wks Bns, 22nd, 33rd, *and* 36th, 252
    Auxiliary Bns, 15th, 276; 17th, 252, 276; 39th, 252; 40th, 252; 42nd, 276; 51st, 252; 55th, 276; 1st Madras Bn, 420
Pipe line operating units, 7, 514
Pipe lines, oil, *Ind*, 12, 248; *B*, 396
Pipe lines, water, *Ir*, 59; *B*, 263, 411; *Ind*, 465
Platt, Maj R. H., 29
Platt, Lt-Gen Sir W., 29, 34, 35, 38, 41, 44, 46
Potts, Capt T. E., 123
Power, Admiral Sir Arthur, 435
Poyser, Lt S. V., 189, 199
Price, Lt-Col D. W., 437
Pringle, Lt, 253
Pringle, Maj K. H. St. C., 457
Prisoners of war, *NE Af*, 44 45; *Ir*, 52; *N Af*, 24-26, 97, 104, 117, 133, 134, 137; *It*, 171-173, *FE* 188; *B*, 379, 387 397, 413-416; *Ma*, 175, 191, 203, 204, 207, 208, 261, 431-435, 504; *SE A*, 442, 445, 447, 448, 451; *Ind*, 473
    Recovery of Allied Prisoners of War and Internees organisation (RAPWI), 434, 451
Pritchard, Maj F. W., 244, 320, 330
Pritchard, Maj-Gen G. A. T., 238, 242, 437, 443
Pritchard, Maj M. I., 251, 325-327, 366 400
Pryde, Maj R. S. A., 375, 448
Public Works Department, *B*, 248, 258, 421; *Ma*, 431; *FE* 462
Pugh, Col L. H. O., 438

Q

Quarrying, *B*, 248, 251, 259, 348; *Ma*, 431
Coys, 7, 503; 442nd, 259, 317
Quinan, Lt-Gen E. P., 51, 54, 60, 63, 65, 66, 70

R

Radcliffe, Maj M. Delmé, 182
Radcliffe, Maj P. A. D., 79
Radcliffe-Smith, Maj H. A. H., 55, 61
Radford, Maj F. F., 157
Radford, Maj J. R., 462
Rahmat Khan, Havildar, 99
Railway construction and repairs, *Ir*, 54-56; *P*, 70-72; *N Af*, 121; *B*, 358, 388, 404, 418, 419
Railway operation, *B*, 216, 226, 358, 359, 382, 407, 412, 416

Railway units
    Bn, 10
    Br Coy, 418, 419
    Coys, 10; 8th, 9
    Const Coys, 6, 25, 503
    25th, 26th, 27th, 28th, *and* 29th, 10
    101st (Madras), 10, 29, 44, 55
    105th, 55, 72
    106th, 120th, 136th, *and* 137th, 55
    Engr Depot No. 2 (later No. 2 TTC), 7, 10, 505, 516
    Maintenance Coys, 121st, 145th, 55
    Operating Coys, 115th, 122
    Workshop Coy, 503
Rajwade, Lt M. R., 360
Ralph, Maj J. E., 328, 329
Ramakrishnan, Lt P. K., 171
Ramasamy, Sapper, 297
Ramree Island, capture of, 303-305
Rane, 2/Lt R. R., *Param Vir Chakra*, 499
Rangoon, evacuated, 217, 222, 224, recaptured, 309-311
Rashid Ali, 51, 52, 56, 58
Rawlence, Maj J. R., 244
Raymond, Lt C., *VC*, 308
Razabil fortress, 284, 286, 287, 294
Razmak, 16
Recruiting, 7, 8, 16, 512
Reed, Maj C. D., 4
Rees, Maj-Gen T. W., 351, 361, 365, 495
Regiments, African, King's African Rifles, 46
Regiments, British,
    Argyll and Sutherland Highlanders, 204
    Buffs, 90
    Cameron Highlanders, 1st Bn, Queen's Own, 39, 458
    Dorset, 2nd Bn, 458
    Duke of Wellington's, 2nd Bn, 498
    King's Dragoon Guards, 90
    Lancashire Fusiliers, 498
    Lincolnshire, 283
    Northamptonsire, 1st Bn, 366, 368
    North Staffordshire, 283
    Seaforth Highlanders, 328
    Somerset Light Infantry, 496, 497
    South Lancashire, 374, 375
    Sussex, R, 133, 137
    Welch Fusiliers, R, 458
    West Kents, 2nd Bn, R, 334
    West Yorkshire, xi, 42, 44, 107, 257, 258, 291, 338
    Worcester, 337
Regiments, Indian
    Assam Rifles, 318, 333, 338
    Burma Rifles, 215, 318
    C. I. H., 90
    Garwhal Rifles, 3/18th R, 42
    Gurkha Rifles, 1/2nd, 118; 2nd, 137; 1/4th, 465; 2/5th, R, 458; 4/10th, 325
    Gurkhas, *Ir*, 53; *P*, 63; *N Af*, 133, 134; *Ma*, 199; *B*, 218-220, 243, 252, 261, 263, 292, 297, 309, 364, 366, 393, 402; *SE A*, 451; *Ind*, 486
    Lancers, 13th, 57, 61
    Light Cavalry (IAC), 7th, 458

Mahratta, 328, 330, 345, 458
Punjab, 266, 442; 3/1st, 40; 5/1st, 458, 460, 461; 3/14th, 39; 4/15th, 375; 16th, 133; 3/16th, 190
Rajput, 440; 7th, 5
Regiments, Malaya; Malaya Volunteers, 181, 205
Regiments, French, Foreign Legion, 57
Regiments, German, Panzer Grenadiers, 137, 160
Regiments, Japanese, 33rd, 450
Railway, 416
Reid, Maj-Gen D. W., 158
Reilly, Maj J. F. C., 29
Rhodes, Lt-Col A. B., xiii, 74, 158, 420, 499
Rhodes, Col Sir Godfrey, 70, 71
Rhodes, Lt, 232
R.I.A.S.C., 123rd Coy, 439
Richards, Col 334
Richards, Lt-Col G. C., 55, 68, 106
Richards, Lt-Col H. C. G., 437, 445
Ritchie, Lt-Gen N. M., 86, 87, 93, 96, 97
Road Roller Platoon, 14, 508
Roads and tracks
  road construction and maintenance, Ind, 12; NE Af, 31, 32, 38, 44; P, 65; Ir, 67, 68; It, 164-166; B, 228, 238, 242-246, 249-259, 277-282, 295, 328, 341, 348, 358, 367, 372, 381, 396, 403, 407, 416; Ma, 429-431, 434; SE A, 445; FE 457
  road surfacing, brick, 282, 399; stone, 348; temporary road surfacing with Sommerfeld Track, mesh, timber, etc, NE Af, 36; N Af, 129, 130; It, 147; B, 228, 282, 303, 308, 369, 372, 381, 389, 399
  tracks for jeeps, mules, or tanks, NE Af, 37, 40-43, 45; P, 69; N Af, 93; It, 152, 159, 162, 166; B, 228, 244, 251, 270, 271, 277, 280, 281, 285, 286, 293, 295, 297, 319-321, 325, 336, 338, 341-343, 349, 367, 429; Ind, 465
Robathan, Maj D., 122
Roberts, Lt-Gen Sir Ouvry, 19, 52, 262, 314, 317, 323, 330, 403, 423, 426
Robertson, Lt-Gen H. C. H., 459
Robertson, Col W. D., 481
Roche, Maj G. T., 95, 100, 157
Rocke, Maj R. P., 459
Rommel, Field-Marshal Erwin, 44, 47-49, 69, 82, 85-87, 91-93, 95-98, 102, 107, 108, 110, 112-114, 116, 117, 121-123, 126, 128, 141, 240
Roome, Maj-Gen Sir Horace, 248, 477, 480
Roorkee (HQ Bengal S & M), vii, xiii, 1, 3, 18, 19, 470-472, 481-483, 489-492
Row, Maj J. W. L., 428
Royal Australian Engineers, 183; 18 Fd Coy, 455
Royal Engineers, 8th Rly Coy, 9; see also Field Companies, and Fortress Engineers, Singapore
Royal Indian Engineers, 15, 419

Royal Indian Military College, Prince of Wales', 4
Royal Marines, 432
Royal Pakistan Centre, 475, 489, 491, 514, 516
Royal Pakistan Engineers, 464, 475, 491
  31st Assault Fd Coy, 464, 491
  68th Fd Coy, 464
Russell, Maj C. C. F., 55, 95, 103, 104
Russia, supplies to, through Persia, 70, 71, 75
Rusted, Maj J. F. W., 320

S

Saegert, Lt-Col J. M., 95, 104
St. George, Maj H. E. G., 29, 32
Sakurai, Maj-Gen, 287
Sampangi Raju, Havildar-Major (later Capt), 41
Sandeman, Lt-Col E. E. N., xii, 391
Sandes, Maj A. H. W., xiii, 301, 302, 304, 310, 311, 424
Sandes, Lt-Col E. W. C., (the Author), vii, viii
Sangro, battle of the River, 146-149
Sankaranarayana Nair, Havildar, 297
Sappers and Miners, re-designated Royal Indian Engineers, and now called the Corps of Engineers,
  before the war, vii, 1, 5, 6, 501, 506, 511
  changes in title, 15, 71, 419, 480, 482, 484
  connections with Burma, 420, 421
  see under Madras, Bengal, Bombay, Burma, and Indian States S & M
School of Military Engineering (SME), now the College of Military Engineering, xii, 4, 469, 470, 472, 476, 490, 491, 499
Scobie, Maj-Gen R. MacK, 80, 85
Scoones, Lt-Gen G. A. P., 241, 260, 262, 268, 314, 323, 339, 351, 355
"Scorpions", 137
Scott, Maj A. E., 123, 286, 335
Selkirk, Maj A., 109, 112, 123
Seymour-Williams, Lt-Col F., 352-354
Shah, 2/Lt K. M., 491
Shamsher Singh, Col, xiii, 103, 171-173
Shave, Maj J. S. R., 446
Shaw, Maj G. W., 462
Shazada Khan, Naik, 155
Shenoy, Maj B. P., 448
Sher Ali, Jemadar, 155
Shibala, Vice-Admiral, 436
Shiv Dial Singh, Col, 2, 72
Showers, Lt-Col L. J., 137
Shrinagesh, Maj-Gen S. M., 460, 461
Sicily, invasion of, 140, 141
Sidi Barrani, battle of, 23-27
Sikander Hayat Singh, Sir, 124
Simson, Brig I., 183
Singapore, defence and loss of, 175-185, 189, 195, 204-209
  reoccupation of, 431-436
Sinzweya, action of, 288-293

INDEX 533

Sirmur State Sappers and Miners, 16
  Fd Coy, 276, 281, 477, 478
Sittang River, action at the, 218-221
Slim, Field-Marshal Sir William, *NE Af,*
  29, 31; *Sy,* 58; *P,* 63; *B,* 224, 225,
  227, 229, 237, 239, 260, 283, 284, 314,
  343, 344, 354-357, 379, 382, 383, 386,
  404; *Ma,* 435
Sloot, Maj P. R., 214, 226, 227
Smith, Capt A. P., 326
Smith, Maj G. V. J. M., 146
Smith, Maj J. Mac C., 214
Smuts, Gen, 108
Smyth, Maj-Gen J. G., *VC,* 212, 213, 218, 221
Snape, Maj J. W., 280
Soerkano, Dr, 438
Sollum, battle of, 83, 84
Somana, Lt K. M., 171
South African Sappers, 106
South East Asia Command (SEAC), 225,
  254, 259, 435, 436
Sourabaya operations, 438-441
Spencer, Capt, 103
Spring-Smyth, Maj T.le M., xiii, 478, 491
Stalin, Marshal, 140
Steed, Brig R. S., 464
Steedman, Maj-Gen J. F. D., 9, 183, 252,
  467, 487, 498
Stenhouse, Lt-Col E. E., 18, 151
Stevenson, 2/Lt, 104
Stewart, Brig A. Mac G., xiii, 79
Stiffle, Maj K. O., xii
Stileman, Brig E. C. R., 335, 349, 424
Stilwell, Gen Joseph, 211, 241, 245, 246,
  260-262, 267, 268, 313, 346, 347, 355
Stopford, Lt-Gen Sir Montagu, 332, 347,
  355, 383, 397, 404, 412, 436
Stuart, Maj N. L., 90
Stumme, Gen Von, 113, 115
Subbiah, Naik, 297
Subramaniam, Subedar, 154, 170, 467
Subramanyam, Maj P. V., 294
Sudan Defence Force, 28, 31, 34
Sultan, Lt-Gen D. I., 355, 356
Sumatra, pacification of, 444-446
Surrender of German Army in North
  Africa, 137, 138
Surrender of Japanese, 412-414, 423, 427,
  432-436, 447, 449
Survey Depot, Group, and units, vii, 7,
  11, 12
Sussex, H. M. S., 432, 433
Sutherland, Maj J. B., 21, 28, 89
Swan, Brig D. C. T., 214, 226, 437, 443
Swinhoe, Col M. R. H. Z., 498
Syria, operations in, 51, 56-58

T

Taj Din, Subedar-Major and Hon Capt, 485
Talwar, Lt A. L., 171
Tanahashi, Col, 280, 287-289
"Tanahashi" Force, 287, 289, 290
Tanaka, Maj-Gen, 339

Tanks, types of, *N Af,* 23, 86, 137; *It,*
  163, 170; *B,* 364, 390-393
  major engagements, *NE Af,* 34, *N Af,*
  25, 26, 96, 111, 117, 121,
  Sapper co-operation with, *N Af,* 26,
  43, 83, 168, 169; *B,* 291, 293, 326,
  336, 341, 342, 410
Taylor, Col H. M., 183, 207
Taylor, Maj I. B. C., 251, 468
Taylor, Lt-Col, (Burma Rifles), 215
Tehri Garhwal Sappers and Miners, 16
  Fd Coy, *B,* 238, 239, 241, 242, 254,
  255, 259, 315, 319, 320, 370, 388,
  389, 394, 395, 413, 416
Terauchi, Field-Marshal, 423, 435, 450
Thailand operations, 447-450
Thimayya, Brig K. S., 305, 435, 458-460
Thoma, Gen Von, 116, 117
Thomas, Capt N. B., 83, 94
Thomas, Lady Shenton, 433
Thomason, College, Roorkee, 4, 470, 490
Thompson, Maj H. F., 389, 434, 440
Thorat, Maj-Gen S. P. P., 500
Thorpe, Maj L. A., 276
Tito, Marshal, 140
Tobruk, capture of, 24, 25
  defence of, 47, 48, 82, 84-86, 88, 95
  fall of, 97, 102
Tollworthy, Maj W. C., 294
Toogood, Lt-Col A. F., xiii, 465
Topham, C. S. M., 202
Towell, Maj W. F., 330
Training Divisions, 283, 466, 469, 476
Transportation Services, 6, 9-11, 300
Transportation Stores Companies, vii, 11
  104th, 55
Transportation Training Centres (TTCs),
  7, 10, 493, 516
Treays, Col W. H., 183, 206, 208
Trigg, Maj J. H., 462
Tucker, Col P. A., 9
Tuker, Lt-Gen Sir Francis, 91, 92, 94,
  128, 132, 133, 137, 138, 485
Tunisia, operations in, 126-139
Tylden-Pattenson, Maj K., 315, 319

U

Ullman, Maj-Gen P. A., 23, 457
Unexploded bombs, 33
Urquhart, Col H. A., 183
Urwin, Maj (later Rev) R. T., xiii, 256,
  265, 271, 342
U Saw, 420
Usher, Maj I. D., 428

V

Veitch, Col W. L. D., 18, 470
Verma, Col A. D., 4, 72
Vichy French, *Sy,* 49, 51, 56-59; *SE A,*
  181
Victoria Cross awards, 35, 36, 308, 513
Volunteers, Federated Malay States,
  Engr Sec, 183, 206
Volunteers, Straits Settlements, Engr Sec,
  183, 206
Vreeden, Col B. Van, 435

W

Wadhera, Lt-Col B. P., xiii
Wadia, Capt L. M. H., 72
Wadi Akarit, battle of, 133, 134
Wakeham, Lt-Col P. O. G., 348
Wakely, Maj W. H. D., 100, 112
Walker, Maj P. A., 315, 388, 494
Waller, Lt-Col D. R. W., 437, 494
Ward, Lt-Col R. S. B., 214, 232, 264, 310 315
Waring, Maj E., 21, 22
Warren, Maj-Gen D. F. W., 334, 350, 371
Water-supply, *Ir*, 53, 54, 59, 60, 69; *N Af*, 23, 26, 88, 124; *NE Af*, 31, 36; *P*, 65, 74; *It*, 165; *B*, 214, 217; *SE A*, 448, 452, 453; *FE*, 457, 460; *Ind*, 465
Watson, Capt J. D., 161
Wavell, Field-Marshal Sir Archibald, *Mid E*, 20-22, 24, 25, 28, 29, 36, 47, 48, 51, 52, 66, 82, 84, 85, 93, 108, 274; *Ma*, 202; *Ind*, 211, 213, 219, 222, 240, 241, 245, 254, 485; *B*, 274, 279
Waziristan, operations in, 15, 16, 465
Weld, Brig C. J., 57
West African Divisional Engineers, 502
Western Desert Force, 24, 25, 82-84; becomes 8th Army, 85
Weygand, Gen, 56
Wheaton, Maj E. B., 80, 134, 137, 151
Wheeler, Lt-Gen R. A., (U.S.A.), 435
Whistler, Maj-Gen L. G., 496, 497
Whitman, Brig B. E., xiii, 183, 202, 203, 480, 499
Williams, Maj C. W., 349, 389, 434
Williams, Lt-Gen Sir Harold, vii, xii, 2, 4, 18, 252, 253 318, 477, 490, 498, 499
Williams, Lt-Col J. H., or "Elephant Bill", 238, 367
Willis, Maj R. M., 325
Wilson, Maj D. S., 360
Wilson, Gen Sir H. Maitland, *N. Af*, 24, 35; *Sy*, 51, 56, 57, 62; *Ir*, 70; *It*, 150
Wilson, Lt-Col J. B., xiii, 187, 188
Winchester, Maj J. C., 68, 94, 105, 112
Wingate, Maj-Gen Orde, 249, 250, 253, 261, 268, 269
Wood, Maj-Gen G. N., 298, 424, 436
Wood, Maj J. G., 55, 157, 491
Works Services, 12; *Ma*, 183, 206; *B*, 252, 253; *FE*, 462
Works units, 443, 452, 460
  107 CRE Wks, 252, 253
  114 Wks Bn, 238, 242, 243
  145 DCE Wks, 348
  907 Ind Wks Sec, 458, 460
Workshops Company, 352
Wren, Maj J. K., 308
Wright, Lt E. J., 367
Wright, Lt J. W., 336
Wright, Lt-Col T., 290, 336, 370, 373, 402

Y

Yamashita, Gen, 207
Yarrow, 2/Lt, 227
Young, Lt, 154
Youngs, Maj M. J., 157

Z

"Z" Craft Operating Companies, 11

www.ingramcontent.com/pod-product-compliance
Lightning Source LLC
Chambersburg PA
CBHW040332300426
44113CB00021B/2729